For Reference

Not to be taken from this room

Mexico and the United States

Volume 2

Film in the United States –
Political Parties in the United States

Marshall Cavendish
New York • London • Toronto • Sydney

Marshall Cavendish
99 White Plains Road
Tarrytown, New York 10591

Website: www.marshallcavendish.com

Library of Congress Cataloging-in-Publication Data
Mexico and the United States / edited by Lee Stacy.
    p. cm.
    Includes bibliographical references and index.
    ISBN 0-7614-7402-1 (set) – ISBN 0-7614-7403-X (v.1 : lib. bdg.) – ISBN 0-7614-7404-8 (v.2 : lib. bdg.) – ISBN 0-7614-7405-6 (v.3 : lib. bdg.)
    1. United States–Relations–Mexico–Encyclopedias. 2. Mexico–Relations–United States–Encyclopedias. I. Stacy, Lee.

E183.8.M6 M4625 2002
327.73072'03–dc21

2002019489

Printed and bound in Malaysia

07 06 05 04 03 02   6 5 4 3 2 1

Academic consultants
David E. Lorey, William and Flora Hewett Foundation, Menlo Park, California.
Héctor Manuel Lucero, University of Southern California.

Brown Reference Group
Project Editor: Lee Stacy
Editors: Chris King, Andrew Campbell, Emily Hill, Mark Fletcher
Designer: Seth Grimbly
Picture Researcher: Clare Newman
Cartographer: Mark Walker
Indexer: Kay Ollerenshaw
Managing Editor: Tim Cooke

Marshall Cavendish
Editorial Director: Paul Bernabeo
Production Manager: Michael Esposito

Contents

Contents

Film in the United States

Since Pedro Esquirel and Dionecio Gonzales's 1894 film *Mexican Duel*, Mexican-origin people have figured prominently in U.S.-made movies. Film representations of Mexicans and Chicanos have reflected prevailing attitudes in U.S. society as well as the struggle to define Chicano identity.

Silent pictures in the early twentieth century presented American audiences with portrayals of Mexicans as, among other things, murderers and thieves. Underlining these stereotypes was the name "greaser," given to Mexicans in many films of this era. Movies such as *Greaser's Gauntlet* (1908), *Tony the Greaser* (1911), and *The Greaser's Revenge* (1914) became known as a distinct genre: "the greaser film." Other pictures, such as *Broncho Billy's Redemption* (1910), featuring a Mexican who pockets the money intended for a dying man's medicine prescription, both reflected and added to racist views of Mexicans in the United States.

In the 1920s and 1930s Mexican actors and actresses such as Ramon Novarro and Dolores Del Rio achieved fame in Hollywood films. However, many of their roles maintained stereotypical views of Mexicans, particularly that of the Latin lover and the Latina seductress, one-dimensional characters who were descendants of the violence-prone greasers and the easily seduced Mexican women of the silent movies. Yet Novarro and Del Rio were very much aware of cinematic racism. Both actors supported Spanish-language newspapers' condemnation of derogatory film images of Mexicans and refused to play roles they believed were ethnically demeaning. In addition, Novarro is often credited as the first Hispanic director at a time when Mexicans were conspicuously absent from the production of films in the United States.

Changing representations

U.S. president Franklin D. Roosevelt's Good Neighbor Policy, inaugurated in 1933 to improve relations between the United States and Latin America, led to a more positive depiction of Mexicans in U.S. films. Hollywood's support of the policy was demonstrated by films such as *Robin Hood of El Dorado* (1935), which can be seen as an antidote to early greaser films. In 1945 Walt Disney embarked on a "goodwill tour" of Latin America to show his support of Roosevelt's policy. That same year Disney released *The Three Caballeros*, an animated feature set in Mexico and starring a sombrero-wearing rooster called Panchito.

From the 1930s through to the 1960s a type of film known as the Hollywood social melodrama helped reveal the stark realities of Mexican American history and society. Movies such as *Bordertown* (1935), *A Medal for Benny* (1945), *My Man and I* (1952), *Salt of the Earth* (1954), and *Giant* (1956) expressed the themes of racial and economic inequality. While these films were usually made with

The Mexican American movie star Dolores Del Rio (1905–1983) was famous for her depiction of Latina seductresses in films such as The Loves of Carmen (1927) and Bird of Paradise (1932).

Directed by and starring Edward James Olmos (center), American Me *(1992) is the story of a Los Angeles street gang leader, his 18 years in prison, and the difficulties he faces after his release. The film was one of several Hollywood movies in the 1990s to be made by Chicanos.*

good intentions, they sometimes reinforced stereotypes in both explicit and implicit ways. An exception, however, was *Salt of the Earth*, which focused on the experiences of Mexican American women and highlighted their role in a real-life zinc miners' strike in New Mexico in the early 1950s.

Film and the Chicano movement

The Chicano movement's 1960s campaign for social justice inspired a number of Mexican American filmmakers to create empowering depictions of Chicano life. Many people consider Luis Valdez's 1969 documentary *I am Joaquín*, based on Rodolfo "Corky" González's epic poem, to be the first film of the movement. Other filmmakers who represented Chicano concerns include Jesus Salvador Treviño, who directed highly political features such as the 1969 *La Raza Nueva* (The new people) and the 1972 *Yo Soy Chicano* (I am Chicano). The filmmakers Esperanza Vásquez and Sylvia Morales conveyed the Chicana feminist perspective in their respective films *Agueda Martínez: Our People, Our Country* (1977) and *Chicana* (1979). Chicanos also created an art form known as "No Movies" to address the difficulties they faced in

making films, particularly the lack of support from major film companies. For example, Harry Gamboa's 1976 *No Movie* consisted of a single image of a gunshot victim lying next to a wall upon which the words "Chicano cinema" were written.

In the 1970s Hollywood films such as *Viva Max* (1970) and *Boulevard Nights* (1979) portrayed Chicano characters as either comical or violent figures. In the 1980s, however, Chicanos began to direct their own major studio productions, including *Zoot Suit* (1981), *Born in East L.A.* (1987), and *Stand and Deliver* (1988), all presenting positive, realistic depictions of Mexican Americans. This trend continued in the 1990s with films such as *American Me* (1992), *My Family* (1995), and *Luminarias* (2000). At the start of the twenty-first century Mexican Americans were still underrepresented in the U.S. film industry and remained vigilant for negative portrayals in mainstream movies. Despite this fact, few people would disagree that the situation has improved since the 1970s.

Richard T. Rodríguez

SEE ALSO:

Chicano Movement; Film in Mexico; Good Neighbor Policy; Stereotypes and Prejudice.

Fisheries

For centuries fishing has provided a vital source of food for Mexican and Mexican American communities on the coasts of the Pacific and the Gulf of Mexico. During the last hundred years fishing has become a massive commercial industry, offering employment to thousands in the fishing fleets and in the support and processing industries on land.

California and Texas are among the top five seafood-producing states in the United States, and both Sonora and Sinaloa are major producers in Mexico. Sinaloa is Mexico's most important state in terms of the commercial value of its catch and fourth by volume. In 1996 California fishers delivered more than 461 million pounds (209 million kg) of fish and other seafood to market. There were then almost 10,000 commercial fishers and many more fish handlers and fishingboat builders. The Pacific coast of southern California, from Point Conception in the north to San Diego, yields mackerel, squid, sardines, and bonito in quantity. Other important California catches include swordfish, shark, spiny lobster, rock crab, rockfish, California halibut, prawns, sea cucumbers, and sea urchins. The California Fish and Game Commission regulates fishing activities within that state's three-mile limit.

In western Mexico there are fisheries on the Pacific coast of Baja California and in the Gulf of California. In commercial terms, at least, Sinaloa is the most important fishing state in Mexico, particularly for its shrimp catch, which constitutes more than one-third of the national total. There has been a spectacular growth in Sinaloan aquaculture (the cultivation of fish or shellfish) since the late 1980s. In 1987 there were 27 shrimp and fish farms in the state, but by 1995 that number had risen to 138. Output from shrimp farms in the same period rose from 576 tons (585 metric tonnes) to 8,587 tons (8,725 metric tonnes). Mazatlan is Mexico's primary Pacific fishing port and is home to the world's largest shrimping fleet. Together with the neighboring state of Sonora, Sinaloa produces 40 percent of Mexico's total catch. Mexico's Pacific fishing grounds produce mainly lobster, shrimp, croaker, albacore, skipjack, and anchovies.

In the Gulf of Mexico shrimp make up at least 90 percent of the value of all Texan fishing products, and the state has consistently been one of the top three U.S. producers. At Port Isabel, near the Rio Grande estuary, shrimping, along with the commercial netting of trout, redfish, and flounder, can be traced back to at least the middle of the nineteenth century. Texas shrimpers typically fish for up to three weeks in the Gulf before returning to port. They have to work at night since brown shrimp are nocturnal creatures. Many crew members are Mexican Americans or undocumented Mexicans. Since 1979 the Texan fleet has had to contend with a ban on fishing in Mexican waters, rising fuel costs, and concerns over the killing of sea turtles caught in nets.

Fishing cooperatives and disputes

In Mexico certain species, such as shrimp, lobster, clam, croaker, and sea turtle, are reserved for the country's 300 fishing cooperatives, which together have more than 39,000 members. The state-owned Mexican Fisheries (Pesqueros Mexicanos) markets about 15 percent of the total catch. Despite an increase in the catch taken by Mexican vessels in the late 1990s, following the introduction of more modern trawlers, it is still less than 10 percent of the total catch taken from Mexican waters by U.S., Canadian, and Japanese boats.

There have been many disputes over territorial fishing rights. In the early 1990s the United States banned imports of Mexican tuna on the grounds that the fish were not caught using environmentally friendly methods. Dolphins were being trapped and killed in the tuna nets. The Mexican authorities argued that the United States introduced the embargo as a measure to protect its own tuna industry and that it had no right to dictate another country's fishing methods. A panel of members of the General Agreement on Trade and Tariffs (GATT) found in favor of Mexico, but in 2001—a decade after the issue was first raised—there was still no permanent resolution to the tuna dispute.

Tim Harris

SEE ALSO:

Ecotourism; Environmental Issues; Gulf of California; Gulf of Mexico; Tariffs; Trade; Wildlife.

Flores Magón, Ricardo

The campaigner and journalist Ricardo Flores Magón (1873–1922) was an outspoken critic of Mexico's government in the period before the Mexican Revolution (1910–1920). His support, first of violent acts of rebellion, later of the notion that political power belonged to the masses, influenced the revolution.

Ricardo Flores Magón was born in San Antonio Eloxochitlán, Oaxaca. His parents had a profound influence on his social and political ideas: his father was an Indian, a veteran of Mexico's War of Reform (1856–1861), and a lifelong liberal. His mother was a mestiza (of Spanish and Indian descent) who instilled in her son a knowledge of the communal values and practices of rural peoples. A student of philosophy and later law, the young man found his political direction through anarchism, the belief that government is unnecessary and harmful. Like other anarchists, Flores Magón felt that capitalist governments—such as that of Mexico's then president Porfirio Díaz (1830–1915)—exploited the poorest in society and fueled inequality.

From 1892 Flores Magón worked as a writer, speaker, and political organizer. One role he undertook at this time was to help establish the Partido Liberal México (PLM; Mexican Liberal Party); he remained its leader for many years. Another role was founding the newspaper *Regeneración* (Regeneration) in Mexico City in 1900, for which he edited and wrote many articles. Both roles brought Flores Magón's criticisms of the Díaz regime and its policies to a wide audience, including the government itself. Between 1900 and 1903 he was frequently imprisoned for his views.

Activism in the United States
In January 1904 Flores Magón and a number of PLM members and supporters, including his younger brother Enrique, crossed the border into Texas. The move was partly the result of government pressure on Flores Magón to leave Mexico and partly because of his belief that the U.S. right of free speech would allow him to express his radical ideas more openly. In Texas he saw firsthand the exploitation of Mexican American farmworkers, whom he encouraged to join the PLM. Many did, and his political party began to forge a presence in the United States. Flores Magón also resumed publication of *Regeneración*, in San Antonio, Texas, and wrote articles attacking the exploitation of Mexico's workforce and the corruption of public offices under the Díaz administration. However, the Mexican government had alerted the U.S. authorities to Flores Magón's activities and the *Regeneración* offices were often raided. He and the PLM group then moved to St. Louis, Missouri, in 1905 and from there to Los Angeles in 1907. Criminal investigators followed Flores Magón wherever he went; in 1907 he was imprisoned for nearly two years on a charge of breaking U.S. neutrality laws, which restricted the United States' involvement in the domestic affairs of other nations.

Encouraging revolution
Between 1906 and 1910 the PLM focused on three main goals: the emancipation of women, developing Mexican American labor organizations, and, most

---

Flores Magón, Ricardo
Revolutionary activist and journalist

Born: September 16, 1873
San Antonio Eloxochitlán, Oaxaca
Died: November 21, 1922
Leavenworth Penitentiary, Kansas

1900	Founds the newspaper *Regeneración*, which publishes views of the Partido Liberal Mexico he also helped found
1902–03	Imprisoned for criticizing government of Porfirio Díaz
1904	Moves to United States, where publication of *Regeneración* continues
1907–18	Between periods in jail, campaigns for revolution in Mexico and for Mexican American laborers
1918	Sentenced to 20 years in jail

importantly, encouraging revolution back in Mexico. In those periods where Flores Magón was in prison he continued to influence the party's direction through his articles and the letters he wrote to his supporters. In advocating women's rights he collaborated with white American radicals such as Emma Goldman, Ethel Duffy Turner, and Elizabeth Trowbridge. The PLM also played an important role in the development of Mexican American labor unions, which organized and represented Mexican workers' views and grievances. The PLM's involvement was significant because most U.S. unions at the time were led by white Americans and were often hostile to Mexicans, denying them union membership.

Flores Magón and the PLM advocated rebellion and revolution in Mexico to overthrow Díaz's regime. At first they encouraged and assisted *focos* (small guerrilla bands) that invaded Mexico from the United States and attacked cities and towns with the intention of sparking a national uprising. Then Flores Magón launched a propaganda campaign throughout northern Mexico, in which he encouraged rural peasants to revolt. In his writings he emphasized that sovereignty belonged to the people—if the government did not reflect this it was illegitimate and should be overthrown. The PLM published two manifestos advocating revolution in Mexico. They received support from Mexican Americans as well as sympathetic white Americans and labor leaders.

The Mexican Revolution

The last two months of 1910 marked the beginning of the revolution as a number of regional uprisings took place against the government of Díaz. In January 1911, PLM forces launched a campaign in Baja California, capturing Mexicali and Tijuana. The PLM forces refused to recognize the revolutionary government of Francisco Madero and continued their fight against the new regime. However, their resistance came to an end in June, largely because a lack of funds made a sustained military campaign unfeasible. Matters were made worse by the fact that the PLM leaders in the United States chose to spend the little money they had on propaganda rather than weapons.

The failure of the PLM's campaign in Baja California has led many historians to question Flores Magón's revolutionary credentials. Some have discounted him as a visionary who was excellent at theorizing but incapable of forging a program to combat injustice. In contrast, other historians point to the role of the *focos* sponsored by Flores Magón in demonstrating to the people of Mexico that a larger insurrection could take place.

The final decade

Between the summer of 1911 and 1918 Flores Magón was largely involved in the publishing of *Regeneración* and public speaking, while the U.S. authorities continued to monitor his activities. Police raided the offices of *Regeneración* in 1911, forcing it to close. The following year he received another jail sentence. Other PLM leaders were also imprisoned and their supporters were discouraged from holding meetings. Consequently, when Flores Magón left prison in 1914 there was little left of the organization he had helped to found.

Undaunted, Flores Magón continued his writing, producing some of his best work. The final issue of *Regeneración* was published on March 16, 1918. Two days later police arrested him, along with the *Regeneración* writer and PLM supporter Librado Rivera, and charged him under the 1917 Espionage Act. The accusation was that both men had conspired to write and publish false statements that adversely affected the operation of the U.S. Army and Navy. Flores Magón received a sentence of 20 years—Rivera received 15 years—to be served at Leavenworth Penitentiary, Kansas.

At Leavenworth, Flores Magón continued to write articles and letters as well as a play for teenagers. He called for unity among radical groups and felt that teaching was the key to making people politically active. Despite his loneliness in prison, he never lost his belief that the world would one day change for the better. On November 21, 1922, he was found dead in his cell. Rumors that he had been murdered by prison guards developed after Librado Rivera reported seeing dark marks around his neck. Others maintained that he died of natural causes—his health was not good during his time in Leavenworth. Flores Magón's body was brought back to Mexico and on May 1, 1945, given a full state reburial in the Rotunda of Illustrious Men in Mexico City. The reburial recognized his role in encouraging the revolution.

Carlos Ortega

SEE ALSO:

Díaz, Porfirio; Exiles; Labor Organizations; Madero, Francisco I.; Mexican Revolution.

Florida

Florida was a Spanish territory for nearly 300 years. The modern U.S. state retains a large Hispanic population, although Mexicans are outnumbered by both Cubans and Puerto Ricans.

Early Spanish exploration in Florida sought to integrate the region into New Spain, the empire based in Mexico. In 1528 Pánfilo de Narváez and 400 men landed in Florida's Tampa Bay and set out to discover how the region was connected to New Spain. Only four of the party survived the eight-year journey to Culiacán in Mexico. Florida's remoteness from the center of Spanish power was emphasized when French settlers began to arrive on the northern coast of the Gulf of Mexico. In 1565 the Spanish commander Pedro Menéndez de Avilés destroyed a French colony at Fort Caroline, near modern Jacksonville. However, French settlers from Canada continued to move south through the Mississippi Valley to Louisiana, separating Florida from the rest of New Spain.

In 1763 Britain took over Florida in return for letting Spain control the Cuban port of Havana. By the 1780s, however, the territory had passed back to Spanish control. Florida then became a focus for the newly formed United States' expansionist aims. These aims were finally realized when the U.S. general Andrew Jackson captured Pensacola in 1818. In the Adams-Onís treaty the following year Spain traded Florida to the United States for recognition of Spanish sovereignty over Texas. Florida became a state of the Union in 1845.

Florida in the twentieth century

Florida remained relatively remote and under-developed until the 1920s, when a series of land booms fueled development and attracted settlers. The state's climate helped the development of fruit and vegetable growing and attracted tourists and, increasingly, retirees from elsewhere in the United States. By the 1980s Florida had become the fourth most populous state in the nation.

Florida has a long history of Hispanic settlement. While people of Mexican origin are a sizable element, Cubans constitute the largest Hispanic community. Cuban immigration to Florida began in the nineteenth century and peaked after the 1959 revolution that toppled Fulgencio Battista's government and brought Fidel Castro to power.

Mexicans and Mexican Americans were first attracted to Florida after the boom of the mid-1920s. Large-scale migrant agriculture began in the 1950s. Mexicans found jobs in the fern, citrus, and sugar-growing industries around Lake Okeechobee, and in the construction industry in cities such as Orlando. In 2001, around 7,000 migrant Mexican farmworkers worked in south Florida in the harvest season. Their equivalent annual wage was only $7,500, which was near the poverty level.

Some Mexicans and Mexican Americans who originally came to the state as migrant farmworkers have put down roots. In southern Dade County, particularly in and around the city of Homestead, Mexicans are the largest Hispanic group and have moved out of the traditional migrant trailer parks into their own properties. Although they originally came to work on the area's tomato farms, significant numbers branched out into running stores and other businesses, such as restaurants, radio stations, and farm-machinery businesses.

Growing Mexican population

According to the 2000 U.S. census, Florida's 2.7 million Hispanics made up nearly 17 percent of the state's population, the seventh highest proportion of Hispanics in the country. In the same census Cubans totaled 31 percent of the Hispanic population, Puerto Ricans 18 percent, and Mexicans and Mexican Americans 14 percent. The Mexican-origin population was growing rapidly, however, and had more than doubled since the previous census in 1990. Furthermore, in 2000 the average age of Florida's Mexicans was a youthful 24 years. Compared with a Cuban population whose average age was rising, this statistic suggested that the state's population would change significantly in the first decades of the twenty-first century.

Tim Cooke

SEE ALSO:

Adams-Onís Treaty; Cuba; Hispanic Americans; Migrant Labor; Spanish Empire.

Folklore

Folklore is the word used to describe traditional poetry, song, dance, stories, festivals, art, food, crafts, and culture. According to the Mexican American folklorist and scholar Americo Paredes (1915–1999), there are at least three kinds of folklore groups of Mexican origin found in the United States today: regional groups (composed of descendants of early settlers on frontiers of New Spain); rural and semirural immigrant groups; and urban groups.

The regional groups are found in New Mexico, western Texas, parts of Arizona, and Colorado, as well as the Mexican state of Chihuahua. Folk groups of the rural type are found in southern Texas from the Nueces River to the Rio Grande. Urban Mexican American folk groups are found in U.S. cities such as Los Angeles, Chicago, and San Antonio. Regardless of its origins, folklore is a timeless tradition, passed from one particular people, place, or time to another in a fixed form that maintains cultural continuity. Folklore, too, is typically anonymous: it is passed along by those who are continually remaking it and authorship is lost in its transmission

Folk crafts

People often see Mexican pottery as the sole representative of Mexican American folk arts and crafts. However, many other crafts specific to the Tejano (Mexican-Texan) culture thrive along the border in rural southern Texas. These include the production of objects including saddles, quilts, roadside crosses, wrought-iron work, ceramics, and yard shrines. Many Mexican American crafts are used solely for interior decoration and are not made to be sold. Other crafts, however, such as guitar and piñata making, can contribute to the livelihood of the artisan.

Probably the best-known product of Mexican-American crafts is the piñata, which, filled with candy, is used to celebrate birthdays and other festive occasions. Piñatas were originally made from clay as a form of pottery. They were later made of river cane (similar to bamboo) and decorated with strips of brightly colored tissue paper. Traditionally the shapes were of Mexican donkeys, stars, and cakes, but today are modeled on virtually any image and are constructed out of papier-mâché. Most piñatas today are mass-produced; the handmade ones are rarely found outside Mexico. Piñatas are often seen at annual Mexican American events and festivities, such as the San Antonio Folk Life Festival, which is held each summer in the grounds of the Institute of Texan Cultures, or at Night in Old San Antonio, an event that commemorates spring. Piñatas are also a popular entertainment at children's birthday parties throughout southern and western Texas. Traditionally children are blindfolded and given turns at hitting the piñata with a stick or bat until it breaks and the candy falls to the ground for the children to gather.

Pottery, leatherwork, metal craft, and weaving are linked to the pre-Columbian, Spanish, and mestizo heritages in Mexico and have developed into a specific Tejano culture. Beginning with the establishment of missions along the Mexico-U.S. border, the involvement of Texas Mexican *vaqueros* (cowboys) on ranches in southern Texas led to the crafting of ranch equipment, which continues today. In addition, the crafts of embroidery and quilting have been part of Mexican American women's domestic arts for several centuries. Mexican women continue to carry on the traditions of knitting, crocheting, and embroidery to decorate their homes and to design their clothing. Yard art and home altars are two other domestically based folk arts found in working-class homes.

Dress making

One of the more popular folk crafts is the embroidered Mexican dress, which is typically a white or bright, solid-colored cotton sheath with elastic, puffed sleeves, and a stitched frontpiece. The embroidery on these dresses is done by hand and traditionally appears in a brightly colored floral pattern or one with Mexican designs that includes parrots or flamingos. In many border towns and cities in southern Texas these dresses are sold both in boutiques and on street corners, in all sizes,

Dancers wearing flamboyant feather headdresses. Throughout the year in Mexico there are festivals and holidays when people dress up in traditional costumes. Many of these festivals have pre-Hispanic origins dating from ancient Aztec or Mayan times.

fetching anything between U.S. $40 and U.S. $120 per dress.

Other family folk-art expressions include roadside crosses (*descansos*) that often consist of a handmade wooden cross surrounded by flowers and a marker with the name of the loved one who has died. The *descansos* are placed at the site of the death to mark the spot where the family believes the person's spirit left the body. These memorials can be spotted along southern Texas roads, from the Gulf of Mexico to the western Texas plains, in Lubbock and El Paso, where people have died in automobile accidents or in other circumstances.

Traditional food and diet

Mexican food is often thought of as a typical fast food—spicy beef and bean concoctions in the form of tacos, burritos, fajitas, and tostados. This food,

however, is very different from traditional Mexican American cuisine, which is a blend of pre-Columbian, Spanish, French, and more recently, American cooking. Even tortillas, a seemingly typical Mexican food, are an American invention.

The typical Mexican diet is rich in complex carbohydrates, which are provided mainly by corn and corn products, beans, rice, and breads. The diet contains good quantities of protein in the form of beans, eggs, fish and shellfish, and a large variety of meats, including beef, pork, poultry, and on very special occasions, goat. Because of the extensive use of frying as a cooking method (the Spanish first introduced pork fat for frying) and the amounts of cheese and cream used, the Mexican diet is also high in fat. The daily meal pattern in the typical Mexican American home varies according to the availability of traditional foods and the degree of assimilation into U.S. society. In Mexico the largest meal was traditionally eaten in the middle of the day, followed by a two or three hour siesta during which everyone rested and avoided the hot sun. This tradition is still followed in some regions of the United States, particularly in border towns in southern Texas.

The flavors and food choices vary from region to region throughout the United States, and many traditional Mexican foods are still eaten. In southern Texas, one is more likely to find a style of cooking referred to as Tex-Mex, which includes homemade flour or corn tortillas (a flat bread) and fajitas (thin strips of beef or chicken). Tex-Mex cuisine has Indian, Spanish, and Anglo-American influences.

In New Mexico, however, Mexican food takes on a special New Mexican or Santa Fe flavor, which includes more whole corn and black bean entrées, reminiscent of the native Indian culture as well as the Hispanic. In general, the farther north a person travels, the less spicy and the more Americanized Mexican food tends to become.

Festivals and events

Most Mexican holidays are celebrated not only in Mexico but also in towns where significant populations of Mexican Americans have settled. Each town or region may choose to commemorate a Mexican event in a specific way, most centering on the concept of a fiesta, or party. In Texas a variety of these festivals occur throughout the year in San Antonio, El Paso, Del Rio, Lubbock, Austin, and Dallas. There is also an abundance of such gatherings of Chicanos in southern California and Chicago, as well as a few in rural midwestern states, such as Nebraska.

Carnival is a five-day celebration prior to the Catholic period of Lent, which begins on Ash Wednesday. Beginning the weekend before Lent, Carnival is celebrated with parades, floats, costumes, music, and dancing in the streets. The festival of Carnival is celebrated as a last indulgence of the carnal pleasures that Catholics must give up for 40 days of fasting during Lent, from Ash Wednesday to Easter Sunday. Strict Roman Catholics will give up eating meat during Lent.

Semana Santa, or Holy Week, is Mexico's second most important holiday season of the year after Christmas, and runs from Palm Sunday to Easter Sunday. In addition to attending Mass on Good Friday and Easter Sunday, many Mexican Americans will also take advantage of the holiday to go on vacation. Semana Santa celebrates the Christian holiday of Easter. People who celebrate this also often stage reenactments of the events leading up to Christ's crucifixion on the cross. The most moving event of Semana Santa is the reenactment of the Passion of Christ, or the Passion Play.

Folk Tales and Legends

The *corrido* is a narrative folk song and is said to be the earliest example of Mexican American folklore. *Corridos* were first heard in Mexico in the sixteenth century, during the Spanish conquest. Later they chronicled the experience of Mexican rebels who were killed or taken prisoner by North American authorities. Names such as Juan Nepomuceno, Juan Cortina, Aniceto Pizana, and Gregorio Cortez were immortalized in these songs and legends.

In these songs and tales Mexicans see themselves and all that they stand for as continually challenging a foreign people who treat them with disdain. The *corridos* relate the feats of the first Mexican American rebels against the North American government. The hero is always a Mexican whose rights or self-respect are trampled upon by North American authority. Older *corridos* deal with the adventures of Mexicans whose work forces them to travel deep into the United States. These *corridos* are always narrated in the first person plural and recount the perils of the journey and the strange things seen by the adventurers. In prose narratives, the legend and the belief tale, as well as the comic anecdote, are used to develop themes of cultural conflict. "La Muerte de Antonio Rodriguez" (The death of Antonio Rodriguez), for example, is a story based on a historical event: the lynching of a young Mexican who was apparently burned alive in a small town in Texas in 1910. In a variant from 1962 the story retains its tone of outrage and indignation but the additions of universal motives have converted the story into a legend.

Día de los Muertos (the Day of the Dead) is the commemoration of dead relatives, both young and old, who are believed to return to the mortal world to visit loved ones. The festival, also known as All Souls' Day or All Saints' Day by Catholics, actually lasts two days, from November 1 to November 2. Spirits are imagined to come down and walk among the living, sampling earthly treats and joining in the festival, which is similar to the Halloween holiday in the United States. However, instead of being frightened by the dead, the Mexican American people welcome the spirits of their families with the delicious smell of food in the air. Gravestones are cleaned and decorated, and the whole family gathers in the graveyard to await and pay respects to their relatives who have died.

Posadas

The Posadas is the Mexican American buildup to Christmas Eve, beginning on December 16. The festival commemorates events in the journey of Mary and Joseph from Nazareth to Bethlehem. After dark, on each night of the Posada, a procession begins, led by two children. The children carry a small pine-decorated platform bearing replicas of Joseph and Mary riding a burro. Other members of the company, all with lighted, long, slender candles, sing the Litany of the Virgin as they approach the door of the house assigned to the first posada (inn). Together they chant an old traditional song and awaken the master of the house to ask for lodging for Mary.

At midnight on Christmas Eve the celebration of Christmas begins when the birth of Christ is announced with fireworks, the ringing of bells, and the blowing of whistles. Following mass, families return home for an enormous dinner of traditional Mexican foods. The dishes vary with the different regions. However, among the more common dishes are tamales (a pork or beef dish), rice, chili *rellenos*, *atole* (a sweet drink), and *menudo* (a popular stew made from intestines).

The Christmas festivals draw to a close on January 6 with the festival of *Epifania* (the Epiphany), when families share a sweet, ring-shaped loaf with a ceramic doll representing the Christ child baked inside. Whoever gets the doll has to throw a party on February 2 (*Día de Candelaría*) for all the others present. In this case, the "winner," who has to find the time and money to arrange the party, is often the loser. On the afternoon of *Día de Candelaría*,

A roadside shrine in Mexico. Memorials such as this are placed at the site of the death to mark the spot where the family believes the spirit left the body.

dancers gather for a performance in the churchyard. Sometimes as many as six different dance groups perform at the same time. The dancers are divided among those portraying Christians and Moors, each competing for the most attention.

Cinco de Mayo (May 5) commemorates the victory of the Mexicans over the French army at the Battle of Puebla in 1862. It is primarily a regional holiday celebrated in the Mexican state capital of Puebla and throughout the state of Puebla, but is also celebrated in other parts of the country and in U.S. cities. It is not, as many people assume, Mexico's Independence Day, which is actually on September 16. Celebrating Cinco de Mayo has become increasingly popular along the U.S.-Mexico border and in parts of the United States that have a high population of people with a Mexican heritage. In these areas the holiday is a celebration of culture, food, drink, music, and customs unique to Mexico.

Folk dance

Almost any Mexican American festival held throughout the United States includes troupes of traditional Mexican dancers who have mastered the ballet *folklorico* or the flamenco dance. Academies and schools teach traditional dance and music (mostly mariachi) in cities from southern Texas along the border to California, and then across the

A Mariachi skeleton doll made for the Day of the Dead. On November 1 and 2 Mexicans not only dress up as the dead using makeup and costumes but they also make decorative items to celebrate the return of their relatives' spirits—sweets, masks, and dolls.

United States to Wisconsin. In folkoric dances, paired troupes of five to seventeen members bring the traditions, ancient folklore, and customs of Mexico to life. Traditional folk dances are a celebration of a variety of Mexican cultures.

Each state in Mexico, as well as specific geographic and cultural regions within states, cultivates a particular dance and folkloric style that is disseminated across the country via community, university, and professional performance groups. These are called *bailes regionales*. Each regional tradition reflects the rich cultural heritage and unique characteristics of the state or region represented. Characteristics unique to each region are reflected in the music (instrumentation), dance (footwork, skirt work, partnering, patterning styles), and costuming. A celebrated example is the *jarabe tapatío* (the "hat dance"), which has become known as the Mexican national dance.

Another form of dance is the mestizo dance, dances that are indigenous in origin but which incorporate European elements. One of the most popular mestizo dances is known as the *danza de los viejitos* (dance of the little old men), which origin-

ated in Michoacán. The music and instruments are Spanish, while the dance is Purépecha.

Mexican music, like Mexican art, has a rich and varied history. Of all the music in Mexico, perhaps the most best known is mariachi. The term *mariachi* has come to mean not just the music but also the musical groups and the individual musicians. Mariachis often play ranch songs (*rancheros*) and narrative folksongs (*corridos*), both of which are early forms of Mexican folk music. They also still perform *sones*, which are instrumental pieces.

In southern Mexico the music centers around the marimba, a xylophone that was probably introduced to Latin America by African slaves. In northern Mexico and southern Texas a traditional, accordion-based dance music known as *conjunto* became popular in the early twentieth century. This music, later adapted by musicians using modern, electric instruments, has become known as Tex-Mex.

J. Marie Doggett

SEE ALSO:

Corridos; Crafts; Dance; Festivals; Food and Drink; Mariachis; Tejanos; Tex-Mex Culture.

Food and Drink

From family-run restaurants to Taco Bells, Mexican restaurants have become a familiar sight in most U.S. cities. While such restaurants all claim to serve authentic Mexican food, visitors to Mexico are often surprised by the range of dishes and at how the food and drink differ from those described as "Mexican" in the United States.

A selection of Mexican fruits, including ripe custard apples (foreground). Mexican jugos (fruit juices) are made from a wide range of fruits, from oranges to mangoes, papayas, and melons.

Mexican food is one of the most popular world cuisines served in the United States. Sometimes, however, the description "Mexican" is misleading. For example, the increasingly popular fajitas (marinated strips of meat, broiled and served with tortillas) are actually "Tex-Mex" rather Mexican. "Tex-Mex" dishes derive from the Indian, Spanish, and Anglo-American influences in Texas's past. Much of the modern Mexican diet dates back to preconquest times. This includes foods eaten by the Aztecs of central Mexico, such as corn (maize), chili peppers, tomatoes, beans, cocoa, and turkey. Dogs and grasshoppers, two once commonly eaten Aztec foods, are no longer eaten.

Historical and regional influences
Mexico's history is reflected in its food and in the development of different dishes. When the Spanish conquered the Aztecs in 1521 they brought with them domesticated animals such as pigs, goats, and chickens. Prior to the conquest there were no dairy products in the Aztec diet and fried food was unknown. However, the arrival of pigs introduced pork fat as a means to fry, and chickens provided eggs, which became a staple part of the Mexican diet. When the French temporarily ruled Mexico in the 1860s they too left an influence on the Mexican diet, in the form of crusty bread rolls and fresh cream pastries.

Because Mexico is a large country, its foods are highly regional and vary from area to area. In the desert and dry regions, plants such as prickly pears and agave cacti are basic foods, as are rabbit and squirrel meat. Along the Mexican coastline a variety of seafood dominates, from fish, such as *huachinango* (red snapper), to crustaceans, such as crab and lobster. Another common dish in the coastal regions is ceviche, raw fish marinated in chili and lemon or lime juice. Regional dishes from the south include avocados, mushrooms, and more unusual foods, such as crickets, maguey worms, and ant eggs.

Many Mexican dishes that are popular today in the United States originated in different parts of Mexico. For example, chimichangas—deep-fried tortillas wrapped around a filling—come from Sonora and Arizona and, while they are known across the United States, are rarely featured on menus in Mexico City. Some dishes are traditional in both northern Mexico and the U.S. Southwest, reflecting the influence that climate, terrain, and history can have on food: until 1848 much of the Southwest was Mexican territory. A good example is chili con carne (originally called chili Colorado), which evolved as a typical cowboy meal throughout northern Mexico and the present-day Southwest.

Basic foodstuffs
Despite regional differences, a number of Mexican dishes involve two staple ingredients: corn and beans. Archaeologists have traced the cultivation of corn in Mexico to around 600 B.C.E. and have discovered its use among the Maya, the Aztecs, and other ancient Indian peoples. Corn was so important to the Aztecs that it became a religious symbol. In present-day Mexico corn accounts for half of all the food eaten each year. Mexican farmers grow more than 35 different varieties of the plant, which is the main ingredient in over 600 dishes, from tamales (ground meat rolled in cornmeal

dough) to popcorn. There are many different ways to use corn, besides the two most common in the United States: served on the cob or as kernels or used as animal feed. Other uses for corn include a thickening ingredient for soups, a source of oil, a food wrapping, and a medicine.

Tortillas and beans

The most common food made of corn in Mexico is the tortilla, a flat, thin pancake cooked on a griddle. In Mexico people either make their own tortillas or buy them fresh from *tortillerías* (tortilla shops) or from supermarkets. Tortillas form the basis of many Mexican dishes. They can be eaten soft, rolled and filled with meat, such as goat or chicken, or vegetables. Tacos, the most common Mexican food available in the United States, are fried tortillas that are then filled. Enchiladas are essentially rolled tortillas that have been covered in sauce. Tostadas are crisp, toasted tortillas, piled with meat and vegetables. Although tortillas are common in the United States, they are usually made of wheat instead of corn and taste quite different. When wheat flour became widely available in the United States in the 1930s, wheat tortillas took over from the corn variety in popularity. Some Mexican restaurants in the United States, particularly along the Mexico-U.S. border, serve corn tortillas, but the majority use wheat flour.

The other staple ingredient in Mexico is beans (frijoles), which serve as a cheap, tasty source of protein. The commonest variety is the black bean and the brown kidney bean. In New Mexico and Texas the dark pink or purple pinto bean is used, while elsewhere in the United States, Mexican dishes contain red beans. There are many different ways of preparing beans. They can be boiled and eaten as *frijoles enteros* (whole beans), which are then reheated and eaten in a soupier form, or they can be fried as *frijoles fritos*. Most common in the United States is the refried bean, cooked and then fried, often with garlic, onion, cilantro, and chili.

Spices and sauces

Chili is probably the most important spice used in Mexican cooking. In Mexico nearly 200 varieties of chili are used as accompaniments in sauces and as an essential ingredient in one of the many versions of salsa that add flavor to dishes. Different types of chili range from mild to extra hot, although the hot varieties are more often used in Mexico than in the United States. Other ingredients commonly used to add flavor to cooking include cilantro, tomatoes, and garlic.

The spicy sauce known as salsa is one of the bases of Mexican food. There are hundreds of different versions of salsa, each combining varying amounts of tomatoes, garlic, onions, chilies, and cilantro. The

Mexican Fast Food

Fast food existed in Mexico long before the arrival of McDonald's, Pizza Hut, and Wendy's. Mexican-style fast food is street food that dates back to the ancient civilizations of the Aztecs and Maya. Street vendors sell a wide variety of hot, freshly prepared foods as well as coffee and freshly squeezed juices, known as *jugos* or *licuados*. Mexican fast food also includes versions of hamburgers and hot dogs, but often with distinctive additions, such as raw chilies.

Eating on the move is not as much a part of Mexican life as it is in the United States. There are few drive-through restaurants in Mexico outside of Mexico City and tourist centers such as Cancún and Acapulco. Mexican meals are more likely to be prepared from scratch and eaten together by families. Furthermore, while some city dwellers follow the U.S. habit of eating three meals a day, the traditional pattern in Mexico is five meals. The first is an early breakfast (*desayuno*) of hot chocolate or coffee and a sweet bun. A second breakfast (*almuerzo*) follows at around 11 A.M., with lunch (*comida*) at around 2 P.M., consisting of soup, a main dish of meat or fish, and a dessert. An early evening snack and a light dinner (*cena*) at around 9 P.M. round off the day.

Mexican fast foods that are popular in the United States include tacos, burritos, and fajitas. These dishes are so popular that they are often found on restaurant menus alongside burgers and fries. Another popular snack in the United States is tortilla chips and salsa. Tortilla chips, however, are an American invention based on the Mexican habit of using up day-old tortillas by frying them.

popularity of salsa in the United States has steadily increased: in the 1990s U.S. consumers bought more jars of salsa than bottles of ketchup. Guacamole is another popular dip in both the United States and Mexico. Made from mashed avocados, chilies, and garlic, the dish is a good way of using surplus avocados.

Another key ingredient of Mexican cooking is the sauce known as mole, thought to have originated from ancient Mayan recipes. It contains ground nuts, raisins, chilies, and bitter-sweet chocolate. *Mole poblano* (turkey served with mole sauce) is a traditional Mexican dish served on special occasions. Authentic Mexican restaurants in the United States serve the meal, but it is rarely on the menu of more mainstream establishments. Prepared *mole poblano* is available in grocery stores in Mexico, but rarely in the United States.

Mexican foods in the Southwest

Mexican food is widely available in the American Southwest. This is due to the region's history as part of northern Mexico and the large number of Mexicans and Mexican Americans who live in the southwestern states of Texas, New Mexico, Arizona, and California. The influence of Mexican food in the region extends beyond Mexican restaurants. Mexican foods are widely available in food stores, and schoolchildren eat Mexican lunches alongside other food. Children grow up eating burritos, tacos, enchiladas, and tamales as well as burgers and hot dogs. Mexican food varies throughout the Southwest. In western Texas and New Mexico, for example, enchiladas are stacked up flat, fried in hot oil, then covered in chili sauce, grated cheese, chopped onions, and fried egg. In other parts of the region, enchiladas are served rolled up, as they are in the rest of the United States. The differences are most pronounced in Texas, where communities from different parts of Mexico eat different foods.

Mexican drinks

Mexican alcoholic drinks—particularly beer and tequila—are very popular in the United States. There are many more types of beer produced in Mexico than in the United States. However, the custom of inserting a wedge of lime in a bottle of beer is a U.S. invention. The tequila-based cocktail called the margarita is another U.S. favorite, although it is hard to find in Mexico outside of tourist destinations. There are more than 500

Mexican chefs preparing thick tortillas with cooked meats, chilies, and beans. While Mexican dishes vary from region to region, tortillas and beans are staple foods that are eaten across the country.

varieties of tequila, which Mexicans tend to drink plain, followed by a piece of lime and a pinch of salt. The drink is made from the juice of the agave cactus and is named after the town of Tequila in Jalisco state, where it is fermented and distilled. Mescal, made from the roots, stalk, and leaves of the agave cactus, is another popular drink, with a stronger flavor and a cheaper price than tequila. The ancient drink pulque is popular, too, but unheard of outside Mexico. The beverage, which is made from the juice of the maguey plant, was a favorite of the Aztecs. During Spanish rule in Mexico (1521–1821) specialized taverns known as *pulquerías* opened. They were segregated by sex and proved very popular into the twentieth century. Folk murals often adorned *pulquería* walls, including one painted by the artist Frida Kahlo in Mexico City in 1943.

Popular soft drinks in Mexico include *jugos* (fruit juices) and *licuados* (fruit juices mixed with water or milk). These juices range from the extracts of oranges and carrots to those from tropical fruits. Other drinks include *horchata* (extract of tiger nuts) and *agua de arroz* (extract of rice). Mexico is a major producer of coffee, and states such as Veracruz are famous for the flavor of the beans they produce. U.S. soft drinks, such as Coca-Cola and Pepsi, are also very popular in Mexico. In the 1990s Mexicans were reputed to have the highest per capita consumption of Coca-Cola in the world.

Anita Dalal

SEE ALSO:

Agriculture; Aztecs; Festivals; France; Kahlo, Frida; Maya; Texas; Tex-Mex Culture; Trade.

Foreign Debt

Traditionally governments have relied on revenue from taxation, but this rarely provides enough money to fund all the programs for which modern administrations are responsible. In today's global economy more and more developing nations, including Mexico, seek loans from wealthier nations, international financial organizations, or even the private sector. While repaying the loans can benefit a nation's economy, it can also lead to serious financial problems.

Setting a nation's budget is a controversial task for any government. In Mexico, as in the United States, the president presents a budget to the congress, which approves it, usually after attaching budgetary amendments. The resulting compromise is a budget that prioritizes public spending based on revenue raised through taxation and borrowing. Sometimes governments prefer accumulating revenue through borrowing rather than through taxes because increasing taxes can disrupt the economy. Modern economies face the challenge of implementing economic policies that strike a balance between their revenue and their spending.

Mexico's foreign debt

Between 1950 and the early 1970s Mexico enjoyed high economic growth, low inflation, and moderate foreign debt. This era of stability came to an abrupt end during the administration of Luis Echeverría, from 1970 to 1976. After taking office, Echeverría attempted to reform the Import Substitution Industrialization policy, which protected Mexican industry through subsidies to domestic manufacturers and high trade tariffs on foreign imports. Echeverría reduced the subsidies available to Mexican manufacturers, which angered Mexican investors and led them to reduce their support for the country's industries. In addition, the Mexican government introduced new laws to restrict foreign investment in 1973. As a result of these measures, intended to improve Mexico's productivity levels, the government's revenues began to lag behind its spending and it began to acquire more foreign debt.

Mexico's economic problems were temporarily relieved by the discovery of new oil fields in the early 1970s. The government's ownership of the oil company Petróleos Mexicanos (PEMEX) provided the government with a major new source of revenue. In addition, a rise in international oil prices in the mid-1970s gave the Mexican

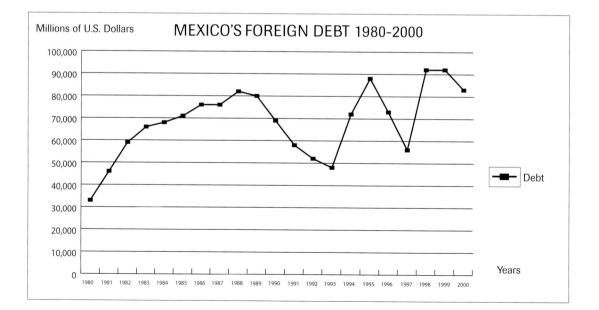

government enough revenue, in theory at least, to regain control of its economy.

The new oil fields proved to be a mixed blessing. The government took on more foreign debt expecting that it could be repaid with future oil revenue. When oil prices collapsed in the late 1970s the government could not find a way to raise the revenue. By the early 1980s Mexico was experiencing soaring inflation and massive capital flight (the loss of foreign investment). Consequently, external creditors refused to grant Mexico further time to repay its foreign debt. The creditors' demands instigated an economic crisis, which lasted from the end of José López Portillo's administration (1976–1982) well into the government of Miguel de la Madrid (1982–1988). During the mid-1980s payment of the interest alone on Mexico's foreign debt consumed most of the government's budget.

The Brady Plan

In February 1989 Mexican president Carlos Salinas started debt negotiations to bring the economic crisis to an end. Mexico obtained a debt restructuring agreement under the Brady Plan, an initiative promoted by the U.S. treasury secretary, Nicholas F. Brady, and strongly supported by the World Bank and the International Monetary Fund (IMF). An agreement in principle was reached on July 23 and the final package was implemented less than a year later. The agreement established favorable terms for Mexico's repayment of the debt it owed to commercial banks, which at the time totaled U.S. $48 billion.

The Brady Plan was set up to resolve the debt problems of all countries in Latin America. Banks and other institutions agreed to cooperate with it on the understanding that debt reduction was essential for the restoration of growth and economic stability in developing nations. The Mexican agreement seemed to bear this out: soon after its implementation the country's interest rates began to fall, private investment increased, and the economy began to grow.

The peso crisis

During 1994 the Mexican government increased its spending to higher than expected levels, causing its foreign exchange reserves to drop from U.S. $30 billion in February that year to $12 billion in early December. The fall alerted foreign investors to renewed instability in Mexico. At the same time,

Mexico owed U.S. $23 billion on its short-term debt, known as *tesobonos* (U.S. dollar-denominated government bonds) but had only $5 billion available to repay the loans. Despite the intention that the *tesobonos* would introduce stability in Mexico's financial market, foreign investors began to lose confidence. Their panic increased the pressure on the Mexican peso. By the end of December the government had little choice but to devalue its currency. As its Central Bank reserves dropped and interest rates and inflation rose, Mexico slipped into another economic crisis.

In 1995 Mexican president Ernesto Zedillo Ponce de León proposed a financial package that included an international short-term credit agreement. In response to his proposal, the IMF, the United States, and Canada assembled a financial rescue package for Mexico worth U.S. $52 billion. The package was intended to convince investors that Mexico had sufficient resources to honor its foreign and national debts. The rescue deal was considered essential in order to prevent the collapse of U.S. private banks and pension funds that had investments in Mexico. Mexican authorities used the money to redeem maturing *tesobonos* and to refinance commercial banks' foreign currency liabilities.

Ending the crisis

Zedillo then set about reducing *tesobonos* liability from U.S. $30 billion to around $9 billion by July 1995, and eliminating it by February 1996. Funds from the international rescue package allowed Mexico to buy back the *tesobonos* as they matured. Once the crisis was over the government was able to focus on developing new strategies for dealing with foreign debt, including negotiations to reduce the costs of borrowing and increasing the repayment periods on loans. In addition, the government accelerated its repayment of the 1995 rescue package. By early 1997 it had repaid the U.S. part of the loan. By April that year it had repaid $3.7 billion of its debt to the IMF. At the start of the twenty-first century Mexico's foreign debt remained high (see chart on page 340) but stood at around 30 percent of gross domestic product and did not represent a threat to its domestic economy.

Miguel Jimenez

SEE ALSO:

Banking and Finance; Devaluation; Globalization; Inflation; Investment; NAFTA; Nationalization; Poverty and Wealth; Presidency, Mexican.

Foreign Policy, Mexican

Historically, Mexico's foreign policy has been defensive, stressing isolationism and nonintervention in other countries' affairs. After its territorial losses to the United States in the mid-nineteenth century, Mexico promoted foreign policies that would shield it and other countries from foreign influence. Since the 1980s, however, this approach to foreign policy has come under pressure from globalization as well as economic and political changes within Mexico.

From the time of Mexico's independence from Spain in 1821 until the election of President Benito Juárez (1806–1872) in 1861, the country's presidency changed hands over 50 times, often through military coups. The resulting political and economic instability did not allow for a consistent or active foreign policy. Instead, the best Mexico could hope for during this period was the extension of central government control over its own territory. Mexico's domestic ambitions did not start well, however. Two years after independence, Central America, then part of Mexico, broke away from the Mexican union and created an independent Central American Federal Republic (also called the United Provinces of Central America). Despite the loss, Mexico demonstrated its power by annexing the state of Chiapas from Guatemala and incorporating it within its southern border.

The threat of U.S. expansionism

In the period after independence relations with the United States remained the most pressing concern for Mexican foreign as well as domestic policy. In response to fears that Texas might be taken over by Anglo-Americans, the Mexican government invited U.S. farmers to settle land in Texas on the condition that they became Mexican subjects and converted to Mexico's state religion of Catholicism. The plan backfired, however. In 1835 the U.S. settlers rose up against what they saw as the oppressive policies of Mexican president Antonio López de Santa Anna (1794–1876), who limited further U.S. immigration and imposed new tariffs on goods the settlers

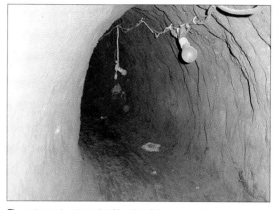

The entrance to a tunnel at Nogales, Arizona, used by smugglers to cross the border. Since the 1990s Mexico's foreign policy initiatives with the United States have cracked down on smuggling.

brought into the state. The following year, after the defeat of Mexican forces by Texan defenders, and to the horror of the political elite in Mexico City, Santa Anna granted Texas its independence. In 1845 the United States annexed Texas and, with its increasingly popular philosophy of Manifest Destiny, considered more ways to increase U.S. territory at Mexico's expense. Through its victory in the Mexican-American War (1846–1848) the United States forced Mexico to sign the 1848 Treaty of Guadalupe Hidalgo, which ceded to the United States most of the present-day states of Texas, New Mexico, Arizona, Utah, Nevada, and California. Five years later, under the terms of the 1853 Gadsden Purchase, Mexico surrendered land to the U.S. government in present-day southern New Mexico and Arizona. As a result of U.S. expansionism and Mexican political weakness, Mexico lost half its territory in the mid-nineteenth century.

Foreign policy in the late 1800s

The Mexican-American War and Mexico's territorial losses taught Mexico's leaders the need to stabilize their government and strengthen their economy in order to prevent additional U.S. encroachment. This concern influenced the policy of Porfirio Díaz's administrations, from 1877 to 1880 and from 1884 to 1911. Díaz encouraged U.S. investment in and ownership of Mexican mining industries and agriculture, which in turn led to improvements in the country's economy and infrastructure. Díaz and Manuel Gonzalez, Mexican president between 1880 and 1884, used U.S. investors to improve Mexico's relations with the U.S. government. Both presidents, for example, appointed foreign investors as Mexican government agents in Washington. Despite the close relationship with investors, Díaz promoted a concept of Mexican nationalism that was, at times, highly critical of U.S. foreign policy. In 1896, for example, he criticized the U.S. Monroe Doctrine, which promoted the United States as the defender of the entire continent against the European powers. Díaz believed that the protection of the Americas was the responsibility of all the nations there.

Noninterventionism

Economic problems in Mexico from 1907 onward highlighted the privileged role of foreign investors in the country and heightened anti-American feelings. These feelings contributed to the Mexican Revolution (1910–1920) and the condemnation of Díaz's foreign policy by the revolution's first president, Francisco I. Madero. Disapproval of growing U.S. economic influence and the need to guard against it became the cornerstones of Mexican foreign policy. Venustiano Carranza, president between 1915 and 1920, rejected the privileges granted to foreign investors by Díaz and outlined a noninterventionist foreign policy that would continue as a theme in Mexico's foreign affairs for much of the twentieth century.

A noninterventionist foreign policy forbids interference in the affairs of other nations, except in the case of self-defense, and balances isolation with high-level international diplomacy. Mexican leaders were able to advocate this approach because the country had no significant foreign investments to protect and did not face major security threats. The weak states of Central America did not pose a security risk, and by the end of the nineteenth century the United States had given up any further territorial ambitions in Mexico.

The foreign policy of Lázaro Cárdenas, Mexican president between 1934 and 1940, was largely non-interventionist. During his administration Mexico became a member of the League of Nations, the international organization established after World War I (1914–1918) to promote world peace. Mexican delegates to the League of Nations in Geneva argued against the interference of one country into the affairs of another, for instance condemning Italian dictator Benito Mussolini's invasion of Ethiopia in 1935. In Mexico itself, Cárdenas rejected foreign interference by taking over control of the holdings of 17 foreign oil companies in March 1938. His action gave the Mexican government control of 90 percent of the country's oil.

World War II (1939–1945)

Mexico's policy of nonintervention changed during World War II, which Mexico entered in 1942. Political maneuvering by Manuel Ávila Camacho, Mexican president between 1940 and 1946, enabled Mexico to make significant economic gains while staunchly supporting the Allied struggle against Germany and Japan. The war led to closer ties between Mexico and the United States, including cooperation between both countries' military forces and both governments' signing of the Bracero Agreement in 1942. The agreement allowed the legal migration of Mexican braceros (fieldworkers) into the United States to help offset U.S. wartime labor shortages. The cooperation led the U.S. government to end its objections to Cárdenas's 1938 oil expropriations. In addition, Ávila Camacho managed to reduce Mexico's foreign debt by 90 percent and obtained U.S. funds to overhaul the country's infrastructure, including major investment to improve its railroads.

Mexico's economic problems following the war led to the return of noninterventionist foreign policies and protectionist economic policies (using tariffs and quotas to protect domestic producers from foreign competition). The start of the cold war between the United States and the Soviet Union resulted in the U.S. government's failure to honor promises to repay Latin American countries for their support during the war. Furthermore, a fall in demand for Mexican braceros in the United States caused many migrants to return south of the border, increasing unemployment levels in Mexico. Consequently, Miguel Alemán Valdés, Mexican president between 1946 and 1952, introduced the economic policy known as import substitution industrialization, which favored state ownership of important industries, high levels of trade protection, and publicly financed industrial policy. Adopted by many countries in Latin America, the approach prescribed economic self-reliance and limited trade with the outside world.

Foreign policy in the 1950s and 1960s

President Alemán and his successor, Adolfo Ruiz Cortines, whose term ran from 1952 to 1958, supported the United States in the cold war, partly out of anticommunist conviction and partly to gain trade concessions through close ties with the United States. Mexican support for U.S. involvement in the Korean War (1950–1953) won Mexico contracts for its mining industries to supply minerals used in U.S. armaments. However, Mexico continued to promote nonintervention in Latin America. In 1954 the United States, fearing the spread of communism in Central America, supported the overthrow of the left-wing president of Guatemala, Jacobo Arbenz. Ruiz Cortines protested the U.S. involvement but failed to openly condemn it, for which he was roundly condemned by ex-president Lázaro Cárdenas.

Adolfo López Mateos, Mexican president between 1958 and 1964, introduced a more assertive foreign policy. While maintaining good relations with the United States, López Mateos was keen to lessen Mexico's dependence on its northern neighbor, and developed political and economic alliances with countries in Europe and Asia. He also defended Cuba's right to pursue the revolutionary policies of its leader, Fidel Castro, despite U.S. economic sanctions. When the United States pressed the Organization of American States to expel Cuba, Mexico was the only country that refused its consent. López Mateos's successor, Gustavo Díaz Ordaz, similarly challenged U.S. dominance by condemning its invasion of the Dominican Republic in 1965.

Guatemalan women in a refugee camp in Campeche, Mexico, in 1990. An influx of refugees from war-torn Guatemala to Mexico in the 1980s led Mexico to seek international cooperation to address the problem.

Foreign policy in the 1970s and 1980s

The Mexican presidents of the 1970s, Luis Echeverría Álvarez and José Lopez Portillo, reverted to the approach of López Mateos. They too sought to reduce Mexican reliance on trade with the United States by forming partnerships with other nations. Echeverría visited 36 countries during his presidency, with the aim of securing trade and investment. He also defied Washington by creating a Latin American trade bloc that included Cuba but excluded the United States, and by negotiating an agreement with the Soviet Union.

In the early 1980s violent conflict in Central America encouraged Mexico to lead a multilateral diplomatic effort to limit U.S. involvement in the region. U.S. president Ronald Reagan viewed the civil wars in Central America as a test of his administration's resolve to fight Soviet influence and supplied arms to the governments of El Salvador and Guatemala as well as to the Contras in Nicaragua, who opposed the left-wing Sandinista government. In an effort to achieve peace and limit U.S. influence, Mexican president Miguel de la Madrid organized a multilateral forum called the Contadora Group. The group called for outside countries—including the United States—to end their military assistance to the warring factions. The negotiations successfully limited foreign interference and marked the peak of Mexico's noninterventionist foreign policy.

The end of noninterventionism

The conflict in neighboring Guatemala, however, forced Mexican foreign policy officials to reconsider the viability of nonintervention. In 1981, while Mexican diplomats pursued efforts to bring Guatemala's military regime and its rebel opposition to the negotiating table, Mexico found itself host to tens of thousands of Guatemalan refugees. Their presence posed a dilemma for policymakers. On the one hand, acceptance of the peasants as political refugees risked damaging relations with the Guatemalan regime and undermining Mexico's role as a peacemaker. The presence of refugees also risked inciting peasants in Mexico's southern state of Chiapas, where there were land-related grievances similar to those in Guatemala. On the other hand, rejecting the refugees would have run contrary to Mexico's long history of accepting Latin American dissidents and would have endangered the lives of the refugees. The Mexican government resolved the dilemma by enlisting the help of the United Nations High Commission for Refugees, the organization set up by the United Nations to provide protection for refugees. Anticipating future changes in Mexican foreign policy, de la Madrid's administration found that international cooperation was better able to solve difficult policy dilemmas than the traditional approach of nonintervention.

Mexico's economic problems, beginning with a recession in 1982, increased the movement toward a new style of foreign policy. De la Madrid's economic reforms—reducing the government's regulation of the economy and lowering tariffs on imported goods—brought the Mexican economy more in line with that of the United States. Mexican presidents of the late 1980s and 1990s, Carlos Salinas de Gortari and Ernesto Zedillo Ponce de León, further aligned Mexico to the United States. Instead of viewing the outside world as a source of interference, Mexico now emphasized the opportunities available from cooperation. The change of approach led Mexico to enter a number of international economic organizations, including the World Trade Organization, the Organization for Economic Cooperation and Development, and the Asia-Pacific Economic Cooperation Forum. The Mexican government also sought new means of influence in its international relations. Instead of relying exclusively on direct channels of communication between Mexico City and Washington, in the 1990s Mexico began to hire lobbyists to advocate its interests with the U.S. government and began to participate in cooperative projects along the Mexico-U.S. border.

Foreign policy and globalization

Keeping pace with worldwide economic change became the first task of the new Mexican foreign policy. Globalization (the international dispersal of production, distribution, and information), together with Mexico's economic reforms, led to an increase in foreign investment. From the 1980s and into the 1990s this investment rose by around 25 percent each year. Most of the capital came from the United States and was geared toward maquiladoras, assembly plants that use low-wage labor in Mexico to create exports from foreign-manufactured components. In 1992, to encourage greater investment and

International Criticism in the 1980s

International criticism of Mexico's domestic affairs contributed to the abandonment of the policy of avoiding international cooperation. Put simply, this policy held that Mexico's nonintervention in other countries' affairs should be matched by other countries' nonintervention in Mexico. The 1985 kidnapping, torture, and assassination of the U.S. Drug Enforcement Administration (DEA) agent Enrique Camarena unleashed a wave of U.S. criticism against corruption and narcotics trafficking in Mexico. Initial suspicions that Mexican police had participated in the murder, later confirmed, redirected U.S. criticism away from the presence of narcotics to an indictment of the entire Mexican political system. Diplomatic protests were followed by temporary closures of U.S. border-crossing points and even by the kidnapping by the DEA of a Mexican citizen in order to pressure Mexico to hand over Camarena's abductors and reform its judicial system. In addition, the U.S. media publicized allegations that Mexican politicians rigged elections and stole public funds. Contradicting the Mexican government's denials, many citizens supplied evidence to support the charges.

International criticism of human rights abuses in Mexico led to another blow to the defense offered by Mexico's traditional foreign policy. In the late 1980s several nongovernmental organizations as well as the Organization of American States echoed the United States' criticisms of the Mexican electoral process and its violations of human rights. While officials initially rebuffed the accusations as the assertion of U.S. values and interference in Mexico's domestic affairs, their arguments became increasingly unpopular with the public. In 1990 President Salinas de Gortari responded to international criticism by creating a National Commission on Human Rights, which advocated recommendations to improve human rights in Mexican law. He also created the independent Federal Electoral Institute to ensure fairer elections and admitted foreign observers to monitor the 1994 elections.

Foreign Policy and Immigration

While the United States and Mexico have liberalized trade and investment policies through the implementation of NAFTA, labor flows remain unregulated and controversial. Every year hundreds of thousands of Mexicans cross the border to find better working conditions in the United States. Past approaches to the issue have been piecemeal: Mexican leaders asked the U.S. government for fair treatment of undocumented Mexican migrants and higher quotas of legally recognized migrants—if they mentioned the issue at all. In a break with the past, President Vicente Fox sought to legalize all migration through an open-border policy and pressed the United States to grant an amnesty for all Mexicans living illegally within U.S. borders. His proposals, guaranteed to generate heated debate in the United States, were temporarily shelved after the terrorist attacks of September 11, 2001, which created a demand for more secure U.S. borders.

add permanency to its trading partnerships, Mexico signed the North American Free Trade Agreement (NAFTA) with the United States and Canada. The agreement planned the eventual elimination of all tariffs on the shipment of goods among the three countries and set investment guidelines that reassured U.S. investors. It also signaled the convergence of the countries' economic policies.

The December 1994 peso crash threatened Mexico's aim of becoming an ever-more important North American trading partner. Mexico's foreign debts and its political instability—including the pro-Indian Zapatista uprising and the assassination of presidential candidate Luis Donaldo Colosio, both in 1994—led investors to sell pesos, driving down their value. Running low on foreign reserves to defend the currency, Mexico appealed to the United States for help. In response, U.S. president Bill Clinton lent Mexico U.S. $20 billion. The loan was repaid ahead of time, although many Mexicans encountered heavy losses as a result of the crisis. One outcome of the peso crash was to signify Mexico's growing vulnerability to international investors and to continue the trend toward further cooperation between Mexico City and Washington.

While President Salinas wed the Mexican economy with its northern counterparts through the adoption of NAFTA, subsequent leaders have attempted to diversify economic links by negotiating trade pacts with other countries. In the 1990s Mexico signed free-trade agreements with other Latin American countries, including Bolivia, Chile, Colombia, Costa Rica, Nicaragua, Venezuela, and the Northern Triangle countries (El Salvador, Guatemala, and Honduras). Outside of the Americas, Mexico created trade agreements with the European Free Trade Association and Israel, and has conducted negotiations with the European Union and several Asian countries. Despite these negotiations, the United States remains Mexico's most important economic partner, accounting for more than three-quarters of its imports and exports at the start of the twenty-first century.

Foreign policy under President Fox

Vicente Fox was elected Mexican president in 2000 and promised to provide Mexico with a strong foreign policy. In contrast to earlier presidents, he supported U.S. efforts in the field of security, including cooperation with campaigns to reduce narcotics smuggling and money laundering. Fox also provided antinarcotics assistance to neighboring countries, such as Belize, and increased funding for narcotics policing in Mexico. Following the September 11, 2001, terrorist attacks, he pledged full support for U.S. president George W. Bush's antiterrorism campaign.

Fox's appointment of the academic Jorge Castañeda as secretary for foreign affairs reflected his foreign policy ambitions. A longtime critic of Mexico's subservient relationship with the United States, Castañeda accepted the job on the condition that he could argue for expanded commercial ties not only with the United States, but also with other countries and international organizations.

Brian Potter

SEE ALSO:

Banking and Finance; Bracero Program; Central America; Foreign Policy, U.S.; Globalization; Maquiladoras; Mexican-American War; Monroe Doctrine; NAFTA; Oil; Presidency, Mexican; Presidency, U.S.; Smuggling; Trade; World War II.

Foreign Policy, U.S.

U.S. foreign policy toward Mexico and the rest of Latin America has changed significantly since the eighteenth century. Initially focused on gaining territory, policy goals shifted to developing a commercial empire, to limiting Soviet influence, and, finally, to encouraging greater political and economic freedom.

Following independence in 1783, the United States was economically and militarily weak compared to its European rivals. British, French, and Spanish possessions in the Americas posed a threat to the new republic's security and its aims of expansion. Since they were unable to rely on economic force or military action, U.S. foreign-policy makers had to find diplomatic ways to counter the European presence. In the early 1800s U.S. diplomacy aimed to prevent Britain and France from gaining control of more colonies in Latin America—including Mexico—then part of Spain's declining empire. To this end U.S. leaders encouraged independence movements in the western territories. While the independent states might forge alliances with the Europeans, at least as independent states they might not belong to a European empire.

The Monroe Doctrine

In addition to encouraging independence movements, the United States promoted the idea that the Americas were different from Europe and should have the freedom to develop democratic governments. This strategy was formalized in 1823 with the declaration of the Monroe Doctrine by U.S. president James Monroe (1758–1831). Monroe declared that the United States would view "any attempt on [the Europeans'] part to extend their political system to any portion of this hemisphere as dangerous to our peace and safety." While the doctrine appeared successful in deterring European interference, in reality the British and French were too preoccupied with developments on their own continent to expend much effort in the Americas. The United States took advantage of its European rivals' preoccupations and pursued territorial expansion in North and South America.

Territorial expansion (1803–1904)

The first major territorial gain for the United States was the Louisiana Purchase of 1803. Fearing further expansion of British power and seeking funds to continue war with Britain, the French leader Napoleon Bonaparte sold to the United States 830,000 square miles (2,150,000 sq km) of land west of the Mississippi River. In exchange for $15 million the United States doubled its size. It then looked to gain control of Spanish-owned Florida. The U.S. Army ocupied Florida, a move that President Monroe and his secretary of state, John Quincy Adams, argued was due to Spain's inability to control the Native Americans in the region. The 1819 Adams-Onís Treaty, signed by Adams and the Spanish ambassador Luis de Onís, recognized this U.S. occupation: Spain ceded control of Florida and all land east of the Mississippi to the United States.

Mexico achieved independence from Spain in 1821 but experienced political and economic uncertainty in the decades that followed. The United States exploited Mexico's weakness to further expand its territory. In 1846, one year after annexing Texas, the United States sent troops to the Rio Grande area in an effort to assert authority over the contested border with Mexico. This action led to the Mexican-American War (1846–1848), in which the United States won a series of battles before capturing Mexico City. Defeat forced the Mexican leadership to agree to the 1848 Treaty of Guadalupe Hidalgo, ceding to the United States much of the present-day Southwest.

The United States expanded its northern frontier, too. In 1846 an agreement with Britain secured U.S. control of the present-day states of Oregon, Washington, and part of Idaho. In 1867 the U.S. Congress purchased Alaska from Russia, while U.S. intervention in Hawaii, beginning in the 1870s, brought it under U.S. ownership by 1900.

Cuba and Panama

U.S. foreign policy toward Cuba and Panama in the early 1900s expanded the United States' sphere of influence. The United States opposed Spain's continuing rule in Cuba: U.S. speculators had invested heavily in the island's mining and farming industries and used force to support a Cuban independence movement. U.S. troops defeated the Spanish in 1898, gaining nominal independence for Cuba. However, between 1901 and 1934 the Platt Amendment to Cuba's new constitution allowed the United States to intervene in the island's affairs. Meantime, U.S. ambitions to become a global naval power focused on the building of a Central American canal to allow quicker passage between the Pacific and Atlantic oceans. One promising site for a canal was Panama, then part of Colombia. However, in 1903 the Colombian legislature refused the United States permission to build the canal, prompting U.S. president Theodore Roosevelt (1858–1919) to support an independence uprising in Panama. The rebellion was a success, and the leaders of the new state allowed the United States to build the canal, which finally opened in 1914.

Expanding economic influence (1904–1934)

In the early decades of the twentieth century U.S. foreign policy moved away from territorial expansion toward increasing its political and economic control over Latin American countries. This policy found greater success in Mexico, Central America, and the Caribbean than in South America, where European powers retained considerable influence through investments and trade. Nevertheless, the U.S. policy of keeping Latin American countries open for U.S. business through military intervention and the support of friendly politicians continued throughout the twentieth century.

In 1904 Theodore Roosevelt justified military intervention in Latin American countries in his Roosevelt Corollary (addition) to the Monroe

This 1896 cartoon shows Uncle Sam defending Latin American countries from European powers, in front of a sign declaring: "Keep Off! The Monroe Doctrine must be respected!" The doctrine was formulated to deter European intervention in the Western Hemisphere.

Doctrine. The corollary was a reaction to the use of force by European nations to collect debts owed by Latin American countries such as Venezuela. Roosevelt declared that any intervention in Latin American nations to ensure that they abided by international law should be carried out by the United States alone. He also declared that international loans to Latin American nations could only be made with Washington's agreement, increasing the United States's economic as well as military influence in the region.

The Mexican Revolution (1910–1920) posed a challenge to the U.S. policy of exerting political and economic influence. The rebellion, led by Francisco I. Madero, threatened the loss of a business-friendly environment for the United States and raised the prospect of political instability across its southern border. Some U.S. diplomats supported the 1913 counterrevolution led by Victoriano Huerta, which aimed to restore to Mexico the policies of Madero's predecessor, Porfirio Díaz. U.S. president Woodrow Wilson, however, favored the promotion of democracy in Mexico and supported the deposition of Huerta in 1914. The United States was able to influence events more successfully in smaller countries, including the Dominican Republic, Nicaragua, Guatemala, Haiti, and Honduras as well as Cuba and Panama. However, while military interventions in these countries successfully protected U.S. investments, they proved to be a major drain on the nation's economy.

The Good Neighbor policy (1933–1945)

Seeking to reduce the costs incurred by interventions in Latin America and to respond to the growing tide of anti-American feeling in South and Central America, in 1933 U.S. president Franklin D. Roosevelt announced the Good Neighbor policy. The new approach led the United States to switch from military interventions to a policy of working with Latin American leaders to encourage economic growth and democracy. The policy also called for U.S. citizens and businesses in Latin America to obey the laws of their host countries and not rely on the protection of the United States. While the policy suggested a reduction in U.S. influence, with the decline of European influence in the region and the rise of authoritarian regimes across Central America and the Caribbean countries, the good neighbor approach actually increased U.S. authority in Latin America.

Trade agreements with countries such as Cuba, Colombia, and Guatemala provided the United States with export markets as well as a source of raw materials. Increased lending to the region, including the creation of the Export-Import Bank of the United States in 1934, allowed the United States to achieve by withholding credit and other forms of economic pressure what had previously been gained through military intervention. When Bolivia expropriated the operations of the U.S.-owned Standard Oil in 1937, the United States withheld loans and pressured other countries in the region to refrain from trade with Bolivia. Resolution of the dispute came without military intervention. The next year Mexican president Lázaro Cárdenas expropriated the holdings of U.S. and British oil companies in Mexico. In response, the foreign oil companies pressed the U.S. State Department to endorse a boycott of Mexican oil but failed to reverse Cárdenas's policy. However, in negotiations after World War II (1939–1945) the Mexican government did agree to let foreign companies provide technology and financing for its oil industry.

The cold war (1945–1990)
After World War II the main security threat to the United States came from the Soviet Union. Consequently U.S. foreign policy became global in scale, and resources were directed primarily to Europe and, to a lesser extent, Asia. While countries such as Mexico greatly felt the impact of these changes, Latin America ceased to be the main concern of U.S. policy makers. With some exceptions—notably the administrations of Dwight D. Eisenhower (1953–1961) and Jimmy Carter (1977–1981)—the general tendency in U.S. foreign policy toward Latin America was to encourage authoritarian regimes to act as a bulwark against Soviet influence. In 1947 the United States asked countries in the region to outlaw national Communist parties and break diplomatic ties with the Soviet Union. In the eyes of U.S. security personnel an authoritarian regime was preferred to left-wing administrations that could result from greater democracy. The United States never questioned the monopoly of power held by Mexico's ruling Partido Revolucionario Institucional (PRI; Institutional Revolutionary Party) and discounted the suspicions of electoral fraud that often circulated in Mexican politics. More significantly still, U.S. intervention in Chile contributed to General

Augusto Pinochet's military coup, which overthrew the elected government of Salvador Allende in 1973 and led to almost two decades of brutal repression.

Influence through investment
In the early period of the cold war, in the late 1940s and 1950s, U.S. economic aid focused on Europe and generally excluded Latin America. However, the Cuban Revolution, which saw Fidel Castro's guerrilla forces overthrow the government of Fulgencio Batista in 1959, nationalize Cuban resources, and sign trade agreements with the Soviet Union, forced U.S. policymakers to reconsider economic development as a means of preventing further communist influence in the region. In 1959 President Eisenhower created the Inter-American Development Bank as a major loan provider for infrastructure projects, such as the development of Cancún as an important Mexican tourist resort in the late 1960s. In 1961 U.S. president John F. Kennedy created the Alliance for Progress, an economic development program to increase economic stability throughout Latin America. The program's charter, which was signed by 22 Latin American countries, stated the goal of achieving social and economic development in Latin America, with the intention that U.S. $10 billion of aid would stimulate greater flows of private capital.

Cold war tensions subsided from the mid-1960s to the mid-1970s but reemerged with the Soviet Union's invasion of Afghanistan in 1979 and the election of the vehemently anticommunist Ronald Reagan as U.S. president the following year. Furthermore, the lack of democracy and land reform in Guatemala, El Salvador, and Nicaragua led to revolutionary conflict in the late 1970s. In Nicaragua the Sandinista movement forced President Anastasio Somoza from power in 1979 and introduced a program of agrarian reform and socialist welfare policies. Fearing the rise of Soviet-influenced administrations across Central America, Reagan pursued a strategy of largely unsuccessful diplomatic punishment and economic sanctions against the Sandinistas. A more effective U.S. tactic was the aid and military assistance given to the Contras, a Nicaraguan guerrilla force opposed to the Sandinistas. Throughout the 1980s the Contras staged attacks on Nicaragua's infrastructure and forced its economy into crisis. The Sandinista government responded with increased force—diverting funds from its successful programs to

A 1970s poster expressing Chilean support for Nicaragua's Sandinista movement. The title translates as "Nicaragua, Chile: two peoples, a single struggle." The United States opposed the left-wing Sandinista government and in the 1980s supported rebellion against it.

improve education and health care in one of the continent's poorest countries. In 1990 voters reacted to their country's economic decline, the Sandinistas' failures to deliver promised social programs, and the prospect of continued U.S. aggression by electing Violeta Chamorro as president over the Sandinistas' Daniel Ortega. Elsewhere, in large part due to the Contadora negotiations established by Mexico, other Central American countries, such as Guatemala and El Salvador, began to experience greater stability. With the collapse of the Soviet Union in 1991 and the rise of democratic politics in Latin America, the cold war era came to an end.

Promoting free trade and democracy

The breakup of the Soviet Union led to the demise of an alternative political-economic model to the U.S. concept of open markets, limited government interference, and democracy. Consequently, after 1991 the United States exercised greater influence in Latin America through the unchallenged status of its own political-economic approach, bolstered by the control over international finance it shared with allies and private investors. At the start of the twenty-first century the objectives of U.S. foreign policy remained those of encouraging demo-

cratically elected governments that pursued market-based economic policies and clamped down on illicit flows of narcotics and on money laundering.

No country better displays the impact of U.S. foreign-policy objectives in the 1990s than Mexico. In the wake of allegations of electoral fraud during the 1988 presidential elections in Mexico, U.S. leaders challenged Mexico to raise the standards of its electoral process. Under a much-reformed system and the watchful eyes of foreign observers, the Partido Acción Nacional's (PAN; National Action Party) Vicente Fox defeated the PRI and won a landmark presidential victory in 2000. Improvements to Mexico's democratic process have encouraged greater levels of foreign investment as well as increasing the role of opposition movements, from the refusal of the Mexican congress to pass some of Fox's initiatives to the Chiapas-based Zapatistas, who campaign for the rights of Indians.

In the 1990s and into the twenty-first century the United States encouraged Latin American nations to adopt free-market economic policies through the use of financial incentives and concerted diplomatic efforts. As a result most countries in the region deregulated their industries, sold state investments, relaxed exchange-rate restrictions, and liberalized trade. Mexico took the most dramatic step toward trade liberalization by signing the North American Free Trade Agreement (NAFTA) with the United States and Canada in 1992. Many Latin American countries would like to follow Mexico's lead, but, despite calls while in office by U.S. presidents Reagan, George H. Bush, and Bill Clinton for a Free Trade Area of the Americas, by 2002 the U.S. Congress stalled any further trade agreements.

At the start of the twenty-first century additional U.S. foreign-policy goals included efforts to stop drug trafficking and money laundering. Along with other Latin American countries, Mexico signed agreements to assist the United States in its enforcement of antinarcotics operations. After the terrorist attacks of September 11, 2001, U.S. leaders increased efforts to achieve international cooperation against money laundering on the grounds that illegal money supplies could fund terrorist networks.

Brian Potter

SEE ALSO:

Adams-Onís Treaty; Central America; Cold War; Cuba; Elections in Mexico; Foreign Policy, Mexican; Good Neighbor Policy; Monroe Doctrine; NAFTA; Oil; Presidency, Mexican; Presidency, U.S.

Fox, Vicente

In 2000 Vicente Fox (born 1942) became the first opposition candidate to win the presidency in Mexico's post-revolutionary era. His victory ended 71 years of rule by the Partido Revolucionario Institucional (PRI; Institutional Revolution Party).

Vicente Fox Quesada was born on July 2, 1942, in Mexico City, the son of a Spanish mother and a father of Irish descent. Fox grew up alongside eight siblings on the family ranch of San Cristobal, in Guanajuato state. His education in Jesuit schools gave him a strong Catholic faith: as a young man Fox even considered becoming a priest. However, he followed his father's wishes and in 1960 entered the Universidad Iberoamericana in Mexico City to study business administration.

After university Fox became a traveling salesman for Coca-Cola. Hard work and determination led to his promotion, in 1975, to chief executive of the company's Mexican operation. In 1979 Coca-Cola offered him a further promotion to head its Latin American operations. Fox turned this down on the grounds that it would have meant living in the United States. He left the company and, with some of his brothers, established the enterprise Grupo Fox, with interests in agriculture and footwear.

Political ambitions

His business prospering, Fox became involved in community issues and, from there, politics. In 1987 he joined the Partido Acción Nacional (PAN; National Action Party), attracted by its right-wing philosophy and mostly Catholic membership. In 1988 he was elected a PAN congressman for his home state of Guanajuato. In 1991 the PAN nominated him to run for the governorship of the state. Fox lost the election, which was nullified after allegations that the PRI committed electoral fraud. In 1995 he ran again and was elected state governor, gaining 60 percent of the vote.

Fox worked relentlessly both as governor and toward his goal of winning the 2000 presidential election. He knew that a conventional campaign would not be enough to defeat the PRI. In order to raise his profile he set up a national network, called

Fox, Vicente
Mexican businessman and president

Born: *July 2, 1942*
Mexico City

1975	Becomes head of Coca-Cola, Mexico
1987	Joins PAN party
1988	Elected congressman for Guanajuato
1995	Elected governor of Guanajuato
2000	Elected president of Mexico

Amigos de Fox (Friends of Fox). By early 1999 he had become a familiar face throughout Mexico. In November that year the PAN nominated him as their presidential candidate. Not everyone in the party was pleased. Fox's unorthodox political style, including his informal manner of speaking and use of irreverent catchphrases, was frowned upon by some party leaders. It proved popular with the Mexican public, however, who viewed Fox as a man of the people rather than a typical politician.

In the run-up to the election in July 2000, opinion polls predicted a close race between Fox and the PRI's Francisco Labastida. The actual result was a clear victory for Fox, who won 42.5 percent of the vote compared to Labastida's 36 percent. On December 1 Fox took office as the first non-PRI president since the Mexican Revolution (1910–1920). His cabinet consisted of business leaders, academics, and politicians, representing a wide range of political beliefs. His main goals were to strengthen Mexico's international image through a strong foreign policy, to improve Mexico's economy and its trade relations with the United States, to end government corruption and the influence of drug cartels, and to calm social unrest in states such as Chiapas, where the Zapatista movement led the struggle to improve the lives of Indians.

Héctor Manuel Lucero

SEE ALSO:

Elections in Mexico; Partido Acción Nacional; Partido Revolucionario Institucional; Zapatistas.

France

France played an important role in the history of Mexico. This involvement reached a climax in 1862, when French emperor Napoleon III (1808–1873) installed a puppet ruler, Maximilian (1832–1867), on the country's throne. The period of Maximilian's rule, which lasted until his overthrow in 1867, is known as the French intervention.

When the French explorer René-Robert Cavelier de La Salle planted a flag at the mouth of the Mississippi River on April 9, 1682, he had Mexico, at the time Spanish colonial territory, on his mind. His charter from Louis XIV read in part "We have the more willingly entertained the proposal, since we have nothing more at heart than the exploration of the country through which, to all appearance, a way may be found to Mexico."

During his next expedition in 1684, taking place at a time of war between Spain and France, La Salle planned to create a colony on the Rio Grande, to serve as a base for expeditions to seize Spanish Mexico's northern silver mines. The expedition failed, and La Salle was killed. However, from this point onward the Spanish government in Mexico would have to deal with a potential threat on its northern border, especially after the permanent establishment of a French colony at Biloxi, in present-day Mississippi, in 1699. The settlement grew into the colony of Louisiana, which separated Mexico from Spanish-owned Florida.

Illegal trade

Although a mission settlement was established in Corpus Christi by 1690, Spanish expansion into present-day Texas was slow at first. An important influence in drawing the Spanish into Texas was the 1713 expedition of the French adventurer Louis Juchereau de St. Denis, who was hoping to establish a trading relationship between Louisiana and Mexico. This was specifically forbidden by viceregal policy, which was firmly aimed at keeping all trade in Spanish hands. Initially invited in by Spanish friars hoping to stimulate a reaction from the Mexican government, St. Denis successfully avoided

imprisonment and established a very profitable trading post on the Red River.

By 1716 a Spanish mission was established on the commonly accepted Mexico-Louisiana border at what is now Robeline, Louisiana. The outpost was known as San Miguel de Lunares de los Adaes and served as the capital of the province of Texas for many years. Although trade was in theory illegal, the inhabitants of the Spanish missions needed French goods and the colony of Louisiana needed Spanish money. Smuggling was therefore an important activity in the region for a long time.

For much of the seventeenth and early eighteenth centuries France, Spain, and Great Britain had been involved in a three-way struggle to achieve hegemony in the Americas. The struggle eventually reached a climax in the French and Indian War (1754–1763), in which Britain defeated France. As a result of this conflict, France ceded all of its North American territory east of the Mississippi River to Britain. Another effect of the conflict was that Louisiana passed to Spain.

Spain was slow to integrate the French colony and the first governor did not arrive until 1769. A passport system was then put in place to regulate the movement of former French subjects into New Spain proper. During the American Revolutionary War (1775–1783), Louisiana briefly passed again into French hands, but the French emperor Napoleon was in no real position to establish imperial authority in the Americas and eventually sold Louisiana to the United States in 1803. Mexico would never again directly border French territory.

After Mexico gained its independence in 1821, French traders began to establish themselves in the region. Although French investment in Mexico did not match that of Great Britain in scale, it led to the formation of a sizable colony of French residents, the welfare of whom would influence French behavior toward Mexico. Because the French monarchy had little sympathy for the Mexican republic, relations between Mexico and France were generally poor between 1821 and 1848. Indeed, during the final stages of the Mexican struggle for independence, several French politicians proposed that a member of the French royal family should take the country's throne. The idea was abandoned because of the opposition of the Spanish king, Ferdinand VII.

Trade disputes nearly led to war in 1830. Also, in 1838, long-running issues of forced loans on French citizens, violations of commercial treaties, and "disrespect" to French warships led to an episode of gunboat diplomacy in which a French fleet blockaded Mexican ports and seized the fort at Veracruz. Peace was finally ratified on July 6, 1839. The conflict had little long-term effect apart from increased disorder within Mexico.

After his country's defeat in the Mexican-American War (1846–1848), the Mexican president, Antonio López de Santa Anna, approached France and Britain for aid in protecting his country from further U.S. expansion, even offering to step down in place of a European-appointed monarch for the sake of stability. This plan came to nothing, but it set a precedent of intervention.

The French intervention

From 1858 Mexico was plagued by civil war waged between liberal anticlerical armies under Benito Juárez (1806–1872) and conservative, proclerical forces headed initially by Felix Zuloaga. In 1861 Juárez managed to take Mexico City but was forced by an empty treasury to suspend payments on all foreign debt. Spurred on by conservative exiles in France, the French emperor Napoleon III took this as an opportunity to intervene. By doing so, he hoped to block U.S. expansion, guarantee French economic interests in Latin America, and improve relations with Austria by offering the Mexican crown to Maximilian, the younger brother of the Hapsburg emperor Francis Joseph.

Initially, Napoleon's plans were not made public. France merely joined Spain and Great Britain in the "Tripartite Convention" of October 31, 1861, in which the three countries agreed to use joint naval action to demand Mexican protection of their subjects and payment of debts.

Spain and Great Britain pulled out of the assault shortly after it started, the result of a disagreement with the French as to the aims of the expedition. The French continued their attack, but in May 1862, French forces were beaten back from the town of Puebla by the Juarist general Ignacio Zaragoza. The French did not finally take the town until a year later. Although the French army entered Mexico City on June 7, Juárez had already withdrawn. He relocated his government to the town of San Luis Potosí, from where he orchestrated a guerrilla campaign against the French invaders.

Maximilian arrived to take the throne of Mexico in May 1864. The new emperor was good-natured but naive and had virtually no experience of government. The little support that the emperor enjoyed in his new country came from ultra-conservative politicians aligned with the church. However, he alienated many of these supporters by declaring that church property nationalized by the Juárez regime would not be returned. Desperate to gain popularity among his subjects, Maximilian toured the country extensively. At the same time, however, the French general Achille-Francois Bazaine carried out a ruthless pacification campaign, pushing Juárez's forces northward.

By late 1865 Maximilian's situation was looking hopeless. The Juarist guerrillas still presented a formidable threat and the emperor's government still had no support from anyone except extreme conservatives. Maximilian now also encountered diplomatic pressure from the United States. Between April 1861 and April 1865 the U.S. Civil War had ensured that the U.S. government had shown little interest in the internal affairs of Mexico. In November, 1865, however, U.S. secretary of state William H. Seward declared that the United States would not recognize any government opposed to that of Juárez. Attempts to link French troop withdrawal to recognition of Maximilian's government failed, and on January 15, 1866, Napoleon sent Maximilian a letter informing him of his decision to pull out all troops by 1867.

Fall of Maximilian

Maximilian was urged to abdicate by members of the French government, but the emperor refused to leave until some sort of national assembly was set up to decide the basis of the new government. Despite the fact that he only had few loyal troops under his command, the emperor took a stand against Juarist forces at the city of Querétaro. He held out for two months but eventually surrendered on May 15, 1867. He was executed by firing squad on June 19. France was never again to play a major role in the history of Mexico.

Bruce Munro

SEE ALSO:

Civil War, U.S.; Juárez, Benito; Maximilian; Spain; Spanish Empire.

Free Trade

Free trade is a policy by which a government does not intervene in any way with the import or export of goods and services by adding duties, taxes, or other trade barriers. However, all governments, including those of Mexico and the United States, regulate overseas trade to a greater or lesser extent, restricting free trade in order to protect the domestic economy.

International free trade is generally regarded as a good policy for the optimal development of the world's output and income levels. Yet, when governments want to control international trade, they usually impose import tariffs, import quotas, and export subsidies (also known as export incentives). This policy is known as protectionism.

At the Bretton Woods conference toward the end of World War II (1939–1945), freer trade policies were recommended in order to stimulate postwar economies. Since World War II, tariffs on industrial products have fallen steeply and were close to an average of 4 percent in industrial countries by 1999.

In the first decades after World War II, the world economy grew at a high rate that was partly the result of lowered trade barriers. Economic growth averaged 5 percent per year while world trade grew even faster, averaging 8 percent. Many economists argue that such figures show a link between freer trade and economic growth.

Free trade and economic growth

The argument in favor of free trade runs as follows: all countries, even the poorest, have assets—human, industrial, natural, financial—which they can use to produce goods and services for their domestic markets or to sell abroad. A country can benefit when these goods and services are traded. The principle of comparative advantage holds that countries prosper by using their assets in order to concentrate on what they can produce best and by trading these products for products that other countries produce best. When it comes to trading in an international market, most companies recognize that the bigger the market the greater their potential profits: they can expand until they are at their most efficient size, while at the same time they

This 1879 engraving shows members of a U.S. trade delegation being entertained after a reception by the Mexican president, Porfirio Díaz.

have access to large numbers of customers. In other words, liberal trade policies—policies that allow the unrestricted flow of goods and services—multiply the rewards that result from producing the best products, with the best design, at the best price.

World Trade Organization

The exceptional growth in world trade in the second half of the twentieth century saw merchandise exports growing by an average 6 percent annually. Total trade in 1997 was 14 times that of 1950. The multilateral trading system was overseen by the General Agreement on Tariffs and Trade (GATT), established in 1948 with the United States as one of the founding members. GATT existed to foster free trade and eliminate trade barriers.

GATT was replaced in 1995 by a permanent body, the World Trade Organization (WTO). By the time the WTO came into being, 125 countries had signed on to GATT, and its agreements covered 90 percent of world trade. The WTO has helped to create and promote a free-trading system that was developed through a series of trade negotiations, or rounds, held under GATT. The first rounds dealt mainly with tariff reductions, but later negotiations included areas such as anti-dumping and non-tariff measures. The eighth round, the 1986–1994 Uruguay Round, led to the creation of the WTO. Some negotiations continued after the end of the Uruguay Round. For example, in February 1997, 69 governments agreed to wide-ranging liberalization measures on telecommunications services. In the same year, 40 governments concluded negotiations for tariff-free trade in information technology products.

Change of economic policy

Mexico joined GATT in 1986. This was part of a radical change in policy during the administration of President Miguel de Madrid (1982–1988). Mexico began to open its economy to trade after 40 years of import-substitution industrialization (ISI). The policy of ISI was designed to encourage the domestic production of previously imported goods through protectionist policies and concessions to domestic manufacturers. Imports were generally restricted by import licensing.

De la Madrid introduced policies geared toward external markets. This involved both a reduction of import-substitution barriers and a relaxation of controls on exports. The government moved quickly, drastically lowering most trade barriers within three years. In 1985 Mexico's average tariff was 23.5 percent, and import-license requirements covered 92.2 percent of national production. By 1987 import-license coverage had been reduced to 25.4 percent of national production and average tariffs were reduced to 11.8 percent with a maximum rate of 20 percent. The government also abolished export controls and devalued the nominal exchange rate. Mexico was the first Latin American country to adopt U.S.-backed, neoliberal trade policies because the country needed U.S. aid to overcome the economic collapse of the 1980s.

Mexico's reduction of import barriers and removal of disincentives for exporting had the effect of opening the economy to trade. International trade as a percentage of gross domestic product (GDP) increased from 24 percent in 1980 to 48 percent in 1995. Mexico's entry into GATT greatly enhanced external trade in both directions, both imports and exports. During the first half of the 1990s there was a strong deficit in the trade balance, mainly caused by the overvaluation of the peso against the U.S. dollar, which partly generated the deep financial crisis of the mid-1990s.

The result of Mexico's signing of GATT can be seen in the sharp growth in the manufacturing sector's share in total exports: from 35 percent to 56 percent in one year. This trend is consistent with the reforms focused on fostering export activity.

Later free-trade policies

During the 1990s Mexico continued to follow policies based on a market-oriented model. Apart from unilaterally reducing tariffs and eliminating other barriers to international trade, Mexico also made several trade agreements. The most significant in terms of volume of trade was the North America Free Trade Agreement (NAFTA), which brought Canada, Mexico, and the United States together in the second largest free-trade area in the world after the European Economic Area (EEA). Other trade agreements included the "Group of Three" trade agreement with Colombia and Venezuela, and bilateral free-trade agreements with Bolivia, Costa Rica, Chile, Israel, and the European Union.

Miguel Jimenez

SEE ALSO:

Banking and Finance; Devaluation; Globalization; Investment; Madrid, Miguel de la; Manufacturing; NAFTA; Protectionism; Smuggling; Tariffs; Trade.

Fronterizos

Today, the term *fronterizos* is roughly synonymous with "borderlanders." It is used to refer to the inhabitants of the strip of land that follows the Mexico-U.S. border along the Rio Grande and across the northern deserts, an area of land that was once part of Mexico and is now part of the United States. The region is home to millions of people and, on the Mexican side of the border, heavy industry. Many of the region's distinctive features were in place by the beginning of the twentieth century.

In the early eighteenth century the inhabitants of present-day northern Mexico and the Southwest United States were not borderlanders because there were no real, clear-cut borders. Instead, these people were *fronterizos*, or frontier people, inhabitants of a thinly populated area that was only tenuously delineated. The area was considered an inhospitable wilderness, distant from the Mexican capital and exposed to the attacks of such tribes as the Comanche and the Apache. The *fronterizos* thus had to achieve a high degree of self-reliance. In particular, they established economic links with traders from the United States.

Regional autonomy
In 1821 Mexico became independent from Spain. In the years following independence, many people in the border region began to resent the control that was being exerted from a capital that lay hundreds of miles to the south. These feelings of resentment were strong enough to inspire several rebellions against the central government.

The most famous, and most successful, revolt occurred in Texas. Shortly before independence Anglo settlers had begun to arrive in the region in large numbers. By the early 1830s many Texans, both Anglo and Mexican, had become angered by the policies of the central government, particularly those regarding taxation and the closing of the border to new immigrants. In 1835 a Texan volunteer force took up arms against the Mexican president, Antonio López de Santa Anna. The Texan

forces proved victorious, and in 1836 Texas became an independent republic.

The Texas Revolution has often been depicted simply as a conflict between Anglos and Mexicans, but in fact it can be more accurately seen as an attempt by the inhabitants of a border state to achieve autonomy from any national government. After Texas's successful secession, there were revolts in other northern areas of Mexico, including California in 1836 and Sonora in 1837, although these proved to be unsuccessful.

In 1848 Mexico ceded much of its northern territories to the United States under the terms of the Treaty of Guadalupe Hidalgo. The decades after the signing of the treaty were marked by great civil unrest, and during this period several border regions became virtually autonomous. For example, in the 1850s and 1860s the military leader Santiago Vidaurri established a powerbase in Nuevo Léon. The state's capital, Monterrey, became an important economic center, its wealth based largely on trade with the United States.

The making of the modern border region
The power of local bosses such as Vidaurri was at least partially contained during the presidencies of Porfirio Díaz (1877–1880 and 1884–1911). Diaz positively encouraged foreign investment in the country, and during his presidency Mexico's northern states became heavily industrialized as U.S. firms invested in the area. At the same time many Mexicans crossed the border to work on the railroads that were being built across the Southwest. Later, during the violent years of the Mexican Revolution (1910–1920), many more Mexicans crossed the border in search of work, mainly serving as agricultural laborers. Thus, by the early twentieth century two characteristics of the border region that are recognizable today were already in existence: heavy industrialization and a Mexican culture that straddles the border.

Bruce Munro

SEE ALSO:

Borderlanders; Díaz, Porfirio; Frontier; Guadalupe Hidalgo, Treaty of; Madero, Francisco I.; Texas Revolution; Villa, Francisco "Pancho."

Frontier

The frontier between Mexico and the United States has been fixed in virtually the same position for almost 150 years, since the Gadsden Purchase of 1853. The border runs from the West Coast between San Diego and Tijuana to the Gulf of Mexico between Brownsville and Matamoros.

Over the course of its 2,079-mile (3,326-km) length, the border constitutes the southern frontier of the U.S. states of California, Arizona, New Mexico, and Texas, and the northern Mexican boundary of Baja California, Sonora, Chihuahua, Coahuila, Nuevo Leon, and Tamaulipas.

From the mouth of the Tijuana River on the Pacific coast, the frontier passes eastward over the mountains of the Sierra de Juárez, then between the twin towns of Calexico, California, and Mexicali, Baja California, before descending into the valley of the Colorado River. For a short distance it doubles back on itself, following the river for 20 miles (32 km) southwest between Arizona and Baja California. Then, near San Luis Río Colorado, it turns east again, climbing gradually through the Sonoran Desert, passing north of the Mexican cities of Nogales and Agua Prieta at the northern end of the Sierra Madre Occidental before meeting the Rio Grande just west of the twin cities of El Paso, Texas, and Ciudad Juárez, Chihuahua.

The eastern half of the frontier's length—1,200 miles (1,930 km)—follows the Rio Grande as it flows southeast until reaching the Gulf of Mexico, passing through the Chihuahua Desert, several deep gorges south of Big Bend National Park, Texas, several pairs of twin cities—Del Rio and Ciudad Acuña, Laredo and Nuevo Laredo, McAllen and Reynosa, and Brownsville and Matamoros—and finally crossing broad sweeps of cultivated land on the alluvial plain of the lower Rio Grande valley.

Northern territories

The border has not always followed this route. For most of the history of the United States it was many miles to the north. The first Europeans to explore the area that now straddles the border were the Spanish—the conquistadores Alvar Nuñez Cabeza De Vaca and Francisco Vázquez de Coronado—between 1535 and 1540. In 1609 Santa Fe, in what is now New Mexico, was established as the capital of the Spanish territory of Nuevo Mexico, and more than 100 years later the colonial Spanish founded about 30 missions in what is now Texas. The Spanish influence continued in the eighteenth century—San Diego, California, was founded in 1769; Tucson, Arizona, in 1776; and San Antonio, Texas, in 1795. By the end of the century the Spanish population of Nuevo Mexico was 20,000.

In 1810 the *Mapa del Virreinato de Nueva España* in the *Atlas Supplementaire Geographie Universelle de Malte-Brun* showed the Spanish viceroyalty of New Spain including the entire present-day Mexico, Florida, and Cuba, plus much of the modern day southwestern states of the United States. The state of Louisiana was the only part of the United States to touch the Gulf of Mexico. The northern boundary of New Spain ran along the 42nd Parallel, roughly where the states of California and Oregon meet today. The 1819 U.S. treaty with Spain set the frontier along the Sabine River running north from the Gulf of Mexico, then along the Red and Arkansas Rivers to the Rocky Mountains, then west along the 42nd Parallel to the Pacific Ocean. Coahuila included much of modern Texas, Nuevo León extended from Durango well into New Mexico, and Sonora reached well into Arizona. Also, New Mexico extended far north of its present boundaries.

Guadalupe Hidalgo

When Mexico gained its independence from Spain in 1821, its border with the United States was defined in the Adams-Onís Treaty of 1819. However, independence opened up a period of border conflicts. During the next 27 years, Mexico lost around half its territory to the United States. Twice, in that period, the United States tried to buy Texas. Significantly, in view of what was to happen later, the southern boundary of Texas followed the Nueces River, well to the north of the modern Texas-Mexico boundary along the Río Bravo del Norte (or Rio Grande as it is known in the United

States), which was then entirely in the Mexican states of Chihuahua, Coahuila, and Tamaulipas.

In the 1830s Texas experienced a massive immigration of Anglo-Americans. The Mexican government's decision to amalgamate the states of Coahuila and Texas—with the state capital of Saltillo several hundred miles away from many of the state's inhabitants—added to the alienation felt by many Texans. In 1836 Texas declared independence from Mexico, and after victory over Mexico at the Battle of San Jacinto, the independent Republic of Texas was established. Inhabitants of other northern states also were unhappy about being governed by a central government in Mexico City. There were unsuccessful revolts in California in 1836, in New Mexico and Sonora in 1837, and in the lower Rio Grande Valley in 1840. The last rebellion resulted in the creation of the short-lived Republic of the Rio Grande, shifting the Mexican frontier to the south.

The government of President Antonio López de Santa Anna (1794–1876) regarded Texas as a rebellious province that would someday be brought back into the Mexican fold, but nine years later, in December 1845, the U.S. Congress voted to annex Texas and sent troops to the Rio Grande to defend the border—despite the fact that the Mexicans regarded the Texan border as being farther north, along the Nueces River. Armed clashes ensued, and Congress declared war on Mexico. U.S. forces took the Mexican city of Monterrey, and—farther west—huge swathes of New Mexico, Chihuahua, and California were occupied by American troops. Effective Mexican resistance ended when Mexico City fell in August 1847.

On February 2, 1848, the Treaty of Guadalupe Hidalgo was signed. Most dramatic of its provisions was the ceding of 525,000 square miles (1,360,000 sq km) of Mexican territory to the United States. In return for U.S. $15 million compensation for war-

The Mexican-U.S. border has changed position many times since the Adams-Onís Treaty of 1819. The most significant change came with the Treaty of Guadalupe Hidalgo in 1848, when Mexico ceded California, New Mexico, Arizona, Utah, Nevada, Wyoming, and part of Colorado.

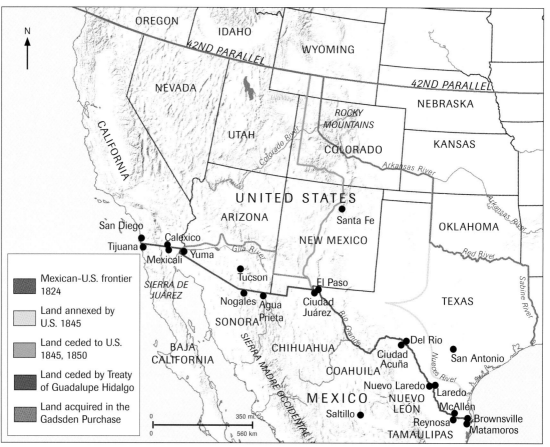

An aerial photograph of the Mexican-U.S. border running along the natural barrier of Río Bravo del Norte (Rio Grande). Here the river separates the state of Texas in the north from the Mexican state of Chihuahua in the south (foreground).

related damage to Mexican property, present-day Arizona, California, New Mexico, and parts of Wyoming, Utah, Nevada, and Colorado were taken from Mexican control and became part of the United States. The *1851 Map of the Republic of Mexico* shows the newly incorporated American states of Texas and California and also the New Mexico Territory occupying all the land between the two. The Arizona Territory did not yet exist.

Gadsden Purchase

Since 1850 the eastern half of the U.S.-Mexico border has changed little, but at that time the western section of the frontier ran along the Gila River, north of the present border in what is now southwestern New Mexico and southern Arizona. The territory between the two lines was mostly poor quality land. The shape of the boundary was to change again, partly as a result of the ambitious plans of James Gadsden (1788–1858), a former soldier, and president of the South Carolina Railroad Company. Gadsden wanted to connect the railroads of the southern states with the Pacific so the West would be commercially dependent on the

South, instead of the North. However, that plan involved the difficult and expensive challenge of constructing a new railroad through the southern Rockies. Gadsden was advised that an easier option was to route the railroad from El Paso, through Tucson to Phoenix—a gentler terrain, but one that was still part of Mexico. As Gadsden had been appointed U.S. minister to Mexico by President Franklin Pierce (1853–1857), he was in a perfect position to broker a deal. Mexico needed money and Gadsden and his business associates wanted the land. In 1853 Gadsden agreed to pay the Mexican government of Santa Anna U.S. $10 million for a strip of territory covering 30,000 square miles (78,000 sq km) south of the Gila River—an area almost as large as Pennsylvania. The Gadsden Purchase, as the deal became known, was deeply unpopular in Mexico, where it was seen as another territorial submission to an increasingly powerful neighbor to the north. Gadsden was recalled as U.S. minister and did not live to see the completion of the South Pacific Railroad. However, by 1854 the newly established territory was marked on a map in Colton's *Atlas of the World*.

In 1889 the International Boundary Commission (IBC) was set up to clarify previous frontier treaties and make recommendations on boundary disputes. With the course of the Rio Grande prone to periodic shifts, the IBC was called into action on many occasions. One long-running dispute concerned El Chamizal, a 437-acre (177-ha) parcel of land near El Paso. Lost to the United States in the nineteenth century, this land was returned to Mexico in 1967 after the two countries signed the Chamizal Convention in 1963, which entailed relocating the river in a fixed concrete channel to prevent any further changes of course.

The modern frontier

For most of its history, rivers have demarcated much of the frontier—notably the Rio Grande and Gila River. Apart from border checkpoints on road crossings, much of the remainder has been unmarked and unguarded. However, in the last decades of the twentieth century undocumented immigration and cross-border drug trafficking emerged as major problems in relations between the United States and Mexico. The U.S. Border Patrol

The metal-tube border wall at Imperial Beach viewed from the Mexican side. The 8-feet (2.5 -m) high wall extends over 300 feet (91.4 m) into the Pacfic Ocean, dividing the two countries.

estimated that it stops about one in every three of those trying to cross the frontier illegally, and maybe one million are successful in getting across, most in the border cities. The United States has responded by making the border more of a physical barrier.

Operation Gatekeeper, a U.S. Border Patrol crackdown on undocumented immigrants, was launched in October 1994. Fences were built to create a barrier against illegal entry in areas where illegal border crossings are particularly common, for example, south of San Diego, California. The 47-mile (75-km) long San Diego-Tijuana fence—constructed from metal landing mats recycled from the Gulf War—was built in response. It proved insufficient, however, for migrants were able to cut their way through it. From 2001 to 2002 a parallel wall was built a few hundred feet to the north. The wall includes 18-foot (5.5-m) high concrete bollard pilings topped with tilted metal mesh screens and an experimental cantilevered wire-mesh fence. As it runs into the Pacific Ocean, the wall becomes eight-foot (2.5-m) metal tube fencing. Miles of stadium night lights, more than 1,000 seismic detectors, numerous infrared sensors, and armed patrols with sophisticated night-vision equipment help detect the movement of people at night. Between 1995 and 2001 along the border fence near San Diego an estimated 340 Mexicans perished, presumably while trying to cross that stretch of the frontier—a rate of one a week; 120 of the dead were never identified.

With no short-term resolution likely to resolve either of the twin problems of human and narcotics traffic across the border, it seems inevitable that the frontier increasingly will become more of a physical presence. Even in Texas, where the Rio Grande provides a natural obstacle, the Border Patrol in 2001 proposed a 90-mile (144-km) fence along sections of its northern shore, complete with 4,000 lights and 165 surveillance cameras. Separate projects in the state include construction of an 8-foot (2.5-m) chainlink fence between the two international bridges in Brownsville, closed-circuit television mounted on tall poles in Laredo, and powerful floodlights along the Rio Grande's northern shore.

Tim Harris

SEE ALSO:

Adams-Onís Treaty; Borderlanders; Border Patrol, U.S.; Boundary Disputes; Chamizal, El; Fronterizos; Gadsden Purchase; Guadalupe Hidalgo, Treaty of.

Gadsden Purchase

The 1853 Gadsden Purchase was the last step in the United States' acquisition of one-half of Mexico's territory. By signing it Mexico ceded territory to the United States in what is today southern Arizona and southern New Mexico.

After accepting defeat in the Mexican-American War (1846–1848) Mexico signed the 1848 Treaty of Guadalupe Hidalgo. Under its terms the United States annexed New Mexico, West Texas, Arizona, California, and parts of Colorado and Utah. However, tensions along the new border made further negotiations between the two countries likely in the early 1850s.

One source of tension was a boundary dispute between New Mexico and the Mexican states of Chihuahua and Sonora, the result of ambiguous wording in the 1848 treaty. American settlers and Mexicans who had been forced out of New Mexico and Arizona claimed their rights to territories and threatened an outbreak of violence in the region. Another conflict arose from Article XI of the treaty, which bound the United States to prevent Native American raids into Mexico from north of the border. The undertaking placed a strain on the U.S. economy. Between 1848 and 1853 the United States spent 12 million U.S. dollars policing the border but failed to prevent further raids.

U.S. transportation links

U.S. transportation needs were the other motivation for the negotiations that led to the Gadsden Purchase. The 1848 treaty had failed to secure U.S. rights of transit across the Isthmus of Tehuantepec on Mexico's southern border. These rights would secure the free movement of U.S. citizens and goods south of Mexico. In addition, the start of the California Gold Rush in 1848 increased demands for a railroad from New Orleans to California. Supporters of the proposed railroad argued that the best route passed through territory on the Mexican side of the border.

In 1853 the U.S. government appointed James Gadsden (1788–1858) as U.S. minister to Mexico, with responsibility for resolving the disputed issues. During negotiations with the Mexican president

The land acquired by the Gadsden Purchase completed the extension of U.S. territory begun in 1848. The new territory facilitated the building of a railroad that brought gold diggers to California in the 1850s.

Antonio López de Santa Anna (1794–1876) Gadsden's ambitious initial proposals to acquire most of the remaining territories in northern Mexico met with fierce opposition. Santa Anna appealed to Spain and Britain for help in resisting the U.S. demands. However, the failure of these appeals and the massive scaling down of Gadsden's proposals, together with the poor state of Mexico's finances, led Santa Anna to sign the Gadsden Purchase on December 30, 1853.

In return for U.S. $10 million Mexico ceded the United States 30,000 square miles (78,000 sq km) of territory in present-day New Mexico and Arizona, as well as agreeing to the removal of Article XI from the Treaty of Guadalupe Hidalgo and granting the U.S. rights of transit across the Isthmus of Tehuantepec. Santa Anna's signing of the agreement increased criticisms of his regime and contributed to his downfall in 1855, while fueling tension between liberals and conservatives.

Carlos F. Ortega

SEE ALSO:

Frontier; Guadalupe Hidalgo, Treaty of; Mexican-American War; Santa Anna, Antonio López de.

361

A Purépecha Indian woman weaving in Angahuan, Michoacán. García Canclini spent time with the Purépecha and attempted to explain the often overlooked meanings behind their traditional crafts and beliefs.

cultures, practices, and artifacts are hybrids, resulting from the intermingling of different societies, languages, and experiences. Nowhere illustrates this hybridization more than Mexico, a developing nation with a history of both ancient Indian cultures and Spanish colonization, and which also shares a border with the world's richest country. García Canclini argues that Mexican American culture demonstrates hybrid forms, too. Chicano lowrider cars, for example, subvert a classic symbol of U.S. culture: lowrider owners lower their cars to be nearer the ground and decorate them with Mexican and Chicano images.

Hybrid Cultures takes as its starting point the modernizing drive most Latin American leaders urged for their countries in the 1990s. This drive involved embracing new technologies as well as new economic and political models, such as globalization—the increased movement of trade, investment, and information between countries. García Canclini questions whether this drive replaces traditional cultural practices. He contends that it does not; rather, hybrids develop as a result of the interaction between the old and the new. For instance, Latin American governments—such as Argentina's—may adopt modern democratic and free market economic systems but may still retain aspects of their authoritarian past.

Diverse roles

In addition to his writing, García Canclini has taught at and advised a number of institutions. He has held visiting teaching appointments at many universities, including the University of Texas at Austin, the University of Buenos Aires, and Stanford University. His knowledge of the interaction of different cultures led to his appointments to both the United Nations Educational, Scientific, and Cultural Organization (UNESCO) and the Organization of American States (OAS). In 1995 he published *Consumidores y ciudadanos: Conflictos multiculturales de la globalización* (published in English in 2001 as *Consumers and Citizens: Globalization and Multicultural Conflicts*), an exploration of the effects of urbanization as well as global media and capital flows on citizens. The following year he received a humanities diploma for achievement in aesthetics, theory, and art history from the Argentine Konex Foundation, which awards academics who serve as role models to young people.

Miguel A. Segovia

SEE ALSO:

Anthropology; Border Studies; Lowriders; Globalization; Indian Policy; Michoacán; NAFTA.

García Canclini, Nestor
Argentine sociologist and anthropologist

Born:	December 1, 1939
	La Plata, Argentina

1968	Publishes study of Argentine poet Julio Cortázar
1974	Teaches at University of Buenos Aires, Argentina
1975	Gains first Ph.D. from the National University of La Plata, Buenos Aires
1978	Gains second Ph.D. from the University of Paris, France
1979	Publishes *La producción simbólica* (Symbolic production)
1982	Publishes *Las culturas populares en el capitalismo* (*Transforming Modernity*)
1990	Publishes *Culturas híbridas* (*Hybrid Cultures*)
1995	Publishes *Consumidores y ciudadanos* (*Consumers and Citizens*)

Globalization

The Organization for Economic Cooperation and Development (OECD) defines globalization as the global dispersal of production, distribution, capital, information, and employment. Supporters of globalization point to the employment it brings to developing nations. Critics, often citing Mexico as an example, argue that it widens the gap between rich and poor nations.

Globalization is a set of processes enabling the international extension of trade and manufacturing through the development of worldwide transport and communication networks. These networks allow ideas, goods, information, money, and labor supply to be quickly diffused around the world. Many people think globalization developed in the 1980s and 1990s, but its origins go back to World War II (1939–1945). Fears of a world recession following the war prompted economists to envisage new forms of production and distribution and to move away from the dominant market system, known as Fordism for the production approach introduced by the car manufacturer Henry Ford. Economists believed Fordism was too rigid to cope with growth in consumer demand. Instead, they wanted more flexible labor markets and the physical fragmentation of production, so that different components of a product could be assembled where materials and labor were cheapest.

The Bretton Woods Conference

The new economic model, termed post-Fordism, was unveiled at the Bretton Woods Conference in New Hampshire in July 1944. The conference, attended by representatives from 44 nations, was called by U.S. and European leaders to make financial arrangements for the postwar world after the anticipated Allied victory over Germany and Japan. The conference resulted in the creation of two international financial institutions: the International Monetary Fund (IMF) and the International Bank for Reconstruction and Development (later renamed the World Bank). Both offered loans to national governments with the aim of stabilizing

A diesel power plant in Mexico. Supporters of globalization argue that it increases employment and investment in developing nations; opponents cite urban overcrowding and pollution among its effects.

exchange rates between countries. The creation in 1947 of the General Agreement on Tariffs and Trade (GATT; later renamed the World Trade Organization) reflected another major pillar of the postwar international economic order: free trade, the encouragement of international exports by reducing countries' trade barriers.

Stablilized exchange rates and free trade paved the way for the development of transnational corporations, which operated across national borders. Two major advantages for transnational corporations are increased access to markets, allowing them to produce more and achieve economies of scale (savings on production costs), and the ability to source materials and labor where it is cheapest. Maquiladoras (assembly plants), introduced in the Mexican border region in the 1960s, demonstrated from the outset the operations of U.S. transnational corporations. Maquiladora workers assemble components shipped from the United States, Mexico, or elsewhere, for generally lower wages than those paid to workers on the U.S. side of the border. According to a survey in *Businessweek* magazine in the mid-1990s, the average Mexican electronics worker received U.S. $1.54 per hour compared to U.S. workers' rates of U.S. $13.95. The finished goods are then sold abroad.

Developments in the 1980s

During the 1980s increasing flows of goods, capital, and ideas across countries gradually weakened many nations' protectionist policies (intended to protect domestic producers from foreign competitors) and set in place conditions for increased globalization. International political and economic events also influenced greater globalization. Events included the debt crisis of the mid-1980s, when developing nations' debts reached colossal levels that consumed much of their export earnings and the introduction of democracy in the Soviet Union, before its collapse in 1991. The debt crisis emphasized a need to stimulate the economies of developing nations, while changes in the Soviet Union led to the decline of an alternative political-economic model to the one being promoted by the United States and western Europe. In 1989 the U.S. government responded to these developments by drawing up the Brady Plan, named for the then U.S. treasury secretary, Nicholas F. Brady. The plan supported the introduction of free-market economic policies in developing countries, particularly in Latin America.

Mexico and globalization

Mexico was the first country to implement the Brady Plan's recommendations. It had long pursued a protectionist economic policy, going back to the Import Substitution Industrialization (ISI) model introduced in the late 1930s by Mexican president Lázaro Cárdenas. The ISI model encouraged the domestic production of previously imported goods. However, following a severe recession in the early 1980s, triggered by the drop in international oil prices and the country's foreign debt, many Mexican politicians and economists welcomed the Brady Plan as a chance to improve their country's fortunes. Their hopes were well-founded: since the late 1980s Mexico's economy has undergone a profound transformation. Changes in economic policy, including the introduction of high levels of competition and efficiency in its manufacturing industries, enabled Mexico to increase its exports and involvement in the global economy. Mexico's

signing of the North American Free Trade Agreement (NAFTA) in 1992, with the United States and Canada, demonstrated its support for free trade and the elimination of trade barriers. In addition to NAFTA, which was implemented in 1994, Mexico has signed free-trade agreements with Colombia and Venezuela (implemented 1995), Bolivia (1995), Chile (1999), and the European Union (2000).

Arguments for and against

Increasing levels of global commercial activity have led to the rise of an antiglobalization movement to protest against the activities of transnational corporations and institutions such as the World Bank. In the late 1990s antiglobalization protests became a feature of summit meetings of world leaders. The San Francisco-based International Forum on Globalization (IFG), an alliance of academics, economists, and activists, represents the views of many people who oppose globalization and proposes alternative economic models for countries to adopt.

The IFG was established in 1994 in response to NAFTA. The organization's arguments against globalization are supported by many people who have witnessed the growth of maquiladoras in Mexico's border region. The IFG believes that globalization diminishes the economic control of local or national regions, widens the gap between rich and poor nations, and leads to large population shifts from rural to urban areas, resulting in environmental damage. Critics of the maquiladoras argue that all these problems are apparent in Mexico, from the removal of limits on foreign ownership of assembly plants through wage differences between Mexican and U.S. workers to the environmental problems caused by overcrowding in border cities such as Ciudad Juárez.

However, supporters of globalization argue that the maquiladoras demonstrate the system's advantages. The assembly plants have created jobs on both sides of the border, including in previously depressed areas of southern Texas, and attracted investment from all over the world. In the 1990s Asian firms such as Sony, Sanyo, and Goldstar built maquiladoras in northern Mexico, taking advantage of the ability to produce goods within easy reach of the enormous U.S. market.

Miguel Jimenez

SEE ALSO:

Border Industrialization Program; Foreign Debt; Free Trade; Inflation; Maquiladoras; NAFTA.

Gold Rush

On January 24, 1848, nine days before Mexico ceded California to the United States by the Treaty of Guadalupe Hidalgo, gold was discovered on the American River at Coloma in the foothills of the Sierra Nevada. The resulting Gold Rush brought thousands to California— Asians, Americans, Europeans, and South Americans—turning it into an ethnically diverse, wild, and violent frontier.

The first gold find was made by a carpenter, James Wilson Marshall, during the construction of a sawmill on land belonging to Swiss-born pioneer John Sutter (1803–1880), at the junction of the American and Sacramento Rivers.

The story appeared in *The Californian* newspaper on March 15, 1848, but it aroused little interest. The Gold Rush was really started by Sam Brannan, who had a store at Sutter's small pioneer settlement. He figured that the more people who heard about the discovery, the more supplies they would buy from him. On May 12 he filled a bottle with gold nuggets and rode up and down Montgomery Street in San Francisco, which was the nearest village, yelling, "Gold, gold from the American River!"

Once the news reached New York it spread like wildfire. An article in the *New York Herald* on August 19 sparked a frenzy of interest, and thousands set out to stake claims in northern California. These prospectors became known as "forty-niners," after the year in which most arrived in the West.

On December 5 President James Polk (1795–1849) officially confirmed the discovery of gold in California. By the end of 1848 a quarter of a million dollars' worth of gold had been extracted. There was then a frenzied drive to improve transportation to California. The first regular steamboat service from the East Coast via Cape Horn was inaugurated on February 28, 1849. Plans were also quickly drawn up for a railroad to the Pacific.

San Francisco grew as a gateway to the area. Between 1848 and 1850 California's population more than trebled, to 93,000 inhabitants. Husbands left wives, sailors jumped ship, soldiers deserted, farmers and businessmen abandoned their livelihoods. While most of the immigrants were from the United States, "forty-niners" also came from China, Australia, many Latin American nations, and all parts of Europe. Among the prospectors were many Mexicans, especially miners from Sonora. Many California coastal settlements saw a major drop in population as most people rushed to the Sierra foothills. Some became ghost towns.

Changing population

The Gold Rush lasted until the mid-1850s, by which time large mining companies had started deep mining. For the 10,000 Spanish-speaking inhabitants of California, known as *Californios*, the Gold Rush was a disaster. Although many prospectors arrived from Mexico and South America, the Spanish-speaking population quickly became a minority, falling to 15 percent by 1850 and 4 percent by 1870.

The *Californios'* land rights were protected under the Treaty of Guadalupe Hidalgo, yet many of them were forced into long-running and expensive legal battles to prove the validity of their Spanish and Mexican land grants. On the lawless frontier they were unable to stop land-hungry miners from squatting on their land, and there was growing vigilantism and squatter violence against *Californio* landowners and other Mexicans. In addition, the Foreign Miners' tax, a monthly fee of $20 introduced in 1850, was imposed on California-born Mexicans as well as foreign immigrants. Around this time stories about a legendary Mexican outlaw, Joaquin Murrieta, began to circulate. Murrieta attacked and robbed Anglo-American prospectors in revenge for his and his family's mistreatment. Whether he really existed is not known.

The great influx of Easterners to the Pacific seaboard during the Gold Rush was instrumental in drawing California into the United States. On November 13, 1849, in preparation for U.S. statehood, voters approved a state constitution, and Peter H. Burnett was elected governor.

Henry Russell

SEE ALSO:

Bandits and Outlaws; California; Californios; Guadalupe Hidalgo, Treaty of; Polk, James.

Gomez-Peña, Guillermo

Guillermo Gomez-Peña is an award-winning Mexican poet, playwright, and performance artist based in San Francisco. His work explores cross-cultural issues and Mexican-U.S. relations through the use of several media: performance art, bilingual poetry, journalism, and video installation.

Gomez-Peña's performance work and critical writings have played an important role in highlighting issues of cultural diversity and identity in Mexican-U.S. relations. He is considered one of the most influential commentators on Mexican and Chicano cultural identity in the United States.

Born in Mexico City in 1955, Gomez-Peña studied linguistics and literature at the the National Autonomous University of Mexico (UNAM), Mexico City, and was influenced by the student movement and counterculture of the time. Interests in experimental art and the Chicano urban experience brought him to California in 1978, where he studied at the California Institute of Arts in Los Angeles.

Border Art Workshop

In 1981 Gomez-Peña and choreographer Sara-Jo Berman founded the Poyesis Genetica performance troupe, whose style was a mixture of Mexican *carpa* (urban popular theater), magical realism, kabuki (a form of traditional Japanese theater), and American multimedia. In 1983 the theater group moved to the San Diego-Tijuana area and eventually became the Border Art Workshop/Taller de Arte Fronterizo (1985–1990), whose work was featured in the 1990 Venice Bienale art fair. The manifesto of the BAW/TAF declared the border region to be an intellectual laboratory and the group staged performances on the Mexico-U.S. border.

In all of his work, Gomez-Peña challenges conventions of race, culture, and class. His performances typically use various notions of "border"—cultural, sexual, and technological—to develop ideas. His aim is to make experimental yet accessible art and he explores themes such as immigration, globalization, the digital divide, censorship, and interracial sexuality.

Guillermo Gomez-Peña with his characteristic "hyper-Mexican mustache and loungy sideburns." Here he is performing as "El Mad Mex," or Mexterminator, one of his many artistic personas.

Gomez-Peña uses his body, languages (English, Spanish, Spanglish), humor, and mixed literary styles in his subversive art form. He creates unique Chicano personas, such as El S&M Zorro, El Webback, and Mexterminator, by dressing up in bizarre costumes and using these characters to dramatize cross-cultural issues. Mexterminator, for example, is a Spanglish-speaking karate expert who carries machetes and guns, sings old Mexican songs, eats jalapeños, and communicates with fellow gangsters through a digital watch. The character's mission is to reconquer the U.S. Southwest. According to the artist, this "Mad Mex" character has replaced the old stereotype of the lazy Mexican in the United States. Several of these dramatic personas, including Mexterminator, were developed using data gathered on an anonymous website. Set up in 1997 by Gomez-Peña and longtime collaborator Roberto Sifuentes, the website asked Americans to express their racial prejudices.

Gomez-Peña's work aims to draw attention to the two worlds that Hispanics inhabit—the present of California and the past of Mexico. When staging monologues and performances, he often appears wearing a colorful mix of traditional and stereotypical Mexican costumes and accessories. For performances of *Border Brujo*, for example, he wears a mariachi sombrero, a necklace of plastic bananas, a wrestler mask, dark glasses, a pachuco hat, skeleton earrings, feathers, and an icon of the Virgin of Guadalupe. Such costumes, according to the artist, are designed to reflect the disjunctive experience of life on and around the Mexico-U.S. border

His performances have taken him throughout the United States, most notably to the Whitney Museum of American Art, New York, the Smithsonian Institution, Washington, D.C., and the Art Institute of Chicago. Further afield, his work has been presented in Europe, Mexico, and Australia.

Gomez-Peña, Guillermo
Mexican poet and performance artist

Born:	1955
	Mexico City

1978	Moves to California to study art
1981	Founds Poyesis Genetica performance troupe
1985	Founds Border Art Workshop/Taller de Arte Fronterizo
1986	Cofounds cultural magazine *La Linéa Quebrada* (*The Broken Line*)
1991	Becomes first Mexican to receive MacArthur Fellowship
1996	*El Naftazteca: Cyber Aztec TV for 2000 AD* wins first prize at Cine Festival in San Antonio, Texas
1997	American Book Award for *The New World Border*
1998	*Temple of Confessions* awarded first prize at Cine Festival, San Antonio
2000	Gains cineaste lifetime achievement award from the Taos Talking Pictures film festival
2001	*Borderstasis* wins the prize for best performance video from the Vancouver Video Poetry Festival

Written works

In addition to his performance art, Gomez-Peña is known internationally for his critical writings, cultural theory, journalism, and poetry. He has written extensively for both American and Mexican newspapers, and in 1986 cofounded a bilingual, experimental magazine, *La Linéa Quebrada* (*The Broken Line*). He has been a contributing editor to *High Performance* magazine and *The Drama Review*, two of the leading magazines dealing with performance art, as well as a contributor to the national radio program *Crossroads* (1987–1990). He is a regular contributor to the national radio news magazine *All Things Considered*. Many of his chronicles and scripts have been published in his books, the best-known of which are *Warrior for Gringostroika* (1994), *The New World Border* (1996), *Temple of Confessions: Mexican Beasts and Living Santos* (1997), *Dangerous Border Crossers* (2000), and *Codex Espangliensis* (2000).

Prizes and awards

Gomez-Peña has received numerous fellowships and awards for his films, videos, poetry, books, and performance art. He was the recipient of the Prix de la Parole at the 1989 International Theatre of the Americas in Montreal, the 1989 New York Bessie Award, and the Los Angeles Music Center's 1993 Viva Los Artist as Award. In 1991 he became the first Mexican artist to be given the prestigious MacArthur Fellowship (1991–1996). In 1997 he received the American Book Award for *The New World Border*.

The film version of his solo performance *Border Brujo* (in collaboration with Isaac Artenstein) was awarded first prize in the 1991 National Latino Film and Video Festival and first prize in the category of Performance Film at Cine Festival (San Antonio 1991). His videos, *El Naftazteca: Cyber Aztec TV for 2000 AD* and *Temple of Confessions* were awarded first prizes at Cine Festival in San Antonio, Texas, in 1996 and 1998, respectively. In 2001, his film *Borderstasis* was awarded the prize for best performance video from the Vancouver Video Poetry Festival. Gomez-Peña's experimental radio works have also received many honors.

Joanna Griffin

SEE ALSO:

Border Studies; Chicano Art; Chicano Theater; Chicano Writers; Literature; Mariachis; Music; Stereotypes and Prejudice.

Gonzales, Richard "Pancho"

Richard "Pancho" Gonzales, photographed restringing a tennis racket in 1962. Gonzales overcame his early experiences of prejudice to become the most famous Mexican American sportsman of his era.

The Mexican American Richard "Pancho" Gonzales (1928–1995) was one of the outstanding tennis players of his era. He won the U.S. Championship in 1948 and 1949 and retained his ranking as one of the top ten U.S. players into the 1970s.

Gonzales was always something of an outsider. As a Chicano in a predominantly white, middle-class sport he was never completely accepted at youth tournaments in his native Los Angeles. Later he was barred from junior tournaments in southern California because of truancy from school. Gonzales left the U.S. Navy in 1946 to concentrate on his tennis career. In 1948, although ranked only 17th nationally, he won the U.S. Championship at Forest Hills, New York, beating the South African Eric Sturgess in the finals. The following year Gonzales retained his title, beating the number-one ranked Ted Schroeder in the finals. In the same year Gonzales helped the U.S. national tennis team beat Australia to win the Davis Cup competition.

Professional crowd pleaser

Gonzales turned professional in 1949, at a time when many tournaments were still for amateurs only. The greatest crowd pleaser of his generation, "Emperor Pancho," or just "Pancho," as he was known, won the U.S. professional singles title a record eight times. When the sport itself turned fully professional in 1968, Gonzales returned to mainstream tournaments, still a powerful opponent. In 1968 he reached the quarterfinals of the first U.S. Open. A year later Gonzales—by now a grandfather—beat Charlie Pasarell at Wimbledon in a famous 112-game match lasting 5 hours, 12 minutes. Until 1992 this was the longest contest in the history of the British grand slam tournament.

An attacking right-hander, Gonzales is best remembered for his strong serve. He was sometimes given to temperamental outbursts against anyone who incurred his displeasure on court, including opponents, officials, photographers, and spectators. These rages were an important part of his game because they helped him concentrate. The Australian champion Rod Laver spoke for many of Gonzales's opponents when he said: "We hoped he wouldn't get upset; it just made him tougher."

In 1972, at age 43, Gonzales became the oldest player to win a tournament in the professional era. From 1973 he became a consistent winner on the Grand Masters tour for the over-45s, bringing his total career earnings to more than one million U.S. dollars. Gonzales was married six times. His last wife was Rita Agassi, sister of tennis star Andre. Gonzales died of cancer in Las Vegas, Nevada, where he worked as a tennis coach, on July 3, 1995.

Henry Russell

SEE ALSO:

Segregation and Integration; Sport.

Gonzales, Richard "Pancho"
Mexican American tennis player

Born: *May 9, 1928*
Los Angeles, California
Died: *July 3, 1995*
Las Vegas, Nevada

1948	Wins U.S. tennis championship
1949	Retains U.S. title; turns professional
1969	Plays 112-game match at Wimbledon

González, Henry B.

Liberal Democrat Henry B. González (1916–2000) was the first Hispanic elected to the U.S. Congress from Texas.

Henry Barbosa González was raised in poverty on the west side of San Antonio, Texas. As a youth he was thrown out of swimming pools and restaurants for being Hispanic, but he battled discrimination to win a place at law school. In 1953 he was elected to the San Antonio City Council. As deputy director of the city housing authority he forged a relationship with the Massachusetts congressman and later U.S. president John F. Kennedy. The two remained close—González was in the motorcade when Kennedy was assassinated in Dallas in 1963.

When González won election to the Texas Senate in 1956, he became the first person of Mexican descent to sit in the chamber for 110 years. As a freshman senator he defied then Texas governor Price Daniel's attempts to pass a range of segregationist bills. González defeated many of Price's measures with a 36-hour filibuster (continuous speech).

When a congressional seat became available in Bexar County in 1961 the Democratic Party nominated González. His subsequent victory was a historic result for Mexican Americans in both Texas and the United States. He won reelection with little or no opposition every two years until 1996. In Congress he devoted much of his attention to helping his hometown, to which he returned from Washington, D.C., every weekend. He secured federal aid for the construction of a medical school in San Antonio, passed measures protecting its drinking water supply, and drafted bills that brought the 1968 HemisFair International Exposition to the city. The exposition celebrated San Antonio's Hispanic and Anglo heritage—from the southern and northern hemispheres—and attracted 6.3 million visitors.

An outspoken congressman

Among the national and international issues that concerned González in the 1980s and 1990s were the savings-and-loan crisis and the United States's sale of arms to Iraq. His concerns led him to call for the impeachment of presidents Ronald Reagan and George Bush and the resignation of Federal Reserve chairman Paul Volcker. In 1994 he won the John F. Kennedy Profiles in Courage Award for speaking out on controversial issues.

From 1989 to 1996 González was chairman of the House Banking Committee, where he won respect for the way he drafted bills to resolve the savings-and-loan crisis and for his stewardship of community development programs. He used the committee's investigative powers aggressively. For example, he arranged hearings to explore the links between five U.S. senators and an Arizona savings-and-loans company. In the 1990s he harshly criticized investigations into President Bill Clinton's alleged financial misconduct that became known as the Whitewater scandal. González felt the investigators were not impartial.

In 1996 González—who was by now seen as old and out of touch by some in the Democratic party—was challenged for his job on the banking committee. Always a strong orator, he held onto the post with a rousing speech at a caucus meeting. By 1998, however, González had developed heart problems and did not seek reelection. His son, Charlie, took over his seat.

George Lewis

SEE ALSO:
Political Parties in the U.S.; Politics, Local.

González, Henry Barbosa
Mexican American politician

Born:	*May 3, 1916*
	San Antonio, Texas
Died:	*November 28, 2000*
	San Antonio, Texas

1940	Marries Bertha Cuellar
1943	Graduates from St. Mary's University School of Law
1956	Enters Texas Senate
1961	Elected to U.S. House of Representatives
1998	Decides not to seek reelection

González, Rodolfo "Corky"

Rodolfo "Corky" González (born 1928) was a boxer who retired from the ring to become one of the leading figures in the Chicano movement. His poem "Yo Soy Joaquin" (I am Joaquin) helped define Mexican American identity in the 1960s.

The son of poor seasonal farmworkers, González was born in 1928 in a Mexican neighborhood in Denver, Colorado. On graduating from high school at age 16 he took a job in a local slaughterhouse. At 20 he began a successful career as a professional boxer. González won 65 of his 75 bouts, became a Golden Gloves champion, and was once rated as the third-ranking contender for the World Featherweight title.

González gave up boxing in 1953 to run a bar and work as a bondsman, taking responsibility for court defendants' bail charges in return for a fee. He also became involved in local Democratic politics. In 1957 he became the first Chicano district captain in the Denver Democratic Party. However, González became disillusioned with established party politics and left the Democrats to become a civil rights activist. In 1966 he helped create the Chicano youth program Cruzada para la Justicia (Crusade for Justice) and the following year led a contingent of Mexican Americans in the Poor People's March on

Washington, D.C., to protest the problems faced by ethnic minorities in U.S. cities. During the campaign he unveiled his Plan of the Barrio, a project to improve educational opportunities for Chicanos, provide better housing, and help set up more Chicano businesses. In 1968 he bought an old school and church in Denver and opened a Cruzada school, theater, gym, nursery, and cultural center.

Promoting Chicano identity

González played a crucial role in defining the aims of the Chicano movement in the 1960s and, more generally, what it meant to be Chicano. In 1966 he wrote "Yo Soy Joaquin," a 502-line epic poem narrating the history and struggle of the Mexican people from preconquest times to the twentieth century. The poem's narrator identifies himself with many of the figures in Mexican history, from the Aztec ruler Cuauhtémoc through the Spanish conquistador Hernán Cortés to the nineteenth-century president Benito Juárez. The poem encouraged a sense of identity among Mexican American youth and helped change the overtones of the word *Chicano*. Originally a derogatory term for Mexicans immigrants, González used it to describe all Mexican Americans and symbolize their ethnic pride.

In March 1969 the Cruzada para la Justicia sponsored the first Chicano National Youth Conference, in Denver. Under González's leadership the conference drew up El Plan Espiritual de Aztlán (The Spiritual Plan of Aztlán), which set out many of the aims of the Chicano movement. The plan also identified Aztlán, the mythical southwestern homeland of the Aztecs, as the symbolic home of Chicanos, a rallying cry that stirred the Mexican American community.

In the late 1960s González was also instrumental in founding El Partido de la Raza Unida (the United People's Party), which officially came into being in January 1970 and represented Chicano aims at the national level.

Henry Russell

SEE ALSO:

Alurista; Aztlán; Chicano Movement; Chicano Writers; Denver.

González, Rodolfo "Corky"
Boxer and Chicano movement leader

Born: *June, 1928*
Denver, Colorado

1948	Becomes a professional boxer
1957	Works for Democrats in Denver
1966	Founds Cruzada para la Justicia; writes "Yo Soy Joaquin"
1969	Sponsors first National Chicano Youth Conference
1972	One of leaders at first national convention of La Raza Unida party

Good Neighbor Policy

The term Good Neighbor Policy dates back to the 1933 inaugural address of President Franklin Delano Roosevelt (1882–1945). In the speech, Roosevelt pledged to be a good neighbor to the countries of Latin America, and the phrase became indelibly linked to U.S. policy in the Western Hemisphere.

In 1823 U.S. president James Monroe declared Latin America off-limits to further colonization by Europeans. The declaration became known as the Monroe Doctrine, and it played a central role in U.S. foreign policy for many years afterward. Following its victory in the Spanish-American War of 1898, the United States began to exercise a more activist policy in Latin America. President Theodore Roosevelt (1858–1919) summarized the new approach in his 1905 corollary to the Monroe Doctrine (known as the Roosevelt Corollary), which stated that the United States had the right to intervene in the internal affairs of other American countries. The early twentieth century thus saw U.S. troops stationed in many parts of Latin America, including Cuba between 1906 and 1909.

Theodore Roosevelt was succeeded as president in 1909 by William Taft, whose own brand of foreign policy became known as dollar diplomacy. The basic idea behind dollar diplomacy was that economic pressure was a more effective way of achieving U.S. national goals than military intervention. In Costa Rica and Honduras the United States was able to exert a substantial degree of control through the United Fruit Company, which had a grip on almost every sector of those countries' economies. The United States tried to establish a similar degree of control in Nicaragua by the offer of loans but was unable to do so, and in 1912 U.S. troops occupied the country.

A changing climate

U.S. foreign policy became less belligerent during the presidency of Herbert Hoover (1929–1933), a trend that became even more marked during the presidency of his successor, Franklin D. Roosevelt. In his inaugural address Roosevelt pledged to

Franklin D. Roosevelt, pictured in 1937. During Roosevelt's presidency the United States pursued a less belligerent form of foreign policy that became known as the Good Neighbor Policy.

"dedicate [the United States] to the policy of the good neighbor, the neighbor who resolutely respects himself and, because he does so, respects the rights of others." In practice, the main components of this policy were an agreement not to interfere in the internal politics of other states, the promotion of trade, and the development of pacts for mutual defense. The first steps toward this new form of foreign policy were taken at the International Conference of American States, which was held in Montevideo, Uruguay, in November and December 1933. There, U.S. secretary of state Cordell Hull formally renounced his country's self-appointed right to intervene in other American countries' domestic politics.

The following year, the United States ended its 19-year occupation of Haiti. Troops had originally been stationed there in 1915, after the country's ruler had been killed during a popular uprising. The occupation was greatly resented by the island's inhabitants and, in keeping with the spirit of the Good Neighbor Policy, Roosevelt withdrew the marines in August 1934, replacing them with a national guard made up of Haitian nationals.

In 1934 the United States also renounced the Roosevelt Corollary and repealed the 1901 Platt Amendment, which had entitled the United States to intervene in Cuba and made the island a virtual U.S. dependency. The 1930s also saw an improvement in the relationship between the United States and Panama. A treaty signed in 1903 had given the United States exclusive use and control of the Canal Zone, a narrow strip of land along the Panama Canal. A new Panamanian constitution had also been drawn up giving the United States the right to intervene militarily in the country's affairs, a right it exercised on four occasions between 1908 and 1925. In 1936, however, a treaty was drawn up in which the United States relinquished the right to intervene and also agreed to increase the amount of money it paid to Panama for the right to use the Canal Zone.

To some extent, the United States simply began to use economic tools rather than military intervention to achieve its national goals. For example, in 1934 the Export-Import Bank of the United States was created. The bank supplied loans to firms and governments in Latin America so that they could purchase U.S. goods. A number of trade agreements were also made that strengthened existing economic ties between the United States and less powerful Latin American nations.

Mexican oil

One of the biggest challenges to Roosevelt's Good Neighbor Policy came in 1938, when Mexican president Lázaro Cárdenas nationalized his country's oil industry, a gesture seen as an assertion of national sovereignty. Before this point the industry had been dominated by British and U.S. firms, most of which had bought oil fields during the second presidency of Porfirio Díaz (1884–1911), when foreign investment was welcomed. Mexico's 1917 Constitution, however, declared that anything found in the country's subsoil belonged to the nation, and after this point foreign oil companies only had the status of concessionaires.

The 1938 expropriation of foreign holdings inspired a furious reaction from U.S. oil firms, which tried to organize an embargo of Mexican oil. Roosevelt, however, decided that maintaining an amicable relationship with Mexico was more important than restoring the oil companies' property. A joint U.S.-Mexican commission was set up to determine the amount of compensation that was to be paid, and in 1942 Mexico paid the oil companies for their seized assets.

Roosevelt was keen to settle the issue of oil expropriation as quickly and peacefully as possible because the world was on the brink of war. The strong relationships built between the United States and its neighbors during the 1930s ensured that most Latin American countries supported or joined the Allies after the Japanese attack on Pearl Harbor in December 1941. The relationship with Mexico was especially close, with about 250,000 Mexicans serving in the U.S. military during the war. Another example of the good relationship between Mexico and the United States during this period is the implementation of the Bracero Program in 1942. The program was designed to combat wartime labor shortages and allowed Mexican citizens to work legally in the United States.

Decline of the Good Neighbor Policy

In the latter half of the twentieth century U.S. relations with Latin America deteriorated, as the United States once again began to intervene militarily in its neighbors' internal politics. During the cold war, U.S. foreign policy was largely dictated by the ideological battle between communism and capitalism, and successive U.S. governments took action to prevent communism from gaining a foothold in the Americas. In the 1950s the CIA engineered the overthrow of the democratically elected government of Guatemala. In 1961 the United States attempted to topple the revolutionary government of Cuba through the abortive Bay of Pigs invasion. Other, later examples of U.S. intervention include overthrowing of the democratic government of Salvador Allende in Chile in 1973, President Ronald Reagan's support of Contra guerrillas against the Nicaraguan government in the early 1980s, and the 1983 U.S. invasion of Grenada.

Joanna Griffin

SEE ALSO:

Bracero Program; Cárdenas, Lázaro; Cold War; Foreign Policy, U.S.; Oil; Roosevelt, Franklin D.; World War II.

Gran Chichimeca, Wars of the

In the 1540s Spanish conquistadores found silver in northern Mexico, leading to a wave of white prospectors settling and digging the region. The attempts to extract this mineral wealth were resisted by several indigenous peoples, collectively known as the Chichimecas, which sparked a long-term conflict in North America, the Wars of the Gran Chichimeca (1550–1590s).

In 1546 Juan de Tolosa, a Basque nobleman, became the first European to find silver in Mexico when some Indians living near the present-day city of Zacatecas gave him several pieces of silver ore as a gift. That same year the town of Zacatecas was founded. In the next few years dreams of wealth brought many prospectors, entrepreneurs, and laborers to the small mining town, which quickly became a major settlement. Rich mineral deposits were discovered around Zacatecas and, between 1556 and 1574, at the nearby towns of Fresnillo, Nieves, and Sombrerete.

The region was already inhabited by several semi-nomadic, semi-agricultural tribes—principally the Cazcanes, the Guachichiles, the Tepehoanes, and the Zacatecos—who were together called the Chichimecas by the Aztecs. *Chichimeca* is a derogatory Aztec term meaning "son of a dog." The Spanish thus named the whole area—which included Aguascalientes, Guanajuato, Jalisco, and Nayarit, as well as Zacatecas itself—La Gran Chichimeca.

As would happen many times over the following 300 years, the white settlers treated the Indians' claims to the land with little or no regard. The Chichimecas viewed their land as a sacred inheritance from their ancestors, and as the mining camps grew in number the Indians became increasingly angry at the European encroachment.

Decades of bloody conflict

In 1550 the Guachichiles and the Zacatecos began to attack merchants along the "silver roads" from Zacatecas to Mexico City. This was the start of the Wars of the Gran Chichimeca. The Spanish soon learned why the Aztecs had failed to conquer these peoples, who fought fiercely and relentlessly, mainly with bows and arrows. They specialized in hit-and-run ambushes, attacking suddenly in short bursts and then disappearing without trace into the desert.

For many years the Spanish colonial government in Mexico left it up to individuals to defend themselves against these attacks. As a result, merchants and miners transporting goods and silver throughout the territory had to travel in armored wagons and pack trains accompanied by mounted armed guards. La Gran Chichimeca gradually became dotted with walled towns and fortified dwellings (originally named *casas fuertes*, literally "strong houses," they later became known as presidios).

It was not until 1568 that Martin Enriquez de Almanza (viceroy from 1568 to 1580), decided to use his authority to defend the Spanish towns, mines, and ranches. He declared "una guerra a fuego y sangre" (war by fire and blood) against the Chichimecas and began to establish Spanish military settlements across northern Mexico.

Peace by purchase

For several decades the Chichimecas kept up their fierce guerrilla war, attacking mining towns and small caravans in the disputed zone. However, in 1585 a new viceroy, Alonso Manrique de Zuniga, Marques de Villamanrique (viceroy from 1585 to 1590), discovered that Spanish soldiers had been raiding Indian settlements and enslaving the inhabitants. Infuriated by this practice, he immediately banned it and freed or placed under religious care those who had already been captured. Shortly afterward he launched a full-scale peace initiative and began negotiations with the principal Chichimec leaders, to whom he offered land, agricultural implements, food, and clothing in return for their renunciation of violence.

This policy of "peace by purchase" worked; by the end of the sixteenth century the Wars of the Gran Chichimeca had ended. The Spanish settlements built during the period became bases for converting indigenous peoples to Christianity.

George Lewis

SEE ALSO:

Aztecs; Catholic Church; Explorers; Missions and Religious Orders; Silver; Spanish Empire.

Great Depression

The Great Depression (1929–1939) was the longest and worst economic downturn in the twentieth century, with consequences for countries around the world. Mexico did not escape its effects, but those living south of the border suffered less than Mexicans and Mexican Americans living in the United States.

The nation that sustained the worst damage during the Great Depression was the United States. This was to some extent predictable—the world's greatest economic power was the most likely to bear the brunt of a steep decline in commerce and industry triggered by the crash in share prices on the New York Stock Exchange on October 24, 1929. Yet few people foresaw the extent of the devastation the economic problems would cause. At the lowest point of the slump, in 1933, one American worker in every four was out of a job, while between 1929 and 1932 the U.S. gross national product (GNP) declined at an average rate of over 10 percent a year.

Mexico, whose fortunes were inextricably linked to the United States, inevitably felt the shockwaves created by the depression. The slump north of the border led to a fall in demand for Mexican services and exports, such as minerals and metals. Between 1929 and 1932 the value of Mexico's exports fell by nearly 65 percent and unemployment began to rise, particularly in the countryside.

Mexican response and recovery

Despite its problems, Mexico was not affected as badly as the United States because it relied less on exports and more on a traditional economy based on agriculture. In addition, a number of structural reforms implemented by President Lázaro Cárdenas (1895–1970) helped Mexico recover from the depression more quickly than the United States. Cárdenas, whose administration lasted from 1934 to 1940, put in place a six-year plan for land reform and the nationalization of Mexican industry. He broke up large haciendas (estates) and redistributed land to rural peasants, who were therefore able to provide for their own needs. In 1936 he passed a law that allowed the government to take control of private properties and enterprises. In 1937 he nationalized Mexico's railroads, and the following year he turned his attention to the foreign oil companies. After they refused to pay a 27 percent wage increase awarded to workers by the Mexican Federal Labor Court, Cárdenas nationalized their holdings on March 18, 1938. Although Cárdenas's oil policy created tensions with the United States— as well as problems for subsequent Mexican administrations—it provided a welcome boost to the Mexican economy.

In the late 1930s the Mexican government began to stimulate economic growth by encouraging the domestic production of manufactured goods that had previously been imported. The system, which relied on tax incentives for domestic industries and tariffs to protect domestic products over imports, was known as Import Substitution Industrialization, or ISI. These measures led, by the mid-1930s, to the steady rise of agricultural production and urban employment in response to increasing domestic demand.

Xenophobia toward Mexican Americans

Meanwhile the plight of Mexicans living in the United States had deteriorated rapidly. This was ironic, given that many had originally left Mexico to escape danger and poverty. In 1910, at the start of the Mexican Revolution (1910–1920), thousands had headed north, attracted by better wages and the demand for workers in U.S. industries, such as agriculture, mining, and transportation. During the economic boom in the 1920s hundreds of thousands more Mexicans crossed the border, most of them settling in Texas, the Southwest, and the Midwest. By 1930 the Mexican population in the United States had reached 1.5 million.

The decline of the U.S. economy led to an increase in anti-Mexican feeling. Many Americans felt that the solution to high unemployment was to get rid of foreigners. Consequently support grew for repatriation, the return of foreign immigrants to their countries of citizenship. When job cuts were made, especially in seasonal and labor-intensive industries, it was usually Mexicans who were fired

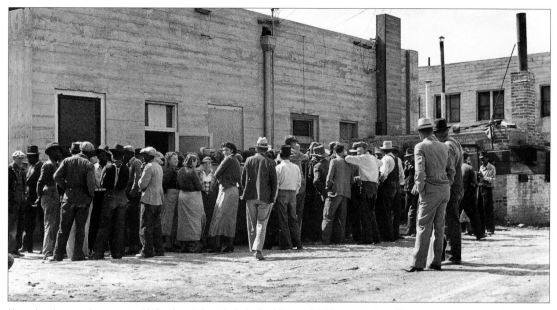

Unemployed men and women stand in line for relief checks in California's Imperial Valley, 1937. One of the arguments in support of the repatriation of Mexicans and Mexican Americans during the Great Depression was the cost of providing them with welfare.

first, before African Americans and other ethnic groups. As more Mexican immigrants became unemployed, penniless, and homeless, U.S. government officials called for the deportation of Mexican-born Americans to save the cost of providing them with public services and relief.

Mass deportations

In March 1929 the U.S. government passed the Deportation Act, which gave counties the power to expel Mexicans. County officials in states such as California and Texas organized deportation trains, and the Immigration Bureau conducted sweeps, arresting people for no other reason than that they looked Mexican. When the authorities started asking questions, many immigrants were unable to demonstrate their U.S. citizenship, either because they did not understand the regulations or because their migratory work made it practically impossible for them to fulfill the residency requirements. Between 1929 and 1939 up to one million Mexicans and Mexican Americans were repatriated to Mexico, a greater forced movement of people than the relocation of Native Americans in the 1800s.

The repatriations were popular with both the American poor and big business, which had lost its enthusiasm for Mexican American workers after they became involved in labor-union activity. In 1933, for example, 18,000 cotton pickers—many of them Mexican or Mexican American—went on strike in San Joaquin Valley, California, protesting employment conditions. Those Mexicans who were not repatriated remained vulnerable to persecution. Lack of documentary evidence to support their claims of U.S. citizenship meant that many found themselves unable to benefit from U.S. president Franklin D. Roosevelt's New Deal policies, such as the creation of public-works jobs.

Although many repatriated Mexicans returned to Mexico with their own farm equipment and livestock, the majority lacked the capital to establish their own farms and were unable to sell their possessions. Similarly, entrepreneurs often left the United States with merchandise so they could reestablish businesses in Mexico, but on arrival they usually found they had insufficient funds to do so.

The end of the Great Depression came with the start of World War II, which the United States entered in 1941. As factories responded to the rise in demand for military equipment, employment levels began to increase. The depression led to greater federal intervention in the U.S. economy to prevent a similar slump occurring again—little consolation for all the immigrants expelled in the 1930s.

George Lewis

SEE ALSO:

Cárdenas, Lázaro; Deportation and Repatriation; Labor Organizations; Roosevelt, Franklin D.

Greater Mexico

Through annexing half of Mexico's territory in 1848, the United States acquired land shaped by over 250 years of Spanish-Mexican culture. This region also became home to growing communities of Mexican Americans. A concept rather than an actual place, cultural critics use the term "Greater Mexico" to describe the impact of Mexican and Mexican American culture on the United States and the relationship between people of Mexican origin and Anglo-Americans.

The Mexican American anthropologist José Eduardo Limón has done much to popularize Greater Mexico, a concept that refers to predominantly Mexican or Mexican American parts of the United States, such as the *colonias* (shanty towns) along the Mexico-U.S. border and the barrios (Spanish-speaking neighborhoods) in cities such as Los Angeles, San Antonio, Phoenix, and Chicago. In his book *American Encounters: Greater Mexico, the United States, and the Erotics of Culture* (1998), Limón examines the relationship between these areas and the rest of the United States. He explores aspects of culture such as literature, film, art, and music to look at the way Chicanos portray themselves and in turn are portrayed by Anglo-Americans.

Impact of immigration

Mexican influence on U.S. culture grew with immigration. In the first decades of the twentieth century Mexican immigrants settled in the Southwest, the northern Midwest, and, in fewer numbers, on the East Coast. They worked in fields, mines, railroads, steel mills, meat processing plants, restaurants, and tanneries. They also faced discrimination due to poverty, skin color, use of the Spanish language, their immigrant status, and their Catholicism. In many border towns, for example, Mexicans were forced to live in segregated communities that often lacked adequate plumbing and municipal services. Despite the problems they faced, Mexicans established their own thriving communities in barrios and *colonias*. They set up restaurants, movie houses, theaters, and saloons in their neighborhoods, and published Spanish-language newspapers, such as *La Prensa* in San Antonio and *La Opinión* in Los Angeles.

By the 1960s Mexican immigrants and their descendants had settled in most U.S. regions but were mainly concentrated in the Southwest and Midwest. However, developments since the 1960s changed the legal status and occupations of many new arrivals. The end of the Bracero Program (1942–1964), which had facilitated the migration of Mexican farmworkers to fill wartime labor shortages in the United States, increased the amount of illegal immigration across the border. The subsequent decline of U.S. manufacturing industries and growth of the service sectors, such as retail and catering, encouraged the employment of low-wage workers throughout the United States, but especially along the border. Furthermore, the rise of maquiladoras (foreign-owned assembly plants) on the Mexican side of the border drew migrants from southern and central Mexico northward. Many who failed to find maquiladora work crossed over into the United States. Population growth along the border gave rise to twin Mexican-U.S. cities, such as Ciudad Juárez-El Paso and Nuevo Laredo-Laredo. These cities became jumping-off points for immigration to other parts of the United States.

Growing confidence

By the start of the twenty-first century Mexican and Mexican American communities existed in every major U.S. city. According to the 2000 U.S. Census there were 20.6 million people of Mexican origin in the United States, with a further estimated 3 million undocumented Mexican immigrants. Mexican Americans' ethnic pride is evident through many aspects of Chicano culture, such as festivals and street fairs. For example, the week-long Mexican Fiesta in Milwaukee, Wisconsin, attracts many Mexican and Mexican American musical acts, as well as performers from the Caribbean. In addition, Mexican American political leaders reflect ethnic pride by sponsoring Spanish street signs, colorful murals painted by local artists, and the renaming of boulevards in honor of famous Mexican Americans, such as the labor organizer César Chávez.

A Chicano mural, featuring the Virgin of Guadalupe, in a shopping center, Los Angeles. Mexican and Mexican American culture is evident in many parts of the Southwest and, through its food, music, film, and literature, across the United States.

The concept of Greater Mexico describes not only the Mexican-origin community but also its influence on the rest of the United States. Spanish-language media has become part of this influence. In 2002 the Univisión television network reached over 90 percent of U.S. Latino households with a diverse range of television programming, and some Univisión stations received better ratings than the major networks in some U.S. cities. Spanish-language radio stations and newspapers are also flourishing in every large city.

Film, literature, and music

Mexican and Mexican American film, literature, and music have left their mark on U.S. culture. As early as the 1920s Mexican immigrants patronized U.S. movie theaters that presented Mexican movies. Since the 1940s Hollywood films have featured Mexican movie stars such as Dolores Del Río, Ramón Novarro, Ricardo Montalbán, Anthony Quinn, and Salma Hayek. José Limón examines the portrayal of Mexicans in Hollywood films in *American Encounters*. In an optimistic assessment of changing attitudes, he argues that representations of

Mexicans and Mexican Americans have become less marginalized. Characters like the prostitute Helen Ramirez in *High Noon* (1953) are being replaced by figures such as the schoolteacher Pilar in *Lone Star* (1995). Since the late 1970s popular U.S. films such as *Boulevard Nights* (1979) and *American Me* (1992) have explored barrio culture, while films such as *The North* (1983) and *My Family* (1995) have focused on the Mexican immigrant experience.

One of the first significant Mexican American novels was José Antonio Villarreal's *Pocho* (1959), describing a Mexican American boy's cultural conflicts growing up in California's Central Valley. Since that time many Mexican American novelists and poets have had an impact beyond their immediate communities. Influential novelists include Victor Villaseñor, Tomás Rivera, Rudolfo Anaya, Sandra Cisneros, Ana Castillo, and Denise Chávez. Poets include Gary Soto, Jimmy Santiago Baca, and Lorna Dee Cervantes.

Mexican music has also had an impact in the United States. Genres such as *corridos*, *rancheras*, and *norteño* music continue to be popular on both sides of the border. Musicians in Texas combine pedal

Pan-Hispanic Identity

As the U.S. Hispanic population has grown and diversified it has given rise to new identities. Many Mexicans and Mexican Americans identify themselves with Mexico, while others see themselves primarily as U.S. citizens. However, many people of Mexican origin also embrace a pan-Hispanic identity and feel a connection to all people from Latin America. Several factors have created this identity, including political pressure to create coalitions between Hispanic communities, and commercial pressure, for example, the marketing of products as simply "Hispanic." Furthermore, wars in Central America in the late 1970s and 1980s brought new groups of immigrants to barrios in U.S. cities, such as the refugees from El Salvador and Nicaragua who moved to San Francisco's Mission District.

As a result of this pan-Hispanic identity, the Cinco de Mayo (May 5th) celebration has grown into a broad expression of Hispanic culture and pride throughout the United States. While the event commemorates the Mexican victory over the French at Puebla in 1862, it has also become a general celebration of all Hispanic culture, much like St. Patrick's Day is celebrated by Irish and non-Irish communities in the United States.

guitar, brass, accordion, and even synthesizers to create a Tex-Mex sound popular among Anglo-Americans and Mexican Americans. Present-day Mexican American bands such as Los Lobos and The Texas Tornados continue the strong tradition of mixing musical genres (rock, mariachi, Tex-Mex) that reflect the cultural intermingling in the border region. Finally, the Mexican musician Carlos Santana has indelibly influenced rock and roll in the United States and beyond, with his combination of Afro-Caribbean percussion and electric guitar.

Murals and architecture

Mexican American murals have long been a feature of Mexican barrios in U.S. cities. Leaders of the 1960s Chicano movement encouraged new murals to depict Chicano culture and identity, a tradition that continues to the present day. One famous example in Los Angeles is Judith Baca's *The Great Wall of Los Angeles* (1984), which depicts the history of that city's communities. The history of David Alfaro Siqueiros's mural *La América Tropical* (1932) demonstrates changing attitudes toward Mexican Americans. Painted in Los Angeles's Olvera Street, the mural aroused controversy for its critical representation of U.S. foreign policy in Latin America. As a result, authorities painted over the mural, but, beginning in the late 1980s, local preservationists uncovered and restored the work.

Spanish-influenced architecture from Mexico's colonial period (1521–1821) has had an important influence on U.S. styles. Since the early twentieth century an Anglo-American preservation move-ment has sought to maintain examples of Spanish-Mexican architecture in the Southwest, including missions and cattle ranches. Spanish colonial architecture continues to influence domestic architecture throughout the Southwest and beyond, in features such as whitewashed walls and red-tiled roofs.

Food and drink

Mexican and Tex-Mex food has become one of the most visible manifestations of Mexican influence on U.S. culture. Its popularity results from the ingredients used (spices, sauces, meats, and cheeses), and because the food is inexpensive, quick to prepare, and easy to eat on the move. Mexican-themed food restaurants, including Taco Bell and Chi Chi's, developed in the 1960s, while more authentic Mexican restaurants continue to operate in many U.S. cities. The popularity of Mexican food has led to the expansion of Mexican food industries in the United States. The Milwaukee-based El Rey, for example, has grown to become a major producer of tortillas and tortilla chips. Larger still is Goya, founded in 1936, which in the 1990s was the largest distributor of Latin American food products in the United States. Alongside food, Mexican beers such as Carta Blanca, Dos Equis, and Corona have also become popular throughout the United States.

Joseph A. Rodriguez

SEE ALSO:

Anglo-Americans; Architecture; Chicano Life; Chicano Writers; Festivals; Film in the U.S.; Food and Drink; Hispanic Americans; Immigration, Mexican; Murals and Muralists; Music; Tex-Mex Culture.

Guadalajara, Jalisco

Guadalajara, the capital of Jalisco state, is Mexico's second largest city, with around three million people living in the metropolitan area. Guadalajara has played an important role in national political and economic history.

Situated almost 400 miles (644 km) west of Mexico City, Guadalajara is located on a plain at an altitude of 5,220 feet (1,570 m), surrounded by mountains. Its elevation and proximity to Mexico's largest lake, Lake Chapala, contribute to a mild, dry climate. For most of the year the city has temperatures of 75–85°F (24–29°C), except in April and May when temperatures can reach 90°F (32°C).

History and culture

Guadalajara was founded in the early sixteenth century by the Spanish conquistador Nuño de Guzmán, a bitter rival of Hernán Cortés. In 1530 de Guzmán ordered a town to be built in present-day Nochistlán, Zacatecas. However, de Guzmán was not happy with the location and moved the town to present-day Tonála in 1533 and again in 1535 to Tlacotlanán. The town was threatened during the Mixton War (1540–1541), an uprising by the Caxcan Indians, partly against de Guzmán's cruelty. After the war a safer location was picked on the San Juan de Dios River, and the town was permanently established in 1542. It was named Guadalajara for the town in Spain where de Guzmán was born.

In 1560 Guadalajara became the capital of New Galicia, and in 1782 it was made the capital of one of the 12 intendencies (administrative regions) into which the Spanish reorganized New Spain. In 1792 the Royal Literary University was established, later known as the University of Guadalajara.

During the Hidalgo Revolt (1810–1811) the city was captured and sacked by the revolutionary priest Miguel Hidalgo y Costilla and his followers. It became a center of reforms, and it was here in 1811 that Hidalgo decreed the abolition of slavery. The revolt was crushed near Guadalajara by Spanish forces. In 1858 during the War of the Reform the city was briefly occupied by Benito Juárez, who was later president of Mexico (1861–1872).

Guadalajara lies in the west of Mexico. The city was sacked in 1810 during the Hidalgo Revolt that sparked the Wars of Independence.

Guadalajara has many examples of Spanish colonial architecture, including the cathedral and the governor's palace. The city was home to the muralist José Clemente Orozco, who painted some of his most highly regarded murals in the governor's palace, the orphanage chapel, and the university.

Economy

Since the implemention of the North American Free Trade Agreement in 1994 Guadalajara has enjoyed a manufacturing and electronics boom. Corporate giants such as IBM and Hewlett-Packard have established operations in the city. Between 1995 to 1999 the number of electronics companies increased from 25 to 125, and the sector's workforce grew from 5,000 to 90,000. Other leading industries are food processing, plastics, and the manufacture of photographic equipment. The surrounding area is a rich agricultural region.

Joanna Griffin

SEE ALSO:

Architecture; Mexican Independence; Orozco, José Clemente; Reform, War of the.

Guadalupe Hidalgo, Treaty of

The Treaty of Guadalupe Hidalgo was signed on February 2, 1848, as a conclusion to the Mexican-American War (1846–1848). Under its terms a vast area of Mexican territory came under the control of the United States. In all, Mexico lost over half its territory.

The Treaty of Guadalupe Hidalgo brought to a close a long and bitter dispute over the status of Texas, which had formerly been part of Mexico. In 1836 settlers in Texas had declared the region to be an independent republic, a stand that soon led to military conflict. After Texan forces defeated him in the battle of San Jacinto, the Mexican general Antonio López de Santa Anna (1794–1876) signed a treaty in which he agreed to withdraw troops from Texas. The treaty effectively recognized the independence of Texas, but the Mexican government denied that Santa Anna had a right to sign it on the country's behalf.

The Texan secession

For the following 10 years the independence of Texas remained disputed. However, in July 1845 the people of Texas voted to become part of the United States. Three months later U.S. president James K. Polk (1795–1849) sent his emissary John Slidell to Mexico. Slidell had two objectives. First, Polk wanted him to renegotiate the boundary between Texas and Mexico. Traditionally it had stood at the Nueces River, but Polk wanted it to move 150 miles (240 km) south to the Rio Grande. Slidell's second objective was to acquire the area covered by present-day California and New Mexico.

When Slidell's negotiations failed, Polk turned to military pressure and ordered General Zachary Taylor to advance to Point Isabel, which lay in the disputed territory just north of the Rio Grande. On April 8 there was a clash between U.S. and Mexican forces, which gave the United States a justification for declaring war on May 13.

Taylor won several important victories in the spring and early summer, and as the war continued, President Polk sent Slidell's nephew to Havana to confer with the now exiled Santa Anna. Santa Anna agreed to help negotiate a treaty favorable to the United States in exchange for U.S. help to reinstate him as president. Santa Anna entered the Mexican port of Veracruz in August 1846 but reneged on his deal with the United States. In November 1846 a new round of negotiations began, with the United States represented by the newspaper editor Moses Beach, but these initiatives failed as Santa Anna regained the presidency.

Negotiations under Trist

In April 1847 U.S. diplomat Nicholas Trist (1800–1874) was appointed as a peace commissioner. In the same month Polk and his advisers prepared the final draft of the treaty that Trist would present to the Mexican government. Considerably enlarging Slidell's original proposals, the United States demanded the cession of New Mexico, California, and Baja California, the recognition of the Rio Grande as the southwestern border of Texas, and the right to travel across the Gulf of Tehuantepec on Mexico's southern border. In exchange, the U.S. government would pay 15 million U.S. dollars.

In May 1847 Trist landed in Veracruz, which had fallen to U.S. forces under the command of General Winfield Scott (1786–1866) two months earlier. Trist was authorized to suspend hostilities if the Mexican government signed the treaty. However, the Mexican government was unwilling to admit defeat and Scott pressed on toward Mexico City. In August 1847, after two decisive battles where Scott defeated Mexican forces, the U.S. general asked for an armistice to discuss peace. Santa Anna appointed four peace commissioners to handle discussions.

Negotiations proved extremely difficult. Talks continued throughout August and September, and when they broke down Scott advanced and took Mexico City itself. Santa Anna resigned and the Mexican government fled north. Negotiations carried on through intermediaries, but the Mexican authorities still refused to recognize the Rio Grande as the boundary of Texas or agree to the annexation of New Mexico. As the talks dragged on, Polk ordered Trist to return home. However, the emissary ignored his president's orders and continued to pursue a settlement.

The opening page of Mexico's copy of the Treaty of Guadalupe Hidalgo, which was signed in February 1848 and ratified three months later. The treaty ceded hundreds of thousands of square miles of land to the United States and was a source of Mexican resentment for years afterward.

With the threat of further military defeats looming, the Mexican authorities gave in to U.S. demands. The two sides signed a treaty on February 2, 1848, in Guadalupe Hidalgo, a small town outside Mexico City. Although Mexico kept control of Baja California, it gave in to most of the other demands that Trist had submitted a year earlier. The Treaty of Guadalupe Hidalgo not only acknowledged U.S. sovereignty over Texas, it also ceded to the United States 525,000 square miles (1,360,000 sq km) of land, covering most of present-day Arizona, California, New Mexico, Nevada, Utah, and western Colorado. In return, the United States agreed to pay a total of 15 million U.S. dollars to Mexico and to protect Mexican territory from Native American raids. The United States also assumed more than three million dollars in claims that U.S. citizens held against the Mexican government. Mexico was to retain everything south of the Rio Grande, which it now accepted as the boundary of Texas. For less than 19 million U.S. dollars, the United States had annexed nearly half of Mexico's territory.

Apart from the far smaller U.S. acquisitions under the 1853 Gadsden Purchase, the Treaty of Guadalupe Hidalgo marked the last major change in the Mexico-U.S. border. Mexico's humiliation at the harsh terms of the treaty soured its relationship with the United States for years to come. In addition, the treaty made tens of thousands of Mexicans inhabitants of a new country, with new and often hostile neighbors. As some Mexican Americans in the Southwest still say: "We didn't cross the border; the border crossed us."

Susana Berruecos García Travesí

SEE ALSO:

Alliances and Agreements; Gadsden Purchase; Mexican-American War; Polk, James; Santa Anna, Antonio López de; Scott, Winfield; Texas Revolution.

Guerrero, Vicente

Vicente Ramón Guerrero was a guerrilla leader who joined forces with Augustín de Iturbide to help achieve Mexican independence from Spain in 1821. He was later briefly president of Mexico.

Vicente Ramón Guerrero was born on August 10, 1782, in Tixtla, near Acapulco, in what is now Guerrero, the state named in his honor, to a poor peasant family of mestizo and African ancestry. He began his military career during Mexico's Wars of Independence (1810–1821). Guerrero distinguished himself in battle and also contributed to the movement by establishing an armory that manufactured artillery and powder.

Guerrero became one of the main leaders of the rebel forces after the execution of José María Morelos y Pavón in 1815. When his father, under pressure from the Spanish viceroy, asked him to lay down his arms, Guerrero famously said "la Patria es primero" (the fatherland is first).

In 1821 the royalist commander, Agustín de Iturbide, invited Guerrero to meet him at Acatempan. In this historic meeting the royalist colonel and the rebel leader agreed to join forces and fight for independence under the Three Guarantees: Mexico would be an independent constitutional monarchy; the caste system would be abolished and all races would have civil liberties; and Catholicism would be the only religion. Iturbide and Guerrero's forces entered Mexico City triumphantly on September 27, 1821. Realizing that it was a fait accompli, the viceroy, Juan O'Donojú, formally recognized Mexican independence, although the Spanish government refused to recognize defeat for several years.

After independence

Guerrero continued to be involved in Mexican politics after independence. He initially supported Iturbide, who declared himself emperor, but soon rebelled against his tyrannical regime. Iturbide was forced to abdicate in February 1823 and Guerrero became a member of the provisional governing junta until Guadalupe Victoria, the first president of Mexico, assumed his post in 1824. Guerrero was a

---

Guerrero, Vicente Ramón
Mexican soldier and politician

Born:	*August 10, 1782*
	Tixtla, Guerrero
Died:	*February 14, 1831*
	Oaxaca, Oaxaca

1810	Joins rebellion against Spain
1815	Leader of independence movement
1821	Proclaims the Three Guarantees with Agustín de Iturbide
1822	Supports Iturbide as emperor
1823	Rebels against Iturbide
1829	President, but then overthrown
1830	Rebels against new president
1831	Captured, tried, and executed

---

liberal and was considered the leader of the disenfranchised masses. He ran for president in the 1828 elections but was beaten by General Manuel Gómez Pedraza.

Guerrero refused to recognize the election results, overthrew Gómez Pedraza, and assumed the presidency himself on April 1, 1829. However, he was less successful as a president than as a general. It was not long before his conservative vice president, Anastasio Bustamante, rebelled against his regime. Defeated, Guerrero headed south to begin an insurrection against Bustamante. However, one of Bustamante's ministers persuaded Francisco Picaluga, a Genoese captain, to betray Guerrero by inviting him onto his ship and taking him prisoner. Guerrero was taken to Oaxaca, court martialed, and executed on February 14, 1831. The harsh treatment Guerrero received, condemned even by his contemporaries, may be explained by the racial and social prejudices of the time toward one of his humble origins and mixed ancestry.

Luz María Hernández Sáenz

SEE ALSO:

Iturbide, Agustín de; Mexican Independence; Morelos y Pavón, José María.

Guillén Vicente, Rafael Sebastián

On February 10, 1995, the Mexican government in a televised message to the nation identified Subcomandante Marcos, the leader of the Zapatista National Liberation Army (EZLN; Ejército Zapatista de Liberación Nacional), as Rafael Sebastián Guillén Vicente.

In the same message President Ernesto Zedillo Ponce de León (1994–2000) ordered Guillén's detention, along with another four EZLN leaders: Fernando Yáñez Germán, Vicente Javier Elorriaga, Jorge Santiago, and Sofía Silvia Fernández. Zedillo claimed that there was sufficient evidence that the EZLN was preparing for violence. Despite army incursions into Zapatista-held territory, all the EZLN suspects eluded capture.

Zapatista rebellion

The Zapatista rebellion began on January 1, 1994, when the EZLN, or Zapatistas, as they became known, rebelled against the Mexican government, capturing four municipalities in the southern state of Chiapas. The rebellion started on the same day as the inauguration of the North American Free Trade Agreement (NAFTA), which Subcomandante Marcos announced was "nothing more than a death sentence for the indigenous ethnicities." EZLN communiqués made it clear that the rebels opposed not only what they saw as the authoritarian regime in Mexico City but also the neoliberal economic reforms followed by President Carlos Salinas's administration (1988–1994). One fundamental issue for the EZLN was the modification of constitutional Article 27, which had given legal rights to Indian settlements, protecting them from ranchers and landowners.

The Zapatista movement, named after the Mexican revolutionary hero Emiliano Zapata (1879–1919), gathered considerable attention and worldwide support. In particular, Subcomandante Marcos attracted people's attention with his passionate writing about the exploitation and injustices done to the indigenous people in Chiapas and due to the mystery long surrounding his identity. Most of his communiqués, signed by the Comité Clandestino Revolucionario Indígena-Comandancia General (CCRI-CG), were published worldwide, along with his personal letters and even some poetry.

Media attention

Subcomandante Marcos, or El Sub, as he is known, became famous in the United States when he was interviewed by Ed Bradley of the CBS *60 Minutes* team in 1994. With his black ski mask and pipe he was an intriguing figure. In addition to the media coverage of his exploits and writing, El Sub used the Internet effectively to promote the Zapatista cause. His interviews—which he gave in English, French, Spanish, and Italian—helped enhance his image as the masked rebel and intellectual fighter opposing the forces of capitalism. High-profile international figures, including the former first lady of France, Danielle Mitterrand, and Uruguayan writer Eduardo Galeano, took an active role in defending the Zapatista cause.

Subcomandante Marcos addressing a crowd in front of the presidential palace in Mexico City on March 11, 2001. The rally marked the end of a 3,000-mile (4,900-km) march from Chiapas.

After nearly 10 years of the Zapatista uprising, there was still no certainty about Subcomandante Marcos's true identity, although there was a strong possibility that he was Guillén Vicente. Everyone was curious about who was behind the *pasamontañas* (black mask). Marcos did not admit to being Rafael Sebastián Guillén, but neither did Rafael Sebastián Guillén Vicente deny that he was Subcomandante Marcos. Meanwhile, for the Zapatistas, Marcos became as much a symbol as a real leader: as the rebels expressed it, "Todos somos Marcos" ("We are all Marcos').

The Zapatista Web site was quoted as saying: "Marcos, as all the other CCRI members, does not know anything and is not anything. Marcos is only one representative more, the same as all the other CCRI, the indigenous and the Chiapas."

Educational background

According to his relatives, Rafael Sebastián Guillén Vicente was born on June 19, 1957, in the port city of Tampico, in the northern state of Tamaulipas. His parents, Alfonso Guillén and María Socorro Vicente, come from a middle-class family of traders and still live in Tamaulipas, where they run furniture shops. Guillén Vicente was the fourth of eight brothers. From 1963 to 1969 he went to primary school at the Colegio Félix de Jesús Rougier, directed by the Eucharistic Missioners of the Holy Trinity. From 1970 to 1976 he attended a high school run by Jesuits—the Instituto Cultural Tampico. During this period he is thought to have made several trips to regions in the Sierra Tarahumara as well as to remote areas in Tampico, becoming aware of the social needs of the indigenous population. After graduating, Guillén moved to Mexico City, where he was awarded two degrees at the National Autonomous University of Mexico (UNAM), one in philosophy and literature and the other in sociology.

In January 1979 he started teaching graphic design in the communications program at the Autonomous Metropolitan University in Mexico City (UAM-Xochimilco). One theory is that Guillén worked on graphic design projects for revolutionary organizations such as the Guatemalan guerrillas. As a part-time teacher, Guillén first resigned in May 1980, was readmitted twice, and left definitely in May 1984, when he apparently disappeared. According to his family he has not been seen in Tampico since 1992.

Guillén Vicente, Rafael Sebastián

Mexican academic and reputed Zapatista leader

Born: June 19, 1957
Tampico, Tamaulipas

1963	Attends Colegio Félix de Jesús Rougier
1970	Studies at the Instituto Cultural Tampico
1976	Studies for a degree at the National Autonomous University of Mexico (UNAM)
1979	Teaches design at the Autonomous Metropolitan University (UAM)
1984	Leaves teaching post
1995	Mexican government claims that he is Subcomandante Marcos

March on Mexico City

When Vicente Fox was elected president in 2000, he indicated his willingness to enter into dialogue with the Zapatistas to find a peaceful solution to the uprising. On February 24, 2001, Marcos and 23 indigenous commanders left Chiapas to march to Mexico City. The march in which they rallied support for the Cocopa initiative—a legislative proposal that would grant Mexico's indigenous groups specific rights—ended in March 2001 with the historic Zapatista presence in the Chamber of Deputies. Despite massive public support—more than 100,000 Mexicans filled the capital's main square to support the Zapatistas—discussions with the new government broke down once again.

Although opinion is deeply divided between those who believe that Subcomandante Marcos is a charismatic and true national leader who speaks for the poor, and those who call him a demagogue with clear political and personal objectives, the Zapatista movement has put the impoverished status of Mexico's indigenous population in the spotlight not only at the local but also at the international level.

Susana Berruecos García Travesí

SEE ALSO:

Fox, Vicente; Land Reform; NAFTA; Zapatistas; Zedillo Ponce de León, Ernesto.

Gulf of California

The Gulf of California is over 900 miles (1,448 km) long from the mouth of the Colorado River to the open Pacific Ocean, and 125 miles (200 km) wide at its southern end. Also called the Sea of Cortés, this massive inlet separates most of the peninsula of Baja California from the remainder of mainland Mexico.

The Gulf of California has long been an important resource for Mexico's fishing industry, and more recently for the country's growing leisure industry. The beautiful Baja California coast of the gulf is arid, rocky, and mountainous. In some places, mountains rise steeply from the sea to peaks of 3,300 feet (1,000 m) or more. There are more than 900 islands and islets in the gulf, including the Isla de Tiburon, the largest off the Mexican coast. Many of these islands are uninhabited. To the east of the gulf, the coast of Sonora and Sinaloa is mostly more gentle, with a broad coastal plain, disrupted in places by highland areas, for example, near Guaymas in Sonora.

Exploration by Cortés
The gulf's alternative name, the Sea of Cortés, derives from that of the Spanish conquistador Hernán Cortés (1485-1547), who was sent by the king of Spain to explore Central America but spent most of his time in the Caribbean Sea and what is now Mexico. One of the regions he visited was present-day Baja California.

In 1535 Cortés and his entourage landed near the present-day town of La Paz, on a stretch of coast at the southern end of the peninsula. One of Cortés's aims in California was the search for the legendary Amazon paradise, which was believed to have been ruled over by the mythical queen Calafia. The Spanish who followed him met with strong resistance from the Native Americans who lived in the area and were unable to gain a foothold. Disillusioned, they christened the area "California" for the queen they had failed to find. However, the Spanish did not colonize the peninsula until 1697, when the Jesuit priest Juan Maria Salvatierra established a Catholic mission at Loreto.

The Gulf of California runs between the Baja California peninsula and the western coast of mainland Mexico. A number of thriving resorts exist on the gulf's shoreline.

Earth movements
The very unusual, long and thin shape of the Gulf of California and the Baja California peninsula are products of massive movements in the earth's crust in the region. Geologists believe that some time around 7 million years ago a slab of the North American continent west of the San Andreas Fault—an area of land that is now the Baja California peninsula—started to move northwest in relation to the rest of the continent. As it did so, the southern part of the moving chunk of land moved directly west, allowing the Gulf of California to open up. Later, more huge faults opened up between Baja California and the Mexican mainland, causing chunks of crust to rise and fall in relation to each other. There has been a long history of volcanic activity in the area, with volcanoes on the islands of Isla Tortuga, Las Tres Virgenes, and Isla Coronada active during recorded history.

Several geological factors combined to create the peculiar character of the seabed of the Gulf of

California. In the southern part of the gulf, the difference in altitude between the seabed and the surrounding mountains is greater than 10,000 feet (3,050 m) in some areas, and west of Los Mochis, Sinaloa, the sea itself is 10,740 feet (3,275 m) deep. However, no part of the northern quarter of the gulf is more than 600 feet (180 m) deep. The shallowness of the northern section is due to the huge quantities of silt that have been swept down the Colorado River and deposited in the gulf over millions of years. The basement rocks there are buried beneath 25,000 to 30,000 feet (7,620 to 9,145 m) of delta sediments.

Fishing and tourism

The Gulf of California is Mexico's most important fishing zone, and towns such as Guaymas, Puerto Peñasco, La Paz, and Topolobampo have been sending out fishing boats for centuries in search of prawns, snappers, groupers, and others. While fishing was once the gulf's most important economic activity, that role is now played by leisure and tourism.

One town that demonstrates the change well is Puerto Peñasco, on the northern Sonoran coast. This town of 40,000 is a long-established fishing port but has developed into a fast-growing seaside resort. Its growth has been helped by its proximity to the U.S. border, which is just 70 miles (115 km) away. Opportunities for sport fishing, snorkeling, and wildlife watching along the long and beautiful Baja California coast draw many thousands of American tourists, as well as Mexicans, every year. Other growing tourist resorts on the Gulf of California coast include Bahia de los Angeles and San Felipe.

Natural riches

The great wealth of wildlife in the Gulf of California is one of its greatest attractions. Cold water upwelling from great depths produces plankton-rich surface waters that in turn provide good feeding for around 900 species of fish, 32 different types of marine mammals, including whales and dolphins, and many thousands of seabirds. Hundreds of islets provide breeding sites for sea lions and seabirds, while colorful coral reefs are home for many fish and invertebrates.

One of the world's rarest and most endangered sea mammals, the vaquita, lives in the upper part of the gulf. Named the little cow by local fishers, the

The view across the Gulf of California, as seen from La Paz on the southeast coast of the Baja California peninsula. The bay of La Paz was one of the areas explored by the conquistador Hernán Cortés.

vaquita is a very small dolphin. In contrast, the two largest types of whales, blue and fin whales, are regular visitors. Large numbers of gray whales also spend part of their year in the gulf, migrating from the Bering Sea to breed. They are estimated to attract 250,000 tourists to the region each year. Less common, but no less spectacular marine visitors are hammerhead and whale sharks. The totoaba fish lives only in the gulf. It is extremely endangered and has been protected by law since the 1970s.

The wildlife of the Gulf of California faces problems, however. The decreasing amount of fresh water entering the sea from the Colorado River affects its ecosystems, and toxins that enter the sea from surrounding agricultural land may be to blame for reduced shrimp catches reported in the late twentieth century. Unless the Gulf of California is kept healthy, tourism and fishing will suffer.

Tim Harris

SEE ALSO:

Baja California; Baja California Sur; Fisheries; Tourism.

Gulf of Mexico

The Gulf of Mexico is an oval-shaped sea, approximately 600,000 square miles (1,550,000 sq km) in area. In the sixteenth century the gulf provided the gateway for the Spanish exploration and domination of Mexico. In the twentieth century the discovery of the gulf's oil reserves both boosted the U.S. and Mexican economies while conversely increasing the risks to its fragile environment.

The south and west of the gulf are bounded by the Mexican coastline, from the Yucatán Peninsula, around the Bay of Campeche and north to the Mexican-U.S. border. The Mexican states of Yucatán, Campeche, Tabasco, Veracruz, and Tamaulipas are exposed to the gulf's waters. The U.S. states of Texas, Louisiana, Mississippi, Alabama, and Florida lie around the gulf's northern coastline. In the southeast, two channels link the gulf with the waters of the Caribbean Sea and Atlantic Ocean: the Straits of Florida, between the Florida Keys and the north coast of Cuba, is about 90 miles (144 km) wide, while the Yucatán Channel, between Cuba and the Yucatán Peninsula, is slightly narrower.

Formation of the gulf

The Gulf of Mexico was formed around 200 million years ago when the continents of North and South America separated. For millions of years after that time, mineral, vegetable, and animal sediments were deposited on the seabed. As the deposits built up, pressure from the waters above transformed the deposits into natural gas and oil. Today the gulf is edged by a continental shelf, or underwater platform, that is up to 200 miles (320 km) wide off the coast of Florida but narrows to 50 miles (80 km) at the sea's most westerly point. The shelf slopes down steeply, with underwater cliffs off Florida, Louisiana, and the Yucatán Peninsula plunging to the deep sea plain. The deepest point in the gulf is the Sigsbee Deep in the Mexico Basin, which is 17,070 feet (5,203 m) below sea level. Two major rivers discharge into the gulf: the Rio Grande on the Mexico-U.S. border and the Mississippi.

The Gulf of Mexico's oil reserves and fishing industries make it hugely important to both the Mexican and U.S. economies.

Spanish exploration

The European discovery of the gulf was made by the Spaniard Sebastián de Ocampo, who sailed around Cuba between 1508 and 1509 before journeying back to Spain. Shortly afterward the Spanish conquered Cuba and the island's governor, Diego Velázquez, was charged with sending out parties to explore the lands and overpower the tribes around the gulf. Francisco Hernández de Córdoba led the first expedition from Cuba in 1517. De Córdoba discovered the Yucatán Peninsula, which he mistook for an island, before Mayans attacked his party and sent it fleeing back to Cuba. The next expedition was led by Juan de Grijalva the following year. It resulted in a fuller exploration of Mexico's gulf coastline, as well as friendlier meetings with other Indian peoples, who told de Grijalva about the Aztec Empire, which lay in the country's interior.

In 1519 a third Spanish party set sail from Cuba, led by Hernán Cortés (1485–1547). Cortés landed at the site of Veracruz, where he founded the city. He then made alliances with various groups of Indians who were opposed to the Aztec's dominance. Through them Cortés learned that the Aztec ruler, Montezuma II, greatly feared him, believing the Spaniard to be a manifestation of the Aztec god Quetzalcoatl. By 1521 Cortés and his men had taken the Aztec capital Tenochtitlán and conquered much of central Mexico.

icans, and was rife among illegal immigrants, the majority of whom had no insurance.

The barriers to health care imposed by a lack of private insurance meant that many Mexican-origin Americans had no regular contact with a doctor for check-ups and did not seek treatment unless in an emergency. The failure to detect diseases at an early stage can lead to complications later on. Diabetes, for instance, is a disease with an extremely high prevalence among Hispanics. Researchers have found that Hispanic diabetics are more likely to experience complications such as eye and kidney disease than Anglo-Americans and that this complication rate is particularly high for Mexican Americans. With earlier diagnosis and treatment these rates could be lowered.

The next generation

In 2002 almost a third of Mexican American children lacked health insurance. The problem was especially severe in the *colonias* (shanty-towns) along the border. In an effort to improve insurance coverage for the next generation, in 2001 the Health Resources and Services Administration (HRSA), a branch of the PHS, launched a campaign in the border region to enroll eligible children in the State Children's Health Insurance Program (SCHIP) and Medicaid. In 1997 Congress created the SCHIP program to provide health insurance for children from families with incomes too high to qualify for Medicaid but too low to make private health insurance affordable. The HRSA's effort was accompanied by a bilingual television and radio campaign with the slogan: *Proteja la salud de su familia con confianza* (Protect your family's health with confidence).

Cutting costs

Federal provision of health care remains a politically sensitive issue that creates tension between Mexican Americans and the white American majority. During the 1980s and 1990s political concern about the cost of providing health care for the uninsured and, particularly, illegal immigrants caused a backlash and led to severe efforts to limit access to health care. In 1994 California passed Proposition 187, which prohibited the use of publicly subsidized health care services by undocumented immigrants. Subsequent court rulings, however, outlawed the proposition. Federal welfare reforms in 1996 again demonstrated a reaction against immigrant communities. These reforms

The U.S.-Mexico Border Health Commission

In 1994 U.S. president Bill Clinton signed the United States-Mexico Border Health Commission Act, which paved the way for the creation of the U.S.-Mexico Border Health Commission (BHC), which came into effect in 2000. Its creation was the result of mounting pressure from medical professionals since the early 1980s for federal and state agencies in both Mexico and the United States, as well as nongovernmental organizations (NGOs), to cooperate on a range of public health issues. The pressure intensified as health care problems along the border worsened. These included drug and alcohol abuse, teenage pregnancy, and the spread of HIV/AIDS.

The main aims of the BHC are to provide a permanent focus on health in the border region, irrespective of changes in U.S. and Mexican politics, and to create a forum for discussing public health concerns that affect people on both sides of the border. Through outreach programs and research the commission also aims to educate the public about health issues and find solutions to a range of health-related problems. The BHC's structure consists of 26 members, 13 each from Mexico and the United States, including Mexico's Secretary of Health and the U.S. Secretary of Health and Human Services. The commission, which has headquarters in Mexico City and El Paso, Texas, aims to work with a range of partners, including universities, businesses, NGOs, and cross-border agencies, such as the Pan American Health Organization and the Border Environmental Cooperation Commission.

In 2001 the BHC published an agenda entitled *Healthy Border/Frontera Saludable 2010*, which contained its major goals for enhancing health in the region. These goals included reducing rates of infectious diseases, improving border residents' access to health and dental care, and tackling environmental factors that cause ill health.

withdrew services previously available to immigrants, including prenatal care for pregnant women and routine doctors' visits for conditions such as asthma. In many states, hospitals and health care providers have ignored the 1996 ruling, leading to court battles. It is likely that the political tension caused by these wranglings has reduced the confidence of many Mexican Americans to access publicly subsidized services.

Health along the border

The majority of the Mexican population in the United States is concentrated in the Southwest and along the 2,000 mile (3,200 km) border with Mexico. As a result of poverty, problems accessing health care, poor working conditions, overcrowding, and environmental pollution, ill health is particularly prevalent in the region. In October 2001 the HRSA declared: "If U.S. territory within 100 km of the border were a state, its 11 million residents would rank last [in the nation] in access to health care, second in deaths due to hepatitis, and third in deaths related to diabetes." Rates of several major infectious diseases are far higher in the region than elsewhere in the United States. In 2002 tuberculosis along the border was six times the national rate, while measles and mumps were twice the national average. In addition, levels of HIV infection continued to rise, particularly in California. Cancer, asthma, and diabetes were also higher along the border than the national average of both Mexico and the United States.

Cross-border cooperation

The health problems in the border region are compounded by the fact that the area is one of the busiest crossroads in the world. The high rate of border crossings means that coordinated policies by the U.S. and Mexican governments are essential in addressing the spread of infectious diseases. Institutions on either side of the border have helped each other informally for many years, for example, in the wake of the flooding at Tampico, Tamaulipas, in 1927. Formal cooperation began in the late 1940s, when health authorities became concerned with the spread of sexually transmitted diseases among U.S. troops stationed along the border.

Monitoring and treating infectious diseases in a migrant population calls for far greater imagination in policymaking than is needed for treating a stable population. Mexicans receiving treatment for a disease often abandon their treatment if they cross illegally into the United States. Furthermore, once in the United States, undocumented immigrants frequently fail to seek treatment for fear of deportation. Interrupted treatment can cause wider problems. For example, any interruption is dangerous in the treatment of tuberculosis, because the pause in taking medicine can lead to a patient becoming resistant to medication. One possible solution that emerged at a 2001 meeting of the U.S.-Mexico Border Health Commission was to issue binational tuberculosis cards. These would allow patients to continue their treatment on either side of the border with confidentiality (see box on page 392).

Learning from Mexico's example

Cross-border communication on health matters has also allowed U.S. policymakers to learn from their Mexican counterparts. Since 2000 initiatives taken by the Mexican government to improve the health of Mexicans on both sides of the border have included immunization campaigns in August and September, when migrants often leave home to work in the United States during the harvest season. Another measure is the *Vete sano, regresa sano* (Go healthy, return healthy) project, launched in Ciudad Juárez in 2001, to offer health care to migrants on their journey from their hometowns to the United States. Also in 2001 California and Mexico staged their first joint "health week," with a range of initiatives aimed at California's migrant population, including vaccinations, check-ups, and bilingual information campaigns.

Joint initiatives may help bring to the United States some of the techniques in caring for Mexicans that have made Mexico's public health system highly regarded. Mexico holds a National Public Health Week three times a year to bring vaccinations to the homes of millions of people. The initiative has immunized 98 percent of Mexicans against a number of major diseases. In one public health week 180,000 volunteers gave 11 million injections to prevent childhood diseases. California health authorities believe they can use some of these techniques to reach the 3 million Mexicans living and working in the state, especially the 1 million agricultural laborers. Many U.S. health authorities also recognize the need for Hispanic-origin staff to provide Spanish-speaking, culturally sympathetic care for Mexican Americans.

Cost Comparison across the Border

Rocketing health costs in the United States have prompted many Mexican Americans and other U.S. residents to cross the border into Mexico for more affordable health care and cheaper prescription drugs. Health care in Mexico is heavily government subsidized and many Mexican-origin people prefer to see doctors who share their culture and language. In the Dallas, Texas, area, for instance, buses, vans, and airline services regularly journey to Zacatecas, Guanajuato, and other Mexican states to provide access to cheaper health care. Their passengers include undocumented workers whose employers do not offer health coverage, those who cannot afford health insurance, and even those with health coverage who find Mexican care cheaper.

In 2002 many newspapers in the U.S. Southwest ran stories about the gap in health care costs between the two countries. One story featured a California woman who could not afford the U.S. $7,000 charged at a local hospital for surgery to remove a cancerous cyst from her womb. On the advice of a neighbor, she traveled 100 miles (160 km) south to Tijuana, Baja California, where the surgery cost U.S. $2,800. Without this option, many border residents would have to go without medical treatment.

It is not only people of Mexican origin who are driven to cross the border for health reasons. The Prescription Express is a service that buses predominantly white, elderly residents from Phoenix, Arizona, to the border town of Nogales, Sonora, solely to visit the pharmacy. The service costs $40 per trip, with an annual membership of $25. However, many passengers save themselves as much as $800 in prescription charges by shopping in Mexico. Big drug companies charge whatever they think the local market will take, so the cost of some drugs can be ten times cheaper on the Mexican side of the border.

Despite measures to improve health care for people of Mexican origin in the United States, at the start of the twenty-first century there were relatively few Mexican American medical professionals. While overt discrimination is rare, a 2002 study sponsored by the U.S. Department of Health and Human Services highlighted the problems that can arise from cultural barriers between doctors and patients. The report showed that all ethnic minorities in the United States tended to receive lower-quality health care than white Americans, even when insurance status, income, and age were comparable. The report concluded that "bias, prejudice, and stereotyping on the part of the health care providers" are still problems in treating ethnic minorities.

Language barriers

Mexican patients explain their symptoms more effectively in Spanish, and do so more freely with someone who shares their cultural experience. Conversely, language and cultural barriers between doctor and patient can prevent accurate and early diagnoses. Hispanic doctors are usually better at understanding culturally specific syndromes that Hispanic patients might present. These syndromes include *susto* (fright), *nervios* (nerves), *mal de ojo* (the belief that suffering is caused by an "evil eye," or curse), and *ataque de nervios* (a nervous attack that may lead to screaming, trembling, and seizure-like episodes). However, non-Hispanic health care providers are slowly beginning to understand more about these common, culturally specific complaints.

Communication difficulties are particularly problematic in diagnosing and treating mental illness. For example, one national study found that only 24 percent of Hispanics with depression and anxiety received appropriate care, compared with 34 percent of Anglo-Americans. In general, Hispanics are less likely to receive a diagnosis of depression than Anglo-Americans. To test this discrepancy, researchers monitored bilingual patients during medical consultations to see if they were evaluated differently when interviewed in English as opposed to Spanish. One small-scale study found that Hispanic Americans with bipolar disorder (manic depression) were more likely to be misdiagnosed with schizophrenia than non-Hispanic white Americans.

Jane Scarsbrook

SEE ALSO:

Colonias; Cross-Border Initiatives; Environmental Issues; Immigration, Mexican; Migrant Labor; Proposition 187; Segregation and Integration.

Hidalgo y Costilla, Miguel

Miguel Hidalgo y Costilla (1753–1811) is considered by Mexicans to be the "father of the nation." The rebellion he led against the Spanish government between 1810 and 1811 developed into the movement to free Mexico from Spanish control.

Hidalgo was born on the hacienda (estate) of Corralejo, near Pénjamo, Guanajuato, to a family of wealthy *criollos*, the term given to the descendants of Spaniards born in Mexico. Hidalgo was an extremely able pupil and went on to study at San Nicolás College and the Royal and Papal University of Mexico, both in Valladolid (present-day Morelia), and Michoacán, where he obtained his bachelor's degree in theology in 1773. He was ordained as a priest five years later and taught philosophy and theology in his old college of San Nicolás, becoming its rector in 1790. Hidalgo's years as a teacher demonstrated the enthusiasm for reform that marked his later career: his support for new teaching methods was one reason why church authorities forced him out of Valladolid. Other reasons included his fondness for gambling and the fact that he fathered several children.

The activist priest

Hidalgo next served as a priest in various parishes, including Dolores, in his home state of Guanajuato, which he took over in 1803. He left most of his clerical duties to other priests and concentrated on advancing the economic and social welfare of his parishioners. He set up workshops for local craftsmen, established a pottery factory, and planted vineyards, olive groves, and mulberry trees to raise silk worms. He also pursued intellectual interests, reading the latest works by European Enlightenment thinkers. The colonial authorities banned these works, and in 1809 a church official denounced Hidalgo for owning such books, although nothing came of the charge.

Hidalgo's intellectual interests were well received at the literary society in nearby Querétaro, one of many such groups in Mexico at the time. Members of these societies discussed politics more than literature and often shared radical views about the

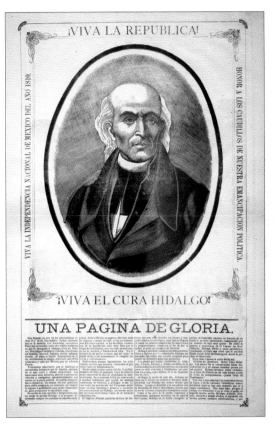

An illustration of Miguel Hidalgo y Costilla, created in the late 1800s. The text around the image reads: "Long live the Republic! Long live Father Hidalgo! In Honor of the leaders of our political emancipation."

nature of government, inspired by the Enlightenment and the revolutions in France (1787–1799) and the United States (1775–1789). The political dissent of the literary societies increased after the French emperor Napoleon invaded Spain in 1808 and imposed his brother on the Spanish throne, causing a change of government in Mexico City and the arrest of a number of *criollo* officials. Hidalgo, along with Ignacio Allende, the Querétaro society's leader and a fellow *criollo*, joined a conspiracy against the new government of Mexico City and in support of the deposed Spanish king. The Querétaro conspirators planned a rebellion for December 8, 1810, but by mid-September the authorities had learned of their plans. Hidalgo and Allende decided to act immediately. On the morning of September 16 Hidalgo incited his Dolores parishioners to rebel by issuing his famous "Grito" (Call to Arms) that is still celebrated on Mexican independence day.

Hidalgo's poorly armed peasant band quickly grew into a mass movement, consisting of a handful of criollos and a vast majority of Indians and mestizos (offspring of Spaniards and Indians). As it moved through Guanajuato, pillaging and destroying the towns of San Miguel and Celaya, the rebel army demonstrated its greatest problem: a lack of discipline. When the rebels arrived at the wealthy mining city of Guanajuato, Hidalgo requested the surrender of the city in exchange for full protection for its citizenry. Knowing that Hidalgo was unable to control his army—by now numbering around 20,000—the inhabitants decided to resist. The city's Spaniards and criollos locked themselves in the *alhóndiga*, or local granary, but the attackers were able to penetrate the building. Within an hour all the defenders were dead. The looting and destruction lasted much longer, however, and caused the deaths of around 2,500 people.

The insurgents split their army into two and moved from Guanajuato to Michoacán state. Within a month the cities of Zacatecas, San Luis Potosí, and Valladolid were in their hands. By late October Hidalgo led 80,000 followers toward Mexico City. On October 30 the insurgent army defeated the government's forces at Monte de las Cruces, in the hills surrounding Mexico City. Then, after three days' encampment outside the capital, Hidalgo

ordered his army to withdraw. Historians have often tried to explain Hidalgo's decision. Some point out that his army had suffered heavy losses and was short of ammunition; others suggest that he was aware of the risks of letting his undisciplined army loose in the capital and may have decided to spare it. Whatever the reason, the withdrawal angered Allende, Hidalgo's second-in-command, and increased the tension between the two men.

Many of Hidalgo's followers became disillusioned following the failure to take Mexico City. The rebels suffered their first defeat at San Jerónimo Aculco, Querétaro, on November 7, and by the time they reached Guadalajara, Jalisco, half had deserted. Nonetheless, Hidalgo entered Guadalajara in triumph and, with Allende, set about reorganizing the insurgent movement. They created a government, established a newspaper, *El Despertador Americano* (The American Awakening), and spent time training their armies. In addition, Hidalgo demonstrated his concern for Indians and mestizos by drafting a number of decrees that called for the abolition of slavery and the establishment of communal lands for the exclusive use of Indians.

Defeat of Hidalgo

Meanwhile the Spanish forces also regrouped and began their advance on Guadalajara. Against Allende's wishes, Hidalgo concentrated his forces at Puente de Calderón and was defeated by a smaller number of government troops on January 17, 1811. The rebel army disbanded and Hidalgo was forced to relinquish command to Allende. Recognizing their precarious situation, Hidalgo and the other leaders fled northward to obtain support from the United States. These hopes were dashed when Spanish forces ambushed them near Monclova, Coahuila, on March 21.

The leaders of the revolt were brought to Chihuahua City, where the bishop of Chihuahua found Hidalgo guilty of heresy and treason, stripped him of his priest's robes, and handed him over to the secular authorities. He was executed on July 30. Despite the failure of his rebel army, Hidalgo was an inspiration behind successive insurgent movements that campaigned for Mexico's independence from Spain from the period after his death until 1821.

Luz María Hernández Sáenz

SEE ALSO:

Constitutions, Mexican; Criollos; Iturbide, Agustín de; Mexican Independence; Morelos y Pavón, José.

Hidalgo y Costilla, Miguel
Priest and independence leader

Born: May 8, 1753
Corralejo, Guanajuato

Died: July 30, 1811
Chihuahua City, Chihuahua

1778	Ordained a priest
1803	Assigned parish of Dolores
1810	Delivers "El Grito;" leads a rebel army toward Mexico City but fails to take the capital
1811	Ambushed by Spanish forces; tried and executed in Chihuahua

Hispanic Americans

Most Hispanic Americans trace their origins to Mexico, Puerto Rico, Cuba, Central America, or South America. Today, Hispanics are one of the fastest growing ethnic groups in the United States. In 2000 the U.S. Census Bureau reported that there were 32.8 million Hispanics in the United States, or 12 percent of the total population.

The largest group (66.1 percent) of Hispanic Americans is of Mexican origin. The next largest group (14.5 percent) includes immigrants from Central or South America. Other significant portions of the Hispanic population have origins in Puerto Rico (9 percent) and Cuba (4 percent). The remaining 6.4 percent of the Hispanics in the United States come from other countries.

Most Hispanic Americans are native born, are naturalized citizens, or have legal residency status. The majority of Hispanics live in urban centers and in the West; there are large concentrations in Arizona, California, Colorado, Florida, Illinois, New Mexico, New York, and Texas. Hispanics tend to live in family units that are larger than those of non-Hispanic whites and earn less. Unemployment and poverty rates are also higher in Hispanic communities than in white communities.

Mexican Americans

Mexicans have been living in what became the southwestern United States since the 1600s, when they began to establish homesteads in the areas that later became New Mexico, Arizona, California, Colorado, and Texas. In the 1800s Mexicans were attracted to the Midwest to work on the railroads and in the steel factories. Immigration continued in the early twentieth century with opportunities to work in rich agricultural areas, such as Imperial Valley in California.

Today, Mexicans continue to immigrate to the United States. However, the majority of Mexican Americans are U.S.-born citizens. In the Mexico-U.S. border region there are large Mexican communities that continue to have strong ties with Mexico. They watch television from Mexico, listen

Most Hispanic Americans live in urban centers and many suffer from poverty and low education standards. In 1996, 37 percent of employed Hispanic Americans did not have a high school degree, compared to 13 percent for all U.S. workers.

to the radio stations playing Mexican or Tejano music, attend churches where Mexican Spanish is spoken, and use stores, bars, and restaurants run by Mexican Americans.

Although there have been incidents of tension between Mexican Americans and other Hispanics, they often work together in business and attend the same Spanish-speaking churches and schools. Indeed, organizations such as the Mexican and American Solidarity Foundation work to bring together Mexicans and other Hispanics in collaborative projects in education, business, and cultural exchange.

Central and South Americans

Hispanics immigrated from Central and South America in the 1970s and 1980s when much of the region was in political turmoil. Civil wars in the late 1970s in Nicaragua, El Salvador, and Guatemala induced people to seek refuge from the unrest. Today, immigration continues from El Salvador, Panama, Honduras, Guatemala, Nicaragua, Ecuador, Bolivia, Colombia, and Peru for various reasons.

Many Central and South Americans now live in California. According to the 1990 census, 49 percent, or 301,000, of Salvadorans, and 52 percent, or 159,000, of Guatemalans in the United States live in Los Angeles. Central and South Americans are attracted to southern California because of cheaper housing and established immigrant services.

Puerto Rican Americans

Puerto Ricans account for the third largest U.S. Hispanic population. They are able to move freely between Puerto Rico and the United States because of the Jones Act of 1917, which made all Puerto Ricans U.S. citizens. However, Puerto Ricans living in their homeland do not have the same rights as other Americans; they are not allowed to vote in U.S. presidential elections.

New York has a sizable, though diminishing, Puerto Rican population. According to the 2000 census, 789,000 Puerto Ricans now live in New York City. This compares to 187,000 Mexicans living in the same area. Where once most Hispanics in New York were Puerto Rican, today Puerto Ricans make up less than half of the population. Many traditions, like Three Kings day, block parties, and having two sets of godparents, remain a part of Puerto Rican American life.

Cuban Americans

When Fidel Castro took control of Cuba in 1959, many middle-class Cubans from the professional, technical, and business sectors migrated to the United States and, in particular, to Miami, Florida. Since 1979 these Cuban immigrants have tended to be less well educated than their predecessors. Despite this, Cuban Americans are the most educated Hispanics, with 70 percent graduating from high school and 25 percent graduating from college, compared to only 50 percent of Mexican Americans graduating from high school and only 7 percent graduating from college. The differences in educational attainment, as well as immigration circumstances, result in differing economic statuses, with Cuban Americans tending to be more affluent than Mexican Americans.

Hispanic American economy and culture

According to U.S. census studies it has been estimated that by the year 2050 Hispanic Americans will make up as much as 25 percent of the U.S. population, possibly making them the largest ethnic group. By 2030 Hispanic students age 5 to 18 will account for 25 percent of the school population. Clearly the Hispanic population will continue to play a significant and important role in U.S. business and society. Already by 1996 there were as many as 1.25 million Hispanic-owned businesses, accounting for revenues of over $50 billion per year.

In politics, public service, entertainment, science, and sports, Hispanic Americans have made considerable contributions to U.S. society. In 2001 Rosario Marin became the first Mexican-born U.S. treasurer when she was asked to serve in George W. Bush's presidential administration. There have been two Hispanic American Nobel Prize winners: Luis W. Alvarez in physics and Severo Ochoa in medicine and physiology. Hispanic writers include Anais Nin and Josephine Niggli and in the entertainment industry Hispanics include the actors Anthony Quinn and Martin Sheen, the musicians Trini Lopez and Joan Baez, and the artist Wilfredo Lam. Hispanic sports stars have included golfer Lee Trevino, footballer Jim Plunkett, pitcher Luis Tiant, and boxer Hector (Macho) Camacho.

Lois Swanick

See also:

Housing in the United States

Of all the social problems faced by Mexican Americans, the lack of affordable and adequate housing is one of the most serious. Shelter is not the only problem; poor housing can affect an individual's health, overall financial stability, and educational opportunities.

Mexican settlement in the present-day Southwest started in 1598, but remained sparse due to the relatively harsh conditions there. The main forms of habitation were missions (religious settlements), presidios (forts), and pueblos (administrative towns); the main activities were ranching, farming, and mining. Widespread immigration of Anglo-Americans to the region started in the early nineteenth century. In Texas, Anglos outnumbered Mexicans by 1830.

After the conclusion of the Mexican-American War in 1848, a large area of former Mexican territory became part of the United States. Today this area forms the Southwest. The Treaty of Guadalupe Hidalgo that accompanied the boundary change granted full rights to Mexicans living in the region. In reality, however, these Mexican-Americans were treated as second-class citizens.

Until the turn of the twentieth century the Southwest attracted only a small number of Mexican immigrants. Their type of work—temporary agricultural labor, mining, and work on the railroads—promoted segregation, as workers lived in employer-owned quarters. These Mexican immigrants were particularly concentrated in Texas. It was there that the first barrios were formed, as families and friends from the same hometowns clustered together in distinct neighborhoods, so establishing the pattern of separate Mexican-American areas. Opportunities for housing outside the barrios were severely restricted.

Immigration to the United States

The massive immigration into the Southwest from Mexico that occurred between 1910 and 1930 dramatically increased the number of urban barrios and rural labor camps in the region. It was not just the turbulent years of the Mexican Revolution that fostered immigration, however. There was also enormous demand for cheap labor in the United States. By the 1920s Mexicans formed large enclaves in the bigger industrial cities.

The condition of housing in these areas was the subject of several official studies. In 1928 the Los Angeles County Health Department showed that the dwellings occupied by Mexicans were the worst in the county. Outside Los Angeles, an inspector of the California Commission on Immigration and Housing reported that the Mexican labor camp he surveyed had the highest infant mortality rate in the whole of the United States.

Mexican immigration intensified after 1941, when the United States' entry into World War II caused labor shortages. A formal program to supply labor was established between the U.S. and Mexican governments. Under the terms of the Bracero Program immigrant workers were to receive free transportation and food, guaranteed wages, safe working conditions, and adequate housing. In practice, however, these contract provisions were often violated and housing failed to meet the contract standards.

Housing in the postwar period

The years following the end of World War II were a time of general prosperity in the United States. The Housing Act of 1949 and the loan programs of the Federal Housing Administration and the Veterans Administration led to a substantial improvement in housing in the United States. The FHA aimed to provide decent homes and a suitable living environment for all U.S. citizens and promoted the ideal of owning a suburban house. These federal policies directly subsidized the migration of the white middle classes to newly formed suburbs. Home ownership became a major form of savings and investment, because interest payments on mortgages and property taxes were income-tax deductible.

Mexican Americans were largely excluded from these programs, however. Discrimination was intrinsic in the codes of practice of both the FHA and real estate agents because of the belief that integration would reduce property values. The FHA thus helped to define the segregation patterns in which city centers were occupied by racial minorities, while the newly created suburbs were dominated by whites.

The late twentieth century

The flight to the suburbs of the white middle-class intensified in the late twentieth century. Successive surveys showed that at all levels of household income Hispanics were more likely than Anglo Americans to reside in cities, with a larger proportion living in central areas. As a result, Hispanics generally lived in older houses located in low-income areas. Often these houses were unsatisfactory in both condition and size.

The housing problems faced by Mexican Americans and other Hispanic groups in the mid-to-late twentieth century can be illustrated by the results of the Annual Housing Survey (AHS; later the American Housing Survey). In 1980 the AHS showed that 16 percent of owner-occupied Hispanic households and 24 percent of houses rented by Hispanics were overcrowded, figures that were eight times greater than for whites. Subsequent reports from the AHS have shown little or no improvement. Other statistics from the AHS show that Hispanics are more likely to live in areas that have poor public facilities.

Historically, Hispanics have tended to be excluded from publicly assisted housing programs, which were originally started in the 1930s for African Americans. However, this situation changed toward the end of the twentieth century, as the number of Hispanics in the United States grew. The Neighborhood Reinvestment Corporation, a national nonprofit agency created in 1978, sponsors a network of more than 170 low and moderate income neighborhoods. At the beginning of the twenty-first century the program covered 2 percent of the total housing stock of the United States. Of the organization's 4.8 million residents, 20 percent were Hispanic.

Traditionally, a large number of farmworkers in the United States have been of Mexican origin. These seasonal and migrant workers form one of the most disadvantaged groups in American society because they are uneducated, unskilled, speak no English, and are often undocumented. Because their employment is temporary, they are ineligible for federal benefits. Due to their low wages and the seasonal nature of their work, they do not have the resources needed to obtain decent housing.

In the mid-twentieth century farmers provided much of the housing for their workers, but due to more stringent health and safety regulations, they later began to find this too costly. The number of state-licensed camps in California dropped from 5,000 in 1968 to 100 in 1994. This trend led to the growth of informal settlements, known as *colonias*. A survey in 1995 showed that more than 340,000 people lived in *colonias* in Texas alone

Life in *colonias*

Typically *colonias* are simply collections of shacks, often with no sewage systems or running water. Because they are usually located a considerable distance outside city boundaries, *colonias* are often not supplied with electricity. Dwellings can be extremely basic and often assembled from wooden crates, with plastic sheets serving as roofs. Disease is a huge problem for the inhabitants of *colonias*, with dysentery particularly prevalent. The United States Department of Housing has recently taken considerable steps to improve living conditions within *colonias*, specifically attempting to ensure that they are all served by adequate sewage systems.

Housing continues to be a serious problem for Mexican Americans. While outright prejudice is illegal, indirect and subtle forms of discrimination continue. Thus Mexican Americans continue to be segregated, concentrated in city centers where buildings are old and services are frequently poor. Mexican Americans are also less likely to own their home and more likely to pay higher prices for their accommodations.

U.S. policy makers have often assumed that Mexicans will obtain better housing as they become more assimilated into the mainstream community. However, the continuous influx of immigrants in the latter half of the twentieth century has reinforced Mexican customs and language. Since the 1970s Mexican Americans have revitalized their ties with Mexico in a way that makes an increase in assimilation unlikely. The means to improve Mexican American housing may instead reside in the growing political power that the Mexican American population is gaining as it increases in size.

Zilah Quezado Deckker

SEE ALSO:

Barrios; Bracero Program; Colonias; Health Care in the U.S.; Immigration, Mexican; Mexican Communities, U.S.; Segregation and Integration.

Houston, Sam

A man of contradictions, Samuel "Sam" Houston (1793–1863) was a slaveholder and a defender of Native American rights, an alcoholic who subsequently embraced the temperance movement, a soldier and a peacemaker. He served as governor of two U.S. states and was the first president of the Republic of Texas.

Born March 2, 1793, in Virginia, Houston was 13 when his father died suddenly. His widowed mother purchased 400 acres (160 ha) near Maryville, eastern Tennessee, and moved her family of nine children to what was then wild frontier territory. Houston, who never had more than a year of formal schooling, took neither to farming nor to working in the family shop. At age 16 he ran away from home to live with the Cherokee, whose lands lay across the Tennessee River. He lived with them for three years, learned their language, and received his Indian name, "the Raven." He wrote later: "My early life among the Indians was a necessary portion of that wonderful training that fitted me for my destiny."

Military and political success
After the United States declared war on Great Britain in June 1812, Houston joined the U.S. Army. In 1814, under the command of General Andrew Jackson (1767–1845), he gained promotion to the rank of third lieutenant. He led a series of infantry charges at the Battle of Horseshoe Bend on the Tallapoosa River against the Creek Native Americans, allies of the British who threatened the United States' southern frontier. During the battle Houston was severely wounded by an arrow in his thigh and two musket balls in his arm. Horseshoe Bend was a U.S. victory, however, and brought Houston to General Jackson's attention.

Houston accepted U.S. Army postings to Washington, New Orleans, and Tennessee before leaving his military career to study law and enter politics. He did this with the support of Jackson, by now his benefactor. After setting up a legal practice, Houston won the election for attorney general of the District of Nashville, a post he held from 1818 to 1821. As part of Jackson's inner circle Houston

Sam Houston is one of the most famous figures in Texan political history. An experienced soldier, he advocated compromise in later life in both U.S. relations with Mexico and in the buildup to the Civil War.

was elected to the U.S. House of Representatives in 1823, the same year Jackson was elected to the U.S. Senate. In 1827 Houston was elected governor of Tennessee while Jackson became U.S. president.

Drink and marriage problems
The governorship made Houston, age only 34, a national figure, and led to speculation about his potential as a future U.S. president. His personal affairs were less successful: his first marriage in 1829 lasted only three months. Its failure caused Houston to resign as governor. He left Tennessee and again went to live with the Cherokee, by now relocated by the U.S. government to Indian Territory, in present-day Oklahoma. Houston drank liquor heavily, as the Cherokee's new name for him, "Big Drunk," suggests. Despite his drinking, Houston

Human Rights in Mexico

Mexican governments have long expressed their commitment to the protection of human rights, despite well-documented cases where people's rights have been abused. Since the late 1980s, however, the pressure to change attitudes and reform laws has grown steadily.

Three years after independence from Spain, Mexico's 1824 Constitution enshrined the rights of individuals to free elections, justice under the law, and freedom from slavery and torture. The nation's concern with human rights was also evident in the 1848 Treaty of Guadalupe Hidalgo, in which Mexico ceded land to the United States only on condition that the new landholders would not reintroduce slavery to the region. However, despite its historical concerns, Mexico had a consistently poor record on human rights throughout the twentieth century. Elections were rigged, numerous arrests made without charge, and citizens persecuted because of their race, political links, religious beliefs, or sexuality.

Political and electoral rights

Mexico's 1917 constitution forbade presidents to serve more than one term, but ways were found around this requirement in the following decade. In 1928 President Álvaro Obregón, who held office from 1920 to 1924, arranged another term for himself but was assassinated before his inauguration. The outgoing president, Plutarco Elías Calles, subverted the rule against holding office again by appointing a succession of weak presidents, through whom he effectively ruled for six more years.

Mexican voting rights were often overlooked in the twentieth century. During the 71-year rule of the Partido Revolucionario Institucional (PRI; Institutional Revolutionary Party) from 1929 to 2000, there were many reported cases of vote-rigging to maintain the party's dominance. During the 1988 presidential campaign, for example, opinion polls showed that an opposition candidate, Cuauhtémoc Cárdenas, was ahead of the PRI's Carlos Salinas de Gortari. However, the final election result gave Salinas an 18 percent margin of

A pro-Zapatista mural hung by human rights campaigners in Mexico City during the 2000 presidential elections. The text reads: "85,000 soldiers in Chiapas, let us stop the war," and refers to the army's presence in that state since the uprising over Indian rights in 1994.

victory. Independent statistical analysis subsequently showed that Cárdenas should have won the election, and there were numerous cases of malpractice at the voting stations, including the removal of opposition voters from the electoral roll, a practice known as *la razurada* (shaving).

Criticism of the 1988 elections led President Salinas to create the independent Federal Electoral Institute to oversee future elections. In the run-up to the 1994 elections he introduced further reforms, such as fairer funding for parties' election campaigns and allowing foreign observers to oversee that year's elections, which were generally regarded as a vast improvement on 1988's. In response to international criticisms of human rights abuses—triggered by the involvement of Mexican police in the murder of a U.S. Drug Enforcement Administration agent—Salinas created a National Commission on Human Rights in 1990. Sponsored by the government, the commission has nonetheless been limited in its influence. However, by the late 1990s it recommended punishments for several thousand Mexican civil servants whom it claimed had abused human rights.

Withholding constitutional rights

The 1917 constitution provides for freedom of expression, association, and religion. It also states that no one may be deprived of life, liberty, or property without the due process of law. In practice, however, arbitrary arrest and the detention of suspects were commonplace throughout the twentieth century. While torture is illegal in Mexico, it was practiced widely by the law enforcement agencies. One of the main reasons for the practice was that, in cases where a witness made more than one statement, Mexican law favored his or her earliest account of events. This encouraged the use of coercion to obtain an initial confession, which was then used to secure a guilty verdict in the courts.

Although there is no overt censorship in Mexico, successive governments exerted pressure on the press and broadcast media. Journalists were bribed to write favorable stories, and *gacetillas*—columns prepared by the government but disguised as ordinary news—were inserted in many newspapers. Independent newspapers, such as *La Reforma*,

refused to publish the *gacetillas*. Others, such as *La Jornada*, identified them as paid insertions and printed them in italics. Many newspapers published the government-sponsored articles and refrained from criticizing local or national officials. To do otherwise could have fatal consequences: from the late 1980s to the mid-1990s a number of reporters who had investigated government-related corruption were found dead in mysterious circumstances.

Workers' rights

The right of workers to strike in protest against working conditions was traditionally limited by the ruling PRI party's control of Mexico's largest union, the Central de Trabajadores Mexicanos (CTM; Mexican Workers' Union). In December 1989 workers at the Ford Motor Company plant in Cuautitlán, Federal District, objected to the PRI-imposed union leadership. The workers insisted on the right to elect their own leaders. The following month CTM gunmen entered the plant and shot workers at random, killing one and injuring several others. Shortly afterward nearly a thousand police officers forcibly removed protesters from the premises. In April 1994 workers at a Sony manufacturing plant in Nuevo Laredo, Tamaulipas, resisted a demand that they work on weekends. In

People at Risk from Rights Abuses

Although only about one in ten Mexicans is white, this small minority has most of the power and influence in the country. The majority most likely to suffer human rights' violations are the mestizos of mixed Spanish-Indian descent, who constitute 60 percent of the population, and the indigenous Indians, who make up 30 percent. In a tradition dating back to the Spanish conquest, Indians are the most likely group to face exclusion and discrimination. In the mid-1990s rates of illiteracy among Indians were three times the national average, while their average wages were half those of other workers in Mexico.

Another at-risk category is gay men and lesbians. Although homosexuality between consenting adults is not illegal in Mexico, authorities have tolerated violence toward gay men and lesbians and persecuted those who campaign for gay rights. In June 1992, for example, AIDS

worker Gerardo Rubén Ortega Zurita criticized the government for its treatment of homosexuals. Three days later he and an associate, José Cruz-Reyes Potenciano, were arrested, charged with rape, and beaten by police. They were then sentenced to nearly 14 years in jail, prompting the human rights organization Amnesty International to classify them as possible prisoners of conscience. Both men were released in July 1993 and cleared of all charges. Other acts of violence carried out on gay men and lesbians include murder. In the early 1990s, 11 gay men were murdered in a series of killings in Chiapas.

In defiance of this atmosphere of hostility, gay and lesbian movements in Mexico have offered support to members of their community and pressured Mexican society to become more tolerant. By 2000 there were approximately 70 gay and lesbian organizations in Mexico.

response the plant's management and the CTM called a vote with only 12 hours' notice and required all the voters to declare their intentions in the presence of executives. When 300 workers put down their tools in protest, the mayor sent in police officers armed with water cannons to evict them.

If CTM- or government-approved union leaders challenged authority, they risked arrest on unrelated charges. A famous case in point was that of Joaquin "La Quina" Hernández Galicia, leader of the Oil Workers Union. In the 1988 presidential election he organized his union's support for the opposition candidate, Lázaro Cárdenas. Following Cárdenas's defeat and Salinas's questionable victory, the new president ordered the arrest of La Quina. The union boss was accused of stockpiling weapons, but witnesses said they had seen the army planting them. Troops then stormed La Quina's home, following government claims that his bodyguards had shot dead a public ministry agent. However, contrary evidence suggested that the agent had been killed elsewhere and his corpse planted at La Quina's house.

Land ownership rights

The Mexican constitution makes extensive provision for small landowners and is opposed to large plantations that monopolize fertile land. In practice, however, peasant farmers' rights have often been overlooked. Abuses of campesinos (rural farmers) by large landowners reached a crisis point in the southern state of Chiapas in the 1990s. Lacking the funds to pursue their cases through the courts, many campesinos took direct action by occupying large estates and claiming squatters' rights. In response, landowners paid for vigilantes to commit acts of violence against the peasants. The situation led to the uprising of the Ejército Zapatista de Liberación Nacional (EZLN; Zapatista Army of National Liberation) in January 1994. A ten-day battle resulted in nearly 150 deaths. About 200 EZLN members were arrested and tortured by police and army personnel. Additional government responses included evicting rural peoples from their homes.

Protests at the government's reaction to the Zapatista uprising included human rights organizations' visits to Chiapas and demonstrations in Mexico and the United States. Other voices remained critical of the campesino movement and the EZLN. The pro-PRI newspaper *Summa* accused the Jesuit priest Jerónimo Hernández López of being the mysteri-

ous Subcomandante Marcos, leader of the EZLN. For a long time liberal priests were highly critical of the PRI and the abuses of power by the government. The Jesuits filed a charge of defamation, but Mexico's attorney general declined to prosecute the newspaper. Shortly afterward posters appeared all over Mexico City threatening the lives of Jesuits.

The Zapatista uprising highlighted the issue of campesino rights. President Salinas initiated a series of peace talks, while his successor, President Ernesto Zedillo Ponce de León, invited the Inter-American Human Rights Commission to visit Chiapas. President Vicente Fox, elected in 2000, pledged to bring about a peaceful solution to the conflict with the Zapatistas. He ordered the Mexican army, stationed in Chiapas since the 1994 uprising, to remain in its barracks. The EZLN responded by announcing its readiness to hold talks.

President Fox and human rights

Chronic abuse of human rights has been both a cause and an effect of divisions in Mexican society. When the Partido Acción Nacional's (PAN; National Action Party) Fox took office, bringing to an end 71 years of PRI rule, he declared: "Mexico will no longer be held up as a bad example in matters of human rights." Fox invited the United Nations Commissioner for Human Rights to help implement or restore long-neglected provisions of the Mexican constitution. Reflecting the desire for change, in December 2000 Oaxaca's state congress passed new legislation that secured the release of 30 political prisoners.

However, in spite of the high-profile initiatives, torture, death threats, and political killings continued to be reported in 2000. Prisoners of conscience remained behind bars, while journalists and human rights activists continued to be harassed. The detention of suspects without trial remained widespread, and many detainees were allegedly tortured. At the start of the twenty-first century, some Mexicans believed Fox could greatly improve Mexico's human rights record, while others feared that corruption was so endemic that change would be a much slower, more painful process.

Henry Russell

SEE ALSO:

Constitutions, Mexican; Elections in Mexico; Foreign Policy, Mexican; Indian Policy; Justice System; Land Reform; Newspapers and Magazines; Zapatistas.

Illegal Labor

Undocumented immigrants come to the United States for the same reasons as their legal counterparts: pushed out of Mexico and other sending-states by the lack of jobs, attracted to better opportunities within the United States, and seeking reunion with (and aided by) friends and family members who migrated previously.

Like legal immigrants, most undocumented migrants successfully find employment in the United States. Economists generally agree that the benefits to the U.S. economy of migrants' low-priced outputs balance the negative effects of falling wages, so that the overall net effect of illegal labor on the U.S. economy is very small. Nonetheless, undocumented immigrants differ from their legal counterparts in at least two important ways. First, undocumented immigrants, especially those from Mexico, have less formal education, less English-language ability, and fewer job skills than legal migrants. One study found that illegal Mexican migrants average only five years of formal education. Second, undocumented migrants lack job security; and many employers use the threat of deportation as a way to limit employee demands and prevent complaints about illegal working conditions or wages. Likewise, employers use the threat of deportation as a way to discourage undocumented migrants from joining labor unions.

For these reasons, undocumented workers are more likely to accept "3D jobs," those that in addition to being low-wage are dirty, dangerous, and difficult. Thus, even though their overall effect on the U.S. economy is small, undocumented migrants are most likely to have a wage-depressing effect on other low-skilled workers. Because of their insecurity these migrants are also least likely to contribute to the U.S. economy as consumers, and they are less likely than their legal counterparts to significantly upgrade their skills or to maximize educational opportunities for their children. As a result, the policy debate about illegal labor is complex. On one hand, employers who depend heavily on undocumented labor actually benefit from the maintenance of an undocumented labor force. On the other hand, even though in the past labor unions have sought to limit inflows and prohibit the employment of undocumented migrants, an increasing number now push to legalize them. Indeed, in 2000, the AFL-CIO adopted a resolution calling for universal amnesty, a policy that would eliminate the category of "illegal labor" and guarantee that all workers living in the United States would enjoy the same legal protections.

Roots of the current trends

These demographic trends and policy debates are the product of a century of legal and illegal migration and labor. Mexican labor in the United States began when the coincidence of U.S. railroad construction, an irrigation boom in the Southwest, and World War I (1914–1918) caused a surge in labor demand in California and Texas. The vast majority of the early Mexican migrants worked in railroad construction, agriculture (especially cotton in Texas and fruit and vegetables in California), mining, roadbuilding, and irrigation projects.

The legal status of these migrants was ambiguous. Although Mexicans could legally enter the United States, the U.S.-Mexican border was largely unpatrolled, allowing a large number of Mexicans to enter without inspection. Moreover, the U.S. authorities assumed Mexican migrants would eventually return home and focused their efforts on regulating unwanted Asian and European immigration. Thus, although many Mexicans lacked formal legal status at this time, they were in no way identified as undocumented or illegal laborers.

This status question changed with the 1917 Immigration Act, which imposed a reading test on adult migrants and an $8 head tax on all legal immigrants. However, growers prevailed upon the government to waive these new requirements for Mexicans to ensure adequate labor flows during the agricultural labor shortages caused by World War I. Although the waivers were initially short-term and limited to agricultural workers, the programs were steadily expanded and extended. Then, in 1921, temporary admission orders were rescinded and thousands of Mexican workers were suddenly "illegalized." Thus, the World War I recruitment program allowed a large number of Mexicans to

Migrants waiting at the roadside to be employed as day laborers. Many migrant workers do low-wage jobs offering little or no job security.

migrate legally. Eventually, however, the program ensured an even larger number of illegal workers as many left their legal agricultural jobs for higher wages elsewhere, failed to leave when the visa waiver program expired, and recruited family members to join them in the United States.

Following the onset of the Great Depression in 1929, officials in Texas and California deported a half-million Mexicans who lacked documents to prove they had migrated legally. In almost every case, Mexicans were denied access to legal counsel or the opportunity to appeal decisions. Strict enforcement became a highly contentious diplomatic issue, contributing to the overall deterioration in U.S.-Mexican relations during the 1930s.

The Bracero Program

When the United States entered World War II (1939–1945), the U.S. and Mexican governments agreed on a program to allow Mexican agricultural workers into the United States on temporary contracts to fill the new labor shortage. Known as the Bracero Program, the plan was loosely based on the previous World War I recruitment effort. As before, although the program facilitated an unprecedented level of legal Mexico-U.S. migration (with over 4 million bracero contracts issued in 22 years), it also created new incentives and capacities for Mexicans to work illegally in the United States.

Specifically, numerous braceros overstayed their contracts or broke contracts to find higher wages; and many also returned to the United States illegally, taking advantage of contacts forged on earlier bracero visits. Illegal labor was facilitated by employers who preferred to operate outside the highly regulated and initially labor-friendly terms of the bracero agreement. By the 1950s, illegal former braceros vastly outnumbered legal current braceros.

The problem of undocumented braceros became highly politicized both within the United States and on a binational level, with each concerned group seeking to shift the cost of enforcement to others. Mexico (and U.S. labor interests) demanded a solution involving fines being levied on U.S. employers who hired illegal braceros, but the Eisenhower administration (1953–1961) demanded that Mexico take greater responsibility for policing its side of the border. Eventually, Mexico was forced to accept a renegotiated agreement strictly on U.S. terms giving braceros fewer guarantees.

As part of these 1954 negotiations, Mexico agreed to allow a U.S. sweep of undocumented braceros. Operation Wetback remains the largest enforcement effort in U.S.-Mexican history, resulting in the deportation of 1.1 million Mexicans in one year—many of whom were in the United States legally. Perhaps as many as half that number again chose to leave to avoid deportation. Although such a crackdown would appear detrimental to U.S. agricultural interests, in combination with the revised Bracero Program, Operation Wetback created a captive audience of braceros who were unable to skip their now more employer-friendly contracts; and the program was thus eventually endorsed by all major grower interest groups.

Nonetheless, the problem of bracero contract overstays resumed, and the program became again a major contributor to undocumented immigration. Moreover, when the program ended in 1964, a large number of Mexicans accustomed to regular U.S. migration were cut off from their legal means to do so. Combined with the migration of friends and family who followed these "seed migrants," the legacy of the Bracero Program was a large, fast-growing population of undocumented Mexicans in the United States. By 1970 there were an estimated 345,000 Mexicans working illegally in the United States; another 219,000 were apprehended trying to enter the country. Apprehensions increased to 867,000 by 1979, but migrants continued to cross the border successfully, and the estimated undocumented population in the United States peaked at 1.076 million in the same year.

Recent responses

There were two responses to these trends. First, the U.S. Congress and public opinion pressed for stronger border enforcement. The budget of the Immigration and Naturalization Service (INS) was increased and a series of operations were carried out along the border, including building fences in urban areas. It is unclear whether border enforcement of this kind has been an effective deterrent.

The second response was the Immigration Reform and Control Act in 1986, which granted an amnesty to around 3 million undocumented workers who had lived in the United States for at least four years. It also made it illegal for U.S. employers to knowingly employ undocumented migrants. Although these employers' sanctions were demanded by labor unions and bitterly resisted by growers, the legislative compromise eventually reached was largely ineffective because of the difficulty of proving that employers knew their workers lacked legal status. Most importantly, over 95 percent of U.S. enforcement efforts are concentrated within 25 miles (40 km) of the U.S.-Mexican border; migrants who slip through this area are unlikely ever to be apprehended.

Despite these moves, there were an estimated 6 million undocumented migrants living and working in the United States by 2000, of which more than 3 million came from Mexico. An additional legacy of the 1970s and 1980s was a substantial geographic and economic diffusion of migrants, including undocumented migrants, throughout the country instead of them being concentrated in the Southwest. The INS estimated that in 1996 roughly half of all undocumented migrants lived in the states of California (2 million) and Texas (700,000), with another 1.5 million living in New York, Florida, Illinois, New Jersey, Arizona, and Massachusetts. The remaining 1.5 to 2 million were scattered across the rest of the country.

In addition, undocumented migrants are no longer concentrated in agriculture, though such work is still a first job for many. They can be found in meat packing, food processing, hotels and restaurants, manufacturing, construction, and cleaning work, as well as virtually all other low-wage sectors. Employers admit in surveys that they value immigrant labor—regardless of legal status—because migrant laborers work hard, complain little, and fill jobs that others will not accept.

Forecasts

Despite the fact that politicians on both sides of the U.S.-Mexico border express a commitment to preventing undocumented immigration, no major new policy responses have been implemented since 1986. With border enforcement and worksite inspections limited in their scope and potential to checking flows without sabotaging the regional economy, many experts agree that a guestworker program has the greatest potential to legitimize a large proportion of currently undocumented flows. Such a program was the subject of intense U.S.-Mexican negotiations in 2001. Resistance to such a program will be mounted by unions and those supporting immigrant rights, who recognize that it may be used to curtail migrants' labor rights at the same time as it legalizes their status; and by others who resist any attempt to legalize migrant flows. Whatever the outcome, inflows of undocumented migrants are likely to continue.

Marc R. Rosenblum

SEE ALSO:

Bracero Program; Deportation and Repatriation; Immigration, Mexican; Immigration Reform and Control Act; Labor and Employment.

Immigration, Mexican

Mexican immigration to the United States has been going on for more than a century. For generations powerful economic and political forces have pushed Mexicans from their native country while others pull them northward. The sensitive issue of immigration has often been at the center of the relationship between the two countries.

Until 1880 there was little immigration from Mexico to the United States. The area that is present-day New Mexico, Texas, Arizona, and California was home to many people of Mexican origin, as the region was part of Mexico until 1848.

First wave of immigration

The first big wave of Mexican immigration to the United States began in the late 1880s and lasted until the early twentieth century. It was propelled by two major factors. The first was the political and economic transformation of Mexico that occurred under the regime of Porfirio Díaz. As president from 1877 to 1880 and again from 1884 to 1911, Díaz pursued government policies that created an increase in private property and built a national railroad system. Changes in land ownership laws consolidated land into haciendas (large estates) and caused a massive displacement of small farmers as entire villages lost their holdings. According to some estimates, nine out of ten rural families in 1910 became landless due to such changes. At the same time, the country's railroad system was being built, and by 1884 it connected Mexico City to the Mexico-U.S. border. The railroads allowed the dispossessed to travel cheaply to the northern border, from where they could emigrate to the United States in search of work.

The U.S. Southwest, meanwhile, was also undergoing dramatic changes. A transcontinental railroad completed in 1869 linked the region to the rest of the nation, fueling a boom in mining and agriculture. These developing industries needed unskilled workers, and employers turned to Mexico to find them. By 1890 only about 78,000 Mexicans had immigrated to the United States. By 1920 the

A Mexican emigrating to Laredo, Texas, in 1912, at a time when Mexican immigration to the United States was unrestricted.

number had reached 222,000. Between 1880 and 1929, more than one million Mexicans entered the United States.

Most Mexican immigrants found work in the U.S. Southwest. They first labored on the railroads, doing the hard, low-paid work of laying track. Later many took jobs in agriculture, mining, and factories. They picked cotton in south Texas and California's Imperial Valley, citrus fruits in southern California and Texas's Lower Rio Grande Valley, and sugar beets in Colorado. By the early twentieth century Mexican immigrants had also moved beyond the Southwest. They worked on railroads and in packing houses, smelters, and auto plants throughout the Midwest.

Before the Mexican Revolution began in 1910 most Mexicans who migrated to the United States had been landless peasants and workers from rural areas. As the revolution shook Mexico, however, hacienda owners, professionals, and intellectuals also crossed the border to flee political and economic chaos. Counterrevolutionary groups loyal to Porfirio Díaz moved to San Antonio and Los Angeles. Entire families made the trip across the border.

World War I (1914–1918) and continued prosperity in the Southwest created an even higher demand for Mexican labor. That demand was intensified by the passing of the federal Immigration Act of 1917, which restricted immigration from Asia and southeastern Europe but did not limit immigration from Mexico. There was plenty of work even for Mexicans immigrating illegally. It was easy to cross the border. The U.S. Border Patrol was organized in 1924, but it had far too few employees to police the entire 2,000-mile (3,200-km) border effectively. By the 1920s some 49,000 Mexicans per year were immigrating to the United States.

The large migration was abruptly shut off by the Great Depression of the 1930s, when unemployment soared. U.S. president Herbert Hoover (1929–1933) blamed Mexicans for the economic problems of the Southwest. Local authorities organized a repatriation program to send Mexicans back to their native country. Although it was meant to be voluntary, in practice many were sent back against their wishes. Some 500,000 Mexican immigrants were expelled from the United States along with their U.S.-born children.

Bracero Program

Only a few years later, World War II (1939–1945) again created an intense labor shortage in the United States, especially in agriculture. To deal with the problem, the United States made an agreement with the Mexican government in 1942 called the Bracero Program. It contracted Mexicans for temporary seasonal agricultural work. They were not allowed to join unions, and they could only stay in the United States for six months. The Bracero Program was the main form of Mexican migration to the United States from 1942 to the early 1960s. In all, some 4.7 million Mexicans worked under bracero contracts until the program ended.

After the end of the war, immigration surged. Most of it was sanctioned under the "legal permanent resident" program of the INS. Between 1940 and 1960 about 360,000 Mexicans settled in the United States permanently and lawfully under this program, which admits most people because of their family ties to someone who is already a legal U.S. resident or U.S. citizen. Changes in immigration law in the 1960s and 1970s allowed more

Restricting Mexican Immigration

Until 1917 Mexicans could freely cross the border into the United States. The requirements of the 1917 Immigration Act (an $8 head tax and reading tests) were waived for Mexicans, who were also exempt from the national immigrant quotas imposed in 1921 and 1924. However, the creation of the U.S. Border Patrol in 1924 had a significant effect on Mexicans. From 1929 it became a crime to enter the United States from Mexico without documents. From then on any Mexican living north of the border could be regarded with suspicion.

The Bracero Program (1942–1964), which gave Mexicans the right to work temporarily in the United States, increased illegal immigration, as braceros overstayed their contracts or absconded to work illegally for better wages and conditions. In 1954 the U.S. government mounted Operation Wetback to remove undocumented immigrants. In one year, 1.1 million Mexicans were deported, many of whom were working legally. Along the border the Immigration and Naturalization Service (INS) and Border Patrol tried to detain would-be immigrants. In 1965 agents made 110,000 arrests (often multiple arrests were made of the same individuals). In

1975 the number of arrests reached 766,000. Four years later it topped one million.

Even as the economies of both Mexico and the United States became increasingly dependent on immigrant labor, U.S. anxiety and resentment grew about undocumented immigrants. As a result Congress passed the Immigration Reform and Control Act (IRCA) in 1986. It legalized 1.2 million undocumented immigrants who had lived in the United States since 1982. It also legalized previously undocumented farmworkers. For the first time in the history of U.S. immigration law, IRCA made it unlawful for companies to hire undocumented workers. The law sounded strict but the INS did not have enough resources to enforce it. Would-be immigrants who were arrested were simply sent back across the border. Many kept trying to return to the United States until they were successful.

In the 1990s there were massive efforts to reinforce the border with programs such as Operation Gatekeeper. Meanwhile, each year, an estimated 300 immigrants die from drowning, thirst, freezing, pedestrian accidents, or violence as they swim rivers, hike through treacherous terrain, cross highways and confront vigilantes.

people from the Western Hemisphere to immigrate to the United States, and the number of newcomers from Mexico increased dramatically: from 300,000 in 1971 to 640,000 in 1980.

In 1964 Mexico and the United States established the Border Industrialization Program (BIP), partly to provide employment for the braceros returning to Mexico. Under the program, plants known as maquiladoras were built in Mexican border cities where low-wage Mexican workers assembled parts into products for U.S. and other foreign companies. The BIP was very successful—maquiladoras spread all along the border and employed hundreds of thousands of workers. However, the program did not succeed in providing employment for braceros. The maquiladoras drew young, ambitious Mexicans from the country's interior. On the border, they worked for U.S. companies and could see the U.S. skyline. Maquiladoras became springboards for illegal immigration into the United States where jobs were waiting—jobs directly related to the globalization of production reflected by the maquiladora industry.

From the 1970s cities in the United States such as Los Angeles, Houston, and New York became enclaves for affluent, educated professionals who managed the emerging global economy. These people were willing to pay for an array of personal services—from restaurant meals to nannies to house cleaners and manicurists. Their needs created a demand for low-paid, unskilled labor. That demand attracted immigrants from countries such as Mexico. In turn, these immigrants sent part of their wages back to their families in Mexico. The money sent home by immigrants is Mexico's third most important source of hard-currency earnings after oil and tourism. By the end of the century Mexicans lived in areas where they had hardly been seen a generation before. In New York City, for instance, only a few thousand Mexicans were counted in the census in 1970. By 2000 an estimated 196,000 lived in the area. Talks in 2001 between Mexico and the United States on the issue of continued undocumented immigration included the possibility of introducing a guestworker program.

Immigration to Canada

Immigration of Mexicans to Canada began later than immigration to the United States and remains small in comparison. A few Mexicans began arriving in Canada in the 1950s, and in the 1970s

This 1964 photograph shows a Mexican farmworker holding a work permit that allows him to cross the Mexico-U.S. border.

their numbers increased as professionals, technicians, and students began to follow. Another group of immigrants from Mexico included the Mexican-born descendants of Mennonite farmers who left Canada for northern Mexico between 1920 and 1940. Drought and economic hardship in Mexico caused some of them to begin returning to Canada in the mid-1980s. The 1996 census counted about 23,000 people in Canada of Mexican descent.

Canada, the United States, and Mexico are parties to the North American Free Trade Agreement (NAFTA) implemented in 1994. One of NAFTA's selling points was its promise to curtail Mexican immigration, predicting more jobs would be created in Mexico as its economy grew stronger. NAFTA, however, has had little effect on immigration. In fact, many researchers believe that NAFTA's support for agricultural modernization and industrial globalization encourages immigration, at least in the short term.

Deborah Nathan

SEE ALSO:

Border Patrol, U.S.; Bracero Program; Canada; Deportation and Repatriation; Illegal Labor; Migrant Labor; Operation Gatekeeper; Operation Wetback; Sending Communities.

Immigration and Naturalization Service

The Immigration and Naturalization Service (INS) is an agency of the U.S. Department of Justice and is responsible for implementing immigration policy. Its enforcement arm is the Border Patrol.

The Immigration Service was set up in the 1890s as immigration law became increasingly complicated. The main duty of the service was regulating the arrival of non-U.S. citizens to the country at various ports of entry, the most important being Ellis Island. From 1906 the agency took on the responsibility of naturalization (granting citizenship to immigrants) and its name was changed to the Immigration and Naturalization Service.

U.S. immigration laws became increasingly complex in the early twentieth century, making it harder to enter the United States. As it became more difficult to qualify for legal status, the amount of undocumented immigration began to rise, especially along land borders. To combat undocumented immigration, the U.S. Congress created the Border Patrol as part of the INS in 1924. Gradually the work of the Border Patrol turned toward deportation, or the returning of undocumented immigrants to their country of origin. Throughout the twentieth century the INS and Border Patrol were primarily concerned with the removal of undocumented immigrants.

The INS and the U.S.-Mexico border

The U.S.-Mexico border includes the world's busiest international land crossing, at San Ysidro linking San Diego and Tijuana. Ninety million people crossed here in 1998. The activities of the INS along the border include inspecting all traffic at ports of entry, apprehending immigrants who commit crimes, investigating cases of forged documents, and excluding or deporting undocumented immigrants. The INS works closely with both U.S. Customs and the Drug Enforcement Agency.

In 1993, under pressure from the U.S. public to reduce the number of undocumented immigrants in the United States, Attorney General Janet Reno implemented plans allowing for major changes in the INS, especially along the U.S.-Mexico border. Between 1993 and 1999 the overall budget of the agency increased by more than 150 percent, and in 2001 was more than $4 billion. During this time, the size of the Border Patrol force increased by over 100 percent, to around 10,000 agents.

The budget funded four specific operations along the border between 1993 and 1997, each covering a different section. Their goal was "prevention through deterrence"; in other words, making the risk of apprehension so high that prospective illegal entrants would be too frightened to attempt entry.

The operations fortified the border, especially in urban areas such as San Diego, California, and El Paso, Texas, with steel fences, ground sensors, and floodlights. Military personnel were deployed to help combat drug trafficking. There was widespread alarm at this militarization of the border in both Mexico and the United States. In 1995 Janet Reno announced that Operation Gatekeeper had resulted in a 32 percent decrease of illegal border crossings in the San Diego area. However, the figure only showed that people were not crossing in that area, not that the numbers of people entering the country without documents were actually decreasing. Indeed, there was no evidence to indicate that the numbers of border-crossers had changed at all. As easier routes were closed off in the cities, border-crossers began to walk through remote and dangerous areas, such as high mountains and wide deserts. The result was an increase in deaths of border-crossers. Since 1995 more than 1,870 have died trying to cross the border, and the figure continues to rise at an average of one per day. After the terrorist attacks on the World Trade Center and the Pentagon in September 2001, the INS stepped up its controls at the border and is likely to increase them further in the future.

Sarah Eriksen Keller

SEE ALSO:

Border Patrol, U.S.; Immigration, Mexican; Migrant Labor; Operation Gatekeeper; Operation Hold-the-Line; Operation Wetback.

Immigration Reform and Control Act

The 1986 Immigration Reform and Control Act (IRCA) was the first major change in U.S. immigration policy since the 1960s. It legalized nearly 3 million undocumented immigrants living in the United States, 70 percent of whom were of Mexican origin.

The IRCA had several goals: to control the number of undocumented (illegal) immigrants in the United States, to ensure that employers check the identification and eligibility documents of those they hire, and to discourage employers from hiring undocumented workers through the imposition of fines and other penalties. It also allocated a 75 percent increase in funds to the U.S. Immigration and Naturalization Service (INS) over two years and an increase of the number of officers in the INS's Border Patrol, which detects and prevents illegal entry along the Mexico–U.S. border.

Granting resident status

The IRCA established two programs to allow undocumented immigrants to become legal U.S. residents: the Legally Authorized Workers (LAW) program and the Special Agricultural Worker (SAW) program. The LAW program allowed those living continuously in the United States since January 1, 1982, to apply for 18-month temporary residence, after which they could apply for permanent status. The SAW program targeted agricultural workers who had worked on U.S. farms for at least 90 days a year for three years. In order to appease farmers who were concerned about losing workers once they were granted legal residency, the SAW applicants were required to remain farmworkers for one more year before applying for permanent status. Both programs required immigrants to have a basic knowledge of English and U.S. law before gaining permanent status.

The IRCA required all U.S. employers to check the identification and work eligibility documents of their employees. Under the act, employers who hired undocumented workers faced possible fines from $250–$10,000 per employee, as well as jail sentences for repeated offenses. The undocumented workers themselves would be deported. Despite the penalties, the IRCA led to a growth in the black market for counterfeit papers such as fake passports, green cards, and driver's licenses.

Effects of the IRCA

The IRCA developed out of the U.S. government's ambitions to greatly reduce levels of illegal immigration. The resulting legislation, however, was a compromise between conservatives and liberals, including Mexican American advocacy organizations, that resulted in an amnesty for those immigrants already living in the United States, as well as laws to crack down on further influxes.

Opponents argued that the amnesty would promote more illegal immigration to the United States, not less. While the legislation briefly slowed the number of people illegally crossing the border, numbers soon began to rise again. At the start of the twenty-first century there were between 3 and 4 million undocumented Mexicans in the United States. Many who became legal residents through the IRCA left their low-wage jobs after the one-year requirement to seek better work elsewhere in the United States, leaving a gap for more undocumented workers to fill. However, the IRCA amnesty alone cannot explain the continued influx of immigrants. A greater stimulus comes from the consistent demand by U.S. employers to hire cheap labor on farms as well as in factories, restaurants, hotels, and shops. In 2001 U.S. president George W. Bush announced plans to introduce one-year permits for immigrant Mexican workers. In contrast Mexican president Vicente Fox called for an open-border policy to allow unrestricted movement between Mexico and the United States.

Margaret Gray

SEE ALSO:
Border Patrol, U.S.; Illegal Labor; Immigration and Naturalization Service; Immigration, Mexican.

Immigration to Mexico

While not on the same scale as immigration to the United States, many people have moved to Mexico since the early nineteenth century. They have come for a variety of reasons, including land acquisition, escape from persecution, or simply to enjoy the Mexican way of life.

Many people immigrated to Texas when it was part of Mexico. During the country's colonial period (1521–1821), few colonists wanted to live in Texas because the vast area was geographically remote from the rest of Mexico. Texas was also home to several Native American tribes who were hostile to colonists and often raided their settlements. The Spanish government was eager to settle the region, however, to secure it from the Native Americans. Shortly before Mexico won its independence from Spain in 1821, the Spanish government gave Moses Austin, a colonist from the United States, permission to bring 300 families to Texas. The conditions imposed by Mexico City were that the families had to follow the Catholic faith and obey Mexican law.

Increasing immigration to Texas
Moses Austin died in 1821, but his son, Stephen F. Austin, took over the founding of the colony. Soon after its establishment, large numbers of U.S. immigrants began to arrive in Texas. Many settled in legal colonies, but many others came illegally. The main attraction was land, which in Texas in the 1820s cost only ten cents an acre, compared to $1.25 for much lower grade land in the United States. Moreover, the Mexican government was generous with its land grants. An immigrant husband and wife could buy 960 acres (388 ha) of land, together with 160 acres (65 ha) for each of their children.

By 1827 Texas was home to around 12,000 Anglo-Americans, compared with only 7,000 Mexicans. Although nominally a Mexican, Catholic, Spanish-speaking province, Texas's majority of Anglo-American, Protestant, English speakers had little interest in adopting another faith or language. Religious, cultural, and political conflict soon developed. The issue of slavery fueled tensions further. Mexico had abolished the practice in 1821, but later laws permitted it in Texas, whose white immigrants were mostly from the slaveholding U.S. South. However, in 1829 Mexican president Vicente Guerrero issued a proclamation aimed specifically at ending slavery in Texas. The following year, worried about Anglo-American unrest, Mexico forbade further immigration to Texas from the United States, but the action came too late, in large part because of the number of U.S. settlers in the region. By the mid-1830s their population had risen to 30,000. In 1836 Texas successfully revolted against Mexico and became an independent republic.

African Americans and Chinese
Slavery remained legal in the new Republic of Texas and also in the territory annexed by the United States in 1845. At the start of the Civil War (1861–1865) Texas seceded from the Union and joined the Confederacy. Until the Confederates' defeat, 30 percent of Texas's population were slaves. However, Mexico and its antislavery laws lay just to the south, and many African American slaves moved there after escaping from their owners. Tejanos (Mexican-origin Texans) often helped runaway slaves by hiding them and pointing out safe routes across the Mexico-U.S. border. Slaves from states other than Texas also headed for Mexico and freedom. Sometimes they did so in large numbers, including a group of hundreds of fugitive African Americans who crossed into Mexico in 1850.

Chinese immigrants came to Mexico as far back as the 1600s, but it was not until the mid-1800s that large numbers arrived. Chinese immigrants mainly settled in northern Mexico and worked as laborers, farmers, and shopkeepers. Their success at business led to resentment in some regions, particularly in Sonora in the 1930s. However, Mexicali, Baja California, remains home to a thriving Chinese community of around 5,000 people.

Commercial and artistic immigration
During the late 1800s and early 1900s President Porfirio Díaz opened up Mexico to foreign investment in industries such as mining and oil exploration. As U.S. companies began doing business in Mexico, engineers and managers immigrated from

the United States, often with their families. Some individuals stayed permanently, and their descendants still live in Mexico. In the 1920s and 1930s several prominent U.S. writers, artists, and intellectuals became fascinated with Mexican culture. They included the photographers Edward Weston and Tina Modotti, the writers Anita Brenner, Katherine Anne Porter, and Hart Crane, and the architect and designer William Spratling. The 1930s were also a period when thousands of people immigrated to Mexico from Spain to escape the turmoil of the Civil War and the repressive government of General Francisco Franco.

Enforced immigration

A wave of involuntary immigration to Mexico occurred during the 1930s. As the Great Depression (1929–1939) ravaged the United States and many jobs disappeared, U.S. states with large Mexican immigrant populations pressured people to return to their native country. Hundreds of thousands of non-U.S. citizens were deported, often with their U.S.-born children in tow. These Mexican

Joan Mark's biography of the designer William Spratling (1900–1967), a famous U.S. immigrant to Mexico. Spratling established Taxco, Guerrero, as the Mexican center for silver jewelry and craftwork.

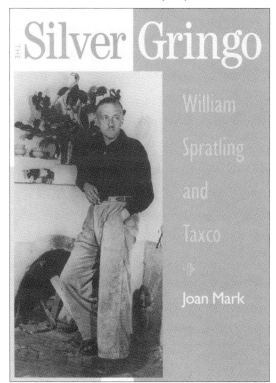

Americans often spent years in Mexico. Many never returned to the United States. Large numbers of illegal Mexican migrant workers in the United States were also deported by the U.S. Immigration and Naturalization Service in the early 1950s.

Further immigration to Mexico from the United States occurred during the McCarthy era of the 1950s. At a time of intense U.S. government suspicion about communist influences from the Soviet Union, Senator Joseph McCarthy and investigators at the Federal Bureau of Investigation (FBI) interrogated and hounded thousands of suspected communist sympathizers throughout the United States. In response, dozens of U.S. citizens and their families sought refuge in Mexico. They included labor organizers, Hollywood activists, "unfriendly" witnesses at anticommunist congressional hearings, and people who maintained an underground organization for the U.S. Communist Party.

In the late 1970s and 1980s wars in Central America resulted in a new wave of immigration to Mexico. Rebellions against authoritarian governments in Nicaragua, El Salvador, and Guatemala forced thousands of people to escape the violence. While many journeyed north to the United States, others stayed in Mexico. Tens of thousands of Guatemalan refugees moved to southern Mexico, where they were housed in U.N. refugee camps.

Present-day immigration

In 2000 the U.S. Embassy in Mexico City estimated that 600,000 U.S. citizens lived in Mexico. Many had dual (Mexican and U.S.) citizenship, grew up on the U.S. side of the border, and maintained close family ties in Mexico. However, since the 1960s large numbers of Anglo-Americans have immigrated to Mexico. Many are former government workers, war veterans, and other retirees on fixed incomes. They move because the Mexican climate is mild and because the cost of living in Mexico is much cheaper than in the United States. Guadalajara, Jalisco, attracts many U.S. immigrants: 50,000 of them lived in and around the city in 2000. The nearby village of Ajijic had more than 4,500 U.S. residents, as well as an English-language movie theater and a supermarket stocking U.S. packaged foods.

Deborah Nathan

SEE ALSO:

Austin, Stephen F.; Chinese; Deportation and Repatriation; Guadalajara; Spratling, William.

Imperial Valley

Imperial Valley, a 50-mile (80-km) depression that runs from southeastern California to northwestern Mexico, is one of the most important agricultural regions of the borderlands. Imperial County, which lies within the valley, is the twelfth most productive U.S. agricultural county.

Imperial Valley is part of the Colorado Desert and receives only around 3 inches (7.5 cm) of rain a year. Despite the arid climate, irrigation from the Colorado River and the All-American Canal has resulted in about a million acres (404,700 ha) of land being cultivated. The fruit and vegetable industry that dominates the valley is an important source of employment for Mexican Americans.

Imperial Valley is part of a long geological depression that stretches from San Gorgonio Pass southeast, including the Gulf of California and stretching beyond the tip of Baja California. The valley has been shaped by the Colorado River, which has spilled into the Salton Sea at various periods throughout history.

Early exploration

European exploration of the region began with Spanish pioneers in the sixteenth century. When Mexico achieved independence from Spain in 1821, it built a fort at Laguna Chapala, northwest of the present-day town of El Centro. However, the harsh conditions of the desert—boiling summers and bitter winters—prevented the development of many permanent settlements. Europeans did encounter various native peoples who lived in the valley for at least part of the year. The Kumeyaay, for example, made an annual migration from their home on the California Coast to plant crops along the shores of Lake Cahuilla. Another people, the Cahuilla, were ancestors of today's 6,000 Torres Martinez Desert Cahuilla Indians.

In the early nineteenth century, the inhospitable region attracted American trappers such as Kit Carson and Jedediah Smith. After the Treaty of Guadalupe Hidalgo was signed in 1848, much of the valley passed into U.S. ownership. In 1849 it became an important route for prospectors on their way west as part of the Gold Rush.

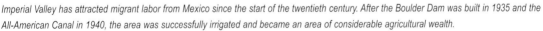

Imperial Valley has attracted migrant labor from Mexico since the start of the twentieth century. After the Boulder Dam was built in 1935 and the All-American Canal in 1940, the area was successfully irrigated and became an area of considerable agricultural wealth.

The Farming Business

Each morning in the peak harvest season, from January to February, around 15,000 to 18,000 Mexican workers, mainly from Mexicali, travel to work in Imperial Valley. They are recruited by farm-labor contractors at the border crossing and bused to the fields. They earn close to the California minimum wage, around U.S. $6.25 an hour in 2001. Most permanent employees in agriculture are U.S. residents, who tend to earn more. Because nonfarm business in the valley is also seasonal—it is often indirectly associated with processing foods or is connected with tourism—laid-off workers are a major drain on welfare systems in the off season.

The midwinter vegetable harvest includes lettuce, cauliflower, broccoli, and cabbage; the asparagus season begins in January and continues to March, but harvesting the vegetable is hard work and workers are reluctant to take it on. Carrots are another important winter crop. In the spring, production in the valley switches to onions, bell peppers, and melons.

Other important crops are animal foodstuffs, such as alfalfa—Imperial Valley is the largest alfalfa growing region in the world—sugar beets, and Sudan grass. Cattle and sheep raising are the major forms of livestock farming.

Under the terms of the Utilization of the Waters of the Colorado and Tijuana Rivers and of the Rio Grande Treaty (1944), signed by Mexico and the United States, Mexico is guaranteed 65.3 million cubic feet (1.85 million cubic m) of water a year. This water supports around 510,000 acres (207,000 ha) of irrigated land in the Mexicali Valley and around San Luis Río Colorado, Mexico. Cotton and wheat are the major crops.

Irrigation

In 1853 Dr. O. M. Wozencraft, who had originally come to the valley for the Gold Rush, first proposed that the valley had immense agricultural potential, if it could be reliably irrigated. Wozencraft's project remained unfulfilled when he died in 1887. In 1900 U.S. developer George Chaffey (1848–1932) excavated the Imperial Canal, bringing water from the Colorado River to Calexico; in 1901 some 1,500 acres (607 ha) came under irrigation. At this time the valley acquired the name "Imperial," from developers eager to attract settlers to the region. By 1905 some 12,000 people lived in the valley; the 80 miles (128 km) of main canals and 700 miles (1,126 km) of distribution canals irrigated an area of 67,000 acres (27,000 ha). Towns such as Imperial and Calexico were founded in the United States, and in Mexico, Mexicali. The Southern Pacific Railroad built a branch line to Imperial and Calexico, linking them to San Diego.

From 1908 to 1925 there was an influx of Mexicans to the area. People from Baja California Sur and Sonora moved to Calexico, though they often worked in the Mexican cotton industry based around Mexicali, where there was opportunity to work in professions or trades. Meanwhile, families from Guanajuato, Jalisco, Coahuila, and Sonora moved to Brawley. They worked in Imperial Valley itself, where their lack of English language meant that they were restricted mainly to low-paid, low-skilled labor. Many of these immigrants saw their stay in the United States as temporary, declining to register as U.S. residents and intending to return to Mexico. As a result there was tension between Anglo-Americans and Mexicans in the valley.

All-American Canal

In the late 1920s the building of the Boulder Dam—now the Hoover Dam—put an end to the Colorado's floods. In 1934, work began on the All-American Canal, which opened in 1940. The whole length of the canal was on U.S. soil, preventing Mexican access to the water and avoiding concerns about international water rights.

With reliable irrigation, Imperial Valley flourished. More than 500,000 acres (202,000 ha) are farmed, and agriculture is worth U.S. $1 billion a year. Geothermal power, aerospace, and manufacturing are other significant industries. Today the valley is home to around 145,000 people; that total is predicted to rise to 300,000 by 2020.

Tim Cooke

SEE ALSO:

All-American Canal; Colorado; Colorado River; Guadalupe Hidalgo, Treaty of; Illegal Labor; Mexicali; Mexicali Valley; Salton Sea.

Indiana

Mexican immigration to the United States has largely been associated with the border states of the Southwest. Mexicans, however, are migrating to other parts of the country and now live in growing numbers in the heartland of the United States.

In Indiana, a midwestern state that has historically been home to few Latinos, Hispanics now comprise 3.5 percent of the population, a 55 percent increase since 1990. According to the 2000 U.S. Census, 70 percent of these Hispanic residents, or 153,000 people, are Mexicans.

In the past Mexicans in Indiana concentrated in Lake County in the northwest corner of the state. Drawn by higher wages and the promise of more stable jobs, Mexicans migrated north during and after World War I to work in the steel-producing cities of Gary and Chicago. Steel companies recruited workers directly from Mexico to help with production and to cross picket lines during the labor strike of 1919. The number of Mexicans working at the Inland Steel Company increased from 90 to 945 at the time. Immigrants from Mexico, however, also included educated and middle-class families escaping economic and social unrest. As professionals and business owners they supplied services to East Chicago's growing community of 4,500 Mexican residents. Throughout the early twentieth century, Mexicans also came to work on the railroads and on farms.

Indianapolis

Indiana's Hispanics still concentrate in the northwestern part of the state, and active communities now exist in Goshen and Elkhart, where Mexicans comprise the majority of the labor force at several manufacturing plants. Hispanics have also migrated to Indianapolis, the state capital, and Frankfort. Since the Immigration Act of 1986, which provided amnesty to workers without legal documents, a small but vibrant barrio has emerged in Indianapolis. Mexicans also play an important role in the corporate-owned vegetable and fruit-growing industries in the southern part of the state.

Historically Mexicans migrated to Chicago, Illinois, or to Gary, which is in the northwest corner of Indiana. Since the 1980s a growing number of Mexicans have migrated to the state capital, Indianapolis.

Although Hispanics make up a tiny proportion of the state's population, their growing influence is notable. The Mexican government, for instance, agreed in 2000 to open a consular office in Indianapolis—the first time that a foreign government has located a consular office in Indiana.

Mexicans seem to be assimilating better in Indiana than in other parts of the country. Indiana's Hispanics experience less difficulty learning English than those in states with more concentrated Hispanic populations. They achieve higher high school completion rates than their counterparts nationally, attain more college education, and enjoy better economic status. Hispanics in Indiana also marry outside their ethnic community far more frequently than in other parts of the country—nearly 60 percent of Hispanics in the state are married to non-Hispanic partners. Although historically Mexicans have experienced discrimination in the state, these indicators suggest that the situation for Mexicans has improved.

Joel Hodson

SEE ALSO:
Barrios; Chicago, Illinois; Hispanic Americans; Immigration, Mexican; Railroads.

Indian Policy

Despite some parallels in their attempts to "civilize," educate, and assimilate the Indian peoples under their jurisdictions, the Indian policies of the United States and Mexico have differed substantially.

After independence, the U.S. government authorized aggressive expansion into the lands west of the Appalachian Mountains. Officially, Native American peoples in these areas were semi-independent nations whose land rights remained intact, but U.S. officials often conducted treaty negotiations without the participation of the tribes who lived on the land in question. In 1824 the Bureau of Indian Affairs (BIA) was created to administer this process. In 1830 Andrew Jackson (president 1828–1836) launched a new policy to keep the peace and solve land disputes. Under the Indian Removal Act the government began the forced removal of the "Five Civilized Tribes"—Cherokee, Chickasaw, Choctaw, Creek, and Seminole—to the new Indian Territory in present-day Oklahoma and Kansas.

The Indian policy of the Mexican government was very different. In the Spanish colonial period, legal distinctions between Indians and Europeans bestowed special rights and limits upon indigenous communities. After Mexican independence in 1821, the constitution of 1824 abolished such differentiation, theoretically giving all Mexican citizens the same legal status. In fact, the elimination of the unique status of Mexico's indigenous communities undercut their ability to maintain traditional communal lands (known as *ejidos*) and their status as ethnically distinct communities.

In northern Mexico many free-roaming native American groups remained outside of government control. Here the interests of the Mexican and U.S. governments converged, as both viewed unassimilated raiding tribes such as the Lipan Apache, the Kiowa, and the Comanche as a threat to their territories. The Mexican government encouraged Anglo-Americans and certain Native American tribes, such as the Shawnee and Cherokee, to settle in Texas in order to secure Mexican control there.

This illustration for Harper's Weekly *in 1870 by Theo R. Davis shows a group of Native Americans being forced to move onto a reservation.*

Texas became independent in 1836 and fierce fighting broke out between Native Americans and European settlers. In 1839 the Texan government drove several tribes, including the Cherokee, across the Red River into Indian Territory and others, including the Kickapoo, Potawatomi, and Seminole, into Mexico, where they were welcomed as a buffer against hostile incursions by other tribes.

Indian policy after 1848

After the Mexican-American War ended in 1848, a series of treaties by the BIA gradually established reservations for Native Americans living on the vast territories that the United States had received from Mexico. This continued the U.S. policy of treating Native American groups as semi-independent nations, although the government responded to any resistance with punitive military expeditions.

A lively trade grew among Native American communities on the border, where raiding parties traded stolen goods and livestock in both Mexico and the United States. The Mexican army was unable to protect Mexican settlements in the border states against these raids, so the state governments of Sonora, Chihuahua, and Coahuila resorted to paying friendly groups large bounties for the scalps of hostile tribes from 1835 until the 1880s.

The ascendancy of Mexico's Liberal Party in the late 1850s unintentionally resulted in a sharp decline in the status of Mexican Indians, even though some Indians were prominent Liberals, such as Benito Juárez (president 1861–1865 and 1867–1872). The Lerdo Law of 1856 endorsed private property rights and dissolved traditional patterns of corporate land ownership. This resulted in many Indian communities losing the land they held under the *ejido* system, as they lacked the money to claim individual properties. Landless Indians were forced to work on vast estates as indebted laborers. During the regime of Porfirio Díaz (president 1877–1880 and 1884– 1911) the policy of privatization was expanded. When the Yaqui Indians of Sonora rose up in protest, the government violently put down the rebellion and forced hundreds of Yaqui prisoners to work as laborers for pro-government landholders.

The U.S. government instituted a momentous shift in its Indian policy after the Civil War. By the 1870s land given to Native Americans was coveted by European settlers. At the same time, reformers wanted Native Americans to have the chance to integrate fully into U.S. society. From 1871 Native American peoples were no longer seen as sovereign and independent. From then on they were considered wards of the government, subject to resettlement and management by the BIA. Apache in Arizona and New Mexico and Comanche in Texas made a last attempt to resist confinement on reservations in the early 1870s without success. Under the Dawes Act of 1887 government authorities began dividing reservation lands into allotments for individual families from tribes considered ready to start a new life as farmers. They sold the remaining land to Euro-American settlers.

Indian policy in the twentieth century

The Mexican Revolution (1910–1920) encouraged a spirit of *indigenismo* in which artists and intellectuals exalted Mexico's native traditions, and the government pursued policies to assist indigenous groups. The revolutionary Constitution of 1917 required the restoration of Indian lands, and in the 1920s and 1930s millions of acres were restored to communal *ejido* ownership, including part of the Yaqui land in Sonora. The government implemented Indian education programs throughout Mexico. Later administrations encouraged the incorporation of Mexico's Indian heritage into the national identity. The National Indigenous Institute, established in 1948, administrated this policy, finally instituting a concrete mechanism for supporting Indian self-government in the 1980s.

In the United States the allotment process of dividing and reducing Native American lands persisted until the Indian Reorganization Act (1934), which rescinded the Dawes Act and allowed for greater Native American self-government. After World War II the government again sought assimilation and integration while attempting to permanently settle land claims and other grievances. In response to changing public opinion brought about by the Civil Rights movement and protest groups such as the American Indian Movement, the U.S. Congress passed an act in 1975, signaling the government's willingness to allow for increased Native American self-government and for the restoration of a measure of sovereignty.

Barry Matthew Robinson

SEE ALSO:

Apache; Aztecs; Caddo; Cherokee; Comanche; Ejido System; Kickapoo; Maya; Mixtecs; Native Americans; Yaquis; Zapotecs.

Inflation

Inflation can be defined as a persistent increase in the general level of prices, which, in turn, devalues the worth of money. Both the United States and Mexico have experienced inflationary crises. In particular, both countries were affected severely by the sudden rise in the price of oil in the 1970s.

Inflation is a recurring but intermittent phenomenon. A crucial feature of it is sustained price increases for all commodities in the marketplace. Prices of individual goods may go up, such as apples after a poor harvest, but this price increase on its own does not constitute inflation. The consequences of the phenomenon can be severe and explain why governments try so hard to avoid it or deal with it when it occurs. Price increases cause salaries to rise as well, but never as fast as the goods consumers purchase, a situation that creates further inflation. Workers on fixed incomes are worst hit by inflation as their ability to purchase is steadily reduced. Banks also suffer because inflation causes the value of loans to go down. Consequently, inflation discourages saving and investment and encourages borrowing and spending, creating problems for governments' economic planning.

Causes of inflation

Accounts of the causes of inflation are numerous. The most popular argument is that it results from an increase in the money supply. This creates excessive demand or, in other words, "too much money chasing too few goods." Heavy government spending—for example, on war or welfare programs—without accompanying tax increases has often induced politicians to print more paper money to pay for government obligations. During the Mexican Revolution (1910–1920) increasing amounts of banknotes were issued to pay for armies and new mechanisms of government. The increase of money contributed to the collapse of Mexico's financial system during the revolutionary period. Other related causes of inflation include voters' pressure on governments to increase expenditure while keeping taxes to a minimum and people's

The circulation of Mexico's coins and banknotes is controlled by the Banco de México, established in 1925. One of the central bank's functions is to prevent inflation from getting out of control.

efforts to protect themselves against the consequences of inflation. For example, in times of inflation workers and unions press employers to increase wages so they can afford the rising price of goods.

Responding to inflation

The causes of inflation amount to an attempt by a nation to live beyond its means or to enjoy a living standard higher than that allowed by its output or borrowing. As a result, attempts to cure inflation are invariably associated with austerity measures that suppress higher living standards. Governments control inflation by restricting demand through tighter control of the money supply or high rates of interest on loans. Restricting demand can often lead to unemployment, when employers cannot raise their sales prices and so must either lay off some of their employees or go out of business.

Central banking institutions aim to prevent inflation by achieving price stability, the condition most conducive to sustained output, steady employment, and moderate interest rates. Economists also believe that stable prices encourage savings and investment. The U.S. Federal Reserve was founded by Congress in 1913 to provide the United States with a safer, more flexible, and more stable monetary and financial system. Its duties fall into four main areas: conducting the nation's monetary policy; regulating U.S. national banks and protecting the credit rights of consumers; maintaining the stability of the financial system; and providing financial services to the U.S. government and other public and private institutions. Following high inflation in the mid-1970s (see below), the U.S. Federal Reserve implemented a tight money policy in 1979. It limited the supply of money which, in turn, led businesses to experience problems obtaining loans. The result was greater unemployment and a recession between 1980 and 1983. Although extremely painful, the Federal Reserve's measures lowered the rate of inflation from 13 percent in 1980 to less than 5 percent in 1983.

In Mexico the government-controlled Banco de Mexico was set up in 1925 to stabilize the economy after the revolution. Like the U.S. Federal Reserve, the national bank's functions include regulating Mexico's money supply and interest rates. In the period following World War II (1939–1945) the Banco de Mexico played an important role in reducing wartime inflation levels. Inflation began to rise again in the 1950s, in response to the growth of Mexico's industries and increased government borrowing from the International Monetary Fund (IMF) and the World Bank. In response, policy makers sought to stabilize prices through currency devaluations and by fixing the exchange rate between the peso and the U.S. dollar.

Inflation in the 1970s and 1980s

In common with many other countries, the United States experienced high inflation in the 1970s as the result of massive increases in world oil prices, growth in the nation's labor force, and the beginning of a decline in its manufacturing base. By the mid-1970s the price of most goods in the United States had more than doubled. The fixed rate of exchange between the peso and the U.S. dollar stimulated inflation in Mexico, too, and led the Banco de Mexico to switch to a flexible rate of exchange in 1977.

However, with the discovery of new oilfields in Mexico in the late 1970s, the country was in a different situation from the United States. Expecting huge oil revenues, the Mexican administration under José López Portillo borrowed heavily from the U.S. government and U.S.-dominated institutions, such as the IMF and the World Bank. The strategy proved disastrous. The U.S. Federal Reserve's anti-inflationary measures reduced the

price of oil and increased the interest rates on loans, including those owed by Mexico. Inflation in Mexico rose while its economic output fell. In August 1982 the Mexican government effectively declared itself bankrupt by announcing its inability to pay its international loans.

Mexico's recovery

The crisis in 1982 forced the Mexican government to consider economic reforms, such as reducing government regulation, lowering trade tariffs, and encouraging greater foreign investment. A second drop in international oil prices in 1986, which reduced Mexico's gross national product (GNP) by approximately 8 percent, caused inflation to rise again, reaching a peak of 159 percent. Responding to the ongoing crisis, in the mid-1980s the Mexican government intensified the process of economic reform in order to receive more credit from the U.S. government, the IMF, and the World Bank. Reforms included stabilizing the economy through a new monetary policy and the privatization of public enterprises.

President Carlos Salinas de Gortari's reforms between 1988 and 1994 further reduced inflation levels and stabilized the Mexican economy. His encouragement of free trade—including his signing of the North American Free Trade Agreement (NAFTA) with the United States and Canada in 1992—won praise from the World Bank and the IMF as well as U.S. presidents George Bush and Bill Clinton. However, shortly after Salinas left office in December 1994, Mexico experienced another severe economic crisis, which was triggered by a devaluation of the peso. Economists believe that a high level of inflation, relative to the value of the peso against the U.S. dollar, was a contributing factor. The Mexican economy was able to recover quickly, however, helped by a U.S. $20 billion loan from the U.S. government. The economy continued to improve in the late 1990s, closing the gap between U.S. and Mexican inflation rates. Between 1990 and 1998 average inflation in the United States stood at 3.09 percent, compared with 20.8 percent in Mexico over the same period. In 2001, however, annual inflation in Mexico was down to 4.4 percent, the lowest figure seen in many decades.

Miguel Jimenez

SEE ALSO:

Banking and Finance; Devaluation; Free Trade; Globalization; Investment; NAFTA; Oil.

InSITE

The inSITE arts project was established in 1991 in the San Diego–Tijuana region. Regarded as the most important cultural event on the Mexico–U.S. border, its name refers to the site-specific nature of the artists' installations and the fact that they are "in sight," that is, visible to the public.

The inSITE festival first took place in 1992 and is held every three years. Teams of curators commission artists from Mexico, the United States, Canada, Brazil, and elsewhere in Latin America. InSITE2000 involved more than 30 internationally acclaimed artists who took up residence in the San Diego–Tijuana region. The residencies, which on average lasted around 100 days, allowed the artists to absorb the character of the region and interpret it in their work. For the 2000 festival, artists' work included genres as diverse as installation art, performance art, films, and new media.

Over the course of each festival, artists' works are exhibited free to the public at specific sites throughout San Diego and Tijuana. The venues chosen are often highly visible, such as airports, parking lots, and train depots. The intention is to make art accessible and enable visitors to view it in new ways. Local schools, neighborhood organizations, and cultural institutions help set up the exhibits, and during "exploration weekends" visitors can discuss the works of art with the artists themselves.

Cross-border collaboration

InSITE involves collaboration between a range of institutions and communities in Mexico and the United States. The festival is jointly organized by Mexico's Instituto Nacional de Bellas Artes (National Institute of Fine Arts) and Installation, a San Diego-based arts organization. The Mexican consulate in San Diego, the state of Baja California, and city authorities in Tijuana and San Diego provide additional assistance. At inSITE97 the artist Marcos Ramiros received assistance from both Mexican and U.S. authorities to position his *Trojan Horse* installation on the San Ysidro port of entry between Tijuana and San Diego. The same festival featured a "virtual" public space where Mexican

Marcos Ramiros's Trojan Horse, *a major exhibit at inSITE97. Ramiros set up the installation at the San Ysidro border crossing and benefited from cooperation from the Mexican and U.S. authorities.*

and U.S. children could use the Internet to communicate with each other. Another example of collaboration was the installation by the Mexican artist Gustavo Artigas for inSITE2000. Artigas turned an area along the border into a giant sports field and invited teams from Mexico and the United States to play soccer and baseball at the same time. The challenge required the teams to find new ways to interact.

Education and exploration

The aim of inSITE's founders is to involve and educate the local public and visitors. In addition to the "exploration weekends" the organizers issue a range of publications to document the artworks and stimulate people to think about the border region. One thought-provoking exhibit in inSITE97 was *Jute Car* by Mexican artist Betsabee Romero. The artist placed a customized lowrider car in a poor barrio (neighborhood) in Tijuana. Subsequent damage to the car by vandals became a central part of the exhibit.

Joanna Griffin

SEE ALSO:
Border Studies; Chicano Art; Lowriders; Murals and Muralists; San Diego; Tijuana.

Internal Migration

Since the 1940s the migration of indigenous peoples from one area of Mexico to another has been caused primarily by the country's gradual change from an agricultural economy to an industrialized economy.

Rapid industrialization in the second half of the twentieth century lowered agricultural production in Mexico's indigenous areas, such as Oaxaca and Chiapas. These and other areas became economically poorer as investment in the agriculturally commercial northwestern part of the country increased. After 1980 the northern regions of the country became increasingly popular as areas in which to find work.

From the 1940s to the 1980s indigenous communities migrated as a result of conflicts, religious traditions, or economic necessity. Internal Mexican migration started with the migration of single male members of the household. The migration soon included other members of the family, initially brothers, sons, and other male kinfolk, and then women as well. In 1980 in Mexico over half a million indigenous people were living in areas other than their place of birth. This represented 10.6 percent of the total indigenous population. The cities of Mexico City, Guadalajara, and Monterrey were the most popular destinations for the migrating peoples of Mexico. By 1980 there were as many as 323,000 indigenous-language speakers living in Mexico City, by far the most popular destination.

Causes of migration

There are a number of causes for internal migration, the most significant of which are damage to the ecology resulting in low land productivity, failing local economies, and conflicts over land. Other causes include the resettlement and involuntary relocation of peoples due to the assignation of lands to new, nonindigenous colonizers, interethnic conflicts, armed conflicts, military occupation, and religious conflicts. A lack of basic social services affects all Mexican regions.

The low productivity of land has affected parts of Oaxaca, Guerrero, and the Tarahumara Sierra. Other environmental factors are droughts, frosts, hurricanes, and soil deterioration due to the introduction of large-scale agriculture. Peoples of Huasteca, Chiapas, and the Huichol region of Jalisco have suffered from lack of land and land conflicts, while large-scale livestock production requiring extensive grasslands has also badly affected Huasteca, Chiapas, and the Totonaca area of Veracruz. The construction of dams, roads, and industrial plants has affected petroleum producing areas. Failing crops, such as coffee, sugar, tobacco, cocoa, tomato, and citrus fruits, is another factor. The decreasing demand for artisan products such as pottery, basketry, and textiles, has had a detrimental effect on the mountain area of Guerrero, the Tarahumara Sierra, and Oaxaca.

The United States and indigenous migrants

Northern Mexico and the southwestern United States are very attractive to immigrants because they offer secure employment. Typically, Mexican immigrants first move to work on vegetable farms or ranches just south of the border. Many became employed as construction workers or ranch hands and incorporated into the service sector or in the formal economy of cities such as Tijuana and Mexicali. From northern Mexico several migrate to California via San Diego and are received by indigenous organizations. The final step for many occurs when they establish themselves in the main cities in California, such as Los Angeles.

Although this migration is often illegal, many immigrants later become official residents in the United States. The Mixtec have a long tradition of emigration and are the most numerous in the United States. Various ethnic groups are attracted to specific regions of the United States. For example, the Mixtec and Mazahua are attracted to California, Oregon, New York, Los Angeles, Florida, and Washington for the purpose of working in agriculture or the service industries. There is also a considerable Zapotec community from Oaxaca in Los Angeles County.

J. Marie Doggett

SEE ALSO:

Illegal Labor; Immigration, Mexican; Immigration to Mexico; Migrant Labor.

Investment

A large and important part of Mexico's economic development results from foreign investment in the country, along with the growth in industrialization, tourism, and exports. The United States has been the biggest investor in Mexico. In 1943 U.S. investments in Mexico amounted to U.S. $286 million; by 1999 the figure had risen to U.S. $11 billion.

Investment is defined as the formation of real capital, such as the production or maintenance of machinery or the construction of buildings, that will in turn produce goods and services for future consumption. Foreign investment is the acquisition of the assets of one country by governments, institutions, corporations, or individuals of another. Foreign investment can take two forms: foreign direct investment (FDI) or foreign portfolio investment. FDI is investment in foreign companies, such as their factories, machinery, and labor. Portfolio investment is the investment in a share of the ownership of a company, usually in the form of stocks and shares.

Foreign direct investment

Since the 1980s FDI has expanded rapidly worldwide. FDI grew by 18 percent in 2000 reaching a record U.S. $1.3 trillion. Developed countries remain the prime destination of FDI, receiving more than three-quarters of global FDI. Within the developed world, the E.U. (the European Union), the United States, and Japan received 71 percent of world FDI and sent 82 percent of total world FDI in 2000. Richer, more competitive economies receive and send more international direct investment than other economies. The main factors that determine FDI are proximity to markets, factors of production, a cheap labor force, specialized skills, innovatory capabilities, and suppliers. Mexico, because of its strategic location, competitive labor force, open economy, and free-trade agreements, is increasingly attractive for FDI. However, this has not always been the case—Mexico has had many economic crises over the last 50 years, which discouraged investment.

Financial reforms

During the 1970s the Mexican government carried out profound financial reforms, introducing a universal banking structure and a unified stock market. In 1970 the government supported a number of regulations authorizing "multiple banking" through mergers of specialized banks, such as mortgage banks, trust companies, and financial companies. In addition, they issued, for the first time, government treasury bills. This issuing of government money-market instruments was officially promoted as part of an effective monetary policy. The financial reforms of the 1970s were interrupted, however, by the rapid sequence of events in 1981 and 1982, when a fall in the price of oil rendered Mexico unable to pay its foreign debt. This in turn led Mexico into a decade of recession. In a drastic reaction to the debt crisis and massive capital flight—U.S. $36 billion from 1978 to 1982—Mexican banks were nationalized in 1982 and austerity measures implemented as a means of stabilizing the financial system.

Globalization

The economic policy adopted by Mexico during the early 1980s coincided with structural reforms all around the world. As the globalization of the world economy took place, Mexico was forced to adapt its trade and financial relations. From 1985 onward, the economic policy implemented in Mexico was intended to make a structural adjustment of the national economy. The Mexican government under President Miguel de la Madrid (1982–1988) introduced economic reforms to try to reduce inflation and stabilize the economy. They encouraged high levels of competition and efficiency in the national productive base through the implementation of an economic policy of trade and financial liberalization. Public enterprises were privatized, a new economic regulation framework, especially in the financial sector, was introduced, and trade tariffs were reduced.

De la Madrid's successor, Carlos Salinas de Gortari (1988–1994), reprivatized the national banking system in 1988, six years after nationalization. He also authorized the operation of

A view of the financial district of Mexico City. Free-trade agreements between Mexico and foreign countries, including the E.U., Israel, Switzerland, Norway, Iceland, Guatemala, Honduras, and El Salvador, will lead to increased foreign direct investment in Mexico.

financial groups as integrated financial-service holding companies (comprising banks, brokerage houses, and other financial firms), continued the privatization of state-owned companies, and promoted the North American Free Trade Agreement (NAFTA) between Canada, the United States, and Mexico, signed in 1992, in an ambitious effort to stimulate investment in the Mexican economy. Changes introduced in October 1989 to the Foreign Investment Act granted greater freedom for foreigners investing on the Mexican exchange. Since then it has been possible for foreign investors to buy shares with full corporate rights of any Mexican company. At the end of December 1993, the balance of foreign investment in the Mexican stock exchange reached a historic high of U.S. $54.6 billion dollars.

In 1993 further changes to the Securities Market Act and to the Mutual Funds Act introduced the possibility of trading foreign securities in the Mexican financial markets. This opened up the possibility for Mexico to become a regional financial center. Despite the collapse of the peso in 1994 and 1995 and the resulting financial crisis (the United States stepped in with a U.S. $40 billion bailout package) Mexico has continued to introduce financial reforms and encourage foreign investment and free trade as part of its ongoing neoliberal economic policy.

Investment opportunities in Mexico

Although the United States is clearly the biggest foreign investor in Mexico in the form of mergers and acquisitions, investment from European companies, particularly from the United Kingdom, is growing significantly. It is foreseen that European investment will further increase as a result of the Free Trade Agreement between the E.U. and Mexico that took force in 2001. Foreign investment has been particularly strong in the gas distribution, transportation, electricity, telecommunications, and automotive industries. Further participation in other industries, such as oil and power (currently legislation allows only Mexican investors in these sectors), may attract additional foreign investment. Already Mexico has allowed foreign banks to take over Mexican banks. For example, U.S. giant Citigroup purchased the Mexican bank Banamex in 2001. This deregulation and privatization of government-owned companies will continue to be a driving force in attracting foreign investment into Mexico. In 2000 foreign direct investment reached U.S. $13.2 billion, a five-fold increase from U.S. $2.5 billion in 1986.

Miguel Jimenez

SEE ALSO:

Banking and Finance; Foreign Debt; Free Trade; Globalization; Inflation; NAFTA; Nationalization; Oil; Trade.

Iturbide, Agustín de

Agustín de Iturbide (1783–1824) was a military leader in the Spanish army during Mexico's Wars of Independence. Although his reign as emperor of Mexico (1822–1823) was short and unpopular, he was instrumental in the transition of Mexico from a Spanish colony to a fully independent country.

Agustín de Iturbide was born in Valladolid (today Morelia, in the state of Michoacán) in 1783. His father was a wealthy, conservative Spaniard and his mother was born in Michoacán. Early in his life Iturbide showed an interest in pursuing a military career. At age 17 he registered in the infantry and soon received a royal commission as lieutenant.

Military career

When Hidalgo's Revolt against the royalists started in 1810, Iturbide received an offer from the rebels to become their general, but he refused. Instead, Lieutenant Iturbide supported the crown for almost a decade, successfully fighting rebel insurgents. By 1813 he had been promoted to commander.

However, in 1816 Iturbide was accused and charged by the army with illegal acts, such as torturing prisoners and stealing land. Although he was cleared, Iturbide decided not to go back to the army. He moved to Mexico City, where he indulged in a decadent lifestyle, spending his money on gambling and women. He also became increasingly disillusioned with Spanish rule.

In 1820 the Spanish viceroy Juan Ruíz de Apodaca invited Iturbide to head a new offensive against the rebel leader General Vicente Guerrero (1782–1831). After some uncertainty, Iturbide began negotiating with Guerrero to make peace. On February 24, 1821, Iturbide proclaimed Mexican independence at Iguala, in the state of Guerrero, and drew up the Plan of Iguala.

The most important part of the plan was the Three Guarantees. The first proclaimed that Mexico's form of government would be a constitutional monarchy and that the national constitution was to be drawn up by congress. The

Portrait of Iturbide in military uniform. He began his military career as a lieutenant and was rapidly promoted to colonel after a series of victories against Hidalgo rebels between 1810 and 1813.

emperor would be chosen from a European dynasty, preferably from the Spanish monarchy. The second guarantee offered security, union, and equal treatment for Mexicans and Spanish citizens. The third promised to preserve ecclesiastical privileges that had been under attack by the Spanish revolutionary regime. Iturbide pledged to protect these guarantees with his Ejército de las Tres Garantías (the Army of the Three Guarantees).

Mexican independence

With all these measures, Iturbide won the support of the old guerrilla fighters for independence, particularly from General Guerrero. Gradually the rebels gained control of the whole country, except Mexico City and the ports of Veracruz and Acapulco. On August 24, 1821, Iturbide met the Spanish viceroy, Juan O'Donojú, to sign the Treaty of Córdoba, recognizing Mexico as a sovereign and independent nation. The treaty, following the lines of the Plan of Iguala, specified that the throne was to be offered to the Spanish King Ferdinand VII and, if he refused, to a prince of the Castilian royal family. If this plan failed, the Mexican congress would select the new emperor themselves.

In September Iturbide marched into Mexico City. Acting as president, Iturbide chose a governing junta dominated by conservative interests, which formally declared Mexico independent and awarded Iturbide a new military title—Generalísimo de Tierra y Mar. Iturbide had hoped for O'Donojú's support in the transition from the Spanish viceroyalty to the future empire under a Spanish monarch. However, O'Donojú died and Iturbide failed to send any commissioners to Madrid to negotiate the settlement agreed upon in the Córdoba Treaty. The Spanish attitude toward independent Mexico became hostile. Some royalists even withdrew to San Juan de Ulúa in Veracruz in order to reconquer Mexico. On February 13, 1822, the courts in Spain rejected the treaty.

Emperor of Mexico

The Mexican congress increasingly began to favor an emperor of their own after Spain's rejection of the treaty. On May 18, 1822, the local army proclaimed Iturbide "Emperor Agustín" and the congress approved his appointment the following day. In a highly elaborate ceremony on July 21, Iturbide was crowned by the president of the congress in Mexico City's cathedral.

Iturbide's empire did not last long. Mexico's economic situation had deteriorated after 11 years of war. Moreover, U.S. president James Monroe (1817–1825) was disappointed that Mexico had not become a free republic. Additionally, the Mexican nobility and other groups, who favored a European prince, charged Iturbide with having violated the Córdoba Treaty. Opposition to Iturbide also grew in response to his arbitrary acts. Just five weeks after his coronation, the new emperor imprisoned several army officers and 19 congressmen. He even dissolved congress and announced confiscatory fiscal measures.

On December 2, 1822, the commander of Veracruz province, Antonio López de Santa Anna (1794–1876), launched a revolt against Iturbide. Santa Anna accused Iturbide of tyranny and called for the reinstallation of congress. He gathered support from other anti-imperial movements and, with the Plan de Casa Mata, established a republic. Ten months after coming to the throne, Iturbide abdicated in February 1823.

Because Iturbide had played a key role in the independence of Mexico, the congress offered him an allowance, provided he resided in Italy. After two years abroad, in Italy and England, however, Iturbide returned to Mexico, unaware that during his absence the congress had declared him a traitor. Immediately after his arrival on the Gulf Coast in July 1824, Iturbide was arrested and executed in Padilla, Tamaulipas.

Susana Berruecos García Travesí

SEE ALSO:

Constitutions, Mexican; Guerrero, Vicente; Hidalgo y Costilla, Miguel; Mexican Independence; Santa Anna, Antonio López de; Spanish Empire.

Iturbide, Agustín de
Mexican soldier and emperor of Mexico

Born: September 27, 1783
    Valladolid, Michoacán
Died: July 19, 1824
    Padilla, Tamaulipas

1813	Becomes colonel in the Spanish viceregal army
1816	Removed from and then reinstated to his command by royalist army
1821	Announces the Three Guarantees in the Plan of Iguala
1822	Approved as emperor of Mexico by congress
1823	Abdicates the throne and goes into exile in Europe
1824	Returns to Mexico, is arrested as a traitor and executed

Jalisco

The state of Jalisco is located in western Mexico and borders the states of Durango, Zacatecas, Aguascalientes, Nayarit, Guanajuato, San Luis Potosí, Michoacán, and Colima. It is famous as the center of Mexico's information technology industry.

The name Jalisco derives from the Nahuatl words *xalli*, meaning sand or gravel, and *ixtli*, meaning face, or plain. Jalisco means, literally, "sandy plain." In 2000 it had a population of nearly six million, about 6.5 percent of Mexico's total population. With its 215-mile (345-km) coastline it is known for its resorts, including the renowned Puerto Vallarta. The state's capital is Guadalajara, which is Mexico's second largest city.

Jalisco has a varied climate because of its geography. It is dominated by the southern end of the Sierra Madre Occidental and the western end of the chain of volcanic mountains traversing central Mexico. Its landscape ranges from fresh pine woods to tropical forest. The country's largest lake, Lake Chapala, is in the center of the state. Jalisco has a semitropical climate: temperatures are warm for most of the year but hot and humid in July and August. The rainy season is from June to October.

Jalisco has a land surface of 30,000 square miles (80,000 sq km). Its geography varies from flat coastline on the Pacific Ocean to the high Sierra Madre Occidental mountain range to the north.

History

The Spanish invaded what was to become Jalisco in 1529, when conquistador Nuño de Guzmán began an incursion into the area. The region was later included in New Galicia. In 1823 Jalisco was declared a state; at the time it also included areas that now form part of the states of Nayarit, Colima, and Zacatecas. In the war against the United States (1846–1848) Jalisco contributed troops that took part in conflicts in Angostura, Nuevo León, and Palo Alto. Shortly before the War of Reform (1858–1861) Jalisco became a leading state in the liberal revolution led by Benito Juárez (1806–1872). Jalisco was occupied by the French during the Wars of Intervention but was recaptured in 1866, and in 1884 Nayarit state was separated from Jalisco. In the years after the Mexican Revolution (1910–1920) the Cristero Rebellion enjoyed its strongest support in the state.

Economy

Agriculture and livestock breeding are two of the most important economic activities in Jalisco. The state is now Mexico's leading producer of corn, milk, sugar, and poultry. Other crops grown include beans, oats, chile, alfalfa, and onions. Jalisco produces internationally renowned handicrafts, including typical products made of brown glass, wrought iron, papier-mâché, and leatherwork. The production of tequila is important in the Los Altos region of the state, which is often referred to as "the most Mexican" state because, in addition to tequila, it is the presumed birthplace of mariachi music. Fishing and tourism are key activities on the coast.

In recent years Jalisco has become known as the Silicon Valley of Mexico because many U.S. electronics firms, taking advantage of the North American Free Trade Agreement (NAFTA), have established operations there. The main electronic products manufactured are computers, cellular phones, and printers. The state's exports are now worth more than U.S. $3 billion annually.

Joanna Griffin

SEE ALSO:

Agriculture; Crafts; Guadalajara; Manufacturing; Mariachis; NAFTA; Tourism.

Jews

Mexico has been home to a small Jewish community since the sixteenth century. Many faced persecution and fled to the northern frontier regions that later became part of the United States. About 50,000 Jewish people live in present-day Mexico, while in the United States a growing number of Mexican Americans are discovering their Jewish heritage.

The earliest Jewish settlers in Mexico arrived with the Spanish conquistadores in 1519. Among them was Hernando Alonso, whom historical sources describe as "the first Jewish jeweler." According to tradition, Alonso was at Hernán Cortés's side when the Spanish leader came ashore at Veracruz. The first Spanish-Jewish settlers were known as *conversos* because they had been forced to convert to Christianity on pain of exile or death.

Escape from persecution

Forced conversion had been carried out sporadically in Spain since 600 C.E., but it was pursued with particular vigor in the late fifteenth century with the establishment of the Spanish Inquisition. This papal institution was designed to root out all heretical (anti-Catholic) beliefs, particularly Judaism. On March 1, 1492, the Inquisition declared that all Jews were to be expelled from Spain or would face death. In addition, it accused the *conversos* of secretly practicing Judaism. Five years later Jews were expelled from Portugal, and in 1506 many Portuguese Jews who had converted to Christianity were killed during a riot in Lisbon.

The New World offered Spanish and Portuguese Jews a refuge from persecution. In 1531 large numbers of them left the Iberian Peninsula for Mexico, where Spanish rule was now firmly established under Viceroy Antonio de Mendoza, whom some historians think may himself have been Jewish. Many of the immigrants were skilled doctors, lawyers, tailors, or teachers, and were therefore welcomed into the community. They settled in Campeche, Guadalajara, Oaxaca, Mexico City, Morelia, and Veracruz. Some Jews assimilated by marrying into gentile (non-Jewish) families or

becoming Catholic priests, but within a generation many felt comfortable enough in their new surroundings to practice their Jewish faith openly.

Further persecution

By 1571, however, the Inquisition had crossed the Atlantic into Mexico, and practicing Jews and *conversos* were once again victimized. They fled north of Spanish Mexico and settled for a while in the kingdom of Nuevo León, a colony that had been granted in 1579 by the king of Portugal to the nobleman Luis de Carvajal. By 1641 the colony had fallen victim to the expansion of the northern Mexican frontier. As a result, the Jewish settlers moved on to areas that were free from the influence of the Inquisition, regions that later became New Mexico, Arizona, Texas, and California.

In Mexico the anti-Semitic edicts of the Inquisition remained in place until the early 1800s. The Catholic Church's control on Mexican society ensured that only those who professed its faith could be citizens of Mexico. From 1825 a few European Jews entered the country, but by 1865, when the French-imposed emperor Maximilian issued an edict of religious tolerance, there was little left to tolerate: a mere 20 Jewish families remained in Mexico City.

New Jewish immigrants

After victory over the French in 1867, Mexican president Benito Juárez (1806–1872) greatly reduced the powers of the Catholic Church. As a result, non-Catholics were free to settle in Mexico. The stage was now set for a new wave of Jewish immigration, which began in 1882, one year after the assassination of the Russian czar Alexander II. Fueled by widespread anti-Semitism, false rumors that the czar's assassin was Jewish led to pogroms (the Russian word for attacks by mobs) throughout Russia, forcing many Jews to flee.

In 1884 the Mexican government invited Jewish bankers to open branches of banks throughout the country. Many other Jewish immigrants became peddlers, traversing the countryside with pack mules and selling household goods and clothing in remote villages.

The next waves of Jewish settlers arrived in the early 1910s and early 1920s. They were refugees from Greece, Lebanon, Syria, and Turkey—all parts of the disintegrating Ottoman Empire. Many of the immigrants were Sephardic Jews (descendants of the Jews who had been expelled from Spain in the 1400s and 1500s), and, since they spoke the Spanish dialect Ladino, had no language problems when they arrived. They tended to form different social groups and worship in different synagogues from the Ashkenazi Jews who had come from Russian and eastern Europe. The new arrivals took over as peddlers because the previous Jewish immigrants had improved their social standing and moved into the towns.

The twentieth century

When another wave of Jewish immigration took place in Mexico after World War I (1914–1918), there was a well-established Jewish community to welcome the newcomers. Some immigrants chose Mexico because they already had relatives there; others arrived after having been deported from the United States, which introduced immigration restrictions in 1921 and 1924. In contrast, the Mexican Catholic Church faced pressure from the anticlerical government of Venustiano Carranza, president from 1915 to 1920, and was therefore too preoccupied with its own struggle for survival to object to the arrival of Jews.

Throughout the 1920s Jews in Mexico prospered, mainly as peddlers and proprietors of small stalls in public markets. They also introduced the system of buying on credit. There was some anti-Semitism during the Great Depression (1929–1939), notably when Mexican labor unions pressured the government to curb Chinese and Jewish immigration, and later when Nazis staged demonstrations in Mexico City. Such incidents forced Jews to abandon their trade in marketplaces and to open private stores.

Jews in present-day Mexico

The precise number of Jews in Mexico today is unknown. Those registered as "Israelites" in the official Mexican census include Protestant sects and mestizos (people with mixed Spanish and Indian descent) with Jewish roots. At the start of the twenty-first century an estimated 40,000 Jewish people lived in Mexico City. The Mexican capital had 23 synagogues, all but two of which were Orthodox. Most other Jews lived in Guadalajara

(200 families), Monterrey (200 families), and Tijuana (60 families). There were perhaps another 300 families in Mexico, notably in towns such as Puebla, Cuernavaca, and Veracruz. The majority of these Jews are Ashkenazi, descendants of the Russian immigrants of the late 1800s.

Over the course of Spanish rule (1521–1821) many Jews either fled Mexico or assimilated into Christian society. Those who became Christians lost touch with their Jewish heritage, although some Mexican Catholic families retain Jewish traditions. The rate of "marrying out" (intermarriage between Jews and non-Jews) is estimated at between 5 and 10 percent. Although in the latter part of the twentieth century there was a marked revival of interest in Mexican cultural heritage and a consequent increase in the number of mestizos who believe they have Jewish antecedents, the documentary evidence in support of these claims is sketchy, and most of these mestizos remain unacknowledged by the country's rabbis.

Mexican Jews in the United States

In the late twentieth century Mexican Americans in the United States began to take a greater interest in their cultural and religious heritage. Some people of Mexican origin have discovered that they are descendants of the Mexican Jewish *conversos* who fled north from Spanish Mexico in the sixteenth and seventeenth centuries. However, the *conversos'* desire to hide their Jewishness was so great that it is often very difficult to establish the truth. Having submerged their identities for so many generations, families have no documentation to prove that they are of Jewish lineage.

A number of organizations, such as the International Federation of Messianic Jews (IFMJ), work to help Mexicans and Hispanic Americans establish their Jewishness. Based in Tampa Bay, Florida, the IFMJ believes that the conversos have many thousands of descendants scattered throughout the United States and Latin America. In Albuquerque, New Mexico, a monthly local radio show called "Mi Seferino" (My little prayer book) is dedicated to raising awareness of many Hispanic Americans' Jewish heritage.

George Lewis

SEE ALSO:

Catholic Church; Chinese; Immigration to Mexico; Juárez, Benito; Maximilian; Mestizos; Spanish Empire; World War I.

Juárez, Benito

Benito Juárez was president of Mexico from 1861 to 1872 during the era of reforms. He led the opposition during French intervention in Mexico (1862–1867). His reforms aimed to establish Mexico as a democratic federal republic.

Benito Juárez was born in the highlands of Oaxaca, on March 21, 1806. His parents, both of whom died when he was three years old, were Zapotec Indians. Juárez moved to the city of Oaxaca to live with an uncle. There he learned to speak Spanish and went to school. Later he entered a Catholic seminary, but lacking a vocation for the priesthood, he obtained a law degree in 1831 from the Oaxaca Institute of Arts and Sciences.

Juárez began to practice law and became involved in politics. He won a seat on the Oaxaca city council in 1831; three years later he was elected local congressman and then state court judge. When war broke out between Mexico and the United States in 1846, Juárez served as provisional governor in Oaxaca and refused to grant the Mexican president Antonio López de Santa Anna (whom he regarded as a traitor) asylum in his state. In 1847 he ran for state governor and held the position until 1853, when Santa Anna was reelected president. Along with other leading liberals, Juárez was arrested and forced into exile in the United States, where he lived in New Orleans until 1854. There he met other Mexican liberals, such as Melchor Ocampo, José Mata, and Ponciano Arriaga. Late in 1854 Juárez heard of a movement against Santa Anna and returned to Mexico, joining the forces of General Juan Álvarez.

Government minister

The Revolution of Ayutla, led by Álvarez, ousted Santa Anna from power in 1855, and Juárez was appointed to his first ministerial post, secretary of justice. He issued the Laws of Juárez, which attempted to bring the clergy and army under civil law by abolishing their special privileges and immunities. Juárez returned to Oaxaca as state governor from 1856 to 1857 and implemented the new liberal Constitution of 1857.

The words on this monument in honor of Benito Juárez read: "The party has guided the people along the path of progress."

President Ignacio Comonfort appointed Juárez secretary of the interior and later president of the supreme court. This post also effectively made Juárez vice president. The removal of Comonfort by conservatives in January 1858 and their annulment of the 1857 Constitution sparked a three-year civil conflict between conservatives and liberals, known as the War of Reform. President Comonfort fled to the United States. Juárez declared that, according to the law, he was the new president. However, conservative forces had named another president in Mexico City. Juárez established a liberal government in Guanajuato under the protection of the state governor, Manuel Doblado. He later moved the government to Guadalajara and then to Veracruz, where it remained until 1861.

While in Veracruz Juárez issued several decrees that became known as the Reform Laws, expressing the ideas of the era of La Reforma (1855–1876). These included the separation of church and state, the nationalization of church property, and the establishment of a civil registry, ending the Catholic church's monopoly of the registry for births, deaths, and marriages. Freedom of religion was guaranteed to all citizens.

As the civil war continued, foreign pressure began to build up due to lack of debt repayment. Both governments lacked funds. Juárez was later criticized for his attempt to secure a U.S. loan in return for granting transit rights across Mexico. However, the treaty was never ratified. In 1860 the liberals won several important military victories and the conservative government collapsed. On his return to Mexico City in 1861 Juárez called a referendum and was elected president.

President of Mexico

As president, Juárez faced several pressing issues. The internal political situation was unstable and European nations were demanding repayment of debts. His main concern was Mexico's serious financial problems. There was also instability along the Mexico-U.S. border due to the American Civil War (1861–1865). Juárez regarded the United States as a model of republican democracy and consistently supported Abraham Lincoln. Juárez began to reorganize the judiciary and to improve the country's transportation infrastructure, especially railroads and steamship lines. He aimed to establish fair electoral laws and freedom of the press, and to reform the prison and welfare systems.

In May 1861 the new congress approved the Reform Laws and authorized Juárez to declare a two-year moratorium on foreign debt payment. This decision provoked an immediate reaction in England, France, and Spain, which decided to invade Mexico to recoup their investment. Spain and Britain soon made agreements with Mexico and withdrew, but the French emperor, Napoleon III, had imperial ambitions. French intervention was supported by conservative groups who wanted a European monarch as ruler of Mexico.

French troops invaded Mexico and on May 5, 1862, they attacked the city of Puebla. Their defeat in the Battle of Cinco de Mayo was celebrated throughout Mexico. However, it did not prevent French troops from pushing into the interior, taking Mexico City and making Napoleon's puppet ruler, Maximilian of Austria, emperor of Mexico.

Juárez was forced to leave the capital and retreat to the northern border, but he remained in the country as a focus of resistance to French intervention. The liberal armies continued to fight until, under General Porfirio Díaz (1830–1915), they won an important victory in July 1867, allowing Juárez to return to Mexico City and regain power. In an act that was controversial both in Mexico and abroad, Juárez ordered the execution of Maximilian and the Mexican generals who supported him.

Juárez then turned his attention to reorganizing state finances, the army, and federal powers. He was reelected president from 1867 to 1871. However, he began to lose political support as he tried to introduce changes to the constitution. His presidential victory in 1871 was declared fraudulent by Porfirio Díaz—by this time a rival presidential candidate—and by many others. In November 1871 Díaz led a rebellion but was defeated. Several months later, however, Juárez died of a heart attack.

Susana Berruecos García Travesí

SEE ALSO:

Civil War, U.S.; Constitutions, Mexican; Díaz, Porfirio; Maximilian; Reforma, La; Reform, War of the; Santa Anna, Antonio López de.

Juárez, Benito
Mexican president

Born:	*March 21, 1806*
	San Pablo Guelatao, Oaxaca
Died:	*July 18, 1872*
	Mexico City

1831	Gains law degree and a seat on the Oaxaca city council
1847	Elected state governor
1853	Two-year exile in the United States
1855	Appointed secretary of justice
1858	War of Reform begins
1861	Elected president
1863	Forced to leave Mexico City when French troops invade Mexico
1867	Returns to power as president
1871	Reelected president
1872	Dies of a heart attack

Justice System

While there are similarities between the structure of the U.S. and Mexican systems of justice, there are also fundamental differences in the application of law in each country.

Both the United States and Mexico divide their justice systems between the state and federal levels. State and federal courts in Mexico and the United States share a similar organizational structure. At both levels there are three tiers of judicial authority, which enforce and interpret the law. These three tiers are the lower courts, the high court, and the supreme court. However, despite this similarity, the United States is a "common law" country, while Mexico is considered a "civil law" nation. The U.S. common law system is based on statutory English law, which emphasizes case law, usage, and customs. In other words, judicial decisions can actually make laws by overturning legislation or previous judicial rulings. In contrast, Mexico's civil law system, which is based on Roman and Spanish colonial law, gives less emphasis to judicial interpretation of the law and stresses strict adherence to legal codes.

U.S. justice system

Article III of the U.S. Constitution establishes the judiciary (justice system) as one of the three separate branches of the federal government, alongside the legislature (Congress) and the executive (presidency). The federal judicial power is vested in the Supreme Court and in the hierarchy of courts below it. The U.S. Congress determines the jurisdiction of these courts and controls the types of cases they can address. It also decides how many judges there should be, where they will work, and approves the courts' budget and the presidential nominations for federal judges.

The federal courts' aim is to protect the rights and liberties guaranteed by the Constitution, as well as resolving disputes through impartial judgments. In 1787 the Constitution's drafters considered an independent federal judiciary essential to ensure equal justice for all U.S. citizens. They attempted to ensure this independence in two ways. First, federal judges are appointed for life and can be removed

A member of the Mexican mafia being taken into custody in Phoenix, Arizona. The process of prosecuting criminals and challenging points of law differs in the Mexican and U.S. justice systems.

from office only through impeachment. Second, the Constitution guarantees that neither the president nor Congress can reduce judges' salaries. Another feature of the U.S. judiciary's independence is the Supreme Court's ability to invalidate laws or presidential actions that, according to its members' judgment, conflict with the Constitution. This power, known as judicial review, was confirmed in the 1803 *Marbury v. Madison* ruling, when Supreme Court chief justice John Marshall decided that both the president and the Congress had acted against the intent of the Constitution.

U.S. Supreme Court

The Supreme Court is the highest judicial tribunal and final arbiter of the law in the United States. It functions as interpreter and guardian of the Constitution, which, in turn, limits the court to dealing with particular types of cases, usually those that involve important constitutional or federal issues. Since its formation in 1790 the number of justices that make up the Supreme Court has changed six times before settling at nine, including the chief justice. In the court's history there have been 16 chief justices and 97 associate justices, serving on average for a period of 15 years. Supreme Court justices, as well as court of appeals and district court judges, are nominated by the president and confirmed by the Senate. The names of potential nominees are often recommended by members of congress who belong to the same political party as the president. The Senate Judiciary Committee usually conducts confirmation hearings for each nominee.

U.S. federal and state courts

The federal justice system in the United States is organized into 94 judicial districts, each with its own district court. These are the trial courts of the federal system: they have the jurisdiction to hear nearly all categories of federal cases, including both civil and criminal matters. There is at least one judicial district in each of the 50 U.S. states, as well as the District of Columbia and Puerto Rico. In addition, three U.S. territories—the Virgin Islands, Guam, and the Northern Mariana Islands—have district courts that hear federal cases, including bankruptcy cases.

There are 12 courts of appeal in the U.S. system with the ability to review decisions made by the district courts. Each court of appeals has jurisdiction over one of 12 regional circuits and all the district courts within that region. For example, the First Circuit in the United States includes Maine, New Hampshire, Massachusetts, Rhode Island, and Puerto Rico. An additional court of appeals for the Federal Circuit, based in Washington, D.C., was created by Congress in 1982. This court has nationwide jurisdiction to hear appeals in special cases, such as those involving patent and copyright laws, and cases decided by the Court of International Trade and the Court of Federal Claims. These last two courts are known as "special trial courts." The Court of International Trade addresses cases involving international trade and customs issues, while the Court of Federal Claims rules on claims against the U.S. government, including disputes over federal contracts and government appropriation of private property.

At the state level, significant variations exist between court systems, including the number and organization of the courts, the number of judges, and the procedure for appointing new judges. The degree to which the state judiciary depends on other branches of government also varies from state to state. However, the nature of the courts' jurisdiction, if not their makeup, is broadly similar. For example, the bulk of any state supreme court's jurisdiction is appellate: it hears appeals from the courts beneath it and has the ability to review and correct the decisions made in those courts.

Mexican justice system

In common with the U.S. Constitution, Mexico's 1917 Constitution established its judiciary as one of the three separate branches of the federal government. One of the main functions of the judiciary is to protect the constitutional rights of Mexicans. It does this mainly through a process known as a *juicio*

U.S. Supreme Court Justices (2002)

Name	Date of Birth	Presidential Appointment	Date Sworn In
William H. Rehnquist	October 1, 1924	Nixon	January 7, 1972★
John Paul Stevens	April 20, 1920	Ford	December 19, 1975
Sandra Day O'Connor	March 26, 1930	Reagan	September 25, 1981
Antonin Scalia	March 11, 1936	Reagan	September 26, 1986
Anthony M. Kennedy	July 23, 1936	Reagan	February 18, 1988
David H. Souter	September 17, 1939	Bush	October 9, 1990
Clarence Thomas	June 23, 1948	Bush	October 23, 1991
Ruth Bader Ginsburg	March 15, 1933	Clinton	August 10, 1993
Stephen G. Breyer	August 15, 1938	Clinton	August 3, 1994

★Appointed Chief Justice by President Ronald Reagan in 1986.

Mexican Americans and the U.S. Justice System

Mexican Americans have often had a difficult relationship with the U.S. justice system. This relationship dates back to the U.S. acquisition of Mexican territories in 1848. Following the U.S. gain, laws in the Southwest were translated into Spanish and a number of Mexican Americans became lawyers and court officials in towns along the border. However, the increasing influx of Anglo-Americans to the region in the late 1800s put an end to the policy of translating laws into Spanish. Many Mexican Americans later lost their land through lack of familiarity with U.S. laws.

Discrimination in the law courts continued in the twentieth century. One notorious example was the 1942 Sleepy Lagoon Case in which a Los Angeles court convicted nine Mexican Americans of murder despite a lack of evidence.

However, by the 1960s U.S. court rulings reflected civil rights campaigns to improve the status of ethnic minorities. Yet whereas Mexican Americans benefited from Supreme Court rulings, such as *Lau v. Nichols* (1974), which affirmed non-English-speaking childrens' right to education, other rulings were less helpful. For instance, in 1973 the Supreme Court ruled that the Texas school finance system was constitutional, even though it spent more on schools in Anglo-American areas than in Mexican American neighborhoods. Despite Mexican Americans' difficult relationship with them, U.S. courts can serve as an effective safeguard of civil rights. After California introduced Proposition 187 in 1994 to severely restrict services to immigrants, federal courts declared it to be unconstitutional.

de amparo (injunction), which allows citizens to appeal to the courts if they consider their constitutional rights have been violated. The process is comparable to the form of common law known as habeas corpus, used in U.S. law to correct violations of individual liberties. The *juicio de amparo* is the most powerful judicial instrument that can be used to challenge actions by the Mexican government. However, unlike its U.S. equivalent, where the judiciary has wide-ranging authority, the Mexican legal system is based upon limited decision making and strict adherence to legal codes. In further contrast to the United States, whose courts may rule on constitutional matters, the Mexican supreme court cannot apply its rulings beyond any individual case.

For most of the twentieth century the main weakness of the Mexican judiciary was the fragile nature of its independence, particularly from the executive branch. Between 1929 and 2000 Mexico's government and political system were dominated by the Partido Revolucionario Institucional (PRI; Institutional Revolutionary Party). Successive administrations abused the courts' independence, for example, through the manipulation of judicial appointments or the application of pressure on the courts to render particular verdicts. However, constitutional reforms in 1994 strengthened the federal judiciary by altering its composition and powers.

Mexican supreme court

Mexico's highest court is the Suprema Corte de Justicia (supreme court of justice), located in Mexico City. Before 1994 the court had 26 ministers, or justices, but the constitutional reforms of that year reduced the number to 11, with each justice serving a 15-year term. Since 1995 the president's nominees for supreme court must be selected by the senate with a two-thirds majority vote. Ministers must be Mexican citizens by birth, hold a law degree, be at least 35 years old, and must have resided in Mexico for 10 years or more before they can be nominated. To ensure that the majority of supreme court nominees are judicial figures, as opposed to politicians, one reform to the Constitution in 1994 stated that candidates must not have held a political position for at least a year before their nomination.

Constitutional reforms in 1988, 1994, and 1999 gave the supreme court new powers to review the actions of the congress, presidency, and government administration. One consequence of the reform has been to relegate many *amparo* functions to the next level of federal courts, the circuit courts. The supreme court meets in plenary sessions, with all 11 ministers, to resolve unconstitutional actions, constitutional controversies, and *amparo* judgments that may have been incorrectly applied in the lower courts. In addition, the supreme court separates into two chambers, each with five ministers, to rule on separate matters. The *primera sala* (first chamber) resolves criminal and civil issues, while the *segunda sala* (second chamber) deals with government and employment affairs. The rulings of both the supreme court's plenary sessions and its separate chambers are made on the basis of majority opinion. Rulings by the separate chambers may be overturned by the court's plenary sessions.

Other Mexican federal courts

There are three levels of federal courts under the supreme court: the collegiate circuit courts, the unitary circuit courts, and the district courts. The federal magistrates and judges for each of these lower courts remain in office for six years and can only be removed under the provisions set out in the Constitution. The federal magistrates and judges are nominated and appointed by the judicial council, which is presided over by the president minister, or chief justice, of the supreme court. Since 1995 the judicial council has had responsibility for the selection, training, and evaluation of all lower-level judges in Mexico.

There are 107 collegiate circuit courts in Mexico, 31 of which are located in Mexico City. The courts' function is comparable to the U.S. courts of appeals. Each court has three judges who deal with the protection of individual rights, most commonly hearing appeals regarding *amparo* judgments. Beneath the collegiate circuit courts are the country's 49 unitary circuit courts. These courts also handle appeal cases but are made up of magistrates, as opposed to judges. Each court has six magistrates.

Below the circuit courts are the 192 district courts, each with one judge. There are 34 district courts in Mexico City alone. In some cities, such as the capital and Guadalajara, district judges specialize in specific areas of law, including criminal, civil, administrative, and employment cases. In other cities and areas with fewer federal courts, judges hear complaints that arise in all types of cases.

An additional federal court is Mexico's electoral tribunal, which in 1996 became the highest judicial authority in electoral matters. Reforms extended the tribunal's powers to include both national and local elections. This reform may be seen in the context of a range of measures to improve Mexico's election process. Widespread allegations of vote-rigging in the 1988 presidential elections led the winner, President Carlos Salinas de Gortari, to instigate electoral reforms in the 1990s. The elec-

---

Mexican Supreme Court Ministers (2002)★

President minister
Genaro David Góngora Pimentel

Primera sala (first chamber)
1. Juventino Víctor Castro y Castro
2. José de Jesús Gudiño Pelayo
3. Humberto Román Palacios
4. Olga María del Carmen Sánchez Cordero Dávila
5. Juan N. Silva Meza

Segunda sala (second chamber)
1. José Vicente Aguinaco Alemán
2. Sergio Salvador Aguirre Anguiano
3. Mariano Azuela Guitrón
4. Juan Díaz Romero
5. Guillermo Iberio Ortiz Mayagoitia

★Approved by the Mexican senate on January 26, 1995.

---

toral tribunal consists of an appeal circuit to oversee national elections and five regional courts for local and state elections. The seven magistrates in the appeal circuit are nominated by the supreme court and elected by the senate.

Mexican state courts

At the state level in Mexico the basic organizational structure resembles that at the federal level. However, as in the United States, in each of the country's 31 states and the Federal District (incorporating Mexico City) there is considerable variation in the performance of the courts and their resources. In terms of their organization and procedures, state courts are independent from the federal system. Supreme courts in each state hear appeals from lower courts but have limited functions to review the actions of government at the state level. Below the state supreme courts are the high and lower courts, which handle smaller civil claims and disputes.

Susana Berruecos García Travesí

SEE ALSO:

Civil Rights in the U.S.; Constitutions, Mexican; MALDEF; Presidency, Mexican; Prison System, U.S.; Proposition 187; Zoot Suit Riots.

Kahlo, Frida

Frida Kahlo (1907–1954) was one of the most celebrated female painters of the early twentieth century. She painted powerful and expressive images of her own life, which was marred by continual ill health. Kahlo was part of the generation of Mexican artists who pursued *Mexicanidad*—a self-consciously nationalistic artistic direction that mixed European avant-garde styles with Mexican cultural and religious themes.

This photograph of Frida Kahlo was taken in 1938. At this point in her career, Kahlo had just begun to establish herself as an artist, stepping out of the shadow of her husband, Diego Rivera.

Magdalena Carmen Frida Kahlo y Calderón was born in Mexico City on July 6, 1907, the daughter of a German father and a Mexican mother. Her father was a professional photographer and amateur painter. Frida grew up in the fashionable middle-class suburb of Coyoacán. She attended the progressive Escola Preparatoria in the center of Mexico City. There she first saw a figure who would become very important in her life: the painter Diego Rivera (1886–1957), who had been commissioned to paint murals at the school.

Kahlo's life changed radically in 1925. On a trip from the Escola Preparatoria to Coyoacán the bus in which she was traveling was hit by a tram. She suffered major injuries to her back, pelvis, and right leg. The accident left her partly crippled and subject to continued surgery. On the other hand, it provided the incentive for her to start painting and the subject matter for her life's work: the pain, boredom, and frustration of long confinement and the inability to bear children.

First paintings

Kahlo started to paint in 1926 during a long period of convalescence. Because they were in no position to support an artist, her family initially thought that she could illustrate medical textbooks. Kahlo, however, began to move in a different direction. In 1928 she met the Italian-born artist Tina Modotti, who introduced Kahlo to the bohemian artistic circles of Mexico City and, in 1929, to Rivera. Kahlo showed her work to the famous muralist, who was immediately impressed by both the art and the artist. They married later in the year.

At that time Mexico City was a vibrant artistic center. The idea of an authentic Mexican culture, *Mexicanidad*, that stood in opposition to the pre-revolutionary, officially sanctioned European culture was extremely important. The idea of *Mexicanidad* was perfectly in tune with Kahlo's own artistic direction. Mexico, for Kahlo, meant life, warmth, and family. She drew inspiration not only from pre-Columbian cultures but also from the Christian imagery seen in *retablos* (altarpieces) depicting pain, suffering, and salvation. Politically, she was a fervent communist and sided with the Mexican people against foreign imperialism.

Despite their differences in age and reputation, Kahlo was not Rivera's pupil. Her work contrasted distinctly with Rivera's in its scale and themes. Rivera depicted epic political themes in large-scale murals. Kahlo's life's work consisted of about 200 small-scale pieces of an intimate nature, mainly self-portraits or depictions of personal experiences.

At the time of their marriage, Rivera was internationally famous and in great demand in the United States as a muralist. In 1930, the pair took a short honeymoon in Cuernavaca. Kahlo and Rivera then moved to the United States. They spent the next three years living in San Francisco, Detroit, and New York City. During this time, Kahlo was known only as the wife of the famous Rivera, but she continued to paint in private.

While in the United States, Kahlo suffered several miscarriages and it soon became apparent that she could not bear children due to her injuries. Her sadness at her infertility is expressed in paintings such as her *Miscarriage in Detroit* (1932) and *Henry Ford Hospital* (1932), in which she showed herself in the hospital with the image of her dead baby floating above in the manner of a *retablo*.

Kahlo and Rivera returned to Mexico in 1933. Their life together was marked by frequent extramarital affairs. Despite being considered ugly, not least by Kahlo, Rivera had a passionate personality that made him notoriously attractive to women. Despite her injuries, Kahlo exerted an almost magnetic sexual attraction over both men and women. Among Kahlo's many lovers were the communist leader Leon Trotsky, who was living in exile in Mexico, and the U.S. artist Isamu Noguchi. Kahlo's affairs made Rivera extremely jealous and the pair divorced in 1939; they remarried in 1940,

but by this time their relationship was mainly one of mutual support and friendship.

Before the divorce, Kahlo had already moved back to the family house in Coyoacán, which became her main studio. It became known as the Blue House because of its cobalt blue walls. The house later became an international artistic center. It was here that Kahlo painted *Two Kahlos* (1939), in which she portrayed her dilemma over her divorce, and *Self Portrait with Cropped Hair* (1940), which symbolized the end of her married status and rejection of femininity.

Growth in reputation

Kahlo eventually began to acquire a reputation as an artist in her own right. In 1938 she exhibited at the Julien Levy Gallery in New York, her first solo exhibition. The French surrealist writer André Breton invited her to Paris in 1939, and she exhibited at the Exposición Internacional del Surrealismo in the Galeria de Arte Mexicano in Mexico City in 1940.

This association with surrealism gave Kahlo a degree of credibility. Her work was selected for the *Twenty Centuries of Mexican Art* exhibition at the Museum of Modern Art, New York, in 1940. In 1942 she became a founding member of the Seminario de Cultura Mexicana and was invited to teach at the progressive Escuela Nacional de Pintura y Escultura La Esmeralda.

By 1950, however, Kahlo's health had deteriorated so badly she spent the next year in the hospital. From then on she was confined to a wheelchair or to bed. Her fame increased, however, and her first major exhibition in Mexico was held in April 1953, which she attended on a stretcher laid on a four-poster bed installed in the gallery. Her last work, *Viva la Vida* (1954), was of bright red watermelons, a symbol of life. She died in Mexico City on July 13, 1954.

Kahlo's reputation grew in the years that followed her death. In the United States, she proved to be an inspiration to Chicano artists as their Mexican heritage became a positive source of pride. On the Day of the Dead in November 1978, the Galeria de la Raza in San Francisco, one of the major Chicano arts cooperatives, organized a show entitled *Homage to Frida Kahlo*, in which 50 Chicano artists were invited to produce works in her spirit.

Zilah Quezado Deckker

SEE ALSO:

Art; Chicano Art; Rivera, Diego.

Kahlo, Frida
Mexican painter

Born:	*July 6, 1907*
	Mexico City
Died:	*June 13, 1954*
	Mexico City

1925	Suffers serious injuries in a bus accident
1926	Begins to paint
1929	Marries Diego Rivera
1938	Holds first one-person show at the Julien Levy Gallery in New York
1939	Divorces Rivera. Paints *Two Khalos*.
1940	Her work forms part of the *Twenty Centuries of Mexican Art* exhibition in New York

Kickapoo

The Kickapoo are a staunchly independent Native American tribe. Originally from central Michigan, they roamed widely across North America, with some bands eventually settling in Mexico.

Like many other Native American peoples the Kickapoo speak the Algonquian language, from which their name derives. "Kickapoo" comes from *Kiikaapoa*, meaning "one who stands about" or "one who moves about." French traders—the first Europeans to come into contact with the Kickapoo in the late seventeenth century—called them "the great travelers." The French also noted the independent and self-sufficient character of the Kickapoo and their seminomadic way of life, divided between settled periods, when they tended crops in their villages, and traveling seasons, when families moved over the prairies, hunting animals and gathering wild foods, such as rice, berries, and nuts.

Resettlement in the 1600s and 1700s

The Kickapoo have endured many hardships and been forced to relocate numerous times in order to remain free of domination by white Europeans, whom they never trusted. Before contact with the white traders and settlers the Kickapoo lived in the area between Lake Erie and Lake Michigan in present-day Michigan. Beginning in the 1640s they came under attack from the east, first by Ottawa and Neutral Native Americans and then by the Iroquois. The cause of these conflicts lay in the need to control hunting grounds rich in animals such as deer, bear, and beaver. By 1658 the Kickapoo had been forced into southwestern Wisconsin. By about 1700 most had moved to the area between Peoria, Illinois, and the Wabash Valley on the western border of Indiana.

In 1819, after a number of wars with white settlers who moved into the Ohio Valley, the Kickapoo signed treaties with the U.S. authorities, ceding their remaining land east of the Mississippi River. Over the next five years they relocated to southern Missouri. Here they soon came into conflict with the Osage and, again, with white settlers who moved onto their land and refused to

leave. In response to these further conflicts, two-thirds of the Kickapoo left and headed for the plains of Kansas, Oklahoma, and Texas.

Some groups of Kickapoo had already been living in Texas since 1775, when the Spanish encouraged bands from Missouri to relocate in order to help secure the frontiers against the Apache and Comanche. However, the Kickapoo who moved to Texas in the 1820s settled in lands that were coveted by white American settlers. After the Texas Revolution (1835–1836), which resulted in the separation of Texas from Mexico, Sam Houston, the first president of the new republic, arranged a land grant to the Kickapoo and other Native Americans. However, the land grant treaty was never ratified, and the deaths of nearly 20 members of an American surveying party in 1838 in a battle with Cherokee and Kickapoo warriors caused Houston's successor, Mirabeau B. Lamar, to expel all Native Americans from Texas. Some Texan Kickapoo had already moved to northern Mexico in around 1836. Two years later, those expelled by Lamar either crossed the southern border to join those in Mexico or moved north to the land set aside by the U.S. government as Indian Territory (now Oklahoma).

Kickapoo in Mexico

While the Kickapoo in Kansas and Oklahoma were generally friendly with the Comanche, those in Mexico took both Comanche and Apache scalps for the bounties offered by local political leaders. Kickapoo resistance to raids by these two tribes prompted the Mexican government in 1849 to offer the Kickapoo territory in the Santa Rosa mountains of Coahuila in return for continued pressure on the Comanche and Apache. One band of Kickapoo, under Chief Papiquan, accepted and moved south in 1850. Two years later the band traded this land for Nacimiento, also in Coahuila.

Pressure from white settlers on the Kickapoo living in Oklahoma and Kansas caused them in the 1850s to move to join those living in Nacimiento. Leaders of the Kansas Kickapoo signed a treaty with the settlers in May 1854, selling 600,000 acres (240,000 ha) of their land for 300,000 U.S. dollars. They also agreed to accept either allotment (the distribution of land to individual tribespeople) or relocation to Indian Territory. These decisions were unpopular with many Kickapoo, who left for Mexico and were joined by dissatisfied Potawatomi and Seminole Native Americans along the way. By the late 1850s there were only 300 Kickapoo left in Kansas.

In the mid-1860s many Oklahoma Kickapoo decided to join their kinfolk in northern Mexico instead of agreeing to allotment, which they felt demeaned their way of life by granting them areas of land organized like white American settlements. However, while crossing Texas in 1865, these Kickapoo were attacked by Confederate cavalry in the Battle of Dove Creek. The attack only added to Kickapoo grievances against Texas. From the 1850s the Mexican Kickapoo had conducted border raids across the Rio Grande, stealing Texan horses and cattle. By the 1870s these had escalated from occasional skirmishes to full-scale raids into central Texas north of the Nueces River. Kickapoo warriors found they could easily elude U.S. Army pursuit by slipping back into Mexico across the Rio Grande.

Relocations in the late 1800s

In 1873 U.S. colonel Ranald Mackenzie led a secret cross-border raid into Indian territory in Nacimiento. The colonel's cavalry killed many Kickapoo and brought women and children, as prisoners, to Fort Gibson in Oklahoma. The attack put an end to most of the Kickapoo raids: during the next five years 800 Mexican Kickapoo and Seminole returned to the United States so that they could be reunited with their captured families. At first they settled near the border, but in the 1880s some Kickapoo agreed to relocate to Indian Territory. Others eventually followed.

However, the majority of the Kickapoo refused to leave Nacimiento. In 1894 many Kickapoo who had relocated to Indian Territory attempted to move back to Mexico. They were unhappy with the allotment settlements, the pressure to send their children to government schools, and the nearby presence of white Americans. However, the community in Nacimiento refused to allow the displaced Kickapoo to return and argued that they had lost their heritage by accepting conditions laid down by white Americans. The rejected Kickapoo eventually returned to Indian Territory, and Kickapoo settlement patterns have remained stable ever since the end of the nineteenth century. In the

Babe Schkit, chief of the Oklahoma Kickapoo in the late 1800s. Two centuries of U.S. expansion, forced relocation, and violence on the Mexico-U.S. border split the Kickapoo into a number of separate bands.

1990s over 2,500 Kickapoo lived in the United States, divided between approximately 500 in Kansas and 2,000 in Oklahoma. In addition, 700 Kickapoo lived in Mexico and Texas. In 1983 the state finally granted them lands near El Indio.

Maintaining Kickapoo culture

Of all the Kickapoo the Mexican branch has remained the most traditional and the most reluctant to admit visitors from outside. Most still speak the Algonquian language and many can trace their pure descent back for many generations. Few have converted to Christianity and instead follow such Native American religions as the Dream Dance or the Peyote religion. The Kickapoo who live in Nacimiento still practice a seminomadic lifestyle, but one that has been adapted to suit modern economic circumstances. Since the 1940s many have worked as migrant farmworkers in the United States, taking advantage of the dual citizenship granted to them by the U.S. government in the late nineteenth century.

Henry Russell

SEE ALSO:

Apache; Comanche; Houston, Sam; Indian Policy; Native Americans; Texas Revolution.

Kino, Eusebio Francisco

Father Eusebio Francisco Kino was a pioneering Jesuit missionary and explorer on the northern frontier of the Spanish empire in the Americas. He founded more than 24 missions in the desert region of northern Mexico and southern Arizona between 1687 and 1711.

Born in 1644 in the Tyrolean village of Segno, Italy, Kino graduated from the University of Fribourg in Switzerland in 1665, then moved to Landsberg in what is now Germany, where he joined the Society of Jesus (also known as the Jesuits), a Roman Catholic order that carried out missionary work around the world. After studying astronomy and mathematics in the German state of Bavaria, he was sent by the Jesuits to teach in his native Tyrol.

In 1678 Kino moved to a seminary in Seville, southern Spain. While there he observed the comet of 1680–1681 at Cadiz and published his account of it in *Exposición astronómica de el cometa* (Astronomical explanation of the comet, 1681).

Missionary in Mexico

Jesuits worked together with the Spanish colonial government in the Americas to extend the frontiers of the empire and bring the indigenous peoples into the Spanish way of life. They sent missionaries out among the indigenous peoples to establish settlements that were eventually meant to become towns. Kino was sent by the Jesuits as a missionary to Mexico City in the spring of 1681.

In 1683 he was appointed royal cosmographer on an expedition led by the conquistador Isidro de Antillón y Atondo to the northern regions of the Spanish domains, including Baja California. The settlement founded on the trip was soon abandoned due to its unhealthy location and local hostility but Kino wanted to continue the work. He made a personal appeal to the Spanish viceroy to be allowed to carry out extensive colonization and missionary activity. His request was granted and in 1687, at age 43, Kino embarked upon the most productive phase of his remarkable career.

Over the next 24 years Kino made more than 40 excursions into the northwest of Mexico and regions that later became part of the southwestern United States. The territory he covered included not only what are today the Mexican states of Sinaloa and Sonora but also the vast desert region known as Pimería Alta, in reference to the Pima Indians who lived there. This is now southern Arizona and northwestern Sonora. Kino's first mission was established among the Indians of

Francisco Kino, as depicted in a twentieth-century mural by Jay Datus at the Arizona State Library in Phoenix.

Sonora at Nuestra Señora de los Dolores. This became the headquarters for all his subsequent explorations, as well as for the founding of other missions, including the most northern ones in Arizona at San Xavier del Bac in 1700 near Tucson, Guevavi, and Tumacacori, which is now a U.S. National Monument.

Kino's work

Kino made many journeys from his base at Nuestra Señora de los Dolores—perhaps as many as 50—often with only local guides as companions. Although he preached to the Indian peoples he encountered and attempted to convert them to Christianity, his work with them was practical as well as spiritual. He taught them new practices in agriculture and introduced them to food and animals they had never seen before, such as seed grain, cattle, horses, and sheep. He encouraged them to leave their scattered settlements (known as *rancherías*) and move to compact centers of population where they would have easy access to the mission for worship and prayer and could contribute to the economy of the new settlement. Each Indian man was given a plot of land in return for three days' work a week for the mission, tending herds of livestock or providing specialized services, such as escorting travelers, constructing buildings, or defending the settlement against Apache raids.

Under the dynamic leadership of Kino, Jesuit influence in the northwest frontier of the Spanish empire reached its all-time peak. Meanwhile he also found time to write and learned several local Indian languages. *Favores celestiales* is the diary of his missionary activities between 1687 and 1710, the year before his death. This was later published under the title *Las misiones de Sonora y Sinaloa*. It was translated into English as *Kino's Historical Memoir of Pimería Alta* and published in 1919. Another work, *Libra astronómica y filosófica* (Book of astronomy and philosophy), features vocabularies of the Cochimi, Guaycura, and Nabe languages.

In 1701 and 1702 Kino made two expeditions down the Colorado River. On the second he reached the head of the Gulf of California and was able to finally prove that Baja California was a peninsula, not an island. He was the first to chart Pimería Alta on the basis of actual exploration, and his map, originally published in 1705 and reprinted many times, was the basis of all maps of the region for more than one hundred years.

Kino died in 1711. The whereabouts of his grave were unknown until 1966, when it was discovered by a team of Mexican and U.S. researchers near the town of Magadalena in Sonora.

Kino's legacy

After Kino's death Jesuit influence in northwestern Mexico declined. Many later missionaries and Spanish settlers dealt dishonestly with the Indians, who suffered such injustice that they eventually rose against the colonists. Their rebellions became so frequent and so violent that by the middle of the eighteenth century the Spanish had abandoned their hopes of frontier expansion and reconciled themselves to a policy of containment and defense based on the construction of a chain of presidios, or fortresses. Many people thought that none of these things would have happened under Kino, who was universally respected for his plain dealing. He treated the indigenous peoples with respect, helped them organize against Apache raids, and opposed their enslavement in the silver mines of northern Mexico. In 1767 the Spanish crown expelled the Jesuits from New Spain.

San Xavier del Bac, a mission opened by Kino near present-day Tucson, Arizona, is still used as a church and a statue of Kino symbolizes the state of Arizona in Statuary Hall of the U.S. Capitol in Washington, D.C.

Henry Russell

SEE ALSO:

Catholic Church; Missions and Religious Orders; Native Americans; Spanish Empire.

Kino, Eusebio Francisco
Missionary and explorer

Born:	*August 10, 1644*
	Segno, Italy
Died:	*March 15, 1711*
	Sonora, Mexico

1669	Joins Society of Jesus (Jesuits)
1681	Arrives in Mexico
1687	Founds mission at Nuestra Señora de los Dolores, Sonora
1691	First expedition into Arizona
1701	Explores Colorado River

Labor and Employment

Employment patterns in Mexico changed enormously during the twentieth century, as the country underwent a transition from a predominantly agricultural to an industrial base. The transition accounts for the growth of foreign-owned maquiladoras (assembly plants) in Mexico as well as the migration of millions of Mexicans to the United States, where they faced a different set of employment challenges.

In 2000 Mexico's labor force consisted of nearly 40 million people out of a total population of 100 million. Employment patterns by sector had changed dramatically since the early twentieth century, from a labor force primarily occupied in agriculture to one primarily occupied in the industrial and services sectors. In 1930, 65 percent of the Mexican labor force worked in agriculture. By 1998 the figure for agriculture was just 20 percent, with industry accounting for 24 percent and services 56 percent.

Changes in agriculture

The Mexican Revolution (1910–1920) had a profound effect on the lives of many rural people. In 1895, during the peak of President Porfirio Díaz's rule, 95 percent of Mexicans were landless and worked as farm laborers on large haciendas (estates) owned by the remaining 5 percent. Between the 1920s and the late 1930s approximately 170 million acres (70 million ha) of land was transferred to around three million peasants. The land was granted in the form of *ejidos*, a communal system of ownership that gave individuals the right to a plot of land where they were able to practice subsistence farming.

However, from the 1940s onward, the Mexican government focused increasingly on developing the country's industrial sector, a policy that affected rural employment. In order to feed the growing urban, industrial workforce, the government began to emphasize the importance of increasing agricultural productivity. Private landholders were given new rights to protect their land against further

A Mexican maquiladora worker sewing pleated shirts. By 2000 maquiladoras employed more than one million people, but an expanding population still left Mexico with a growing unemployment problem.

Crossing the Border for Work

In addition to the people who migrate from Mexico's southern and central states to the maquiladoras in the north of the country, many workers end up in the informal employment sector that exists along both sides of the Mexico-U.S. border. This sector includes work related to the trafficking of illegal drugs, prostitution, personal services such as house cleaning and babysitting, and selling items on city streets. Migrants also find employment in the agricultural sector on both sides of the border.

Increased militarization of the border in the 1990s had little effect on the flow of migrants into the United States, in part because the U.S. economy depends on cheap migrant labor. Successive operations to increase the presence and arrest rates of the U.S. Border Patrol included Operation Blockade and Operation Gatekeeper. While the efforts failed to stop undocumented migration, one political effect may have been to address concerns of the U.S. working class regarding competition with Mexicans.

redistribution. Farm owners responded to the need to improve output by investing in new farming equipment, such as tractors, that replaced centuries-old farming techniques with mechanization. Changes in agricultural policy in the 1950s and 1960s forced more peasants to work on private farms or for agribusiness concerns, while new farming equipment reduced the number of jobs available. Numbers of the landless and unemployed began to rise in the countryside once more, resulting in migration to seek work in Mexico's cities and in the United States.

Developments in the 1990s threatened a greater decline in agricultural employment. In 1992 the Mexican government amended Article 27 of the 1917 Constitution, allowing private companies to buy *ejido* lands. In addition, Mexico's adoption of free trade policies, including the implementation of the North American Free Trade Agreement (NAFTA) in 1994, required that the government no longer protect its domestic crops, such as beans and corn, from cheaper U.S. and Canadian imports. Both measures increased concerns that rural jobs would decline further and influenced the Zapatista uprising in Chiapas in 1994.

Industrial employment in Mexico

Industrialization in Mexico took off during World War II (1939–1945), when the country experienced difficulties obtaining imports from the United States and began to improve its own manufacturing base and infrastructure. The government was helped in its industrialization policy by a generally harmonious relationship with organized labor, in particular the Confederación de Trabajadores de México (CTM; Confederation of Mexican Workers), which was created by President Lázaro Cárdenas in 1936. In the 1950s and 1960s the Mexican economy developed rapidly as the result of growth in sectors such as petrochemicals, steel, construction, and transport. While workers' salaries remained fairly low, the relationship between the government and the unions kept strike activity to a minimum. However, during the economic crises that began in the 1970s, labor militancy increased as wages failed to keep pace with rising inflation.

Employment in maquiladoras

The border region grew in importance for Mexico's industrial labor force with the start of the maquiladora program in 1965. The program allowed foreign companies to bring parts or raw materials duty-free into Mexico for assembly by low-wage workers. The aim was to reduce unemployment in the border areas, in large part caused by the termination of the Bracero Program, which had encouraged Mexican braceros (field-workers) to fill labor shortages on U.S. farms between 1942 and 1964. The end of the program left many braceros jobless and stranded in northern Mexico.

The maquiladora program grew into a major source of employment. In 1980, 113,897 people worked in the plants, which ranged from low-tech woodworking shops to high-tech electronics firms. By 2000 the total number of employees in the maquiladora industry was 1,307,982, an increase of more than 1,000 percent over 20 years. However, maquiladora work typically involves low wages—in 2001 the average worker earned about U.S. $4.80 a day—few benefits, little job security, and high exposure to toxins. Toxins constitute a particular risk to the health of female workers and their children—born and unborn. In 1980, 77 percent of maquiladora workers were women. Although this figure had fallen to 55 percent by 2002, women still predominated in many sectors, such as electronics.

Employment problems in Mexico

While the demand for workers in the maquiladora industry is high, it does not keep up with the growth in Mexico's labor supply. Nearly one million new workers enter Mexico's labor force each year; in contrast, the maquiladora industry took over 30 years before it employed one million people. Furthermore, employment levels in the nonmaquiladora manufacturing sectors have sharply declined since the implementation of NAFTA. One reason for this has been the Mexican government's policy of promoting exports while focusing less on the domestic market as a source of growth and development. In addition, Mexico's increasing reliance on trade with the United States, both as a market for Mexico's exports and as the main supplier of Mexican imports, makes Mexico more vulnerable to the ups and downs of the U.S. economy. This vulnerability translates into job insecurity. When the U.S. economy fell into recession in March 2001, Mexico suffered a similar economic downturn. Its gross domestic product fell 1.6 percent between 2000 and 2001, and the number of people in work dropped by 382,000. Vicente Fox's successful presidential election campaign in 2000 included a pledge to create 1.5 million new jobs. Two years into his administration Fox had yet to deliver on his promise.

Employment in the United States

Attracted by the higher wages paid in the United States, many Mexicans have migrated across the border in search of work. This migration dates back hundreds of years and is one reason for the existence of Mexican American communities throughout the United States—the other reason being the incorporation of northern Mexico into the U.S. Southwest in the mid-1800s. Traditionally, the labor undertaken by Mexican migrants tended to be the menial jobs that U.S. citizens avoided, including work in steel mills, packing houses, and garment factories, and on construction crews on canals or railroads. During the twentieth century the work available to migrant workers in the United States changed, but the low pay and poor conditions generally remained. Many workers are illegal residents and refrain from joining labor unions or voicing their demands for fear of being deported to Mexico. Since the 1960s increasing numbers of Mexican migrants have found work in service industries, such as retail and catering, alongside the more traditional jobs as farm laborers, warehouse packers, and garment workers.

The cheap labor provided by Mexican workers is enormously important for the U.S. economy. However, discrimination against Mexican workers continues to be a major issue in the United States. In both the 1920s and 1940s employers actively encouraged Mexicans to cross the border and work in the United States. In the 1930s and the 1950s Mexicans became the scapegoats for the country's economic and social woes, leading to huge deportation and repatriation programs that transported Mexicans back across the border.

In 1994 a backlash against illegal immigrants in California caused a majority of the state's voters to approve Proposition 187. Although it was outlawed by federal court rulings, the proposition aimed to prevent illegal immigrants from receiving education, health care, and other social services. Despite the problems involved in representing workers who are not legal residents, many labor and advocacy organizations do much to counter discrimination toward Mexican-origin workers.

Mexican Americans' employment patterns vary widely. Many urban Mexican communities experience the same limited employment opportunities and the same problems of exploitation as migrant Mexican workers. Employment in these communities is often supplemented by home-based work, such as catering, car repairs, or dressmaking. However, an increasing number of Mexican Americans have well-paid middle-class jobs, working as doctors, lawyers, accountants and computer programmers. In 2002 the U.S. Public Broadcasting Service (PBS) received praise for its authentic depiction of a Mexican American family in its drama *American Family*. The central characters included a doctor, a lawyer, a filmmaker, and a social worker.

Janet M. Tanski

SEE ALSO:

Agriculture; Deportation and Repatriation; Ejidos; Illegal Labor; Labor Organizations, U.S.; Maquiladoras; Migrant Labor; NAFTA; World War II.

Labor Organizations, U.S.

Mainstream U.S. labor unions were slow to support Mexican Americans in their struggle for better working conditions, and Mexicans often had to fight their own battles, a trend that ccontinued well into the twentieth century. Union successes in organizing Mexican Americans in the late 1960s and 1970s were undermined in the 1980s by a general decline in union power, but achievements in the 1990s demonstrated that many Mexican Americans still looked to the organized labor movement to improve their lives.

Throughout the late 1800s and early 1900s Mexican immigrants and Mexican Americans made up a large part of the workforce in the Southwest but were largely excluded from white-dominated labor unions. The umbrella organization for these unions, the American Federation of Labor (AFL), represented skilled craftworkers. It claimed that, because many Mexicans worked in "unskilled" jobs such as farm laboring, they could not join their unions. Unofficially, the unions also feared that Mexican immigrants worked for low wages and stole U.S. jobs, a view that led unions to discriminate against Mexican nationals and Mexican Americans.

Organizing Mexican labor

While Mexicans rarely relied on support from mainstream unions, they had a long history of coming together in groups where they could find mutual support. Mexicans in Texas, for example, joined *mutualistas* (mutual aid societies) as well as political parties, such as the Texas Socialist Party and Mexican revolutionary Ricardo Flores Magón's Partido Liberal Mexicano (Mexican Liberal Party). They also formed their own unions. These included the Unión Federal Mexicanos (Mexican Federal Union), representing Mexican railroad workers, and La Unión de Trabajadores del Valle Imperial (The Imperial Valley Workers Union), which organized a successful strike of cantaloupe pickers in California's Imperial Valley in 1928 to gain higher wages.

In the early decades of the twentieth century, some U.S. unions made efforts to organize Mexican workers. The Industrial Workers of the World (IWW) recruited Mexicans who worked in the fields of southern Texas and southern California. The IWW instigated a number of strikes in these regions, starting in 1903 with a strike by Mexican American sugar-beet pickers in Ventura, California. After two months workers won the right to negotiate terms directly with farmowners, rather than indirectly through labor contractors. In 1913 Mexican Americans also struck against the owners of Durst Ranch in Wheatland, California. The strike led to a riot in which four workers were killed, but the tragedy led the state government to regulate living and working conditions in farm labor camps. Away from the fields, in Arizona, the Western Federation of Miners (WFM) began a drive to recruit Mexican American mine workers.

However, Mexicans continued to face discrimination and mistreatment. In 1917, during a WFM strike in Bisbee, Arizona, more than one thousand Mexican strikers were rounded up and dumped in the New Mexican desert in a vigilante operation supported by local mine owners. Mexicans were routinely given the worst, most dangerous jobs for much lower wages than Anglo-Americans. Evidence also shows that employers hired Mexican American and African American strikebreakers to encourage racial tension. The situation deteriorated further with the Great Depression (1929–1939), which caused hundreds of thousands of white Americans to move from the Great Plains to the Southwest and compete with Mexicans for jobs. The depression also led to a growth in anti-Mexican feeling, with many Mexican workers scapegoated for the country's economic failure.

Increased activism in the 1930s

In response to extreme difficulties in the 1930s, Mexican Americans became more involved in labor union activity. A number of organizations played important roles in this decade, ensuring that Mexican labor activity became better organized. The U.S. Communist Party and unions with communist links, such as the Cannery and Agricultural Workers Industrial Union (CAWIU), became involved in organizing Mexican labor. In 1933 the CAWIU

Women's Involvement in Unions

At the end of the 1800s large numbers of Mexican women entered the U.S. labor market, particularly California's food-processing industry. By 1939, 75,000 women worked in the state's canneries and food-packing houses. Guatemalan-born Luisa Moreno helped found the United Cannery, Agricultural, Packing, and Allied Workers of America (UCAPAWA) to represent these workers. She became the union's vice president in 1937 before setting up El Congreso del Pueblo de Habla Española (The Spanish-Speaking Congress). While not a union, El Congreso encouraged Hispanic workers to join unions and called for greater Mexican American union representation. Other Mexican women labor leaders in the 1930s and 1940s included Josefina Fierro de Bright, who helped establish El Congreso, and Emma Tenayuca, who organized Mexican pecan shellers in Texas in the 1930s.

In the 1950s and 1960s Dolores Huerta played a leading role in representing Mexican American workers. From her involvement organizing workers in the Mexican American Community Service Organization she cofounded the National Farm Workers Association with César Chávez in 1962. Her efforts coordinating national consumers' boycotts helped ensure that grape producers improved working conditions for

This UFW poster shows migrant workers in the fields. The UFW was founded in 1962 by Dolores Huerta and César Chávez.

migrant fieldworkers. Since the 1980s Mexican American women have played leading roles in establishing unions for workers in sectors such as garment manufacturing, cleaning, and catering.

initiated a strike involving 12,000 cotton pickers in California's San Joaquin Valley. The strike held for some months but was lost due to government repression and vigilante violence.

Other institutions helped organize Mexican workers. From the mid-1930s the Congress of Industrial Organizations (CIO) unionized huge numbers of Mexican Americans in the Southwest. One union affiliated with the CIO, the International Union of Mine, Mill, and Smelter Workers (Mine Mill), organized thousands of Mexicans who worked in the metal smelting and refining industries in El Paso, Texas. Mine Mill used a variety of tactics to win support: it collaborated with Mexican unions, used Spanish speakers to inform Mexican laborers of the benefits of membership, and liaised with Mexican consuls in the United States, who openly supported Mexican laborers'

right to strike. In 1946 Mine Mill strikers won important concessions from El Paso's refining companies for increasing wages and ensuring equal pay and conditions in all their factories.

New opportunities and threats

The United States' entry into World War II in 1941 gave Mexican Americans new employment opportunities, from enlisting in the U.S. Army to working in factories producing defense equipment. A considerable level of discrimination continued to exist, however, and Mexican Americans often struggled to gain wartime jobs. The Pan-American Union was one organization whose campaigning persuaded the U.S. government in 1941 to set up the Committee on Fair Employment Practice, which called for an end to discrimination in the hiring of workers.

Mexican Americans played a significant part in World War II and emerged from it more confident about their status as U.S citizens. More Mexican Americans joined unions, a trend that occurred generally in the population across an increasingly industrialized United States. Mexican American unions continued to face difficulties, however, not least from the Bracero Program (1942–1964). The program was set up by the U.S. and Mexican governments to encourage Mexican migrant fieldworkers to make up the wartime labor shortage in the United States. Migrant workers who signed contracts under the program were not allowed to join unions, and U.S. farmers who rejected the program's conditions encouraged millions more Mexicans to work illegally. U.S. labor organizations criticized the U.S. government for refusing to allow bracero workers to join unions, but to no avail. The influx of illegal Mexican workers also led to further anti-Mexican sentiment from Anglo-American workers, employers, and white-dominated unions.

Community involvement

The termination of the Bracero Program in 1964 increased the ability of unions to organize Mexican American farmworkers. In 1962 César Chávez and Dolores Huerta founded the National Farm Workers Association (NFWA), later the United Farm Workers (UFW) union. The NFWA broke new ground in representing migrant farmworkers and, in a series of actions beginning with the Delano Strike in 1965, championed their grievances against California's grape growers. Chávez's nonviolent tactics gained his union enormous media attention and support. He received help from a range of institutions, including the now-merged American Federation of Labor and Congress of Industrial Organizations (AFL-CIO), church groups, and student and civil rights organizations. He also urged the U.S. public to boycott all wines and grape juices produced by companies that did not accept the NFWA's demands for improved working conditions. In the late 1960s 17 million U.S. citizens participated in the NFWA boycott, forcing the grape growers to recognize the union. The NFWA's strategy was successfully mirrored by that of the Amalgamated Clothing and Textile Workers Union (ACTWU). In 1972 the ACTWU engineered a boycott against the Farah Manufacturing Company, resulting in improved conditions for the firm's female garment workers.

Unions face new challenges

Unions in the United States declined in the 1970s and 1980s. Numbers of workers fell in industries that traditionally had strong unions, such as mining, construction, and manufacturing. This was the result of globalization and increasing automation in manufacturing, which led U.S. companies to seek cheaper labor in other countries. In contrast, the number of workers in sectors with little union representation, such as retail, catering, finance, and technology, had grown. Many Mexican workers, including most illegal Mexican immigrants, worked at the lower end of this employment scale. The temporary nature of these jobs, and the fact that illegal immigrants often made themselves as invisible as possible, stood in the way of labor organizing. By 2000 union membership in the United States had dropped to 9 percent, and membership of Mexican American unions also declined. In 1995 membership of the UFW had fallen from its mid-1970s' peak of 70,000 to 26,000.

Despite the problems of the 1980s, Mexican Americans have continued to achieve victories in the struggle to improve their working lives, particularly in the nonunionized service industries. In 1985 the Service Employees International Union began the national Justice for Janitors campaign in Denver, Colorado, to improve pay and conditions for office cleaners, many of whom are Mexican American. The campaign, which inspired the film *Bread and Roses* (2000), continued into the 1990s and involved around 100,000 cleaners in campaigns across the country. Another campaign occurred at the New Otani Hotel in Los Angeles. In 1995 Mexican American staff belonging to the Hotel and Restaurant Employees Union were dismissed by management in an attempt to prevent union activity. Although the National Labor Relations Board backed the dismissals, there were strikes and demonstrations. Ironically, a decline in overall union membership, and the success of Mexican-dominated unions, has led the AFL-CIO to switch from its earlier hostile stance on migrant workers. In 2001 the AFL-CIO called for an amnesty for all illegal Mexicans in the United States.

Andrew Campbell

SEE ALSO:

Bisbee; Bracero Program; Chávez, César; Civil Rights in the U.S.; Flores Magón, Ricardo; Galarza, Ernesto; Huerta, Dolores; Migrant Labor; United Farm Workers Union.

Laguna Madre

Laguna Madre is a coastal lagoon that stretches 277 miles (443 km) along the coasts of northern Tamaulipas and southern Texas, broken only by the delta of the Rio Grande. The lagoon is separated from the Gulf of Mexico by a chain of narrow, sandy barrier islands, including Padre Island in Texas.

Laguna Madre is saltier than the open sea. In fact, it is the only hypersaline coastal lagoon in North American and one of only five in the world. The surrounding region, with its combination of shallow estuaries, tidal flats, barrier islands, impenetrable thorn scrub forests, cattle ranches, and agricultural land, provides habitats for several species of scarce mammals, birds, and reptiles. Endangered Kemp's ridley turtles swim in Laguna Madre's waters and nest on the sandy beaches of Padre Island.

The coastal plain along Laguna Madre is one of Mexico's most important agricultural areas, with cotton, cereals, and vegetables, all valuable crops. Cattle ranching is also important, both north and south of the border. In Texas, the King Ranch, one of the biggest in the world, stretches across Laguna Madre's western shore. It covers 825,000 acres (334,000 ha) and has 60,000 cattle.

In Mexico Laguna Madre extends south along the Gulf coast to the mouth of the Soto La Marina River just north of Tampico, while in Texas it runs north as far as Corpus Christi.

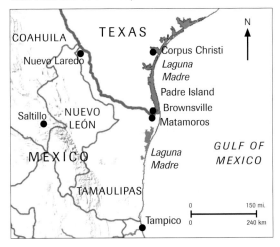

Agriculture has brought environmental problems to the region, however: pesticides, herbicides, and fertilizers have entered runoff from the land and polluted Laguna Madre's waters. Urban wastewater and fuel spills from boats have added to the problem, damaging populations of invertebrates and the fish and birds that feed on them. This environmental degradation has had an effect on the local economy. Fishers from ports such as Port Isabel and Port Mansfield in Texas have witnessed declining productivity of shrimp, and crab catches have fallen in the Laguna Madre of Tamaulipas.

History

Up until the eighteenth century the Laguna Madre region was inhabited by Native Americans. There is evidence from marine archaeology that Spanish ships were shipwrecked along the coast. In 1554 a massive Spanish fleet, loaded with treasures plundered from newly conquered Mexico, was hit by a hurricane. It was wrecked on the shore of Padre Island, near what is now Mansfield Cut. About 250 men, women, and children who survived the ordeal were attacked and killed by local Karankawa Indians. Only a few of the Spaniards made their escape to the south.

In 1791 Padre (Father) Nicolas Balli established a settlement on the barrier island, now known as Padre Island. After the Mexican-American War (1846–1848), the United States took control of the island, and the land speculator Henry Lawrence Kinney (1814–1862) set up a trading post at its northern end. The shelter afforded Laguna Madre by the barrier islands allowed several small ports to develop along its inland coast. During the U.S. Civil War the ports of Brownsville, Corpus Christi, and Port Isabel prospered as they shipped supplies to the Confederacy. Padre Island became a protected National Park when it received federal recognition as a National Seashore in 1962. It is now the longest remaining undeveloped barrier island in the world, receiving an average 800,000 visitors per year.

Tim Harris

SEE ALSO:

Agriculture; Brownsville; Fisheries; Mexican-American War; Ranching; Texas.

Laguna San Ignacio

One of the biggest Mexican environmental controversies of the late 1990s was centered on a remote stretch of the Pacific coast of Baja California called Laguna San Ignacio.

In 1995 one of Japan's richest corporations, Mitsubishi, announced plans to build the world's largest saltworks at Laguna San Ignacio, near the town of Punta Abrejos on the west coast of the Baja California Peninsula. Opposing this plan was the Coalition to Save Laguna San Ignacio, a group of scientists, local Mexican communities, and environmentalists from around the world.

Whale sanctuary

The plan was controversial because the area was part of the whale sanctuary of El Vizcaino, which was established by the Mexican government in 1972 in recognition of its importance for migratory gray whales. Gray whales swim each year from the Bering Straits, near Alaska, to its saline lagoons to give birth to and nurse their young. The sheltered waters of Laguna San Ignacio offer protection from winter storms, enabling the whales to calve their young with a high success rate. In addition, the area also provides breeding grounds for green, hawksbill, and olive ridley turtles and the endangered pronghorn antelope, and is an important hatchery for commercially valuable fish and shellfish species. World recognition for the site came in 1993 when the United Nations environmental agency, UNESCO, declared it a World Heritage Site.

Saltworks

Mistubishi's partner for the saltworks project was ESSA, a Mexican government-owned business. The Japanese corporation already operated a saltworks a little farther north on the Baja California coast at Laguna Guerrero Negro. This factory was operating at full capacity, and Mitsubishi wanted to increase operations in the area. Laguna San Ignacio seemed the ideal solution. There was a saline lagoon and plenty of land on which to build the saltworks, and the construction of a 1-mile (1.6-km) pier would enable large cargo vessels to berth and collect the salt. Mitsubishi claimed that gray whale numbers at Guerrero Negro had increased since the company had been making salt there. Conservationists, on the other hand, agreed that while the whales still visited, the disturbance prevented them from breeding. Scientists explained that gray whales need extra buoyancy when they are nursing young whales, something that high levels of salinity provide. The saltworks would decrease the lagoon's salinity, making it less attractive to the whales.

In addition to environmentalists, local people were opposed to the plan. Many local people earned a living from fishing in the lagoon, and some supplemented this income by taking visitors out in boats to view the whales. Thousands of ecotourists came to Laguna San Ignacio each year, many of them from the United States. The fishing communities worried that if the whales disappeared so would the tourists, and they were fearful that the disturbance could damage fishing stocks.

The Coalition to Save Laguna San Ignacio

The Coalition to Save Laguna San Ignacio, which included more than 50 Mexican environmental organizations, lobbied Mitsubishi and the Mexican government, mounted a high-profile publicity campaign, and encouraged investors to divest holdings in Mitsubishi until the corporation abandoned its plans. In the late 1990s more than one million people in the United States and Mexico signed petitions against the scheme. At least 40 California cities passed resolutions opposing Mitsubishi's plans, and 15 of the world's top mutual funds, representing U.S. $14 billion in potential investment funds, pledged not to invest in the company until it scrapped its plan for the lagoon.

In a decision that surprised most people, Mitsubishi and the Mexican government announced on March 2, 2000, that plans for the salt plant at Laguna San Ignacio were being abandoned for environmental reasons. The interests of the gray whales and local fishers had won the day.

Tim Harris

SEE ALSO:

Baja California; Ecotourism; Environmental Issues; Gulf of Mexico; National Parks; Wildlife.

Land Reform

Conflicts over the ownership of land and attempts to reform its distribution have underscored much of Mexican history. Population growth, rural poverty, greed, modernization of agriculture, and international pressures have complicated the efforts at reform.

At the end of the colonial era there were three main landholding groups, the church, the hacienda owners and ranchers, and the Indian village communities, which held communal lands called *ejidos*. Most of the communal lands were cultivated by peasants. Often it was not the best land; but it played a vital role in supporting Mexico's rural majority. Even before Mexico gained independence from Spain in 1821, the 1812 Constitution de Cádiz called for the privatization of the community lands. Although this policy was not implemented in Mexico for many years, it was to become one of the key conflicts of Mexican society. Peasants demanded community lands to sustain their families and communities, while liberal and conservative politicians alike increasingly called for their privatization and use as marketable commodities.

Successive Mexican governments found themselves under pressure to produce agrarian policies that increased production in the face of an increasing population and competition from abroad. It proved impossible to do this without alienating either the large landowners, who fought to maintain ownership of their haciendas (estates), or the peasants and small landowners whose support was needed to remain in office.

The Ley Lerdo

In 1856 the Liberal government led by President Benito Juárez (1806–1872) passed a law known as the Ley Lerdo. It aimed to reduce the power of the Catholic Church and encourage the growth of small to medium-sized landholders by ending all forms of community landholding. The communal lands would become the property of the individual villagers that had cultivated them. The peasants protested that they should not have to pay for land that they already farmed, and in any case, few could

afford to buy it as individuals. Even so, the privatization of community lands was incorporated into the 1857 Constitution. The seizure of church land met with opposition from the conservatives, but in 1859 Juárez nationalized all church property, auctioning it off to the highest bidder.

Land reform and revolution

Huge changes in land tenure continued during the administration of president Porfirio Díaz (1877–1880 and 1884–1911). The privatization of communal land was accelerated and almost 96 million acres (39 million ha) of untitled land (*terreros baldíos*) was brought into private ownership. The government's stated aim was that this land would go to the peasants, but most ended up in the hands of wealthy landowners. The Díaz years witnessed the flowering of commercial ranching and agriculture for export in Sonora, Coahuila, and Chihuahua, while rural communities grew increasingly impoverished. Peasant uprisings accompanied the commercialization of agriculture. Díaz's policies fueled the resentments that led to the Mexican Revolution in 1910. By the time of the revolution the number of haciendas had doubled from 6,000 to 12,000, large ranches had increased from 15,000 to 30,000, and 1 percent of the population owned 97 percent of the cultivable land.

When Francisco I. Madero replaced Porfirio Díaz as president in 1911, rural Mexico was seething with discontent. Some 90 percent of peasants had become landless during Díaz's administration. They wanted land and improved working conditions. In Morelos, Mexican revolutionary Emiliano Zapata (1879–1919) led a peasant army that destroyed properties, took landowners prisoner, and seized their lands. In his Plan of Ayala of November 1911, Zapata demanded the restoration of the *ejidos* through the expropriation of one-third of the private estates. He argued that the large estates could coexist with *ejidos*, but if the estate owners resisted, their lands should be turned over entirely to the peasants. Zapatista armies occupied many estates and established collectives. In the north, the peasant army of revolutionary leader Francisco "Pancho" Villa (1878–1923) also seized many estates, but unlike Zapata, Villa did not distribute the land to peasants but to his supporters.

Under pressure from the rural majority, President Venustiano Carranza (1915–1920) issued his Law of January 6, 1915, giving Indian communities the right to petition for either the restoration or the granting of *ejido* lands. Article 27 of the 1917 Constitution declared that the state could seize land to create communal holdings and restricted the amount of land an individual could own. Carranza also reduced foreign land ownership in Mexico.

After Zapata was assassinated and Villa was confined to Chihuahua, Carranza's successor, Álvaro Obregón (1920–1924), put the brakes on land reform. Large landowners were given more legal protection and estates seized during the revolution were handed back. *Ejido* holdings were limited to 7.2 irrigated acres (2.9 ha), whereas privately owned ranchos could be 360 irrigated acres (145 ha).

The Cárdenas program

The biggest changes in land ownership in Mexican history took place during the presidency of Lazaro Cárdenas (1934–1940). He understood the need to modernize agriculture while promoting a fairer distribution of the land. He advocated collective *ejidos*, with land expropriated from big landed estates to be run by elected committees that would share land, labor, credit, and technical resources. Land reform proceeded more quickly than even Cárdenas could have expected. Many unemployed peasants, victims of the economic depressions of the 1930s, organized themselves with the help of the Confederación de Trabajadores de Mexico (CTM; Mexican Labor Federation) to seize land. In May 1936 thousands of agricultural workers in the cotton-growing Laguna region near the Coahuila-Durango border demanded ownership of the land they worked; they threatened to strike if their demands were not met. In just six weeks Cárdenas took 75 percent of Laguna's irrigated land from the foreign companies that owned it and gave the land to 30,000 peasants in 226 *ejidos*. Similar actions followed in the Yucatán, Michoacán, Sonora, Sinaloa, and Chiapas.

By the end of 1940 the Cárdenas administration had overseen the redistribution of over 50 million acres (20 million ha) to 800,000 agricultural workers. In four years, twice as much land had been redistributed as in the period from 1917 to 1934. Almost half of Mexico's cultivable land was held by

20,000 *ejidos*. The Banco de Crédito Ejidal was set up to provide finance for the cooperatives so they could compete on a more equal footing with bigger private farms. Of course, these large expropriations were not popular with the estate owners, so Cárdenas encouraged *ejido* workers to organize militias for self-defense. From 1940, when Manuel Camacho replaced Cárdenas as president, the finance so vital to the success of the *ejidos* was virtually cut off, marking the beginning of the end of the *ejido* system.

The end of land reform

As a result of massive growth in population in the 1950s and 1960s, successive governments strove to modernize agriculture. Modern, highly capital-intensive wheat and cotton developed in northwestern Mexico. Large, privately owned farms were able to invest in the new machinery and fertilizers that increased productivity and profits. Between 1950 and 1960, for example, there was a 22 percent growth in irrigated land, but the figure for the northwestern states of Sonora, Sinaloa, and Baja California was 63 percent. In the 1970s and 1980s land reform wound down as many more private landowners were given exemption from expropriation. The World Bank made new loans to Mexico conditional on privatization of state-owned agricultural enterprises and the elimination of price subsidies, so by 1989 farmers received a guaranteed price for only two crops, corn and beans. As a result many small landowners were not able to compete with cheap foreign imports.

Land reform officially ended when President Carlos Salinas de Gortari (1988–1994) made fundamental changes to Article 27 of the 1917 Constitution, ending the right of peasants to petition for land redistribution and allowing the sale of *ejido* land to private owners. In some areas, peasants resisted the government's attempts to demarcate each one of the 2.5 million *ejido* plots. The changes to Article 27 helped spark the 1994 Zapatista revolt in Chiapas, where rural communities feared that they would lose their land, especially as there were many outstanding land claims.

Tim Harris

SEE ALSO:

Agriculture; Constitutions, Mexican; Creel Family; Díaz, Porfirio; Ejido System; Mexican Revolution; Ranching; Reforma, La; Zapata, Emiliano; Zapatistas.

Language

Mexico is the largest Spanish-speaking country in the world, and is also home to over 60 prehispanic languages. In the United States, Spanish speakers constitute the country's fastest growing minority.

The mother tongue of 92.5 percent of the Mexican population is Castilian Spanish: the Spanish dialect spoken in the province of Castile in central Spain. There are a few differences in vocabulary and pronunciation between the Spanish spoken in the Americas and in Europe—notably the American "s" sound where Castilian has "th"—but in general the languages are remarkably similar.

Before the Spanish arrived in Mexico, there were many indigenous languages spoken in the region. A recent survey suggested that 6.4 million Mexicans spoke an indigenous language. However, survey data on indigenous languages and their classification is notoriously complex and unreliable, so this figure can only be taken as a guide. The majority of those who speak indigenous languages today are bilingual or multilingual: in addition to their own mother tongue, they speak Spanish and sometimes other indigenous languages as well.

Indigenous languages in Mexico

Most speakers of indigenous languages live in rural areas, with more than 93 percent of them resident in the central and southern parts of Mexico. There are particularly high concentrations of indigenous language speakers in Oaxaca, Chiapas, Veracruz, Yucatán, and Puebla. Other states, such as Colima, Zacatecas, and Aguascalientes, have very few speakers of indigenous languages.

The most widely spoken indigenous language is Nahuatl, part of a group of languages that were spoken as far north as Oregon and as far south as Nicaragua at the time of the Spanish conquest of Mexico. At the end of the twentieth century there were over 1.6 million people who spoke Nahuatl in Mexico, mainly in the south-central part of the country around Mexico City. Nahuatl was the language spoken by the Aztecs. It was used as a lingua franca (common language) by many other peoples. *Nahuatlato*, meaning "one who speaks Nahuatl,"

As these roadside signs in Tijuana suggest, English and Spanish coexist throughout the border region.

came to mean "interpreter" even after Nahuatl ceased to be used as an intermediary language. Many Mexican place-names are Nahuatl words even though the places are in other linguistic areas because the Spanish dealt mainly with Nahuatl speakers who told them the Nahuatl versions of place-names. Words that have reached English from Nahuatl (via Spanish) include *(xi)tomatl* (tomato) and *xocolatl* (chocolate).

Other major language families in Mexico are Mayan languages, with around 1.5 million speakers (Mayan languages are also spoken throughout Guatemala); Otopamean languages, with 600,000 speakers; Zapotec languages, with 530,000 speakers; and Mixtec languages, with 360,000 speakers. These figures show indigenous language speakers, regardless of where they live, and not the total number of people in each ethnic group.

Spanish in Mexico

The Spanish arrived in Mexico with the conquistadores in 1519. Indians were taught Spanish by the missionaries who converted them to Christianity. The local languages were marginalized but not entirely suppressed. Nahuatl absorbed many words from Spanish as a result of colonial contact. At first mainly Spanish nouns were borrowed; in around 1650 Spanish verbs, particles, and expressions found their way into Nahuatl. Other indigenous languages, such as Yucatec Maya and Mixtec, were similarly affected by Spanish but at a slower rate. The evidence for this lies in the many documents dating from the colonial period that were written in indigenous languages but using the Latin alphabet. Spanish missionaries taught indigenous elites the Latin alphabet writing system, which they quickly adapted to write in their own languages. Mexican Spanish borrowed words and sounds from indigenous languages, mainly Nahuatl, especially words for plants, animals, and local artifacts. Despite the efforts of the missionaries, as late as the start of the Mexican Revolution in 1910 up to 38 percent of the population still did not speak Spanish. The first revolutionary government promoted Spanish as part of the attempt to unify the country.

Spanish in the United States

The Spanish arrived in the United States in 1513, when Juan Ponce de León claimed the peninsula of Florida for Spain. The first permanent European settlement, St. Augustine, was founded in Florida in 1565, 40 years before the English colonists arrived in Jamestown. By 1820 the Spanish had established colonies and missionaries in Florida, New Mexico, Texas, and California. After the Mexican-American War (1846–1848), Mexico ceded almost half its territory to the United States under the Treaty of Guadalupe Hidalgo. The treaty promised that Spanish speakers in the new U.S. territory would be protected in the free enjoyment of their liberty and property, and secure in the free exercise of their

Spanglish

Many Hispanic Americans switch back and forth between English and Spanish in the same conversation, a technique called code-switching, signaling that they live in two cultures. The mixing of the two languages has been called Spanglish. In the United States Spanish is at least partially excluded from the public domain, and many Hispanics use Spanish more to speak than to write. As a result, Spanish is more informal, fluid, and subject to change and experimentation.

Spanglish is created using several different methods: bilingual speakers might adopt words directly from English, for example, *OK*, *baby*, *rock*, *sexy*. Sometimes they will borrow a shorter English word for speed and efficiency, for example, *el parquin* instead of *estacionamiento* (parking). Some English verbs are given Spanish forms, *shootiar* (to shoot), *frikiar* (to freak out), *cuquear* (to cook). Some words are simply cognates, or literal translations, from Spanish, for example, *educación* (instead of *pedagogía*) for "education," or *computadora* (instead of *ordenador*) for "computer."

Spanglish has been used since the 1960s by Chicano writers such as Luis Valdez but has recently become fashionable among many young people in the Southwest. Several radio stations broadcast in Spanglish, writers use it, Hispanic rappers combine it with Ebonics (Black American speech), and Latina women's magazines feature Spanglish headlines.

The hybrid language has also stirred controversy. Although it requires a high level of understanding of both languages to use Spanglish successfully, educators are worried about its implications for both Spanish and English. Spanglish has even fueled xenophobia in border regions, where some see it as part of a wider movement by Mexican Americans to attempt to reclaim territories in the Southwest ceded to the United States in 1848.

At a conference on Spanish in the 1990s the Mexican author Carlos Fuentes declared the new hybrid language as "a fascinating border phenomenon. Sometimes dangerous, always creative, as necessary or fatal as the old encounters between Spanish and Nahuatl." Many believe that Spanglish is merely the latest example of the long exchange between English and Spanish, and that it uniquely expresses the cultural experience of life in the border regions of the United States.

religion without restriction. Protection of their language rights was implied but was not always upheld. The English language in the Southwest absorbed a certain amount of Spanish during the eighteenth century, when Anglo settlers relied on Spanish-speaking communities to teach them farming and ranching methods and to familiarize them with local plants and animals. Spanish words adopted into English include charro, bronco, adobe, chaparral, and burro.

The original Spanish-speaking communities in the United States have been reinvigorated over the years by steady immigration from Mexico and other Latin American countries. The 2000 U.S. census confirmed that there were 35 million Hispanics in the United States. Owing to their high birth rate and immigration, Hispanics have overtaken African Americans as the country's largest minority. Most Spanish-speaking immigrants come from Mexico, Puerto Rico, and Cuba. Since 1980 the number of Hispanics has grown at a rate five times faster than the rest of the population.

Hispanic cultural identity

There is an ongoing debate on how to describe the Spanish-speaking communities in the United States. The U.S. census describes all Spanish-speaking communities as Hispanic, but this does not reflect their widely differing origins and experiences. A Texan with Mexican roots may call himself Tejano, or refer to himself as being part of La Raza (the race). Mexican Americans often use the name Latino to describe non-Mexican Spanish speakers. The name Chicano, which was originally used to describe Mexican Americans in a derogatory sense, was reclaimed during the civil rights movement of the 1960s as a term of pride. To Hispanic groups of various origins the ability to speak Spanish is the most important aspect of their cultural identity. Those who have lost their language are sometimes called *vendidos* (sell-outs) or *Tío Tacos* (Latino Uncle Toms) by Spanish speakers.

Immigrants to the United States usually follow a three-generation pattern in regard to language. The first generation is largely monolingual. The second generation is bilingual in the parental language and English, and the third generation speaks English and perhaps just a few words of the grandparents' language. Hispanic communities are unusual in that they have largely maintained the use of their minority language. Bilingualism and codeswitching are very common (see box on page 458). The variety of Spanish spoken in different parts of the United States is determined by the origin of the majority of immigrants: for example, in Miami, Cubans; in New York, Puerto Ricans.

Use of Spanish in education

Schools have been a major battleground in the promotion and suppression of Spanish in the United States. In 1855 California mandated English-only teaching in schools, but as late as the 1870s its legislature operated mainly in Spanish, with laws later translated into English. In Texas in 1919 it was made a criminal offense to teach in any language other than English. In some areas, punishment for speaking Spanish at school persisted well into the 1960s. During the first half of the twentieth century Spanish speakers often suffered de facto segregation by being placed in separate schools, which were usually inferior.

In response to the civil rights movement, many schools began to introduce bilingual education programs in the 1960s. In 1968 the Bilingual Education Act was passed by Congress, providing for first-language instruction to those students whose English was not good enough to understand the content of classes. The bilingual education system was introduced so that students would not be held back in their studies in math, history, and other subjects by their lack of knowledge of English.

In recent years there has been a backlash against such programs. In California, an initiative to end bilingual education programs was passed in 1998, known as Proposition 227. In fact, even before the proposition was passed, first-language instruction in California had been severely cut back. Other states have followed in scrapping bilingual education programs, regardless of their success rate.

Bilingual education continues to be a hotly debated topic. Critics say bilingual education has enabled many Spanish speakers to simply survive in their own communities without learning English. Supporters cite higher success rates in English acquisition and the better educational achievement of students in bilingual programs.

Joanna Griffin

SEE ALSO:

Bilingual Education; Chicano Writers; Civil Rights in the U.S.; Education; Immigration; Literacy; Literature; Media, Spanish Language; Television and Radio.

La Paz Agreement

In 1983 the presidents of the United States and Mexico, Ronald Reagan and Miguel de la Madrid, signed an agreement on the Cooperation for the Protection and Improvement of the Environment, known as the La Paz Agreement. The agreement, signed in La Paz, Baja California, was aimed at improving bilateral efforts to address environmental concerns in the border area.

This abandoned maquiladora in Tijuana has a wall around it to prevent people walking in the sulfuric acid that contaminates the old factory. The La Paz Agreement was set up to stop similarly hazardous waste materials from polluting the environment.

The foundation of the La Paz Agreement was the 1972 Declaration of the United Nations Conference on the Environment, which urged nations to collaborate to resolve environmental problems of common concern. Under the auspices of La Paz, the United States and Mexico have coordinated initiatives to improve the environment along their 2,000-mile (3,200-km) shared border, involving nongovernmental organizations, national agencies, academics, and others.

The Mexico-U.S. border area underwent unprecedented economic development in the second half of the twentieth century. Many U.S. companies established assembly plants south of the border, known as maquiladoras. The number of maquiladoras grew from a handful in the 1960s to hundreds by the 1980s. Rapid industrialization and population growth caused serious pollution of water, air, and soil in the border area. Maquiladoras were a particular problem because they pumped heavy metals, acids, solvents, and other hazardous wastes into communities without providing an adequate infrastructure to deal with them.

Implementation

The Border XXI Program is the binational framework for the implementation of the La Paz Agreement. The U.S. Environmental Protection Agency and Mexican Ministry of the Environment, Natural Resources, and Fisheries (SEMARNAP) are the main agencies in charge of the program. Border XXI operates through nine binational workgroups that address the following issues: water, air, natural resources, pollution prevention, hazardous and solid waste, cooperative enforcement, environmental information resources, and contingency planning. The workgroups develop future plans and exchange scientific information.

One major transborder environmental issue is the shipment and disposal of hazardous wastes. Annex III of the La Paz Agreement seeks to ensure that the transboundary shipments of hazardous wastes and substances between the United States and Mexico are conducted in such a manner as to reduce or prevent risks to public health, property, and environmental quality. Often, wastes dumped in Mexico return to the United States through the air or water. U.S. waste dumping in Mexico has been linked to abnormal cancer rates and high rates of child and infant mortality. Through La Paz the Consultative Mechanism was set up in 1999 to coordinate the exchange of information between Mexico and the United States on hazardous and radioactive waste sites within 62 miles (100 km) of the border. La Paz also paved the way for action in other areas. For example, air-monitoring networks have been established in Tijuana, Mexicali, and Ciudad Juárez.

Joanna Griffin

SEE ALSO:

Border Environmental Cooperation Commission; Border Industrialization Program; Border Studies; Border XXI Program; Environmental Issues.

Laredo/Nuevo Laredo

The Texas city of Laredo faces its Mexican sister, Nuevo Laredo, across the Rio Grande. Los dos Laredos (the two Laredos) are located in a flat area of dry mesquite scrub in the Rio Grande Valley. With July temperatures typically exceeding 100°F (37°C), Laredo is one of the hottest towns in Texas.

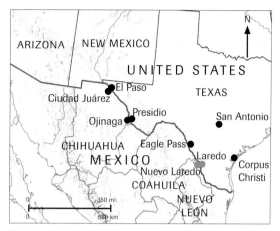

The twin cities of the two Laredos lie on either side of the Rio Grande River, which forms the border between Mexico and the United States.

Laredo's population of 160,000 is 90 percent Hispanic. Most people in Laredo, Texas, are bilingual, and Mexican Independence Day is celebrated as fervently there as on the Mexican side of the border. Laredo has a unique brand of Tex-Mex cuisine, including a tacos breakfast called mariachis and a goat-tripe sausage, *machito*. South of the river, Nuevo Laredo is well-known for the northern Tamaulipas speciality, fajitas.

Laredo's San Agustin Plaza is on the site of the original Spanish settlement of 1755. At one end of the plaza is the nineteenth-century church of the same name; a small stone building on the plaza served as the capitol building of the Republic of Rio Grande during its brief existence in 1840. This building now houses a museum of memorabilia from that time. Two road bridges and a railroad across the Rio Grande carry more tourists into Mexico than any other route. Nuevo Laredo's three leafy plazas are popular meeting places, surrounded by shops and restaurants. The Parque Arqueologico Morelos exhibits a selection of replicas of historical artwork from Mexico City's Museum of Anthropology. There is also a 9,000-seat stadium where bullfights are held on one Sunday each month.

Complex history

Originally founded as Villa de San Agustin de Laredo by Don Tomas Sanchez in 1755, the town became the center of the Spanish colonial province of Nuevo Santander, which included parts of what is now southern Texas and northern Mexico. During Mexico's Wars of Independence (1810–1821) most inhabitants remained loyal to the Spanish. Texas gained independence from the new republic of Mexico in 1836, but the people of Laredo decided that as neither Mexico nor Texas would protect them from marauding bandits or hostile Native Americans, they would establish their own state. In 1840 the Republic of the Rio Grande was founded. During its 10-month existence, the new republic's citizens elected a president and even designed their own flag. At the end of the Mexican-American War in 1848, the Treaty of Guadalupe Hidalgo declared the border between the two countries to be the Rio Grande. Inhabitants of Laredo who wanted to remain Mexican citizens moved south of the river and founded Nuevo Laredo in 1848.

Railroad links to Corpus Christi and Mexico City gave Laredo/Nuevo Laredo a new importance as a trading center, and in 1935 the Pan-American Highway created a link between the cities and the Panama Canal. The advent of maquiladora industries and NAFTA, implemented in 1994, added to the importance of the cities. Long-established economic activity in the area includes cotton farming, ranching, and oil production; tourism has grown in importance. Maquiladoras have given the Nuevo Laredo economy a big boost; in 1999 there were 53 enterprises, employing over 20,500 workers, a figure likely to grow.

Tim Harris

SEE ALSO:

Maquiladoras; Mexican Independence; NAFTA; Rio Grande/Río Bravo; Twin-Cities Phenomenon.

Las Vegas, Nevada

Las Vegas is situated in Nevada, one of the U.S. Southwest's largest states. A colorful center of entertainment, the city attracts millions of tourists each year from around the world who come to gamble, witness major boxing events, or even get married at one of a cluster of wedding chapels. The neon-lit main street, the Strip, is home to many of the world's most spectacular casinos and hotels.

Las Vegas's natural springs (Las Vegas means "the meadows" in Spanish) were first discovered in 1829 by an 18-year-old Mexican named Rafael Rivera. Rivera had been traveling on the Old Spanish Trail to Los Angeles with the Mexican trader Antonio Armijo when he ventured out alone into the Las Vegas Valley. For years following his discovery of the springs, Las Vegas was a minor stop-off point to ease the journey of those following the Spanish Trail. In 1844 the explorer John C. Frémont (1813–1890) set up camp at the springs. He is remembered in the city today; both a hotel and casino complex and a street have been named for him. Soon after, Mormon settlers from Salt Lake City built a fort that can still be visited.

Arrival of the railroad

The first established industries in Las Vegas included mining, cattle ranching, and the manufacture of leather goods. Hispanic settlers played an important part in the development of all three. Like many American towns, Las Vegas was transformed by the railroad. It grew in both size and importance when a railroad was built between Los Angeles and Salt Lake City in 1905. Further construction work helped raise the profile of Las Vegas to those in the surrounding areas, as employment was offered not only by the development of the railroad but also by the construction of the nearby Hoover Dam. The Hoover Dam on the Colorado River provided Las Vegas with inexpensive electricity and water. Lake Mead, an immense reservoir formed by the Hoover Dam, is a popular attraction for tourists all year round.

By the time the dam was completed in 1935, Las Vegas had forged its reputation as a gambling town. By the 1940s, the first hotel and casino complexes were established. Infamous organized crime figures such as Bugsy Siegel, owner of the Flamingo Hotel, became associated with the town. Subsequently, Las Vegas was associated with mob figures until the early 1980s, gaining a reputation for its glitzy musical acts along the way. Elvis Presley, Frank Sinatra, and Liberace all performed there.

Gambling and Mexicans

Although Las Vegas is known for its elaborate recreations of other cities, such as New York and Paris, it still has a strong Mexican American heritage. Many of the street names reveal the early Hispanic influence, and Mexican American cuisine, music, and festivals remain popular with locals and tourists alike. There is a growing Mexican area around North Eastern Avenue, and the Mexican population of Nevada increased significantly in the 1990s. The 2000 U.S. census figures show that 14.3 percent of the state population is Mexican in origin.

Las Vegas is a popular tourist destination for the large Mexican American population in the United States (21.7 million in 2000) as well as Mexicans from Mexico. According to the Las Vegas Convention and Visitors Authority, 225,000 Mexicans flew into Las Vegas from Mexico in 1999. Indeed, Mexican politicians and business leaders are eager to develop legalized gambling in Mexico itself to benefit from this market. Gambling has been banned in Mexico since the 1930s, when President Lázaro Cárdenas (1895–1970) introduced anti-gambling legislation. However, President Vicente Fox has favored opening legalized casinos in resorts such as Cancún, Acapulco, and Mazatlan. Mexico and Brazil are the only Latin American countries without resort casinos and the National Council of Business and Tourism in Mexico estimated that casinos in Mexican resorts could generate as much as U.S. $1.3 billion annually.

Christopher Wiegand

SEE ALSO:

Cárdenas, Lázaro; Fox, Vicente; Hispanic Americans; Mormons; Nevada; Railroads.

Legorreta, Ricardo

Ricardo Legorreta, an award-winning Mexican architect who works mainly in his own country and the United States, is famous for the integration of landscape, building, and color in his designs. These and other elements infuse each of his structures with a tropical, playful resonance that is at all times sensitive to the building's surroundings.

Ricardo Legorreta was born in Mexico City on May 7, 1931. He studied architecture at the Universidad Nacional Autonoma de Mexico (UNAM) from 1948 to 1952. From 1948 to 1955 he was a draftsman and project manager for the architect José Villagrán Garcia. In the late 1950s Legorreta formed a partnership with Villagrán Garcia that lasted until 1959. In that year Legorreta began his own practice, Legorreta Arquitectos, in Mexico City, and in 1985 he branched out into the United States with Legorreta Arquitectos U.S.A.

What first brought Legorreta to the attention of the international architectural community were his designs for the Camino Real Hotels, located in Mexico City (1968), Cancún (1975), and Ixtapa (1981). Like in all of his work, these hotels stress the Mexican architectural traditions of privacy, simplicity, and brilliant color. In the hotels' lobbies Legorreta incorporated water features. A common element of his designs is his use of courtyards, patios, pools, and fountains. Humor is another aspect of Legorreta's buildings, and in the Ixtapa hotel he designed large architectural features in the shape of watermelon slices.

Perhaps Legorreta's most famous building is the Renault factory (1985) in the Mexican state of Durango. There the landscape and the building are well integrated, and his signature use of thick textured walls, bright saturated colors, and mysterious, light-filled spaces—elements that have earned him an international following especially in the United States—are clearly evident. His first project outside Mexico was the Montalbán House in Hollywood, California, in 1985, for the Mexican actor and Hollywood film and television star Ricardo Montalbán.

Legorreta, Ricardo
Mexican architect

Born: *May 7, 1931*
            Mexico City

1959	Establishes Legorreta Arquitectos
1968	Designs Camino Real Hotel, Mexico City
1985	Designs his first work in the United States, the Montalbán House
2000	AIA Gold Medal recipient

Legorreta has earned numerous honors and awards throughout his career, including the Premio Nacional de las Artes, awarded by the president of Mexico, and the Gold Medal of the International Union of Architects. Legorreta has also been an honorary member of the American Institute of Architects (AIA) since 1979, and in 2000 he was awarded the AIA Gold Medal award, the highest honor the AIA confers on an architect. Past recipients include Frank Lloyd Wright and I. M. Pei.

In the United States Legoretta's most notable projects are the Children's Discovery Museum, San Jose, California (1989), with certain rooms and spaces designed only for children; Pershing Square, Los Angeles, California (1994); San Antonio Main Library, San Antonio, Texas (1995); and the Mexican Museum, San Francisco, California (completion scheduled for 2003).

In 2000, when asked about where he saw the future of architecture, Legorreta replied: "I think [what] we architects have to do now is to really devote our time and effort to do better cities, not only outstanding buildings. So the first thing is to react to the environments." Following the Mexican Museum in San Francisco, Legorreta planned to take on the challenge of designing large-scale, affordable public housing.

Héctor Manuel Lucero

SEE ALSO:
Architecture.

Lemon Grove Case

In 1930 the school board in Lemon Grove, California, built a separate school for Mexican American students to educate them apart from Anglo-American students. The Mexican American students and their parents went to court to challenge this attempt at segregation. The Lemon Grove case was the first successful legal challenge to the segregation of Mexican American children in U.S. public schools.

Lemon Grove is a small town near San Diego where most of the employers in the earliest twentieth century were citrus growers. In 1930 Mexican American students in the Lemon Grove Grammar School had become almost half of the total enrollment, and some Anglo-American parents started blaming them for overcrowding and unsanitary conditions. Following these complaints, one morning in January 1931, Mexican American children were suddenly barred from attending the school. As Anglo-American students watched, the Mexican American children—most of them native-born Californians and English speakers—were led to another building known as "La Caballeriza" (the barn). There they were to be taught separately from their Anglo-American classmates. The students went home in protest, and their parents refused to agree to send them to the separate school.

Background of segregation

Lemon Grove's move to segregate Mexican American students was typical policy in the Southwest at that time. Mexican Americans were considered inferior to Anglos, and although segregation was not mandated by law, educators and school administrators were allowed to separate children based on "special educational requirements." The need for Mexican schools was often ascribed to Hispanic students' poor knowledge of English or because they felt uncomfortable going to school with Anglo-American children.

The real reasons for segregation were often not the stated concern for the welfare of the children but racism and greed. In El Paso, Texas, in the 1920s,

for example, a researcher was told that Anglos wanted to "separate the Mexicans." An area superintendent said that "Education may spoil labor... Mexicans are regarded as a servant class." A 1930s survey found that 85 percent of school districts in the Southwest segregated Mexican children. Compared with schools for Anglo children in the same districts, Mexican schools were usually underfunded, with substandard buildings and high teacher turnover. In 1930 it was legal in California to segregate Native Americans, African Americans, and Asian Americans but not Hispanics. However, that year a bill was pending in the legislature to permit segregation of Hispanics.

The fight for integration

The Lemon Grove parents immediately opposed the segregation and organized to sue the school board to prevent their children from being forced to attend the separate school. They received assistance from the Mexican consul in San Diego, who found lawyers for them. Ultimately the Lemon Grove parents and students won their case, and the community school stayed open to all students.

Lemon Grove was not the first community where Mexican Americans fought attempts to segregate their children in public schools. Protests occurred in cities in Texas and California before World War I and in Kansas, California, and Arizona in the 1920s. Later, community leaders would challenge school district policies throughout the Southwest.

The case helped defeat the statewide bill to segregate Mexican American students. However, it did not set a precedent, and other school districts continued to place Mexican American students in separate schools. More important, the case provided key precedents for the historic 1954 U.S. Supreme Court ruling that finally ended school segregation nationwide. The Lemon Grove case was the first successful desegregation case in the country, 33 years before the landmark *Brown v. Board of Education* case in 1954.

Deborah Nathan

SEE ALSO:

Civil Rights in the U.S.; Education; Immigration, Mexican; Segregation and Integration.

Literacy

The ability to read and write was mainly a concern for people at the top of society in colonial Mexico (1521–1821). Since that time, however, efforts have been made to improve literacy rates in both Spanish and Indian languages. In the United States discrimination against Mexican Americans in the early twentieth century contributed to low average literacy rates. While the problem has not been completely resolved, community-based literacy programs demonstrate a way forward.

In preconquest Mexico writing systems developed as a way to record the dates, names, and genealogies of rulers. From the earliest times reading and writing were elite activities. For example, while schooling was compulsory in Aztec society, different social classes received different types of education. Children of lower-class parents received basic military or vocational training (for boys) and mothering skills (for girls). Meanwhile children of the upper classes attended the *calmécacs* (religious colleges), and learned picture writing alongside history, poetry, astronomy, and other disciplines.

After the Spanish conquest, which introduced a written alphabet to Mexico, literacy was taught primarily through the Catholic Church. However, reading and writing remained upper-class activities. In an effort to "hispanicize" the Indian population as quickly as possible, Spanish priests taught religious instruction and the Spanish language. It was only in schools for the children of Aztec nobles, however, such as the school of Santa Cruz de Tlatelolco, that reading and writing were taught, as well as Latin, philosophy, and logic. The Spanish thought that their European culture would diffuse through the elites down to ordinary people, and the

Mexican American children in a one-room school in Ojo Sarco, New Mexico, in 1943. In the early twentieth century Mexican Americans contended with educational segregation and discrimination, which had a negative impact on their literacy levels.

Literature

Mexican American literature flourished in the 1960s, drawing on a century of ethnic minority experience in the United States. Chicano and Chicana authors tackled issues of discrimination and inequality, conscious of their role as social activists in the wider protest movement of the time. Mexico and the borderlands of the Southwest, as well, have long been featured in the work of many U.S. writers.

The modern generation of Chicano and Chicana writers has celebrated the diversity of Mexican American culture, writing in Spanish, English, or a mixture of the two to echo the patterns of Mexican American speech. In the words of novelist Sandra Cisneros, "There's a lot of good writing in the mainstream press that has nothing to say. Chicano writers have a lot to say. The influence of our two languages is profound."

The Quinto Sol writers

The Chicano publishing house Quinto Sol, set up in Berkeley in 1967, spearheaded a renaissance of Chicano literature. The major Quinto Sol novelists include Rolando Hinojosa-Smith, Tomás Rivera, and Rudolfo Anaya. Anaya's *Bless Me, Ultima*, one of the best-known Chicano novels, tells the story of a Mexican American boy, Antonio Márez, growing up in 1940s New Mexico. Written in conventional English, the novel nevertheless has a distinctively Mexican atmosphere that has been described as elegiac and lyrical. Like many works of Mexican American authors, the novel makes frequent reference to Mexican folk tales and tradition. Antonio speaks of the legends of La Llorona (the weeping woman) and the Virgin of Guadalupe, stories told to children growing up in Mexican families both south and north of the Rio Grande.

Cultural dilemma

Many works of the 1950s charted the pull of mainstream U.S. culture on Mexican Americans coming of age in the era. *Bless Me, Ultima*, like a number of Chicano works, focuses on the impact of World War II as a harsh instrument of assimilation.

Antonio's older brothers, having fought in the U.S. forces, return with little interest in their Mexican heritage. To guard against Antonio becoming similarly distanced, his parents entrust him to Ultima, a *curandera* (healer), who teaches him the gifts that can come from honoring his culture without allowing it to trammel his individual spirit.

It is a hard lesson, however, and Antonio struggles with the burden of honoring his culture and family while suffering personal shame by standing out in everyday U.S. life. The experience of feeling shame is a pervasive theme in Mexican American work and draws on the distinctive meaning of pain in Mexican speech as a synonym for shame. Mexican American authors share many cultural reference points such as this with their Mexican counterparts. For example, the Mexican author Carlos Fuentes, in his novella "Pain," from his book *The Crystal Frontier*, follows Juan Zamora from his home in Mexico to university in New York. While there, the protagonist disguises his meager home life, ashamed of his poverty and reproaching his father for it, "I feel pain for my father's useless morality which no one remembers or values."

Antonio, in *Bless Me, Ultima*, experiences the pain of dishonor when he is singled out at school by his packed lunch of "green chili wrapped in tortillas." The laughter of the other children strikes Antonio deeply: "The pain and sadness seemed to spread to my soul, and I felt for the first time what the grownups call *la tristeza de la vida*. I wanted to run away, to hide.... but I knew that if I did I would shame my family name."

Literary heritage

The shared values of characters in Mexican and Mexican American novels links the two traditions. Mexican American and Mexican authors share a literary heritage that dates back to the Golden Age of Spanish literature in the sixteenth century and to the Nahua literature of the Aztecs.

In the late sixteenth century, Spanish conquistadores pushed north from Mexico into the present-day Southwest. Back in Spain, this was the era of epic works by the novelist Cervantes and the poet and dramatist Lope de Vega. In the Americas, the conquistadores celebrated each wave of colonization with chronicles, songs, and plays, planting the language and literary tradition of their culturally confident nation. The first major Spanish-American work of the Southwest was *Historia de la Nueva México* (1610), an epic poem in 34 cantos by Gaspar Pérez de Villagrá, a Spanish settler in New Mexico.

Mexican *corridos*

From the seventeenth to the nineteenth centuries the Southwest was a frontier environment, an unstable society in which formal education and literacy were luxuries. Oral and dramatic literary forms flourished, drawing on the strong traditions of songs and spoken poetry in Mexico and Spain. The Mexican *corrido* (ballad) is a uniquely vibrant tradition that has enriched the literature of both Mexican America and Mexico. Related to the Spanish epic ballad named the *romancero, corridos* were composed to mark important events and celebrate heroes. The *corrido* reemerged from its early history during the conquest as a means of chronicling the Mexican Revolution and conflict along the Texas-Mexico border at the beginning of the twentieth century. The songs were composed by those involved in events and also by detached observers. *Corridos* remain a living tradition on either side of the border and have been likened to African American blues by the Mexican American scholar Raymund A. Paredes. In recent decades *corridos* have been written to mark the assassination of John F Kennedy and to commemorate the death of the Mexican American union leader César Chávez in 1993.

The influence of oral tradition

The narrative form of the *corrido* can be seen clearly in the work of Mexican and Mexican American authors today. The *corrido* typically opens with a stanza in which the singer speaks directly to the audience. The device of speaking directly to a "listener" rather than a "reader" distinguishes much Mexican American work. For example, the Chicano author Rolando Hinojosa-Smith uses this technique. In *Becky and Her Friends,* a novel from his Klail City Death Trip series of the 1970s and 1980s, Hinojosa-Smith tells the story from the viewpoint of a number of friends and onlookers of a young Texas Mexican woman who leaves her husband. Like the *corrido* singer, the author maintains a discreet

Some Important U.S. Works about Mexico and the Borderlands

Bellow, Saul	*The Adventures of Augie March* (1953)
Burroughs, William	*Queer* (1984)
Cain, James M.	*Serenade* (1985)
Cather, Willa	*Death Comes for the Archbishop* (1927)
Flandreau, Charles Macomb	*Viva Mexico* (1908)
Ford, Richard	*Ultimate Good Luck* (1981)
Gelhorn, Martha	*The Lowest Trees Have Tops* (1967)
Grey, Zane	*Riders of the Purple Sage* (1912)
Kerouac, Jack	*Desolation Angels* (1965)
	On the Road (1957)
McCarthy, Cormac	*All the Pretty Horses* (1992)
	The Crossing (1994)
	Cities of the Plain (1998)
McMurtry, Larry	*Lonesome Dove* (1985)
Michener, James	*Mexico* (1992)
Nichols, John	*The Milagro Beanfield War* (1994)
Olson, Charles	*Mayan Letters* (1953)
Porter, Katherine Anne	*Ship of Fools* (1962)
	Collected Stories (1965)
Steinbeck, John	*Sea of Cortez* (1941)
Traven, B.	*Treasure of the Sierra Madre* (1935)

distance: "What are we to do with Becky? What should we think of such a woman?"

Homelands

Mexican American authors have employed folk themes and the forms of Mexico's oral tradition to place their work in the body of Latin American literature. However, their relationship with Mexico itself is more complex. Celebrated British Asian author Salman Rushdie has written that ethnic writers, or writers in exile from their home country, "are haunted by some sense of loss, some urge to reclaim, to look back" but, in so doing, "create fictions... imaginary homelands."

In much Mexican American writing, Mexico symbolizes home more powerfully than the Southwest. However, the arid Southwestern landscape is used as a living character with a powerful, distinctive ambience by authors of all ethnic backgrounds, including U.S. authors such as Barbara Kingsolver and Cormac McCarthy. Many Mexican American authors have used the politically powerful concept of Aztlán (the ancestral home of the Aztecs located somewhere in the Southwest) to identify more strongly with the area. However, Mexico remains the homeland.

For some Mexican American authors, the pull of Mexico is the pull of their culture, religion, language, and people. This "nostalgia of the blood" (Josephine Niggli; *Mexican Village*) and the theme of homecoming is ever present in various guises. The poet Gary Soto, for example, writes in "Black Hair" of the elation of a young Mexican American boy in the bleachers at a ball game. The dream of sporting triumph becomes entwined with a deeper longing:

> "In my mind I rounded the bases
> With him, my face flared, my hair
>   lifting
> Beautifully, because we were
>   coming home
> To the arms of brown people."

Arm in arm with a powerful but undefined longing for Mexico and Mexican culture comes panic at losing this connection. In *The Autobiography of a Brown Buffalo* Oscar Zeta Acosta charts the effects of this fear. He has forgotten virtually all his Spanish and knows few Mexican Americans intimately. To compensate for this loss of his racial identity, Acosta throws himself into the Chicano protest movement, railing against all aspects of U.S. culture in a vitriolic attack.

A Mexican American voice

By sharing the distinctive mix of Spanish and Mexican Indian culture that shaped Mexican literature, Mexican American writers have created a distinctive body of work. The experience of maintaining and celebrating their language, religion, and values in the clash with mainstream U.S. society has given Mexican American writing a unique sense of purpose and vitality. This sense is also found in the work of writers from other Latin American communities in the United States and in the work of African Americans. However, the ambience and form of Mexican American literature is nonetheless unique and strongly shaped by the Mexican love affair with the *corrido*.

American writers on Mexico

Mexico and the borderlands of the Southwestern United States have attracted many U.S. and other writers. For some Americans, such as Jack Kerouac and Hunter S. Thompson, Mexico is a playground of plentiful booze and cheap drugs. For the beat novelists, the country south of the border represented escape, anarchy, and freedom from the cultural norms of the United States.

The tradition of lawlessness is a strong literary one. The German-born U.S. writer B. Traven portrayed Mexico as a country for adventure in *Treasure of the Sierra Madre*. The fascination of American writers with traditions of the Wild West also manifests itself in a fascination with the borderlands and their history. The tradition begun by writers such as Zane Grey around the end of the nineteenth century was continued at the end of the twentieth century by novelists such as Larry McMurtry. Cormac McCarthy explored physical and emotional borders in his *Border Trilogy*, which was a bestseller in the 1990s. Meanwhile, writers such as Katherine Anne Porter and Martha Gellhorn have explored, respectively, the position of Indians and women in Mexican society and the effects of living in Mexico in a disparate community of expatriate Americans and Europeans.

Jane Scarsbrook

SEE ALSO:

Chicano Literature; Cisneros, Sandra; Corridos; Crane, Hart; Niggli, Josephine; Paz, Octavio; Porter, Katherine Anne; Romano, Octavio.

López Mateos, Adolfo

Adolfo López Mateos was president of Mexico between 1958 and 1964. Known for his abilities as a negotiator, diplomat, administrator, and orator, he defined a new international position for his nation.

Adolfo López Mateos was born on May 26, 1909, in Apatzingan de Zaragoza in the state of Mexico, the fourth child of Mariano López, a dentist, and Elena Mateos, a schoolteacher. His father died while he was still a young boy. In 1929 López Mateos took an active part in the presidential campaign of José Vasconcelos, who ran unsuccessfully as an independent candidate against Pascual Ortiz Rubio, the candidate of the governing party. López Mateos graduated from law school and was a lawyer for a time before becoming the personal secretary of the governor of the state of Mexico. He married Eva Samano in 1937 and held several public posts over the following years.

In the early 1940s López Mateos impressed Isidro Fabela, a powerful politician, with his fine oratory. Fabela became López Mateos's political mentor and was responsible for him becoming first an alternate federal senator, and then senator for the state of Mexico in 1946. In 1952 López Mateos was appointed minister of labor and social welfare in the government of his good friend Adolfo Ruiz Cortines. In this difficult period, which saw many strikes, López Mateos displayed his considerable skills as a negotiator by successfully settling hundreds of labor disputes.

His outstanding performance as minister led him to obtain the presidential nomination of the Partido Revolucionario Institucional (PRI; Institutional Revolutionary Party), and in 1958 he was elected president. During his administration he promoted a number of measures that brought considerable economic liberalism to Mexico. As a result of these measures, wages rose faster than prices, and exports increased at a faster rate than imports.

López Mateos had several notable achievements as president: he nationalized the electric industry in 1960 and asserted Mexico's control over its airspace. His many social measures included creating the Social Security Institute for State Employees and the building of over 50,000 units of low-income housing. In 1964 he oversaw the completion of the Museo Nacional de Antropologia (National Museum of Anthropology).

International relations

López Mateos distinguished himself in the international arena. A remarkable diplomat, he managed the difficult feat of maintaining good relations with the United States and Cuba at the same time. Stressing the principles of nonintervention and a nation's right to self-determination, his government maintained an embassy in Havana after the Cuban revolution, opposed Cuba's exclusion from the Organization of American States, and refused to impose economic sanctions or break off diplomatic relations with Cuba. He also managed to negotiate the return of the long-disputed territory of El Chamizal from the United States.

At the end of his presidential term in 1964, López Mateos was elected president of the organizing committee for the Olympic Games of 1968, which took place in Mexico City. He died shortly after the Games on September 22, 1969.

Héctor Manuel Lucero

SEE ALSO:

Cuba; Chamizal, El; Political Parties in Mexico; Ruiz Cortines, Adolfo.

López Mateos, Adolfo
Mexican president

Born:	*May 26, 1909*
	Apatzingan, state of Mexico
Died:	*September 22, 1969*
	Mexico City

1946	Becomes senator
1952	Appointed minister of labor and social welfare
1958	Elected president
1964	Appointed president of Mexican organizing Olympic committee

López Portillo, José

José López Portillo was president of Mexico from 1976 to 1982. His presidency was notable for its expansionist economic policy—increased government spending and industrial production funded by Mexico's growing oil exports.

José Ramón López Portillo y Pacheco was born in Mexico City on June 16, 1920. He received all his formal education in Mexico City, including a professional education at the Law and Social Sciences School of the Universidad Nacional Autónoma de México (UNAM; National Autonomous University of Mexico). In 1945 he joined the Partido de la Revolución Mexicana (PRM; Party of the Mexican Revolution). After receiving his law degree, he became a professor at his alma mater between 1947 and 1958, teaching general theory of the state and public administration.

After showing very little interest in politics in his youth, especially in comparison to his close friend Luis Echeverría (born 1922) who preceded him as president, at age 40 López Portillo began to work in the government. At first he held minor positions in the administration of Adolfo López Mateos (1958–1964). He then occupied several technical positions during the presidential terms of Gustavo Díaz Ordaz (1964–1970) and Luis Echeverría (1970–1976), including undersecretary to the president's office and director of the Federal Commission of Electricity (CFE). Halfway through the Echeverría administration he was made minister of finance, earning a reputation as a tough administrator.

Economic policy

In 1976 López Portillo was selected as the PRI presidential candidate by outgoing president Luis Echeverria and duly elected. Once in office, he was determined to strengthen the country's economy by increasing both government spending and industrial production. This program was to be paid for through industrial loans secured against anticipated oil revenues. Abundant oil fields in Chiapas, Tabasco, and Campeche had been discovered in the late 1970s. His social policy was intended to raise wages and reduce poverty.

López Portillo, José	
Mexican politician, author, and president	
Born:	*June 16, 1920*
	Mexico City

1945	Joins PRM (later the PRI)
1947	Becomes professor at UNAM
1976	Elected president of Mexico
1978	Reestablishes diplomatic relations with Spain
1981	Price of oil falls
1982	Nationalizes banking system

The fall of the price of oil in 1981 precipitated a major economic crisis at the end of López Portillo's term from which it took the country more than a decade to recover. Poor government administration, in part caused by nepotism and corruption, added to the crisis. In a desperate attempt to alleviate the damage, he reacted by nationalizing the banking system, giving the state control and ownership of all banking institutions in September 1982. Three months later his term finished. He was succeeded as president by Miguel de la Madrid Hurtado.

In foreign policy, López Portillo strengthened Mexico's relationship with the Cuban government and supported the Sandinista revolution in Nicaragua. In 1978 he had reestablished diplomatic relations with Spain, which had been interrupted for 38 years. In addition, he supported the guerrilla opposition movements in El Salvador and welcomed political asylum seekers from Chile, Argentina, Uruguay, and Guatemala to Mexico.

López Portillo is an established author of both nonfiction and fiction. His many published books include *El Valor del Estado* (The value of the state), *Quetzalcoatl*, and *Don Q*. He has also written a memoir, *Mis Tiempos* (My times).

Héctor Manuel Lucero

SEE ALSO:

Díaz Ordaz, Gustavo; Echeverría, Luis; López Mateos, Adolfo; Oil; Presidency, Mexican.

Los Angeles, California

Mexicans have long been associated with the city of Los Angeles. By the 1960s successive waves of immigration had made it home to the largest Mexican American community in the United States. In the 2000 U.S. census, 30 percent of the city's 3.7 million inhabitants were Mexican or Mexican American, while 84 percent of residents in East Los Angeles—the heart of the city's Hispanic community—were of Mexican origin.

The original site of Los Angeles was home to the Gabrielino Native Americans who cultivated the fertile lands on either side of the Los Angeles River. In 1769 a Spanish expedition led by Gaspar de Portola laid claim to the Gabrielino's land. Two years later the Spanish built the San Gabriel Mission near the Gabrielino's village of Yang Na. In 1781 the mission settlers gained permission from the Spanish government to establish a city, which they named El Pueblo de Nuestro Señora de Los Angeles (The city of our lady of the angels). In common with other settlements along Spanish Mexico's northern frontier, the majority of the settlers were *criollos* (Mexican-born Spaniards), mestizos (off-spring of Spaniards and Indians), and Indians.

From Mexican to U.S. control

By the time of Mexico's independence from Spain in 1821, Los Angeles's population included settlers from the United States and Europe, as well as its growing Mexican community. The city's inhabitants initially opposed independence, but, by the outbreak of the Mexican-American War (1846–1848), loyally fought against the U.S. forces. Nevertheless, the U.S. Army captured the city and its surrounding area in 1847. That year, one year before Mexico would formally grant it the territory, the United States declared its ownership of Los Angeles and California in the Treaty of Cahuenga.

Thousands of Mexicans in Los Angeles found themselves citizens of a new country. They were soon surrounded by large numbers of new settlers, drawn to the region by the California Gold Rush that began in 1848. Among the Mexicans who

Until 1847 Los Angeles was part of Mexico. The city has always had a large Mexican-origin population. Successive waves of Mexican immigrants have added to this community.

arrived during the gold rush were many from mining communities in Sonora. The city's Mexican inhabitants were initially helped with the transition to U.S. citizenship by regulations enforcing the protection of their property, the provision of bilingual education, and the translation of state laws into Spanish. In addition, newly formed Mexican barrios (Spanish-speaking neighborhoods) helped maintain Mexican culture in the city, as did the city's Mexican American newspaper, *El Clamor Publico* (The people's voice), founded in 1855.

Ethnic relations

The building of a transcontinental railroad to Los Angeles and the growth of industry in the city brought a new influx of non-Mexican settlers in the 1870s and 1880s. Surrounded by increasing numbers of white Americans, Mexicans experienced new levels of discrimination in the form of new taxes and an end to the policy of translating laws into Spanish. Mexicans were also forced out of their traditional areas of the city and into East Los Angeles, where city planners built new housing, water, and transportation connections in developments such as Boyle Heights and Lincoln Heights.

The skyscrapers of downtown Los Angeles were built on the city's original Mexican neighborhood. Chicano culture is ever present, however, in nearby barrios, as well as in markets and restaurants.

During the Mexican Revolution (1910–1920) thousands of Mexicans fled the violence in their homeland and settled in East Los Angeles. They were joined by large numbers from other ethnic groups, such as African Americans, Italians, Japanese, and Jews, who came to work in the city's factories and, in the case of the Jews in the 1930s, escape persecution in Eastern Europe. As a result Los Angeles, and East L.A. in particular, became one of the most vibrant, multicultural communities in the United States.

Anti-Mexican sentiment among white Americans in Los Angeles increased, however, during the Great Depression (1929–1939), when Mexican immigrants, as well as other ethnic groups, were blamed for taking jobs from American citizens. Many were deported from Los Angeles and transported across the border to Mexico. Hope for the city's Mexican community rose with the U.S. entry into World War II (1939–1945) in 1941, which brought recruitment opportunities in the defense industries and the military. However, discrimination continued against Mexicans. One example was the Sleepy Lagoon Case of 1942, in which 24 young Mexican Americans were tried for a variety of violent offenses and subjected to abuses of the law. Another was the city's Zoot Suit Riots, which took place over 10 days in June 1943. During the riots U.S. servicemen attacked Mexican American pachuco gangs, whose members wore baggy zoot suits.

Community resurgence

Los Angeles's Mexican Americans who had served their country in World War II felt a new level of confidence in the postwar period. This was demonstrated by the growth of community organizations in the city, from the Mexican American war veterans' G.I. Forum to the League of United Latin American Citizens (LULAC). The movement of other ethnic groups out of East L.A. and into West L.A. and the suburbs in the 1950s added to the strength of the Mexican community in East L.A. Proof of Mexican Americans' power in the city came with the election of the Mexican American Ed Roybal to the city council in the late 1950s, followed by his election to the U.S. Congress.

Mexican Americans in Los Angeles were in the vanguard of the 1960s Chicano movement, campaigning for greater civil rights and recognition for Mexicans and Chicanos in the United States. Chicano activism was evident in many different ways: in 1968 the largest ever demonstration of its kind occurred when more than 30,000 Mexican American high school students protested the state of their education, achieving a number of concessions from the local school board. The Chicano movement also encouraged the appearance of murals throughout the city, depicting scenes from Mexican and Chicano history as well as more recent events, such as in Judith Baca's *The Great Wall of Los Angeles*, which commemorates the Zoot Suit Riots.

In the closing decades of the twentieth century tensions emerged between the city's population of Mexican Americans and Mexican nationals, as well as between people of Mexican origin and African Americans. However, Los Angeles continues to foster the communities and traditions of a range of different groups, not least Chicanos, whose culture is evident throughout the city in the form of music, food, theater, art, and festivals, such as Mexican Independence Day and the Day of the Dead.

Christopher Wiegand

SEE ALSO:

African Americans; Barrios; California; Chicano Movement; Chicano Life; Festivals; Zoot Suit Riots.

Los Lobos

The Mexican American rock group Los Lobos was founded in East Los Angeles in the early 1970s. Three decades later it had achieved international fame for its original combination of traditional Mexican styles and driving rock and roll.

In 1973 David Hidalgo, Conrad Lozano, Louie Perez, and Cesar Rojas, friends from Garfield High School in East Los Angeles, met in the backyard of Cesar Rojas's parents' home to form a new music group. The young men had played in local rock-and-roll bands but had become increasingly interested in the Chicano movement for the social empowerment of Mexican Americans. Beginning in the 1960s, the movement had achieved a national presence. It was particularly strong in East Los Angeles, which by that time had the largest concentration of Mexicans outside of Mexico City. The young musicians' interest in the Chicano movement stimulated their enthusiasm for the traditional Mexican music to which older Mexican American generations listened.

Developing a distinctive sound

Hidalgo, Lozano, Perez, and Rojas decided to call themselves Los Lobos del Este de Los Angeles (the Wolves of East Los Angeles) and began to study various Mexican styles and instruments, including the accordion, the *bajo sexto* (a 12-string guitar), and the *guitarrón* (a bass guitar used by mariachi musicians. The band began to play at weddings, colleges, and restaurants, and over an eight-year period their repertoire grew to around 150 traditional songs. In 1978 Los Lobos recorded an album of traditional Mexican music, self-deprecatingly entitled *Just Another Band from East L.A.*

In the late 1970s the band grew tired of playing the same material night after night and began to incorporate electric instruments. The musicians' audiences continued to request traditional Mexican pieces, but in addition began to ask for cover versions of songs by artists such as the Beatles and Little Richard. The band responded, but the increasingly diverse nature of its sound made it difficult to continue playing at local restaurants.

In 1980 Los Lobos sent demo tapes to various established artists in the hope of performing in major venues beyond East L.A. In May that year the band's debut supporting performance was for the British punk band Public Image, Ltd., at the Olympic Auditorium in downtown Los Angeles. While the punk audience was generally unappreciative of Los Lobos's sound, the band greatly impressed one person in the crowd, Steve Berlin, a saxophonist with the L.A.-based group the Blasters. The following year Los Lobos supported the Blasters at a number of high-profile venues, such as the Whiskey-A-Go-Go, Club 88, and the Music Machine. Los Lobos's shows were so exciting that Dave Alvin, the Blasters' lead singer, claimed that at times he was afraid to follow it on stage. Through its performances Los Lobos developed a driving rock-and-roll style to accompany the traditional music it had perfected in the 1970s. One quality that music critics emphasized was the band's ability to reach out to Anglo-American audiences, as African American performers such as Sly and the Family Stone and Jimi Hendrix had done in the previous decade.

In 1982 Los Lobos signed a recording contract with Slash Records, an emerging label distributed by Warner Brothers. In addition to its members' musical talent and skill at performing, the band's growing popularity benefited from a reaction against punk and new wave, musical styles that some people felt had moved too far away from earlier influences. The reaction to punk and new wave came to be known as the roots-rock movement, which brought about a return to the guitar-driven sound of groups such as the Blasters and the Stray Cats. Los Lobos fitted in with this trend, combining traditional and contemporary styles and incorporating a variety of influences, from Tex-Mex music through rock and rhythm and blues to traditional Mexican rhythms.

Mexican influences

By 1983, the year of Los Lobos's first album on the Slash label, Steve Berlin had left the Blasters to join Los Lobos as a fifth member. Los Lobos's album entitled *And a Time to Dance* had a distinctive

Chicano sound. The first track, "Let's Say Goodnight," featured David Hidalgo's accordion playing, while "Anselma" was a traditional Tex-Mex polka song. The following year the group won a Grammy Award for the album in the newly created category "Best Mexican American Performance."

National and international success

The group's next two albums, *How Will the Wolf Survive?* (1984) and *By the Light of the Moon* (1987), continued its rise to national prominence. Both albums reached the U.S. Top 50 and received praise from critics. *How Will the Wolf Survive?* showed Los Lobos's ability to play in a range of styles, including western swing ("Our Last Night"), New Orleans rhythms ("The Breakdown"), 1950s-style rock-and-roll ("I Got Loaded"), and polkas ("Corrida #1"). It also featured the classic Mexican American ballad "Prenda del Alma" (Token of the soul). As a sign of the band's growing renown, the highly respected country-music singer Waylon Jennings covered the album's title track, "How Will the Wolf Survive?" By the time the group released *By the Light of the Moon* it had undertaken national and international tours, and its annual concerts at Los Angeles's Greek Theater had become one of the highlights of the city's musical calendar, attracting audiences of white Americans, Mexican Americans, and people from other ethnic groups.

In 1987 Los Lobos achieved international recognition for its cover version of "La Bamba." The band recorded the soundtrack to the film of the same name, about Ritchie Valens (1941–1959), the first Mexican American rock-and-roll star, who died in a plane crash alongside the musician Buddy Holly. The 1987 film was directed by Luis Valdez, the founder of the Chicano theater group El Teatro Campesino. While the movie was a box-office success, Los Lobos's soundtrack album did even better, selling more than 2 million copies. The band's version of "La Bamba" outsold Ritchie Valens's original recording and charted at number one in the United States and many other countries.

Change of direction in the 1990s

In the late 1980s and 1990s Los Lobos changed musical direction, reflecting both its maturity and its desire not to be typecast as the band that had a hit with "La Bamba." Consequently, the 1988 album *La Pistola y el Corazon* (The gun and the heart) featured acoustic songs. Critics acclaimed the next two albums, *The Neighborhood* (1990) and *Kiko* (1992), as more introspective and experimental than previous recordings. Both albums revealed the group's Mexican and Chicano influences in new ways. One track on *Kiko*, "Río de Tenampa" (Tenampa river), featured a Spanish and English chorus, while a song on *The Neighborhood*, "Be Still," drew on a Mexican rhythm known as a *huasteco* and used a large Mexican eight-stringed guitar called a *huapangueras*. The album's title track, "The Neighborhood," dealt with the problems faced by many people in barrios (Hispanic districts in U.S. cities): poverty, drug addiction, and the struggle to survive with dignity.

As the 1990s progressed Los Lobos worked on a diverse range of projects. It collaborated with a number of internationally acclaimed musicians, including Bob Dylan, Elvis Costello, and Paul Simon. In 1998 the group joined forces with other Hispanic musicians to release *The Super Seven*. This was followed in 2001 with another recording, *The Super Seven: Canto*. After its success with the soundtrack for *La Bamba*, demand grew for the band to contribute music to other films. Soundtracks featuring work by Los Lobos include *The Mambo Kings* (1992), *From Dusk Til Dawn* (1996), and *Miss Congeniality* (2000). The group also composed the score to the 1995 film *Desperado*, directed by the Mexican American Robert Rodriguez.

Community contribution

Los Lobos has retained strong links with East Los Angeles and has worked to develop the local Mexican American community. The group established a scholarship fund to help graduates from Los Angeles's high schools and adult education centers go to college. In 2001 Los Lobos received a Lifetime Achievement Award at the U.S. *Billboard* Latin Music Awards. In presenting the award, Leila Cobo, head of the *Billboard*'s Latin bureau, praised the band for "breaking ground in both Spanish- and English-language music [and] effortlessly crossing cultural and language divides." Reflecting its involvement in the Chicano movement, the group called its 2002 album *Good Morning Aztlán*. Aztlán is the name of the mythical Aztec homeland, believed to be in the present-day U.S. Southwest, as well as a symbol of Chicano empowerment.

Carlos F. Ortega

SEE ALSO:

Film in the U.S.; Los Angeles; Mariachis; Martinez, Narciso; Music; Teatro Campesino, El; Valens, Ritchie.

Lowriders

A lowrider is any vehicle—car, truck, or bike—that has been customized by its owner to ride lower on its wheels than factory models. The term also refers to the people who create, own, and drive the cars. On both sides of the U.S.-Mexico border and throughout the Southwest, lowriders and their cars—known as *carritos*, *carruchas*, or *ranflas*—are an important expression of Mexican-American identity.

Lowriders originated among Mexican-Americans in East Los Angeles, from where they spread throughout Hispanic American communities in the Southwest. The majority of owners of lowriders are still Hispanic Americans, but the popularity of the phenomenon is also growing among other racial groups, such as young African Americans, thanks to rap videos and movies.

The origins of lowriders probably lie in the importance of the horse as a status symbol in colonial Mexico. Owners spent their money on luxurious leather saddles, or silver bits and spurs. Today Chicanos have replaced the horse with its modern equivalent, the automobile. In the 1940s the pachucos, members of a Chicano youth movement, began lowering their cars. Such customization subverted a powerful symbol of U.S. values, the automobile. The careful handcrafting that went into the cars was a contrast to the mass production techniques of U.S. industry. The intentional slowing of a vehicle designed to travel quickly turned its back on the contemporary American emphasis on speed. Decoration also stressed the lowriders' position outside mainstream U.S. culture. The early cars were painted with Mexican symbols such as the Virgin of Guadalupe. The cars cruised each Sunday, in a parallel to the *paseo*, a ritual in Mexican plazas in which men and women promenade in opposite directions, establishing eye contact but not speaking.

Making a lowrider

Lowriders are lowered, usually with hydraulic lifts at each wheel, so that any corner of the car can be raised and lowered by hydraulic switches and pumps

Enthusiasts examine a lowrider at a car show in Kearny Park, Fresno, California. The negative image of lowriders overlooks the cultural pride reflected by their careful customization.

that create a hopping effect. The cars are given customized paint jobs and their interiors are luxuriously decorated. Metal-flake paint, murals, deep-pile upholstery, and tiny steering wheels made of chrome chains are typical features, as is a powerful stereo system. One particularly favored model for customizing was the 1964 Chevy Impala.

Culture

Lowriding has a negative image in the mainstream U.S. press because of its association with Hispanic youth gangs. The phenomenon also has many positive associations, however. The cars are seen by their fans as works of art. Some scholars see them as contemporary statements of an impulse toward the baroque that is deeply seated in Mexican and Mexican American culture. Lowriding also allows Hispanic youths to express pride in their skills: handcrafting techniques are learned through community apprenticeship and mechanical work in the military and auto shops. *Low Rider* magazine, first published in San Jose in 1976, became a forum for a general debate about Mexican American identity. Today, lowriding remains a focus for clubs formed for mutual assistance and social activities.

Joanna Griffin

SEE ALSO:
Chicano Art; Cholismo, El.

477

Madero, Francisco I.

Francisco Indalécio Madero (1873–1913) was a key figure behind the Mexican Revolution (1910–1920) and the first president of the post–revolutionary era. However, once he assumed the presidency, his policies alienated both supporters of the revolution and conservatives who were faithful to the old regime.

Francisco Madero was born on a hacienda in the northern state of Coahuila on October 30, 1873. Madero belonged to a family of wealthy landowners and businessmen. At age 12 he entered the Jesuit school of San José in Saltillo, where he obtained a profound sense of morality that would stay with him throughout his life. He later studied in both the United States and France.

Madero returned to Mexico in 1892, when he took charge of his family's hacienda in San Pedro de las Colonias. Soon after he returned, however, he developed an interest in politics. He wrote articles on the subject for a variety of publications and in 1905 he founded the Partido Democrático Independiente (PDI; Independent Democratic Party), a local political party based in Coahuila.

Díaz and the presidency

In 1908 President Porfirio Díaz (1830–1915), who had been in power for almost three decades, declared that he would retire from office in 1910 and that Mexico was ready for truly democratic elections. Díaz's declaration inspired Madero to write a book titled *La sucesión presidencial en 1910* (The presidential succession in 1910). In this book, Madero proposed that the democratic system envisioned in the Constitution of 1857 should be reinstated. He also called for the creation of a political party to participate in the presidential elections of 1910 and defended the Constitution of 1857 as a triumph of liberal ideas over conservative interests.

In 1909 Díaz changed his mind and decided to run for reelection. In response Madero founded the Centro Antireeleccionista de México (Mexican Antireelectionist Center), whose motto was "sufragio efectivo, no reelección" (effective suffrage,

Francisco I. Madero pictured in 1911, the year he assumed the Mexican presidency. His right arm is in a sling, the result of a wound suffered in a battle against the forces of President Díaz.

no reelection). The Partido Anti-Reeleccionista (Antireelectionist Party) was formed to stand against Díaz in the forthcoming elections, and Madero became its presidential candidate. Madero enjoyed much popular support, but on the eve of the election he was taken into custody under Díaz's orders and imprisoned under accusations of inciting a rebellion against the government. Madero won the popular vote, but Díaz manipulated the results and declared himself the winner.

On October 4, 1910, Madero escaped from prison and fled to the United States. Hiding in San Antonio, Texas, Madero issued the San Luis Potosí Plan. The plan called for an insurrection against the Díaz regime, to begin on November 20. The uprising gradually spread across the country under the leadership of military leaders such as Francisco "Pancho" Villa, Pascual Orozco, Jose de la Luz

Blanco, and Jose Garibaldi. Madero returned to Mexico in February 1911 to join in the rebellion. In May, Villa and Orozco captured the key city of Ciudad Juárez, and Díaz resigned.

This particular chapter of the Mexican Revolution came to a close on May 21, when the Treaty of Ciudad Juárez was signed. Under the terms of the treaty Díaz agreed to leave office before the end of May. Madero entered Mexico City in triumph on June 7, cheered on by a crowd of around 100,000 people. Francisco Leon de la Barra, Díaz's secretary of foreign affairs, was named interim president and given the task of supervising a legitimate election. In October Madero duly won the contest as the head of the newly formed Partido Constitucional Progresista (PCP; Progressive Constitutional Party).

Madero's presidency

Once president, Madero embarked on an ambitious political program that reflected his liberal views. During the course of his presidency he abolished the death penalty, freed political prisoners, passed laws that permitted workers to form unions, lifted restrictions on press freedom, and reduced the length of the working day.

From the very outset of his presidency, however, Madero faced fierce opposition from both the left and right. Conservative supporters of the old Díaz regime saw Madero as too radical, while some of the revolutionary leaders who had helped him gain

power believed that he was not radical enough. For example, the revolutionary Emiliano Zapata refused to disband his troops until the land distribution promised in the San Luis Potosí Plan was implemented. A series of armed rebellions broke out almost immediately after Madero gained the presidency. In November, Zapata took up arms against the new government, demanding that a far-reaching agrarian progam was carried out. The following month, the conservative Bernardo Reyes led another armed insurrection.

In the months that followed, other revolts began to surface under the command of local leaders. Emilio Vázquez Gómez, the brother of Madero's former running mate Francisco Vázquez Gómez, began a revolt in Ciudad Juárez, Chihuahua. In March 1912 Pascual Orozco, who had been commissioned by the government to fight against the rebels, turned against Madero. Madero's ability to deal with these rebellions was hampered by his own liberal ideals. Despite advice to the contrary, he refused to have any of the rebels executed because of his opposition to the death penalty.

Huerta's coup

Madero's clemency was to prove his undoing. On February 9, 1913, Felix Díaz escaped from prison. Díaz was the nephew of the former dictator and had recently led a rebellion against the government. Díaz conspired with the U.S. ambassador, Henry Lane Wilson, and Madero's general Victoriano Huerta to mount a coup against Madero. On February 18 soldiers entered the National Palace and ordered the president to resign. Madero agreed to do so on the condition that he and his family would be permitted to leave the country. However, on February 22, Madero and his vice president, Jose Maria Pino Suarez, were murdered while being transferred between prisons.

Despite the brevity of his reign, Francisco Madero is remembered as one of the most important figures in Mexico's history. Through his courage and commitment to democracy, Madero helped Mexico to escape from a long dictatorship. In the end, however, his administrative inexperience and lack of pragmatism prevented him from fulfilling his aims for the country.

Héctor Manuel Lucero

SEE ALSO:

Díaz, Porfirio; Huerta, Victoriano; Mexican Revolution; Villa, Francisco "Pancho"; Zapata, Emiliano.

Madero, Francisco I.
Mexican revolutionary and president

Born: October 30, 1873
Coahuila

Died: February 22, 1913
Mexico City

1910	Runs for president against Díaz, but is imprisoned by government shortly before the election. Escapes and flees to the United States.
1911	Returns to Mexico and takes part in rebellion against Díaz. Wins presidency in new election.
1913	Forced out of office by military coup and later murdered

Madrid, Miguel de la

Miguel de la Madrid became president of Mexico in 1982, in the middle of a deep economic crisis that continued during his term in office.

Miguel de la Madrid Hurtado was born in Colima, capital city of Colima state, on December 12, 1934. He was educated at private schools in Mexico City and then at the Universidad Nacional Autónoma de México (UNAM; National Autonomous University of Mexico). After graduating from law school in 1957 he worked at the Bank of Mexico and was involved in the Mexicanization of the mining industry, which was largely foreign-owned at the time. In 1964 the Bank of Mexico sponsored him to study for an M.A. in public administration at Harvard University.

Political career

De la Madrid joined the Partido Revolucionario Institucional (PRI; Institutional Revolutionary Party) in 1963 and in 1965 he was appointed vice director of credit in the ministry of finance and public credit. Throughout his political career he remained interested in the academic field, and from 1959 to 1968 he was a professor of constitutional law at UNAM.

Madrid Hurtado, Miguel de la
Mexican president

Born: *December 12, 1934*
Colima, Colima

1963	Joins PRI
1965	Receives M.A. from Harvard; appointed vice director of credit in the ministry of finance and public credit
1976	Appointed minister of planning and budget
1982	Elected president
1988	Ends presidential term

From 1970 to 1972, during the presidency of Luis Echeverría, de la Madrid was the vice director of finance of Petróleos Méxicanos (PEMEX), the state-owned oil company. In 1972 he was appointed general director of credit in the ministry of finance and public credit, a position that gave him valuable experience in public finance.

During the López Portillo administration (1976–1982) de la Madrid was minister of planning and budget. This important appointment enabled him to gain his party's nomination for the presidency in 1981, and on July 4, 1982, he won the presidential elections, taking office on December 1 of that year.

Presidency

De la Madrid took over the presidency in a very difficult economic situation that persisted throughout his term of office. The main causes of the crisis were rampant inflation, the drop in international oil prices (particularly harmful since the previous administration had based its entire economic model on oil production), and a large budget deficit. The situation provoked a flight of international capital from Mexico, which in turn deepened the crisis.

De la Madrid tried to alleviate the situation by implementing several programs to fight inflation. He began a program that forced a structural change in the economy by removing trade barriers and privatizing nationalized industries. At the same time, government spending, which had been very high in the two previous administrations, was reduced in an effort to decrease the budget deficit.

His relations with the United States were troubled by soaring undocumented immigration and an increase in drug trafficking, two issues that the U.S. president Ronald Reagan had made a focus of his administration (1981–1989).

Although his presidential term existed in a permanent state of economic hardship, de la Madrid's policies did manage to bring a certain level of stability to the country, which would lead to the economy's recuperation in later years.

Héctor Manuel Lucero

SEE ALSO:

Inflation; Partido Revolucionario Institucional; PEMEX; Political Parties in Mexico.

MALDEF

The Mexican American Legal Defense and Educational Fund (MALDEF) is the most important nonprofit Hispanic litigation, advocacy, and educational outreach group in the United States. MALDEF works to create public policy, laws, and programs to protect Hispanics' civil rights and to empower them to participate in society.

MALDEF focuses on six key issues: education, immigration, employment, language, access to public resources, and access to the political system. The organization is best known for filing lawsuits, although it also does a good deal of other work, including offering law school scholarships.

Pete Tijerina

MALDEF was the brainchild of Pete Tijerina, a San Antonio lawyer of Mexican American descent. After World War II, Tijerina became active in LULAC (the League of United Latin American Citizens). LULAC was founded by Mexican Americans early in the twentieth century to fight discrimination against their community. LULAC spent decades helping set up Mexican American organizations, mainly in the Southwest. By the 1960s, the group had concluded that Chicanos needed to mount a sustained legal attack against institutional racism. However, LULAC did not have the funds to launch such an attack.

In 1966 Tijerina was involved in a key court case that led him to mount a major challenge to end discrimination in Texas. That year he worked on a case in south Texas involving a Mexican American woman who had lost part of her leg in an accident. Tijerina wanted to sue the party responsible for the accident and get $50,000 in damages for the injured woman. When the time came to choose members for the jury, Tijerina found that not one person on the panel had a Spanish surname. Fearing that an all-Anglo jury would not sympathize with his client, he dropped the lawsuit and instead settled the case for less than $50,000. At this point Tijerina realized that if he was to successfully file a legal challenge to jury discrimination in Texas he needed the support of a powerful national organization.

In 1967 Tijerina and other influential Chicanos went to New York City to meet with the Ford Foundation and argue the need for a Mexican American civil rights organization. The Ford Foundation is an international, independent, nonprofit, nongovernmental group. One of the foundation's aims is to help reduce poverty and injustice. The foundation responded by granting the Mexican American Legal Defense and Educational Fund $2.2 million to be spent over five years. The Legal Defense Fund of the National Association for the Advancement of Colored People (NAACP) also promised support. In 1968 Tijerina became MALDEF's executive director.

MALDEF's first national office was in San Antonio, but the Ford Foundation felt that some of the staff were too militant and recommended that the headquarters be moved and Tijerina replaced. MALDEF complied and moved its headquarters to San Francisco. It also chose Mario Obledo as executive director and general counsel. The national office was later relocated to Los Angeles. MALDEF now has regional offices in Atlanta, Los Angeles, San Antonio, Chicago, and Washington, D.C., a satellite office in Sacramento, and program offices in other southwestern cities.

First successful lawsuit

MALDEF filed its first winning lawsuit before the U.S. Supreme Court in 1973, in a case called *White, et al. v. Regester, et al.* Before this case, political officials in many Texas county, city, and school governments were elected at-large. This meant that if a candidate from a Mexican American or black neighborhood ran for office, everyone in the city—including white people who often lived far away and were opposed to minorities holding office—got to vote on every candidate. As a result, it was almost impossible for a black or Hispanic candidate to win a political race. *White, et al v. Regester, et al* led to the creation of single-member districts, permitting voters in a certain part of town to vote for candidates from their area. The suit helped bring Texas in line with the 1965 Voting Rights Act. MALDEF also joined a project to challenge policies that kept Mexican Americans from voting. From

1974 to 1984, MALDEF filed a total of 88 lawsuits. These lawsuits led to increased voter registration among Mexican Americans.

Education laws

In 1982 MALDEF took a landmark education case to the U.S. Supreme Court, challenging a Texas public school district that had refused to let undocumented immigrant children attend classes unless they paid tuition. MALDEF won the court case when the Supreme Court ruled that all children living in the United States have the right to a free public education, regardless of their immigration status.

In 1987 MALDEF filed a lawsuit charging the state of Texas with discrimination against Mexican Americans living in south Texas because public colleges there were poorly funded. The jury found the state to be innocent, but noted that the legislature had failed to establish a first-class university and college system in south Texas. As a result of this MALDEF case the Texas legislature in 1993 created measures to improve University of Texas schools and Texas A&M branches in several south Texas cities—where the population is mostly Mexican American.

In yet another important education case, in 1989, MALDEF won a victory in *Edgewood Independent School District v. State of Texas*. In this suit, the Texas Supreme Court found that the state's way of funding public schools was unconstitutional because it was based on using property taxes from local communities to pay for schools in those same communities. The problem was that schools in well-off areas received a lot of money, while schools in poorer areas got much less. As a result of the MALDEF suit, the Texas high court ordered the legislature to change this arrangement.

Immigrants' rights

MALDEF also focuses on protecting the rights of immigrants. The organization contested California's Proposition 187, which aimed to deny education, education, health care, and social services to the state's undocumented immigrants. As a result of MALDEF's efforts, the state of California agreed not to challenge an earlier court ruling that Proposition 187 was unconstitutional. MALDEF also supported restoring food-stamp eligibility to legal immigrants, who had been cut off from welfare aid by Congress in 1996.

The right of Hispanics to speak Spanish is another issue on which MALDEF campaigns. In a successful legal case brought by the group, a city in Georgia was sued because it passed a law prohibiting the use of any language except English on public signs. The case was brought after a Hispanic minister had put up signs in Spanish outside his church, advertising religious services.

MALDEF also campaigns for worker rights. In one famous example the group brought a case against a restaurant in Beverly Hills, California, that had maintained an entirely non-Hispanic staff of servers, but an entirely Hispanic bussing staff. MALDEF represented plaintiffs who were fired from the restaurant after they signed a petition protesting the inequality. MALDEF challenged the restaurant's discriminatory practices and the firings.

Beside going to court on behalf of Hispanics, MALDEF runs educational programs, directs research, and advocates policy change. MALDEF's leadership and development program was established in 1980. By 1992 it had trained 1,300 people. Of these, more than half were later appointed to local, state, and national public-policy boards.

2000 U.S. census

When the federal government was preparing to undertake the national census in 2000, MALDEF noted that unusually high percentages of Latinos are not counted when interviewers go from door to door, or when applications are sent back in the mail. This happens because many poor Hispanics move often, never see an interviewer, or fail to get their forms in the mail. Many Hispanics fear talking to authorities because they may not have the correct documentation. MALDEF and other groups pointed out these facts and lobbied for the government to take them into account. As a result, the Census Bureau issued two sets of statistics for the 2000 census: the actual door-to-door and mail figures, and a statistical estimate that claims a more accurate count of Hispanics in the United States. A higher count ultimately leads to more representative voting districts, increased social services, and additional resources that help Hispanics participate fully as citizens in the United States.

Deborah Nathan

SEE ALSO:

Affirmative Action; California; Civil Rights in the U.S.; Hispanic Americans; Immigration, Mexican; Population; Proposition 187; Texas.

Malinche, La

La Malinche, or Doña Marina as she was also known, was an indigenous translator and guide for Hernán Cortés during his conquest of Mexico. Since her death in 1527, facts about her life have been mixed with myth to create a powerful symbol mirroring the country's deepest cultural and political passions.

In 1519 a 14-year-old indigenous girl was given as as a gift to the Spanish conquistador Hernán Cortés (1485–1547). Historians are unsure of her original name or where she came from. She was a gift from the Chontal Maya, who lived on Mexico's Tabasco coast. The girl was a slave of the Chontal, but it is not clear how she came into their hands. According to one account by the sixteenth-century Spanish historian Bernal Díaz del Castillo, she was born perhaps in 1505, the daughter of an Aztec ruler and a princess. When she was a child her father died, and her mother remarried and bore a son. As an unwanted stepchild, her family sold her into slavery to the Maya.

Linguistic skills

The girl was bilingual: Nahuatl (the language of the Aztecs and other peoples) was apparently her first language, and she learned the Mayan language, spoken by peoples living across the Yucatán, as a slave. She was presented to Cortés by the Maya as part of a group of 20 indigenous young women. Cortés gave one young woman to each of his captains, and La Malinche, who was later baptized Doña Marina, was given to Alonzo Hernando Puertocarrero. When Cortés learned she was bilingual, he realized she would be useful in his planned conquest of Mexico and took her for himself. He gave Puertocarrero another girl and later sent him to Spain to serve as Cortés's messenger to the Spanish crown.

Cortés had another bilingual assistant: a Spaniard named Jerónimo de Aguilar. He was a priest who had been shipwrecked in the Yucatán and had lived among the Maya, during which time he learned their language. At first the translation process was protracted. When Cortés wanted to communicate

The multilingual Doña Marina is shown translating between Spanish and Nahuatl in this sixteenth-century Tlaxcalan painting.

with indigenous people who spoke Nahuatl, he would first talk to Aguilar in Spanish. Aguilar would speak to Doña Marina in Mayan and she would translate the Mayan to Nahuatl. The process was reversed when Nahuatl speakers wanted to talk to Cortés. Doña Marina gradually learned Spanish and became Cortés's primary translator, guide, confidante, and mistress. She acquired several names, depending on who was talking about her. Nahuatl speakers called her "Malintzin," a direct Nahuatl translation of "Doña Marina," (-*tzin* being a title roughly equivalent to the Spanish *doña*). Spanish speakers, hearing her being called "Malintzin," mispronounced the name in Spanish as "La Malinche."

Career during the conquest

Doña Marina became one of Cortés's greatest assets. Although Cortés mentions her very rarely in the accounts of the conquest he sent back to Spain, she was often depicted in indigenous pictorial records standing next to him and translating for him. Two Spanish historians also wrote about her: López de Gómara and later Bernal Díaz del Castillo, who had been in Mexico during the conquest. Díaz del Castillo emphasizes her importance in the Spanish conquest of Mexico. She was key to convincing other indigenous peoples to unite with the Spaniards to destroy the Aztecs. She translated between Montezuma II and Cortés. She helped interrogate Cuauhtémoc, the last ruler of Mexico, while he was imprisoned and before he was executed by Cortés. She also learned about a plot by the Cholula Indians to ambush the Spaniards. According to Díaz del Castillo, she could have taken the opportunity to leave Cortés and join the Cholula. Instead, she told Cortés about the plot, which enabled him to massacre the Cholula and occupy Tenochtitlán.

In 1522 Doña Marina and Cortés had a son, whom they called Martín. However, they never married. Instead, Cortés arranged for Doña Marina to marry the conquistador Juan Jaramillo. Doña Marina had a daughter, Doña Maria, with her husband and died soon afterward in 1527. Cortés married a Spanish woman after Doña Marina's death and eventually took Martín to Spain, where he succeeded in having him legitimized. Martín became a knight and served the Spanish king.

Malinchismo

As "La Malinche" Doña Marina became a legend in the sixteenth century and was portrayed by both Spaniards and indigenous peoples as a powerful woman who deserved respect. These favorable depictions, however, changed as Mexico struggled for its independence from Spain in the nineteenth century. La Malinche began to be described as a traitor who had betrayed indigenous Mexico to the Spaniards and the conquest. Her interrogation of Cuauhtémoc before his execution and telling Cortés about the Cholula plot were given as examples of her treachery. Instead of being respectable, she was seen as sexually voracious, filled with lust for European men, and wanting her children to be fathered by a white man rather than an indigenous father. A new concept arose, that of *malinchismo*—the rejection and betrayal of one's indigenous roots and country and the worship of Europeans and all things foreign.

These increasingly negative images mirror the development of Mexican nationalism. La Malinche became a powerful symbol in Mexican culture, rivaling other mythological female figures from both Western and indigenous cultures, such as the Virgin of Guadalupe and the Aztec goddess Tonatzin. As a symbol La Malinche took on the characteristics of Old Testament Eve—a woman to blame for the destruction of paradise. La Malinche was seen as the betraying whore, responsible for European colonization.

In the early twentieth century, the symbol of La Malinche was partially rehabilitated by the legend—which was not true—that she had given birth to the first mestizo children in Mexico and thus was mother of the modern Mexican people. Once that legend was established another followed: that Cortés had separated La Malinche from her mestizo children by taking them to Spain; in fact, the children did not leave until after her death. To some, La Malinche became a tragic figure: a mother grieving for her lost children, who in turn represented all the victims of colonialism. In this tragic role, La Malinche came to be identified with La Llorona, the Weeping Woman of Mexican folklore—a dangerous ghost who cries at night for her dead children.

The twentieth century produced additional dramatic depictions of La Malinche. In 1926 Mexican artist José Clemente Orozco painted her and Cortés, both naked, resting their feet on a corpse as Cortés's arm lies possessively across La Malinche's body. This image inspired paintings, comic books, calendars, and murals showing a semi-naked Indian woman with a domineering man.

The most influential literary depiction of La Malinche occurs in Octavio Paz's *El Laberinto de la Soledad* (1950; *The Labyrinth of Solitude*, 1961). In this extended essay, Paz describes the Mexican national male character as violent, lonely, and woman-hating. He blames these problems on male shame, caused by La Malinche's treachery in letting herself be sexually used by Cortés, thereby giving birth to the Mexican nation.

In the United States, La Malinche has become a symbol of Chicano culture, lamenting children lost by assimilation into Anglo culture. Many Mexican Americans—particularly feminist artists and writers—have recognized La Malinche as a misogynist symbol and have tried to find positive qualities in her. Feminist imagery shows her as violated, abandoned, and vengeful, but also as strong, intelligent, and, above all, a survivor.

Deborah Nathan

SEE ALSO:

Chicana Feminism; Cuauhtémoc; Folklore; Maya; Orozco, José Clemente; Spanish Empire.

MANA

**MANA–A National Latina Organization
is a nonprofit advocacy group
that aims to empower Hispanic women in
the United States by developing leadership
skills and encouraging educational
achievement and community service. It is
the largest U.S. pan-Latina organization.**

MANA was founded in 1974 by Mexican American women as the Mexican American Women's National Association. In 1994 the organization was renamed MANA–A National Latina Organization, to reflect the fact that its membership had expanded to include a wide variety of Hispanic women, not just Mexican Americans. MANA was founded during a period of growing Chicano political and social awareness in the United States. Inspired by the wider Civil Rights struggle and the black power movement, Chicanos began to organize politically during the mid-1960s. Universities were a focal point of the campaign for Chicano rights, in which Chicana women played a very active part. Hispanic women came to the fore in promoting their communities in many different fields: for example, Dolores Huerta was a cofounder of the United Farm Workers union; journalists Betita Martínez and Enriqueta Longeaux Vasquez founded the bilingual newspaper of the Chicano movement, *El Grito del Norte,* in New Mexico; and Alicia Escalante, a welfare rights expert, organized the Chicano National Welfare Rights Organization.

Hispanic women

One of the main goals of Hispanic women's organizations such as MANA is to address disparities in education and the professional attainment of Latinas in the United States. Although they are the fastest-growing group in the United States, Hispanic women lag behind other women in the United States in several important areas. For example, they have lower rates of participation in the workforce than Anglo- or African American women. In 1993 3.7 million Hispanic women had jobs. The largest proportion (39 percent) worked in technical, sales, and administrative support posts. Hispanic women

are much more likely to be employed as operators, fabricators, laborers, and service workers than non-Hispanic women. They are more likely to work in low-wage jobs that require little training and are much less likely to be hired in management roles than non-Hispanic women.

According to the U.S. Bureau of the Census, Hispanic women employed full-time had average annual earnings of $16,244 in 1991. This was 78 percent of what similarly employed non-Hispanic women earned. Of the 6.2 million Hispanic women age 25 and over in the United States, 46 percent had not finished high school. Among Hispanic women 25 to 29 years old, only 60 percent had completed 12 or more years of school by 1990, while the numbers were 81 and 91 percent for African American and Anglo women respectively.

MANA's activities

MANA organizes educational programs and conferences, offers scholarships to Latina students, and publishes information of interest to women in the Hispanic community. MANA has chapters in communities and colleges throughout the United States. The organization is funded by membership dues, corporate donations, government grants, and foundations.

Among the programs run by MANA to benefit Latinas are AvanZamos, a leadership development program for Latina community leaders, and Hermanitas, a counseling and mentoring program for teenage Latinas. The program is designed to help them develop self-confidence, excel academically, and realize their full potential. A core part of the Hermanitas program is the National Hermanitas Summer Institute, which offers participants cultural and social activities and workshops to help them understand their life choices.

MANA also runs Project Esperanza, which publishes personal case histories relating to physical and emotional health, and organizes local events to recognize the achievements of Latinas.

Joanna Griffin

SEE ALSO:

Advocacy Organizations; Chicana Feminism; Chicano Movement; Huerta, Dolores.

Manifest Destiny

Belief in the divine right of the United States to expand its territory was known as Manifest Destiny. The phrase was first used in 1845, but the concept behind it existed throughout early U.S. history. The belief fueled the United States' westward expansion, with profound consequences for both Native Americans and Mexicans.

The phrase Manifest Destiny first appeared in the July 1845 edition of the *United States Magazine and Democratic Review*, in which its editor, John O'Sullivan, described "the fulfillment of our manifest destiny to overspread the continent allotted by Providence for the free development of our multiplying millions." O'Sullivan believed that, by expanding U.S. territory, U.S. settlers were carrying out God's will. Manifest Destiny represented nationalistic pride in the United States and the belief that it was God's chosen land. Moreover,

many white Americans believed that their ethnicity, the Protestant religion, and the republican system of government made them superior to every other people. Many U.S. expansionists believed they had a duty to establish their religious and political ideals throughout North America.

Declarations and expansion

Actions taken in the spirit of Manifest Destiny occurred long before the phrase came into being. In an address to the U.S. Congress in 1823, President James Monroe proposed what became known as the Monroe Doctrine, an attempt to weaken European influence in the Western Hemisphere in order to strengthen the position of the United States. In his speech Monroe warned that the United States would view "any attempt on [the Europeans'] part to extend their political system to any portion of this hemisphere as dangerous to our peace and safety."

The airborne figure in John Gast's 1872 painting American Progress *embodies the concept of Manifest Destiny. The telegraph wire in the figure's hands, the railroad, stagecoach, and other images in the painting represent the triumph of progress over the fleeing Native Americans.*

Manifest Destiny reflected the belief of many Anglo-Americans in the historical inevitability of their expansion throughout North America. The nineteenth-century expansion got underway with the Louisiana Purchase from the French in 1803, from where the United States extended its control into Florida. Exploration of the Far West began soon after with the expedition of Meriwether Lewis and William Clark to find the source of the Missouri River. Lewis and Clark's reports encouraged further western exploration, including expeditions by fur trappers and missionaries. These groups gradually established trails to the Far West, such as the 2,000-mile (3,200-km) Oregon Trail to the Pacific Northwest. In the 1840s more than 300,000 settlers traveled the trail, with one in ten dying during the journey.

Domination of other peoples

The negative side of Manifest Destiny was its justification for white Americans to overcome anything and anyone that got in their way, particularly Native Americans. In the 1820s the U.S. government began to develop a specific Indian Policy, making treaties with Native American tribes to exchange their territories for land in Indian Territory, in present-day Oklahoma. The 1830 Indian Removal Act authorized Congress to buy the desirable southeastern lands of the so-called Five Civilized Tribes: the Cherokee, the Chickasaw, the Choctaw, the Creek, and the Seminole. In return, Congress granted them land in Indian Territory. Many Native Americans refused to move and were forcefully evicted by the U.S. Army. Within 10 years of the act, around 100,000 Native Americans had moved west to Indian Territory. As many as 25,000 died on the journey, which became known to Native Americans as the Trail of Tears.

Manifest Destiny also encouraged the United States to seek expansion into Mexican territory. U.S. settlers began moving into Mexican-owned Texas in the 1820s. By the following decade white Americans outnumbered Mexicans in the region and rose up against Mexican control to establish the Republic of Texas in 1836. Many settlers wanted the United States to incorporate Texas into the Union. They achieved their aim in 1845, when the newly elected president, James K. Polk (1795–1849), declared Texas the 28th U.S. state. Mexico reacted angrily to the announcement, and skirmishes along the Mexico-Texas border between U.S. and Mexican troops sparked the Mexican-American War (1846–1848). The war was driven by the United States's desire to gain control of Mexico's northern provinces. This control would provide U.S. settlers with huge areas on which to establish farms and look for mineral wealth, and would eliminate foreign influence between U.S. territory and the Pacific Ocean. The end of the war came with the signing of the Treaty of Guadalupe Hidalgo in February 1848, in which Mexico surrendered Arizona, California, New Mexico, Nevada, Utah, and western Colorado to the United States in return for U.S. $15 million.

From territorial to political domination

In the late 1800s Manifest Destiny drove the United States' imperial ambitions of expansion beyond its immediate borders. In 1867 the U.S. government purchased Alaska from Russia for just over $7 million. Three decades later, as a consequence of the Spanish-American War (1898–1902), the United States took control of Guam, the Philippines, and Puerto Rico. The U.S. justification for its actions was summed up by the British poet Rudyard Kipling in his 1899 poem "White Man's Burden." The poem encouraged the United States to pursue imperial policies, explaining that it shared Europe's duty to bring Christian religion and society to the so-called inferior peoples of the world.

Belief in Manifest Destiny began to decline in the twentieth century as the United States turned away from territorial expansion and toward political and economic control in the Western Hemisphere. The nationalism that fueled Manifest Destiny asserted itself in different ways. For example, in 1904 U.S. president Theodore Roosevelt put forward the Roosevelt Corollary to the Monroe Doctrine, declaring that the United States had the sole right to intervene in the affairs of Latin American countries if it believed they were not abiding by international law. However, in contrast to nineteenth-century attitudes, belief in a God-given right to U.S. territorial expansion dwindled. In the twentieth century the United States became home to many peoples who were themselves victims of other countries' territorial expansion.

Joanna Griffin

SEE ALSO:

All-Mexico Movement; Filibusters; Foreign Policy, Mexican; Foreign Policy, U.S.; Indian Policy; Mexican-American War; Monroe Doctrine.

Manufacturing

Both the U.S. and Mexican economies are strongly dependent on manufacturing, and since 1987, a year after Mexico joined the international General Agreement for Trade and Tariffs (GATT), manufacturing output in Mexico has increased substantially. During the same period, however, manufacturing has declined in terms of its share of Mexico's total gross domestic product (GDP), whereas the trade and service sectors have grown. Manufacturing today stands at one-fourth of GDP and one-tenth of the total workforce.

Mexico's economy prior to the 1940s was largely agricultural. During World War II the government introduced programs that successfully developed the country's manufacturing and industrial sector, diversifying the economy. Since the 1980s—and especially since the mid-1990s when the special trading relationship began among the NAFTA countries of Mexico, Canada, and the United States—productivity and employment have risen in Mexico's manufacturing sector. These productivity gains have resulted in rising incomes and higher standards of living for many Mexicans.

Manufacturing in the United States

During the same period in the United States productivity in the manufacturing sector increased, but employment declined. In 2000 manufacturing in the United States accounted for about 25.2 percent of GDP (the service sector accounted for 73.2 percent and agriculture for only 1.6), and there were shipments, both domestic and exports, of around U.S. $3.9 trillion. The products of manufacturing range from foods, clothing, household goods, and motor vehicles purchased directly by consumers to metal, chemicals, lumber, concrete, computers, instruments, and heavy machinery used by other industries in their own production process.

Wages, number of employees, and contribution to total economic output vary widely among the different manufacturing firms in the United States. The profile of the U.S. manufacturing sector, according to the 1998 Organization for Economic Cooperation and Development (OECD) industrial data, is that the chemical industry led in total production and net profit, followed closely by food and transportation equipment. The machinery industry, albeit no longer the largest employer, had the largest payroll. Printing and publishing, where

A skilled factory worker in Mérida, Yucatán, assembling dental braces for both the domestic and export markets. Mexico's diverse manufacturing base has vastly expanded since the mid-twentieth century, when areas such as Yucatán were mostly agricultural.

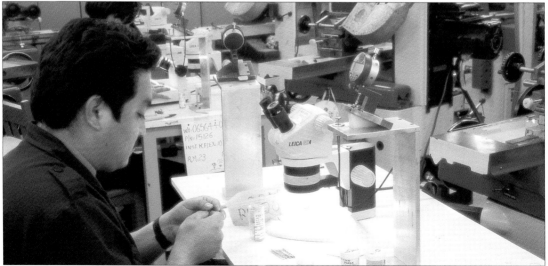

small companies still predominate, had the largest number of establishments and jobs.

Employment in U.S. manufacturing reached its recent peak in 1989 at 19.4 million workers, then dropped to 19.1 million in 1992–1993 due to a recession. Although the industry has improved over all, employment numbers have not returned to what they were in 1989. On the contrary, the U.S. Bureau of Labor Statistics expects a continuing decline in employment, and that by 2005 there will be just under 17 million people working in manufacturing, compared with 18 million in 1993. There are exceptions to the trend, however, and those industries where employment is set to rise include computers, food and beverages, furniture and fixtures, paper and allied products, printing and publishing, and rubber and plastics.

Manufacturing in Mexico

In contrast to the U.S. economy, Mexico's principal manufacturing industries are metal products, food and beverages, textiles, garments, and leather. Most manufacturing firms are located in or near Mexico City, followed by a high concentration of maquiladoras (foreign-owned assembly plants) in towns near the U.S. border.

Employment in the different industries varies greatly. Metal products, for example, had nearly 1.3 million employees in 1998, or almost 36 percent of the total manufacturing workforce. This industry is more broadly defined than its U.S. counterpart and includes fabricated metals, industrial and computer equipment, electronics, and transportation parts and vehicles. Food and beverages employed 663,000 workers in 1998 and remains Mexico's second largest employer. The third largest industry group in terms of employment is the textile, garment, and leather industry, which employs 583,000 workers, or 16.6 percent of the manufacturing total.

As in the United States, average earnings vary widely by industry; tobacco, chemicals, petroleum, and base metal industries are at the top of the scale and the textile, garment, leather, and wood product industries are at the bottom.

The 1994–1995 peso crisis plunged the Mexican economy into a recession, and employment in manufacturing dropped by more than 200,000, or about 7 percent, from 1993 to 1995. While the recession was sudden and severe, reducing wages and prices across the board, the ensuing recovery, including in manufacturing where strong gains were made in exports, was vigorous. In 1996 manufacturing output recovered to levels higher than before the recession, and employment in manufacturing also increased, experiencing 6.9 percent average annual growth between 1995 and 2000. However, the economic slowdown in the United States during 2001 hit Mexican manufacturing hard because of the economic integration of NAFTA, implemented in 1994: in 2001 the growth rate of the Mexican economy was zero.

One sector that seems to have been aided by the peso devaluation of the mid-1990s is the maquiladora industry. Maquiladoras have experienced a boom in productivity and exports following the implementation of NAFTA. The peso devaluation also made the price of Mexican products highly competitive abroad.

U.S.-Mexico trade

In U.S. terms, total U.S. exports of manufactured goods rose 61 percent between 1989 and 1996. During the same period, global imports to the United States rose 67 percent, increasing the U.S. trade deficit on manufactured goods. The U.S. manufacturing trade balance within NAFTA has varied widely from year to year, from a surplus of U.S. $14 billion in 1992 to a deficit of almost $13 billion in 1996. Mexico's trade balance within NAFTA has shown a dramatic change in the last few years, from deficits in excess of U.S. $5 billion in 1994 into a surplus of $11.5 billion in 1996. Trade between Mexico and the United States increased dramatically between 1989 and 2000, with especially large gains in 1995, 1996, and 2000. U.S. exports to Mexico have more than doubled since 1989, while Mexican exports to the United States more than tripled.

In the 1990s virtually all manufacturing industries in both Mexico and the United States invested heavily in modernizing their plants. The improvements ranged from updating antiquated facilities and equipment to purchasing new computers and software. The cost involved in such actions was necessary in order to boost productivity and remain competitive with other industries in both the domestic and international markets.

Miguel Jimenez

SEE ALSO:

Border Industrialization Program; Free Trade; Investment; Labor and Employment; Labor Organizations, U.S.; Maquiladoras; NAFTA; Trade.

officials, in part because it was anticipated that maquiladora plants, with their U.S. counterparts in the U.S. border region, would have a positive impact on the region's economic development through an increase in U.S. supply, warehousing, and distribution facilities.

From a more negative U.S. perspective, this is seen as a back door to the U.S. market that foreign manufacturers could use to bypass import laws and tariffs. Transnational companies from other countries with maquiladora operations are aware of the sensitivity of the issue and generally use their U.S. subsidiaries to establish maquiladora plants. This also gives them legal protection. So, for example, Sony-USA, Matsuhita-USA, and Nissan-USA are legally entitled to all the privileges that General Motors or Ford can claim before the customs law.

Recent developments

In the 1980s and 1990s several developments dramatically affected the maquiladora industry. One such development was the rapid growth of maquiladoras in the interior of Mexico. In the early 1980s the Mexican government revised the original laws governing the industry that restricted maquiladoras to operating within 15 miles (24 km) of the border. This step was taken to reduce overcrowding in the border region. Maquiladoras in the interior lessened the incentive for workers to travel north in search of employment. Reduced migration to the north had the benefit of alleviating the pressure on the already overused infrastructure on both sides of the border.

One city that benefited considerably from the new legislation was Guadalajara, in the west of Mexico, more than 400 miles (650 km) from the U.S. border. The city has since become a magnet for international maquiladora manufacturing because of its qualified workforce, modernizing infrastructure, and close proximity to manufacturing materials and customers.

A second important development was the rapid growth of maquiladoras owned by companies from Europe and Asia (especially Japan, Korea, and Taiwan) rather than the United States. This development has been welcomed by successive Mexican government, which have viewed ownership of maquiladoras by other countries as a means of diversifying Mexico's sources of foreign capital, thus reducing its overwhelming reliance on the United States.

With the successful use of the maquiladora program by U.S. companies, Mexico has gained international attention and has rapidly become a world-class manufacturing center. Previously Asia was the most competitive center of manufacturing, but goods made there take a long time to reach the U.S. market, while products made in Mexico are only hours away by road. For example, the new Samsung Electronics plant, set up in Ciudad Juárez, Chihuahua, in 1995, cuts transportation time to all areas of the U.S. market from four days by plane or eight days by ship from plants in the Philippines, Malaysia, and Taiwan to as little as two days. Increased interest in maquiladora production by foreign companies has stimulated a growth in local suppliers in Mexico's interior.

Effects of NAFTA

The third important development is the implementation of the North American Free Trade Agreement (NAFTA) in 1994. This agreement bound the economies of the United States and Mexico much closer together. There were some regulations that specifically affected maquiladoras. For example, the restriction that allowed only 50 percent of a maquiladora's products to be sold in Mexico was lifted. Preferential tariffs were given to goods manufactured with a specified percentage of components originating within the NAFTA area, but the duty-free advantages, which were the original impetus to the maquiladora program, disappeared as duties were phased out over a period of seven years.

However, despite the disappearance of one of the key aspects of the maquiladora program, maquiladoras continued to thrive because of the twin advantages of a cheap labor force and a close proximity to U.S. markets. These provide a strong incentive for transnationals from countries outside NAFTA to relocate their production to Mexico, which combines low wages with increasingly high productivity levels. The maquiladora industry has thus continued to expand since NAFTA. In addition, as the result of protests by pressure groups, side agreements to NAFTA have been made to address environmental problems caused by industrialization in the region.

Miguel Jimenez

SEE ALSO:

Border Industrialization Program; Border Studies; Bracero Program; PRONAF.

Mariachis

Since the 1930s the mariachi has been widely considered the quintessential Mexican musical ensemble. Today mariachi is also popular in many parts of the United States.

Mariachi has come to refer to an ensemble (musical group), individual musicians, or the music itself. There are many theories about the origins of the word *mariachi*. Despite claims that mariachi is derived from the French word *mariage,* dating from the French occupation of Mexico in the 1860s, it is more likely that the word originates from a native Indian language. Recent evidence suggests that the word may originate from the Coca Indians' language of the 1500s in central Jalisco state, where it referred to a folkloric musician.

When the Spanish invaded present-day Mexico in the sixteenth century they brought professional musicians with them from Europe. These musicians' instruments, including the harp and the *vihuela* (similar to a guitar, but with a convex back and five strings), were the prototypes of instruments later used by mariachis. The European traditions were soon mastered by the Indians, who had their own traditions. At the same time, African rhythms were being introduced to Mexico by black slaves, and a fusion of these indigenous and foreign musical traditions eventually evolved into what became known as mariachi music.

However, the modern mariachi ensemble has more recent roots. It dates from as late as the end of the nineteenth century, when a distinctive form of Spanish theatrical orchestra began playing a hybrid music form—a mixture of indigenous roots and Spanish guitars, *vihuelas,* and harps—from areas along the Pacific coast and elsewhere. For a long time this music was thought to have originated in the state of Jalisco, but it is more likely that it developed over a larger area in the west of Mexico, from Sinaloa in the north to Guerrero in the south.

At the end of the nineteenth century a mariachi ensemble was made up of four musicians. The most typical arrangement used two violins, a *vihuela,* and a *guitarrón* (a six-string bass version of the *vihuela*). By this time the harp was no longer being used.

Typically a mariachi ensemble consists of a guitarist, violinists, trumpeters, a vihuela player, and a guitarrón player. However, there are no set rules to a mariachi group: in this photograph the guitarist, dressed in traditional costume, is accompanied by an accordion player.

After 1910 mariachi ensembles added the modern classical guitar and, frequently, wind instruments. With the rise in popularity of jazz and Cuban music in the 1920s, first the cornet and then the trumpet were introduced. In the early 1950s the Mariachi Mexico de Pepe Villa group popularized the two-trumpet combination. The contemporary instrumentation is typically two trumpets, three or more violins, a *vihuela*, a guitar, and a *guitarrón*. Modern-day ensembles can be expected to perform regional *sones* (instrumental pieces), polkas, waltzes, boleros, and *rancheras* (ranch songs).

Twentieth-century developments

Documentation in the nineteenth century shows mariachi ensembles as a rural phenomenon of central Mexico. As early as 1905 the music was linked to official functions, with several bands performing at state occasions under Porfirio Díaz. During this period the musicians traveled in search of work and usually performed at haciendas. They wore peasant clothing of cotton shirts, wide-legged pants, and sandals.

It was not until after the Mexican Revolution (1910–1920) that mariachi music became associated with Mexican nationalism. After the revolution many haciendas were no longer able to pay mariachis, and the musicians were forced to play in public places for a small fee, as well as to expand their repertoire to include popular polkas and waltzes. They adopted the clothes of a *charro,* or cowboy, as a sort of uniform: tightly fitting, ornamented pants, short jackets, embroidered belts, high boots, and the wide-brimmed sombrero.

Despite its rural origins, it is the post-revolutionary mariachi of Mexico City that has remained the dominant model since the 1930s. In 1920 Cirilo Marmolejo's band became the first mariachi ensemble to establish itself permanently in Mexico City. By the mid-1920s Cantina Salon Tenampa, situated on what is now Plaza Garibaldi, became the center of mariachi performances in Mexico City.

The arrival of the radio, the movies, and the phonograph in the 1930s popularized mariachi music and propelled it to international prominence. During the golden age of Mexican cinema (1936–1957) mariachis appeared in hundreds of films. In the 1940s and 1950s recording contracts were signed and musicians were paired with singers such as Pedro Infante and Jorge Negrete.

Mariachi Vargas

The Mariachi Vargas de Tecalitlán is the most famous mariachi band of all time. Formed by Gaspar Vargas in 1898 in Jalisco, and later taken over by his son, Silvestre Vargas, the band has a long history of working with many of the most influential musicians of the mariachi genre. Silvestre himself is considered one of the greatest mariachi musicians, and collaborators have included Ruben Fuentes, who was hired to arrange the group's music, and the singers Lola Beltrán and Jose Alfredo Jiménez. In 1936, when President Lázaro Cárdenas was striving to unify different regions with a common cultural tradition, he invited Mariachi Vargas to accompany him on his presidential campaign. He was the first Mexican president to subsidize the music during his term of office (1934–1940). Mariachi Vargas moved to the United States in the late 1930s.

The United States

Mariachi has become firmly established in the United States, where it has taken on unique characteristics and even influenced its Mexican counterpart. Mariachi music first became well-known in the country when Mexican immigrants began moving to the United States at the start of the twentieth century. By the 1950s Los Angeles had become a mecca for fans of the genre. In 1961 Nati Cano formed the band Los Camperos, and in 1969 La Fonda restaurant was opened in Los Angeles to showcase its music.

The first famous Mexican American group was Mariachi Cobre, which was formed in Tucson, Arizona, in 1971. More recently, well-known popular musicians such as Linda Ronstadt have helped popularize the music, and bands such as Campanas de America, based in San Antonio, Texas, and Sol de Mexico, based in Los Angeles, have experimented with the genre. Most large cities in the Southwest border states have large mariachis, while small groups can often be found playing in Mexican restaurants throughout the United States. Today in Texas mariachi ensemble music is taught at universities, colleges, and public schools. Mariachi conferences and workshops are held regularly in San Antonio, Texas, and Tucson, Arizona.

Joanna Griffin

SEE ALSO:

Cárdenas, Lázaro; Dance; Festivals; Film in Mexico; Jalisco; Music; Ronstadt, Linda.

Marin, Rosario

As well as being the Treasurer of the United States, Rosario Marin is a strong advocate for the rights of the disabled and their families.

Mexican-born Rosario Marin was the 41st Treasurer of the United States. She was the first immigrant to hold the post and the highest placed Latina in the George W. Bush administration.

Rosario Marin was sworn in as Treasurer of the United States on August 16, 2001. Her responsibilities included overseeing the U.S. Mint and the Bureau of Engraving and Printing; she also served as the National Honorary Director of the Savings Bonds Program.

One of six children, Marin spoke no English until age 14 when her father, a janitor, brought his family to California from Mexico. After finishing high school she worked to help her family and went to college at night. Seven years later she graduated with a business degree from California State University in Los Angeles and went on to the John F. Kennedy School of Government Programs for Senior Executives in State and Local Government at Harvard University.

She then worked for two banks, where promotions came fast and frequently. After seven years she moved to AT&T as public relations manager for the Hispanic market in southern California. Then she married and gave birth to the first of her three children, Eric, who suffers from Down syndrome. The struggle of coping with his disability propelled Marin into politics, initially as a child advocate. As she wrote: "I don't know why my son was born with Down's syndrome. I don't know why we were given the challenge, but I welcome the opportunity to serve people like my son and I look forward to helping create policies and procedures that will enable them and their families to live 'ordinary' lives." When asked once what inspired her, Marin replied: "Eric: he is the wind beneath my wings."

In 1994 Marin was elected to the council of Huntington Park, California. She stood out as a Republican in a predominantly Democratic blue-collar community, and her political career took off. She served as assistant deputy director of the California State Department of Social Services and later became deputy director of the governor's office of community relations in Los Angeles, in Governor Pete Wilson's administration. In 1999 she was re-elected by the voters of Huntington Park.

Marin served as California's Chair of the State Council on Developmental Disabilities, and her commitment to the disabled has earned her many awards, including the distinguished Rose Fitzgerald Kennedy Award given by the United Nations in June 1995.

George Lewis

SEE ALSO:
Bush, George W.; Chicana Feminism; Political Parties, U.S.

Marin, Rosario
Treasurer of the United States

Born:	*August 4, 1958*
	Mexico City

1962	Emigrates from Mexico to the United States
1994	Elected to Huntington Park, California, City Council
1995	Wins the United Nations Rose Fitzgerald Kennedy Award
1999	Re-elected to Huntington Park City Council
2001	Appointed Treasurer of the United States

Marriage

For Mexican Americans, who are predominantly Roman Catholic, marriage is both a sacred and sociologically important institution. Marriage is not only more common than in other U.S. ethnic groups, it is expected. The average age for Mexican American men at the time of a first marriage is about 22, and for women, about 20. The primary purpose of marriage, according to the Catholic Church, is procreation, and Mexican American families tend to be larger than those of the general population.

The size of Mexican American families is declining slightly, although it has remained high compared to that of other Hispanic American subcultures. In the 2000 U.S. census there were nearly 22 million Hispanics who categorized themselves as being Mexican American, and within the families of that large group 33.1 percent had more than five members sharing a single household, compared to less than 14 percent as the national average. Over 7.5 percent of Mexican American families had over seven members.

Because the census focused on households instead of nuclear families, these numbers could represent extended or multigenerational families, as was common for Mexican families until the early twentieth century. By the early twenty-first century, however, it is widely believed that a growing number of Mexican American households were made up of nuclear families.

The wife's role
The most significant change in marriage in the twentieth century was occasioned by the introduction of Mexican American women to the workforce and the rise of Chicana feminism in the 1970s. Both changes altered women's expectations for their role within marriage and family. Gender roles have long been considered very strictly defined among Mexican Americans. For many Mexican American men, being virile, aggressive, and answerable to no one is how they perceive their role, whereas for the same men women are supposed to be submissive to husbands and fathers and be the primary caregiver for the family. Although it is a cultural ideal for men to have a dominant decision-making role and for women to help husbands carry out their decisions, this, as in most patriarchal cultures around the world, is not the day-to-day reality.

Mexican American women wield far more influence in the family than many men acknowledge. Themes of patriarchy remain in the modern Mexican American family, but the nature of male dominance is different. Children may be taught to respect their fathers as authority figures, but in practice parents more often share decision-making responsibilities.

Surveying attitudes among Chicanas
In a recent study that surveyed Mexican American women who worked in cannery factories, the concept of the family was found to be very highly valued. However, there was a trend toward less traditional values. Of the women surveyed, 94.6 percent agreed that children are the essence of the family, and 83.8 percent agreed that children give women identity within the family. The significance of children to the family, a traditional value, has remained in this group, whereas values regarding adult relationships have changed. About 37 percent did not think a woman should live with her parents until she was married, and 40.5 percent did not agree that an adult's word should not be questioned. Both attitudes would have been much more rare two generations ago.

None of the married women surveyed reported going out alone with their husbands and thought that an unusual question. However, the unmarried women reported ascribing to an ideal of a more balanced couple relationship, and wanted to marry a man who would be their equal. This is in sharp contrast to a study conducted of 118 Mexican American families at the beginning of the twentieth century, in which women said they preferred to marry older men because they wanted to look on their husbands as father figures and to have respect for their husbands rather than be seen to be their marital equal.

Gender divide

Marriages in Mexican American families are strongly affected by the division of household tasks, which has remained segregated by gender. This gender divide is rooted in a long history of female virtue having been based on motherhood and domesticity. Recent studies have shown that Mexican American men living in urban areas are largely exempt from household chores despite the lack of outdoor tasks that a rural lifestyle would require. In the twentieth century work and wage earning gave women more rights within the family. However, in Mexican American families, outside jobs were considered extensions of household labor and as a way of supplementing the family income, thus less important than the husband's wage and work. Nevertheless, it is often the case that women working outside the home are still entirely responsible for the management of the household.

In a recent study comparing Mexican American families in Los Angeles, California, and San Antonio, Texas, the majority of respondents over the

The Traditional Mexican Wedding Ceremony

Many elements of a modern Mexican American wedding—including the bride's white dress, the groom's hat, and the open carriage—reflect traditions that have developed over centuries.

Throughout most of Latin America, including Mexico, the ritual surrounding and including marriage follows a similar set of customs. A marriage proposal traditionally follows a long period of courtship. To request the hand of a woman in marriage, the prospective groom asks permission from the woman's father or male head of the woman's family. For the wedding ceremony the groom is responsible for all costs, sometimes having to cater for hundreds of guests. At the wedding there is a full meal, a mariachi band, and a dance where male guests ask the new husband's permission and pay some money to dance with the bride. These "dollar dances" are intended to help out the new couple financially.

The bride and groom select sets of godparents, a tradition known as *compadrazgo*. It is common to have four sets of godparents, each of whom supplies the young couple with specific gifts, such as the white silk scarf worn around the couple's shoulders during celebration of the sacrament, or 13 pieces of silver, which represent family values.

After the wedding the groom's family supports the couple until the newlyweds can afford to live on their own, or the couple lives with the groom's family until the couple can buy their own house.

Although gender roles in Mexican American marriages are more equal today than they were a generation ago, with wives working in full-time jobs outside the home, in most Mexican American marriages traditional domestic chores, such as preparing meals, remain within the wife's domain.

age of 50 felt that a man should have complete control over a family's income (59 percent in Los Angeles and 75 percent in San Antonio). However, among those under the age of 30, only 38 percent in Los Angeles agreed with the statement and 53 percent in San Antonio. Within the same study, however, slightly more than half of those interviewed in both cities felt their mothers had more influence over them than did their fathers, and the majority of the subjects reported that their mothers had been in charge of the family.

In a survey of Mexican American women who worked in cannery factories, domestic chores such as car repairs, garbage removal, and paying bills were all found to be most often within the male domain, while women primarily did the house cleaning and laundry and prepared meals. The women in this study did not find this arrangement unsatisfying, however they did desire greater respect from their spouses for their responsibilities and role within the family. Data from a Los Angeles–San Antonio comparative study suggest that in tasks more significant than dishwashing, the modern Mexican American male has ceded some control and assumed more traditionally female roles.

Interracial marriage

Exogamy (marriage outside one's own cultural group), as opposed to endogamy (marriage within a cultural group), is an indicator of a minority or immigrant group's assimilation into a majority culture. In the case of Mexican Americans, urbanization and movement into middle-class status and less-segregated communities have contributed to this assimilation into American culture. Increased opportunity for social interaction, especially among the young, has resulted in higher rates of interracial marriages. Mexican Americans have often been portrayed as a self-enclosed group with a strong tendency to maintain cultural separateness, and Mexican Americans are the least likely Hispanic subculture to marry exogamously. However, second generation Mexican Americans are consistently shown to have much higher rates of marrying into another ethnic group.

Endogamy among Mexican Americans exists for many reasons, ranging from cultural pressure to ethnic population density or size of barrio. For example, in both southern Florida, where there is a large concentration of Cubans, and in New York City, where many Puerto Ricans live, endogamy in both subcultures is extremely high. Mexican Americans have recently begun to show similar trends of high endogamy in some densely populated barrios of California and Texas, for what appear to be similar reasons.

There is also a gender and age difference between endogamy and exogamy. Mexican American women between the ages of 18 and 34 are slightly more likely to marry outside of their culture than either younger or older women. In California and Texas, Mexican American women tend to marry endogamously more often than Mexican American men do.

Generational and class differences

In 1991 a study in New York City exposed the trend that Mexican American men were more likely than women to marry non-Mexican Americans. The overall lower rates of exogamy among Mexican American women are low in part because many are new arrivals to New York City. This new-arrival or first-generation low rate of exogamy is consistent with nationwide trends among Mexican immigrants.

Exogamy among second- and third-generation Mexican Americans, however, is generally higher nationwide. Whereas the rate of exogamy rises dramatically among the third generation of most ethnic groups, especially for those who have well-paid or high-profile jobs, the shift is not so evident among Mexican Americans of similar status.

Among third-generation Mexican Americans, those who come from working-class backgrounds tend to marry outside of their ethnic group more often than those from middle-class families. Researchers have yet to understand fully why the marriage trends for third-generation Mexican Americans from different socioeconomic backgrounds are not the same. One explanation is that working-class Mexican Americans have a higher divorce and subsequent marriage rate than do middle-class Mexican Americans. When marrying for the second or third time, Mexican Americans, like most ethnic groups in the United States, are more likely to marry someone from outside their ethnic group.

Divorce

Because the vast majority of Mexican Americans are Catholic, and because marriage is seen by the church as sacrosanct, the divorce rate among

Mexican Hollywood movie star Dolores del Río and her husband, art director Cedric Gibbons, in 1933. For a famous actress like del Río, marrying outside her own culture in the early twentieth century was far less difficult than it would have been for most Mexican women.

Mexican Americans is low compared to other ethnic groups. However, rates of desertion are high. In 1998 only 7.2 percent of Hispanics were divorced, as compared to 9.3 percent of the total population. However, 6.9 percent reported being married but with their spouse absent, which is about twice the rate reported within the total population (3.5 percent). Additionally, in 1999 Mexican Americans had the lowest divorce rate among Hispanics (5.8 percent), but one of the highest rates of desertion. Also, according to the 2000 U.S. census, over 1 million Mexican American households, or around 21 percent, were headed by a single female parent, compared to 17.6 percent for other ethnic groups.

Catharine Inbody

SEE ALSO:
Barrios; Catholic Church; Chicana Feminism; Chicano Life; Family; Festivals; Hispanic Americans; Housing in the U.S.; Mexican Communities, U.S.; Rural Life; Segregation and Integration.

Martinez, Narciso

Narciso Martinez (1911–1992) was born in Reynosa, Tamaulipas, across the border from McAllen, Texas. An exceptionally influential accordian player, Martinez was known as the father of *conjunto* music. *Conjunto* is a vibrant style of dance music that has its roots in Mexican American culture; Martinez set the stage for the development of the style in the mid-1930s.

Though he lived most of his life in the United States, Martinez never became a citizen of the country, always stressing his pride in his Mexican heritage. Like many *conjunto* musicians both before and after him, Martinez was raised in a rural setting. The need for regular work caused his family to move from place to place. As a result, Martinez received almost no schooling, simply because the conditions under which rural Mexicans lived at the time were not conducive to formal education. Because of his poor literacy, Martinez found that his labor opportunities as an adult were severely limited. Over the course of his life he worked as a truck driver and an agricultural laborer, working both in the fields with a shovel and driving tractors. In his later life he also worked for a number of years at the Gladys Porter Zoo in Brownsville, Texas.

Martinez began playing accordion in 1927, the year before his marriage to Edwina, with whom he had four daughters. He learned to play on a cheap instrument and was entirely self-taught, although he was influenced by other players such as Jose Rodriguez, Lolo Cavazos, and Alejandro Aguire. Martinez soon started to perform at local dances and bought his first new instrument in 1930. In 1935, he gave up the one-row accordian for the more flexible two-row model.

Collaboration with Santiago Almeida

In the mid-1930s Martinez began his long-time collaboration with Santiago Almeida, who played the *bajo sexto*, a 12-string guitar. Almeida used the *bajo* to add a bass rhythm and countermelody to the part played by the accordion. Previously, accordionists were accompanied only by a simple drum beaten by a stick.

Between them Martinez and Almeida were able to establish the accordion and *bajo sexto* as the key instruments in the developing style of *conjunto*. Martinez came to ignore the left-hand bass accompaniment that most accordionists played, focusing instead on the right-hand melody notes. He thus relied on Almeida to provide the bass part on *bajo*. Martinez's technique was considered snappier than other accordionists of his day. Although his approach was unique at the time, many other accordionists eventually copied his style.

Martinez's association with Almeida led to a contract with Bluebird, an important record label during the Depression years. The accordionist's

Conjunto Music

The style of music known as *conjunto* first appeared in Texas and northern Mexico in the early 1900s. *Conjunto* music was primarily played at dances and was distinguished by the fact that the main instrument was the cheap and versatile accordion. Its rhythms were influenced by central European dance forms, such as the polka.

Narciso Martinez's main contribution to the music's development was his establishment, with Santiago Almeida, of the accordion and the *bajo* as the core of the *conjunto* ensemble. Subsequent generations of musicians added bass guitars, saxophones, and synthesizers to the mix.

Modern *conjunto* music is divided into two sub-genres—norteño from northern Mexico and Tejano from Texas. Norteño tends to consist of ballads, often sung in a high-pitched voice by duos and accompanied by a saxophone. The more upbeat Tejano style has absorbed elements of rock music and can be grouped according to the areas where it is played: San Antonio, Corpus Christi, and southern Texas.

recording career began in 1936, when a local furniture-store owner took him to San Antonio to make his first record. He recorded 20 tracks on that day and was paid a total of U.S. $150, a third of which went to his accompanist, Almeida.

The recording session led to the release of "La Chicharronera" (The crackling). The record was a success, and shortly afterward Bluebird started to use both musicians for regular sessions. Martinez remained with Bluebird from 1935 until 1940.

Martinez's music was heavily influenced by the dance styles of central Europe. In 1928 he had moved to Bishop, Texas, which was home to many German and Czech immigrants; when he started recording for Bluebird, most of his pieces were either polkas or *redowas*, both dances that originated in Bohemia, the present-day Czech Republic. Martinez also recorded other European dances, such as schottiches, waltzes, and mazurkas, which were distinguished from one another by differences in pace and rhythm.

Martinez and the polka

Martinez's most popular recordings, however, were polkas, which soon became the main *conjunto* dance style. Martinez's polkas carried titles that reflected his Texan surroundings: "La Parrita" (The little grapevine), "La Polvadera" (The dustcloud), and "Los Coyotes" (The coyotes). Martinez's music appealed to many different nationalities, but his record company sometimes disguised his Mexican roots when they were marketing his recordings to other ethnic groups. When Bluebird wanted to appeal to the Cajun market they released his records under the name "Louisiana Pete." For Polish customers, Martinez and his band were presented as the "Polski Kwartet."

In 1946 Martinez left Bluebird to record for the Ideal label, where he backed some of its most popular singers, including the vocal duo Carmen and Laura. However, over the course of his career the vast majority of Martinez's recordings were instrumental. The accordionist primarily considered himself a dance-hall performer, and instrumentals were the main type of music played at these venues.

As his recordings became popular, Martinez's reputation grew. He gained the nickname "Hurricane of the Valley," a title that hinted at both his presence as a musician and the speed of his playing. He found himself in regular demand to play at weddings and on holidays. Martinez could rarely afford to turn down such employment. Like other *conjunto* and blues musicians in the South at that time, Martinez did not collect royalties for either his compositions or his records. He was thus forced to play on weekends if he wanted to supplement his wages as an agricultural worker.

Martinez made little money as a musician but still built up an enthusiastic following. He continued to record throughout the 1950s and in 1952 became one of the first *conjunto* musicians to tour beyond the state of Texas, playing in New Mexico, Arizona, and California. At the same time many of Martinez's compositions were entering the repertoires of other *conjunto* musicians.

In the 1960s Martinez's popularity waned as a new generation of Mexican American musicians appeared. Although he continued to perform live, Martinez recorded only sporadically. His profile grew higher, however, when he was featured in the 1976 film *Chulas Fronteras* (Beautiful borders), a documentary about Tex-Mex music. In 1982 he was inducted into the Conjunto Music Hall of Fame, and in 1989 Arhoolie Records released a compilation of his best work, which was nominated for a Grammy award. Three years later Martinez died in San Benito, Texas.

Carlos F. Ortega

SEE ALSO:
Music; Tex-Mex Culture.

Martinez, Narciso
Mexican musician

Born:	*October 29, 1911*
	Reynosa, Tamaulipas
Died:	*June 5, 1992*
	San Benito, Texas

1927	Learns to play accordion
1928	Moves to Bishop, Texas, where he is influenced by central European dance styles
1936	Makes first recordings, later released on Bluebird label
1946	Hired by Ideal to serve as house accordionist
1982	Inducted into the Conjunto Music Hall of Fame

Matamoros, Tamaulipas

One of the four largest cities on the Mexico-U.S. border, Matamoros has often played center stage in conflicts between the two nations, but today it is linked by the Gateway International Bridge to its twin city of Brownsville, Texas.

Cattle ranching has been a part of Matamoros since the early eighteenth century. In 1793 the settlement of Congregacíon de Nuestra Señora del Refugio was founded, which was renamed Matamoros in 1826 in honor of the Mexican independence hero Mariano Matamoros. It is one of only four Mexican cities with the prefix "H," which stands for "Heroica," a title given to the city by the government after its courageous defense against a rebellion in 1851.

The town was laid out close to the Rio Grande in a traditional Spanish grid system around a main square, Plaza Hidalgo. The cathedral of Nuestra Señora del Refugio faces the square. The cathedral was originally built in 1831 but had to be rebuilt after a damaging storm a century later. Many Spanish colonial-style buildings dating from the eighteenth and early nineteenth centuries survive in the city.

Role in historical events
Matamoros became a city in 1834, before its sister city, Brownsville, which did not develop until Texas was annexed to the United States in 1845. The United States and Mexico disputed the border between the two countries, and Fort Taylor (later renamed Fort Brown, for its commanding officer) was built where Brownsville now stands. Matamoros prospered during the U.S. Civil War (1861–1865), when Texas cotton was shipped through the town and out to Europe via the nearby Mexican port of Bagdad, at one time the only port open to the Confederates.

Matamoros witnessed one of the most dramatic episodes of the Mexican Revolution (1910–1920) when a small garrison of troops loyal to the dictator president Porfirio Díaz defended the city against Constitutionalist rebels. On June 3, 1913, General Lucio Blanco and his rebel forces managed to

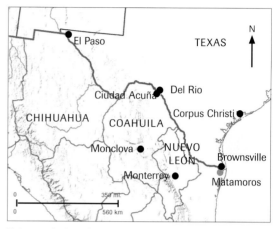

Matamoros is situated near the Rio Grande and the Texas border. It is connected to the United States by three major bridges.

capture the garrison. Casualties, mostly among the defending forces, numbered more than a hundred deaths and several hundred injured.

Growth and development
In the last three decades of the twentieth century, Matamoros grew rapidly. The city was home to Mexico's first maquiladora (assembly plant) enterprise in the 1960s. From then on the population grew in tandem with the growth of industry. By 2000 the population had reached 500,000, and it was the third largest maquiladora center; by 2002 there were about 62,000 workers in more than 120 maquiladora enterprises. About 30 percent of U.S.-Mexico trade passes through the city, contributing to its economic importance. Growth has brought environmental problems, such as shortages of clean water from the Rio Grande and increased air and water pollution.

Matamoros attracts an increasing number of tourists. Sites of interest include the Museo del Maíz (the Maize Museum) and the Casa Mata fort, which played a key role in the Mexican-American War (1846–1848) and houses memorabilia from the Mexican Revolution.

Tim Harris

SEE ALSO:

Brownsville; Maquiladoras; Mexican Revolution; Ranching; Twin-Cities Phenomenon.

Maximilian

Ferdinand Maximilian von Hapsburg was a European prince who was emperor of Mexico from 1864 to 1867. He was installed with the backing of the French emperor, Napoleon III (1808–1873), who wanted to curb the expansionism of the United States and extend his own power in North America.

Maximilian was born on July 6, 1832, in the castle of Schonbrunn, near Vienna, Austria, the second son of Archduke Francis Karl and Archduchess Sophie. He served in the Austrian navy and as governor-general of Lombardy-Venetia in Italy before retiring from public life in 1859. He took a trip to Brazil in 1860 and on return moved to his castle of Miramar near Trieste in Italy, with his wife, Charlotte, daughter of King Leopold of Belgium.

At the time Mexico was in upheaval. The War of Reform between liberals and conservatives broke out in 1858. The liberals won in 1861 and Benito Juárez was elected president. After their defeat, the conservatives looked to France for support. Napoleon III, who had become emperor of France in 1852, seized the opportunity to extend his influence in the Americas.

When Juárez suspended foreign debt payments in May 1861, Napoleon used the act as a pretext to send an armed French expedition to Mexico. By this point, the U.S. Civil War had begun and the United States was in no position to resist European encroachment in the Americas. Spain and Britain joined the invasion but soon reached an agreement with the Juárez government. By February 1862 only the French forces remained. Napoleon's goal was to set up a monarchy under a European prince who would be pliable to his wishes. His candidate was Archduke Ferdinand Maximilian.

A new emperor for Mexico

French troops began to move into the interior in early 1863. Juárez and his government fled to the north of Mexico, and in July 1863, a month after the French occupied Mexico City, the provisional government announced that the country would become a monarchy. Many in the government

Maximilian's short reign as emperor of Mexico was violently opposed by liberal Mexicans, who overthrew and executed him in 1867.

believed that closer ties with Europe would strengthen Mexico's position against the United States. In October a delegation went to Europe and offered the crown to Maximilian. He made it clear that he would accept only if invited by the Mexican people to rule over them, so a mock plebiscite was organized in the French-controlled parts of the country and the favorable results sent to Miramar, Spain, where Maximilian waited. Maximilian signed the Treaty of Miramar and accepted the crown, believing he had the support of the Mexican people. By the terms of the treaty, 25,000 French troops were to remain in Mexico until they were replaced by a Mexican army. They were complemented by 8,000 men of the French Foreign Legion, who would stay in Mexico eight years. In exchange for full command over the French expeditionary forces, Maximilian had to pay the expenses of the occupying troops. Napoleon extended a loan to Maximilian to cover the cost, tripling Mexico's foreign debt.

Maximilian and his wife, known in Mexico as Carlota, arrived in Veracruz on May 28, 1864. Their initial reception was cold, but as they traveled into

Maximilian
Emperor of Mexico

Born: *July 6, 1832*
Vienna, Austria
Died: *June, 1867*
Querétaro, Mexico

1860	Retires to Miramar, Trieste, Italy
1863	Signs the Treaty of Miramar and agrees to rule Mexico
1864	Arrives in Mexico with his wife and is crowned emperor in June
1866	Napoleon III begins to withdraw the French army from Mexico
1867	Maximilian is captured, tried, and executed

central Mexico and conservative territory the people's enthusiasm increased, and their solemn entry into Mexico City was accompanied by the cheers of enthusiastic crowds. The empire was recognized by most foreign governments, with the exception of the United States, which opposed any European influence in the Americas because it violated the principles of the Monroe Doctrine.

Soon after they arrived, Maximilian and Carlota set up residence in Chapultepec Castle in Mexico City. Maximilian remodeled the eighteenth-century building to suit the needs of his court. An extra wing was added and an Italian-style garden created for Carlota. Chapultepec became the center of court life. Maximilian and Carlota made an effort to adapt to their new country. For example, they spoke only Spanish, even to foreign diplomats.

Maximilian's rule
From the beginning Maximilian faced immense obstacles: an economic crisis resulting from years of civil war, an enemy determined to defeat the empire, and supporters that opposed his liberal reforms and ideology. His support for the separation of church and state and his continuation of the sale of church properties earned him the enmity of the clergy, who had originally been among his strongest supporters. Maximilian's views were too liberal for his conservative backers; but he was still considered a foreign usurper by the liberals.

By 1865 the imperialist French-Mexican troops controlled most of the national territory and Juárez and his followers were forced to retreat to Chihuahua and later to El Paso, on the northern border. However, civil unrest and guerrilla warfare continued. Maximilian was informed, incorrectly, that Juárez had fled to the United States in October. From then on all rebels were deemed simple criminals by the imperialists. The emperor was persuaded to issue a harsh decree, making execution mandatory for all captured republicans who refused to give up the fight. Despite legislation and reprisals, the republican guerrillas continued to fight, making pacification of the country impossible.

When the Civil War in the United States ended in April 1865, the U.S. government increased pressure on Napoleon to withdraw from Mexico. In January 1866 the emperor announced that all troops would be withdrawn within a year. Carlota traveled to Europe in an effort to convince Napoleon not to recall his troops. His refusal and the pressures of her mission took their toll, and Carlota went insane. Maximilian never saw his wife again.

The end of the empire
The withdrawal of the French troops allowed the republicans to advance rapidly into the imperial territories. Maximilian's effort to raise a strong local army failed and the empire began to crumble. Instead of abdicating, Maximilian decided to fight on. In February 1867 he traveled north of the capital, to the loyal city of Querétaro, and prepared to make his last stand. The imperial armies were unable to resist republican attacks, and on May 15 Querétaro fell. Maximilian was captured on the nearby Hill of the Bells. A trial was held to give the appearance of due process of law, but the emperor's fate had already been decided. On June 19, 1867, Maximilian was executed by firing squad on the hill where he had surrendered.

Although Maximilian may be accused of naiveté and financial irresponsibility, his good intentions and his desire to rule his adoptive country fairly cannot be denied. His efforts to reorganize the country's administrative, educational, and health boards set the stage for the centralization of power by later governments.

Luz María Hernández Sáenz
SEE ALSO:
Civil War, U.S.; France; Juárez, Benito; Monroe Doctrine; Reforma, La; Reform, War of the.

Maya

The Maya are a group of Indian peoples living in southern Mexico, particularly in the states of Campeche, Chiapas, Quintana Roo, Tabasco, and Yucatán. They also inhabit parts of the neighboring countries of Belize, Guatemala, and Honduras.

The Maya first came to North America from Asia more than 20,000 years ago during the last Ice Age when they crossed the land bridge across what is now the Bering Strait. By 5000 B.C.E. they had migrated south and settled in fishing communities along the Caribbean and Pacific coasts of southern Mexico. By 2000 B.C.E. they had moved inland and turned to agriculture for their livelihood. Then, as now, the staple ingredients of their diet were beans, squash, and maize (corn). The Mayan word for maize is the same as their word for food.

By 200 C.E. the Maya had built great cities with stone palaces, pyramids, and temples decorated with elaborate sculpture and relief carving. They developed their own hieroglyphic writing and a complex calendar system. They practiced advanced agricultural techniques of irrigation and terracing.

Early Classic period

Between 250 and 550 C.E. (a period known as the Early Classic), the Maya came into contact with warriors and traders from Teotihuacán in central Mexico, the largest and most powerful state of the era. There is no evidence of conquest, but the Maya adopted some Teotihuacán deities, styles of art, architecture, and clothing.

By the end of the Early Classic the Maya had established numerous cities and city-states, becoming one of the greatest civilizations of the Western Hemisphere. Tikal, their largest center, may have had a population of as many as 100,000. Their other main cities were Bonampak, Uaxactun, Palenque, Rio Bec, Tikal, and Copan. At this time there may have been as many as two million Maya.

After 900 C.E. the Mayan civilization fell into rapid decline as a result of either famine, chronic warfare, or disease. By the end of the tenth century it had largely collapsed, although Uxmal and Mayapan in the highlands of Yucatán continued to thrive until the early sixteenth century. The strongest remaining Mayan enclave was at Chichén Itzá, which was ruled by speakers of Itzá or Putun Maya from the Tabasco coast.

Chichén Itzá

In 987 C.E. Chichén was taken over by Toltecs from central Mexico, who were led by a man named Kukulcan, the Maya name for the Toltec deity Quetzalcoatl (Feathered Serpent). Aided by the Itzá, a Mayan people from the gulf coast, the new rulers quickly dominated northern Yucatán and rebuilt Chichén into a hybrid Toltec-Maya capital. They consolidated a powerful state sustained by trade, tribute, and war. Some historians believe they developed a new system of administration in which three or four brothers ruled jointly.

At the end of the twelfth century Chichén Itzá was sacked and abandoned. In the thirteenth century the Itzá founded a new Mayan capital at Mayapan, 62 miles (100 km) west of Chichén Itzá. Unlike most other Mayan cities, Mayapan was walled; it had a population of about 15,000. In the mid-fifteenth century, Mayapan, too, was sacked. The Maya of Yucatán then broke up into tiny states and became mainly village-dwelling farmers.

Spanish conquest

From the moment in 1502 when Christopher Columbus (1451–1506) first sighted Mayan traders in canoes filled with cloth and other goods off the coast of Honduras, invasion became inevitable. At the time of the Spanish conquest the Maya were wracked by wars and quickly succumbed to European diseases. The Spanish took control of Mayan territory in 1542, establishing their capital at Mérida, on the site of the Mayan city of Tiho. The last Mayan kingdom, Taytasal, in Lake Peten Itzá, fell in 1697. During the colonial period Spanish slaveholders dealt harshly with the Maya, forcing thousands to work in the mines of northern Mexico, where most died. Their deaths led to the depopulation of large areas of the tropical lowlands. Although the Spanish quickly established themselves after the conquest, Mayan rebellions were common until the twentieth century.

The entrance to the Temple of the Warriors at Chichén Itzá. The entrance is guarded by two serpents and a reclining figure known as a chacmool, believed to represent the Mayan rain god. It may have served as an altar for human sacrifices.

In 1902 the Mexican government established a separate territory for the Maya in Quintana Roo on the east side of the Yucatán Peninsula, where many rebels took refuge. Quintana Roo was made a state in 1974 and is now the location of Mexico's prosperous Caribbean resorts of Cancún, Cozumel, and Isla Mujeres.

Modern Maya

Modern Maya live in roughly the same areas as their ancestors did 2,000 years ago. Some 4 million or so Maya speak one of the 30 or more Mayan languages. Some have adopted an urban life, particularly in Mérida and Cancún, but most still live in rural areas.

The Maya have maintained many of their ancient customs in diet, dress, and housing. Traditional Mayan methods of naming children, marriage and burial customs, agricultural practices, the treatment of illness, and even foretelling the future are still much the same as they were thousands of years ago. In the northern lowlands, the rain god Chaac is worshiped, and in times of drought a *chachaac*, or

rainmaking ceremony, is performed. Before the Spanish conquest, the *uayeb* (the last five days of the year) were regarded as a dangerous time; most Maya now identify the period with Christmas. Carnival is also carefully observed.

In recent years many Maya in Mexico, Guatemala, and Belize have moved to the tropical lowlands in search of property. Before this development, only the Lacandon, a small group of 350 people living in a handful of communities, had lived in the jungle in the twentieth century. Now many Tzeltal, Tzotzil, Chol, and Yucatec Maya have been granted new *ejidos* (collective farms) by the Mexican government, where they grow coffee or raise cattle. In Guatemala, civil and racial strife during the 1970s and 1980s forced many Maya to flee across the border to Mexico. The Mexican government moved a large number of these refugees to a permanent settlement near Edzna, Campeche.

Henry Russell

SEE ALSO:

Agriculture; Archaeology; Architecture; Cancún; Indian Policy; Spanish Empire.

McAllen, Texas

The city of McAllen sits 8 miles (13 km) across the Rio Grande from its larger and older Mexican sister city, Reynosa, Tamaulipas. McAllen began as a ranch and grew to become a major port of entry into the United States.

McAllen lies on ranching land granted to settlers by the Spanish government of Mexico in the mid-eighteenth century. Salomé Ballí, the great-granddaughter of one of the settlers, inherited the land in the 1800s and married the Anglo-American settler John Young in 1848. After Young's death, Ballí married the ranch manager, John McAllen. Ballí and McAllen continued to acquire new land and renamed their estate McAllen Ranch. By 1904 a community had developed in the region, named for John McAllen. Despite the building of a railroad that passed through McAllen, the new town was eclipsed by another community that was founded in 1907 by rival landowners two miles to the east. The older community became known as West McAllen; the newer one East McAllen. By 1911, however, West McAllen had ceased to exist and East McAllen changed its name to McAllen.

Segregation

In the early decades of the twentieth century the number of white American farms increased around McAllen, displacing Mexican American ranches in the region and attracting an influx of Mexican migrant laborers from across the border. Segregation between the Anglo and Hispanic communities became a fact of life, occurring in schools, hospitals, and housing as a result of the sales policies of the McAllen Real Estate Board. Many local landowners welcomed Mexican migrants because they provided cheap labor. According to a 1950 study, cotton growers in the Rio Grande Valley received half the wages of fieldworkers in other parts of Texas. In 1953 a local newspaper demanded action against illegal immigrants from Mexico, dubbed "wetbacks." In 1954 the U.S. Immigration and Naturalization Service responded with Operation Wetback, which it claimed forced more than one million immigrants to leave Texas.

McAllen has been an important border-crossing point since the completion of the McAllen-Hidalgo-Reynosa International Bridge in 1941. As well as tourism, the city relies on agriculture and industry.

Industrialization

Since the 1980s more companies have relocated to the McAllen-Reynosa area than to any other in southern Texas. The establishment of the McAllen Foreign Trade Zone in the late 1970s encouraged companies such as General Electric and Whirlpool to move into the area. The zone, a small-scale forerunner of the North American Free Trade Agreement (NAFTA) implemented in 1994, allows companies to transport goods and materials across the border free of charge. The companies set up maquiladoras (assembly plants) around Reynosa, and warehousing and distribution operations on the McAllen side of the border. Agriculture continues to boost the local economy—McAllen is the center of the Rio Grande's citrus industry—while tourism has increased in importance. Many McAllen residents travel to Reynosa to eat in its restaurants and thousands more travel across the Rio Grande to shop in McAllen's retail district. McAllen's annual Texas Square Dance Jamboree is one of the largest in the world, drawing visitors from far and wide.

Harry Star

SEE ALSO:

Maquiladoras; NAFTA; Operation Wetback; Segregation and Integration; Tourism; Twin Cities.

Media, Spanish Language

The rapid growth of the Hispanic population in the United States has been accompanied by a corresponding increase in Spanish-language and bilingual media serving the Hispanic community.

The U.S. census of 2000 estimated that there were around 35 million people of Hispanic origin in the United States, with a purchasing power of more than $500 billion. Although newspaper circulation in general is declining, many newspapers aimed at the Hispanic community have increased their circulation. The main radio and television networks serving the Hispanic community have experienced growth in advertising revenue, and there has been a sharp increase in the number of U.S.-based Spanish-language or bilingual Web sites.

Newspapers and magazines

The first Spanish-language newspaper published in the United States was *El Misisipi*, published in 1808 in New Orleans and aimed at colonial merchants and traders. During the nineteenth century the number of Spanish-language newspapers grew to more than 150. El Paso and San Antonio were two of the most important publishing centers.

At the beginning of the twenty-first century Spanish-language newspapers and magazines were growing fast. Not only were leading dailies serving the Hispanic community increasing their circulation but also the number of new newspapers and magazines was increasing: in 1990 there were 355 Hispanic newspapers and 177 magazines, and in 2000 there were 540 newspapers and 346 magazines. Hispanic newspaper circulation rose from 420,000 in 1970 to 24.1 million in 1996.

The biggest Spanish-language newspaper is *La Opinión*. Published in Los Angeles, it is among the country's top 100 newspapers. It is distributed through southern California and reaches more than 679,000 readers every day. A Mexican immigrant, Ignacio Lorenzo, founded *La Opinión* in 1926, and his family still owns a 50 percent stake in Lorenzo Communications, making it one of the longest-running Hispanic newspapers with Hispanic ownership in the United States. Another leading

Spanish and English magazines are sold side-by-side on this newsstand, an indication of the huge demand for Spanish newspapers and magazines in the southwest United States.

daily is *El Nuevo Herald*, based in Miami. *El Nuevo Herald* was founded in 1987 and was the first Spanish-language counterpart of a major U.S. newspaper (*The Miami Herald*).

In New York the market is split between *El Diario–La Prensa*, launched in 1963 and now owned by El Diario Associates Inc., and its rival *Hoy*, which was launched by *Newsday* in 1998. *Hoy* has overtaken the older newspaper by appealing to Hispanics with diverse origins, while *El Diario–La Prensa* is aimed mainly at Puerto Ricans. Other leading Spanish-language newspapers are *El Sol de Texas*, a weekly published in Dallas; *La Raza*, a bilingual Chicano newspaper published in Chicago; *El Diario de las Americas*, published in Miami; and *Hispanos Unidos*, based in San Diego. Many Spanish-language newspapers have been launched by English-speaking media companies, such as *People en Español*, published by Time Inc., and *Exito*, published by the *Chicago Tribune*.

Radio

Spanish-language radio started out broadcasting in the early morning hours on mainstream stations in the 1920s and 1930s. Radio personalities of the time included the actor Rodolfo Hoyos and the singer Pedro González. Gradually these programs increased in popularity, and by 1941 an estimated total of 264 hours of Spanish-language radio were broadcast per week in Arizona, Texas, California, and New York. In 1946 Raoul Cortez set up KCOR-AM, the first full-time Spanish-language radio station owned and operated by a Mexican American. Cortez developed a highly acclaimed series of radio theater programs that was broadcast across the country. From the 1970s, when new marketing techniques and the rise of specialized Spanish-language advertising companies increased advertising revenue, Spanish-language radio began to expand.

At the beginning of the twenty-first century the biggest Spanish-language broadcasting corporations in the United States were the Hispanic Broadcasting Corporation, with 55 radio stations, and the Spanish Broadcasting System, with 24 radio stations. In addition, many cities had independent Spanish-language radio stations, such as New York's La Mega97 and Wojo in Chicago.

Television

Raoul Cortez was also responsible for the first Spanish-language television station, KCOR-TV, in the United States, which he set up in San Antonio in 1955. KCOR-TV (later renamed KWEX-TV) became part of a nationwide Spanish-language network by 1970, with stations in New Jersey, California, and Florida. This network eventually became Univisión, one of the two biggest Spanish-language television broadcast networks in the United States. Univisión Communications, Inc., consists of three television networks—Univisión, TeleFutura, and Galavisión—48 broadcast television stations, and a television production business.

Together Univisión and its closest rival, Telemundo, reach 90 percent of Hispanic households. Telemundo, owned by NBC, owns and operates 23 television stations in the United States and Puerto Rico. Spanish-language television in the United States is heavily dependent on imported programs

from Mexico and Venezuela. The bulk of programming consists of *telenovelas* (Latin American soap operas), musical variety shows, and sports programs. Viewers complain that there is insufficient documentary and dramatic programming, and little variation across the country to accommodate the interests of different Hispanic groups.

According to a 2001 study, each week 74 percent of Hispanics report watching Spanish-language television and 82 percent English-language television. Younger Hispanics, particularly, switch between languages. Univisión and Telemundo have both recognized the importance of catering to the Hispanic youth market: Telemundo launched Mun2, and Univisión launched TeleFutura for young bilingual Hispanics.

The 2001 study also indicated that 60 percent of Hispanics report listening to Spanish-language radio and 67 percent to English-language radio; 29 percent of Hispanics read Spanish-language newspapers, 67 percent read English-language ones; 53 percent read Spanish-language magazines, and 63 percent read English-language magazines.

The Internet

The Hispanic community has been slow to make full use of the Internet, and there are relatively few U.S.-based Spanish-language Web sites. In 2001 the Commerce Department reported that its research showed 31.6 percent of Hispanics use the Internet, compared to 60 percent of Asian Americans and 60 percent of Anglo-Americans. According to the Online Computer Literacy Center, less than 3 percent of all online content in 1999 was in Spanish. However, Hispanic use of the Internet is steadily growing, and a number of key players are active in this market, including Univisión, AOL Latino, Terra, and YupiMSN.

The Hispanic market is attractive to advertisers, particularly because of the growing number of young Hispanics. One in five teens in the United States is of Hispanic origin. The Hispanic advertising industry has been growing at an average rate of 19 percent for the three last years. Spending for this group ranged from $25 to $51 million.

Joanna Griffin

SEE ALSO:

Chicano Art; Chicano Theater; Film in Mexico; Film in the U.S.; Language; Literacy; Literature; Music; Newspapers and Magazines; Television and Radio.

Mestizos

Mestizos, from the Spanish word "to mix," are the children of a Spanish (or European) parent and a noncaucasian parent. The blending of ethnic groups, miscegenation, is known in Spanish as *mestizaje*. It began in Mexico when the Spanish conquistadores took Indian, African, and other peoples as partners and conceived children with them.

Mestizos and the process of *mestizaje* that created them have not always been well regarded. During the early colonial era in Mexico (1521–1821) mestizos were a low-status caste compared to *peninsulares* (people born in Spain) and criollos (people born in Mexico to Spanish parents). However, after the Mexican Revolution (1910–1920) the new government praised mestizos as the social and cultural backbone of the nation. This new stance was vastly more democratic than the earlier attitude that mestizos were racially inferior to those of pure Spanish descent. This cultural shift proved oppressive, however, for Mexico's many indigenous peoples. In the name of *mestizaje*, Indians were pressured to blend with the rest of the nation by abandoning their languages and customs.

Mestizos and the Spanish conquest

As soon as the Spanish arrived in the New World in 1519 they began the process of *mestizaje*. The conquistador Hernán Cortés, for instance, took several Indian women as partners, including his translator Doña Marina (also known as La Malinche) with whom he had a son. Such liaisons were common, particularly from 1520 to 1540, when only about 6 percent of Spanish immigrants to New Spain (colonial Mexico) were female. As a result, the conquistadores had sex with and sometimes married Indian women, with or without the women's agreement. Spanish men prized Indian women from noble families; in turn, some Indian men from royal backgrounds married Spanish women. One example is Diego Luis Montezuma, grandson of the Aztec emperor Montezuma II (1466–1520). Diego Luis married a Spanish woman and founded the powerful dynasty of the counts of Montezuma.

When Spaniards had children with high-status Indians, their mestizo offspring sometimes received honors from the Spanish side of the family. Don Martín Cortés, for example, the son of Hernán Cortés and Doña Marina, was granted a knighthood in Spain and became a soldier in the royal army. However, Don Martín was denied the right to inherit his father's estate, which went to Cortés's legitimate son by his Spanish wife. So many mestizos during Mexico's early colonial period were illegitimate that the word *mestizo* was equated with "bastard." Most of these children were raised by their Indian mothers; few were recognized or cared for by their Spanish fathers.

Most mestizos occupied a low position in the ethnic caste system that developed in New Spain. At the top of the system were *peninsulares*, followed by criollos. Indians and Africans, brought to Mexico as slaves, occupied the lowest rungs. Mestizos were only slightly better off than those at the bottom. Like other low-status groups, mestizo women could not wear expensive clothes or jewelry. Mestizos were also banned from becoming soldiers or priests. New Spain had no laws forbidding marriage between the castes, but it was a social taboo to wed a person of lower status.

The Spanish conquistador Hernán Cortés (seated) and the Indian Doña Marina (to his left), from a copy of the Spanish cloth painting the Lienzo *of Tlaxcala (c.1550). Cortés and Doña Marina (also known as La Malinche) had a mestizo son, Martín Cortés.*

Changing attitudes

In 1821, the year it gained its independence from Spain, Mexico had a population of about 6 million. Of that total, half were Indians, 30 to 40 percent were mestizos, and between 10 and 20 percent were of Spanish extraction, the vast majority of whom were criollos. The liberal reforms of the 1850s and 1860s technically gave all Mexican citizens equal rights before the law, regardless of their class or race. Even so, Mexico's late nineteenth-century elites still looked to Europe for ideas about race, which meant that they continued to believe that darker-skinned peoples were inferior to those with lighter skins. These ideas affected mestizos, including the few who wielded political and economic power. Mexican president Porfirio Díaz (1830–1915), for instance, was a mestizo who often put white powder on his face to look less Indian and more Spanish.

At the end of Díaz's regime, on the eve of the Mexican Revolution, mestizos made up half of Mexico's population, with Indians, criollos, and foreigners comprising the balance. By this time some writers praised mestizos as the future of Mexico. Justo Sierra, for example, a supporter of the Díaz regime, wrote that "We Mexicans are the sons of two countries and two races.... This fact rules our whole history; to it we owe our soul." However, Sierra also thought Mexico needed to "whiten" itself by allowing more immigration from Europe.

He also believed that Mexico's Indians should be "mestizo-ized." Sierra argued that all schoolchildren should be taught exclusively in Spanish, even though the country's 56 Indian groups spoke their own languages. Sierra believed that the Indians' languages must be destroyed in order to achieve national integration. The ensuing revolution adopted and glorified his ideas.

José Vasconcelos (1882–1959)

The status of mestizos and *mestizaje* was raised again when the philosopher and writer José Vasconcelos became head of Mexico's Secretaría de Educación Pública (SEP; Department of Education) in 1921. In an age when Europe and the United States considered mixed-race people to be both mentally and morally deficient, Vasconcelos defended Mexico's majority mestizo population, of which he was a member. He argued that mestizos were the best people in the world, lacking in prejudice, blessed with abundant intelligence, and always ready to take up a challenge. Vasconcelos believed that "Mexico would be the cradle of this higher civilization, and *mestizaje* would form the basis of the country's identity."

With Vasconcelos at its head the SEP demanded that Indians integrate into the nation by becoming as much like mestizos as possible. Indian children in public schools were to learn Spanish as their only language and to abandon their native dress and

Rise and Fall of Mexico's Caste System

Miscegenation in colonial Mexico involved not only Europeans and Indians. Sexual liaisons also took place between Europeans and people of African descent. During the colonial period an estimated 200,000 Africans entered the country. The vast majority were slaves who worked in silver mines or on sugar plantations. By the late sixteenth century there were almost as many Africans as Spaniards in Mexico. The offspring of Spanish and African parents were called mulattos, while those born to African and Indian parents were known as zambos. Slaves in Mexico were allowed to buy their freedom and often were freed after their owners died. As a result, by the late 1500s there were many free Africans, mulattos, and zambos in the country.

By the end of the colonial period, miscegenation was so widespread in Mexico that the caste system was becoming unworkable. It began to be replaced by a class system that placed no legal restrictions on people's ability to move up the social ladder if they had money, property, and education. As a result, an individual who occupied a particular place in the older caste system could "pass" to another category. Well-off Indians who spoke Spanish and dressed like mestizos were able to pass for them and so avoid the forced labor and taxes that Indians faced. By the mid-1800s the caste system became increasingly fluid: the Indian Benito Juárez became president of Mexico in 1861; in 1880 the mestizo Porfirio Díaz became head of government.

A *mestizo selling* elote *(corn on the cob) in Mexico City's Chapultepec Park. After the discrimination of the colonial period, the status of mestizos grew in the late nineteenth and early twentieth centuries.*

other customs. Ironically, at the same time as muralists such as Diego Rivera were celebrating Mexico's indigenous past, attempts to destroy the country's ethnic culture were taking place in its classrooms. "Mestizo-izing" schools opened in many rural areas with large Indian populations, but few Indians chose to attend them.

Moderating Indian policy

In 1948 the Mexican government created the Instituto Nacional Indigenista (INI; National Indigenous Institute). The measure was part of a new approach to encourage Indians to assimilate into mestizo culture by recognizing indigenous culture instead of trying to destroy it. The approach included new teaching methods geared to Indians' needs, such as bilingual education in both Spanish and Indian languages. The policy increased respect for indigenous culture, but Indians continued to suffer considerable economic, political, and social inequality compared to other Mexicans.

In the late 1970s Indian groups in Mexico began demanding greater legal and political rights, forcing the INI to abandon its policy of "mestizo-ization." In 1992 the Mexican government reformed Article 4 of the 1917 Constitution, with the stated aim of protecting and promoting Indian languages, cultures, customs, and access to resources. In addition, the reform guaranteed Indians effective access to Mexico's legal processes. Although Article 4 sounded powerful, it remained a symbolic gesture since no laws were passed to implement it.

Zapatista movement

The most recent and dramatic Indian challenge to the ideology of *mestizaje* has come from the Zapatista movement in the southern Mexican state of Chiapas. The Zapatistas are an Indian group who staged an armed rebellion in 1994, demanding equal rights and self-governance for Mexican Indians. The movement won worldwide publicity. It increased awareness, in Mexico and internationally, that although mestizos may dominate their country numerically, other groups also demand a voice in how Mexico defines and develops itself.

Deborah Nathan

SEE ALSO:

Criollos; Díaz, Porfirio; Human Rights in Mexico; Indian Policy; Juárez, Benito; Malinche, La; Rivera, Diego; Sierra, Justo; Zapatistas.

Mexicali, Baja California

Mexicali is one of Mexico's most dynamic and fast-growing cities. It is located in the northwestern corner of the country on the Mexico-U.S. border and is the capital of the northern state of Baja California.

Mexicali lies just across the border from its neighboring city, Calexico, California. The names of both cities are a combination of the words *Mexico* and *California*. Both cities were founded in the first years of the twentieth century as a result of the irrigation works that took place in a vast, largely uninhabited part of the Colorado Desert. Mexicali officially dates from March 14, 1903. Early in the administration of governor Esteban Cantú (1915–1920) it became the capital of the Northern District of Baja California, now the state of Baja California.

Water from the Colorado River has made it possible for Mexicali to flourish despite its natural environment. The city prospered as the commercial center for a growing agricultural community in the Mexicali Valley as a result of investment by the U.S.-based Colorado River Land Company. Cotton became the most important crop. Mexicali's development depended on U.S. investment and interests during the first three decades of the twentieth century. This was mainly due to the isolation of the entire peninsula from the rest of Mexico. It was not until the 1930s that Mexican migrants from other parts of the country began to settle in the area.

Prosperity and growth

During the 1950s the valley experienced its most productive agricultural boom, becoming the third largest cotton-producing region in the country. As a result, the city's population almost tripled from 65,000 to 179,000 during this period. Mexicali was the largest urban center in the state until the 1960s, when it was surpassed by Tijuana.

Despite its strong agricultural beginnings, the city has evolved into a dynamic urban manufacturing center. As the agricultural era began its decline in the 1960s, the first maquiladoras (assembly plants) were built in the region. As elsewhere in the border region, this industry has become an important part

Mexicali has historically had close ties with the United States, partly as a result of its geographical isolation from the rest of Mexico.

of the city's economy, with maquiladoras providing a large percentage of local jobs.

Mexicali suffers from extreme weather. Lying in one of the continent's most hostile desert regions, the city has long, hot summers and short, cold winters. Mexicali is the third largest Mexican border city after Tijuana and Ciudad Juárez, with a population of 765,000. It has become a major educational center in northwestern Mexico, with one of the leading public universities in the country, Universidad Autonoma de Baja California, as well as CETYS Universidad, an equally prestigious private institution. Mexicali is also home to the Cerro Prieto plant, the largest geothermal energy plant in Latin America.

The popular beach resort of San Felipe in the Gulf of California lies 124 miles (198 km) south of Mexicali in the same municipality. Thousands of U.S. tourists make their way through Mexicali every year as they head for San Felipe.

Héctor Manuel Lucero

SEE ALSO:

Baja California; Border Studies; Cantú, Esteban; Colorado River Land Company; Maquiladoras; Mexicali Valley; Twin-Cities Phenomenon.

Mexicali Valley

Located near the U.S. border in the northeastern corner of the Mexican state of Baja California, the Mexicali Valley is part of a vast plain that became one of Mexico's most productive agricultural regions in the twentieth century.

The area now called the Mexicali Valley, named for its largest urban center, the city of Mexicali, was part of the Colorado Desert and largely uninhabited and infertile until the early 1900s. A group of U.S investors, realizing the agricultural potential of the area, formed the California Land Company and began to build an irrigation system. Using the waters of the Colorado River to irrigate the rich soil of the valley, thousands of acres of dry land were transformed into prime farming land, attracting a steady stream of farmers and settlers to the area. The region, which had been divided by the Treaty of Guadalupe Hidalgo in 1848, came to be called the Mexicali Valley to the south of the Mexico-U.S. border and the Imperial Valley to the north. Esteban Cantú, a military commander, took control of the area during the second half of the Mexican Revolution (1910–1920), establishing himself as its de facto governor.

Colorado River Land Company

Early in the twentieth century the Colorado River Land Company (CRLC), formed by investors from the Los Angeles area, acquired the settlement rights for much of the land in the Mexicali Valley. For the following 30 years, the company played a key role in the development of the Mexicali Valley.

World War I (1914–1918) gave the CRLC the opportunity to develop the cultivation of cotton in the valley on a large scale, consolidating the area's agricultural potential. In a few years a series of small settlements appeared along the railroad that ran through the valley, forming a system of rural communities whose activities revolved around the city of Mexicali.

In 1929 the Mexican government decided to end the CRLC's monopoly over the productive lands of the Mexicali Valley. The company had failed to comply with the agreement by which it had originally obtained possession of the land: that it would soon settle Mexicans there. In 1936 President Lázaro Cárdenas (1934–1940) signed an agreement forcing the CRLC to complete settlement of the land by Mexicans within 20 years. The government began a program of expropriating and redistributing the CRLC's land. In 1946 the government purchased all remaining land owned by the CRLC. By then more than half the land owned by the company had already either been sold and distributed or expropriated by the government to create communal landholdings known as *ejidos*.

Regional transformation

The region's new structure of land ownership permanently transformed it. Waves of Mexicans from different regions were attracted to the valley by the promise of extensive land distribution. Since the early 1930s migration to the region had been fueled by laborers brought from the interior to work in the Mexicali cotton fields, and by the thousands of Mexican farmworkers, repatriated from the United States during the Great Depression, who found a permanent home in the region.

In the second half of the twentieth century, patterns of settlement in the Mexicali Valley showed it gradually shifting from being predominantly rural to becoming increasingly urban. In the 1950s half of the valley's population lived in the city of Mexicali, the rest was distributed among the other 166 settlements. By 1970 the city of Mexicali had 66.5 percent of the population, and by 1990 the figure had risen to about 73 percent.

After the 1950s, when the Mexicali Valley experienced its biggest agricultural boom, agricultural production began to decline. As an increasingly urban economy developed, the importance of the agricultural sector fell behind both the industrial and commercial activities of the growing city of Mexicali. However, agriculture and the industries that derive from it remain an intrinsic part of the valley's economy, culture, and way of life.

Héctor Manuel Lucero

SEE ALSO:

Cantú, Esteban; Colorado; Colorado River Land Company; Ejido System; Imperial Valley; Mexicali.

Mexican-American War

The Mexican-American War lasted from May 1846 to February 1848. Its root cause was the United States' annexation of Texas in 1845. Settlers in the area had declared it independent from Mexico nine years earlier, but the Mexican authorities still regarded it as part of their country.
A dispute over the location of the Texas border added to the tension between the United States and Mexico.

The incident that sparked the war was a skirmish between Mexican and U.S. troops that occurred on April 25, 1846. The engagement took place near the disputed southern border of Texas along the Rio Grande when 11 U.S. dragoons were killed. The exact location of the incident has never been clear, and while it is possible that the Mexicans crossed the river, some people doubted the claim of U.S. president James K. Polk (1795–1849) that Mexico "invaded our territory." Among the most prominent skeptics was Abraham Lincoln (1809–1865), who suspected that the incident had taken place on Mexican soil and was the result of a deliberate attempt to start a war.

Mexican president Mariano Paredes y Arrillaga (1797–1849) believed that the United States would be demoralized by internal opposition to a war and spoke grandly of recapturing Texas. The Mexican army of about 32,000 men was well armed, disciplined, and experienced, and it was four to six times larger than the U.S. border force. On May 1 Mexican forces crossed the Rio Grande from Matamoros. They fought and lost at Palo Alto on May 8 and at Resaca de la Palma the next day. The two quick defeats shocked the Mexican leadership, which ordered immediate withdrawal to the south.

Polk signed the official declaration of war on May 13, 1846. U.S. general Zachary Taylor (1784–1850) advanced across the Rio Grande and occupied Matamoros on May 18 but then waited there for several months. Taylor was reluctant to strike out south across the desert until the arrival of the reinforcements he had been promised by the U.S. government. Polk, however, maintained that the army could live off the land.

By August the number of U.S. troops who were stationed near the Rio Grande had increased to 20,000. However, their mortality rate from dysentery was so high that a determined Mexican attack in July or August might have proved decisive.

The Mexicans did not attack because their government was collapsing. Rather than uniting Mexico, the war had given the Federalist faction, which opposed the Mexican president, an opportunity to rebel. There were major uprisings at Acapulco and Guadalajara, and on July 28 Paredes went into hiding. The military garrisons of Veracruz and Mexico City were taken by rebels on August 3 and 4, and the government fell on August 6.

The return of Santa Anna

On August 16 former president General Antonio Lopéz de Santa Anna (1794–1876) returned to Mexico from Cuba, where he had been exiled since 1844. Having promised Polk that he would bring about a settlement of the war, he was allowed to pass through the U.S. naval blockade and land at Veracruz. Soon he regained command of the Mexican army. At this point he reneged on his earlier pledge, and prepared to drive the Americans out of Mexico.

Taylor, meanwhile, attacked Monterrey on the morning of September 21. After a short siege the Mexican general Pedro de Ampudia requested and was granted a truce. On September 25 he was permitted to withdraw his forces from the city, and an eight-week armistice was agreed. Polk rebuked Taylor for agreeing to cease hostilities, and the general therefore informed Santa Anna that the armistice would be terminated early. On November 16 Taylor occupied Saltillo.

In January 1847 Santa Anna's army moved north to confront Taylor. The two forces met on February 22 at Buena Vista, where Taylor's troops won a hard-fought victory. There was no further fighting in northern Mexico. By this time the area today covered by California and New Mexico had also been subdued, largely because of the efforts of U.S. general Stephen Watts Kearney. The final victory in Kearney's campaign came on January 9 at the Battle of the Mesa, after which he occupied Los Angeles.

This contemporary lithograph shows Mexican and U.S soldiers clashing at the Battle of Resaca de la Palma in May 1846. The battle was one of the first encounters of the Mexican-American War. The U.S. forces, under the command of Zachary Taylor, won an emphatic victory.

While Taylor was fighting Santa Anna at Buena Vista, another U.S. general, Winfield Scott (1786–1866), was preparing an amphibious assault on Mexico from the east. His troops landed near Veracruz on March 27, capturing the port shortly afterward with a minimum number of casualties. After his defeat at Buena Vista, Santa Anna moved south to meet Scott's troops at the mountain pass of Cerro Gordo, where he established a strong position. Although they were outnumbered, the U.S. troops managed to inflict a heavy defeat on Santa Anna's forces. About 1,000 Mexicans died in the battle, compared to only 63 U.S. troops.

On May 15 U.S. forces moved on to Puebla, where they routed about 2,000 Mexican cavalry. During June and July 1847 Santa Anna prepared to defend Mexico City. On August 7 Scott began his advance from Puebla, following an unprotected route to the south of Lake Chalco. Santa Anna eventually fell back about 5 miles (8 km) to Churubusco, where he took up a defensive position in a fortified convent. Advancing under fire on August 20, Scott's men forced the convent's surrender, although Santa Anna and much of his command escaped.

Scott might have moved straight into the capital, but instead on August 24 he granted an armistice to permit the negotiation of a peace treaty. Santa Anna used the time to muster his forces and prepare a last defense of the capital. Fighting was renewed on September 7 at Molino del Rey. The final battle for Mexico City was fought on the fortified hill of Chapultepec. An American artillery bombardment on September 12 was followed the next day by a decisive infantry assault. The U.S. Army entered Mexico City that afternoon.

The war was formally concluded by the Treaty of Guadalupe Hidalgo, signed on February 2, 1848. Mexico renounced all claims to Texas above the Rio Grande, and ceded much of the present-day Southwest to the United States. In return the United States paid Mexico U.S. $15 million and took over more than U.S. $3 million worth of claims by U.S. citizens against Mexico.

George Lewis

SEE ALSO:

Buena Vista, Battle of; Cerro Gordo, Battle of; Guadalupe Hidalgo, Treaty of; Niños Héroes; Polk, James; Santa Anna, Antonio López de; Scott, Winfield; Taylor, Zachary.

Mexican Communities in the United States

An estimated one sixth of the 120 million people who comprise the population of Mexico are resident in the United States. These numbers do not include Mexican Americans, but only those who identify Mexico as their country of birth: first-generation immigrants.

It is common for native-born Mexicans to maintain a close affinity to their country of origin. The last decade of the twentieth century saw many new immigrants from Mexico settle in areas of the United States that had previously not had appreciable numbers of Mexican residents. Mexican communities are now found in all the U.S. states and territories. Particular concentrations are along the Mexico–U.S. border, especially in California.

Mexican American population figures

The 2000 U.S. census registered the total U.S. population at 281,421,906. The Hispanic population count was 35,305,000, representing an increase of 12,951,759, or 57.9 percent, over the previous decade. The Hispanic population accounted for 12.5 percent of the total population.

The increase included 7,144,773 persons listing Mexico as their country of origin. The Mexican population continued to be the largest of the Hispanic subgroups, although the percentage of the total diminished by 1.9 percent in that decade. In 1990 the Mexican subgroup accounted for 60.4 percent of the Hispanic population, while in 2000 the proportion was 58.5 percent.

Immigration from Mexico

Experts who trace immigration patterns indicate that the number of towns (*municipios*) in Mexico registering zero migration to the United States is now as low as 93. Thus, 2,350 municipalities in Mexico, or 96.2 percent, have families with relatives in the United States. Of these, 461 municipalities report high and very high migration; 408 register medium to high migration; and 1,481 towns show low or very low migration. As with the dispersion of the Mexican newcomers to the United States, the sending regions (regions from which the immigrants originate) have also increasingly diversified. However, the states with established migration patterns to the United States continued to be the main places from which Mexicans immigrated. Zacatecas, Jalisco, Michoacán, Guanajuato, and Durango are states in which more than half of the towns register high or very high rates of migration *al otro lado* (to the other side).

Another part of Mexico that saw considerable migration to the United States was the metropolitan area of the Valley of Mexico, which includes the towns in the southern part of the state of Mexico and Morelos. Other regions in this category include the northern area of Guerrero, the southeastern part of Puebla, and the Mixtec area of Oaxaca, Guerrero, and Puebla. Two other southern Mexico areas that increased their migration to the United States notably in the past decade were central Oaxaca and south-central Veracruz.

Sending money back home to Mexico

An important feature of Mexican communities in the United States, especially those with recent immigrants, is their relationship to their families in their region of origin. One of these relationships is financial. Between 1992 and 2000, the number of homes receiving funds from relatives in the United States doubled, from just over 600,000 to 1,252,000. In particular, the economic crisis in Mexico in 1995 helped increase the number of family members going *al norte* (north) in search of work. The number of homes receiving funds in 1994 was 600,000, and by 1996 this number had increased to 1,076,000. The Banco de México has provided figures indicating that between 1990 and 2000, Mexican families received around U.S. $45 billion from relatives in the United States. In the year 2000 alone, U.S. $6.5 billion entered Mexico.

Economists divide family members who send funds to Mexico into two groups, though the members are not necessarily exclusive of each other. One group consists of heads of the household, who come to the United States for part of the year or settle permanently, establishing residence. In this group one spouse, generally the mother, is left with young children in Mexico, although sometimes both parents go to the United States, leaving their young children in the care of grandparents or other relatives. The children may later join them. The members of this group are usually determined to face the challenges of the journey and of finding work once out of Mexico.

The second economic group is composed of family members who have been in the United States longer, perhaps sons or daughters, or other family members, who have been living in the country for years. Grandchildren born in the United States fall into this second category. The group with longer residency in the United States often helps older relatives in Mexico, possibly because those relatives may no longer be able to work or may have been widowed.

Funds received from the United States are used primarily to cover basic necessities, and to a lesser extent are used for improving the quality of life for the families, such as repairing or improving family homes. However, 40 percent of these Mexican homes are wholly dependent on funds from the United States for day-to-day expenses.

The total amount sent to Mexico is impressive—some U.S. $17 million a day, although 75 percent of the funds go to only 100 municipalities, with most of these being in the states of Guanajuato, Zacatecas, and Michoacán. The average amount received is U.S. $250 a month, and 85 percent of these funds are used for basic needs.

Hometown associations

Voluntary associations of same-country immigrants are a common occurrence throughout history and across the world. There are records of their existence in Mexican communities in the United States that date from the 1910s. These associations are mutual aid societies, pooling funds for burials or natural disasters, such as floods, and organizing celebrations for Mexican holidays. Even in those early days these clubs were also aware of their potential political power on both sides of the border.

For example, in 1938 hometown associations sent money to Mexican president Lázaro Cardenas (1934–1940) to support his expropriation of the oil industry. Another good example is from the 1930s and 1940s when a small southwestern town in

Texas, called Sanderson, had a population of 1,500, two-thirds of which were either Mexican or Mexican American. The town had two clubs composed of men born in Mexico: El Club Civico Patriótico and El Club Atlético Católico. In addition, there was a third club, El Club México Tejano, whose membership was Mexican American men with Texas ancestry predating the Mexican-American War (1846–1848). Each club had its own identity; the Patriótico made sure all the Mexican holidays were properly observed, and the Atlético Católico organized the big pageants for Easter Week and Christmas. All three had baseball teams that played against each other. In times of economic crises or when faced with racial discrimination, all of the clubs would join forces.

Today hometown associations are composed of members from the same hometown or home state in Mexico. In 2000 more than 400 were registered with Mexican consulates across the United States, and there were many that were not counted in those rosters. Large cities have numerous clubs of this sort. In 1997 Los Angeles had 170 of these associations. This count included 51 clubs from towns in Zacatecas, 49 from Jalisco, 11 from Michoacán, 11 from Sinaloa, nine from Nayarit, eight from Oaxaca, five from Puebla, four from Durango, one each from Guanajuato and Guerrero, and 20 from towns in other states. The clubs from Jalisco, Zacatecas, Sinaloa, Durango, Nayarit, and Oaxaca have formed statewide federations.

Association leaders

The leaders of these hometown associations in most cases are first generation immigrants who have been in the United States for a least one or two decades. They are usually individuals who have reached a certain level of economic security. In the cities members could be owners or managers of businesses, such as restaurants, supermarkets, insurance companies, or car dealerships. Typically leaders who live in small towns or rural areas may include owners of ranches and farms. A growing number of the younger leaders, who arrived in the United States when they were children or teenagers, now hold professional positions: lawyers, teachers, dentists, doctors. An important feature of this group is that most have obtained their economic stability through their jobs.

Over time the hometown associations have enhanced their agendas and strengthened their

People of Mexican Origin by U.S. State, 1990 and 2000

Mexican Population Rank	State	2000 Mexican total	2000 Mexican percent	1990 Mexican total	1990 Mexican percent
1	California	8,455,926	25	6,118,996	21
2	Texas	5,071,963	24	3,890,820	23
3	Illinois	1,144,390	9	623,688	5
4	Arizona	1,065,578	21	616,195	17
5	Colorado	450,760	10	282,478	9
6	Florida	363,925	2	161,499	1
7	New Mexico	330,049	18	328,836	22
8	Washington	329,934	6	155,864	3
9	Nevada	285,764	14	85,287	7
10	Georgia	275,288	3	49,182	1
11	New York	260,889	1	260,889	1
12	North Carolina	246,545	3	246,545	0
13	Michigan	220,769	2	220,769	1
14	Oregon	214,662	6	214,662	3
15	Indiana	153,042	3	153,042	1
16	Kansas	148,270	6	148,270	3
17	Utah	136,416	6	56,842	3
18	Oklahoma	132,816	4	63,226	2
19	Wisconsin	126,719	2	57,615	1
20	New Jersey	102,929	1	57,615	0
21	Minnesota	95,613	2	34,691	1
22	Ohio	90,663	1	57,815	1
23	Idaho	79,324	6	43,213	4
24	Missouri	77,887	1	38,274	1
25	Tennessee	77,372	1	13,879	0
26	Virginia	73,979	1	33,044	1
27	Nebraska	71,030	4	29,665	2
28	Arkansas	61,204	2	12,496	1
29	Iowa	61,154	2	24,386	1
30	Pennsylvania	55,154	0	24,220	0
31	South Carolina	52,871	1	11,028	0
32	Alabama	44,522	1	9,509	0
33	Maryland	39,900	1	18,434	0
34	Louisiana	32,267	1	23,452	1
35	Kentucky	31,385	1	8,692	0
36	Connecticut	23,484	1	8,393	0
37	Massachusetts	22,288	0	12,703	0
38	Mississippi	21,616	1	6,718	0
39	Wyoming	19.963	4	18,730	4
40	Hawaii	19,820	2	14,367	1
41	Alaska	13,334	2	9,321	2
42	Delaware	12,986	2	3,083	0
43	Montana	11,735	1	8,362	1
44	South Dakota	6,364	1	3,438	0
45	Rhode Island	5,881	1	2,437	0
46	District of Columbia	5,098	1	2,981	0
47	New Hampshire	4,590	0	2,362	0
48	West Virginia	4,347	0	2,810	0
49	North Dakota	4,295	1	2,878	0
50	Maine	2,756	0	2,153	0
51	Vermont	1,174	0	725	0

power. From the onset these groups were mutual aid societies, maintainers of the traditional hometown holidays, and sponsors of athletic teams. They also fought against ethnic and language discrimination aimed at people of Mexican origin. Further, through these groups the members maintained visibility in Mexico, with occasional involvement in the politics of their sending towns or of the nation itself. Their efforts were initially felt only locally. By the end of the twentieth century, however, these associations had become formidable economic and political forces on both sides of the border. No longer limited to activities such as repairing the hometown church and sending deceased family members home for burial, these groups now raised money in the United States for major improvements such as building schools, community halls, clinics, and sports fields or drilling wells, installing drinking water systems, and paving roads.

Economic and political activities

The economic strength of the Mexican communities in the United States and the political strength of their numbers have increased the importance of the Mexican hometown associations to the governments of both countries. In Mexico, the municipal, state, and federal governments have begun courting these hometown associations, taking an interest in the investment of the collective funds they are sending to their home country. In 2001 both the World Bank and Banco Interamericano de Desarrollo (BID) held conferences in Washington, D.C., to suggest ways of using these funds for national development in Mexico. There is an effort to promote projects that would not only improve the infrastructure of the localities receiving these funds, but also to change the economics of local structures, developing projects that would create jobs and thus stem the flow of people leaving the country.

In the United States these associations have turned to political activism during campaigns against legal initiatives that would turn back the clock on rights and services for the immigrant communities. A good example is the case of Proposition 187 of California. In 1994 Californians were asked to to vote for Proposition 187, which authorized excluding undocumented students from public schools and denying medical services to those families. The hometown association from Mexico joined immigrant's rights groups in education campaigns and in massive demonstrations denouncing the proposed initiative.

The law passed nevertheless and was seen as a statement of anti-immigrant sentiment among the California voters at the time. The negative sentiment was particularly aimed at immigrants from Mexico and Central America. An indirect consequence of the new law was that Mexican immigrants recognized the need to become U.S. citizens and participate in elections at all levels. The notorious law was subsequently overturned in the courts, and California gained hundreds of new Mexican-origin voters.

The associations also have important political influence in Mexico. Chicago and Los Angeles are now regular stops for all candidates for the national presidency of Mexico. Both of these cities have more Zacatecans than does Ciudad Zacatecas, the capital of that state. Other cities with large Mexican communities are also courted by candidates running for office in Mexico. In 1996 laws were approved by the Mexican Congress that permit retention of Mexican nationality upon becoming naturalized in the United States and allow the recovery of Mexican nationality by children born in the United States of Mexicans living in the United States. The interest of these communities to become binational agents in the political process of the two countries is frequently very effectively channeled through these important organizations.

Indigenous Mexicans in the United States

Many Mexican communities in the United States are made up of indigenous populations from Mexico. Often these indigenous migrants are attracted by the possibility of finding secure work on ranches or farms around the border area or working in the service sector in cities such as Los Angeles and Chicago. The largest numbers of indigenous Mexicans in the United States are from Oaxaca, Michoacán, and the Central Valley of Mexico. Estimates place some 250,000 Oaxaqueños in Los Angeles County alone, while the total count is close to half a million for the the United States. The indigenous community from Oaxaca that has settled in Los Angeles is primarily Zapotecs from the Sierra Norte and from the central valleys of that state in southeastern Mexico. The Chicago area has large numbers from the Mixtec sending region.

These Mexican communities have also formed hometown associations with functions that are very

People of Mexican Origin, Selected U.S. Cities, Year 2000

Mexican Population Rank	City	State	Total Population	Total Mexican
1	Los Angeles	CA	3,694,820	1,091,686
2	Chicago	IL	2,896,016	530,462
3	Houston	TX	1,953,631	527,442
4	San Antonio	TX	1,144,646	473,420
5	Phoenix	AZ	1,321,045	375,096
6	El Paso	TX	563,662	359,699
7	Dallas	TX	1,188,580	350,491
8	San Diego	CA	1,223,400	259,213
9	Santa Ana	CA	337,977	221,719
10	San José	CA	894,943	221,148
11	New York City	NY	8,008,278	186,872
12	Austin	TX	656,562	153,868
13	Tucson	AZ	486,669	145,234
14	Fresno	CA	427,652	144,772
15	Laredo	TX	176,576	133,185
16	Ft. Worth	TX	534,694	132,894
17	Long Beach	CA	461,522	127,129
18	Anaheim	CA	328,014	126,017
19	Denver	CO	554,636	120,664
20	East Los Angeles CDP	CA	124,283	104,223
21	Brownsville	TX	139,722	103,297
22	Oxnard	CA	170,358	101,264

similar to those of their mestizo compatriots. However, linguistic and human rights tend to be more explicit in their political projects. Often the indigenous groups do not speak Spanish fluently, in addition to not speaking English, so upon arriving in the United States they face even greater challenges than Spanish-speaking immigrants.

For instance, in many cities and towns where there has been a Spanish-speaking Mexican immigrant community for several decades, the school and health systems may have Spanish-English translation assistance. On the other hand, it is less likely that there will be interpreters for Zapotec-English or Mixtec-English, although many of these groups have begun to arrive in the United States in large numbers. The indigenous groups are very aware of the importance of their native identity. As these families settle into their new towns they often express the desire to maintain their traditional indigenous roots and culture. Their community organizations endeavor to preserve their traditions and overtly support the maintenance of their indigenous languages. The stated goal for these families is to be trilingual, adding Spanish and English to their first languages.

Transnationalism of Mexican communities

The Mexican communities in the United States have the potential to achieve a truly transnational identity. It is now much easier than it was in previous periods for first-generation immigrants to travel to and from Mexico, even though their American communities may be farther away from the Mexican border.

The economic and political power of Mexican American communities allows them access to the governments of both countries. Collective ties are continually being enhanced by philanthropic projects, binational festivals, sports tournaments, and even shared community publications. The children of these immigrants, many born in the United States, are shaping the world views, languages, and identity of both Mexico and the United States. Both neighboring countries have much to gain from the invaluable economic and, most especially, cultural contribution of the Mexican communities in the United States.

Concepción M. Valadez

SEE ALSO:

Bilingual Education; California; Hispanic Americans; Illegal Labor; Immigration, Mexican; Mixtecs; Proposition 187; Zapotecs.

Mexican Independence

Mexico's Wars of Independence were sparked in 1810 by a revolt in the Bajío region of Mexico, then the Spanish colony of New Spain. Led by a priest named Miguel Hidalgo y Costilla, the revolt spread across the country. Eleven years of warfare followed, culminating in Mexico's independence from Spain in 1821.

The movement for Mexican independence was influenced by events outside the country, including U.S. independence in the late eighteenth century. In 1808 the French emperor, Napoleon, invaded Spain, deposing King Ferdinand VII and appointing his own brother Joseph Bonaparte as ruler. The Spanish revolted and promulgated a liberal constitution in the king's name in 1812, incorporating many ideas from the U.S. and French constitutions, such as the idea of a representative government.

The turbulence in Napoleonic Europe left a power vacuum in the Spanish colonies, and confusion grew as to who was to rule them. Instability increased when a group of *peninsulares* (European-born Spaniards) led a coup against the viceroy, José de Iturrigaray, in September 1808. Fearing a foreign invasion and suspicious of the *peninsulares*, the *criollos* (Mexicans of Spanish descent) organized themselves under the guise of literary societies in which they discussed radical political ideas, including New Spain's independence.

Hidalgo's revolt

An active member of the literary society in Querétaro was Miguel Hidalgo (1753–1811), the parish priest of the small village of Dolores in the present-day state of Hidalgo. There he met Ignacio Allende, a cavalry captain and revolutionary thinker. Allende introduced him to another soldier, Juan de Aldama; Miguel Domínguez, a former *corregidor* of Querétaro; his wife Josefa Ortiz de Domínguez, better known as La Corregidora; Epigmenio González; and Marino Galván. Allende and Hidalgo planned an uprising for December 1810, but Galván betrayed them to the Spanish authorities. The Spanish found arms in Epigmenio's house and ordered the arrest of the conspirators, but La

Corregidora warned Hidalgo, who decided to launch an uprising for independence immediately.

On the morning of September 16 Hidalgo rang the church bells in Dolores and promulgated *El Grito* (The Call to Arms), an appeal for an end to rule by the *peninsulares*, the introduction of land reforms, and equality for all Mexicans. His band of Indians and mestizos (people of mixed Spanish and Indian ancestry) set out for San Miguel, poorly armed and with little organization. When they stopped in Atotonilco, Hidalgo adopted the symbol of the Virgin of Guadalupe as the emblem of the crusade, urging the insurgents to fight in her name. Thousands of recruits joined along the way.

On September 28 the rebels arrived at the wealthy mining city of Guanajuato. The city's residents decided to resist the insurgents and opened fire on them, killing hundreds. The insurgents attacked the *alhóndiga de granaditas*, a local granary in which many Spanish and *criollo* citizens had barricaded themselves, and killed everyone inside. The undisciplined rebels then went on to pillage the city. Although this was a victory for the rebels, many were shocked at the atrocities directed against the *criollos* and Spanish, and switched to support the royalist side. Meanwhile, Hidalgo and Allende divided the army in two, and within a month had conquered Zacatecas, San Luis Potosí, and Valladolid. By the end of October 1810 around 80,000 marched with Hidalgo on Mexico City to defeat the Spanish troops at Monte de las Cruces. For reasons that remain unclear, Hildalgo did not press his advantage and occupy the capital.

Royalist successes

The royalists, led by the newly appointed Spanish viceroy Francisco Venegas and military commander Félix Calleja, took some weeks to respond effectively to the uprisings. However, in January 1811 rebel forces were routed in a serious defeat at Puente de Calderón outside Guadalajara. The insurgents had the advantage of large numbers and strong conviction, but they were no match for the better trained and equipped royalists. Hidalgo and Allende turned toward the northern provinces to regroup their forces. The royalists moved north to

The words of a corrido (Mexican ballad) called "100 años despues" (100 years later) celebrate a hundred years of Mexican independence, with a picture of Miguel Hildalgo below the title.

crush resistance, and uprisings were confined to Coahuila and Texas (then part of Mexico). On March 21, 1811, Allende, Hidalgo, and others were ambushed in Coahuila. They were taken to Chihuahua, where Allende and the other nonclerics were immediately executed as traitors. Hidalgo was tried by the Inquisition and found guilty of heresy and treason. He was defrocked and executed on July 30.

The movement under Morelos

After Hidalgo's death the rebel leadership was assumed by Hidalgo's commander in the south, the mestizo parish priest José María Morelos y Pavón (1765–1815). Morelos trained a small but effective army in guerrilla tactics. By spring 1813 the insurgents had almost completely encircled Mexico City. With confidence inspired by military successes, Morelos called a congress to meet in Chilpancingo to discuss plans for the nation. The congress formally declared independence and agreed on a series of principles to be incorporated into a new constitution, which was later drafted at Apatzingán. Among the 23 principles were the abolition of slavery and the caste system. However, while

delegates discussed these issues, General Calleja began a new military offensive. In the fall of 1815 Morelos was captured, tried, and executed on December 22.

After Morelos's death the movement split into various independent guerrilla forces operating without any central coordination. The two most effective leaders were Guadalupe Victoria in Puebla and Veracruz, and Vicente Guerrero in Oaxaca. Over the next five years, the situation reached stalemate: the guerrillas were unable to capture any major cities, and the royalists were unable to clear the countryside of the rebels.

In the end, independence came about after a rebellion in Spain in 1820 forced the king to restore elements of the liberal 1812 Constitution. When conservative *criollos* heard this news, many decided to support the independence movement to prevent the introduction of liberal reforms in Mexico. Among them was a royalist commander, Agustín de Iturbide. He formed an alliance with the guerrilla leader Vicente Guerrero to bring about independence. On February 24, 1821, they issued the Plan de Iguala, which proclaimed the Three Guarantees: independence, equality of all Mexicans, and preservation of the Catholic faith. Their forces would merge in the Army of the Three Guarantees. Mexico was to be an independent nation with a limited constitutional monarchy. The Spanish royal family, the Bourbons, had first right to the throne, but if they declined, an emperor would be elected.

With these measures, Iturbide gradually gained control of the whole country except Mexico City, Veracruz, and Acapulco. On August 24, 1821, Juan O'Donojú, the newly appointed Spanish viceroy, signed the Treaty of Córdoba recognizing Mexico as a sovereign and independent nation. A month later the Army of the Three Guarantees marched into Mexico City, and Iturbide chose a governing junta dominated by conservatives that formally declared independence. Iturbide was proclaimed emperor and the congress was dissolved in 1822. The United States reluctantly recognized Mexican independence in 1823. Later that year Washington issued the Monroe Doctrine, a statement of U.S. territorial ambitions in the Americas.

Susana Berruecos García Travesí

SEE ALSO:

Constitutions, Mexican; Guerrero, Vicente; Hidalgo y Costilla, Miguel; Iturbide, Agustín de; Morelos y Pavón, José María; Spanish Empire.

Mexican Revolution

The Mexican Revolution was a period of civil war and social transformation that is generally seen as lasting between 1910 and 1920. It was a time of bloodshed and constant upheaval. A number of revolutionary leaders rose to power only to be challenged and overthrown themselves.

By the beginning of the twentieth century people from many different parts of Mexican society were beginning to express dissatisfaction with the repressive government of General Porfirio Díaz (1830–1915). Díaz had held the presidency since 1877, with the exception of a single term spent out of office between 1880 and 1884. The continuous reelection of Díaz, ensured by his control of the electoral process, caused political discontent among both a rising urban middle class and the rural poor. Although Mexico had experienced considerable

economic growth under the Díaz regime, very few people had benefited from the influx of wealth into the country, and a large number of Mexicans were living in miserable conditions. In 1908 the situation was made worse by a famine that struck the northern states of the country particularly badly.

Rise of Madero

In 1908 opponents of Díaz were given encouragement when the president declared in an interview that the Mexican political system needed to be invigorated by the inclusion of new political parties. Díaz also hinted that he would not run in the 1910 presidential election. Díaz's declaration inspired the publication of the book *La sucesión presidencial en 1910* (The presidential succession in 1910). The book's author was Francisco I. Madero (1873–1913), a wealthy landowner with an interest in politics. Despite his background, Madero held liberal political views and was deeply concerned

Pancho Villa (front center, with black mustache) with a band of his soldiers. Villa provided much of the military force behind Francisco Madero's ascension to the Mexican presidency in 1911. His capture of the city of Ciudad Juárez signaled the end of Díaz's regime.

about both the widespread poverty within Mexico and the undemocratic nature of its political system. Madero also argued that a political party should be created to participate in the presidential elections of 1910. He proposed a political compromise by which Díaz would keep the presidency while Madero took the position of vice-president. From there he would oversee a reform process.

Madero's ideas found support in a wide cross section of Mexican society. Among the people opposed to Díaz's presidency were industrial workers angry at the low wages and poor working conditions imposed by foreign firms, regional politicians opposed to the centralization of power under Díaz, and middle-class liberals who objected to the lack of democracy in the political process. There was also considerable opposition among poor peasants who had lost land during Díaz's presidency.

Buoyed by messages of support, Madero founded the Centro Anti-reeleccionista de México (Mexican Anti-reelectionist Center). The organization's motto was "sufragio efectivo, no reelección" (effective suffrage, no reelection). In the summer of 1909 Madero began to travel across the country to spread his organization's message.

Initially the government greeted Madero's movement with skepticism. However, by the time that Madero made his second trip across the country in December, Díaz had begun to view him as a serious challenge. Madero's position had also changed. His goal was no longer that of electing a vice-president to accompany Díaz. He was convinced of the necessity of changing the entire executive office.

Madero runs for the presidency

Shortly after a third trip, a convention was held on April 15, 1910, to create the Partido Nacional Anti-reeleccionista (National Anti-reelectionist Party). Madero was overwhelmingly elected as the party's candidate to contend for the presidency.

Support for Madero increased strongly in the following months. A few days before the election, however, Madero decided to make one final campaign trip. While in the city of Monterrey he was taken into custody and imprisoned, almost certainly on the orders of Díaz. Madero was accused of inciting a rebellion against the government. He was later moved to a prison in the city of San Luis Potosí in central Mexico, where he awaited the results of the presidential election. Even though

Madero earned more votes than his opponent, Díaz was declared the winner.

Thanks to the influence of powerful friends, Madero was allowed to move around the city of San Luis Potosí by day, although his movements were closely monitored. On October 4, 1910, however, he managed to escape his captors. Three days later Madero crossed the U.S. border. From the safety of the United States he issued the Plan de San Luis Potosí (San Luis Potosí Plan), which denounced the election results as fraudulent and called for an armed insurrection against the Díaz regime.

Madero's first attempts at armed insurgency were a failure. When he crossed the border on November 19, the day before the revolt was supposed to begin, Madero was met only by a handful of supporters and was forced to return across the border. Elsewhere, however, local leaders were taking matters into their own hands. On November 21, the northern bandit leader Francisco "Pancho" Villa (1878–1923) captured the city of San Andrés. In Chihuahua, Pascual Orozco, Jr., took command of a group of several hundred men and attacked a federal garrison. Other local leaders began revolts in Veracruz, Tlaxcala, and Guerrero. Later Emiliano Zapata (1879–1919) led a peasant rebellion in the the south of the country.

The fall of Díaz

The Díaz regime soon began to show signs of weakness, as federal troops were not able to control the revolts that were springing up throughout the country. A key moment in the struggle came on May 10, 1911, when forces led by Villa and Orozco took Ciudad Juárez, acting directly against the orders of Madero. The city's fall marked the beginning of the end of Díaz's regime. On May 21, Díaz resigned as president. In return, he was permitted to leave the country. On June 7, Madero entered Mexico City in triumph.

On Díaz's resignation, Francisco Leon de la Barra temporarily assumed the presidency. De la Barra had been secretary of foreign affairs under Díaz. His principal task was to supervise a fresh election. Madero soon dissolved his party and created a new one, the Partido Constitucional Progresista (PCP; Progressive Constitutional Party). Madero became its presidential candidate, while Jose Maria Pino Suarez ran for the vice-presidency. The party subsequently won the new election, which was held in October of 1911.

Madero's government faced many challenges. Although he had been elected by an overwhelming majority, Madero had been reliant on support from diverse sectors of Mexican society, each with different goals, interests, and expectations. Now all these groups expected their demands to be met by the new regime. To a large extent, Madero found himself isolated. He still faced enemies on the right, from among the conservative supporters of the old Díaz regime. On the other hand, many of the people who had taken part in the revolution were impatient for change and were not prepared to wait long for their grievances to be resolved.

Unleashing the tiger

On leaving the country, Díaz is alleged to have said: "Madero has unleashed a tiger. Now let us see if he can control it." The comment proved to be an accurate prophecy of the difficulties that Madero would face. After the fall of Díaz, Madero demanded that all rebel forces should demobilize. Emiliano Zapata, however, refused to dissolve his troops until the land distribution that was promised in the San Luis Potosí Plan was carried out. He responded to Madero's presidency by issuing the Plan de Ayala (Ayala Plan) on November 28, 1911.

In the document Zapata refused to recognize Madero as president of Mexico and demanded the return of all peasant land seized illegally during the presidency of Díaz. The plan found support among rural communities across Mexico.

The new government faced opposition from other quarters as well. Bernardo Reyes, a supporter of Díaz who had stood against Madero in the 1911 election before fleeing to the United States, returned to lead an armed uprising. In the spring of 1912, meanwhile, Madero's former ally Emiliano Vazquez Gomez began a revolt in Ciudad Juárez. Pascual Orozco was commissioned by Madero to fight against the rebels but soon turned against the government. In October, Felix Díaz (1868–1945), the nephew of the former president, launched a rebellion in Veracruz.

The federal army was able to subdue all the uprisings but by the end of 1912 Madero's government was politically weak. In addition to the armed rebellions, Madero had to face constant criticism from the press, which undermined his standing with the public at large. More and more sections of Mexican society, which had generally not supported the initial rebellions, began to grow discontented with Madero's policies.

Henry Lane Wilson

Among the many enemies the government of Francisco I. Madero faced during its 15-month duration, U.S. ambassador to Mexico Henry Lane Wilson (1857–1932) proved to be one of its most dangerous. Many of Wilson's actions were never officially approved by the U.S. government, which for the most part demonstrated support for Madero's administration.

Wilson was appointed ambassador to Mexico in 1909. Closely allied to U.S. business interests in Mexico, Wilson was a natural supporter of the regime of Porfirio Díaz. He was thus suspicious of Madero from the very start of his presidency. Wilson's feelings of antipathy for Madero and his government only grew as time progressed. In his communications with the U.S. State Department, Wilson attempted to portray Mexico as a country in a state of anarchy. He constantly exaggerated the problems experienced by U.S. citizens. The

tone of the messages made even President William H. Taft doubt their veracity.

From February 1913 onward Wilson participated directly in attempts to overthrow Madero. To begin with, he pressurized the Spanish ambassador to try to persuade Madero to resign. When this failed he arranged for a meeting to take place between Madero's general Victoriano Huerta and the conservative politician Felix Díaz. Wilson drew up a pact by which the pair agreed to remove Madero from office and then share power between them. It was signed in the U.S. embassy. In the end Huerta betrayed both Díaz and Madero.

Wilson's efforts to attain official recognition from the United States for Huerta's government proved unsuccessful. In July 1913 the newly elected President Woodrow Wilson appointed a new ambassador.

This contemporary broadside (handbill) was published to celebrate the victory of Francisco Madero's forces in the Mexican Revolution. The text describes Madero's triumphant march into Mexico City.

Madero's liberal ideals prevented him from executing his political enemies and his principles soon cost him dearly. On February 9, 1913, generals Manuel Mondragon and Gregorio Ruiz set free Bernardo Reyes and Felix Díaz, who were being held in prison after their unsuccessful attempts at rebellion. The rebel forces attacked the National Palace and a period of intense hand-to-hand fighting followed, which became known as the Decena Tragica (the Tragic Ten Days).

U.S. intervention

The federal forces were led by Victoriano Huerta, who had ambitions of his own. Throughout the uprising the U.S. ambassador Henry Lane Wilson remained in contact with both Díaz and Huerta, trying to broker an agreement by which Madero would be removed from office. His hopes were fulfilled on February 18 when Huerta betrayed his president, sending troops into the National Palace to arrest Madero. Madero resigned on condition that he and his family be allowed to leave the country. However, four days later both Madero and his vice-president, Pino Suarez, were dead, murdered while being transferred between prisons.

By the time of Madero's death, Huerta was already the new president. Upon Madero's resignation, Huerta had called for a general assembly of congress, which had proceeded to accept the resignation and name the minister of foreign affairs, Pedro Lascurain, as interim president. Lascurain held the post for a mere 45 minutes, during which time he named Huerta as minister of the interior. Once this was done he offered his own resignation, thus paving the way for Huerta to legitimately claim the presidency. A fraudulent general election confirmed Huerta's position.

Huerta's presidency

In the early months of his brief presidency Huerta made attempts to answer the grievances of the trade union movement, giving unions the right to strike.

He also distributed a small amount of land to the rural poor. However, Huerta had inherited a country beset by huge problems. The military conflicts of the past few years had left much of the country devastated, a situation that led to severe food shortages. There were high levels of unemployment in industrialized areas, while the fact that Huerta's government was not recognized internationally made it difficult for the country to acquire loans from abroad.

In these circumstances, a broad-based military movement arose to oppose Huerta in the spring of 1913. At its head was Venustiano Carranza (1859-1920), the governor of the state of Coahuila. Another important figure in the movement was Álvaro Obregón (1880–1928), the mayor of the town of Huatabampo, Sonora. Carranza's forces were known as the Ejercito Constitucionalista (Constitutional Army) because of the movement's

Emiliano Zapata (right) pictured with one of his supporters. Zapata's call for land reform drew support from the rural communities in states such as Guerrero and Morelos.

aspiration to restore the constitutional order violated by Huerta. Other military uprisings against Huerta occurred under Villa in Chihuahua and Zapata in Morelos.

Faced by such challenges, Huerta's presidency became more dictatorial in nature. He suspended congress and ordered the murder of several political rivals. The worsening situation in Mexico alarmed politicians in the United States, and U.S. president Woodrow Wilson offered support to Carranza, first by ordering U.S. companies to suspend payments to the government, then by allowing guns to be sold to the rebel forces. Finally, on April 21, a large U.S. force landed at Veracruz. The U.S. occupation of the port deprived Huerta's government of customs duties. Huerta resigned the presidency three months later. In August, 1914, Obregón and Carranza entered Mexico City.

As long as the main objective of the movement was the removal of Huerta, Carranza was able to maintain unity among the different factions under his control. However, once Huerta had resigned the movement began to fall apart. The main military leaders met in a convention in the city of Aguascalientes in October 1914. Its purpose was to elect a new government and define the future direction of Mexico. By this point, however, a mutual hatred had grown up between Villa and Carranza, and this personal rivalry made the creation of a successful coalition government impossible.

The various parties at the convention eventually decided that Eulalio Gonzalez should serve as an interim president. Carranza refused to recognize the government, and responded by immediately establishing his own government in the port of Veracruz. Villa and Zapata supported the new president. Obregón remained loyal to Carranza.

Civil War

Over the next few months Carranza established himself across the center of the country, while Villa and Zapata created strongholds in the north and the southwest respectively. Eventually, in the spring of 1915, Obregón and Villa, the two outstanding military leaders of the Ejercito Constitucionalista, met on Mexico's central plateau. Villa's forces began by gaining important victories. Slowly but surely, however, Obregón recovered ground. He defeated Villa at the battles of Celaya and Leon, both in the central state of Guanajuato. The defeats cost Villa many men and large quantities of ammunition.

Obregón then inflicted a decisive defeat on Villa at Aguascalientes. After Obregón's overwhelming victory, the Gonzalez government was dissolved and Venustiano Carranza became president.

In October 1915 Carranza moved his government from Veracruz to Mexico City, where it was soon given formal recognition by that of the United States. Villa, meanwhile, retreated to the extreme north of Sonora with the remnants of his army, living the life of an outlaw. Angered by U.S. president Wilson's support of Carranza he began to carry out raids across the border. In one raid in March 1916 on the town of Columbus, New Mexico, 18 U.S. citizens were killed. The raid prompted the Pershing Expedition, a punative expedition carried out by U.S. troops. The soldiers remained in Mexico for almost a year but were unable to achieve their principal objective, the capture of Villa.

A new constitution

While Villa was evading U.S. troops in the north, his old rival Carranza was trying to establish a new constitution for Mexico. Between November 1916 and February 1917 a congress was held in the city of Querétaro, where a new constitution was drafted. One area that the new constitution addressed was that of workers' rights. It also had a strong nationalistic aspect: Article 27 declared that all subsoil materials were the property of the Mexican state, a challenge to the many foreign oil firms operating in the country.

After the new constitution came into effect, Carranza won a general election and officially assumed the presidency. A new congress was also elected. The government then began the task of rebuilding a country that had been badly injured by years of armed conflict. Carranza's main objective when he took office was to ensure that peace prevailed from that moment on. He reorganized the army, decreasing it in size, and began the construction of dams, roads, and railroads.

Despite such investment in the country's infrastructure, levels of unemployment remained high, a problem that caused protests among the general population. Another source of discontent was Carranza's agricultural policy, which was relatively conservative. The situation was made even worse when Emiliano Zapata was assassinated in an ambush in 1919. Carranza was widely held to be responsible for Zapata's death.

Until this point Álvaro Obregón had continued to support Carranza. By 1919, however, he had begun to disagree with Carranza's policies, believing that the government was becoming increasingly reactionary. With a presidential election due to be held in 1920, Obregón decided to return to the political arena, and in 1919 he began his campaign for the presidency.

Carranza had already announced his backing for a separate candidate, Ignacio Bonilla, and viewed Obregón as a threat. In 1920, in the middle of the presidential campaign, Obregón was charged with being involved in a conspiracy against the president. He was forced to leave Mexico City and flee to Guerrero, where he formed an anti-Carranza alliance with Adolfo de la Huerta, then governor of the state of Sonora. Another key member of this group was General Plutarco Elías Calles (1877–1945), who had fought in Carranza's army during the revolutionary war but had also turned his back on him as his government became unpopular.

The Plan de Agua Prieta

In April 1920, Obregón, Calles, and de la Huerta announced the Plan de Agua Prieta, which refused to recognize Carranza's presidency. When senior figures in the army also turned against him, Carranza attempted to flee to Veracruz, but found the way blocked. Instead, he headed for Puebla. On May 21, 1920, in the town of Tlaxcaltongo, he was assassinated by one of his own guards. The federal congress named Adolfo de la Huerta as a temporary president to finish out Carranza's term.

In the subsequent general election, Obregón ran for president and won. Once in office, he attempted to establish institutional stability to end the decade-long tradition of presidential successions being decided through military coups and assassinations. From 1920 onward military revolts and sporadic acts of violence continued, but the degree to which the government and presidency were threatened lessened. Obregón's administration marked the beginning of a transition of Mexico's political system, a movement away from the violence of the immediate past.

Héctor Manuel Lucero

SEE ALSO:

Carranza, Venustiano; Calles, Plutarco Elías; Columbus Raid; Díaz, Porfirio; Madero, Francisco I.; Obregón, Álvaro; Pershing Expedition; Veracruz Occupation; Villa, Francisco "Pancho."

Mexico City

As the capital, Mexico City is the center of Mexico's political, economic, and cultural life. It is also one of the largest metropolitan areas in the world. About a quarter of the country's population, an estimated 21 million people, live in Mexico City, and it is one of the world's fastest-growing cities.

Mexico City, simply called México by Mexicans, lies in the central Mexican plateau in the Valley of Mexico, a basin with an average altitude of 7,500 feet (2,300 m). The Valley of Mexico is located in the south of the country and is surrounded by mountains: the Sierra de las Cruces to the southwest; Monte Alto and Monte Bajo to the west; and Ajusco and Chichinautzin to the south. Across the plain to the east of the city, two volcanoes, Iztacihuatl (17,342 ft; 5,286 m) and Popocatépetl (17,883 ft; 5,452 m), are visible when air pollution is not too thick. Tepeyac Hill and the Sierra de Guadalupe once marked the city's northern boundary, but the city has spread beyond them. The wall of mountains around the city traps air in the valley, worsening the pollution caused by automobile traffic.

Mexico City has a relatively cool climate, despite being located in a tropical climatic zone, due to its high altitude of 7,347 feet (2,239 m). The average annual temperature is 64°F (18°C) and there are only a few degrees of seasonal variation. The coolest month is January, and the warmest period is from April to June. The rainy season lasts from late May through October, which moderates the dry air.

The site of the city
Present-day Mexico City was built on the ruins of the Aztec capital of Tenochtitlán in the 1520s by Spanish explorer Hernán Cortés. The Valley of Mexico was already a populous region when the Aztecs arrived there in the mid-thirteenth century, and they had difficulty in finding somewhere to settle. Eventually they built Tenochtitlán on an island in Lake Texcoco. The exact date of the founding of the city is unknown but it was probably built between 1325 and 1375. The city grew to be the military and administrative center of the Aztec Empire, with a population of 200,000 to 300,000 by the sixteenth century.

When the Spanish first saw Tenochtitlán in 1519 they marveled at the beauty of the stone-built city on the lake linked to the shore by great causeways. Two years later they destroyed it, having conquered the city in an 85-day siege. The Spanish colonial city was built on the ruins around a central square or *zócalo* (now called the Plaza de la Constitución), with the viceroy's residence on the site of the Aztec emperor's palace. The streets followed the grid pattern of the Aztec city. The original Indian inhabitants were confined to four areas on the outskirts. During the colonial period, Mexico City became the most important capital in the Americas but did not reach the previous Aztec population level until the twentieth century.

Political organization
After Mexican independence from Spain (1821), a new republican constitution was adopted. The new national congress created by the Constitution of

Mexicans usually call their capital city simply México or "el DF" (pronounced "day-effay"), referring to the Distrito Federal (Federal District).

1824 designated Mexico City as the capital and created the boundaries of the Distrito Federal (Federal District). The Federal District is the state and local government for Mexico City and is divided into 16 areas called *delegaciones*. Until the 1990s it was governed by a regent appointed by the Mexican president. The regent in turn appointed delegates for the 16 *delegaciones*. Under this system the city's residents could not vote for their own local government. As a result, for 60 years the ruling Partido Revolucionario Institucional (PRI; Institutional Revolutionary Party) controlled the administration of the Federal District and Mexico City because the president always appointed a PRI member as head. Protests in the 1980s and 1990s led eventually to the creation of an elected head of the Federal District (often referred to as the mayor of Mexico City) accountable to the city. The first election was held in 1997 and was won by Cuauhtémoc Cárdenas of the Partido de la Revolución Democratica (PRD; Democratic Revolution Party).

Mexico City was officially equated with the Federal District in 1970, although the urban area extends beyond it in the north and does not extend into the southern part. Mexico City covers an area of 570 square miles (1,480 sq km). The Federal District occupies an area of 597 square miles (1,547 sq km), extending into the states of México and Morelos.

Growth and development

Mexico City began to expand during the regime of Porfirio Díaz (1877–1880 and 1884–1911) as Mexico began to industrialize. Despite an increase in unemployment and social unrest, many new buildings were constructed; electricity was introduced in 1880, and electric trams in 1896.

Development was halted during the Mexican Revolution (1910–1920), but the city's population grew rapidly over the decades following the revolution, as people moved from the countryside in search of work. The population doubled twice between 1920 and 1960, reaching 8 million by 1970 and 14 million by 1980.

As the population grew the city engulfed towns that had originally been outside of it, and illegal settlements known as *ciudades perdidas* (lost cities) expanded in the northeast of the city. These settlements lack essential services such as drains and electricity. One such settlement, Ciudad Nezahualcoyotl, one of the poorest areas, is so vast that it would be one of the largest cities in Mexico if measured on its own.

Environmental problems

Mexico City has always suffered from water-related problems. There is no natural source of water nearby, so finding enough water to supply the expanding city has been a continuing problem. At the same time, the city suffered from flooding until the twentieth century, when a permanent drainage system was completed. The soft sedimentary clay of the lakebeds on which the city was built, and the removal of groundwater have led to serious subsidence in some parts of the city.

Mexico City lies in a seismically active zone. Moderate earthquakes damaged the city in 1957 and 1979. In 1985 a major earthquake measuring 8.1 on the Richter scale caused extensive damage in the city. An estimated 10,000 people died and 50,000 were injured. The citizens organized themselves to carry out rescue efforts that contrasted with the ineffectiveness of the authorities.

Economy

Mexico City's metropolitan area dominates the nation's economy. It is responsible for over 30 percent of the country's industrial production and is the center of one of Mexico's most important manufacturing areas, stretching from Guadalajara in the west to Veracruz in the east. Main products are yarns and textiles, chemicals and pharmaceuticals, and electrical and electronic items.

To try to stem pollution and overcrowding in the city, the government encouraged heavy industrial and manufacturing development in other areas of the country in the 1980s. As a result, Mexico City lost about 25 percent of its industrial jobs and the service sector grew in importance. The country's banking and finance services are overwhelmingly concentrated in the capital. Overcrowding and pollution continue to be major problems: harmful levels of air pollution occur on more than half the days of the year. Like many large cities, Mexico City's other pressing problems include poverty, unemployment, and crime.

Joanna Griffin

SEE ALSO:

Architecture; Aztecs; Earthquakes and Natural Disasters; Mexican Revolution; Political Parties in Mexico; Spanish Empire.

Miami, Florida

With its art deco architecture, large beaches, and tropical climate, Miami is one of the most popular tourist resorts in the United States. The cosmopolitan city has a large Hispanic population made up mostly of Cubans who fled their homeland to escape Fidel Castro's communist regime. There is, however, a small yet vibrant Mexican American community in Miami that at times is at odds with local Cubans.

The city of Miami is home to a large Hispanic community, attracting immigrants from both Central America and the nearby Caribbean.

Miami has looser ties to Mexico than many similarly sized cities in the Southwest mainly because of the city's history. The first European to explore Florida was Juan Ponce de León, in 1513. By the late sixteenth century the region had become a Spanish colony, but in the early eighteenth century it was cut off from much of New Spain by French colonization of Louisiana. In 1763 Florida came under the sovereignty of Britain, which retained control of the region until the end of the American Revolution (1775–1783), when the region once again passed to Spain. The second period of Spanish rule was marked by conflict between Seminole and U.S. forces, and in 1821 Florida was ceded to the United States. Thus, unlike the states of the Southwest, Florida was never a part of Mexico.

Foundation and growth

In 1835, during a second period of conflict between the U.S. authorities and the Seminole, Fort Dallas was built near the site of the present-day city of Miami. Over the course of the next 60 years, settlers slowly began to come to the area, but in 1896 the arrival of the Florida East Coast Railroad provided the impetus for large-scale migration. The city of Miami was incorporated in the same year.

In the early twentieth century the city went through a series of difficult periods, including the harsh Florida Depression of 1926 as well as severe hurricanes in the late 1920s, but by the mid-1930s, when most of the city's art deco landmarks were built, the economy picked up. The boom continued through World War II with the establishment of military bases in the area, and in the postwar years the city became a center for gambling. At the start of the twenty-first century Miami continued to prosper—it had become the third most popular U.S. city to visit for non-American tourists.

In the 1950s many Mexicans and Mexican Americans migrated to Florida to take jobs as agricultural workers. Although most remained in rural areas, such as Homestead, many moved to Miami, where they joined a large community of Cuban exiles. After Fidel Castro took over Cuba in a military coup in 1959, thousands more Cubans fled to the city. Today Miami is home to a varied Hispanic community that includes large numbers of Nicaraguans, Puerto Ricans, and Colombians.

There are often tensions between these various groups, however. One source of ill feeling between Mexicans and Cubans is the Mexican government's traditionally amicable relationships with the Castro regime. For example, in February 2002 a group of Cubans sought refuge in the Mexican embassy in Havana. The Mexican government allowed Cuban police to enter the embassy to arrest the asylum seekers and their decision prompted anti-Mexican protests by Cuban exiles on the streets of Miami. Commentators on a local radio station serving the Cuban community called for a boycott of Mexican products and for undocumented Mexican workers to be reported to the authorities.

Christopher Wiegand

SEE ALSO:

Cuba; Earthquakes and Natural Disasters; Exiles; Florida; Hispanic Americans; Seminole.

Michoacán

Michoacán is located in central western Mexico and has a population of just over 3.5 million. The state's name is said to derive from the Nahuatl words for fish (*michin*), those who have (*hua*), and place (*can*), meaning fisherman's place. The state has an area of 23,202 square miles (60,093 sq km), and its capital is Morelia.

Michoacán extends from the Pacific Ocean northeastward into the central plateau. It is dominated by the Sierra Madre Occidental mountains and the volcanic chain of central Mexico. The Lerma River and Lake Chapala form part of its southern boundary with Jalisco, and the Rio de las Balsas marks the southern border with Guerrero. In addition to Jalisco and Guerrero, it neighbors Guanajuato to the north, Querétaro to the northeast, Mexico to the east, and Colima and the Pacific Ocean to the west. Owing to its topography, the state's climate varies from tropical with rain all year round to hot with low rainfall.

Most of the state's inhabitants are native Tarascan Indians, who were known as the Purépecha people before the arrival of the Spanish. The Tarascans, who were enemies of the Aztecs, had established themselves in Michoacán by the twelfth century C.E. After the Tarascans were defeated by the Spanish in 1522, the conquistadores developed the Lake Patzcuaro area into a series of villages specializing in particular crafts. Traces of this utopian experiment can still be seen today: the area is home to many skilled craftsmen and women.

Throughout its history Michoacán has played an important role in fomenting ideas that led to rebellion in Mexico, particularly Mexico's Wars of Independence. At the end of the eighteenth century Jesuit colleges in Zamora and Valladolid (now Morelia) spread the ideas of European philosophers, including René Descartes, Isaac Newton, and Galileo, and the notion of independence began to take hold. After the Roman Catholic priest and revolutionary Miguel Hidalgo y Costilla raised the cry for independence in Dolores, Guanajuato, on September 16, 1810, José Maria Morelos y Pavón, another priest and a native of Michoacán, met with

Michoacán is rich in natural resources, and the state's economy thrives on its agriculture, fishing, and mining industries.

Hidalgo and pledged allegiance to the rebellion. After Hidalgo was captured in 1811, Morelos y Pavón became de facto leader of the uprising. He was later captured and executed; Valladolid was renamed Morelia in his honor.

Another native of Michoacán whose progressive ideas changed the face of Mexico was Lázaro Cárdenas, president from 1934 to 1940. Before becoming president Cárdenas had fought in the revolutionary wars and been governor of Michoacán. Both as governor and as president, Cárdenas built schools, roads, and irrigation projects, but he is perhaps best remembered for nationalizing Mexico's oil industry in 1938.

Economy

Michoacán is a diverse agricultural state because of variations in soil and climate. Its main products include cereals and many fruits and vegetables, including avocados, chickpeas, and strawberries. Along with the states of Veracruz and Jalisco, Michoacán is one of the leading producers of cattle in Mexico. Also important are fishing and mining: 32 municipalities have considerable ore deposits. Gold, silver, zinc, and coal are all mined in the state.

Joanna Griffin

SEE ALSO:

Aztecs; Cárdenas, Lázaro; Mexican Independence; Mining and Minerals; Morelos y Pavón, José Maria.

Migrant Labor

Although the phenomenon of migrant labor has a long history, until the twentieth century it was almost invariably internal; workers from one part of a country would move, sometimes in large numbers and over great distances, to another part of the same nation in order to find work. It was not until about 1910 that such movements became external—in other words, they began to be made across borders. The world's first and most significant wave of external migrant labor was that of Mexicans into the United States.

Migration between bordering countries is affected to varying degrees by two main considerations: the migrants' need to leave their country of origin (typically because of poverty, unemployment, or persecution) and the new country's economic need to add to its existing workforce. These are known respectively as push and pull factors. Both have been important stimuli in the migration of Mexicans to the United States.

Early twentieth-century guest workers

During the Mexican Revolution (1910–1920), U.S. states in the West and Southwest were rapidly developing. The need for semiskilled laborers in agriculture and manufacturing opened thousands of job opportunities, many of which were taken by Mexican guest workers. Although large numbers of these immigrants crossed the border illegally, few were sent back, and by 1911 U.S. farm owners had become so dependent on Mexican labor that they lobbied successfully for Mexicans to be excluded from the literacy requirements for U.S. citizenship.

Subsequent events created a need, or at least a perceived need, for even more unskilled labor, with the result that immigration from Mexico began to be formally encouraged by the U.S. government. The catalyst for this new policy came after 1917, when the United States entered World War I (1914–1918). The predominantly agricultural states of the South and Midwest lost nearly 8 percent of their population, as farm laborers moved to the large industrial cities of the Northeast to take jobs in munitions factories. This migratory trend from rural areas to towns continued in the United States throughout the 1920s.

As a result there was a labor shortage on U.S. farms, and more hands were needed quickly. Meanwhile there were great social divisions and economic privations in Mexico, constituting the push factor. The pull factor came from wage differentials between Mexico and the United States that made it advantageous for Mexicans to seek work north of the border. The U.S. government soon gave its approval to this form of economic migration with the first of a series of temporary worker or sojourner programs through which Mexicans were welcomed to undertake hard agricultural labor. Mexican workers were allowed into the United States on the understanding that they would be sent back to Mexico when the work was finished.

During this period some Mexicans entered legally; others slipped over the border and remained in the United States. For the time being, at least, the U.S. authorities again turned a blind eye to the latter because it was expedient for them to do so. That all changed, however, during the Great Depression of the 1930s, when immigration restrictions were imposed and Mexicans were periodically deported. Since then, persecution and repatriation of Mexican migrant workers has come and gone in waves. The greatest antipathy has always coincided with periods of economic adversity, during which some Americans have felt that, if there is too little work to go around, foreigners should be deported. The deportees have not always been illegals. Many had been encouraged to come to the United States and had entered the country legitimately.

Collusion of the farm owners

Few of the Mexican workers who entered the United States during and after World War I actually reached their intended destinations on the East Coast where there existed a greater number of industrial jobs. Most got no farther than California or Texas. The reasons for this were complex. Even though there had been a loss of population in the rural areas and therefore a decline in the agricultural labor force, it turned out that there were still just about enough Americans available to reap the harvests. However, the reduction in the surplus of labor threatened the profits of the farm owners, who were faced with the possibility of having to pay higher wages because there were fewer people to do the necessary work. As a result, the influx of cheap labor, even into another part of the United States, helped employers keep wages down.

A similar situation arose in 1941, when the United States entered World War II (1939–1945). Many American railroad workers and farmhands in the South went off to fight in Europe and the Pacific. Again farmers worried that they would be faced with a significant decrease in the labor supply and would have to pay higher wages. The U.S. government acted quickly to replenish the workforce by reaching in 1942 an agreement with Mexico known as the Bracero Program (*bracero*

Mexican farmworkers cross the U.S. border at Calexico. The farmworkers receive a green card, which allows them to work legally in the United States.

means "farmhand" or "laborer" in Spanish), under the terms of which Mexicans could work in the United States but would be exempt from military service. By 1943 around 4,000 Mexicans had been transported to gather harvests in Arizona and California. After the end of World War II, the integration of Mexican migrant workers into the U.S. workforce was slowed as the United States went back to peacetime production. Nevertheless, millions of temporary Mexican migrants had crossed the border to work in the fast-expanding agribusiness. Although many took their earnings back to their families in Mexico, others stayed on in the United States.

The benefits of migrant labor were to some extent mutual. Mexicans could earn more in the United States than in their own country, while American employers could get away with paying migrant laborers less than either native workers or other immigrants. Yet the farm owners had been dealt a much stronger hand than their employees, and many migrants suffered injustices. Although the Bracero Program had clearly defined ways of helping U.S. agriculture, it was vague on the subject of labor rights and did little to help the workers organize trade unions.

Working without protection and rights

Mexican migrants were not U.S. citizens, so they could be exploited and their services easily dispensed with whenever they became surplus to requirements. For unscrupulous employers and politicians, Mexican migrant laborers had the same advantage as immigrants—they were cheap—but not the disadvantage of being in the United States to stay. Consequently, during periods of economic contraction, Mexican migrant workers were victimized and laid off, often before other workers such as blacks and Asians.

Since the 1940s thousands of workers each year have been brought into the United States, principally from Mexico but also from other foreign countries. Migrant labor, which remains almost exclusively agricultural, continued to receive little legal protection. Mexican and other migrants were often forced to work much more than the statutory eight-hour day and were used as scab labor to break strikes

Whenever there was economic adversity, migrant laborers were among the first to suffer a backlash. In 1954, for example, "Operation Wetback," a campaign to remove all undocumented Mexican workers from the United States, was a response to ethnic violence in the Southwest that had been sparked by economic recession. This initiative was not only unfair, it was also paradoxical: the Bracero Program was still in effect and would remain so until 1964. Mexicans were being encouraged to enter the United States and then thrown out soon after.

Gaining support and solidarity

In the late 1960s and 1970s a dangerous combination of high inflation, unemployment, and fear of recession if the Vietnam War should be brought to an abrupt end caused an upsurge of anti-Mexican sentiment among many Americans. Racism was inflamed by right-wing politicians and certain interest groups blamed all immigrants, not just Mexicans, for the country's economic and social problems.

In a backlash militant unions of undocumented workers sprang up to protect the rights of the migrant and immigrant workers. One of the most notable leaders of these movements was César Chávez (1927–1993), who helped found the National Farm Workers Association (NFWA) in 1962. He organized a nationwide boycott of grapes, wine, and lettuce in an attempt to bring pressure on California growers to sign contracts with the NFWA and the Agricultural Workers Organizing Committee (AWOC). The protest was popular with Mexicans, and after the NFWA and AWOC merged to form the United Farm Workers union (UFW) they had, by 1972, more than 60,000 members. The Teamsters then began to organize farmworkers in competition with the UFW. This led to many strikes and some

violence, and also significantly reduced the UFW's membership, which fell from a peak of 100,000 members in the late 1970s to 24,000 in 1996.

As Mexican guest workers became politicized and militant, their employers asked the government for help, which came in the form of the 1986 Immigration Reform and Control Act (IRCA). IRCA granted legal status to a large proportion of unauthorized immigrant farmworkers but helped break the unions by making the possession of a work permit a condition of union membership. At the same time, to make up for a predicted labor shortfall of up to 20 million workers by 2000, IRCA reintroduced "contract labor," which permitted companies to recruit foreign workers by paying for their passage to the United States and then recouping their investment out of the immigrants' wages. Almost identical legislation had been repealed in 1868.

IRCA's compensatory amnesty provisions, which legalized some of the undocumented workers, were only partially successful. Some aliens who sought legal entry were penalized by deportation anyway, while sanctions against employers for hiring them were rarely enforced. In 1990 President George Bush signed further legislation that allowed an increased number of specially trained workers. In the early 1990s the U.S. Immigration and Naturalization Service was still deporting more than a million "undocumented" workers a year.

George Lewis

SEE ALSO:

Agriculture; Bracero Program; Chávez, César; Illegal Labor; Immigration, Mexican; Immigration Reform and Control Act; Operation Wetback.

Migrant Farm Laborers

In the early twenty-first century, although there remained a steady flow of migrant labor from Mexico to the United States, there was a discernible decline in the proportion of Mexican migrant laborers who worked as crop harvesters, the traditional occupation of Mexican migrant workers in the United States. In 1990 an estimated 46 percent of migrant laborers from Mexico worked as crop harvesters. By 1998 the proportion had dropped significantly, to 32 percent of the migrant workforce, and the number continued

to decrease. During the same period there was a corresponding increase in the proportion of semiskilled workers from Mexico who made the same journey into the United States in search of employment. This change reflects the increase in mechanization in the U.S. economy. It is also worth noting that in Mexico during the twentieth century the migration of the best farm laborers from Mexico's largest farms to the United States has had a detrimental effect on the agricultural competitiveness of Mexico itself.

Mining and Minerals

Mexico contains a vast array of minerals. The most valuable are petroleum and silver, both of which make significant contributions to the national economy. Mexico exports many of its minerals to the United States, Europe, and Japan.

Petroleum is Mexico's principal mineral resource and leading export; more than half the nation's foreign earnings come from fuel exports to the United States. The first successful prospectors were two Americans, Charles A. Candfield and Edward L. Doheny, whose Mexican Petroleum of California company made a strike in 1901 at Ebano in the state of San Luis Potosí. The following year there was another major oil find near San Cristóbal de las Casas on the Isthmus of Tehuantepec, and shortly afterward a pipeline was built from there to a refinery at Minatitlán in the state of Veracruz.

Petroleum production

Petroleum production was nationalized in 1938. Further refineries were built in the 1950s at Poza Rica, Salamanca, and Ciudad Madero. The industry was placed under the control of the government agency Petróleos Mexicanos (PEMEX). The most abundant oil fields are offshore in the Gulf of Campeche, where deposits were discovered in 1978 and 1981. These, together with the Reforma field in the states of Chiapas and Tabasco, which was first developed in 1972, have made Mexico the fifth largest producer of oil in the world. Further oil fields were discovered in 1984, and at the end of the 1980s annual production of crude oil had reached 920 million barrels. In 2000, Mexico's known oil reserves were almost 57.7 billion barrels.

Crude oil is often found in association with natural gas, and this is also an important Mexican mineral resource. Annual production has reached 804.8 billion cubic feet (22.8 billion cubic meters). In 2001 over 70 percent of Mexico's electricity was derived from oil- or gas-fired generators, with 25 percent from hydroelectricity.

Silver mining

The growth and development of Mexico are inextricably linked with the discovery of silver beneath the surface of its land. Hernán Cortés (1485–1547) owned the first silver mine in New Spain at Taxco (Taxco de Alarcón), about 70 miles (112 km) southwest of Mexico City. The first major find by the Spanish was made in 1546 to the northwest of the capital, in what is now the state of Zacatecas. Numerous other finds led to the development of an area that became known as the Silver Belt, which runs between Guanajuato,

Leading Producer of Silver

Silver has always played an important part in Mexico's economy. Today Mexico is the leading producer of silver, about 15 percent of total world output being extracted from the country's mines annually. The United States is the major importer of Mexico's silver. Mexico also has vast reserves of the metal, an estimated 40.7 million tons (37 million metric tons). The most abundant deposits are at San Luis Potosí city, in San Luis Potosí state, where in the 1980s a single mine produced 2,805 tons (2,550 metric tons) of the metal in a year.

Some Mexican cities owe their very existence to this precious metal. Aguascalientes, for ex-ample, was founded in 1575 as the last stop on a road from the capital to a number of remote silver mines. Most Mexican silver is found in association with various other elements, especially sulfur, and in many parts of the country silver is often extracted as a gangue, which is any mineral taken from the earth fortuitously while digging for something else. Indeed, this is characteristic of many Mexican mineral deposits—the range of valuable materials in any given mine is typically so great that extraction is carried out with exceptional care so that nothing with economic potential is wasted or lost.

A miner operating a drill in the Torres gold and silver mine in Guanajuato in 1991. Silver mining is the second most important mining industry in Mexico, after petroleum production. Mexico's silver production accounts for 15 percent of total world output.

Zacatecas, and Chihuahua. During the Spanish colonization of Mexico silver was used primarily in the minting of coins; silver made up a large part of the colony's mineral output.

Mining metals

In terms of weight, more iron ore is mined in Mexico than any other metallic mineral: about 6.16 million tons (5.6 million metric tons) a year. The largest iron mines are in the northeastern state of Durango, chiefly at Cerro del Mercado, and near the mouth of the Balsas River. The tonnage of rock salt (mineral halite) produced in Mexico almost matches that of iron ore; most of the salt is taken from evaporation lagoons on the east coast of Baja California. The Japanese company, Mitsubishi Corporation, has invested heavily in salt mining in Mexico and currently runs a large saltworks on the Baja California coast at Laguna Guerrero Negro.

Mexico leads the world in the production of strontium, a soft, silvery metal extracted from the mineral celestite. The nation is also among the top five producers of arsenic, baryte, fluorspar, graphite, and sodium sulfate. About 858,000 tons (780,000 metric tons) of fluorspar have been produced

annually in recent years. This mineral has a wide range of industrial uses—as a flux in iron smelting, as a source of fluorine and hydrofluoric acid, in ceramics, and in special optical lenses. The finest crystals make rare and attractive collector's items.

In addition, Mexico is among the top 10 producers of antimony, cadmium, copper, gypsum, lead, manganese, mercury, molybdenum, salt, sulfur, and zinc. Most of the copper mined at Cananea in the northwest and near Santa Rosalia in Baja California is exported to Arizona for smelting. Mexico is one of only two countries in the Western Hemisphere that produces manganese in significant quantities; the other is Brazil.

Today most of Mexico's significant deposits of lead and zinc are found in and around towns that were built originally to mine silver. Chief among these is Guanajuato, founded by Spanish prospectors in 1554; there are further rich ore veins at La Paz, Pachuca, Parral, San Luis Potosí, Taxco, and Zacatecas. The majority of Mexico's valuable minerals are found in the north of the country. The main exception to this general rule is sulfur, most of which has been mined since 1956 at Jáltipan in Veracruz. Every year Mexico produces about 1.6 million tons (1.44 million metric tons) of this element, which is used in the commercial production of sulfur dioxide, sulfuric acid, and hydrogen sulfide. Sulfur is also essential in the vulcanization (hardening through heating) of rubber and in the production of chemicals used in detergents. Elemental sulfur is used in a finely divided form to treat certain skin diseases. It is also used in the manufacture of insecticides, fungicides, and plant fertilizers. In addition to all these minerals, there is much coal in the Sabinas fields north of Monterrey.

Precious stones and gems

Although gems are less important to the Mexican economy, many individual specimens of great value have been found. Among the most precious stones unearthed there are danburite and topaz from Charcas, San Luis Potosí. Magnificent crystals of amethyst have been unearthed in Veracruz, while specimens from Guerrero are the most expensive in the world by weight. Elsewhere raspberry garnet, a precious variety of grossular garnet, is found in Coahuila; andradite and olivine are mined at Chavira in Chihuahua; fine crystals of apatite have been extracted with iron ore at Cerro Mercado. Opals are widespread throughout the country and occur in pockets in volcanic rocks such as rhyolites and basalts. Some of the world's best fire agate comes from Mexico. Amber is found at Chiapas.

Economic effects of mining

The effects of all this mineral wealth on the Mexican economy, though generally beneficial, have not been without a downside. In the late 1970s the Mexican government borrowed billions of U.S. dollars at high interest rates in anticipation of increased oil revenues, but when oil prices dropped sharply in the early 1980s, Mexico's currency earnings plummeted with them. This led to large foreign debt, and the nation fell behind on its loan payments. Mexico soon faced a severe recession, forcing the government to reschedule repayment of its debts and begin instituting austerity measures. These included devaluation of the peso.

It was this devaluation, together with a general upturn in world metal prices in 1995, that inspired the confidence needed to go ahead with plans for new mines and increased production. Minerals priced in pesos became very cheap, and this attracted many foreign buyers. Export revenues shot up as a consequence. In 1996, this trend continued, with particular gains in the output of gold and ferrous (containing iron) metals. The quantity of minerals produced increased throughout 1996: this was true of cement, as the construction industry recovered; baryte, used in petroleum drilling operations; and sulfur extracted from crude oil.

In the late 1980s, during the presidency of Carlos Salinas de Gortari (1988–1994), the Consejo de Recursos Minerales (Mineral Resources Council) began the privatization of Mexico's mining properties. As a consequence of this initiative, private sector businesses were for the first time allowed to extract coal, iron ore, phosphorus, potassium, and sulfur—minerals that had previously been government monopolies. In addition, foreign companies were allowed to own 100 percent of the stock in any domestic venture. These developments attracted significant investment from Canada and the United States. By 1996, Mexico had 372 registered international mining enterprises, almost 300 of which were Canadian or American. In 1999, Canada and the United States supplied respectively 43 and 39 percent of the U.S. $800 million spent on Mexican mining. Of this amount, U.S. $111 million was spent on mineral exploration.

Today, of the 440 foreign companies that invest in Mexican mining, 360 are either Canadian or American. Responsibility for national mining policy and the promotion and regulation of the industry is undertaken by the Secretaria de Comercio y Fomento Industrial (Ministry of Commerce and Development). There are four major domestic producers: Industrias Peñoles, which mines precious and base metals and is the world's largest producer of refined silver; Grupo Industrial Minera México, which produces 90 percent of the nation's copper; Empresas Frisco, which is involved in the extraction of silver and nonferrous metals; and Luismin, a major gold producer. The main mining provinces are Baja California Sur, Chihuahua, Coahuila, Durango, Guanajuato, San Luis Potosí, Sonora, and Zacatecas. As technology has improved, the number of workers involved in mining has diminished. It is estimated that in 1995 there were about 75,000 miners working in Mexico compared to more than 100,000 miners a hundred years earlier.

Henry Russell

SEE ALSO:

Cananea Mines; Energy; Environmental Issues; Investment; Laguna San Ignacio; Manufacturing; Nationalization; Oil; PEMEX; Silver.

Missions and Religious Orders

From the 1560s to the 1820s Spain had a system of missions on the frontiers of its empire in the Americas. These missions protected and extended the frontier and converted Native Americans to Roman Catholicism.

Several religious orders were involved in the mission movement, including the Jesuits, Franciscans, Dominicans, and the Augustinians, all of which were instrumental in the exploration and early colonization of the Spanish frontier. The religious orders cooperated with the Spanish colonial authority, who paid the costs of founding the missions, decided where and when a mission would be established, and determined how many missionaries and soldiers (if any) the mission would have.

The system was designed to be self-supporting. Each mission was built a day's ride from the next, to make communication and defense easier as well as to encourage permanent settlements. The mission system was to be temporary, with the missions developing into secular towns once Catholicism and the Spanish way of life had been established.

Life at the missions

Mission life revolved around the establishment of a church. Workshops, storerooms, dining areas, and schools were often built around the church courtyard. Many missions owned and operated farms and ranches, relying on the newly converted local people to provide the workforce. They taught new converts carpentry, metalworking, and other skills. Typically each day began with church services and religious instruction. The rest of the day included times for prayer, work, meals, and relaxation. The Native Americans were not forced to enter the missions. They agreed to stay and work in exchange for food, clothing, and religious teaching. One of the major attractions of the mission system to the Native Americans was that Spanish soldiers provided protection from other hostile peoples. In larger mission towns, new converts often helped to defend the missions. However, soldiers were sometimes used to coerce the converts to stay or to return to the missions.

This church at Mission Conception was built in 1755 near San Antonio, Texas.

Along the lower Rio Grande, the Franciscans had a different arrangement. Local peoples, such as the Carrizos and Garzas, joined Spanish settlements, with the priests as local pastors. Several local peoples became Christian and assimilated, to varying degrees, into Spanish society. In the El Paso district, Native Americans controlled their own economic and political life in several towns, with the approval of Spanish officials. These towns eventually adopted a great deal of Spanish culture and Christianity.

Impact on Native Americans

Many Native Americans, used to a seminomadic life, hated the highly structured, sedentary mission life. They viewed working in the missions as virtual enslavement. Resentment against the Spanish for the diseases they brought and their attacks on native religion and traditions grew. An uprising in 1680 by the Pueblo Indians of New Mexico resulted in 400 deaths and the withdrawal of the Spanish to the area of present-day El Paso, Texas. In California in 1781 a Yuma uprising resulted in the deaths of priests and the capture of the mission's women and children.

Spanish settlers and soldiers often lived near the missions. Missionaries sometimes had to defend their converts from exploitation by the Spanish settlers. Overall, the dangers of frontier life forced the missions, settlers, soldiers, and local peoples to cooperate and share precious land, water, labor, and other resources. The mission priests often acted as local pastors to the settlements. In the early years, missions often controlled the best lands and the labor supply. The mission also supplied the local military with food and other goods, if it was prosperous. As settlements grew and the native population declined, the missions were forced to look to the settlers for their workforce. This increased local pressure to secularize mission property over the years.

The Jesuits

Although the Augustinians, Dominicans, Franciscans, and Jesuits all affected Latin America in different ways, it was the latter two orders that had the greatest impact.

The Jesuit order, also known as the Society of Jesus, was founded by Ignatius Loyola in 1540. Its members went out as educators, scholars, and missionaries throughout the world. The first Jesuits arrived in Mexico City in 1572. They gradually established missions, explored, made maps, wrote histories, and learned local languages. The Jesuits had authority over the soldiers who accompanied them, which caused deep resentment. One outstanding Jesuit was Eusebio Francisco Kino, who established many missions and explored widely throughout northern Sonora and southern Arizona between 1687 and 1711.

As time passed the Jesuits aroused much hostility in Europe because of their power and influence at royal courts and in the Catholic Church, because of their strong defense of the papacy, their work in the missions on behalf of the indigenous peoples, and their reputation for intellectual arrogance. In 1767 the king of Spain, Charles III, expelled the Jesuits from all Spanish dominions.

The Franciscans

The Jesuits and Franciscans had agreed to work in different areas and among different local peoples, but after the Jesuits' expulsion the Franciscans continued the Jesuits' work in the Arizona region. They rebuilt San Xavier del Bac, which Kino had founded near Tucson in 1700. The mission system continued to function under the Franciscans until the late 1820s. Most missionaries along the Spanish frontier were Franciscans, that is, members of the Order of Friars Minor, founded by Saint Francis in 1209. As well as establishing missions in the present-day Southwest, Franciscans also operated in what are now Florida and Georgia.

Colonial authorities and Franciscan missionaries introduced the mission system into present-day Texas between 1682 and 1793, with varying results. In all, 26 missions were established within the present boundaries of the state. To these can be added the easternmost colonial outpost, San Miguel de los Adaes, in what is now Louisiana, and several missions in northern Mexico whose influence extended into Texas. Although most of these missions fell short of their goal, all played a key role in establishing the European foundation of Texas. In 1769 the Franciscan Junípero Serra established the first California mission.

End of the mission system

By the 1770s the mission system had fallen out of favor. The number of new converts declined steadily due to high infant mortality, European diseases, hostile pressure from Indians, and assimilation into Spanish society. Missions were seen as economic liabilities and contrary to the growing spirit of liberalism, which championed individual rights, a capitalist economy, and private rather than communal property. The growth of private ranching and agriculture and the government's search for more revenue through taxes on cattle also adversely affected the missions. There was pressure from the growing civilian population to take over mission lands, particularly those with a declining Indian presence. Many civilians were already working on mission properties at the invitation of the missionaries, and this entailed increased labor costs. In addition, mission converts had sometimes assimilated into local Spanish society.

From the 1790s the government began to secularize several missions. In 1833 and 1834 the new independent Mexican government seized and redistributed the remaining properties that belonged to the missions, ending their involvement in the borderlands.

Lois Swanick

SEE ALSO:
Catholic Church; Kino, Eusebio Francisco; Native Americans; Spanish Empire.

Mixtecs

The Mixtec Indians are one of 16 indigenous groups that originated in Oaxaca in southern Mexico. Prior to colonization of Mexico by the Spanish the Mixtec culture flourished in Oaxaca from the ninth to the early sixteenth centuries. After the arrival of the Spanish the Mixtecs and other native American groups coexisted with their new rulers, though not on equal terms. In modern times there has been widespread migration of Mixtec Indians from their now impoverished homeland as they seek work in the southern United States.

Mexican history prior to the arrival of the Spanish can be divided into three distinct periods: pre-classical (3500 B.C.E. to 300 C.E.), classical (300 to 900 C.E.), and postclassical (900 to 1521 C.E.). For some 3,000 years, spread over these three periods, Oaxaca in southern Mexico was home to 16 ethnic groups. Of these, two groups, the Zapotecs and the Mixtecs were to proliferate, with the Mixtecs becoming one of the most influential ethnic groups in Mesoamerica, an area that covered most of modern-day Mexico, all of Guatemala, Belize, and El Salvador, and parts of Honduras.

Surviving Mixtec manuscripts allow scholars to trace Mixtec history back to the middle of the tenth century, early in the postclassical era, though the origins of the Mixtecs predate this. During the earlier classical period they lived in the hilltops of northwestern Oaxaca. The location of their settlements is reflected in the name they are given in their own language, Ñuudzahui, which literally means "people of the rain."

Like other indigenous people of the region, Mixtec society was originally composed of villages made up of extended family groups. These people lived on the food they grew, such as corn, beans, pumpkins, and squash, on domesticated turkeys, and on hunted game. The villages themselves would usually include a ceremonial center. However, as the population grew and societies became more complex, new political structures developed. During the postclassical period the Mixtecs started

to expand rapidly into other parts of the region. By this time they had developed great building skills and during the course of their expansion into new lands they left behind a number of settlements, as yet properly unexplored, all over Oaxaca.

In the thirteenth century the Mixtecs arrived in the Central Oaxaca Valley and conquered the Zapotecs, who had already established a civilization there dating back to around 500 B.C.E. The two most important Zapotec cities were Monte Albán and Mitla. The Mixtecs took over these Zapotec centers, and evidence of their art and culture is present at both these sites. Mixtec culture became increasingly widespread, and the influence of Mixtec art can be seen in other ethnic art across large areas of Mexico. Mixtec artisans produced beautiful manuscripts using a combination of hieroglyphic writing and pictures. For example, a memorable battle might have been depicted by a picture that would have then been annotated using hieroglyphic symbols. They had a 260-day sacred calendar, which, using a system of identifying days by a name and a number, made it possible to pinpoint any day in a 52-year cycle. The Mixtecs were masters at metalwork, using gold and silver to make beautiful decorative objects. Trade, which already linked relatively remote Oaxaca to other parts of Mexico and to Central and South America, carried on under Mixtec rule. Long before the arrival of the Spanish, the marketplaces of Oaxaca were full of merchandise from people living throughout Mesoamerica.

Invasion

In the mid-fifteenth century, the Aztecs came south to Oaxaca in search of gold and conquered the local population, including the Zapotecs and Mixtecs. That the Aztecs ruled with an iron fist ultimately led to the downfall of the Aztec empire. Like most of the Aztecs' subjects, the Oaxacans were virtually enslaved and forced to pay huge taxes to their conquerors. When the Spanish arrived in 1519, led by Hernán Cortés, they found it relatively easy to recruit allies among the local populations to fight the Aztecs, though this did not include the Oaxacans. Following a two-year stuggle, the Spanish defeated the Aztecs, finally taking Tenochtitlán, the Aztec capital, on August 14, 1521. After the defeat of the Aztecs, the Zapotecs and Mixtecs sent delegations to the Spanish in the hope that they would be able to forge an alliance with them. The Spanish immediately sent a party to Oaxaca looking for gold, and, later, an envoy to lay claim to the region. The Mixtecs, in particular, resisted fiercely, and never surrendered their armed struggle against the new invaders. However, Oaxaca finally fell to religion rather than armed force: large numbers of Roman Catholic priests and settlers flooding the region led to wholesale conversions.

The arrival of the Spanish brought great changes. Wheat was grown, and within 30 years the region was exporting plants, seeds, and precious gems. The local elite enjoyed some of the benefits of this new wealth. They enjoyed new types of food such as the meat of cows and pigs, and wore Spanish clothes. However, trade between them and the Spanish was often one-sided. All in all, this was an uneasy peace. Though the actions of the church and settlers were less brutal than those of the conquistadores, the indigenous peoples were still subject to a system of rule that treated them as inferiors; they were organized into *pueblos indianos* governed by special laws that favored the Spanish. The Mixtecs were made to work for little or no money and had to pay tribute, whereas their customs and religion were rarely acknowledged and their graves were often desecrated by settlers looking for treasure. Most catastrophically, the Europeans brought diseases with them for which the local population had no immunity, and large numbers died.

The Mixtecs that survived retained their ancestral lands for more than a century, but by the 1800s were living in virtual servitude on haciendas owned by criollos (Mexicans of European descent) who formed an elite at this time. By the 1890s the Mixtec population began to grow steadily. However, their traditional homelands were too badly eroded to support their new numbers, and they were now forced to lived in rural poverty, conditions that prevail to this day.

Migration in the twentieth century

Primarily since the 1960s, Mixtec Indians have been migrating to the southern United States. This exodus peaked in the mid-1980s when social welfare and wages were cut in Mexico. A 1991 census by the California Institute for Rural Studies found that Mixtecs made up 5 to 7 percent of the agricultural labor force. The census did not take into account the number of Mixtecs living in urban areas, such as Los Angeles, San Diego, or San Francisco. Several factors converged to force Mixtecs low in the pecking order of migrant workers in the southern United States. Few new Mixtec migrants spoke Spanish, making them a target for go-betweens and contractors who only paid them in cash and did not grant them sick leave or vacation pay. Because they spoke many different languages Mixtecs were sometimes unable to communicate with one another. Many Mixtecs arrived in the United States financially worse off than other Mexican mestizo migrants, and they became known as a group willing to work for almost any wage and under any conditions. This led to discrimination from other Mexicans, who were trying to establish a guaranteed minimum wage and better working conditions. Mixtecs often took temporary jobs and had trouble establishing a permanent footing in the United States.

Results of migration

In the United States, many Mixtecs still lack decent housing and live in shanties. They celebrate traditional festivals and preserve strong links with their communities in Mexico. Back home, however, migrant Mixtecs may often clash with other members of their community. Migration has had an impact on family traditions in general: wives of migrant Mixtec men often return to their own parents or accompany their husbands on the migration trail, rather than live, as tradition demands, with their spouse's parents. Aging relatives are left behind as the young seek a better life in the United States. Migrants send money home to pay for projects such as a new sports field or a festival, but supporting community causes in this way does not benefit the local economy much. The latest research, carried out by the California Institute for Rural Studies, seems to indicate that since the 1990s, some Mixtec families have begun to live full-time in the United States returning only for short visits to Mexico. They have children who were born and attend school in the United States and speak Spanish, English, and sometimes Mixtec.

Joanna Griffin

SEE ALSO:

Aztecs; Criollos; Immigration, Mexican; Mestizos; Oaxaca; Spanish Empire; Zapotecs.

Modernization Period

The modernization period in Mexico was a time of radical economic progress that lasted from 1867 to 1906. Modernization was fueled by a demographic boom: the population nearly doubled in 35 years to reach 15 million by 1910. Mexico's infrastructure grew: the railroads, for example, expanded from 150 miles (241 km) in the 1860s to about 15,000 miles (24,100 km) in 1911. Foreign trade increased from 50 million pesos in 1876 to about 488 million pesos in 1910.

When Benito Juárez resumed the Mexican presidency in 1867 after the French intervention ended with the execution of Emperor Maximilian, Mexico struggled to emerge from a period of political instability and economic stagnation that had lasted more than 50 years. While president (1861–1872), Juárez planned modernization and stability to promote a more positive image of Mexico in the international community.

Juárez and his finance minister immediately began an overhaul of Mexico's tariff system intended to attract foreign investment. Juárez funded the rurales, a mounted rural police force, to help curb criminal activity. He also encouraged the completion of the railroad line connecting Mexico City and Veracruz, a project that had started under Maximilian but stopped when the British construction company ran out of funds. Juárez subsidized the completion of this first major line of the Mexican railroad, which opened late in 1872, and negotiated with the United States to settle both sides' outstanding claims for damages after the Mexican-American War (1846–1848). He was largely unsuccessful in his attempts to introduce mandatory primary education, though the number of schools did increase slowly, especially in the large towns and state capitals.

In 1871 Juárez won a third term as president. His electoral opponents were his secretary of foreign relations, Sebastián Lerdo de Tejada, and General Porfirio Díaz, who had earned distinction fighting the French. Díaz revolted against Juárez's victory, and proposed the Plan de la Noria, which argued that no federal officeholder should be allowed to continue in office for two consecutive terms. In July 1872, when Díaz was almost completely defeated by the federal army, Juárez died of heart disease. As chief justice of the Supreme Court, Lerdo de Tejada became acting president. He defeated Díaz in elections held in October.

Lerdo continued Juárez's basic policies, negotiating contracts for the construction of two major railroad lines. Telegraph companies, meanwhile, built over 1,600 miles (2,575 km) of telegraph wires. The number of schools doubled, and by the end of Lerdo's term in 1876 some 349,000 pupils attended school. The figure, however, remained a small proportion of the school-age population. Lerdo continued tariff reform and finally received France's diplomatic recognition of his government.

Díaz comes to power

In 1876 Lerdo announced his intention to run for reelection. Díaz, who had regrouped and formed new alliances, revolted and issued the Plan de Tuxtepec, calling for greater states' rights, increased suffrage, and no consecutive reelection for the president. Lerdo went into exile in the United States with little struggle. In November Díaz occupied Mexico City and took power. He wielded it, directly or indirectly, for the next 25 years.

Despite the efforts of Juárez and Lerdo, Díaz took over a country that was still mostly rural, composed of Indian pueblos, their *ejido* (communal) lands, and small mestizo towns. The cities were home to an enormous, deprived underclass. Díaz needed capital to modernize mining and agriculture: Mexico's railroad and telegraph systems were limited; its ports were in disrepair; and sanitation and health facilities were lacking, even in Mexico City. Rural lawlessness continued to discourage foreign investment.

Díaz at once set out to change Mexico's image in order to attract foreign capital. He significantly increased the number of rurales to combat lawlessness. Recognizing that U.S. support was crucial, he agreed to pay almost U.S. $4 million in claims from the Mexican-American War. After a number of prompt payments, his government finally won U.S. diplomatic recognition in 1877.

This photograph shows a hacienda in Mexico sometime between 1884 and 1900. The hacienda had long been a traditional form of landholding in Mexico, but the growing dominance of commercial haciendas in the late 1800s was a major cause of the revolution that broke out in 1910.

Because Díaz had come to power on the platform of no consecutive reelection, he had to give up the presidency in 1880, when he supported the election of the military hero Manuel González. Díaz was reelected in 1884; he then remained president until forced out by the Mexican Revolution in 1911.

During the 1880s and 1890s Díaz attracted foreign investment to build telephone and telegraph lines. A British engineering firm solved Mexico City's chronic drainage problem. Díaz sponsored public works on a grand scale, creating jobs and encouraging foreign confidence. New railroads opened new markets for agriculture, which modernized in turn. Díaz passed new laws allowing foreign companies to extract minerals, leading to a dramatic increase in the production of gold, silver, oil, and steel, by British and American companies. Mexico's trade deficit was quickly eliminated.

The price of modernization

In the view of Díaz's supporters and advisers known as the *científicos* (scientific ones), his dictatorship was a necessary step in Mexico's progress. Many Mexicans saw few benefits of modernization, however. Díaz allowed no criticism; he strictly censored newspapers and spent almost a quarter of the federal budget on the military to ensure the support of the army.

Opposition to Díaz was aroused most by the increase in haciendas and the power of *hacendados*

(hacienda owners) during the last decades of the nineteenth century. In 1883 Díaz passed a law designed to encourage foreign investment and settlement in Mexico, authorizing land companies to survey public lands. The law rewarded the companies with up to one-third of the land and the right to buy the rest of it at a low price. More and more of Mexico's territory was obtained by land companies and absorbed into large haciendas. Small landholders, who could not prove their legal title to land their families had farmed for generations, and Indian pueblos, which lost most of their *ejidos*, were exploited. In 1894 the law was modified to be even more favorable to the land companies.

By 1910, largely as a consequence of the changes in land distribution, which had resulted in about 95 percent of Mexicans being landless, over one-half of all rural Mexicans worked as peons (landless peasant laborers) on large haciendas. Their wages had stayed more or less constant throughout the nineteenth century, during which time the price of corn and chilies doubled. The utterly wretched condition of the peasants, Díaz's responsibility for it, and his refusal to help rural Mexicans ignited the revolution.

Ellen Hoobler

SEE ALSO:
Agriculture; Communications; Creel Family; Díaz, Porfirio; Investment; Juárez, Benito; Land Reform; Mexican Revolution; Railroads.

Monroe Doctrine

The relationship between Mexico and the United States has been dominated since Mexico's independence in 1821 by the mutual conviction that the Americas should be free of European domination. This idea, later to become known as the Monroe Doctrine, was articulated by President James Monroe in a speech to the U.S. Congress in 1823.

The Monroe Doctrine came to mean, in practice, that the more powerful United States sought to control Latin American countries for its own benefit. The troubled relationship among neighbors was exacerbated by widening economic inequality and different political aspirations. Mexico's close proximity and long border with the United States has led to more intense and complicated relations between the United States and Mexico than with any other Latin American country.

Background to the Monroe Doctrine

In the first quarter of the nineteenth century a large number of Latin American countries, including Mexico, Argentina, Venezuela, and Chile, gained independence from Spain. By 1823, however, both the U.S. and British governments were concerned that France, Spain, and Russia were planning to recolonize the newly independent nations. These former colonies were potentially important markets for British goods, while the U.S. government was concerned about European encroachment in its hemisphere. The British foreign minister George Canning thus suggested that Britain and the United States should issue a joint statement forbidding any future European colonization in the Americas.

However, the U.S. secretary of state John Quincy Adams was opposed to such a move. He argued that the United States should take a strong, independent stance rather than appear as a weak ally of Britain. His argument eventually convinced the U.S. president James Monroe (1817–1825), and on December 2, 1823, Monroe proclaimed in his annual presidential message to the U.S. Congress that: "the American continents, by the free and independent condition which they have assumed and main-

James Monroe (1758–1831) was the fifth U.S. president. His 1823 statement, which came to be known as the Monroe Doctrine, deeply influenced U.S. foreign policy over the following century.

tained, are henceforth not to be considered as subject for colonization by any European powers.

Monroe pointed out that the American continent and Europe had different systems. As well as calling for an end to European colonization of the Americas, Monroe declared that the United States would not become involved in European politics, that European countries should not intervene in Latin American governments, and that any attempt to do so would be regarded as a hostile act by the United States. These policies were referred to as the Monroe Doctrine after 1852.

Monroe's policies met with considerable sympathy in Latin America and popularity in the United States in the early nineteenth century, but these policies remained more a set of ideas than a functioning inter-American system based on a community of interest. They were largely ignored outside the Americas.

The Monroe Doctrine, however, came to shape U.S.–Latin American policy definitively; the United States later called upon the doctrine to justify both its military interventions in other American republics and the defense of the Western Hemisphere against non-American nations.

U.S. territorial expansion

The Monroe Doctrine was soon invoked against Mexico during the U.S. phase of territorial expansion during the 1840s, popularized as Manifest Destiny by U.S. president James K. Polk (1845–1849). This territorial expansion had several causes: popular pressure to increase the settled territory across Indian and Mexican lands; the desire of slave and nonslave states to acquire allies in the Union (which was to lead in 1861 to the U.S. Civil War), and the desire to reach California before Britain, France, or Russia. U.S. expansion into Mexican territories caused great disruption there.

In 1845 Polk annexed the independent Republic of Texas and proclaimed a broader interpretation of Monroe's policies in which the joining of any independent state to the United States would be a matter of mutual agreement without any foreign intervention. Mexico had forcibly opposed the secession of Texas from Mexico a decade earlier. U.S. annexation of Texas led to war between Mexico and the United States in 1846. The United States was already the stronger force militarily and achieved an easy victory against the Mexican army,

eventually occupying Mexico City. In the subsequent Treaty of Guadalupe Hidalgo (1848), New Mexico, Arizona, Nevada and California were also annexed to the United States and the border was established along the Rio Grande. It was after these events that Monroe's policies achieved the status of doctrine.

The French occupation of Mexico between 1862 and 1867, while the U.S. Civil War (1861–1865) raged, was the first major test of the Monroe Doctrine. The French emperor, Napoleon III, sent an army to overthrow President Benito Juárez (1806–1872) in favor of the Archduke Maximilian of Austria (1832–1867), with the intention of checking the growing political and economic power of the United States in Latin America. The U.S. secretary of state William H. Seward (1801–1872), who favored the Monroe Doctrine, and Juárez's ambassador to the United States, Matías Romero (1837–1898), combined to put pressure on Napoleon to withdraw his army. The Archduke Maximilian was then captured and executed. Although Mexico welcomed the United States' assistance against the French at the time, this period in fact marks the beginning of large-scale U.S. involvement in Mexico, which was to erode Mexican sovereignty.

Wider interpretation

By 1880 the United States was a world power, and the Monroe Doctrine was used to define Latin America as within the U.S. sphere of influence. Economic growth and industrial development in

Woodrow Wilson and Mexico

Woodrow Wilson, president of the United States from 1913 to 1921, was opposed to "Dollar Diplomacy" and the misuse of the Monroe Doctrine. However, his enthusiasm for democratizing Latin America led him to become a major interventionist. Whenever diplomacy failed he was ready to use military force.

In the middle of the Mexican Revolution (1910–1920) Wilson abandoned his earlier policy of "watchful waiting." Following an incident in 1914, which involved the arrest of U.S. sailors in the port of Tampico, Wilson sent troops to occupy the port of Veracruz. He intended to use this

action as an invasion threat to force President Victoriano Huerta (1854–1916) out of office.

One of the rebel leaders of the revolution, Francisco "Pancho" Villa (1877–1923), opposed both Huerta and his successor Venustiano Carranza (1859–1920). In 1916 Villistas, supporters of Pancho Villa, seized the town of Columbus, New Mexico, as a protest against Wilson's support of Carranza. This action led to a fruitless retaliatory invasion of Chihuahua by the United States. Wilson's patronizing attitude and ill-advised interventions left a long legacy of anti-American sentiment in Mexico.

the United States had led to a new type of interest in Latin America, as North American industrialists looked for raw materials and markets for their goods. The Monroe Doctrine remained powerful thanks to Dollar Diplomacy, the promotion of U.S. industrial, commercial, and financial interests protected by military power.

U.S. economic expansion was followed by political imperialism—the creation of "protectorate states," including Cuba, Nicaragua, Haiti, Panama, and the Dominican Republic. President Theodore Roosevelt added the Roosevelt Corollary to the Monroe Doctrine in 1904. This stated that the United States could intervene in the internal affairs of a Latin American country if there was obvious mismanagement by the government.

During the administrations of Porfirio Díaz (1877–1880 and 1884–1911), relations between Mexico and the United States improved as U.S. economic expansionism was matched by Díaz's belief in Mexico's economic development through massive foreign investment. However, when U.S. secretary of state Richard Olney declared in 1895 that the United States was "practically sovereign" on the American continent, he provoked a strong defense of Mexican sovereignty. Díaz proclaimed the Díaz Doctrine, in which the principles of the Monroe Doctrine should be upheld by all American countries, not only the United States. This statement was directed against U.S. expansionism. Díaz also refused offers to become involved with the United States in the extension of its control among smaller Latin American countries. The Mexican Revolution began in 1910, mainly as a reaction to the Díaz dictatorship, which was perceived to be supporting the interests of capitalists, often foreign, against those of the indigenous population.

Good Neighbor policy

During the 1920s public opinion opposed the direct involvement of the United States in Latin America, which led to a third phase in their relations. A movement toward nonintervention, which had sprung up among Latin American nations, combined with widespread opposition within the United States to the continued misuse of the Monroe Doctrine to stress "good neighborhood" among American nations. This new approach was fostered by the Great Depression of the 1930s and the coming of World War II (1939–1945). The Good Neighbor policy was announced by President Franklin D. Roosevelt at the beginning of his administration (1933–1945); the United States gave up direct intervention in favor of more subtle forms of domination, using culture and education as instruments of foreign policy. Roosevelt accepted the policies of the Partido Revolucionario Intitucional (PRI; Institutional Revolutionary Party), which had been to the detriment of U.S. interests in Mexico through actions such as the nationalization of oil. He believed that a stable government, however hostile, was preferable to a further period of instability.

After the Monroe Doctrine

After the end of World War II in 1945 the conditions that had originally led to the Monroe Doctrine no longer applied. Europe had been impoverished by the war, while the United States had emerged, with the Soviet Union, as a global superpower. Trade increased enormously between Mexico and the United States and a much greater interchange of populations took place, which led to greater political interdependence. Although the United States continued to invoke the Monroe Doctrine to interfere frequently in the smaller Latin American states, it was never used directly against Mexico, even though Mexico supported the Soviet Union and Cuba during the cold war. Since the cold war, U.S. attention has focused on issues such as drug trafficking.

The North American Free Trade Agreement (NAFTA), which linked Mexico, the United States, and Canada in a trading bloc in 1994, has had several conflicting effects. Despite offending Mexican nationalist feelings, increased economic stability has helped to normalize political relations and has led to greater democracy in Mexico. The ruling Partido Revolucionario Institucional (PRI; Institutional Revolutionary Party), which had become stagnant and corrupt, was overthrown in 2000. Greater interdependence has meant that the Monroe Doctrine, in effect, ceased to be part of diplomatic relations between Mexico and the United States, although it remains an ever-present symbol of U.S. imperialism.

Zilah Quezado Deckker

SEE ALSO:

Dollar Diplomacy; Foreign Policy, Mexican; Foreign Policy, U.S.; Good Neighbor Policy; Guadalupe Hidalgo, Treaty of; Manifest Destiny; Polk, James.

Monterrey, Nuevo León

Monterrey is Mexico's third largest city and the capital of the state of Nuevo León. It is one of the most modern of Mexico's big cities, with a young and growing population. Three-quarters of its 2.8 million residents are under the age of 45, with 44 percent under 20.

Monterrey sits in the Santa Catarina Valley, surrounded by dramatic mountains, including Cerro de la Silla at 5,711 feet (1,740 m) and Cerro de la Mitra at 7,811 feet (2,380 m). The Santa Catarina River is almost dry for much of the year, but when it floods the results can be devastating. In 1988 Hurricane Gilbert brought disaster to Monterrey: the Santa Marina became a raging torrent after heavy rainfall, killing at least 142 people and forcing thousands of people to abandon their homes.

Early history
The nomadic pre-Columbian inhabitants of the Santa Catarina Valley left little evidence of their presence, but in 1584 the Spanish established a garrison called Ojos de Santa Lucia to defend against Native American attacks. Eleven years later, 12 Spanish families settled the area and named the settlement Ciudad de Nuestra Señora for the viceroy of the time, the Count of Monterrey. Monterrey developed slowly. Work began on constructing its cathedral in 1603, only to be completed 250 years later, in 1851. In 1775 the city had a population of only 258.

Despite its modest size until late in the nineteenth century, the city was in a strategically important valley on the main route between Mexico City and San Antonio, which was a part of Mexico until Texas's independence in 1836. Monterrey's location greatly influenced its history. In 1846, during the Mexican–American War (1846–1848), it was occupied by U.S. troops, and in 1864 it was occupied by the French during their war of intervention. The arrival of the railroad connecting Laredo and Mexico City in 1882 changed everything and set Monterrey on course to become one of the powerhouses of the Mexican economy.

Modern city
The largely modern city center has less of a Spanish colonial feel than many other Mexican cities. It is dominated by the magnificent Gran Plaza, opened in 1984, complete with its centerpiece, the huge Fuente de la Vida (Neptune Fountain). Monterrey also boasts the Museum of Contemporary Art and the Mexican architect Luis Barragan's dramatic 249-foot (76-m) tall Point of the Night monument.

Monterrey is Mexico's second industrial center, after the capital itself. The Instituto Tecnologico is one of the largest technological universities in Latin America and has contributed to the skills of Monterrey's workforce. A combination of the city's proximity to the U.S. border and its skilled labor have attracted major large investment. There are around 8,000 industrial enterprises in the city, including brewing, glass, cement, and meat processing. The famous Bohemia beer is manufactured at the massive Cuauhtemoc brewery.

Tim Harris

SEE ALSO:

Manufacturing; Mexican-American War; San Antonio; Texas; Texas Revolution.

Monterrey's location on the route between Mexico City and San Antonio, Texas, caused the town to develop into an important strategic center in the eighteenth century.

Morelos y Pavón, José Maria

José Maria Morelos y Pavón (1765–1815) became the most important leader of Mexico's Wars of Independence after the death of Miguel Hidalgo in July 1811.

Morelos was born on September 30, 1765, in the city of Valladolid (now Morelia), about 125 miles (200 km) west of Mexico City. Born into a poor mestizo (mixed Spanish and Indian) family, Morelos had an unhappy childhood. His father abandoned the family and the young Morelos worked on the sugarcane hacienda of Tahuejo as an accountant or a scribe. He studied at night and in 1790, at age 25, he entered the College of San Nicolás Obispo in Valladolid, where Miguel Hildago (1753–1811) was rector. Morelos then attended the Tridentine Seminary, where he studied theology. He received a Bachelor of Arts degree in 1795 from the Real y Pontificia Universidad de México (Royal Pontifical University) and was ordained as a priest two years later. Despite his vow of celibacy, Morelos fathered several children. The eldest, Juan Nepomuceno Almonte, born in 1803 to Brígida Almonte, became a leading Conservative politician.

Independence movement

When Morelos learned of the rebellion against Spanish colonial power initiated by Hidalgo, he decided to join the movement. Hidalgo put him in charge of the rebellion in southern Mexico. Despite his deep admiration for Hidalgo, Morelos followed completely different and far more effective military tactics. Instead of accepting anybody willing to join, he formed a small, disciplined, and well-trained army skilled in guerrilla warfare. His long-term plan was to control the areas around Mexico City, thereby isolating the center of Spanish power.

Apart from his military activities, Morelos also contributed political and social innovations to the independence movement: he abolished slavery and the caste system (which classified individuals based on their racial origins) in the areas under his control and ordered the minting of copper coins. He was the first insurgent to announce his intentions to fight for Mexico's complete independence from Spain rather than for the restoration of the Spanish monarch Ferdinand VII, who had been deposed by the French emperor Napoleon.

Initially, and with just a few followers, Morelos marched toward the important port of Acapulco on the southern Pacific coast. When his attempt to seize Acapulco failed, Morelos led his troops to Tixtla (now Tixtla Guerrero), where he was joined by Vicente Guerrero (1783–1831), the man who would become one of the main rebel leaders after Morelos's death. Morelos then continued to Chilpancingo to aid the insurgent chiefs besieged by royalist forces. After defeating the royalists, he marched on Chilapa, capturing 400 prisoners in addition to numerous weapons, three cannons, and a vast amount of ammunition. By the time his first campaign ended in October 1811, all of southern Mexico, apart from Acapulco, was in rebel hands.

Later campaigns

Morelos's second campaign lasted seven months. It began in November 1811 with the capture of the towns of Chiautla and Izúcar, where a local parish priest, Mariano Matamoros, joined the movement. Matamoros became Morelos' closest collaborator and a hero of the wars of independence. They continued to Cuautla, Tenancingo, and Cuernavaca and soon took control of these cities. Morelos then divided his army into three forces. The first, under the leadership of Nicolás Bravo, headed to Oaxaca, while the second, under Hermenegildo Galeana, was sent to the wealthy mining town of Taxco. Morelos led the third force, which hurried to defend Cuautla from the approaching royalist army. Morelos held off the royalists for two long months. Eventually, suffering from the intense heat, without provisions and water, Morelos and his men broke the siege and managed to escape from the city in early May 1812. The royalist general Félix Calleja was so impressed by Morelos that he called him "a second Mohammad" because of his determination and ability to inspire intense loyalty and religious conviction among his followers.

Morelos began his third campaign in June 1812, and after Miguel Hidalgo's execution in July, became the leader of the independence movement. After several battles he arrived at the city of

Tehuacán, where he reorganized his army and named Matamoros his second-in-command.

Morelos also organized the military and political arms of the revolutionary movement, keeping in contact with the rebel leaders of various provinces as well as sympathizers in Mexico City. He lost several battles, culminating in the Battle of Acultzingo. Nonetheless, the insurgent army continued to Oaxaca, one of the main cities of the Spanish viceroyalty. The city fell on November 25, leaving the rebels in command of the whole province. This marked the apex of Morelos's military career. He had almost achieved his original military goal, the encirclement and isolation of Mexico City. In February 1813 Morelos and his army marched on Acapulco in his fourth campaign. This time his attack on Acapulco was successful.

Meanwhile, the revolutionary governing body, the Suprema Junta Americana, set up in Zitácuaro in 1811 to coordinate the insurgent movement, was becoming ineffective due to constant disagreements among its members. Morelos began to realize that a new governing body was needed to replace the Suprema Junta. On June 28, 1813, he called all regions under insurgent control to hold elections so a congress could be formed to take charge of future government and administration. Representatives were elected and the congress was inaugurated in Chilpancingo on September 14. On November 6 the congress issued the first Independence Act of Mexico. Mexico's ties with Spain were now partly severed. Satisfied with the work of the congress, Morelos left for Valladolid to continue the military struggle for independence.

The Constitución de Apatzingán

The fifth and final campaign began in November 1813. By then Morelos's fortunes were in decline. He suffered two humiliating defeats on his march to Valladolid. However, he continued to fight a guerrilla campaign in what is now the state of Guerrero until October 1814, when he went to Apatzingán to join the new congress. The congress drafted the Decreto Constitucional para la Libertad de la America Mexicana (Constitutional Decree for the Liberty of Mexican America), better known as the Constitución de Apatzingán. Morelos was closely involved in writing the document, which was partly based on his *Sentimientos de la Nación* (1813; Sentiments of the nation) calling for increased social and racial equality. Although never

Morelos y Pavón, José Maria
Mexican priest and revolutionary leader

Born: September 30, 1765
Morelia (Valladolid), Michoacán
Died: December 22, 1815
Mexico City

1810	Joins independence movement led by Miguel Hidalgo
1811	Begins four years of military campaigns for Mexican independence
1814	Helps to draft the first constitution of an independent Mexico
1815	Captured and executed as independence movement starts to falter

implemented, it was the first attempt to write a constitution for an independent Mexico.

Harassed by the royalist army, the congress was forced to relocate several times. The insurgent movement began to crumble under pressure from Calleja's disciplined troops, and in the fall of 1815 Morelos was captured and taken to Mexico City for trial. Forced to undergo lengthy interrogations and show trials, he was declared guilty of heresy, defrocked on November 27, and condemned to death. He was executed by firing squad on December 22, 1815, in San Cristóbal Ecatepec prison.

Morelos's death was a terrible blow to the independence movement. After his capture, the movement fragmented into numerous guerrilla groups without central coordination. Morelos was the first rebel leader to articulate the idea of a completely independent country and worked hard to establish the first national government and constitution. The Mexican government declared Morelos a hero of the nation in 1823. The old city of Valladolid, where he was born, was renamed Morelia in 1828, and one of the areas where he fought to achieve his dream, now the state of Morelos, was named for him in 1869.

Luz María Hernández Sáenz

SEE ALSO:

Guerrero, Vicente; Hidalgo y Costilla, Miguel; Mexican Constitutions; Mexican Independence.

Mormons

The Mormon church (also called The Church of Jesus Christ of Latter-Day Saints) was founded by Joseph Smith on April 6, 1830, at Fayette, New York. Since then the church has sent missionaries all over the world, and there are now sizable Mormon communities in Mexico and the Mexico-U.S. border area.

According to Mormon belief, in 1815 in upstate New York, Joseph Smith, age 14, became troubled by religion. After seeking guidance through prayer, God revealed to him that in time God would reestablish the ancient church through Smith. Following this epiphany, Smith entered a period of testing and preparation. Part of that preparation included the translation of a collection of ancient texts: the *Book of Mormon.*

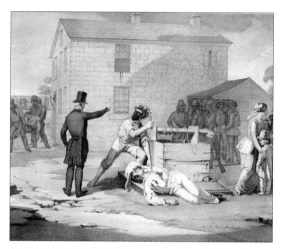

A lithograph from 1851 depicting the death of Joseph Smith at Carthage, Illinois, on June 27, 1844. An anti-Mormon mob stormed the prison where he was being held and murdered him.

Mormon texts and Mesoamerica

Claiming divine assistance, Smith translated into English ancient Hebrew narratives written on metal plates. The original editor of these writings was said to be a fifth-century Native American prophet named Mormon, after whom the book and church became known. Expounding the exodus of a group of Israelites whom God commanded to flee the impending Babylonian destruction of Jerusalem (583 B.C.E.), the record's principal time span is from 600 B.C.E. to 400 C.E., although some sections are dated earlier. Its author describes an overland and oceanic journey to, and colonization of, parts of the Western Hemisphere. Although the exact landing site is still uncertain, some Mormon scholars have proposed that this first contact of Israelites with the New World was in southwest Mexico.

The Mormons believe in the second coming of Jesus Christ to ancient Israel and, following his resurrection, to his worshipers in the Western Hemisphere. As millenarians, they believe that the second coming will usher in 1,000 years of peaceful rule. Some anthropologists have found parallels between the numerous Mesoamerican accounts of visitations of a "white bearded God" to that region and the accounts given of the coming of Christ in the *Book of Mormon.*

Mormons and Mexico

From its inception, the Mormon church sent missionaries around the world. Nearly half of the church membership now lives in Latin America. Mexico has attracted Mormons for over 150 years. The first Mormons immigrated to the northern state of Chihuahua in the late 1870s to escape persecution in the United States. There they set up isolated colonies for ranching and farming. During the Mexican Revolution (1910–1920) they remained neutral, but they were unable to prevent Mexicans invading their lands. Rather than fight back, many abandoned their properties and returned to the United States.

After the revolution Mormons returned to Mexico and by the end of the twentieth century there was a considerable Mormon community in the country. According to the 2000 Mexico census there were 205,229 members. The Mexican Mormon Church was established in 1961; 12 temples have been built or are planned in Mexico; and the country has the fastest growing membership outside the United States.

Dan Wood

SEE ALSO:

Catholic Church; Chihuahua; Immigration to Mexico; Mexican Revolution; Texas.

Morrow, Dwight W.

As U.S. ambassador to Mexico from 1927 to 1930, Dwight W. Morrow settled many outstanding oil, debt, and claims disputes between the two nations. His subtle diplomacy helped lay the foundation of the U.S. Good Neighbor Policy in Latin America that was later introduced by President Franklin D. Roosevelt.

Dwight Whitney Morrow was born in Huntington, West Virginia, on January 11, 1873. His father was a teacher and in 1875 the family moved to Allegheny (now part of Pittsburgh), Pennsylvania, where the young Morrow attended school. He graduated magna cum laude from Amherst College in 1895, then studied law at Columbia University. Admitted to the bar in 1899, he became a highly regarded corporate lawyer in New York City.

Banking career

In 1903 Morrow moved into banking and served as director of many industrial and financial corporations. He helped draft a workmen's compensation law in 1911. In 1914 he became a partner in the banking house of J. P. Morgan & Company, and two years later negotiated a U.S. $500 million loan to Britain and France to finance their fight against Germany in World War I.

Later Morrow became chairman of the New Jersey Prison Inquiry Commission, and the New Jersey State Board of Institutions and Agencies. When the United States entered World War I in 1917 he was made director of New Jersey's National War Savings Committee. Early in 1918 he went to Europe, where he was adviser to the Allied Maritime Transport Council, a member of the Military Board of Allied Supply, and chief civilian aide to General John J. Pershing (1860–1948).

After the war Morrow helped Cuba solve its financial troubles, representing an international banking syndicate that made a U.S. $50 million loan to the Cuban government in 1921. In 1925 he was appointed chairman of the Aircraft Board created by U.S. president Calvin Coolidge and took a leading role in the formulation of national military and civil aviation policy.

Morrow, Dwight W.
U.S. ambassador, businessman, politician

Born: January 11, 1873
Huntington, West Virginia
Died: October 5, 1931
Englewood, New Jersey

1895	Graduates from Amherst College
1899	Graduates from Columbia Law School
1903	Marries Elizabeth Reeve Cutter
1914	Becomes partner in J. P. Morgan Bank
1918	Advises Allied Maritime Transport Council in Europe
1927	Appointed U.S. ambassador to Mexico
1931	Elected senator from New Jersey

Ambassador to Mexico

Two years later Coolidge appointed Morrow ambassador to Mexico in succession to James R. Sheffield. Once installed Morrow worked hard to restore harmony between the Mexican church and state, relations between which had reached an unprecedented level of bitterness. Morrow arrived in the middle of the Cristero Rebellion (1926–1929), in which Catholics fought the forces of the anticlerical government of Plutarco Elías Calles (1924–1928). Calles was determined to remove every trace of Catholicism from Mexico; immediately after his inauguration as president on November 30, 1924, he plunged his country into the most severe religious crisis of its history.

The 1917 Constitution contained articles that practicing Catholics considered intolerable, including provisions outlawing monastic orders, prohibiting religious organizations from owning property, and denying clergy the right to vote. On June 14, 1926, Calles signed a decree known officially as "The Law Reforming the Penal Code" and unofficially as the "Calles Law." Designed to put teeth into the constitutional articles, it spelled out the penalties for transgression. These included fines of 500 pesos for wearing clerical garb and five years' imprisonment for criticizing the law or inducing a minor to join a monastic order.

Catholic revolt

The flashpoint came when Calles attempted to enforce these laws in the strongly Catholic west-central states of Colima, Guanajuato, Jalisco, Michoacán, and Zacatecas. Shouting their battle cry of "Viva Cristo Rey!" ("Long live Christ the King!"), a ramshackle alliance of ranchers, Catholic students and workers from Guadalajara, and Indians from the Los Altos ranch country of northeast Jalisco held off the federal army for three years. The army hit back by victimizing innocent Roman Catholics, and government officials turned the strife to their own political advantage.

In the end the issue was decided not by force of arms but by the timely intervention of Morrow. Calles completed his term of office in 1928 and his successor, Emilio Portes Gil (1890–1978), was

Dwight W. Morrow (left), the U.S. ambassador to Mexico, leaving the Carlton Hotel in Washington, D.C,. with the U.S. ambassador to Great Britain, Charles G. Dawes, in June 1930.

flexible enough to cooperate with the U.S. ambassador in arriving at a settlement. Meanwhile Morrow skillfully manipulated the Mexican political hierarchy, the Vatican, and the U.S. State Department. He prepared drafts for both sides and delivered them personally.

Agreement was finally reached on June 21, 1929. Under this pact, which became known as *los arreglos* (the arrangements), worship was resumed in Mexico and the Catholics were granted minor concessions: religious instruction was permitted in churches (though not in schools) and all citizens, including members of the clergy, were allowed the right of petition for the reform of any law. On June 27, 1929, for the first time in almost three years, church bells rang out across Mexico.

Mexican-U.S. relations

Relations between Mexico and the United States had been strained by events in other parts of Latin America, particularly Nicaragua, where U.S. troops had been evacuated in 1925, but to which they returned a year later upon the outbreak of civil war. In 1927 the Coolidge administration had negotiated an agreement for American-supervised elections, but one rebel leader, César Augusto Sandino, held out, and U.S. marines eventually stayed in the country until 1933.

The troubles in Nicaragua increased tensions between Mexico City and Washington. Relations were already tense because of repeated Mexican threats to take over U.S. oil properties. In 1928, however, Morrow negotiated an agreement protecting American economic rights. This new spirit of cooperation in U.S. relations with Latin America lasted until 1938, when the Mexican government expropriated U.S.-owned properties, promising to reimburse American owners.

On September 30, 1930, Morrow resigned as ambassador. On his return to the United States he was elected as a Republican to the Senate in 1931 representing New Jersey. However, he attended only one session of Congress before his death. He was buried in Brookside Cemetery, Englewood, New Jersey. His second daughter, Anne Spencer Morrow, married aviator Charles A. Lindbergh in 1929.

Henry Russell

See also:

Calles, Plutarco Elías; Catholic Church; Constitutions, Mexican; Foreign Policy, Mexican; Foreign Policy, U.S.; Good Neighbor Policy.

Murals and Muralists

In the wake of the Mexican Revolution (1910–1920) an artistic movement of Mexican muralists began. Although many artists were involved in the movement, the most significant were "Los Tres Grandes": José Clemente Orozco (1883–1949), Diego Rivera (1886–1957), and David Alfaro Siqueiros (1896–1974).

The three great muralists, from different backgrounds, did not share the same beliefs and remained politically and artistically independent from one another. During the Mexican Revolution, Rivera, influenced by the Cubist movement, visited Europe. Siqueiros fought for the revolutionary leader Francisco "Pancho" Villa, whereas Orozco supported Villa's opponent, Venustiano Carranza, and did not take part directly in the fighting. In addition to creating murals in Mexico all three painted murals in the United States at some point in their careers.

Murals were generally painted on public buildings, thereby redefining public space. The muralists aimed to create an art accessible to the general public and not just the privileged elite. Since the murals were painted directly onto a wall they could not be bought or sold but remained in the public domain. In 1929 Orozco wrote: "The highest, most logical, purest, and most powerful type of painting is mural painting. It is also the most disinterested, as it cannot be converted into an object for personal gain, nor can it be concealed for the benefit of a privileged people. It is for the people. It is for ALL."

The artistic output of Orozco, Rivera, and Siqueiros spans five decades, from the early 1920s until, in the case of Siqueiros, the 1970s. The work started in the post-revolutionary administration of President Álvaro Obregón (1920–1924), who hoped to create a new Mexico that was a complete break from the era of the dictator Porfirio Díaz, under whose rule (1877–1880 and 1884–1911) the three painters had grown up. In pre-revolutionary Mexico, a tiny elite controlled the country's wealth, while the indigenous majority lived in abject poverty. The revolution aimed to create a new equality. José Vasconcelos, the minister of education

(1921–1924), wanted this equality expressed by an indigenous Mexican cultural movement. He invited muralists to take part in a government program for popular public art.

An exhibition held in 1910 was an early inspiration for the muralist movement. During Mexico's centennial celebrations an artist known as Dr. Atl mounted an exhibition of Mexican artists as a direct challenge to a government-sponsored exhibition of Spanish art. Dr. Atl's exhibition was the first to celebrate the Mexican worker, Indians, and peasants. These themes were taken up by the muralists a decade later.

Themes and styles of the murals

The major theme of the murals was Mexican history. The muralists concentrated on the experiences and struggles of the ordinary Mexican worker, rather than depict past generals and rulers. With the exception of Siqueiros, the artists' aim was not pictorial innovation but the creation of a dialogue with the Mexican people—the majority of whom were illiterate—to bring them into contact with their glorious history. Siqueiros only rarely used themes from pre-Columbian and colonial history, preferring instead to focus on the contemporary struggles of the worker and peasant.

Vasconcelos commissioned Orozco, Siqueiros, and Rivera, among other artists, to paint murals in Mexico City. The first completed mural, by Rivera, was *The Creation*, painted at the Bolivar Amphitheater of the National Preparatory School between 1922 and 1923. The work was strongly influenced by the Italian and Byzantine frescoes Rivera had studied on his trip to Europe. Similarly, the early murals of Orozco and Siqueiros used European themes and ideas. It took several years for each painter to discover his uniquely Mexican vision.

Orozco, always the most individual and marginal of the group, was influenced by Mexico's innovative printmaker, José Guadalupe Posada (1852–1913). Like Posada, Orozco frequently used scenes from the darker side of daily life in his early paintings. After the terrible reviews of one of his exhibitions in 1917 he left for the United States. He spent three years there, struggling to find his own style. One of

This mural depicting the history of Mexico is by Diego Rivera. It shows pre-Columbian Tarascans dying cloth and writing codices.

his early murals, *Christ Destroying His Cross*, painted at the National Preparatory School, was defaced by conservative Catholic students, and Orozco had to repaint it between 1923 and 1926. He destroyed and later repainted many of his early murals until he was satisfied with the images they portrayed. With his later murals for the National Preparatory School, such as *Cortés and Malinche*, *Destruction of the Old Order*, and *The Trench*, all painted after 1926, Orozco created his own style, which had as a major theme the repercussions of the Spanish conquest. Orozco depicted the social, political, and historical realities of his country as he saw it since the conquest.

In 1924 there was a change in government. With the more conservative administration of Elías Calles (1924-1928), Vasconcelos' resignation, and negative public reaction to the murals, the more radical muralists found their commissions terminated. Unable to get work in Mexico, Orozco left for the United States, where he lived between 1927 and 1934. During that time he undertook a number of important commissions that established his international reputation. As well as mural commissions in Claremont, California, and New York, he painted murals at Baker Library, Dartmouth College, New

Hampshire, between 1932 and 1934. His theme was the mythical Mexican hero, Quetzalcoatl.

Such was the success of Orozco's North American murals that he returned to Mexico triumphant in 1934. He continued to paint both in Guadalajara and Mexico City and his last great work was *National Allegory*, painted in 1947 at the Normal School, Mexico City. In that year he was awarded a prize as the outstanding figure in Mexican arts and sciences of the preceding five years.

David Siqueiros

The most politically active of the three, Siqueiros, wanted his art to reflect his Marxist ideology. He organized and led unions of artists and working men as well as working as an artist. An active member of the Mexican Communist Party, Siqueiros was periodically jailed or exiled for his political beliefs. A less prolific early muralist than either Orozco or Rivera, Siqueiros founded, along with Xavier Guerrero and Rivera, the Syndicate of Technical Workers, Painters, and Sculptors in 1922. Siqueiros used the syndicate's magazine, *El Machete*, to express his political views and criticize the government. Writing for the magazine helped him to develop his beliefs, which are evident in his later murals. After the government stopped commissioning his work Siqueiros moved to Guadalajara where he worked on a mural at the former chapel of the city university.

When the Spanish Civil War broke out in in 1936 Siqueiros traveled to Spain and fought on the side of the Republicans between 1937 and 1938. On his return to Mexico he was again exiled, this time for an attempt to assassinate the Russian political exile Leon Trotsky in 1940, whom he considered anti-Soviet. Despite banishing Siqueiros to Chile, the Mexican government commissioned him to paint a mural there in Chillán. Unable to get a visa to the United States, Siqueiros instead traveled to Cuba before returning to Mexico.

Back in favor with the government, Siqueiros spent the rest of his life fulfilling commissions for murals, predominantly in Mexico City. He completed work for the National Autonomous University of Mexico, and the National History Museum in Chapultepec Castle, among others. Much of his later life was devoted to the creation of the Polyforum Cultural Siqueiros, a cultural center in Mexico City. It contained his last and largest mural, *The March of Humanity*, which took seven years to complete. He increasingly experimented with his murals, including applying industrial paint with a spray gun, a technique the U.S. artist Jackson Pollock, who attended a workshop Siqueiros once held in New York, would later use.

Diego Rivera

Rivera was the only one of the three great muralists to stay in Mexico during Calles's rule. From 1923 to 1928 Rivera worked on his murals for the Ministry of Education and the National Agricultural School at Chapingo, which were perhaps his most significant contributions to the movement. He created a vision of Mexico that both belonged to and was a product of the people. Rivera was a prolific worker. By the time he and his assistants had finished the commission they had painted 235 fresco panels, of which 116 were major paintings. The frescoes showed Mexican history from the peasant and worker's viewpoint and Mexico's strong cultural tradition and customs.

Rivera made the first of several trips to the United States in 1930. At the height of the Great Depression, in 1932, Henry Ford commissioned Rivera to paint a mural to the American worker at his factory in Detroit. Rivera completed the mural in 1933, but it was criticized for its Marxist themes. However, the storm that greeted Rivera's completion of a mural for Rockefeller Center in New York City in 1933 was much greater. *Man at the Crossroads* was criticized by the newspapers and picketed because Rivera included the figure of the Russian Bolshevik leader Lenin next to that of John D. Rockefeller. Rockefeller ordered the mural to be destroyed. Rivera later repainted it at the Palace of Fine Arts in Mexico City. By the late 1930s Rivera was considered too radical for commissions in the United States. He had, however, inspired President Franklin D. Roosevelt with the idea of public art in public places. Roosevelt incorporated it into his Works Progress Administration program, through which the government commissioned thousands of artworks to decorate public buildings.

In Mexico, Rivera concentrated on his greatest mural series, mainly painted between 1929 and 1935 but still unfinished at the time of his death in 1957, at the National Palace in Mexico City. The murals depicted Mexico's history from Aztec times and depicted Indian customs and traditions.

The movement's legacy

Despite long careers that included many commissions, both in Mexico and the United States, the muralists and the movement they created in Mexico City were only at their peak for a period of some six years in the 1920s. Later murals were often painted in government buildings without public access, which negated one of the original aims of the movement. However, the impact of the murals was profound, not just in Mexico but across Latin America. A large number of the Mexican murals survive and can be visited.

The Mexican muralists inspired a mural painting tradition among artists of the Chicano movement in the United States during the 1960s. The first mural was painted at El Teatro Campesino in Del Ray, California. Murals were painted on the walls of shops, garages, and schools in Hispanic neighborhoods across the United States, often by collectives. As in Mexico, they concentrated on themes to educate the population, depict recent events, and express pride in Mexican history.

Anita Dalal

SEE ALSO:
Art; Chicano Art; Barrios; Mexican Revolution; Orozco, José Clemente; Rivera, Diego.

Music

Throughout the twentieth century Latin music has been one of the greatest influences on popular music styles in the United States. Tin Pan Alley, stage and film, jazz, rhythm and blues, country music, and even rock have been influenced in their development by musical elements from Mexico, Cuba, Brazil, and Argentina.

Latin music is not new to the United States. As early as 1857 the American Creole pianist Louis Moreau Gottschalk (1829–1869), influenced by the Cuban *habanera* (a dance), composed "Ojos Criollos" (Creole eyes). His performances introduced Latin music to the United States for the first time. In 1896 American composer and conductor John Phillip Souza (1854–1952) composed *El Capitan* (The captain) for the Broadway stage, long before he penned his now-famous marching tunes. Jelly Roll Morton (1890–1941), who helped pioneer modern jazz in the early 1920s, often exclaimed that ragtime music needed the "Spanish tinge" in order to be ragtime. He was referring to the "cakewalk" rhythm, played by the left hand on a piano, which was derived from the tango rhythm found in the *habanera*.

The *corrido* and *ranchera*

The most important influences to reach the United States from Mexico were the *corrido* and *ranchera* styles. *Corridos* have been described by the U.S. music writer John Storm Roberts as, "pure folk ballads in their simplicity, their detail, their deadpan performing style.... They chronicled the whole of the Mexican civil war [Mexican Revolution], almost all notable crimes, strikes, and other political events...." *Corridos* have much in common with the American ballad of the early twentieth century in their delivery, their concern for detail, and their themes. In the nineteenth century, wagon trains from Mexico would often meet up with wagon trains from Texas or New Mexico. In the evenings, singers from both sides would perform ballads and *corridos*. "Buffalo Skinners" by renowned folk- and country- singer Woody Guthrie (1912–1967), for example, sounds very much like a *corrido*.

*Ranchera*s, on the other hand, are "ranch songs" that were originally sung as interludes between acts in the theater around 1910 and are characterized by medium-tempo waltz rhythms. The style is equivalent to U.S. commercial country music. In 1922 and 1923 in the United States a number of songs appeared that were either Mexican in origin or influenced by the Mexican *ranchera* styles, including "Rose of the Rio Grande" by Edgar Leslie, Harry Warren, and Ross Gorman, and "Cielito Lindo" (Pretty Cielito). In 1926 these influences made their way to Broadway with *Rio Rita,* which told the story of Captain Jim Stewart, a Texas Ranger who falls in love with a Mexican girl. In 1934 "Alla en el Rancho Grande" (Back on the great ranch), a traditional *ranchera,* and "La Cucaracha" (The cockroach), a song of the Mexican Revolution, also became popular.

Mexican influences were also evident in other ways. The founder of western swing, Bob Wills, referred to the style as a combination of mariachi, jazz, and country. Country music from the Southwest took both guitar techniques and songs from Mexican sources in songs such as "San Antonio Rose" and "Alla en el Rancho Grande." Texas bluesman Huddie Ledbetter's (Leadbelly; 1885–1949) guitar runs were like those used by Tex-Mex *bajo sexto* (12-string guitar) players, and Woody Guthrie's *corrido*-like playing was clearly Latin influenced.

Tin Pan Alley

Tin Pan Alley refers to a group of music publishers who were responsible for shaping the popular ballads and musical styles of the 1920s, 1930s, and 1940s. The relationship between these publishers and Mexico began as the popularity of various ballads such as "Mi viejo amor" (My old love), "Estrellita," and "Cuando vuelva a tu lado" (When I return to your side) in the Mexican community led to an increased purchase of records influenced by radio play. By sending agents to Mexico and other parts of Latin America, it became possible to obtain licenses to record the music in the United States. Tin Pan Alley publishers would then hire lyricists to create English lyrics.

In the early 1940s, for example, a number of Mexican songs become popular: "Perfidia" by Alberto Dominguez, "Solamente una vez" (You Belong to My Heart) by Agustin Lara, and "Mar"/"Stars in Your Eyes" by Gabriel Ruiz. The highly popular "What a Difference a Day Makes" from 1944 originated in 1934 as "Cuando vuelva a tu lado."

Rock music

Latin music was extremely popular in the United States and Mexico during the first half of the 1950s. After 1955 rock and roll became extremely popular, performed by such musicians as Buddy Holly (1936–1959) and Ritchie Valens (1941–1959). Even so, Mexican music still had an influence on this new music: one of Valens's most famous records was "La Bamba." The influence of rock in Mexico had more to do with adults than youth. In fact, rock music in Mexico was popularized by jazz orchestras who performed for adults. Moreover, while white American parents in the United States felt the sexually suggestive dancing associated with rock and roll would affect the morals of the country, in Mexico dancers related to the African beats of rock. The first recording in Mexico of this new genre was made by bandleader Pablo Beltran Ruiz, titled (in English) "Mexican Rock and Roll." In the late 1950s and 1960s, Mexican performers were combining music from popular U.S. rock songs with Spanish lyrics.

The 1960s were important musically because U.S. pop music underwent a Latinization process. This influence was not always clearly evident because mass pop music also engaged other musical styles. Examples include the bossa nova craze from 1962 to 1964 and occasional novelty hits such as "Twist Twist Señora," by Gary "U.S." Bonds.

Herb Alpert posing with his band the Tijuana Brass in 1968. Alpert and his band achieved worldwide fame in the early 1960s and helped popularize Mexican-based music with their live performances and new sound. Their 1963 record "Lonely Bull" sold close to a million copies.

Tex-Mex music

Conjunto, a style of dance music from northern Mexico (called *norteño*) and from Texas (called Tejano or Tex-Mex), continued to play its part in popular music. In particular, Tex-Mex music was popular in the Mexican community due to the availability of records and live performances. Musicians such as Flaco Jimenez and Los Pinguinos del Norte were popular. Many of the younger musicians were influenced by the larger musical scene, particularly rock. These musicians began to "electrify" the Tex-Mex sound in what became known as *la onda nueva* (the new wave). Music groups such as Little Joe y la Familia and Sunny Ozuna and the Sunglows, both from Texas, played this style. It was characterized by one or two guitars; drums; bass guitar; and farfisa organ, which replaced the traditional accordion sound; and a horn section. In 1963 Sunny Ozuna had a crossover hit with a song entitled "Talk to Me."

Although not always relying on Mexican-based music, mainstream singers such as Johnny Rodriguez and Freddy Fender (Baldemar Huerta) continued to influence pop music. Rodriguez, originally from Texas, did straight country and always sang in English, and his music reflected a Tex-Mex sound. During the 1960s and early 1970s he had hit albums on the country charts and, during the 1980s, his music became more pop-oriented with a country feel. In the 1990s, Rodriguez released a bilingual CD titled "Coming Home."

Freddy Fender was a farmworker in the early 1950s when he began singing country music in roadside honky tonks (dance halls). He sang rock and roll, the blues, and traditional *corridos* and *rancheras*. In the late 1950s he released an album that brought him to the attention of a wider audience. During the 1960s he had a series of hit songs such as "Until the Last Teardrop Falls" and "Wasted Days and Wasted Nights." He continued to sing in Spanish, bringing traditional *corridos* and *rancheras* to a new audience. Throughout the 1990s he was a member of the Texas Tornados, whose members reflected diverse Mexican American musical traditions. The members included Doug Sahm and Augie Meyers, who played rock, country, and blues; Flaco Jimenez, who played *conjunto*; and Fender, who played rhythm and blues and *rancheras*.

During the early part of the 1960s, folk music was extremely popular. Artists such as Pete Seeger, Woody Guthrie, and Bob Dylan helped influence numerous musicians, including the Mexican American Trini Lopez. Lopez, from Dallas, Texas, began performing traditional *corridos*, *rancheras*, and ballads while still a boy. In his early twenties he put together a nightclub act incorporating pop and folk standards; what became known as urban folk music. While performing at PJ's in Beverly Hills, California, he came to the attention of Frank Sinatra, who signed Lopez to his Reprise label. The ensuing album contained two hits that brought Lopez into the spotlight: "America," from the Broadway musical *West Side Story,* and "If I Had a Hammer," an uptempo version of the Peter, Paul, and Mary hit. After the British pop invasion of the Beatles in 1964, he never again experienced the same degree of success.

Another mainstream performer who popularized Mexican-based music was the trumpeter and band leader Herb Alpert. In 1963 he formed the Tijuana Brass, basing its music on the mariachi sound. The same year he released a record, "The Lonely Bull," that became an enormous success. For the remainder of the 1960s both Alpert and his band were extremely successful in the pop field.

Latin rock and jazz

During the 1960s rock music did not display much Latin-based influence. Despite the strength of the new British pop, certain Latin musicians were successful. Mexican-born guitarist Carlos Santana began recording salsa and blues numbers after he moved to San Francisco. This resulted in the development of Latin rock through records such as "Jingo" and "Evil Ways." As a result of his work, San Francisco became a major crossover center for many Latino musicians. Chicano musicians who could not identify with the traditional *corrido* and *ranchera* sounds took to Latin rock or Latin jazz. There were also elements of Cuban black music that influenced many of these musicians.

By the late 1970s folk, country, and rock bands turned increasingly to Mexican music for inspiration. Most noticeable was the use of popular Mexican mariachi rhythms to express a romantic (and sometimes slightly sleazy) atmosphere. The guitar was also utilized for this purpose, following from early examples such as Marty Robbins's 1959 recording of "El Paso." Songs that reflected these developments include The Amazing Rhythm Aces' "Third-Rate Romance," "Low-Rent Rendezvous" (1975); Capt. Hook's "Making Love and Music"

Roc en Español

In the 1990s, another trend demonstrated the influence of U.S. rock while at the same time showing the diversity and originality of Mexican rock musicians. *Roc en Español* (Spanish rock) emerged from Latin America and took North America by storm. Blending rock styles derived from Queen, Led Zeppelin, and Pink Floyd with Mexican and Latin tinges, *roc en Español* demonstrated diversity in the broadest sense of the word. Its popularity was spread by a growing, young Hispanic population on both sides of the border.

After the success in Mexico in the 1960s of groups like Enrique Guzmán y Los Teen Tops and Los Locos del Ritmo, there came a period of resistance among musicians toward the political structure of the country. The 1968 killing of student protesters by the police and military in Mexico City and the closure of the 1971 Avándaro rock festival forced rock underground in the country.

Thirty years later *roc en español* became one of the fastest growing and popular genres in the world. With top record labels and MTV pushing *roc*, the once underground music became acceptable. The group Maná toured with Carlos Santana; the virtuoso guitarist Adrian Belew produced an album for the group Caifanes; and the group Maldita Vecindad opened shows for Jane's Addiction.

There are now bands with popular appeal from all over Latin America: from Argentina there are Los Fabulosos Cadillacs, Charly Garcia, Los Dividios, and Soda Stereo; from Chile, Sexual Democracia and Los Tres; from Venezuela, Desorden Publico; and from Spain, Seguridad Social, Negu Gorriack, and Heroes del Silencio. However, the greatest impact has come from Mexico with bands such as Café Tacuba, Maná, and Caifanes.

The musical interchange between Mexico and the United States can be understood by considering the diversity of musical styles that have been heard on both sides of the border. As Cosme, lead singer of Café Tacuba, said, "All of this [music] is attacking your brain at all times. So we try to represent this moment in which we live." Considering the history of Mexican and U.S. music, it leaves us with the sense that musically, borders do not exist.

Carlos F. Ortega

SEE ALSO:

Baez, Joan; Corridos; Los Lobos; Mariachis; Martinez, Narciso; Ronstadt, Linda; Santana, Carlos; Valens, Ritchie.

A typical modern mariachi ensemble consisting of violinists and guitarists. Mariachi musicians always wear tight-fitting ornamental pants, short jackets, and wide-brimmed sombreros.

(1977); Maria Muldaur's "Say You Will" (1978); Michelle Phillips's "There She Goes" (1978); Hoyt Axton's "When the Morning Comes," "The No No Song," and "Flash of Fire" (1974–1976); and Kris Kristofferson's "The Taker" (1971).

The impact of Latin or Mexican-based music set the stage for the 1980s, when two important albums were released: *Canciones de Mi Padre* (Songs of my father) by Linda Ronstadt and *La Pistola y El Corazon* (The pistol and the heart) by Los Lobos. Additionally, the release of the film *La Bamba* brought the music of Ritchie Valens to the attention of the wider public.

Throughout the 1980s, Latin music in general continued to be influential in popular music in the United States, with the pop/salsa sounds of the Miami Sound Machine and, on the other hand, the Mexican-based music of Los Lobos. In addition to their roots-rock sound, Los Lobos also performed traditional Tex-Mex music, which was driven by *rancheras*. At the same time in the early 1980s, punk music was also reaching out to young Mexican Americans. It was no surprise when Mexican American punk bands started to become popular; most notably, Los Cruzados. Roots-rock bands like Los Lobos, the Blasters, and the Iguanas continued to include Mexican music in their recordings.

Mythology

In all cultures and civilizations, myths do much more than simply tell stories. More often than not myths reflect values relevant to culture and attempt to provide answers to mysterious or philosophical questions such as why are we here. Myths, which were originally passed orally from generation to generation, can also be didactic, teaching the younger members of a society everything from morals to a culturally accepted version of history, usually combining fact and fiction.

In general there are six types of myths: creation myths, which deal with the creation of anything from the universe to a lake; origin myths, which can cover the origins of either the human race or a specific people; hero myths; apocalyptic myths, which can tell of either death and the afterlife or of the end of the world; renewal myths, such as those which deal with the renewal of the seasons; and morality myths, which often are animal tales and fables. Each of these have existed in every civilization that has occupied Mexico, from those of pre-Columbian times to that of the modern day. However, since the Catholic conversion of Mexico that began in the late sixteenth century, most of the pre-Columbian myths have been either adapted or superseded by Christian myths. Since the emergence of the Chicano movement in the 1960s Chicano-identity myths have also become politically significant.

The trickster Coyote

In many cultures around the world morality myths are built around a central multipersonality character known as a trickster. The trickster is usually an animal, and in many Native American cultures of the U.S. Southwest and northern Mexico, the trickster is known as Coyote. At times cunning and mean and at other times helpful to humankind and other animals, Coyote has magical powers and enjoys playing pranks and making mischief.

Coyote is one of many animal characters that find their way into Mexican American fables. He is often the subject of *corridos* (ballad songs), stories, and folk narratives. Since the 1920s a person who smuggles people across the border into the United States has been called a coyote. The parallel with the mythical being derives from the paradoxical nature of the task that these people perform. They give people hope, but at the same time they profit from the dreams of those they transport.

Catholic characters

Christian myths, which can include creation and other major types of myths, are another source of lessons in morality. Many Catholic characters have been either adapted to fit the Mexican landscape and culture or are seen as being uniquely Mexican, combining Indian and Spanish characteristics. The most sacred Mexican Catholic character is the Virgin of Guadalupe, who is said to have appeared to a peasant named Juan Diego in 1531 on a hillside outside Mexico City. The vision directed Diego to tell the bishop she wanted a chapel built for her at that spot. The bishop doubted Diego, whom he considered too lowly to be a holy messenger. Diego returned to the hillside and was directed by the Virgin to return to the bishop with his cape full of roses, which did not readily grow there, as proof. When Diego did this, the bishop found that the *tilin*'s (cape's) rough surface miraculously contained an image of the Virgin herself. Juan Diego later became Mexico's first indigenous saint for his devotion to the Virgin Mary, although there is no evidence that he ever actually existed.

Miraculous appearances of saints are not uncommon in Mexican American folktales. One story from New Mexico has remained so well loved through the years that it still draws hundreds of visitors to the Loretto Chapel in Santa Fe, New Mexico. The Miraculous Staircase in the Loretto Chapel was built sometime between 1877 and 1881. It has two 360 degree turns with no visible means of support, nails, or dowels. The story behind the staircase goes back to the building of the chapel. When the chapel was completed, there was no way to access the choir loft 22 feet (6.7 m) above. Carpenters were called in to address the problem but concluded that access to the loft would have to be via a ladder, because a staircase would interfere with the interior space of the small chapel. To find a solution to the problem, the nuns made a special prayer to Saint Joseph, the patron saint of carpenters. Not long afterward a man showed up at the chapel with a donkey and a toolbox looking for work. Months later, after completing the elegant circular staircase, the carpenter disappeared without pay or thanks. The nuns believed the stranger had been Saint Joseph himself.

Another indigenous Mexican Catholic myth that emphasizes the significance of religious devotion, as well as female purity and the special value placed on obedient young women, is the Kneeling Nun rock near Silver City, New Mexico. The rock is said to resemble a nun kneeling in prayer. Several legends surround the rock, including one associated with Juan Diego. One myth tells of a young nun from a convent who fell in love with a wounded Spanish soldier brought in from a battle with Indians. Torn between her devotion to God and love of the young man, she prayed to the Virgin Mary for help. After the prayer the nun was turned into stone to preserve her from sin.

Apart from the Christian Virgin of Guadalupe the most famous female character in Mexican American mythology is Doña Marina, more popularly known as La Malinche. La Malinche was a historical character who was the Indian guide and mistress of the conquistador Hernán Cortés. Over the centuries she has featured in many legends and has come to embody different political and sexual ideals. During the colonial period she was seen as a powerful and good woman who was loyal to Spain. As the struggle for Mexican independence grew in the early nineteenth century Mexicans came to see her as a traitor to her people.

However, at the start of the twentieth century, after the mestizos (descendants of Spanish and Indians) had held political power in the republic of Mexico for several decades, the perception of La Malinche, who had supposedly been the mother of the first mesitzo, changed again. This time she was seen, like the Virgin of Guadalupe, as a symbol of Mexico. Because legend related that Cortés had abandoned her and taken their child with him back to Spain, she was also seen as a victim of colonialism.

Hero legends

Both hero and morality myths can teach about courage and bravery and at the same time promote certain figures from history, such as La Malinche, as symbols of pride or victimization. In the early

A modern statue in Mexico City of the sixteenth-century bishop of Mexico, Juan de Zumárraga, kneeling before the peasant Juan Diego who holds a cape imprinted with the image of the Virgin of Guadalupe. Both Juan Diego and the Virgin are symbols of Mexican national identity.

The Weeping Woman

Mexican American folklore is often characterized by chilling and didactic ghost stories. These supernatural legends often serve to warn young children and to express cultural ideals. La Llorona (the Weeping Woman) is a ghost who wanders along canals and rivers at night crying for her lost children. When she comes across children on their own she abducts them in replacement of her own children. In the most popular version of the myth a wealthy man and a poor woman fall in love and have several children out of wedlock, until eventually the young man is persuaded by his parents to marry a wealthy girl they have chosen. When he confesses to his lover that he will marry someone else, Llorona becomes enraged, kills their children and hides their bodies, and then kills herself. However, she is not allowed into heaven until she tells God where she hid her children's bodies. In her grief she has forgotten and returns to earth crying for them, *"Ayyy, mis hijos!"* ("Oh, my children!").

For many Mexicans, La Llorona is a bad woman because she has failed in one of the most significant female roles, motherhood. This version of the myth does two things. One is to encourage young women to remain virgins until marriage and to not be seduced by young men unwilling to marry them. The other lesson is a warning to young children that they should not roam around on their own after dark.

twentieth century, when Mexican nationalism was entering a phase of revolutionary defiance in the face of U.S. intervention, mythic heroes featured in traditional folk ballads called *corridos*. Some of the more popular examples of these types of heroes include the revolutionary leaders Francisco "Pancho" Villa and Emiliano Zapata and the murdered rancher from south Texas, Gregorio Cortez. Cortez was falsely accused of having stolen a horse and was pursued by Texans until he was caught and killed. In "El Corrido de Gregorio Cortez" the folk hero is seen as a defender of Mexican values and fighter against injustice.

As the century wore on other concerns gripped Mexicans living in the border region, such as immigration and discrimination, and these issues were also depicted in *corridos*. Also known as victim *corridos*, they featured a character who was the victim of injustice. For example, the *corrido* "Discriminación a un Mártir" (Discrimination against a martyr) features the true story of Felix Longoria, a Mexican American soldier who was killed in World War II but whose body was denied burial in his hometown in Texas.

Myths of Chicano identity

Since the 1960s Mexican American mythology has focused on the sociopolitical climate in the United States and used the legendary homeland of Aztlán for myths of identity. Aztlán is believed to be the place in the U.S. Southwest where the ancestors of the Mexican Indians originated. During the Chicano civil rights movement in the late 1960s Aztlán became a symbol of Chicano identity.

A descriptive view of this relationship between a mythical land and Mexican Americans is found in a parable describing two migrant workers, a mother and son, walking with Aztlán in the background. In the tale the mother, Evangelista, is showing the way to her son, Christian. They are fleeing from a city of destruction and "fields of death," which represent the oppressive existence of capitalism and racism in the United States.

La Malinche emerged once again, this time as a central mythological figure of Chicano identity. La Malinche in this period was heralded by both supporters of the Chicano movement and Mexican American feminists. For feminists Malinche is seen as a woman who was violated and abandoned but was strong, intelligent, and a survivor.

The Chicano movement also employed *corridos* that appealed for solidarity, such as "Yo Soy Tu Hermano" (I'm your brother) and "El Corrido de César Chávez," about the Mexican American labor organizer and cofounder of the United Farm Workers union.

Catharine Inbody

SEE ALSO:

Catholic Church; Chicano Art; Chicano Writers; Corridos; Folklore; Literature; Malinche, La; Murals and Muralists; Villa, Francisco "Pancho"; Virgin of Guadalupe.

NADBank

The North American Development Bank (NADBank), like its sister organization the Border Environmental Cooperation Commission (BECC), was established in connection with the passage of the North American Free Trade Agreement (NAFTA), which was implemented in 1994. Both organizations were planned as concessions to those who opposed NAFTA on the grounds of its potentially harmful environmental consequences.

NADBank represents a unique experiment in that it is the world's first development bank established to finance nothing except environmental infrastructure projects. NADBank is bilaterally funded, with Mexico and the United States participating as equal partners. NADBank's authorized capital is U.S. $3 billion, with equal commitments from the United States and Mexico. The bank is scheduled to be fully funded by 2006.

Management

NADBank is managed jointly by the United States and Mexico. The bank is governed by a board of directors consisting of six members—three from Mexico and three from the United States. The chair of the board alternates between the two nations. Likewise, the managing director and the deputy managing director, elected by the board of directors, are drawn from both nations; the deputy managing director must be a citizen of the country not represented by the managing director.

Lending practices

There are numerous restrictions on lending by NADBank. All NADBank-financed projects must be certified by the BECC; they must also be directly related to potable water supply, wastewater treatment, or municipal solid waste management. All projects must also lie within a 62-mile (100-km) north-south region of the U.S.-Mexican border. Under the NADBank's charter, it is required to make loans at an interest rate high enough to compensate for the cost of funds and the risk associated with lending on border infrastructure.

These restrictions make it difficult for NADBank to find qualified projects, which has compromised its mission and its effectiveness. In particular, many border communities have limited economic resources. Projects proposed to the bank by these communities that qualify on environmental grounds often do not qualify on economic grounds because of a community's limited ability to repay. NADBank's difficulty in finding projects eligible for funding has subjected the bank to criticism.

NADBank has made efforts to overcome the problem, however. It has aggressively sought out grant funds from donors that can be used to subsidize loans to deserving projects. For example, the Border Environmental Infrastructure Fund (BEIF), funded by the U.S. Environmental Protection Agency, has been used to subsidize loans to U.S. and Mexican environmental projects. BEIF provides grants to communities to reduce the total cost of necessary works. BEIF funds have been critical to the success of many of the projects funded by NADBank.

NADBank has also set up a low interest lending facility, through which up to U.S. $50 million of NADBank funds are made available at low interest rates. Communities with limited resources are able to borrow at below market rates.

Outreach programs

To ensure the long-run viability of its projects, NADBank has been involved in several programs to assist communities in the proper development and management of utility systems. For example, the Institutional Development Cooperation Program (IDP) aids borderland communities in identifying strengths and weaknesses in their current management practices and in developing plans for improvement. The Utility Management Institute, part of the IDP, provides the management and staff of border utilities with the opportunity for ongoing professional development.

Christopher A. Erickson

SEE ALSO:
Alliances and Agreements; Banking and Finance; Border Environmental Cooperation Commission; Cross-Border Initiatives; Environment; NAFTA.

NAFTA

The North American Free Trade Agreement (NAFTA) is a treaty between Mexico, the United States, and Canada to liberalize trade and create an economic region within the larger world economy. It came into effect on January 1, 1994.

As a trade agreement NAFTA is unusual in that it pairs two highly developed countries, Canada and the United States, with a developing one, Mexico. Although Canada has less than one-third of Mexico's population, the Canadian economy is twice as large as Mexico's, while the U.S. economy is twenty times larger. Two theories exist to explain how NAFTA will affect this considerable disparity of wealth. Either Mexico will catch up with Canada and the United States (convergence) or the North-South divide will continue to widen (divergence). Whatever happens, analysts view NAFTA as an efficient way to marshal the potential of all three countries—rich Canadian resources, low-cost Mexican labor, and advanced U.S. technology—to compete in the global economy.

NAFTA may soon expand beyond North America to bring other nations in the Western Hemisphere into a Free Trade Area of the Americas. This expanded trading bloc could be seen as a competitive response to the European Economic Area (EEA), which includes the European Union plus the European Free Trade Association. The EEA came into effect in the same year as NAFTA and is currently the world's largest free-trade zone. NAFTA is the second largest zone, bringing together in a single market over 400 million consumers in Canada, Mexico, and the United States.

NAFTA provides for the gradual elimination of tariffs (duties on imported or exported goods) and other trade barriers on most goods produced and

Representatives of Mexico, the United States, and Canada at the NAFTA signing ceremony at San Antonio, Texas, in 1992. Standing from left to right are Mexican president Carlos Salinas de Gortari, U.S. president George H. W. Bush, and Canadian prime minister Brian Mulroney.

sold in North America. NAFTA began with a 1988 bilateral free-trade agreement between Canada and the United States designed to ease protectionism and regulate trade between the two. In 1990 Carlos Salinas de Gortari, president of Mexico (1988–1994), proposed his own free-trade agreement with the United States to stimulate foreign trade with Mexico. Canada then joined the discussion for a comprehensive North American agreement, and all three signed an accord in December 1992.

NAFTA committed Mexico to the same general principles of trade as Canada and the United States. Side agreements addressed problems arising from issues such as labor, the environment, and intellectual property rights (patents, copyrights, and trademarks). About 60 percent of existing tariffs between member nations were eliminated in 1994, with the rest scheduled to be phased out by 2008.

NAFTA regulations

NAFTA contains hundreds of provisions. The text of the agreement spans five volumes, including separate tariff schedules for each country. Two particularly important provisions are the "rule of origin" and equal treatment for investors. To qualify for reduced NAFTA tariff rates, products must be made in one of the member countries. This rule of origin is important because products made in a NAFTA country may contain parts from nonmember nations, so the agreement stipulates how much of a product can be produced outside the NAFTA area and still qualify for lower tariff rates.

NAFTA requires that member nations give comparable status to investors from other NAFTA countries. In effect, this means that one member country cannot treat companies from another any differently than it treats its own. This rule promotes foreign direct investment between member nations, but it also includes unprecedented investment rights and protections. It means that a company can sue the government of a NAFTA country if that company believes a government regulation or decision adversely affects its interests and conflicts with its NAFTA rights. In other words, corporate interests may in some circumstances take precedence over a government's right to regulate in the public interest. Arguably, such provisions weaken the power of the nation-state under NAFTA.

Opposition to NAFTA

During the ratification of NAFTA there were acrimonious debates in individual countries, not only along party political lines but also over fundamental issues, in particular labor and environmental issues. For example, environmentalists in Canada and the United States argued that pollution control and food safety were uneven under NAFTA because Mexico had lower standards in these areas. In response to these criticisms, side agreements were added to the original accord to address environmental standards and labor issues, although they remain difficult to enforce.

By far the most politically charged argument against NAFTA has been the issue of job losses. U.S.

NAFTA and the Freedom of Trade

NAFTA's aims are to strengthen cooperation among the participating nations and to enhance trade by creating, expanding, and securing future markets. Additional goals include establishing fair rules of trade, creating new job opportunities, promoting development, and strengthening environmental regulations. Other significant challenges outlined in the agreement include lessening distortions to trade between the member nations and enhancing the competitiveness of North American companies in global markets.

Tariff concessions include lower restrictions in key sectors of the individual economies: automobiles, textiles and clothing, energy, and agriculture. Guidelines provide for areas traditionally not covered in trade agreements, such as cross-border investment, financial services, and telecommunications. In addition, procedures exist for the settlement of disputes.

There are grandfather clauses, or exceptions to the regulations for preexisting conditions, to address federal laws and regulations that cannot easily be changed. The Mexican Constitution, for instance, mandates state control of certain sectors of the economy: those dealing with energy, public transportation, and communication, such as the postal system. Therefore Mexico reserves the right to review business arrangements in these areas.

A U.S. customs official oversees the x-raying of a truck from Mexico as it enters the United States. This detection method can check vehicles for contraband goods, illegal drugs, firearms, and undocumented migrants in under an hour, speeding up waiting time at the border.

government analysts anticipated significant export-related job growth because of NAFTA, but many U.S. and Canadian workers were not convinced. It was feared that Canada would lose U.S. investment to Mexico, especially in manufacturing, because Mexican wages and production costs are much lower. In the United States, where the minimum wage is much higher than in Mexico, workers also feared job losses because NAFTA made it easier for U.S.-based companies to outsource production south of the border. In other words, U.S. corporations could take advantage of the lower wages and more lax environmental and labor laws in Mexico. Opponents of NAFTA argued there would be a "race to the bottom" for America workers because of pay cuts and lost jobs.

NAFTA has indeed affected American manufacturing jobs as U.S. companies moved production south of the border. In 1998, for instance, such U.S. icons as Huffy Bicycles in Celina, Ohio, once the world's largest bicycle manufacturer, and Bass Shoes, which had been in Maine for over 120 years, laid off their workers and shifted manufacturing to Mexico.

Other companies, such as Thomson Consumer Electronics in Bloomington, Indiana, followed. Of the 1,200 workers laid off by Thomson, only 8 percent found jobs comparable to or better than those they had held before Thomson moved to Mexico.

Canadian and Mexican concerns

Canada and Mexico were concerned about U.S. cultural hegemony and economic annexation. Canadians are especially worried about the influence of the all-pervasive U.S. media on Canadian culture and identity. Canada has won some tariff concessions from the United States but is nevertheless being flooded by the sheer volume of U.S. media. Mexicans, too, fear the influence of the U.S. economy. Small farmers in Mexico have protested the importation of American agricultural products under NAFTA. They argue that they cannot compete with American agribusiness. Consequently, the Mexican government has won a 15-year exemption from the NAFTA tariff elimination schedule for corn, Mexico's national staple, but in exchange has given the United States concessions for its tomato growers, who compete with farmers in Mexico. As over 20 percent of Mexican jobs are in agriculture, and Mexico's only competitive agricultural products are coffee and vegetables, NAFTA and Mexican-U.S. relations will be seriously tested once the tariff concession on corn ends in 2009.

Effects of NAFTA

When NAFTA came into effect in 1994 U.S. opponents soon noted that Mexican exports to the United States increased while the U.S. trade surplus with Mexico showed a deficit. NAFTA was therefore a major campaign issue in the 1996 presidential election, and in 1997 Congress refused to grant President Bill Clinton (1996–2000) the right to shorten the approval process in future trade deals. A 1996 opinion poll in *Business Week* showed only 26 percent of the U.S. population believed that the United States benefited from NAFTA. Polls in Mexico and Canada yielded similar results.

While proponents contend that NAFTA is a win-win situation for growth and jobs, critics note that the effect of increased trade on job creation during this period has actually been negative rather than positive. Relying on U.S. Department of Commerce statistics, they argue that, while trade exports created about 4.1 million jobs between 1992 and 2000, rising imports during the period accounted for the loss of 7.3 million jobs, for a net effect of 3.2 million lost jobs. In addition, they maintain that increased trade has forced workers out of manufacturing into services and lower-paid jobs. In 1999, for instance, 11.4 million workers (about 9 percent of the total U.S. labor force) either gained or lost a job due to trade. In Canada, too, jobs in export industries rose while in areas affected by imports they fell. The overall result was job displacement. In the 1990s unemployment in Canada was higher than the 1980s, averaging nearly 10 percent.

In Mexico, too, there seems to have been a decline in real wages and stable, well-paid jobs. NAFTA has benefited a few sectors of the Mexican economy, mostly maquiladora industries, but it has not decreased inequality or enhanced incomes and job quality for the majority of Mexicans. Many individual workers in Canada, Mexico, and the United States have been disadvantaged by NAFTA.

NAFTA appears to favor transnational corporations and large investors over individual workers, farmers, small businesses, and the environment. However, it remains strategically important for its member countries. It has provided a much needed improvement in North-South relations, and has the potential of integrating the Americas and becoming the largest trading bloc in the global economy. Without NAFTA, its advocates contend, North American nations would revert to protectionism and forgo the benefits of a large regional market.

An overlooked but important result of NAFTA has been the increase in the crossborder flow of people. Border officials in the United States now handle over 500 million border crossings per year, more than the combined populations of Canada, the United States, and Mexico. Although NAFTA does not explain all of this activity, it accounts for much of the increase since 1994. The interaction between North American nations caused by NAFTA is bound to change people's attitudes and ideas as people from different member nations come into contact with one another more frequently. A common economic community will likely lead to increased convergence, resulting in shared goals, values, and institutions. The political, economic, social, and cultural impact of NAFTA, however, cannot be adequately measured until after the agreement is fully operational in 2009.

Mixed results

During its first eight years NAFTA yielded mixed results. Canada and the United States experienced trade deficits, manufacturing declines, and job losses in key industries, but they also enjoyed considerable growth and wealth creation in others. Mexico, too, was faced with uneven results. NAFTA markedly benefits the northern part of the country, along the border with the United States, in comparison to the rest of Mexico. In addition, Mexican workers face a continued risk of being exploited.

However, Mexico as a nation stands to gain the most. Whereas Canada and the United States already had their own free-trade agreement, NAFTA forces Mexico, a relatively poor country with high import duties and trade and investment restrictions, to sink or swim in the competitive North American economy. Finally, the creation of a single market makes all three NAFTA countries larger players in the world economy.

Joel Hodson

SEE ALSO:

Agriculture; Border Environmental Cooperation Commission; Free Trade; Manufacturing; Maquiladoras; NADBank; Tariffs; Trade.

Nationalism

The concept of *nation* may be defined as the aggregation of a group of people with a shared cultural, historical, and linguistic identity. By extension, *nationalism* may be explained as pride in and devotion to the nation by its members. Nationalism can also be accompanied by the desire to celebrate the group's shared identity and to defend the group (nation) from external threats, both of which can lead to prejudice, xenophobia, and wars.

The relationship between Mexico and the United States has often been an uneasy one. There are vast differences between the cultural identities of each country, and this, in part, has fanned the nationalistic tendencies each country has sometimes displayed, and continues to display, when referring to the other. Because the two countries share a long border, the subject of nationalism is further complicated by immigration issues and the existence of borderland peoples (known as borderlanders) whose identity is neither wholly Mexican nor American but rather a combination of the two.

Nationalism in the United States stems from a belief in the country's political, cultural, economic, and military superiority. The United States is made up of people from multiple and diverse ethnic backgrounds, but at the same time there is an expectation within the United States that ethnic minorities will assimilate into the greater American popular culture. However, as many other countries see it, U.S. nationalism is often expressed as aggressive and self-serving. Non-Americans, perhaps most often Mexicans and Canadians, can feel the full weight of this "America-first" nationalism in terms of anti-immigration sentiment, hostility to internal bilingualism, the exportation of U.S. consumerism, and the export of American popular culture through, for example, merchandise, fast-food restaurants, fashion, and Hollywood movies.

Mexican nationalism

Mexican nationalism, on the other hand, has traditionally been far more defensive and inward looking than that of either the United States or the major European nations, such as Great Britain, France, and Germany. For the most part Mexico's history—from the pre-Columbian civilizations, such as the Aztecs and the Maya, to the revolutionary movements and widespread social reforms in the nineteenth and early twentieth centuries—has formed the basis of the country's nationalism. However, there is far more to Mexico's nationalism than an expression of pride in its own history. During the past two hundred years Mexico's nationalism has gone through four distinct stages: colonial (leading up to Mexico's Wars of Independence, 1810–1921), pre-revolution and revolution (leading up to and including the revolution of 1910–1920), post-revolution (includes most of the twentieth century up to the economic crisis of the 1980s), and modern (from the 1980s to the present).

Colonial nationalism

In the late eighteenth century the criollos (those of purely Spanish descent who were born and raised in Mexico), many of whom resented the economic power and privilege enjoyed by the *peninsulares* (people from Spain who governed in Mexico), came up with the idea of a Mexico politically and culturally independent from Spain. For them Mexico was a place with a specific history and culture that had long outgrown its dependence on Europe. It was also during this early pre-independence, nationalistic movement that the Virgin of Guadalupe became a political symbol of Mexico.

In September 1810 a Catholic criollo priest, Miguel Hidalgo y Castilla, made his call for freedom in the city of Dolores, signaling the beginning of the wars of independence. Between 1810 and 1821, when Spain formally recognized Mexico's independence, the criollos, mestizos (of Spanish and Indian descent), and Indians of Mexico expressed a growing hatred of the Spanish. Following independence this resentment of foreigners grew to include the French, British, and Americans.

Pre-revolution and revolution-era nationalism

For most of the nineteenth century Mexico's nationalism was ill defined and despondent as the country endured dictatorships and political upheavals, lost the Mexican-American War (1846–1848), and was forced to give up vast territory to the United States. The nationalistic highlight during this period, however, was the liberal leadership of Benito Juárez and the expulsion of the French in 1867.

Under the rule of Porfirio Díaz (1877–1911) foreign investment in and immigration to Mexico were encouraged in order to boost the nation's economy, although few Mexicans actually benefited. In the climate of foreign involvement, a new wave of xenophobia emerged that led to the revolution: in part a political, economic, and xenophobic movement against the rule of Díaz. Eventually, however, the xenophobia that sparked the revolution led to a new sense of nation-building, out of which emerged Mexico's most important phase of nationalism.

During the revolution there were many different political factions—the Maderistas, Hueristas, Carranzistas, and Villistas—each claiming to be the true representative of Mexican patriotism and each criticizing the others as being "un-Mexican." However, some of these competing groups were able to unite when faced with an external threat, such as from the United States. More significantly, the revolutionary period was a source of nationalistic folklore in the form, for example, of the resistance of the Mexican naval cadets during the U.S. siege of Veracruz in 1914 and the success of the Villistas in eluding the U.S.-led Pershing Expedition (1916–1917).

Post-revolution nationalism

After the revolution, the Mexican government began rebuilding the economy in a way very different from the Díaz era. The most dramatic economic reforms included greater state control of the oil industry and changes to agrarian policies, such as the *ejido* system. In order to popularize these changes, governments, beginning with that of Plutarco Elías Calles (president 1924–1928) and peaking with that of Lázaro Cárdenas, who nationalized the petroleum industry in 1938, promoted economic nationalism. This new nationalism also glorified the country's indigenous past and its contemporary political leaders. The paintings and murals by Diego Rivera, José Clemente Orozco, and David Alfaro Siqueiros, portrayed in public spaces the splendor of Mexico's pre-Columbian civilizations and the achievements of its national heroes. Additionally, the concept of the *raza cosmica* (cosmic race), forged by the writer and philosopher José Vasconcelos, exalted the Mexican mestizo as the repository of a great civilization.

It was during this era that Mexican nationalism began forming a collective consciousness of shared cultural identity binding all Mexicans together under a common notion of "nationhood." There were practical political motivations behind this new sense of unity. The Partido Revolucionario Institucional (PRI; Institutional Revolutionary Party), the sole governing political party for most of the twentieth century, relied on the concept of single nationhood in order to maintain its dominance. Consequently Mexican nationalism has evolved into something more than pride in a shared cultural identity. Mexican nationalism, especially in the postrevolutionary period, has also functioned as a tool for muting public criticism of the state, for resolving conflict, and for promoting a specific vision of the revolutionary society.

Mexico's modern nationalism

In the 1980s and 1990s Mexico became more integrated into, and dependent on, the world financial market and economic system. The neoliberal and proglobalization policies during this era redefined the country's sense of its own place in the world. However, this change of direction did not sit well with all Mexicans. The late twentieth and early twenty-first centuries witnessed Mexico continuing to promote a type of nationalism wrapped in the cultural symbols of the past, as was evidenced by the popularity in all parts of Mexico of the Zapatista movement.

It is possible to say that nationalism in Mexico, as an expression of shared cultural identity and revolutionary political ideology, is both a celebration of what Mexico is and a fervent denunciation of what it is clearly not. Mexican nationalism can be defined by its indigenous and colonial legacies; by its struggles for independence and freedom not only from Spain but also from relationships with other imperial powers; by its twentieth century social revolution; and by all the attendant heroes, myths, and symbols associated with the forging of its "cosmic race."

James D. Huck, Jr.

SEE ALSO:

Bilingual Education; Foreign Policy, Mexican; Foreign Policy, U.S.; Greater Mexico; Mexican Revolution; Nativism, U.S.; Pershing Expedition.

Nationalization

During the twentieth century in Mexico the government took ownership of many businesses and industries, including the oil industry, the telephone company, and the banking system. This process is called nationalization. However, pressure has been growing from inside the country and abroad to sell off these companies.

For many years after the Mexican Revolution (1910–1920), most Mexicans, including business-people, agreed that nationalization was good for the country, and that the government had a right, if not an obligation, to run many industries. Since the 1980s, however, pressure has been growing, both domestically and internationally, for Mexico to sell off, or privatize, its nationalized industries.

Even though twentieth-century Mexico did not develop into a socialist state, the Mexican Revolution was inspired by socialist ideals, so it is not surprising that the Constitution of 1917 described the state as the rector, or main regulator, of the economy. Even so, during the first years after the revolution, the state intervened in the economy more for practical than theoretical reasons. The first government-run corporations helped jump-start the economy after years of war and devastation. They included the Bank of Mexico, the National Development Bank, and the Federal Electricity Commission. These nationalizations were welcomed by workers and peasants who stood to benefit from cheap electricity brought to rural areas, and from cheap agriculture credit. Nationalization met little resistance from the Mexican business community, which realized that state-run banks and utilities would make it easier to start and manage private companies. By 1930 the state had nationalized 12 companies.

Nationalization under Cárdenas

The government truly became rector of the Mexican economy during the administration of President Lázaro Cárdenas (1934–1940). Cardenas's most significant step toward this goal was the nationalization of the oil industry, which until then had been almost completely owned by U.S., British, and other foreign companies. Cárdenas began expanding the state's role in the economy in order to promote Mexico's economic development. By 1940 some 57 businesses had been nationalized, including the national railroads.

By the end of Cárdenas's term, Mexico was on the way to nationalizing hundreds more businesses: some 470 by 1970. The phase in Mexican history from 1940 to 1970 is known as the era of miracle growth. The state intervened in the economy with other methods besides nationalization, including price controls, which set fixed prices for certain products, and protectionist tariffs, which blocked foreign imports and encouraged Mexicans to buy products made in their own country. The government also created mixed public-and-private companies and took control of businesses that were going bankrupt. The business community generally agreed that all this government involvement in the economy was good for business.

Increasing state intervention

In the 1970s the countrywide consensus on the benefits of nationalization started falling apart. Luis Echeverría (president 1970–1976) greatly expanded state intervention into the economy. He thought doing so would help develop Mexico, strengthen its economic and political independence, and distribute the country's wealth more equally among the rich and the poor. Echeverría created hundreds of new state enterprises. His successor, José López Portillo (president 1976–1982), continued Echeverría's policies and even nationalized the banks in 1982. The number of enterprises owned mainly by the government had more than tripled since 1972 and state participation in the economy was the highest it had ever been in Mexican history.

Even during Echeverría's administration, however, the business community and others had started to complain that the government was gaining too much influence over the economy. When the country experienced a major economic crisis during a world collapse of oil prices during López Portillo's administration, critics became even more opposed to the government's expanding role in the economy. Powerful businesspeople began deserting the long-standing ruling party, the Partido Revolucionario Institucional (PRI; Institutional Revolutionary Party) and shifted their allegiance to the Partido Acción Nacional (PAN; National Action Party), a conservative, probusiness party.

Move toward privatization

When Miguel de la Madrid became president, his administration (1982–1988) began to reduce the state's role in the economy. Nationalized industries were privatized, merged with private firms, or closed down. At first this restructuring was simply a response to the ongoing economic crisis and an attempt to make the government more efficient, but soon neoliberalism, the idea that the state should have as little as possible to do with the economy or social welfare and that private enterprise should play the major role, began to take hold in Mexico.

During the 1980s the business community in Mexico supported the international trend toward neoliberalism. Mexico's economic troubles were blamed on its large public sector. The Mexican Employers Confederation, Coparmex, joined the United States and other foreign investors in demanding that more state enterprises in Mexico be privatized. By the end of de la Madrid's term in 1988, the government had privatized or closed down almost 750 state-run enterprises.

The next president, Carlos Salinas de Gortari (1988–1994), continued the privatization of state-owned industries and announced that he would seek a "redefinition of the role of the state." He told Mexicans that money earned from selling nationalized businesses could be spent on education and other social projects such as providing clean water. In 1990 Salinas showed international financiers that he was serious about privatization by selling off the banking system and Teléfonos de México, the national telephone company. Both industries were very profitable, but they needed massive investment in order to modernize, and foreign investors were eager to intervene. Salinas then privatized very profitable steel, mining, and airline companies. By mid-1991, the state was left with only about 260 companies, down from 1,155 in 1982. Salinas also passed laws in 1995 for the privatization of the railroads, a complex project that met with little success.

During the last two decades of the twentieth century the Mexican government transformed itself. It had defined itself as broker between the interests of the business sector and the workers and farmers. From then on, however, the government operated on the assumption that private business was good for everybody.

Effects of privatization

Privatization of previously state-owned firms did indeed bring some benefits: increased efficiency in many industries and more money for the national treasury. However, it also had disturbing consequences. Increased efficiency often came at the expense of public welfare. In the late 1980s, for instance, more than 110,000 jobs were lost because of cost-cutting measures at the four biggest public enterprises. One was the national airline, Aeromexico. To make it more attractive to buyers, the government declared the company bankrupt in order to cancel labor union contracts. This worsened conditions for the workers. When jobs were cut at privatized companies, private sector investment did not compensate for the losses. People who had worked for the government usually ended up out of work.

Privatization also caused an alarming concentration of wealth, since bidders for enterprises put up for sale were generally already Mexico's biggest conglomerates. Private buyers gained monopoly control of enterprises such as copper, soft drinks, telecommunications, transport, lumber, and paper. Privatization also generally took place behind closed doors, with much political wheeling and dealing but little public input, and no chance for small businesses and workers to buy the companies. Privatization also opened the way for more foreign domination, since Mexico did not have enough domestic capital to buy the enterprises. In 2000 foreign investment reached U.S. $13.2 billion, a five-fold increase from U.S. $2.5 billion in 1986.

Some national enterprises were considered too symbolic of Mexican sovereignty to privatize: the oil company (PEMEX), the electricity company, and the health care agency. No Mexican president has suggested selling off these industries. International pressure to do so, however, is increasing. If the government eventually moves to privatize these companies, there may well be strong public protest.

Deborah Nathan

SEE ALSO:

Cárdenas, Lazaro; Comision Federal de Electricidad; Echeverría, Luis; Investment; Madrid, Miguel de la; PEMEX; Railroads; Salinas de Gortari, Carlos.

National Parks

The borderland region of Mexico and the United States has some of the world's most varied landscapes, fashioned by millions of years of tectonic convulsions, volcanic activity, and the action of rivers and seas. Today much of these natural landscapes in both Mexico and the United States are protected as national parks and biosphere reserves.

The coastal plains bordering the Pacific Ocean and the Gulf of Mexico boast national parks having superb wetlands and many unspoiled coastlines, while protected areas along the Gulf of California provide habitat for a variety of marine wildlife. Inland, the vast deserts of Sonora and Chihuahua offer varied and often spectacular scenery, while large areas of forest survive, despite extensive logging, in the mountain ranges of the Sierra Madre Occidental, the Sierra Madre Oriental, and the smaller ranges at the southern beginnings of the Rockies in the United States.

The United States has a long history of affording protection to areas of outstanding natural beauty or rich wildlife. Many of these have national park or national monument status, and a good proportion are in the border states of California, Arizona, New Mexico, and Texas. The Mexican national park network is more recent, but the border states have some of the country's most important parks, some every bit as important as their more famous equivalents north of the border. They are either national parks (places of historic or aesthetic importance) or biosphere reserves (large areas of genuine biological diversity). Increasing numbers of people use these resources for exercise, study, and leisure. Ecotourism has long been an important source of revenue and jobs in the United States, and indications are that this industry is growing fast in Mexico; if this trend is to continue, much will depend on the success of Mexico's national parks and biosphere reserves.

Not far from the northern Mexican city of Monterrey is Cumbres de Monterrey National Park, at 609,000 acres (246,500 ha) Mexico's largest. It has rugged terrain, with gorges and canyons carved in the Sierra Madre Oriental mountains. Spectacular caves, waterfalls, and forests of pine and oak offer a wide range of leisure activities and opportunities to see pumas, coyotes, white-tailed deer, and black bears.

El Vizcaino Biosphere Reserve

The sparsely populated state of Baja California in northwest Mexico has several major national parks. El Vizcaino Biosphere Reserve is the largest biosphere reserve in Mexico. Afforded biosphere reserve status in 1988 by Mexico and given international recognition five years later, El Vizcaino covers 6.18 million acres (2.5 million ha) of coastal Baja California, including two saline lagoons on the Pacific coast of the peninsula, areas of sand dunes and mangrove forest, and the arid mountains of the Sierra San Francisco. This reserve includes the Desert of Vizcaino, San Sebastian Vizcai Bay, Bahia Tortugas, Bahia Ballenas, and many small islands.

Laguna San Ignacio, one of the lagoons in the reserve, is of major international importance as a calving ground for gray whales. Each year about 900 calves are born in the protected waters. During the 1990s the lagoon was at the center of a battle between Mitsubishi and conservationists. The Japanese corporation planned to construct a salt production plant adjacent to the lagoon, but after protests it abandoned the scheme. The reserve's beaches are important nesting grounds for green, hawksbill, and olive ridley turtles, and elephant seals also breed on the coast. The arid interior of the reserve is outstanding for its variety of endemic species of cacti and reptiles. Interesting mammals include the endangered Cedros mule deer.

Also within the reserve, the ancient rock murals of the Sierra San Francisco are some of the largest prehistoric paintings on earth. Examination of the murals using carbon dating techniques puts the oldest at around 2,000 B.C.E., evidence that this part of the Baja California peninsula has a very long history of human settlement. When Jesuit missionaries first visited the area in the late seventeenth century they found the area occupied by the seminomadic Cochini people, but few Native Americans live in El Vizcaino now.

Santa Elena Canyon in the Big Bend National Park in Texas. With the Rio Grande and striking mountains and canyons, the park has one of the most dramatic landscapes along the Mexico-U.S. border.

Other Mexican reserves

East of the Baja California Peninsula, the Gulf Islands Special Biosphere Reserve covers 53 islands in the Gulf of California. The vegetation of the islands is typical of desert environments but with a wide variety of unique cacti. The majority of the islands host breeding seabirds. The islands are accessible from several ports in the states of Baja California, Sonora, and Sinaloa.

Constitucion de 1857 National Park, in the south of the Baja Peninsula, covers 12,370 acres (5,000 ha) in the Sierra de Juarez and peaks at 4,600 feet (1,400 m). One of the main attractions of the park is the fish-rich Lake Hanson. The park is noted for its granite outcrops and dense scrub. Farther south, Sierra San Pedro Martir National Park features desert highlands, granite peaks, canyons, and coniferous forests. The highest peak of Baja California, Picacho el Diablo, lies in the park.

In northern Mexico, Cascade de Basseachic National Park, Chihuahua, is named for Mexico's highest waterfall, at 1,017 feet (310 m). The Cascade de Basseachic can be accessed only after a day-long hike through the pine and oak forests of the Sierra Tarahumara. Besides hiking, many people visit the park to camp and climb.

In northeastern Mexico, El Cielo Biosphere Reserve, Tamaulipas, was created in 1985 when the federal government gave protected status to a 356,000-acre (145,000-ha) swathe of the Sierra Madre Occidental near Ciudad Victoria, 200 miles (320 km) south of Brownsville. Ranging from 650 to 7,500 feet (200 to 2,300 m) above sea level, the reserve's four different habitat types—tropical rain forest, mountain forest, pine-oak forest, and dwarf-oak forest—contain magnificent plant and animal life. The creation of the reserve began a conflict that has been encountered elsewhere between the interests of conservation and those of local people. Logging was banned, depriving many people of a livelihood, and in 1995 the unemployment rate within El Cielo Bioshphere was 70 percent. The park authorities are hopeful that a growth in ecotourism in the reserve will create new jobs and offset this disadvantage.

Big Bend National Park

Farther west in Coahuila, Boquillas de Carmen National Park protects one of the most spectacular canyons through which the Rio Grande, or Río Bravo as it is known in Mexico, flows. Facing the reserve across the river is Big Bend National Park, Texas. According to one Native American legend, the Great Spirit placed all the leftover rocks in Big Bend after making the Earth. One of the most dramatic national parks of the border region, Big Bend is so named because the Rio Grande follows a massive loop, interrupting its southeastward flow to head northeast for 80 miles (130 km) and carve its way through three ranges of mountains. Tectonic movements on a gigantic scale raised the mountains, and the river continued to cut them down, creating canyons such as Boquillas de Carmen and Santa Elena.

Surrounded by the huge expanse of the Chihuahua Desert, the Chisos Mountains are the centerpiece of Big Bend National Park, their upper slopes cloaked in pine and oak forest. The highest of the Chisos peaks, Emory Peak, rises 7,835 feet (2,389 m) above the surrounding desert, affording superb views over the Mexican border. In recent years the views have deteriorated as a result of air pollution, something many blame on Mexican coal-burning power plants. Despite boasting dramatic canyons, beautiful flowering cacti, and a host of interesting wildlife, Big Bend is one of the United States' least-visited national parks, with fewer than 400,000 visitors in 1993, one-tenth of the number visiting Arizona's Grand Canyon National Park.

Carlsbad Caverns National Park

About 100 miles (160 km) northwest of Ciudad Juárez/El Paso in southeast New Mexico is Carlsbad Caverns National Park. Underneath the Guadaloupe Mountains, which straddle the border between the states of New Mexico and Texas, are the Carlsbad Caverns. These limestone caves were formed by the action of water over many thousands of years. Visitors to one these caverns, the Big

Room, descend in an elevator 900 feet (274 m) to approach a cave 1,800 feet (548 m) long and 250 feet (76 m) wide. The Big Room contains some remarkable stalactites and stalagmites, including the Hall of Giants, the Temple of the Sun, and the Rock of Ages. Each is lit with electric lights of various subtle colors to enhance its beauty. There are also underground pools, again illuminated artificially. The natural entrance to the caves provides a home for around 400,000 Mexican free-tailed bats from April to September; during the winter months they remain in Mexico.

Organ Pipe Cactus National Park

Between the Ajo Mountains, Arizona, and the Mexican border lies Organ Pipe Cactus National Monument, a 330,000-acre (133,500-ha) section of the Sonoran Desert, rich in cacti and other plants. Apart from being the only place in the United States where the distinctive large organ pipe cactus grows, the reserve has 25 other cactus species and impressive blooms of golden poppies and pink owl clovers. Between May and July the white flowers of the organ pipe cacti attract visitors, but the reserve's inaccessibility keeps large crowds away.

Joshua Tree

In 1994 a large area of the Mohave Desert in southern California received national park status. Formerly called Joshua Tree National Monument, this area was named for a species of distinctive, spiky tree that is characteristic of the area. Human civilization has a long history in Joshua Tree National Park, stretching back to the Pinto people, one of the earliest cultures of the border region. The reserve has two distinctive characters: the eastern and southern parts are more Sonoran in character—relatively low-lying, very hot, and very arid—while the western section is higher, cooler, and wetter, with some areas of dense forest. Joshua Tree is less than 100 miles (160 km) from both Los Angeles and Mexicali, just south of the Mexican border, and is popular with hikers, bikers, and rock climbers, as well as naturalists.

Tim Harris

SEE ALSO:

Baja California; Border Environmental Cooperation Commission; Chihuahua Desert; Climate; Ecotourism; Environmental Issues; Laguna San Ignacio; Rio Grande/Río Bravo; Sonoran Desert; Tourism; Wildlife.

Native Americans

The postconquest history of Native Americans living in the present-day border region is marked by conflict. This conflict was largely caused by European and Anglo advances into territory that was previously occupied by Indian peoples.

One of the earliest encounters between Native Americans and European settlers in the border region came in 1540 during Francisco Coronado's expedition along the upper Rio Grande in present-day New Mexico. Coronado was looking for the fabled Seven Cities of Cíbola when he came across the Tiwa people. By the time his expedition left in 1541, 10 out of 12 Tiwa villages had been abandoned due to fighting between Coronado's men and the Indians. While spending the winter in the area, the Spanish soldiers demanded that the Tiwas provide them with food, clothing, and women. When the Tiwas resisted 200 were captured and executed. Most were burned at the stake.

Spanish incursions
By the mid 1600s the Spaniards had made moderate headway in present-day New Mexico among the Pueblo Indians. As the missionaries and Spanish government officials expanded their control, there were severe abuses by church officials against the more resistant Native Americans. There were also civil abuses in the use of Native Americans as a labor force. In 1680, the Indians rebelled, provoked by public whippings, mutilations, severe labor practices, and condemnation of their religions. The Pueblos attacked the Spanish town of Santa Fe and killed missionaries in the outlying areas. The Spanish retreated to El Paso and did not fully return to New Mexico until 1692.

In the eighteenth century the Spanish continued their efforts to convert the native American inhabitants of present-day Texas to Christianity. A number of Spanish missions were established. Among the most famous was San Juan de Valero, also known as the Alamo, at present-day San Antonio. Most, if not all of the Spanish missions were constructed with forced Native American labor.

In the more remote areas of southern and western Texas the Apaches, now being pushed by the encroaching Comanches and Kiowas from the north, increased their raids into Mexico, attacking isolated settlements. Some missions, such as San Saba in west-central Texas, were brutally attacked or destroyed by the Apaches. To provide greater security Spain established a line of presidios (forts) along the Mexican side of the Rio Grande.

Shortly before Mexican Independence in 1821 the Spanish government agreed to allow Anglo empresarios (directors of colonial efforts) to come into Spanish Texas to help serve as a buffer against Indian attacks or other foreign incursions. The first of these colonists were Moses Austin and his son, Stephen F. Austin, who arrived in 1821. By this time Texas was also home to large numbers of Cherokee, who had been driven west from their original home near the Appalachian Mountains.

In 1836 Texas became an independent republic, and although the first president of Texas, Sam Houston, was close to the Indians of the Cherokee Confederation led by Chief Bowles, his successor, Mirabeau B. Lamar, was not. Lamar offered the Indians life on the reservation or removal. The Cherokees refused both options. Lamar ordered their removal, an action that resulted in open warfare. Bowles was killed and many tribes of the Confederation were removed to Indian Territory in Arkansas and Oklahoma. The Kickapoo nation, meanwhile, which was not part of the confederation, migrated southward to South Texas and Tamaulipas, Mexico.

The Seminole nation
In the 1840s a band from the Seminole nation in Florida also migrated to Texas. The leader was Coacachee. Between 1846 and 1849 Coacachee traveled across southern Texas and northern Mexico looking for land where his people could settle and be free from U.S. rule. During this time he forged an alliance with a Kickapoo band, led by Papequah, who had moved to Morelos, Coahuila, just south of present-day Eagle Pass, Texas. Other Indians seeking a home were the Potawatomis, Lipan Apache, and some Tonkawas of central Texas.

Between July 1850 and February 1851 Coacachee, Papequah, and a third Indian leader, Cohia, negotiated an agreement with the Mexican Government in which 70,000 acres (28,000 ha) were set aside for the Indians under the supervision of the military colony of Guerrero. Coacachee's people were expected to provide security against Indian and other invasions into northern Mexico. The Indians were later relocated about 100 miles (160 km) southward to Nacimiento, Coahuila, on 17,000 acres (6,880 ha) in the eastern foothills of the Sierra Madre Occidental. After Coacachee died during a smallpox outbreak in 1857 most of the Seminoles left for Indian territories in the United States. However, a number of Kickapoos remained.

The Apache wars

In the second half of the nineteenth century, as waves of Anglo settlers swept westward, the government of the United States intensified its policy of removing Native Americans to reservations. In the Southwest, the main opposition to this policy came from the Apache, many of whom refused to give up their nomadic ways to live on crowded plots of land where food was scarce. Over the course of about 25 years, from around 1861 onward, small bands of Apache warriors carried out raids across Arizona, New Mexico, Texas, and northern Mexico. The end of significant Apache resistance came in 1886, when the rebel leader Geronimo surrendered to a U.S. force of 5,000 men. Geronimo, in contrast, had only 24 men under his command.

A year later the U.S. government passed the Dawes General Allotment Act, under which reservation land was divided up and sold to individual Indians. The aim of the act was to integrate Native Americans into U.S. society by turning them into farmers. In reality, the main effect of the act was the transferral of Indian land into the hands of white property speculators. As a direct result of the legislation, Native American reservations became more crowded and poverty stricken.

In the early twentieth century the governments of Mexico and the United States began to pursue more humane policies regarding the treatment of Native Americans. In the United States the 1934 American Indian Reorganization Act was a first step in the process of giving Native Americans the right to self-determination. The act gave Native Americans sovereignty over their reservations and allowed them to create their own constitutions. After the revolution of 1910–1920, Indians in Mexico were given similar powers of self-government, as they were given *ejido* lands to work communally. In 1948 a National Indian Institute was organized that allowed the Mexican government to work alongside native groups to address the problems that they faced.

Native Americans today

The 2000 U.S. census revealed that at the beginning of the twenty-first century the U.S. border states of California, Arizona, New Mexico, and Texas were home to around 900,000 people of Native American descent. Today many are integrated into mainstream society. However, others still live on reservations. For example, around 8,000 Apache are based on the Fort Apache reservation in eastern Arizona, which covers 1.6 million acres (650,000 ha). Like the inhabitants of many such reservations, those of Fort Apache depend heavily on gambling and tourism for their income. Among the reservation's attractions are the Hon-Dah Casino and the Sunrise Park Ski Resort. Despite the economic opportunities presented by tourism, unemployment and poverty are still serious problems for the reservation's residents.

In response to such difficulties, another branch of the Apache tribe has pursued a more controversial way of exploiting the lands under its control. In 1994 leaders of the Mescalero Apache, who live in central New Mexico, agreed to allow a power company to bury nuclear waste in their soil. The scheme has met considerable opposition from environmental pressure groups.

Other, smaller reservations in the border region include Ysleta del Sur near El Paso, which is home to the Tigua tribe, and the Alabama-Coushatta reservation near Livingston, Texas. Both tribes rely heavily on tourism to generate revenues. Another tribe to occupy land in the border area is the Kickapoo Traditional Tribe of Texas. The Kickapoo were only recognized as a separate people in 1983 and live in lands near the town of El Indio, Texas, 2 miles (3.2 km) from the Mexico-U.S. border. The Kickapoo cross the border frequently; they effectively enjoy a form of dual citizenship.

E. John Gesick, Jr.

SEE ALSO:

Apache; Caddo; Cherokee; Comanche; Indian Policy; Kickapoo; Pueblo; Seminole.

Nativism, U.S.

Nativism is the belief that foreigners represent a threat to Anglo-American culture and values. It affected U.S. attitudes toward Mexican immigrants in the twentieth century, but its origins lie in an earlier era, when certain Americans were reacting against others whom they deemed "undesirables."

By the time Andrew Jackson became U.S. president in 1829, Americans in the relatively newly formed United States defined their identity and nationality largely in terms of Anglo or northern European ancestry, Protestantism, and the speaking of English. Nativism was born during the 1840s, when Irish and German Catholic immigration threatened this narrow self definition. Many Americans shared a determination to prevent the newcomers from polluting what they termed Americanism. Formed in 1852 to counter inroads made by Catholics in urban politics, the Know Nothing Party, also known as the American Party, became the flag bearer of the nativist crusade. The party got its name because, if questioned about their nativist beliefs, its members were supposed to respond that they knew nothing. The party's main objective was to reverse Catholic political gains. Divisions over slavery, among other things, led to the party's demise shortly before the outbreak of the Civil War (1861–1865), but nativism remained an integral ideology for many Americans.

Nativism in the late nineteenth century

After the Civil War Americans responded less harshly to Irish and German Catholics. Many of the newcomers had served bravely on the Union side, while others had acquired social mobility and a greater social acceptance. The fuel that had ignited nativism in the past became diluted temporarily.

The end of the Civil War, however, also encouraged industrialization of the North, which in turn led to renewed antiforeign sympathies. The burgeoning industrial centers required vast amounts of labor that could not be provided by local sources. In the 1890s industrial employers looked to eastern and southern Europe to provide workers. In the West, Asians and Mexicans became major sources of labor.

This packaging label for soap, created in Boston in 1864, draws on the popularity of the Know Nothing cause, even though the party itself was effectively defunct by then.

For nativists this new influx posed an even greater threat. Not only did immigrants who did not speak English and were not Protestants arrive in greater numbers than before; they also possessed an array of customs and values that seemed diametrically opposed to an Anglo-American culture derived from the British Isles and northern Europe.

While industrialism and economic growth created numerous jobs, immigrants received very low wages and were often laid off during the numerous downturns that characterized early industrial capitalism. This resulted in extreme poverty, a circumstance that nativists and social reformers alike associated with the immigrants who crowded into slums that were plagued by crime, disease, and other social problems. The incursion of unwelcome workers coincided with the rise of eugenics, a pseudoscience based on the study of racial characteristics. Eugenics asserted that northern Europeans were superior to other racial groups. This belief further tainted immigration in the eyes of the supporters of Anglo-Americanism.

Nevada

Once part of Mexico, Nevada passed into U.S. hands under the Treaty of Guadalupe Hidalgo in 1848. Although it was never home to as many Mexicans as present-day California or Texas, people of Mexican origin comprised 14 percent of Nevada's population in the 2000 U.S. census.

Nevada has always been sparsely populated: in 2000 its population stood at only 1.2 million inhabitants. The state's low number of residents is mainly due to its remote and difficult terrain. The greater part of Nevada lies in the Great Basin region, a series of valleys separated by approximately one hundred isolated mountain ranges, many of which are between 50 and 75 miles (80 and 120 km) long, with peaks up to 13,000 feet (3,960 m) above sea level. Glaciers exist on 14 of the mountain ranges, which explains the origins of the name Nevada, from the Spanish for "snow covered."

Early inhabitants

The earliest residents of Nevada were Native Americans who entered the Great Basin around 20,000 years ago. Their descendants dominated the region until relatively recently, because it was the last part of the present-day United States to be explored by Europeans. The Native Americans settled near the region's limited water sources. Apart from the Colorado, Columbia, and the Humboldt, Nevada has few permanent rivers. Most of its streams are short-lived and flow only after heavy storms. However, the area contains more than 200 lakes, most of which are small reservoirs.

The three main Native American peoples who settled in Nevada were the Paiute (divided into northern and southern bands), the Shoshone, and the Washo. The Northern Paiute inhabited the area around Pyramid Lake, near Reno. The Southern Paiute occupied the Moapa Valley. The Shoshone led a foraging existence in the western part of the region, spreading out in summer to search for food and coming together in groups of about 60 in fall for festivals and rabbit hunts. The Washo similarly occupied the western part of the territory but lived in the Sierra Nevada mountain range. Scattered food resources required Washo families to forage and hunt individually, although they gathered as a tribe for seasonal fishing at Lake Tahoe.

Among the other Native American tribes were the Walapai and the Mohave. Both peoples occupied territory that in 1935 became Lake Mead, an enormous artificial lake east of Las Vegas, formed by the construction of the Hoover Dam in the same year. Another tribe, the Chemeheuvi, spoke a different language from the Paiute but lived near their territory and had similar lifestyles, as their pottery and basket-making techniques demonstrate. Around 500 C.E. the Pueblo first entered Nevada, where archaeologists believe they remained for three or four centuries.

One of the first Europeans to see Nevada was Francisco Garcés (1738–1781), a Spanish Franciscan priest who reached the Colorado River while traveling from New Mexico to California between 1775 and 1776. The territory was incorporated into Mexico, but the Spanish did not discover mineral resources as they did in other frontier regions and established fewer missions and presidios (forts) in Nevada than in New Mexico, Arizona, or California. Much of the region's exploration was left to Britain and the United States. In the 1820s the British-owned Hudson's Bay Company sent fur trappers to explore the region. In 1825 the U.S. trapper Peter Skene Ogden crossed the Humboldt and Carson river valleys, while the following year Jedediah Strong Smith reached the Walker River and central Nevada. The first systematic observations of the region were made by John C. Frémont, from 1843 to 1845. By the 1840s many U.S. settlers passed through Nevada on their way to the Pacific coast; their numbers rose sharply with the California Gold Rush in 1849.

From U.S. territory to U.S. state

Mexico lost Nevada under the terms of the Treaty of Guadalupe Hidalgo in 1848. The region first became part of California before its incorporation into the Utah Territory in 1850. The Mormons founded the first permanent settlement, at Genoa in Carson Valley in 1849, and established a mission in Las Vegas Valley in 1855. Monthly mail services across northern Nevada began in 1853.

The discovery of silver and gold at the Comstock Lode near Virginia City in 1859 led to major population growth in Nevada. Between 1860 and 1870 the number of Nevadans rose from 7,000 to 42,000. In 1864 U.S. president Abraham Lincoln persuaded Congress to make Nevada a state of the Union. Lincoln saw the advantage of an additional, mineral-rich state in helping the Union against the Confederacy in the U.S. Civil War (1861–1865).

Developments in transport and agriculture in Nevada included the building of a transcontinental railroad across the northern part of the state in 1869 and the growth of cattle ranching and sheep raising in the 1870s. These changes dealt a blow to the region's Native Americans. In 1863 the U.S. government seized Paiute lands in Nevada without making a treaty. The Paiute took up arms and there were several skirmishes in the 1860s and 1870s. The last Native American battle on U.S. soil was fought at Little High Rock Canyon in Washoe County, Nevada, on March 1, 1911, between U.S. officers and a band of renegade Shoshone-Paiute Indians. The Washo were dealt with less harshly. Under the terms of the 1887 Dawes General Allotment Act, 160 acres (65 ha) of land were granted to the head of each family. Nevertheless, Washo culture was severely disrupted. Lacking their own reservation, the Washo were forced to form scattered settlements around ranches and towns.

Nevada in the twentieth century

Nevada's mining and ranching businesses did well in the 1920s but suffered during the Great Depression (1929–1939). The state was quick to diversify its interests, however, and local entrepreneurs took advantage of the relaxation of gambling and divorce laws in the early 1930s to develop the region as a center for casinos, weddings, and divorces. Nevada's tourism industry continued to expand throughout the twentieth century. Modern industrial development began with the completion of the Hoover Dam in 1935, which provided manufacturers in southern Nevada with low-cost hydroelectric power.

Although the histories of Nevada and Mexico have diverged, there remain thriving trade links between the two. In 2001 Mexico had become the second largest export market for goods produced in Nevada, up from the ninth largest in 1996. The main reason for this development was the implementation of the North American Free Trade Agreement (NAFTA) between Mexico, the United States, and Canada in 1994, which was intended to eliminate trade barriers

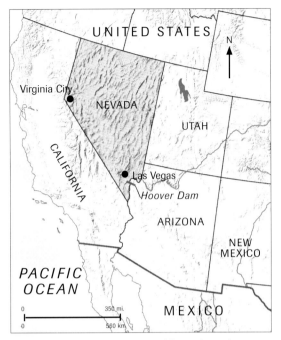

The Spanish did not explore Nevada as fully as other northern territories in Mexico, and it was not until after the region passed into U.S. hands that large deposits of gold, silver, and copper were found.

to exports in each of the three countries. At the start of the twenty-first century two-thirds of Nevada's exports consisted of electrical equipment. Other exports included cement, lime, plaster, and rock salt.

In 2000 Anglo-Americans constituted 75 percent of Nevada's 2 million inhabitants, African Americans made up 6.8 percent, and Hispanics 18 percent. Those of Mexican descent accounted for 14.3 percent of the total population. Most of the Hispanic population was concentrated in and around Las Vegas. Migrant workers were drawn there during the 1990s because of the growing housing market. In 2000, over 83,000 people of Mexican descent lived in the city, about 17 percent of the total population.

Nevada's Hispanics are not only manual workers. In 1998 there were over 1 million Hispanic-owned businesses in Nevada generating $200 billion in annual revenues. Until the 1980s Hispanics would have found it nearly impossible to obtain bank loans to start businesses, but today banks in Nevada are targeting small businesses, specifically those run by Hispanics.

Henry Russell

SEE ALSO:

Guadalupe Hidalgo, Treaty of; Las Vegas; Mining and Minerals; NAFTA; Native Americans; Ranching.

New Mexico

The fifth largest U.S. state, New Mexico is bordered by Arizona, Colorado, Texas, Oklahoma, and Mexico, of which it was a part until 1848. One of the newest states, New Mexico's capital, Santa Fe, is the oldest European settlement in the West.

New Mexico is sparsely inhabited, with just over 1.8 million inhabitants. About 42 percent of the state's population is Hispanic, the highest concentration per capita of Hispanics in the United States. In some northern counties Hispanics constitute a large majority. The state is one of the few, along with California, where Anglos make up less than 50 percent of the population. Around half the Hispanics are Mexican Americans and the other half are descendants of the original Spanish settlers. Spanish remains the dominant language in those areas and is spoken widely throughout New Mexico. It is one of the few U.S. states with two official languages—English and Spanish. About half of the total population is Roman Catholic. The urban areas of Albuquerque, Santa Fe, and Las Cruces are home to about one half the population. Albuquerque is the most populated metropolitan area, with a third of the state's inhabitants.

Native Americans constitute about 9 percent of the population. Most of them are Pueblo, Navajo, or Apache and reside primarily on five reservations and in 19 pueblos; they are concentrated in the northwest counties of McKinley and San Juan. The Bureau of Indian Affairs controls over 12,000 square miles (19,500 sq km) of land.

After a population increase of 6.9 percent in the 1960s, an influx of white Americans raised the New Mexico immigration rate to 28.1 percent in the 1970s and 16.3 percent in the 1980s. This increase was due to a rise in more federal spending on government programs, mainly in defense industries.

Early inhabitants

The earliest known inhabitants of New Mexico were Paleo-Indian hunter-gatherers. Tools and weapons of the Clovis and Folsom cultures have been found in New Mexico, where these cultures flourished about 10,000 years ago.

New Mexico is a state of plains and mountains, with most of its land at least 4,000 feet (1,200 m) above sea level.

Around 1000 C.E. the greater part of New Mexico was inhabited by a culture known as the Basket Makers. Their oldest remains have been unearthed in the Four Corners area, where the states of New Mexico, Arizona, Colorado, and Utah meet. These people are known as Anasazi (from a Navajo word meaning "the ancient ones"). At about the same time, another culture, the Mogollon, flourished farther south. The stone-built villages of the Anasazi and Mogollon can be found across New Mexico. By 1500, however, both groups had migrated and were replaced by other Native Americans. These were the Apache, Comanche, and Navajo, who came to the region from the north. Later the area was settled by Pueblo, descendants of the Anasazi, who cultivated corn, beans, and squash along the Rio Grande.

European exploration

From the 1540s Spanish explorers set out from Mexico in search of gold. They were inspired by the stories of Alvar Nuñez Cabeza de Vaca (1490?–1557?), a Spanish conquistador who was lost in the Southwest for eight years, and who had probably reached New Mexico in 1536. Among the many of his compatriots who followed in his footsteps was

Francisco Vazquez de Coronado (1510?–1554), who explored much of what is now New Mexico.

In 1595 the conquistador Juan de Oñate (1550?–1630) was granted the right by Spain to conquer and govern the territory of New Mexico. He entered the area along the Rio Grande from Mexico. The first settlement at San Juan Pueblo was soon eclipsed by Santa Fe. Founded in 1610 by Don Pedro de Peralta as a mission, the city is one of the oldest in the United States. It has served as the administrative hub of the region since its foundation, and is today the state capital of New Mexico.

Under colonial rule, the lands along the Rio Grande were used for grazing cattle and sheep, but the area was otherwise largely neglected by the Spanish. The Pueblo were often exploited by the Spanish. They reacted by rebelling and in 1680 taking over Santa Fe, which they held for 12 years before it was retaken by the Spanish. After the rebellion, relations with the colonists remained poor.

By 1800, however, trade with the Comanche had started to flourish, and the Spanish population of New Mexico had grown to about 25,000, more than lived in either California or Texas. The region first came to the attention of the United States in the early nineteenth century. In 1806 Lieutenant Zebulon Pike led a detachment of U.S. soldiers into New Mexico. The Mexicans regarded this as a hostile act and imprisoned him for illegal entry. When he was released he went home and spread the news of the area's rich potential.

From Spanish province to U.S. state

In 1821 Spanish rule ended and New Mexico became a state within the Mexican Republic. The following year, the U.S. trader William Becknell and others made the New Mexican capital the western terminus of the Santa Fe Trail, which ran from Independence, Missouri. Along this trade route silver and fur were carried east and manufactured goods moved west. Wagons traveled in convoys to protect themselves against attacks by Native Americans. The trail opened up New Mexico to increased trade and settlement. Mexico attempted to prohibit settlement by U.S. citizens in an effort to prevent a repeat of what happened in Texas, where U.S. settlers gradually outnumbered Mexicans. However, the United States' territorial ambitions became increasingly obvious. Santa Fe was occupied in 1846, at the start of the Mexican-American War, by U.S. troops under General Stephen W. Kearny.

New Mexico was part of the territory ceded to the United States by Mexico in 1848. It became a U.S. Territory in 1850, and the Gadsden Purchase of 1853 added a strip of land to its south, fixing the present boundary with Mexico. Early in the U.S. Civil War (1861–1865), Confederate forces captured the state, but they were defeated at Glorieta Pass near Santa Fe in 1862 and withdrew soon afterward. In 1863 the state assumed its current shape when the Arizona Territory was created. On January 6, 1912, New Mexico became the 47th state of the Union.

Twentieth-century development

With the completion of the southern transcontinental railroad from Kansas City to Los Angeles in the early 1880s, New Mexico was more easily accessible than ever before to the rest of the United States. Cattle ranching expanded, irrigated commercial agriculture began, and petroleum and potash were mined in large quantities. Tourism also became economically important.

In the twentieth century new industries were attracted to New Mexico by its vast expanses of open land and good climate. Military weapons were developed and tested here during World War II (1939–1945); the first atomic bomb was exploded at Trinity Site on July 16, 1945. The Los Alamos National Scientific Laboratory is devoted to the applications of nuclear energy; during the cold war it concentrated on national defense, but its program has now been extended to the peaceful uses of atomic energy and basic research in physics, biology, chemistry, geothermal energy, and medicine.

Today's Hispanics in New Mexico are embracing their cultural heritage through art and the revival of cultural traditions. In parts of northern New Mexico murals depicting famous historical events, such as the appropriation of the state by the United States from Mexico in the 1848 Treaty of Guadalupe Hidalgo, adorn many walls. Also the Spanish Market in Santa Fe is a large venue that promotes traditional Hispanic arts, such as tin working. The state has also produced some prominent Hispanic politicians, including the former mayor of Santa Fe, Debbie Jaramillo, and Congressman Bill Richardson, who was the energy secretary in President Bill Clinton's administration.

Henry Russell

SEE ALSO:

Albuquerque; Gadsden Purchase; Native Americans; Oñate, Juan de; Pueblo Dwellings; Rio Grande/Río Bravo; Santa Fe; Water Management.

New Orleans, Louisiana

Known alternately by such names as The Crescent City and The Big Easy, the atmospheric city of New Orleans is home to as many myths, mysteries, and musical styles as it is to different ethnic groups. It has developed a reputation for fine cuisine, jazz, voodoo customs, and its annual Mardi Gras.

Built on a marsh, the city of New Orleans is situated near the mouth of the Mississippi River opening onto the Gulf of Mexico. The area was explored—and first settled—by Frenchman René-Robert Cavelier de La Salle, who arrived in the region in April 1682, having traveled down the Mississippi from Canada. He claimed the area, naming it Louisiana in honor of the French king, Louis XIV, and his bride Queen Anne. New Orleans itself was founded 36 years later by another Frenchman, Jean-Baptiste Le Moyne, who named it for the regent of France, Philippe, duke of Orléans.

In the eighteenth century French-speaking Acadians arrived in southern Louisiana from Canada, having been driven out of their homes by the British. The Acadians became known as the Cajuns, and today there remains a large Cajun population in Louisiana.

Spanish colony

Louisiana remained a French territory for almost 80 years until it was ceded to Spain in 1762. Spaniards had previously explored the region as early as the sixteenth century. As a Spanish colony, New Orleans became a much visited port. Surrounded by swampland, the city was considered an oasis by its settlers and visitors. The arrival of increasing numbers of Spanish settlers added to a growing mixture of cultures. The French who first settled in New Orleans had brought with them African slaves; other early settlers came from Germany.

In the early nineteenth century Louisiana came under U.S. ownership with the Louisiana Purchase (1803). Several years later, New Orleans suffered a British attack but was successfully defended in the 1815 Battle of New Orleans, under the leadership of General Andrew Jackson. In the late nineteenth century New Orleans was a major center for both the slave trade and the South's cotton industry. Civil rights arrived in 1868 with the Louisiana Constitution, but by the end of the century segregation and racism had returned.

The twentieth century saw New Orleans's profile raised first through its celebrated tradition of jazz and then through its involvement in the profitable oil industry. The city felt the effects of oil slumps in the 1950s and 1980s. Its trade relationship with Latin America, responsible for the city's reputation for fine coffee, also faltered in the 1960s. Nevertheless, this most distinctive of American cities is still a major tourist destination.

Hispanic history

Today the New Orlean's Hispanic population is relatively small—3.1 percent of the total population according to the 2000 U.S. census—but the city has long Hispanic links. The city's Creole population comes from a mixed Spanish and French ancestry, dating back to the late eighteenth century when Louisiana was ceded to Spain from France. The city has a wide range of Creole architecture. Close to Bourbon Street, the Hermann-Grima House is a restored nineteenth-century Creole building. Spanish-influenced architecture can be seen in the distinctive cemeteries, in the famous French Quarter, and in Jackson Square, where the Cabildo, former seat of the colonial government, forms part of the Louisiana State Museum.

During Mexico's long history many political refugees have fled to the United States. In the nineteenth century New Orleans attracted many such Mexican exiles, the most famous of whom was the future Mexican president, Benito Juárez (1806–1872), who fled to the city after he was forced out of the governorship of Oaxaca in 1853 by President Antonio López de Santa Anna. While in New Orleans Juárez plotted his revolutionary junta with fellow liberals Melchor Ocampo, José Mata, and Ponciano Arriaga.

Christopher Wiegand

SEE ALSO:

Gulf of Mexico; Hispanic Americans; Juárez, Benito; Oil; Spanish Empire; Trade.

Newspapers and Magazines

According to data from the National Chamber of the Publishing Industry, more than 320 newspapers and 1,600 magazines are published in Mexico. There are as many as 30 daily newspapers in Mexico City, with the majority of magazines published there as well.

Although Mexico publishes a vast number of newspapers and magazines, new publications frequently appear and then close down. There are, however, a number of leading newspapers. The oldest influential newspapers are *El Universal*, launched in 1916, and *El Excélsior*, which was established in 1917. The daily financial newspaper *El Financiero* was established in 1981. In 1985 *La Jornada* was launched, and in 1993 the independent *Reforma* was founded.

Publishing in Mexico City

In Mexico City there is strong competition between different newspapers. As a result, each newspaper has a relatively small readership; not one of the most politically influential Mexico City newspapers has a circulation of over 200,000. Added to this, since the year 2000 newspaper circulations have fluctuated as a result of a change in the political climate. The 30 newspapers published in the capital account for 50 percent of national circulation.

El Universal, with a circulation of more than 150,000, is the largest circulation broadsheet. *El Financiero*, with a circulation of more than 135,000, is the main financial paper, while *Reforma*, with a circulation of 120,000, covers national and international politics and news. *La Jornada* is an independent daily covering national and local politics and has a circulation of 50,000. *El Excélsior*, traditionally pro-government, has adopted a more independent line in recent years.

Other popular newspapers in Mexico City include *Ovaciones*, *Novedades*, *El Heraldo de Mexico* and *Esto!*, a sports daily with a circulation of 450,000. Several important magazines are also published in Mexico City, including the left-of-center weekly magazine *Proceso*, and the intellectual periodicals *Vuelta* and *Nexos*.

Despite the concentration of publishing in Mexico City there are other important newspapers published elsewhere. One of the most widely read newspapers in Mexico is *El Norte*, published in Monterrey in northern Mexico. In the 1970s and 1980s, under the directorship of Alejandro Junco de la Vega, *El Norte* gained a reputation for publishing articles highlighting government corruption. Today the independent daily has a circulation of 165,000. Other important newspapers published outside Mexico City include *Siglo 21–Publico* in Guadalajara and *El Imparcial* in Hermosillo.

Press freedom

In theory Mexico is guaranteed a free and independent press according to its 1917 Constitution, but in reality press censorship has existed in Mexico since the start of the twentieth century. Article VII of the 1917 Constitution prohibits censorship, and an amendment to Article VI in 1977 states that "the right to information will be guaranteed by the state." However, during its 71-year reign the Partido Revolucionario Institucional (PRI) was widely considered to have withheld information and promoted self-censorship of newspapers. The election to the presidency of Partido Acción Nacional (PAN) candidate Vicente Fox in 2000, ending PRI rule, raised hopes that the ties between the press and successive PRI governments would be loosened, paving the way for a more professional, competitive, and independent media. For example, soon after President Fox was sworn in, he announced that the Center for Information and National Security would no longer spy on journalists.

PRI governments tried on several occasions to censor the print media by withholding government advertising, which accounted for 20 to 30 percent of press revenue during the 1980s. The Mexican government and politicians bought advertising space in the form of news stories to reproduce speeches or publicize their actions. These stories were not distinguishable from ordinary news stories. Because most journalists received low salaries, they became dependent on bribes from government officials or politicians and are thus vulnerable to coercion.

In the 1980s PRI governments threatened to withhold advertisements if newspapers or journalists refused to print what they were told to print. For example, PRI president Miguel de la Madrid (1982–1988) withdrew all government advertising from *El Financiero* because officials disliked the way it covered his debt negotiations. Later, President Salinas de Gortari (1988–1994) excluded reporters employed by the same paper from almost all presidential trips.

Today there are signs that the corruption and self-censorship are breaking up. The new political climate has been helped by several developments, including the launch of *Reforma* by U.S.-trained journalist Alejandro Junco de la Vega. He has made sure that his journalists are well paid and has banned them from accepting bribes. Since then other newspapers, notably *El Universal* and *El Excélsior*, have modified their content and raised journalists' salaries. Subjects such as drug trafficking, human rights, and corruption are now being covered, although this has led to an increase in attacks on and abductions of journalists by members of drug rings.

Historietas

The most widely read publications in Mexico are *historietas*, pocket-sized comic books with graphic images and dramatic tales that often feature sex and violence. It is estimated that the weekly titles sell five million copies combined. The genre first appeared toward the end of the nineteenth century with the development of the printing press and political cartoons. In 1880 the cigarette manufacturer El Buen Tono began including miniature lithographs with texts in cigarette packs and the *historieta* was born. At first the stories were included in weekly newspapers, but by the 1930s they were appearing as separate publications.

The best known is a series entitled *El Libro Vaquero*, featuring Wild West cowboys. Published by Novedades, it sells 800,000 copies weekly. In its failed campaign for the 2000 presidential election the PRI tried to capitalize on the popularity of the genre by publishing a *historieta* featuring the biography of its candidate, Francisco Labastida. Written and illustrated for the working classes, the comic books are intended to fit in the pockets of workers who must commute long distances each day. Many stories urge people to follow their dreams and romanticize the simple life. Others are lurid tales of sex and violence, breaking many taboos in Mexican society. *Historietas* also have a strong following in the Southwest, where their themes are adapted to appeal to Mexican Americans.

Joanna Griffin

SEE ALSO:

Communications; Constitutions, Mexican; Echeverría, Luis; Fox, Vicente; Madrid, Miguel de la; Media, Spanish Language; Partido Revolucionario Institucional; Salinas de Gortari, Carlos.

Alejandro Junco de la Vega

Alejandro Junco de la Vega is one of Mexico and Latin America's most powerful publishers, with daily newspapers in Mexico's three largest cities. Originally from Monterrey, Junco de la Vega studied journalism at the University of Texas. On his return to Monterrey in 1969 he began working for his family's struggling newspaper business as publishers of the local *El Norte* (morning) and *El Sol* (afternoon).

In 1973 Junco de la Vega was made publisher of *El Norte* and he took the radical step of employing his former journalism professor from the United States, Mary Gardner, to train his young, inexperienced journalists in journalistic techniques and ethics. The result was a newspaper that would not tolerate corruption.

Since its launch *El Norte* has published articles criticising the Mexican government. In 1974, for example, it ran a series of articles attacking president Luis Echeverría (1970–1978) for allowing his government to expropriate land in Sonora. In 1985 the newspaper revealed a blatant voting fraud in Monterrey by the ruling Partido Revolucionario Institucional (PRI).

In 1993 Junco de la Vega launched *La Reforma*, a new daily newspaper for Mexico City. It featured multiple sections, commentary expressing different political views, and bold use of color. In 1990 he founded Infosel to provide real-time financial information, he runs the largest Web access provider in Mexico, and he is the country's major Internet content provider.

Niggli, Josephine

Born in Mexico and raised in Texas, the dramatist and novelist Josefina María Niggli's work reflects life on the Mexico-U.S. border. Although bilingual, Niggli wrote in English in order to make her work available to as wide a North American audience as possible.

Josephine Niggli was born on July 13, 1910, in Monterrey, Nuevo Léon, to Texan and Virginian parents. She was christened Josephine but later changed the spelling to the more Latino "Josefina." An only child, Niggli was removed by her parents from Monterrey to San Antonio, Texas, in 1913 to avoid the Mexican Revolution (1910–1920). Her early years were spent between San Antonio and Monterrey. At an early age Niggli started to write poems and short stories, and her first book of poems about her Mexican village, *Mexican Silhouettes*, was published privately by her father in 1928. The book sold out and a new edition was published in 1931.

Through the late 1920s and early 1930s, Niggli published poems and short stories in magazines such as *Mexican Life* and *Ladies Home Journal* and built up a reputation as an author of radio scripts at the local radio station KTSA in San Antonio. In 1935 she went to the University of North Carolina at Chapel Hill to study playwrighting. She joined the Carolina Playmakers where she acted, directed, wrote, and designed costumes. Her one-act plays all had Mexican themes, including those dealing with history: *The Cry of Dolores* (1935), *Soldadera* (1936), *Azteca* (1936), and *This Is Villa* (1939). These plays dealt with issues such as women fighting in the Mexican Revolution, the Mexican revolutionary Francisco "Pancho" Villa, and the Aztecs.

Niggli's most successful plays of the period were the Mexican folk comedies: *Tooth or Shave* (1935), *The Red Velvet Goat* (1936), and *Sunday Costs Five Pesos* (1936). Probably the most popular of Niggli's comedies was *Sunday Costs Five Pesos*, which described Mexican village life at its most vibrant. Her characters live simple but happy lives temporarily overturned by some event that leads them to be jealous, greedy, or proud until events right themselves.

Mexican Village

Niggli's 1945 play *Singing Valley* (1945) tells the story of a father who brings his son and daughter back to Mexico from the United States. The son finds everything charming while the daughter finds life backward and boring. Finally, she comes to understand the village's understated beauty as much as her brother and father. The play is a precursor of Niggli's novel *Mexican Village* (1945), which became a bestseller, remained in print until 1978, and was turned into a Hollywood movie called *Sombrero*.

Niggli's subsequent two novels, both about Mexico, *Step Down, Elder Brother* (1947) and *A Miracle for Mexico* (1964), were not as successful as *Mexican Village*. In the 1940s Niggli went to Hollywood where, as well as writing the screenplay for her novel, she worked on movies such as *The Mask of Zorro*. Her later years, until her death in 1983, were spent traveling between the United States and Europe.

Anita Dalal

SEE ALSO:

Chicano Theater; Chicano Writers; Literature; Mexican Revolution.

Niggli, Josephine
Mexican American novelist and dramatist

Born: July 13, 1910
Monterrey, Nuevo Léon
Died: December 17, 1983
Cullowhee, North Carolina

1928	Publishes first book of poems, *Mexican Silhouettes*
1935	Studies at the University of North Carolina
1945	Publishes bestselling *Mexican Village*
1950	Awarded fellowship by Abbey Theater, Dublin, Ireland
1956	Starts teaching English and drama at Western Carolina University

Niños Héroes

The last great conflict in the Mexican-American War (1846–1848) was the Battle of Chapultepec, which took place just outside Mexico City on September 13, 1847. The most distinctive feature of the battle was the bravery of a group of young military cadets defending their academy. They became known as the Niños Héroes (the young heroes).

The war between Mexico and the United States had begun in May 1846, the precipitating cause being the U.S. annexation of Texas in 1845. After months of battles, most of which ended in decisive U.S. victories, and unsuccessful attempts at negotiation, U.S. general Winfield Scott (1786–1866) made a final advance on Mexico City in September 1847. Scott won a crucial victory at Molino del Rey on September 8 and then marched toward the capital. Between Scott's forces and the capital lay the heavily fortified Chapultepec Hill, which was home to the National Military Academy.

Scott attacked the hill on September 13. It was defended by about 5,000 Mexican troops. After a heavy artillery bombardment failed to force the Mexicans to surrender, fierce hand-to-hand fighting ensued. The 50 military cadets stationed in the academy, some still in their teens, earned particular praise for their bravery.

Eventually, on the night of September 13, the Mexican forces withdrew. According to legend, however, six young cadets fought to the bitter end. They were Juan Escutia Apascasio, Juan De la Barrera Insaurraga, Agustín Melgar, Fernando Montes de Oca, José Vicente de la Soledad Suárez, and Francisco Márquez Paniagua. Most famously, Juan Escutia wrapped himself in the Mexican flag and threw himself from the highest part of the castle rather than surrender to the enemy. After the victory at Chapultepec, Scott marched directly to Mexico City, occupying it the following day. Its capture effectively marked the end of the war.

Although there are some versions of these events that downplay the heroism of the young cadets, the Niños Heroes have become symbols of Mexican pride. Today a monument to them stands at the entrance to Chapultepec Park. Every year on September 13 a pilgrimage is made to the site.

Susana Berruecos García Travesí

SEE ALSO:

Mexican-American War; Santa Anna, Antonio López de; Scott, Winfield.

This contemporary lithograph shows U.S. troops besieging Chapultepec Hill in one of the last engagements of the Mexican-American War. The battle is famous for the heroism displayed by the young military cadets stationed at the National Military Academy there.

Nogales, Arizona

The town of Nogales, Arizona is located on the Mexico–U.S. border near the Santa Cruz River. Across the border lies its twin town of Nogales, Sonora. The towns are so closely integrated that they are often collectively referred to as Ambos Nogales ("both Nogales"). The name is derived from the Spanish word *nogal*, used to describe a walnut tree found in the region.

Before the arrival of the Spaniards in the late 1490s the area around Nogales was home to the Hohokam people. Later, the Nogales Pass became a shortcut off the Old Spanish Trail between Tucson, Arizona, and Guaymas, Sonora. In 1853 the region to the north of Nogales was absorbed into the United States as a result of the Gadsden Purchase. The accompanying treaty established a border that ran near the Nogales Pass.

In the late nineteenth century a transcontinental railroad was constructed connecting Los Angeles, California, and New Orleans, Louisiana. The railroad passed through Nogales and large numbers of Mexicans traveled north to work on the project. Many remained on the northern side of the border after work on the railroad was completed.

The town of Nogales, Arizona, is located on the Mexico-U.S. border. Economically, it is closely tied to its Mexican twin.

The two towns grew steadily, helped by the actions of Mexican president Porfirio Díaz, who established a *perimetro libre* (tax-free zone) around the Sonoran town so that residents could purchase basic goods in the United States without having to pay import taxes. This decree led to the proliferation of retail businesses and grocery stores in Nogales, Arizona, that catered to the residents of Nogales, Sonora. People crossed from one community to the other with complete freedom and without the need for any legal documents. During the 1920s, prohibition in the United States led to the establishment of many bars and nightclubs on the southern side of the border. The bars supplied alcohol to U.S. citizens who crossed the border to circumvent the law.

In 1965 the implementation of Mexico's Border Industrialization Plan led to the construction of maquiladoras, or U.S.-owned manufacturing plants, on the southern side of the border. The U.S. town also benefited to some extent from the maquiladora presence because Mexican shoppers spent part of their income in the United States.

Nogales today

Compared to other pairs of towns on the Mexico-U.S. border, Ambos Nogales is a well-integrated community, thanks partially to the relatively small size of the two towns and partially to their close proximity. Many people cross the border two or three times a day to shop or visit family and friends. The situation is gradually changing, however, as increased traffic and national security issues have limited interaction between the two communities.

Among the most important issues facing Ambos Nogales today are environmental problems such as air pollution and limited water resources. One source of tension between the two communities is the way in which wastewater from Nogales, Sonora, finds its way into Nogales, Arizona. The fact that this wastewater contains high levels of toxic waste has created health concerns north of the border.

Irasema Coronado

SEE ALSO:

Arizona; Border Industrialization Plan; Environmental Issues; Maquiladoras; Prohibition.

Nongovernmental Organizations

Nongovernmental organizations (NGOs) are independent of governments and government agencies and generally do not engage in commercial activity. NGOs play an important role in the United States and Mexico, offering advice and support to communities and often pressing for social and political change.

NGOs operate in many important sectors in society, including business, the environment, culture, and health and safety. While they focus on different issues, NGOs' main concerns are usually humanitarian: they exist principally to help people. They encourage citizens to voice their concerns and help them gain solutions to their problems. NGOs operate on a number of different levels. The smaller ones often have a predominantly regional purpose, while some of the larger organizations work at a national or international level. Many larger NGOs work alongside the United Nations (UN), which works toward international peace and security. The UN's Conference of Non-Governmental Organizations (CONGO), founded in the late 1940s, is an association that helps many NGOs gain an international voice.

National Council of La Raza

Many general NGOs cater to all U.S. residents, but some organizations are more community-specific. Mexican Americans and other Hispanics can make use of a number of NGOs that are designed to support their needs. One of the leading Hispanic NGOs is the National Council of La Raza (NCLR), established in the late 1960s with the goal of improving the lives of Hispanic Americans. Principally targeting both poverty and discrimination, the NCLR has offered comprehensive support to organizations across the nation, particularly in the areas of community management and governance.

The organization's headquarters is in Washington, D.C., where it lobbies the U.S. government to reflect Hispanic needs in its policies and legislation on issues such as education, housing, immigration, health, and employment. The NCLR also has offices in several major cities, including Los Angeles,

Phoenix, and San Antonio. It publishes reports analyzing relevant issues for Hispanics in the United States. In addition, the NCLR's quarterly newsletter, *Agenda*, and its Web site offer information on its policies, programs, campaigns, and affiliated groups, which in 2002 numbered more than 240.

Diverse aims and methods

Two organizations that represent the diversity of NGO activity are the Mexican American Legal Defense and Educational Fund (MALDEF) and the Society for the Advancement of Chicanos and Native Americans in Science (SACNAS). MALDEF was founded in 1968 to empower Hispanics in the United States and to protect their civil rights in areas such as education, employment, immigration, political access, and the distribution of government resources. MALDEF's concerns with political representation led it to establish a national campaign to ensure that as many Hispanic people as possible were counted in the U.S. census in 2000. In addition, the organization runs leadership programs that aim to encourage greater Hispanic presence in politics and business management.

SACNAS was formed in 1973. From its base in Santa Cruz, California, the organization strives to improve education in math and science and to open up career prospects for graduates in these subjects. As its name suggests, the organization exists not only for Mexican Americans, but also for other minority groups in the United States. Its members include science academics, industry-based scientists, and students. SACNAS uses diverse methods to achieve results. It offers the opportunity for further education through its fellowship programs, and its national conference runs for several days each year, offering reflection on scientific subjects through career-oriented workshops, exhibits, talks from guest speakers, and other activities. Students are invited to present their research at the conference and exhibitors in turn promote educational opportunities for students.

A number of NGOs represent communities in both the United States and Mexico. One such organization is the Mexican and American Solidarity Foundation, set up in order to strengthen bonds between people living in Mexico and Mexican Americans in the United States. The organization also aims to improve relations between the two countries. In 2002 its president was Raul Yzaguirre, who since the late 1970s has also been president of the National Council of La Raza. Another organization, the Mexico-U.S. Advocates Network, has similar aims to the Mexican and American Solidarity Foundation. The network focuses on Mexico-U.S. migration and the associated aspects of human and labor rights.

Human and women's rights in Mexico

Some of the most active NGOs in Mexico are those concerned with the promotion of human rights and equal opportunities for women. Human rights NGOs developed in Mexico in the 1970s as people became more critical of governmental abuses of power. One incident that inspired public criticism more than any other was the police shootings during a student protest in Mexico City in 1968. One early organization was a women's group, founded by Rosario Ibarra de Piedra in the early 1970s, which campaigned for the release of husbands and children imprisoned for antigovernmental activities. At the start of the twenty-first century there were around 250 human rights NGOs, but their proliferation did not occur without a challenge. In the 1980s and 1990s police and other authorities intimidated and harassed organizations' members. In May 1990 police shot dead the president of the Sinaloa human rights NGO, Norma Corona Sapiens. Her organization campaigned for the rights of farmworkers in the western state of Sinaloa to land and adequate health care.

Mexican human rights NGOs grew in stature in the 1990s as the government began to acknowledge the need for improvement of its human rights record and international image. NGOs helped mobilize thousands of electoral observers to ensure that the 1994 presidential elections were free and fair, motivated by the allegations of fraud levied at the ruling Partido Revolucionario Institucional (PRI; Institutional Revolutionary Party) after the 1988 vote. In addition, NGOs criticized the ineffectiveness of the National Commission of Human Rights, set up in 1990 by President Carlos Salinas de Gortari. The NGO's pressure resulted in an enhanced role for the commission. NGOs also played a crucial role in the period after the Zapatista uprising in Chiapas in January 1994, which protested the government's treatment of Indians. In response to the uprising, Salinas initiated a series of peace talks, inviting human rights NGOs to advise both the government and the Zapatista movement.

Women's rights NGOs became increasingly active in the 1980s. Groups such as Mujeres en Lucha por la Democracia (Women's Struggle for Democracy) and the Coordinadora Benita Galeana (the Benita Galeana League, named for the political activist Benita Galeana) pressed the government to legislate for better pay and working conditions for women, as well as for improvements in urban housing and social welfare. The organizations also initiated campaigns on women's health and, of particular relevance in a traditional Catholic society, women's right to use contraception. Many women's NGOs in Mexico began to obtain funding from other countries, such as women's groups in the United States. In common with human rights NGOs, in the 1990s the status of women's NGOs increased: many began to play an important role in Mexico's Foro de Organizaciones no Gubermentales (Forum of Nongovernmental Organizations).

Increasing role of NGOs in Mexico

Some commentators believe that Mexico's signing of the North American Free Trade Agreement (NAFTA) in 1992 led to an increase in the number and significance of NGOs in the country. While large businesses welcomed the aim of eliminating trade barriers to U.S. and Canadian imports, as well Mexican exports, other sectors of society were less in favor. These sectors, including people involved in organized labor, small businesses, agriculture, and government administration, had traditionally been loyal supporters of Mexico's political system. Their disapproval of established politics led to a proliferation of new organizations. NAFTA had two additional effects on NGOs. It led to greater international scrutiny of Mexican affairs, which in turn led the Mexican government to acknowledge the role of NGOs in its desire to be perceived as a modern democracy. In addition, many NGOs were inspired by NAFTA to seek new partnerships with organizations in the United States, in particular labor and environmental groups.

Christopher Wiegand

SEE ALSO:

Advocacy Organizations; Civil Rights in the U.S.; Human Rights in Mexico; Labor and Employment; MALDEF; MANA; NAFTA.

North American Agreement on Labor Cooperation

The North American Agreement on Labor Cooperation (NAALC) is a proviso to the North American Free Trade Agreement (NAFTA) between Mexico, the United States, and Canada, to protect workers' rights in the member countries.

NAFTA originally had no provision for labor rights. However, before NAFTA was ratified in 1993, labor rights became an important political issue, and President Bill Clinton (1993–2001) promised to support NAFTA only if it included side agreements on labor and the environment. The North American Agreement on Labor Cooperation (NAALC) was adopted in September 1993.

The NAALC seeks to improve working conditions and living standards in the NAFTA free-trade area and to protect, enhance, and enforce basic workers' rights. It also aims to ensure that domestic labor laws are adhered to. It does not, however, establish supranational labor law enforcement mechanisms or common labor standards between signatory countries. Each country retains the right to establish its own labor standards and to modify its labor laws and regulations accordingly.

Institutions and practices of the NAALC

The NAALC creates mechanisms for cooperative activities and intergovernmental consultations, as well as for independent evaluations and dispute settlement related to the enforcement of labor laws. The NAALC set up a commission consisting of a ministerial council and a secretariat. The staff of the Washington-based secretariat is drawn equally from each NAFTA country. It includes labor economists, lawyers, and other professionals with experience in labor affairs. The secretariat provides information and serves as the commission's administrative arm. The NAALC requires each government to maintain a National Administrative Office (NAO) within the ministry of labor in each country. The NAOs serve as points of contact and sources of information for all interested parties.

The NAOs deal with alleged failures to comply with labor laws in another NAFTA country. Each NAFTA member allows for reviews of labor law issues by each other's NAOs. There are several levels of investigation. Any matter within the scope of the agreement may be the subject of ministerial consultations. Following consultations, any party may request that an independent Evaluation Committee of Experts (ECE) be established. The ECE examines patterns of practice in enforcement related to the specific labor law matters listed in the NAALC. If after consideration of a final ECE report a country believes that there is still noncompliance, it may request further consultation and, eventually, the establishment of an independent arbitrating panel. The panel may issue a ruling and agree on an action plan. If the action plan is not implemented, the panel may impose a fine.

Effectiveness of the NAALC

The most visible result of the NAALC so far has been over 20 public communications submitted to the U.S., Mexican, and Canadian NAOs by labor unions from all three countries. They have alleged lack of enforcement for diverse workers' rights such as freedom of association, minimum employment standards, protection of migrant workers, labor protection for children, and the right to strike.

Although the NAALC is a treaty that is binding for all three countries, the governments seem to distrust it, perceiving it as a form of economic interventionism. Labor unions criticize its lengthy processes and lack of effectiveness. It seems unlikely that the NAALC as it stands will be extended to cover the labor-social aspect of the trade agreement that will expand NAFTA principles across the entire continent. To be useful in this larger context the NAALC will need major changes, otherwise some new institution or approach will be needed.

Luis Miguel Diaz

SEE ALSO:

Alliances and Agreements; Labor and Employment; Labor Organizations; NAFTA.

Nueces River

The Nueces River flows through Texas for 315 miles (505 km) in a south-southeasterly direction from twin sources to its mouth at Corpus Christi on Nueces Bay in the Gulf of Mexico. For many years the river represented Mexico's northern border.

The Nueces first appeared on a map in 1527, when it was identified as the Rio Escondido (Hidden River), so named because of the obscure location of its mouth behind a barrier island in the Gulf of Mexico. It was explored in 1689 by Alonso De León, who named it Río de las Nueces (River of Nuts) for the pecan trees growing along its banks.

Early in the nineteenth century, Fort Ramírez was built on the south bank of the Nueces. After 1821 the Mexican government made numerous grants in the Trans-Nueces area to the south of the river. In 1830, a Mexican fort, Lipantitlán, was established on the Nueces near San Patricio. In 1842 the Republic of Texas used these buildings for defense against Mexican invaders. Two frontier posts of the U.S. Army were later built on the right (southern) bank: Fort Merrill and Fort Ewell.

The Nueces River runs through southeast Texas, flowing into the Gulf of Mexico at the busy port of Corpus Christi. The area between it and the Rio Grande was once disputed territory.

The city of Corpus Christi was founded at the river's mouth in 1832. It was originally a trading post, and its growth into a city was catalyzed by its occupation in 1845 by the army of U.S. general Zachary Taylor. From the Texas Revolution of 1836 to the end of the Mexican-American War the area to the south of the river was disputed territory, but in 1848 the boundary between Mexico and the United States was finally established at the Rio Grande by the Treaty of Guadalupe Hidalgo.

Geographical features

The Nueces rises in two forks just to the northeast of the town of Del Rio. The upper course of the river runs through a rural agricultural area noted for the rearing of sheep and production of wool, and then descends past Crystal City. Through much of its course, the river runs through an inhospitable area where mesquite and prickly pear have traditionally presented a challenge to farmers. However, large tracts of this land have now been cultivated by modern methods, and diversified farming and ranching enterprises developed.

The upper Nueces is of great scenic interest and very popular with anglers. Farther downstream the river and its surrounds become more industrial in character. There is significant oil and gas production, and in Uvalde County there are asphalt works and stone quarries. Corpus Christi, meanwhile, is the second largest port in Texas, handling the shipment of petroleum and natural gas.

Among the artificial lakes on the Nueces are Choke Canyon Reservoir and Lake Corpus Christi. The Choke Canyon Reservoir, 4 miles (6.5 km) west of the town of Three Rivers, was created in a multipurpose project undertaken jointly by the city of Corpus Christi and the U.S. Bureau of Reclamation. It serves to control flooding on the land below it, provides water for municipal and industrial use, and is used for watersports. Lake Corpus Christi, 4 miles (6.5 km) southwest of Mathis, was formed by the construction of the Wesley E. Seale Dam and hydroelectric power station.

Henry Russell

SEE ALSO:

Corpus Christi; Guadalupe Hidalgo, Treaty of.

Nuevo León

Of the six states in Mexico that border the United States, Nuevo León has by far the shortest shared boundary: only 12 miles (19 km) from just west of the city of Nuevo Laredo. Economically and politically, Nuevo León is one of the most important border states in either country. It contains the city of Monterrey, a metropolis whose influence extends throughout Mexico and beyond.

Nuevo León is situated in the northeast of Mexico and is traversed by the Sierra Madre Oriental in the south and the west. Much of the north is arid land, while the plains on the eastern border with Tamaulipas have several large rivers and are good agricultural lands.

Spanish conquest

Monterrey was founded after an expedition in the 1570s, led by the Spaniard Alberto del Canto. He explored northeastern Mexico and discovered mines in what is today the city of Monclova, and also in the valleys of Extremadura and Saltillo. During the same decade and in the same area, Luis de Carvajal was given a commission to pacify the Chichimeca Indians. Because he was successful, in 1579 he received royal authorization to settle the regions explored by del Canto. Carvajal brought 100 Spanish families to colonize 600 square miles (555 sq km).

The region they settled was named the New Kingdom of León, or in Spanish: El Nuevo Reino de León. Finding little silver or other mineral wealth, the settlers made money by capturing local Indians, enslaving them, and selling them to miners who took them to north-central Mexico. Amid the growth of this economy, Carvajal founded the town of Monterrey in an area surrounded by the high peaks of the Sierra Madre Oriental. He also managed the colonization of other towns in the New Kingdom of León.

Carvajal and most of the families he brought to the New Kingdom of León were *conversos*—former Jews who had converted to Catholicism, especially after Spain expelled its entire Jewish population in

The state of Nuevo León is dominated by the Sierra Madre Oriental mountain range in the west and the south. The Mexican state shares a very short common border with the United States.

1492. Many *conversos* were genuine converts to Christianity. Others continued to practice Judaism secretly. Both groups brought many cultural practices with them to the Kingdom of New León. These may have included the breeding, herding, and eating of goats, and may explain why *cabrito*, or goat meat, has for long been a favorite food in northeast Mexico. By all accounts, Carvajal was a sincere Catholic, but his sister, nephew, and other relatives practiced Judaism in secret. They were denounced by the Inquisition in the 1580s, and Carvajal himself was accused and jailed in 1587. He died behind bars. The charges against him led the Spanish settlers to almost totally abandon the New Kingdom of León. Many resettled in Saltillo, which was part of Nueva Vizcaya, a region covering the current states of Sinaloa, Durango, and Chihuahua. In 1596, however, the new province of Nuevo León was founded in the region originally settled by Carvajal. A new capital for the province was established in Monterrey.

Under Spanish rule, Nuevo León was a colonial backwater. Its economy was based on cattle ranching, but development was difficult because of constant attacks by indigenous groups who continued to resist the Spanish. After Mexico won its independence from Spain, Nuevo León had to deal with border disputes and war with the Republic of Texas and later the United States.

In 1846, U.S. Army general Zachary Taylor (later U.S. president) and his army entered Monterrey and occupied important parts of the city at the start of what became the Mexican-American War (1846–1848). This provoked furious demonstrations, but Mexican troops were unable to dislodge the U.S. forces. In 1864, when French forces installed Maximilian as emperor, President Benito Juárez (1806–1872) moved the national government from Mexico City to Monterrey for several weeks. The following year, the French captured Monterrey. Control of the city shifted back and forth for months between the French and the Republicans.

Monterrey

Monterrey's economy and population boomed during the late-nineteenth-century presidency of Porfirio Díaz (1830–1915). Under his regime, massive foreign investment and industrialization were encouraged. Monterrey profited dramatically from the policy, as well as from its location at a mountain pass near the U.S. border on the route between Mexico City and San Antonio. In 1890 José Schneider, a Mexican of German ancestry, founded the Cervecería Cuauhtémoc, the Cuauhtémoc Beer Company. It became the biggest, most important brewery in Mexico, manufacturing Carta Blanca, Mexico's top-selling beer. In 1900 the Iron and Steel Smelting Company, Companía Fundidora de Fierro y Acero, was also founded. Other turn-of-the-century industries included the production of cement, flour, textiles, cigarettes, cigars, soap, bricks, and furniture. Monterrey had so many factories that it was known as the industrial heart of the country, the "Mexican Chicago."

Today Monterrey continues to be an economic powerhouse. Its success is due to well-developed transportation connections (it is the second biggest rail center in Mexico), access to energy sources such as natural gas, and to a skilled, educated workforce. In addition, new technology enables faster communication between Monterrey and the United States. New highways, for instance, have reduced the road trip to San Antonio to less than five hours. According to the 2000 Mexican census, 2.8 million people live in Monterrey. This makes it Mexico's third largest urban area, after Mexico City and Guadalajara.

Industry and politics

Thanks to Monterrey, Nuevo León is now the fourth largest producer of cement in the world, and the fourth biggest manufacturer of glass in the Western Hemisphere. Other industries include production of air conditioners and cellulose, as well as the more traditional beer, cigarettes, and glass. Before oil became a major factor in the Mexican economy in the 1970s, Monterrey produced 25 percent of Mexico's gross national product (GNP) and almost a third of its exports. Education also plays an important part in the local economy: per capita, Monterrey has Mexico's largest number of colleges, universities, and institutes of technology, including the famed Instituto Tecnológico de Estudios Superiores de Monterrey, popularly known as Monterrey Tec.

Parts of Nuevo León remain agricultural—sugarcane, vegetables, corn, cotton, and citrus fruits are all grown in the state. The area around the towns of Allende, Montemorelos, and Linares, in the southwest part of the state, is Mexico's biggest citrus-producing zone. Mainly, though, Nuevo León is urban and high-tech. Residents of the state own a fifth of the computers in Mexico. Commerce is also very important, as evidenced by the fact that two-thirds of all stock brokers licensed in Mexico since 1975 have been from Nuevo León.

Due to the importance of commerce, it is not surprising that Nuevo León is a stronghold of the conservative, pro-business Partido Acción Nacional (PAN; National Action Party). The PAN won the presidency in 2000 with Vicente Fox, defeating the Partido Revolucionario Institucional (PRI; Institutional Revolutionary Party), which had ruled Mexico continuously since 1929. Monterrey's largest daily newspaper, *El Norte*, has for years been influential in promoting PAN politics to the local community and to the rest of Mexico.

Deborah Nathan

SEE ALSO:

Díaz, Porfirio; Education; Fox, Vicente; Jews; Juárez, Benito; Mexican-American War; Monterrey; Partido Acción Nacional; Texas.

Oaxaca

Oaxaca is Mexico's fifth largest state, covering 36,275 square miles (93,950 sq km), but it has a population of only 3.4 million. It has some of the most varied landscapes in Mexico, ranging from sandy beaches to mountains and arid plains. In the late twentieth century the flow of migrants from Oaxaca to the United States began to increase steadily.

Oaxaca is bordered by the states of Guerrero to the west, Chiapas to the east, and Pueblo and Veracruz to the north. Two major mountain ranges run east to west through the state, the Sierra Madre del Sur and the Sierra Madre Oriental, whose highest peak is Cempoaltepetl at 11,159 feet (3,400 m). Sandwiched between the two sierras is the broad Oaxaca Valley, which has evidence of human activity stretching back thousands of years. The state capital, Oaxaca, lies in the bottom of this largely agricultural valley. Oaxaca's coastal plain has a different character; much of this sparsely inhabited region is covered with dry thorn forest.

Oaxaca is one of the poorest states in Mexico, despite a wealth of mineral resources, including silver, gold, coal, and uranium. The main activity in the fertile Oaxaca Valley is agriculture. Oaxaca is the largest producer of mangos in Mexico; other crops include sugarcane, lemons, oranges, alfalfa, avocados, pineapples, and rice. Coffee is grown in the cooler highlands. Oaxacan coffee *fincas* (plantations) account for 15 percent of Mexico's total coffee production. Fishing provides income for small communities dotted along the Pacific coast, and the port of Salina Cruz in the southeast of the state has a major oil refinery. Tourism is of growing importance for the state's economy. The main tourist attractions are Oaxaca's magnificent beaches, rich pre-Columbian archaeological heritage, Indian cultural traditions and crafts, and the Spanish colonial architecture of the city of Oaxaca. Regular flights and a new highway from Mexico City have made Oaxaca more accessible.

Seventy percent of the state's inhabitants are Indians. Oaxaca is the state with the largest indigenous population in Mexico, with nearly 20 percent

Although economically one of the poorest states in Mexico, Oaxaca contains a great richness of scenery and pre-Columbian remains.

of the total. Oaxaca is home to 17 different indigenous groups, including around 300,000 Zapotecs; 200,000 Mixtecs; 100,000 Mazatecs; 60,000 Mixes; 55,000 Chinantecs; 25,000 Amuzgos; and 20,000 Triques.

The capital of Oaxaca

The city of Oaxaca lies in the Oaxaca Valley 5,085 feet (1,550 m) above sea level, with a population of around 250,000. The city retains much of its colonial character. It has a pleasant central *zócalo* (square) with a bandstand, fine old trees, and restaurants. Nearby are the cathedral, parts of which date to the sixteenth century; the old market building; and the beautiful church of Iglesia de Santo Domingo, founded in 1575.

The city was originally an Aztec military base built in 1486. In 1521 the Spanish, under the conquistador Francisco de Orozco, seized the base and built a settlement, which was elevated to the status of the royal town of Oaxaca by the Emperor Charles V in 1532. Much of the city's fine architecture dates from the period that followed.

Two prominent Mexican presidents are associated with Oaxaca. In 1830 Porfirio Díaz (president 1877–1880 and 1884–1911) was born in the city, and Benito Juárez (president 1861–1865 and 1867–1872) lived there for much of his early life and was state governor from 1847 to 1852.

Oaxaca Valley

While the city's history is a long one, that of the Oaxaca Valley is much longer. Early Indian peoples had settled the valley by 6000 B.C.E. Around 1500 B.C.E. the valley's most important settlement was San José Mogote, 6 miles (10 km) northwest of the present city. Existing remains include a stone and adobe building with the oldest stone sculptures found in Oaxaca—a jaguar's head, vultures, and a naked figure dating to 800–600 B.C.E.

Around 600 B.C.E. Monte Albán became the most important center in Oaxaca. The ruins of Monte Albán cover an area of 15 square miles (40 sq km), though the core area is much smaller. The settlement served several peoples for almost 2,500 years as a place of worship. The central part of the ruins, constructed on an artificial mound 1,300 feet (400 m) above the valley floor, is one of Meso-america's most impressive pre-Columbian sites. Visitors can see the central plaza, ruins of a palace, a pyramid, and a ball court. Monte Albán became the

Monte Albán, the largest and most important pre-Columbian site in the Oaxaca Valley, attracts thousands of visitors each year.

capital of the Zapotec empire between around 100 C.E. and 800 C.E., when the core area was home to probably 35,000 people. In the ninth and tenth centuries the Mixtec people drove the Zapotecs from Monte Albán.

At Zaachila, 7 miles (12 km) south of the city of Oaxaca, are the remains of the last Zapotec capital. Only discovered in 1962, much of the site has still to be excavated, but the several buildings and a large central pyramid have been uncovered. Carved jaguar heads, owls, priests, and other figures adorn the stonework. Although the movement of the Zapotecs from Monte Albán signaled the beginning of their decline in power, their direct descendants continue to live in many towns in the state, along with the Mixtecs and other smaller Indian groups.

Oaxaca's Pacific coast

Salina Cruz is Mexico's most important Pacific Coast port. It is situated at the southern end of the railroad that crosses the Isthmus of Tehuantepec from the north coast and has a major oil refinery. A few miles northeast of Salina Cruz, the market town of Juchitán lies on the Pan-American highway linking Mexico City and Guatamala. It has an attractive *zócalo*, the church of San Vicente, and a gallery exhibiting paintings of Diego Rivera and Salvador Dalí. Farther along the coast the major resort of Puerto Escondido attracts thousands of visitors annually to its beaches. Among them is Playa Zicatela, which is considered to be one of the world's finest surfing beaches. It hosts the World Masters surfing championship each November. The town's sport fishing is also renowned.

The sandy beaches of Oaxaca have some of the world's most important turtle nesting beaches. This area is a conservation success story. A museum at Mazunte, near the fishing village of Puerto Angel, is devoted to turtle conservation. Mazunte was a center of a turtle industry for which turtles and their eggs were harvested to such an extent that they were reaching dangerously low levels. In 1990 the industry was outlawed by the government. Since then, the number of turtles has risen and the focus of the local economy has become ecotourism, with local fishermen offering tourists boat trips to watch the seagoing turtles.

Tim Harris

SEE ALSO:
Archaeology; Díaz, Porfirio; Ecotourism; Festivals; Juárez, Benito; Mixtecs; Zapotecs.

Obregón, Álvaro

After the Mexican Revolution (1910–1920) Mexico needed to replace civil unrest and chaos with a more stable political system. When Álvaro Obregón (1880–1928) became president in 1920, his main goal was to establish institutional stability in order to end the tradition of presidential successions being decided by violence.

Álvaro Obregón was born on February 19, 1880, into a family of seventeen children, in the hacienda of Siquivisa in the town of Navojoa, Sonora. His formal education was limited to finishing elementary school. By age 13 he was cultivating tobacco and had started a small cigarette-manufacturing company. As he grew up, agriculture became his main activity. He bought a small farm and established himself as a very successful *garbanzo* (chickpea) farmer. He was also a skilled mechanic, and invented a *garbanzo* seeder that he exported to the United States.

Political career

Obregón was elected mayor of Huatabampo in his home state in 1911. In 1912 he organized an armed movement to support Francisco I. Madero (1873–1913), who was being threatened by a revolt led by Pascual Orozco. In 1913 Madero was deposed and assassinated by General Victoriano Huerta (1854–1916), and Obregón joined the forces led by Venustiano Carranza (1859–1920) opposing Huerta. Obregón demonstrated great military skill and by September of that year, Carranza named him division general, a rank he held while he led the Ejercito del Noroeste (Army of the Northwest). After a series of important victories Obregón entered and occupied Mexico City on August 15, 1914, effectively defeating Huerta and ending his attempted dictatorship.

After Huerta was deposed, Carranza assumed the presidency. During his administration Carranza used Obregón to oppose and stop his enemies within the revolutionary movement: Francisco "Pancho" Villa (1878–1923) and Emiliano Zapata (1879–1919). Obregón defeated Villa a number of times, curtailing his power and influence throughout the

country. Despite having his right arm amputated as a result of being wounded at the Battle of Santa Ana Del Conde, Obregón continued his military campaigns. In 1915 he led his army north and, in Ciudad Juárez, forced what was left of Villa's revolutionary army to surrender.

In 1917 Mexico adopted a new constitution, known as the 1917 Constitution, and Obregón played an important part in its conception. It gained worldwide recognition as one of the most progressive documents of its time. Its radical measures included rights of labor, a restriction of the power of the Catholic church, and sovereign rights to natural underground deposits such as oil.

After serving in Carranza's cabinet for a time as Secretary of War and Marine, Obregón retired from politics and returned to farming. However, he soon grew disillusioned with Carranza's policies and felt that the government was becoming increasingly reactionary. He returned to politics in 1919 and began his campaign for the presidency. Carranza was unhappy with Obregón's decision, and during

Obregón was known for having a quick wit and a photographic memory, both of which helped him in his political and military careers.

Obregón, Álvaro

Mexican revolutionary and president

Born:	*February 19, 1880*
	Navojoa, Sonora
Died:	*July 17, 1928*
	Mexico City

1911	Elected mayor of Huatabampo
1913	Named Division General of the Army of the Northwest
1914	Troops march into Mexico City
1915	Defeats Francisco "Pancho" Villa at Ciudad Juárez
1916	Appointed Secretary of War and Marine in Carranza's government
1917	Resigns cabinet post and retires to private life
1919	Returns to politics in opposition to Carranza
1920	Elected president of Mexico
1924	Replaced as president by Elías Calles
1928	Elected president and assassinated

the presidential campaign of 1920, the government charged Obregón with being involved in a conspiracy against the president.

Obregón was forced to flee Mexico City. Meanwhile, his supporters—Adolfo de la Huerta (1882–1955), the governor of Sonora, and General Elías Calles (1877–1945)—published the Plan de Agua Prieta to overthrow Carranza. The opposing forces defeated the government, and Carranza, who had to abandon the capital, was deposed and later assassinated. The federal congress named Huerta substitute president and he called for a general election. Obregón once again decided to run for president and won.

Presidency (1920–1924)

As president, Obregón attempted to improve the country's finances. He promoted education, instituted agricultural reform, and restructured government institutions. The army was cut back— the number of active members fell to fewer than 60,000. He celebrated the centenary of the country's independence by substituting the paper

currency with coins. Extensive work was done to repair telegraph lines and railroad tracks. The system and rules by which Mexico's diplomatic and consular corps would be selected and operated were established.

In education, Obregón's major initiative was to make José Vasconselos (1882–1959), one of the most respected authors in Latin America, Secretary of Public Education. Vasconselos gave great support to education at all levels, establishing schools in rural areas that lacked them. He was also responsible for encouraging the Mexican muralist movement.

Foreign policy

Obregón was instrumental in restarting the payment of Mexico's foreign debt. The policy brought him international praise, especially from the United States. In 1923 a series of meetings known as the Bucareli Treaties took place between representatives of Mexico and the United States. The main subject of discussion was compensation owed to American nationals for damages suffered during the Mexican Revolution and foreigner's rights of ownership to and use of underground natural resources, which had been denied by the 1917 Constitution. This treaty, although unpopular among many Mexican politicians, led to the official recognition of the Mexican government by the United States. In 1924 Mexico established diplomatic relations with the Soviet Union; the first country in North America to do so.

In 1924 Elías Calles succeeded Obregón as president. Calles and Obregón had formed a partnership through which they planned to maintain government control. Calles had the constitution modified by congress so Obregón could be elected once again in the 1928 elections. In July 1928 Obregón won the presidential election. However, before he could take office he was shot on July 17 in Mexico City by a religious fanatic and caricaturist, José León Toral, who was opposed to the government's anticlerical policies. Obregón, although at times a ruthless leader, is remembered as the man who began the transition of Mexico's political system from one of violence to one of institutional stability.

Héctor Manuel Lucero

SEE ALSO:

Carranza, Venustiano; Huerta, Victoriano; Madero, Francisco I.; Mexican Revolution; Villa, Francisco "Pancho"; Zapata, Emiliano.

Ohio

Ohio is a midwestern state in the Great Lakes region of the United States. It has an area of 41,222 square miles (106,765 sq km), and in 2000 it had a population of 11,353,140. The state has a small but steadily increasing Hispanic population.

Ohio is bordered to the northeast by Pennsylvania, to the southeast by Virginia, to the south by Kentucky, to the west by Indiana, and to the north by Michigan and Lake Erie. The state capital is Columbus; other major cities are Cleveland, Cincinnati, and Toledo.

The state has extensive farmland, producing large amounts of corn, soybeans, hay, wheat, and dairy products. Despite industrial decline since the 1960s, Ohio retains many manufacturing centers and ranks third in the United States in the value of its manufacturing products. Leading products manufactured in the state include metals, auto parts, rubber, machinery, and transportation equipment. The state also diversified its economy in the last decades of the twentieth century, establishing several important centers for industrial research and expanding the service sector.

History

The area was first explored by Frenchman Sieur de la Salle in 1669, but there was little interest in the Ohio Valley until the 1750s, when the British and French fought for control of it. In 1749 a settlement was established by the Ohio Company of Virginia. The area was captured by the French in 1754 and then recaptured by the British in 1758. Britain gained control of the Ohio River after the French and Indian Wars in 1763, but settlement was not permitted.

After the Revolutionary War (1776–1783), the United States acquired the area from Britain, and the first permanent settlement was established in 1788 at Marietta, the capital of the Northwest Territory. Ohio became part of the Union in 1803, and in 1816 Columbus became the permanent capital. During the first decades of the nineteenth century the state grew steadily, aided by the Erie Canal and other canals and toll roads. After the Civil War (1861–1865) industry boomed as a result of increased shipments of iron ore from the upper Great Lakes region and the development of the petroleum industry. The Great Depression of the 1930s hit farms and industries hard, but World War II (1939–1945) returned prosperity to the region through renewed industrialization.

Hispanic Population

Hispanic migrants have been arriving in Ohio since the beginning of the twentieth century. Originally, migrants came from Texas and Mexico to northwestern Ohio for seasonal farm work, settling permanently when jobs opened up at canning and auto plants. Elsewhere, migrants came to work in the meat-packing industry, slaughterhouses, and factories. Second and third generation Hispanics are now making their mark in business and government in the state. In addition to the growing number of prosperous Hispanics living in the area, Mexicans still continue to migrate to the region, often illegally, to work as cheap labor on farms.

In 2000 the U.S. census showed a marked increase in Hispanic populations throughout the cities of the Midwest, a phenomenon that has been called the "browning of the Midwest." The Ohio statistics reflect the fact that Hispanic populations are no longer just growing in the Mexican-U.S. border regions, such as California and Texas, but in other areas with established Hispanic communities. According to the U.S. census, there were 139,696 people of Hispanic origin in Ohio in 1990, a number that increased to 217,630 in 2000, comprising 1.9 percent of the population of the state.

A closer look at areas around Ohio indicates the impact that Hispanic migration is having on the demographic profile of the region. Between 1990 and 1998 the Hispanic population of Wood County grew by 35 percent; in Fulton County by 37.9 percent; in Ottawa County by 25.7 percent; and in Sandusky County by 25.6 percent. The areas in Ohio with the most Hispanics are Cuyahoga, Franklin, Lucas, Lorain, and Hamilton.

Joanna Griffin

SEE ALSO:

Agriculture; Hispanic Americans; Immigration, Mexican; Indiana; Migrant Labor.

Oil

Ever since the federal government took over the oil industry from U.S. and British companies in 1938, Mexicans have seen oil as a symbol of freedom from foreign domination. Mexico's ranking as an oil-producing nation has fallen since the early twentieth century, and its petrochemicals industry has suffered from inefficiency. However, oil remains a huge contributor to the country's economy.

The modern oil industry began in Mexico in 1904, during the presidency of Porfirio Díaz (1830–1915). That year a U.S. oilman, Edward L. Doheny, opened the first producing oil field in El Ebano, San Luis Potosí. British entrepreneurs also developed a field at about the same time. In 1908 a well blowout in Dos Bocas, Nayarit, revealed enormous deposits. It became one of the most prolific wells in the world, churning out almost 105 million barrels of crude oil in its nine years of existence. The surrounding area came to be known as La Faja de Oro (the Gold Belt) because of the value of its vast oil resources. Mexico exported its first shipment of oil

in 1911. By 1915 the country was producing one-quarter of the world's oil. The only bigger producer at the time was the United States.

From foreign to national control

The management of Mexico's oil industry in the early twentieth century was almost exclusively in the hands of U.S. and British companies, including giants such as Standard Oil, Sinclair, and the Texas Company, as well as hundreds of smaller operations. In the late 1800s Díaz's government had changed Mexico's property laws to grant foreign investors ownership of Mexican oil fields and mines. Díaz also gave foreign oil companies generous tax breaks during their first years of operation. Later, however, he imposed heavy taxes, as did the governments that followed both during and after the Mexican Revolution (1910–1920). Moreover, the revolutionary Constitution of 1917 restored the principle that all minerals found in the ground belonged to Mexico. Under this principle, Mexico made its oil fields national property and the foreign companies concessionaires, meaning that although they no longer owned the land, they could still pump oil and take

An oil refinery in Tula, in the central Mexican state of Hidalgo. Mexico sits on the second largest oil reserves in the Western Hemisphere, after Venezuela. The government-controlled Petróleos Mexicanos (PEMEX) company is the fifth largest oil company in the world.

a profit. The foreign companies were unhappy with concessionaire status and argued that other parts of the constitution protected their property rights. The argument led to a diplomatic problem between Mexico, the United States, and Great Britain.

Mexican oil workers further aggravated the foreign companies. The workers formed their first unions in 1915 and organized strikes to demand wage increases and conditions equal to those enjoyed by U.S. workers, who generally occupied more senior roles. The workers' demands, which the oil companies grudgingly accepted, injected the goals of labor unionism into the ideology of the revolution. By 1936 some 20 oil workers' unions had united into the Sindicato de Trabajadores Petroleros de la República Mexicana (STPRM; the Union of Petroleum Workers of the Mexican Republic). Today the STPRM has over 130,000 members.

In 1937 and 1938 the STPRM staged a series of strikes for higher wages and benefits. The Mexican supreme court ordered the oil companies to fulfill the union's demands, but most refused. In response, the STPRM urged the government of Lázaro Cárdenas (1895–1970) to seize the companies' assets. On March 18, 1938, Cárdenas nationalized the oil industry. The government subsequently created the state-run company Petróleos Mexicanos (PEMEX). In 1942 Mexico paid the foreign companies for their seized properties. The government asked ordinary Mexicans to contribute what they could. In what historians regard as the high point of Mexican nationalism, girls and women turned in their gold earrings and married couples gave up their wedding bands to help meet the costs.

Developments and problems

The nationalization of Mexico's oil industry led it to produce less crude oil for export and more for the country's domestic needs. In its early years PEMEX faced a number of problems, including the failure to locate new oil fields, which led to new agreements between the government and foreign oil companies in 1947. The agreements allowed foreign companies to assist PEMEX, both financially and in terms of technological expertise, in return for a share of the profits. In the 1950s the Mexican oil industry again looked for financial aid to expand its production from crude oil to refined petrochemicals. By this time, however, with the discovery of new oil fields in Venezuela and, more significantly, in the Middle East, foreign oil

companies were less interested in assisting Mexico. Instead, the Mexican government obtained funds from international banks.

PEMEX's failure to fund its own development needs resulted from inefficiencies, its unique range of expenses, and the use of its revenues to pay for government activities. By the late 1950s PEMEX was overstaffed. The STPRM controlled the hiring of workers, which increased by 258 percent between 1938 and 1958. Inefficiency continued throughout the twentieth century; in the 1990s sales per worker were a tenth that of international firms like Exxon or Royal Dutch. However, unlike private oil companies, PEMEX's expenses included hospitals, schools, and other social services for its workers, while the federal government took nearly 100 percent of its earnings. Because PEMEX could not afford to refine more oil, by the start of the twenty-first century Mexico imported more than a quarter of its gasoline. Meanwhile, old-fashioned plants and broken equipment caused pollution and fatal accidents, such as the death of a four-year-old girl near Mexico City in 2001. She was killed after a 50-year-old pipeline exploded near her house.

Modernizing Mexico's oil industry

Since the 1980s the Mexican government has tried to reform the country's oil industry. President Vicente Fox, elected in 2000, promised to modernize PEMEX by allowing increased foreign participation. However, nationalist forces, including the STPRM, accused Fox of selling out to foreign exploitation. Additional efforts by Fox to change Mexico's tax system to lessen its reliance on PEMEX and to let the company spend more of its earnings on its own operations, faced opposition from the Mexican congress.

Oil is still immensely important to the Mexican economy. In 2001 about 3.5 million barrels of crude oil were pumped each day, with half the total going toward exports. Taxes and duties on Mexican oil financed more than one-third of the country's national budget. Yet increasing the efficiency of oil production requires solving the issue of allowing greater foreign participation in an industry that remains a powerful symbol of Mexico's independence from foreign domination.

Deborah Nathan

SEE ALSO:

Cárdenas, Lázaro; Díaz, Porfirio; Inflation; Labor and Employment; Nationalization; PEMEX.

Oñate, Juan de

Juan de Oñate (ca. 1550–1626 or 1630) was a Spanish explorer who led expeditions throughout much of the American Southwest, and who also founded New Mexico. Oñate's attempts to discover the legendary wealth of the southwestern Native Americans failed, however, as to a large extent did his attempts at colonization. His career eventually ended in disgrace.

Juan de Oñate was born around 1550 in Zacatecas, Mexico, where his father, Cristobal, was one of the early European owners of the region's silver mines. In his early twenties Oñate took part in campaigns against the Chichimec Indians around Zacatecas and prospected for silver. He gained considerable social status when he married Isabel de Tolosa Cortés Moctezuma, a descendant of Hernán Cortés and reputed descendant of the Aztec emperor Moctezuma (also known as Montezuma II).

First expedition

On September 21, 1595, Oñate received a contract from King Philip II of Spain to lead an expedition to explore and settle the area to the north of Zacatecas. Oñate was an experienced campaigner, now in his mid-40s, and his wife had recently died. Like many other Spaniards, he was possibly encouraged as much by the prospect of great riches to be gained from the mineral wealth of what is now the American Southwest, legendary home of the fabled Seven Cities of Cíbola, as he was by the glory to be gained by founding a new Spanish colony. In the contract made with Philip II to settle New Mexico, Oñate demanded payment of 6,000 ducats a year, a large land grant, and the title of *adelantado*, or civil governor.

In return, Oñate was to provide the supplies and livestock for the expedition north and recruit and equip 200 soldiers. Many of his Spanish recruits took their families to settle the area; many also hoped to strike gold or silver, as had happened in Zacatecas. One of the main aims of the expedition was also to bring Christianity to the Indians. Philip ll gave this duty to the Franciscan order.

After three years of bureaucratic delay, Oñate set out in January 1598 from the frontier settlement of Santa Barbara in southern Chihuahua. The expedition numbered about 600 people and included settlers and their families, soldiers, and priests, along with Africans and Tlascal Indians to do the manual labor. The procession of 83 wagons and more than 7,000 animals stretched over a distance of 4 miles (6 km).

The Rio Grande

Oñate crossed the Chihuahua Desert and reached the Rio Grande at El Paso del Norte, near the present-day city of Ciudad Juárez. On April 30 he ceremonially claimed possession of the area for the King of Spain. The event was also commemorated by celebrating mass and holding a great feast.

Oñate moved up the Rio Grande to its junction with the Rio Chama, where he took over a former Indian village, which he named San Juan de los Caballeros in honor of the hospitality shown by the local O'ke Indians. He proclaimed the pueblo to be the headquarters of New Mexico, which included the present-day states of New Mexico, Arizona, Colorado, and parts of Texas. Oñate later moved the capital to San Gabriel, where there was more scope for expansion. In September the first church in New Mexico, San Juan Bautista (St. John the Baptist) was finished.

Acoma uprising

Oñate's fledging colony faced problems. Many of the Spaniards were disillusioned because they did not immediately discover mineral wealth. The cold of the approaching winter and the shortage of food also undermined morale. Many settlers threatened to return to Mexico. Oñate refused to countenance such desertion. He remained busy exploring Indian settlements in the region, and other members of the expedition explored as far as the San Francisco mountains in Arizona, where they discovered silver.

Problems mounted in December 1598, when a food-gathering party led by one of Oñate's nephews, Juan de Zaldívar, was attacked by Pueblo Indians at Acoma. Twelve Spaniards died, including Zaldívar. Oñate sent a punitive campaign to avenge the killings, led by Zaldívar's brother. On January 22, 1599, Vicente de Zaldívar and his men attacked Acoma and killed several hundred Indians. The captured surviving Indians were given severe punishments, including having their hands or feet cut off and being condemned to up to 20 years of penal servitude. Two Hopi Indians captured at Acoma had their right hands cut off and were released to return to their villages with warnings of the Spaniards' harsh discipline. In 1601 Vicente de Zaldívar led another punitive expedition against the settlement of Abo, east of the Rio Grande, again killing several hundred Indians.

Eastward to Kansas

In June 1601 Oñate led an expedition across the present-day Texas Panhandle to the plains around Wichita, Kansas, in search of Quivira, an Indian province first mentioned by an earlier explorer, Francisco Vasquez de Coronado, in 1541. Coronado reported that the great cities of Quivira were full of gold. When Oñate reached his destination, however, he found only peaceable villages of grass huts and an economy based on agriculture and hunting. There was no gold.

When Oñate returned to San Gabriel in November he found the colony empty apart from a few dedicated supporters. The harvest had failed and many of the settlers had left, finding conditions too hard. Others left because they disapproved of Oñate's harsh discipline; when they arrived back in New Spain they spread word of his actions.

Down the Colorado

Still eager to retrieve some success from his New Mexico venture, in 1604 Oñate led 30 soldiers west to find a route to the Pacific Ocean. He crossed the Gila River region of Arizona and reached the Colorado River, which he followed to its mouth on the Gulf of California. He mistakenly believed that he had reached the Pacific Ocean. Oñate also continued to search for mineral wealth; there was gold and silver in the area, but he failed to find either.

Meanwhile, complaints about Oñate's behavior in New Mexico reached the Spanish authorities in Madrid. The Council of the Indies wanted to abandon the province but was dissuaded by Franciscan monks who claimed to have converted 8,000 Indians and wanted to carry on the work. Spain's new king, Philip III, decided to continue supporting the colony, but without Oñate. Oñate resigned, a new governor was appointed, and in 1608 Oñate was summoned to Mexico City. On his way there, his son was killed by Indians.

In 1613 Oñate finally faced charges of using excessive force during the Acoma rebellion, hanging two Indians, and executing mutineers and deserters. Found guilty, he was fined, permanently banished from New Mexico, and banished from Mexico City for four years. He spent much of the rest of his life trying to clear his name, traveling to Spain in order to do so. He seems to have been at least partly successful because, before his death, the king gave him the position of mining inspector. Oñate died in Spain in either 1626 or 1630.

Lawrie Douglas

SEE ALSO:
Explorers; Mining and Minerals; New Mexico; Silver; Spanish Empire.

Oñate, Juan de
Spanish explorer and colonizer

Born: *c. 1550*
Zacatecas, New Spain
Died: *June 3, 1626 or 1630*
Spain

1595	Oñate is asked by the government of New Spain to lead an expedition to explore lands north of Zacatecas
1598	Leads expedition into Texas and New Mexico; claims New Mexico for Spain; becomes first governor of New Mexico
1601	Begins series of eastward expeditions in search of fabled Seven Cities of Cíbola
1604–05	Explores west from the Rio Grande through modern Arizona and descends the Colorado River to the Gulf of Mexico
1609	Resigns as governor of New Mexico
1613	Charged with cruelty and mismanagement
1614	Exiled from New Mexico
1624	Has sentence overturned after traveling to Spain to plead his case

Operation Gatekeeper

Operation Gatekeeper was one of a series of initiatives by the Immigration and Naturalization Service (INS) along the Mexico–U.S. border. Launched in October 1994, it was an effort to deter illegal immigrants from attempting to cross the border in the San Diego area.

Wooden crosses have been attached to the border fence near Tijuana in memory of the migrants who died attempting to reach the United States. Deaths along the border rose sharply in the 1990s.

Mexican migration into the United States rose dramatically during the mid-1990s because of the economic crisis caused by the devaluation of the peso in 1994. The United States responded to the increase in attempts to cross the border illegally with a raft of new operations. Operation Gatekeeper was the result of several developments. First, Operation Hold-the-Line, a Texas border operation that began in 1993, was believed to have successfully deterred large numbers of illegal immigrants by posting highly visible agents every quarter of a mile in the El Paso border zone. Second, the passage of the Violent Crime Control and Law Enforcement Act in 1994 appropriated funds for an increase in Border Patrol agents and use of military-style equipment, enabling the Border Patrol to implement more sophisticated operations. Third, Gatekeeper was created amid an atmosphere of hostility toward immigrants in California: Proposition 187, which called for the denial of public services to immigrants, was an example of this hostility.

Phases of the operation

Operation Gatekeeper dramatically increased the number of agents stationed along that part of the border, and a 14-mile (23-km) wall was built, stretching to the Pacific Ocean. The operation was implemented in three phases. The first focused on the Imperial Beach area, which begins in the Pacific Ocean and extends inland for 5 miles (8 km). This area had traditionally accounted for a quarter of all border crossings nationwide. Illegal immigrants immediately began to shift to areas with less surveillance, namely the Otay Mountains. Phase two extended surveillance to include the entire 66 miles (106 km) of the San Diego sector. During this time more illegal immigrants began crossing through the Tecate Mountains, a range that reaches as high as

6,000 feet (1,830 m) and experiences freezing temperatures for much of the year: many border crossers perished in this area, including 16 in one month during the winter of 1996/1997.

Much of phase three was aimed at exposing smuggling rings that arose in the eastern part of the state due to increased Border Patrol surveillance in San Diego and the Tecate Mountains. Gatekeeper also expanded existing structures to keep out illegal immigrants: multi-tiered fencing and stadium-style lighting were introduced.

Operation Gatekeeper has successfully driven illegal immigrants away from traditional migration routes in the San Diego area. However, critics of the operation point out that it has not dented would-be border crossers' determination to enter the United States: they have simply moved into more desolate areas. The figures produced by the INS have also come under attack. The operation ran into controversy in June 1996, when border agents claimed they were being ordered not to apprehend border crossers so that it would appear that fewer illegal immigrants were attempting to cross because they had been deterred by Gatekeeper.

Joanna Griffin

SEE ALSO:

Border Patrol, U.S.; Immigration, Mexican; Immigration and Naturalization Service; Migrant Labor; Operation Hold-the Line; Proposition 187.

Operation Hold-the-Line

Operation Hold-the-Line was an initiative by the Immigration and Naturalization Service (INS) implemented in 1993. It cracked down on illegal immigrants entering the United States along the Mexico-U.S. border at El Paso, Texas.

The U.S. public was concerned by the sharp rise in the number of illegal immigrants crossing the border from Mexico into the United States in the 1990s. When Attorney General Janet Reno visited the Mexico-U.S. border in August 1993, she noted the chaos and lack of control along the border. It was clear that the Border Patrol needed additional resources and a new strategy. In response, President Bill Clinton's administration (1993–2000) committed more resources to policing the border. The number of agents was increased, and they were equipped with motion sensors, night-vision goggles, and infrared scopes. The infrastructure along the border was also improved, with fences, stadium lighting, and all-weather roads.

The Immigration and Naturalization Service (INS), whose agency, the U.S. Border Patrol, is responsible for policing the border, introduced a new strategy that aimed at prevention through deterrence: prospective illegal entrants would be deterred from from attempting to cross the border because the risk of apprehension was so high.

Details of the operation

Operation Hold-the-Line was a new departure in controlling the border. In September 1993, without warning, the Border Patrol in the El Paso sector closed breaches in the border fence that had been major entry points for illegal immigrants. The two-week operation, originally called Operation Blockade, used border agents in a new way. Four hundred agents were stationed along the border itself, at quarter-mile (400-m) intervals, within sight of each other and clearly visible to would-be border crossers. They used line of sight to maintain a vigil against would-be migrants.

During the two-week operation, the head of the El Paso Border Patrol, Silvestre Reyes, announced that the program would continue indefinitely and would be renamed Operation Hold-the-Line. The blockade was set for 20 miles (32 km) but was later extended 10 miles (16 km) into southern New Mexico. According to the INS, apprehensions for illegal entry along the El Paso border dropped to about 150 from an average daily level of 800 to 1,000. The INS considered the operation a success, believing that the drop in apprehensions showed that would-be border crossers were being effectively deterred. The strategy prevented day-crossers from attempting to enter the United States in the El Paso sector, but the estimated number of crossings east and west of this area increased.

In 1994 Attorney General Janet Reno and INS Commissioner Doris Meissner announced a comprehensive long-term program to cut dramatically attempts to cross the border. Operation Hold-the-Line was incorporated into the new strategy, providing the model for several other major border operations, such as Operation Gatekeeper in San Diego and Operation Rio Grande in McAllen.

Public reaction to Hold-the-Line

A survey in 1994 by the *El Paso Times* found 78 percent of Hispanic respondents in favor of the policy and just 17 percent opposed to it, despite the fact that 70 to 75 percent of El Paso citizens are of Hispanic descent and mistaken arrests by border agents have resulted in lawsuits. The strategy has also been criticized by Ciudad Juárez residents who work legally in El Paso and were accustomed to crossing the border easily. The INS has claimed that Operation Hold-the-Line is particularly successful because it has not disrupted legal crossings, the normal rate of which is 120,000 a day. Human rights groups have led the protest against the new border enforcement strategy. As it becomes more difficult to cross the border near urban centers, illegal immigrants are forced to make their attempts in remote and dangerous areas. As a result, there has been a steady rise in deaths among those attempting to cross the border since the early 1990s.

Joanna Griffin

SEE ALSO:

Border Patrol, U.S.; Illegal Labor; Immigration and Naturalization Service; Operation Gatekeeper.

Operation Wetback

In July 1954 the U.S. Immigration and Naturalization Service (INS) launched Operation Wetback to repatriate illegal immigrants. Its particular focus was on Mexican "wetbacks," so named for having swum the Rio Grande in order to enter the United States. Although the INS claimed to have deported more than a million Mexicans, or to have encouraged them to leave voluntarily, the operation caused protest because it denied illegal aliens any right of appeal.

Operation Wetback was the INS response to what was perceived as a dangerous level of illegal Mexican immigration. Illegal workers threatened to take jobs from Anglo-Americans; Mexican culture threatened to swamp U.S. communities in Texas and the Southwest. From 1944 to 1954 the number of Mexicans crossing illegally into the United States rose by 6,000 percent. In 1949 the INS seized 280,000 illegal immigrants; four years later that number had risen to more than 865,000.

Part of the cause lay in the changing U.S. relationship with Mexico. Since the Bracero Treaty of 1942 the United States had imported temporary Mexican labor, initially to fill jobs left by U.S. service personnel fighting in World War II. Their labor continued to be valuable in the boom years that followed the end of the conflict. When the end of the Korean War contributed to an economic slowdown in the United States, however, the braceros were no longer welcome. To some extent, Operation Wetback also reflected a change in U.S. government attitudes toward Mexicans. Officials such as Attorney General Herbert Brownell obliquely suggested that Mexicans were a danger to the well-being of the United States.

The U.S. response to the situation was led by the new commissioner of the Immigration and Naturalization Service. Joseph Swing was a retired army general who had been at West Point with future president Dwight D. Eisenhower. Swing's approach to his new position reflected his military experience. Under Swing's guidance, the U.S. Border Patrol became a semimilitary organization, with green uniforms and a Mobile Task Force whose role was to target the high-traffic areas of illegal immigration. Swing intended to give the Border Patrol a deterrent effect, falsely suggesting that it was bigger and more effective at detaining immigrants than was probably the case.

Strong criticism

Operation Wetback was launched in the summer of 1954. About 700 government personnel (the Border Patrol, assisted by federal and state authorities) began searching barrios in border communities for illegal immigrants. On the first day of the operation in Texas, 4,800 people were detained; later the total was about 1,000 per day. Those seized were deported by bus, truck, or train, and later by ships, to the Mexican interior to discourage their return. American-born children, who were U.S. citizens, were deported along with their parents.

The government tactics drew criticism in both the United States and Mexico. Mexico objected when seven deportees drowned jumping ship. Mexican Americans protested that they were routinely being asked for identification simply on the basis of their looks. Farmers in the borderlands, on the other hand, objected that they were being denied access to cheap labor.

Operation Wetback tapered off late in 1954, when protests against its methods grew and INS funding ran out. The effectiveness of the operation remains open to question. The INS claimed to have forced 1.3 million illegal aliens to leave the United States, either by deporting them directly or by making them too afraid of being apprehended to remain.

For its supporters, Operation Wetback was a success, though it only temporarily reduced the number of illegal immigrants. For its opponents, however, it rode roughshod over human rights and encouraged a damaging atmosphere of confrontation that colored future relations between illegal immigrants and U.S. authorities.

Joanna Griffin

SEE ALSO:
Border Patrol, U.S.; Bracero Program; Illegal Labor; Immigration and Naturalization Service; Immigration, Mexican; Stereotypes and Prejudice.

Orozco, José Clemente

José Clemente Orozco was one of Los Tres Grandes, along with Diego Rivera (1886–1957) and David Alfaro Siqueiros (1896–1974): the three great Mexican artists who pioneered the muralist movement of the early twentieth century.

Orozco was born in Ciudad Guzmán, Jalisco, but grew up in Mexico City. He first studied agriculture then turned to art at the San Carlos Academy of Fine Art, which was also attended by Rivera. Influenced by the grotesque caricatures of the leading Mexican printmaker, José Guadalupe Posadas, Orozco worked as a political cartoonist and illustrator for the magazine *El Hijo de Ahuizote* and the newspaper *La Vanguardia* during the Mexican Revolution (1910–1920). In 1917 he went to the United States for three years following critical reviews of one of his exhibitions.

After the revolution the new government commissioned Orozco, Rivera, Siqueiros, and others to paint murals on public buildings in Mexico City. This was the start of the muralist movement. The artists were encouraged to paint murals to communicate the new revolutionary ideals to the poor and illiterate. The murals often featured elements of pre-Columbian art and celebrated the Mexican worker and peasant, but the artists were not given any specific political directives and each one's work was unique. Many of the murals dealt with themes of social justice and episodes from Mexico's history. Unlike the other leading muralists, Orozco was not political, writing that: "No artist has, or has ever had, political convictions of any sort. Those who profess to have them are not artists."

Orozco lost his left hand in an accident at age 17. Afterward, hands featured prominently in his work, as did dark colors, intense emotions, and heavy muscular figures that stood out against geometric backgrounds. His work drew strong reactions, and some of his early murals were defaced by students.

International reputation

In 1927 Orozco was again forced to leave Mexico after more critical attacks and his loss of government patronage. He went to the United States, where he managed to establish an international reputation. One of his best-known works was painted at the Baker Library of Dartmouth College in New Hampshire (1932–1934). The *Epic of American Civilization* is the story of the Americas, from the migration of the Aztecs to the development of modern industrial society.

On returning to Mexico in 1934 he completed a large panel, *Catharsis,* for the Fine Arts Palace. From 1936 to 1939 he worked at the University of Guadalajara, where he painted several fine murals. Perhaps his best work was the series of frescoes he painted at the Cabañas Orphanage (now the Cabañas Cultural Institute) representing a historical panorama of Mexico, from the pre-Columbian world to conquest, revolution, and beyond. In 1946 he won the National Arts Prize.

In contrast to the gregarious Rivera, Orozco was a private man intensely involved with his work. He kept apart from the other muralists. Like Rivera, his central subject was Mexico, although he did not idealize it in the same way. Some of Orozco's drawings and paintings can be seen at his former studio, now a museum in Guadalajara.

Joanna Griffin

SEE ALSO:

Art; Murals and Muralists; Rivera, Diego.

Orozco, José Clemente
Mexican artist

Born: *November 23, 1883*
Ciudad Guzmán, Jalisco
Died: *September 7, 1949*
Mexico City

1905	Attends San Carlos Academy of Art
1920	First commission by the Mexican government to paint murals
1927	Exiled to the United States
1934	Returns and paints murals in Guadalajara and Mexico City
1946	Wins the National Arts Prize

Overseas Aid

Mexico is both a recipient and a donor of overseas aid, most of which is channeled through joint cooperation programs with agencies from other countries. Economic aid to Mexico was running at more than U.S. $1.5 billion a year in the late 1990s and came from a range of sources, not just from the United States.

The donor nation making the most generous contributions to Mexico is not the United States but Japan (over U.S. $200 million annually). Following Japan in order of amount of donations are Germany, Spain, France, and then the United States. The European Union and Canada are also major donors. In addition, the World Bank and the Inter-American Development Bank (IDB) provide about U.S. $1 billion a year to help the Mexican economy, particularly in the provisioning of social services for impoverished Mexicans. In the 2001 financial year the World Bank's Global Environmental Fund donated U.S. $30 million to help provide renewable energy resources for rural areas of Mexico, and the IDB made a large loan to the Mexican Development Bank, with U.S. $500,000 earmarked for helping small businesses.

Cooperation programs involving Japan and Mexico include early detection, prevention, and rescue schemes for natural disasters. Both countries have suffered dramatically from the effects of earthquake damage, and Japan has shared its technical expertise in earthquake-proof building and highway construction.

Funding for health problems

Mexico has the second highest reported number of HIV/AIDS cases in Latin America, and Japan has donated substantially to help Mexico combat the spread of the disease. Japanese financing and expertise made available through this HIV/AIDS program have helped Mexican health agencies in their prevention and treatment campaigns. In addition, the United States Agency for International Development (USAID) in 2002 helped to fund AIDS-awareness programs in seven Mexican states where the incidence of HIV/AIDS is most severe.

Another health program partly financed by USAID is the fight against tuberculosis, commonly known as TB, which is a serious and growing problem in Mexico and also in the U.S. border states. The TB program involves fostering collaboration between health agencies in Mexico and the United States in order to introduce modern technology for detecting and treating the debilitating disease. The TB program also ensures that there are more health personnel in the Mexico-U.S. border region and establishes health facilities to deal specifically with TB cases in areas of high incidence rates throughout Mexico and the southwestern United States.

Other USAID programs in 2002 include financing for the Mexican government's program to encourage small enterprises as a way of countering poverty, help to modernize and streamline the Mexican judicial system, and the development of pilot programs for production technologies based on renewable and nonpolluting energy sources, such as solar and wind power. The last is particularly important in a country where industrialization has degraded so much of the environment.

Aid to Central America

Mexico is not just a recipient of aid, it also provides aid to less well-off countries. With the help of USAID's South-South program, Mexico's development experience is channeled through the Mexican Assistance Agency to help less well-developed economies in Central America and the Caribbean. For example, between January and April 2002, U.S. $62,000 was spent on making repairs to 62 schools in Central America; help was given to provide books for schools in Cuba, Guatemala, and the Dominican Republic; and training courses were provided for teachers. Technical expertise and financimg were offered through a variety of environmental and health programs relating to water cleanliness, wildfire prevention, and TB and AIDS prevention.

Tim Harris

SEE ALSO:

Canada; Central America; Cuba; Earthquakes and Natural Disasters; Foreign Policy, Mexican.

Pan-American Highway

The Pan-American Highway is a road system linking the main cities of South and Central America with the highway system of the United States and Canada. The highway system is around 16,000 miles (25,750 km) long and stretches from Alaska to the southernmost tip of Argentina.

The Pan-American Highway varies greatly along its length. It passes through many different landscapes, from tropical rain forest to high mountains, and some parts are only accessible in the dry season. The United States financially assisted most Latin American countries to build and pay for their sections of the highway. However, Mexico financed and constructed its part independently.

History of the highway

The idea of building a road linking the countries of the Americas has a long history. As early as the sixteenth century Charles V, Holy Roman emperor and king of Spain, wanted to build a road linking the colony of New Spain (now Mexico) with his other territories in South America. In 1884 a proposal was made in the U.S. Congress to construct a Pan-American railroad. The railroad project never came to fruition, but it led to the idea of a Pan-American Highway.

In 1923 a resolution was passed at the Fifth International Conference of American States in Santiago, Chile, calling for the creation of a congress to study the possibility of building a network of highways across the Americas. The Pan-American Highway Congress met for the first time in Buenos Aires in 1925, where it was established as a permanent organization with responsibility for the development of the highway. It became a branch of the Organization of American States (OAS) and continues to meet every four years to consider the progress of the highway's development.

Many routes

The original idea was to have a single road linking North and South America, but now the Pan-American Highway includes several routes in each country. In 1967 the United States chose the Interstate Highway System for inclusion in the system (each country designates the routes to be included in the Pan-American Highway within its borders). The four major U.S. terminals of the Pan-American Highway are Nogales in Arizona and Eagle Pass, El Paso, and Laredo in Texas.

The Alaska Highway, 1,523 miles (2,450 km) long, running from Fairbanks to Dawson Creek, British Columbia, forms the northernmost section of the Pan-American Highway. It connects with highways to other cities in Alaska and with highways to the cities of Edmonton and Prince George in Canada.

The Inter-American Highway is the section of the Pan-American Highway that runs from Nuevo Laredo, Tamaulipas, to Panama City. Construction of this 3,400-mile (5,470-km) section began in 1935. It travels due south to Mexico City from Laredo, Texas, then down through Guatemala City, San Salvador, Managua, and San José, Costa Rica, to Panama City. An important link in the system was completed in 1962 when the one-mile (1.6-km) long Thatcher Ferry Bridge spanning the Panama Canal at Balboa was opened.

The Darién gap

The only break in the Pan-American Highway lies on the border between Panama and Colombia, dividing Central and South America, where lush rain forest forms an almost impenetrable barrier. The 54-mile (90-km) stretch goes through two national parks, the Darién National Park in Panama and Los Katios National Park in Colombia. It is a region of exceptional biodiversity and home to around 30,000 indigenous people. The area has been declared a biological and cultural World Heritage Site. The completion of this section of the highway was opposed by environmentalists who feared the destruction of the rain forest and by local peoples who feared the highway would destroy their culture. The Panamanian government also opposed the completion of the highway because it feared an increase in drug-related violence from Colombia.

Joanna Griffin

SEE ALSO:
Alliances and Agreements; Transportation.

Partido Acción Nacional

The Partido Acción Nacional (PAN; National Action Party) is the oldest political party in Mexico. For the second half of the twentieth century, it represented the only significant opposition to the Partido de la Revolución Mexicana (PRM; Party of the Mexican Revolution) and its successor, the Partido Revolucionario Institucional (PRI; Institutional Revolutionary Party).

The PAN was created in September 1939 at a convention held in Mexico City. Its founder was a lawyer named Manuel Gómez Morín. During the 1920s Gómez Morín had occupied several important government positions, including undersecretary of finance. He was also the founding president of the Banco de México, the country's central bank. Gómez Morín was opposed to the left-wing policies of President Lázaro Cárdenas, who had extended state control of the economy. Gómez Morín set up the PAN to give a voice to all those who opposed the government.

The convention that spawned the new party brought together a diverse group of individuals that included former revolutionaries, university students, landowners, and business leaders. It also attracted many influential lay Catholics who felt threatened by Cárdenas's antipathy to the church. The men and women who became the new party's supporters tended to come from the higher echelons of Mexican society. However, they were bound together more by their opposition to the government than by any common ideology.

The party soon began to contest elections but had little impact, mainly because of the firm grip that the ruling PRM, and later the PRI, had on the political process. From the 1940s onward first the PRM and later the PRI blatantly manipulated election results and intimidated opposition politicians. When this happened, the PAN could only appeal to institutions that were themselves under the control of the ruling party. The PAN was also handicapped by the fact that it did not have widespread appeal, since it was widely seen as representing only a small, middle-class elite.

In the four decades after its founding, the PAN's only real effect was to inadvertently legitimize the PRI's dominance of the Mexican political system. Indeed, many PAN members did not see the party as one that could seriously compete for power, but merely as a channel through which opposition to the government could be voiced.

The PAN's rise to prominence

The role that the PAN played in Mexican politics began to change in the 1980s. Halfway through the decade a new breed of politician emerged. Known as the Barbaros del Norte (Barbarians of the North), a group of businessmen from states such as Chihuahua, Nuevo León, and Baja California took the party by storm. In the early 1980s Mexico had experienced a profound economic crisis, and the new generation of PAN politicians attracted the support of middle-class voters worried about their financial security. Ideologically, these politicians combined social conservatism with an opposition to state control of the economy and government corruption.

In 1988 Manuel J. Clouthier gained the largest number of votes that had yet been obtained by the PAN in a presidential election. The new movement kept gaining ground and in 1989, in the state of Baja California, the PAN candidate Ernesto Ruffo became the first opposition candidate ever to defeat the PRI in a gubernatorial election. This victory gave both the PAN and other opposition parties the hope that the PRI could be defeated.

The PAN continued to gain support throughout the 1990s, particularly in the more prosperous states of northern Mexico. Mayoral and gubernatorial victories, and an increasing number of seats in the federal congress, made the PAN a real threat to the stranglehold that the PRI had maintained over federal government. The climax to this process came on July 2, 2000, when the PAN politician Vicente Fox became the first opposition candidate to win a presidential election since the revolution.

Héctor Manuel Lucero

SEE ALSO:

Cárdenas, Lázaro; Elections in Mexico; Fox, Vicente; Partido Revolucionario Institucional; Political Parties in Mexico; Ruffo, Ernesto.

Partido de la Revolución Democrática

The Partido de la Revolución Democrática (PRD; Democratic Revolution Party) was born on May 5, 1989. It was the offspring of a reformist movement within the ruling Partido Revolucionario Institucional (PRI; Institutional Revolutionary Party).

In 1987, as Mexico's political parties were getting ready to start the campaign for the 1988 elections, a group within the PRI proposed major changes to the party's outlook and structure. Calling itself the Corriente Democrática (CD; Democratic Movement) the group advocated radical changes to the government's economic policy and pressed for internal reform, in particular for the democratization of the party's system for selecting election candidates. The PRI had dominated Mexican politics at all levels for over 70 years, and its outgoing presidents traditionally nominated their successors without consulting members of the wider party.

Breaking from the PRI

The leaders of the CD were Cuauhtémoc Cárdenas (born 1934) and Porfirio Muñoz Ledo. Both were important members of the PRI, especially Cárdenas, who was the son of former president Lázaro Cárdenas. Despite their prominence, the leadership of the PRI resisted their calls for reform, prompting the CD to break with the party completely. Cárdenas and Muñoz Ledo formed the Frente Democrático Nacional (FDN; National Democratic Front), an alliance of their followers who had also left the PRI as well as left-wing political parties and organizations. The FDN nominated Cárdenas as its candidate for the 1988 presidential election.

Although the subsequent election was won by the PRI's Carlos Salinas de Gortari, rumors flew that electoral officials, at the PRI's behest, had destroyed thousands of votes for Cárdenas. The rumors were never proven, but many believe the real winner was Cárdenas. However, even in defeat the movement gained strength and reestablished itself as the

A PRD rally in Mexico City during the 1990 local elections. The PRD won the mayoral election in Mexico City in 1997 and retained it in 2000 with the victory of Andres Manuel Lopez Obrador.

Democratic Revolution Party (PRD). In the 1990s its membership grew with the influx of ex-PRI members who were either disenchanted with the political situation in Mexico or who had lost political influence within the ruling party.

In the federal elections of 1991 and 1994 the PRD won some seats in the Mexican congress. Yet its first major victory came in 1997, when Cárdenas won the mayoral election in Mexico City. This was the first time that the mayor of the capital was democratically elected, following reforms implemented by President Salinas in the wake of criticisms of his 1988 election. In 2000 Cárdenas came third in the presidential election. The disappointment was offset by victory in the local elections of Mexico City and the maintenance of a strong presence in congress.

Support for the PRD is uneven across Mexico. It is stronger in the south, where left-wing politics are generally popular, and weaker in the industrialized north. Despite this, the party has become the third most influential political force in Mexico and the most important left-wing voice in the country.

Héctor Manuel Lucero

SEE ALSO:

Cárdenas, Lázaro; Elections; Political Parties, Mexican; Salinas de Gortari, Carlos.

Partido Revolucionario Institucional

The Partido Revolucionario Institucional (PRI; Institutional Revolutionary Party) molded twentieth-century politics in Mexico by holding presidential power, as well as most other institutions of government, for 71 years.

Toward the end of 1928 President Plutarco Elías Calles proposed the creation of a political party that represented the ideals of the Mexican Revolution (1910–1920). Several months later, on March 4, 1929, the Partido Nacional Revolucionario (PNR; National Revolutionary Party) was founded. While the party was intended to end the era of military leaders holding absolute power, in reality Calles remained the force behind successive presidents for six years. His control came to an end with the election of Lázaro Cárdenas, who exiled Calles in 1936 for criticizing the new administration.

Changing names, increasing power

In an attempt to erase Calles's influence on Mexican politics, Cárdenas proposed a new party, the Partido de la Revolución Mexicana (PRM; Party of the Mexican Revolution), to replace the PNR. The new party was founded in 1938 and had a broader organization than the old PNR, with separate sections for laborers, farmers, and the military. The new structure served to boost the power of its leader, the president. This power revealed itself in the 1940 presidential election. In the run-up to the election, growing support for the opposition candidate and writer José Vasconcelos threatened the PRM. As a result the governing party used the army to intimidate voters on election day. The PRM's strong-arm tactics worked and its candidate, Manuel Ávila Camacho, became president.

On January 18, 1946, the party's name changed for a second time, to the Partido Revolucionario Institucional (PRI). In the 1950s and 1960s the PRI maintained its tight grip on power, winning all federal and state elections. During this period Mexico experienced considerable economic growth, but although most people seemed happy with the PRI's management of the country, criticism of its lack of regard for Indians and its authoritarian tactics began to grow. One event that fueled the governing party's detractors more than any other was the killing of student protestors in 1968 in Mexico City.

Loss of support

In the 1970s and 1980s heavy government borrowing and spending contributed to Mexico's decline from a potential world power to a developing nation. Accusations of corruption, including electoral fraud, added to the PRI's misfortunes and led to increasing public discontent. Before the 1988 presidential election the left-wing opposition candidate, Cuauhtémoc Cárdenas, led the race in a number of opinion polls. Strong suspicions that the government committed electoral fraud were never confirmed, and the PRI's Carlos Salinas de Gortari became president. The allegations of fraud weakened the party, however, resulting in its first major defeat in 1989, when the Partido Acción Nacional (PAN; National Action Party) won Baja California's gubernatorial election. The PAN's Ernesto Ruffo became the first opposition-party governor in Mexico.

The PRI suffered further defeats in state and federal elections, but managed to hold on to the presidency in 1994 as a result of public approval for Salinas's management of the economy. Only days after newly elected president Ernesto Zedillo Ponce de León took office, an economic crisis hit Mexico, devaluing the peso. Zedillo's presidency was a difficult time for most Mexicans.

By 2000 many people were ready for a different political party to lead Mexico. On July 2, after 71 years, the PRI finally lost the presidency to the PAN's Vicente Fox. The defeat led to a period of turmoil within the PRI, which began to consider changes to its structure and policies. The ensuing clash of views within the party caused it further losses in a number of state elections. By 2002 the PRI was still struggling to come to terms with Mexico's changed political landscape.

Héctor Manuel Lucero

SEE ALSO:

Calles, Plutarco Elías; Cárdenas, Lázaro; Elections in Mexico; Fox, Vicente; Political Parties in Mexico; Ruffo, Ernesto; Student Movement in Mexico City.

Paz, Octavio

Octavio Paz (1914–1998) was a Mexican poet, writer, and diplomat, regarded as one of the major writers of the twentieth century. He received many of the world's most notable prizes for literature, including the Nobel Prize in 1990.

Octavio Paz was born in Mexico City in 1914 into an intellectual, literary, and politically active family. His father was a political journalist who joined the agrarian uprising led by Emiliano Zapata (1879–1919) during the Mexican Revolution (1910–1920). His grandfather was one of the first authors to write a novel with an indigenous Indian theme. Paz developed his passion for books and writing in his grandfather's extensive library.

Paz studied law and literature at the National University but did not complete his degree. From his youth Paz's ambition was to be a poet, and he started to write at an early age. He published his first poem at age 17, and his first book of poems, *Luna Silvestre* (1933; Wild Moon), when he was age 19.

In 1937 Paz married writer Elena Garro, and that same year they went to Spain to support the left-wing Republican government as noncombatants in the civil war against the Nationalists. They took part in the Second International Congress of Anti-Fascist Writers in Valencia, Spain, where they met, among others, the French communist writers André Malraux and André Gide.

Before returning to Mexico, Paz visited Paris, where he had his first encounter with surrealism, which influenced his later work. This literary and artistic movement emphasized the use of dreams, magic, and accident to liberate the subconscious.

Early career

From the late 1930s Paz worked as a journalist. He founded and edited several important literary reviews, including *Taller* and *El Hijo Prodigo* (The prodigal son). In 1943 Paz traveled to the United States on a Guggenheim Fellowship, which allowed him to spend two years studying Spanish American poetry in San Francisco and New York.

At the end of World War II (1939–1945), at age 31, Paz entered the Mexican diplomatic corps. He

This photograph of Octavio Paz was taken in 1990, when he won the Nobel Prize for Literature.

considered his diplomatic role to be "the best thing that could have happened to me. It is very good for a writer to be something else, to have a profession. To be only a poet is not too good."

Diplomatic travels

Paz was first posted to France, where he wrote his famous study of Mexico, *El labarinto de la soledad* (1950; *The Labyrinth of Solitude*, 1961), and became involved in activities with the surrealists. He served as a diplomat in several other countries, including Japan, where he became interested in Buddhism and the works of the poet Basho, whose poems he later translated. He divorced Elena Garro in 1959. He was sent as Mexican ambassador to India in 1962, where he stayed for six years. This appointment was important for Paz because it enabled him to study another ancient culture that he could compare with his native Mexico. South Asian thought and religion had a strong influence on his work. While he was in India he met his second wife, Maria-José Tramini. In 1968 he resigned from the diplomatic service in protest against the government's violent suppression of student demonstrations in the Plaza de Tlatelolco shortly before the Olympic Games.

Later career

After his resignation from the diplomatic corps, Paz lived the rest of his life in Mexico City. He continued his work as an editor and publisher, having founded two more magazines dedicated to the arts and politics: *Plural* and *Vuelta*. His later collections of poetry included *Blanco* (1967), *Ladera Este* (1971; East slope), *Hijos del aire* (1979; *Airborn*, 1981) and *Arbol adentro* (1987; A tree within). From 1968 to 1970 he was a visiting professor of Spanish American Literature at several universities, including the University of Texas, Austin; the University of Pittsburgh; the University of Pennsylvania; Harvard; and Cambridge University, England.

In 1980 he was given an honorary doctorate by Harvard. The following year he received the Cervantes Award, the most important award in the Spanish-speaking world. In 1982 he was awarded the American Neustadt Prize and in 1990 the Nobel Prize for Literature.

His greatest poem is generally considered to be "Piedra del Sol," published in a collection of the same name in 1957 (*Sun Stone*, 1962). This work was inspired by an Aztec calendar stone, where the calendar was based on the conjunctions of Venus and the sun. The 584 days of this cycle are matched by the 584 lines of the poem.

While primarily a poet, Paz also wrote volumes of essays and literary criticism. He won international recognition for his examination of Mexicans and Mexican culture, *El labarinto de la soledad*. In this influential essay he traces the "invisible history" of Mexico, which is the history of the pre-Columbian cultures that continue to influence the modern state. "Mexicans," he wrote, "are instinctive nihilists who hide behind masks of solitude. They do not know who they are and they are suspicious of others because they are suspicious of themselves."

His other works include discussions on themes such as cultural attitudes in *Conjunciones y disyunciones* (1969; *Conjunctions and Disjunctions*, 1974); language and the borders between prose and poetry in *El mono gramático* (1974; *The Monkey Grammarian*, 1981); and international politics, focusing on the United States and Latin America, in *Tiempo nublado* (1983; *One Earth, Four or Five Worlds: Reflections on Contemporary History*, 1985).

Paz, Octavio
Mexican poet, writer, and diplomat

Born: *March 31, 1914*
Mexico City
Died: *April 19, 1998*
Mexico City

1931	First poem published age 17
1937	Marries writer Elena Garro and travels to Spain during its civil war
1943	Receives Guggenheim Fellowship
1945	Enters diplomatic service
1950	Publishes *El labarinto de la soledad*
1959	Divorces Elena Garro
1964	Marries Maria-José Tramini
1968	Resigns from diplomatic service
1990	Receives Nobel Prize for Literature

Paz had strong views on contemporary life, which he wrote about at length in his essays and articles. He was concerned about the lack of spirituality in the modern world. In addition, he thought that beliefs and ideas were no longer collective but private. He feared this privatization would lead to the destruction of society and that people would become possessed by ancient religious fury or fanatical nationalism. He also considered that belief in the market economy was a symptom of the contemporary spiritual wilderness. He accepted that the mechanism of the market was efficient, but as it was just a mechanism, it lacked both conscience and compassion. Paz was concerned about the environment as well. "Pollution," he wrote, "affects not only the air, the rivers, and the forests but also our souls. A society possessed by the frantic need to produce more in order to consume more tends to reduce ideas, feelings, art, love, friendship, and people themselves to consumer products. No other society has produced so much material and moral waste as ours."

His *Obras completas* (Complete works) was published in 1994. He died at his home in Mexico City at the age of 84 after suffering from cancer for more than a year.

Lawrie Douglas

SEE ALSO:

Language; Literature; Spain; Student Movement in Mexico City.

PEMEX

The enormous oil company known as PEMEX—short for Petróleos Mexicanos— is an overwhelming economic and political presence in Mexico. It is also a powerful national symbol throughout the country. At the end of the twentieth century, however, the company's financial performance worsened. Efforts to reform the company have become bound up in the symbolic role of the oil industry in Mexican nationalism and with the large influence wielded by vested political and financial interests.

PEMEX is everywhere in Mexico. All gas stations throughout the country are franchises of the company. Every factory uses PEMEX fuel. One hundred and thirty thousand people belong to an oil workers' union whose sole employer is PEMEX. More than one-third of Mexico's entire national budget is financed by taxes and duties on the company's products.

Unlike oil companies in the United States, PEMEX is not a private enterprise but is wholly owned by the Mexican government. It was created after Lázaro Cárdenas (president 1934–1940) nationalized Mexico's oil industry in 1938. Before 1938 foreigners, mainly Americans, controlled every bit of oil in Mexico, which at Mexico's peak output represented one fourth of the world's production. Nationalization was accompanied by changes to the federal constitution to forbid foreign exploitation of the country's petroleum resources. Soon after, PEMEX was organized. Mexican schoolchildren are still taught that the creation of PEMEX marked the highpoint of Mexican independence from foreign economic and political domination.

Mexico's oil industry

Mexico sits on the second largest oil reserves in the Western Hemisphere; only Venezuela has more. The oil fields lie in the Gulf of Mexico and along its coast. There are also natural gas fields near Reynosa, Veracruz, and in the Chiapas-Tabasco region.

PEMEX pumps about 3.5 million barrels of crude oil every day, and almost half of its output is

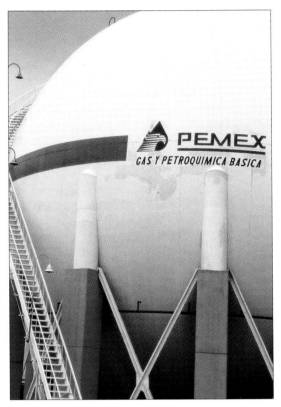

The name PEMEX is found all over Mexico, as on this tank at a refinery in Poza Rica, Veracruz. The company's position as a national symbol, however, has been undermined by poor performance.

exported. The United States buys one-sixth of its imported petroleum from Mexico. PEMEX earns enormous amounts of money, the majority of which is claimed by the Mexican government. This arrangement was begun by the Partido Revolucionario Institucional (PRI; Institutional Revolutionary Party), which governed Mexico from 1929 until it was voted out of power in 2000. The PRI also had a close relationship with the giant oil-workers' union. Together, the union and PEMEX have been called the PRI's "right arm." They played a vital role in the government for seven decades.

By the end of the twentieth century, PEMEX's performance no longer lived up to its reputation. It was increasingly referred to as the least efficient oil company in the world, and one of its own directors described it as "a combination of an oil company and a bureaucracy." PEMEX suffered from corruption, patronage, and financial crisis. The result was that the company had become very inefficient. In terms of laborers versus productive output, for example, PEMEX employed twice as many workers as the oil industry of Venezuela, yet turned out the same amount of oil. PEMEX sales per worker, meanwhile, were only a tenth of those achieved by rival international firms such as Exxon or Royal Dutch.

The company's overstaffing and inefficiency can be blamed at least partly on bureaucratic management by the oil workers' union, which controls all hiring for PEMEX. Mexico's enormous economic dependence on the company is another contributing problem. The government routinely takes all of PEMEX's earnings, and sometimes even more than it earns, a situation that forces PEMEX to borrow in order to pay its taxes. In 2001, for example, the company earned U.S. $20.9 billion in the first nine months of the year. Over the same period its taxes and other duties amounted to U.S. $22.1 billion. As a public rather than private company, PEMEX also has remarkably high overheads. It pays much of its income to provide hospitals, schools, stores, and other social services for its employees.

Raising funds

The net result of mismanagement and inefficiency has been to leave PEMEX with virtually no funds to invest in searching for new oil fields, modernizing equipment, or increasing its capacity to refine oil. A shortage of refining capabilities meant that Mexico was not even self-sufficient in gasoline: it had to import more than a quarter of its gasoline. Meanwhile, old plants and broken equipment have caused pollution and serious accidents. One such tragedy occurred in 2001. A four-year-old girl in a town near Mexico City was killed after a 50-year-old PEMEX pipeline blew up near her house.

Modernizing PEMEX would cost billions of dollars that the company does not have. PEMEX's director observed that the money could come only from foreign investment. He predicted that by 2010 the company would need $20 to $30 billion in outside capital. For many Mexicans, however, PEMEX is still a powerful symbol of the country's sovereignty. Even though many other industries in the country are highly financed and controlled by

foreign investment, oil's unique role as a symbol of Mexican nationalism makes the industry very hard to restructure. To invite foreign investment would be to risk popular resentment.

Attempts at reform

The Mexican government has tried to reform PEMEX since the 1980s. The attempts continued after the Partido Acción Nacional (PAN; National Action Party) defeated the PRI in 2000, bringing to power President Vicente Fox. Fox promised to modernize the company. He intended to break the hold of the oil workers' union on politics and to sever the government's dependence on PEMEX earnings. Fox said that he wanted PEMEX to be not only successful and competitive but "transparent." By this he meant that its operations and finances should be open to public scrutiny. Controversially, Fox intended to allow foreign investment in PEMEX, and to let foreign companies run operations in Mexico's biggest natural gas fields.

Fox's efforts faced strong resistance from the oil unions and from nationalist elements in the government, which accused him of selling Mexico's sovereignty to foreign exploitation. During his first year in office, Fox tried to change Mexico's tax system to reduce its reliance on PEMEX so that the company would be able to spend money on its own operations. However, the Mexican congress blocked this effort. In 2001 Fox appointed an outside board of businessmen to oversee PEMEX. Congress objected to the board, which was dissolved. Fox's government also charged the PRI with illegally taking $120 million from PEMEX to help campaign against Fox in the 2000 presidential campaign. PRI leaders denied the charges, which they claimed were an attempt by Fox to increase foreign investment in PEMEX.

PEMEX remains a problem for the Mexican government. One former energy official remarked that it was unfortunate that the oil industry is so symbolically connected with Mexican nationalism. He argued that such symbolism tends to block rational discussion and significant reform, as well as necessary changes that could protect Mexico's sovereignty even as they help save PEMEX.

Deborah Nathan

SEE ALSO:

Cárdenas, Lázaro; Fox, Vicente; Gulf of Mexico; Nationalization; Oil; Partido Revolucionario Institucional; Political Parties in Mexico.

Pershing Expedition

The Pershing Expedition was an 11-month incursion into Mexico by U.S. forces in retaliation for the Columbus Raid in March 1916.

After the attack on Columbus, New Mexico, by Villistas (supporters of Francisco "Pancho" Villa) U.S. president Woodrow Wilson (1856–1924) asked his Mexican counterpart, Venustiano Carranza (1859–1920), for permission to pursue those responsible into Mexico. Carranza agreed; given the power of the United States he had no choice. On March 10, General John Joseph "Black Jack" Pershing (1860–1948) was ordered to organize an expedition against Villa (1878–1923) and others who had carried out the Columbus Raid.

On March 16 Pershing led two columns across the border into Chihuahua. His force included infantry, cavalry, field artillery, engineers, the First Aero Squadron with eight airplanes, field hospitals, wagon and ambulance companies, and signal detachments. He had 11,000 men in all, including Buffalo Soldiers (African American troops) and Apache Scouts.

Wilson also called up the state militias, and by the end of August 1916 there were almost 140,000 regular army and National Guard troops patrolling the vast border between Mexico and the United States to discourage further raids. The Pershing Expedition eventually advanced as far south as the city of Parral, 400 miles (645 km) into Mexican territory. U.S. troops did encounter Villistas along the route, but Villa himself was never captured. The Pershing Expedition ended on February 14, 1917, when the last of the U.S. troops crossed back over the border from Palomas, Chihuahua, into Columbus, New Mexico.

Although the expedition failed in its main objective, the capture of Villa, the mission was not entirely unsuccessful. It ensured that the Villistas became too fragmented and disorganized to cause further trouble north of the border. It also left Villa a fallen idol, and he had no choice but to come to terms with the Carranza government.

Henry Russell

SEE ALSO:

Carranza, Venustiano; Columbus Raid; Villa, Francisco "Pancho"; Wilson, Woodrow.

Company A, 6th Infantry, of the U.S. Army in a defensive trench at the American Army Field Headquarters in 1916 during the Pershing Expedition. The expedition never achieved its ultimate objective of capturing Francisco "Pancho" Villa.

Phoenix, Arizona

The largest city in the Southwest, Phoenix is the state capital of Arizona. Home to the Grand Canyon National Park, Arizona has particular relevance for Mexican Americans since they were among the first to establish homesteads in the region.

Located on the upper edge of the Sonoran Desert, the city of Phoenix was named to commemorate its rise from the ashes of the Hohokam, the Native American people who lived there before white settlers arrived. The city's ancient past is celebrated by the Heard Museum, which houses an extensive display of Native American artifacts. The city is also associated with the architecture of Frank Lloyd Wright (1867–1959), who worked on the Biltmore Hotel. He also built a winter studio there, now the architecture school known as Taliesin West. In the 1940s elderly and sick Americans would visit the city for its clean, dry air and its warm winter climate. These days the city no longer offers a suburban idyll, although there are still retirement communities in nearby towns such as Sun City.

Arizona is a very hot state and much of the region is desert. The state capital, Phoenix, was founded in the nineteenth century in the middle of what was then a mining area.

Mexican American communities

Until 1848 Arizona was part of Mexico. A wave of Mexican immigrants settled in Phoenix in the mid-to-late nineteenth century. At this time Phoenix was still a farming town. Many Mexicans had originally been recruited to southern Arizona to work as miners. For this work the Mexicans drew on their own culture's well-established tradition of mining. Their expertise in dry washing and patio processing, and the fact that they provided a cheap labor force, made it easy to find work. Other Mexican settlers found work as ranchers and as farm laborers.

Mexican American communities soon developed in the nearby towns of Tempe and Wickenburg, while the booming mining towns of Globe, Clifton, Metcalf, and Morenci also provided employment. As more Mexicans arrived these communities began building their own churches, such as the Immaculate Heart of Mary Catholic Church, completed in Phoenix in 1928.

Although some Mexicans returned home, many stayed in Phoenix. Throughout the twentieth century Mexican Americans worked hard for equal rights. In the early twentieth century, the efforts of Mexican Americans proved integral to miners' strikes. Later, during the 1960s, as Hispanic civil rights leader César Chávez (1927–1993) increased Mexican American unity, organizations were set up to offer support to Mexican Americans. Several of these, including the nonprofit Chicanos Por La Causa (Chicanos For The Cause), were based in Phoenix, as were several Chicano institutions, including the Latin American Club of Arizona.

Evidence of Phoenix's Mexican heritage can today be seen throughout the city, thanks in part to its colorful murals. The Chicano Mural Movement of the 1960s helped keep the Mexican tradition of painting alive in major cities in Arizona, including Phoenix. Today the city, with nearly 30 percent of its residents claiming Mexican descent, sponsors Mexican American festivities, including an annual Cinco de Mayo (May 5) celebration.

Christopher Wiegand

SEE ALSO:

Chicano Movement; Festivals; Hispanic Americans; Labor Organizations, U.S.; Mining and Minerals.

Political Parties in Mexico

For much of the twentieth century Mexican politics was characterized by an unusual form of single-party rule. The political system was dominated by the Partido Revolucionario Institucional (PRI; Institutional Revolutionary Party) and its predecessors the Partido Nacional Revolucionario (PNR; National Revolutionary Party) and the Partido de la Revolución Mexicana (PRM; Party of the Mexican Revolution). Opposition parties were allowed to exist but did not represent a genuine challenge to one-party rule until the late 1980s and 1990s.

The PRI was created as the National Revolutionary Party in 1929. Between then and 1988 elections were held at all levels, but the PRI never lost a presidential, gubernatorial, or senatorial race. However, a series of electoral reforms from 1977 onward eased the requirements for new party registration and the situation started to change at the end of the 1980s. Two opposition parties began to challenge PRI candidates for local, state, and even national offices. They were the Partido Acción Nacional (PAN; National Action Party), which was founded in 1939 and occupied the center-right of the ideological spectrum, and the center-left Partido de la Revolución Democrática (PRD; Party of the Democratic Revolution), which was founded in 1989. In the last decade of the twentieth century, the Mexican political system gradually evolved from one dominated by a single party into a competitive system in which the three main parties had substantial representation at federal, state, and local levels.

The Partido Revolucionario Institucional

On March 4, 1929, President Plutarco Elías Calles founded the PNR as a loose group of local political bosses and military commanders allied with labor unions, peasant organizations and regional parties. In its early years, it served primarily as a means of organizing political competition among the major revolutionary leaders, assuring the principle of no reelection and the continuity of governmental plans. Presidential elections were first held in 1929, but Calles managed to control Mexican politics until 1934, weakening the regional military commanders who had operated with great autonomy throughout the 1920s.

The selection of Lázaro Cárdenas as the PNR presidential candidate in 1934 resulted in a shift of ideological emphasis within the party, with Cárdenas advocating more radical policies than his predecessor. Between 1934 and 1940 an intense struggle for political control developed between Cárdenas and Calles. As part of his strategy to defeat his rival, Cárdenas formed the National Peasant Confederation (CNC) and the Confederation of Mexican Workers (CTM). Using these organizations as the bases of his support, Cárdenas reorganized the PNR in 1938, renaming it the Partido de la Revolución Mexicana (PRM). The PRM was organized into four sectors: labor, agrarian, popular, and military, transforming it from an elitist organization into a more inclusive party.

The chamber of deputies, the lower house of the Mexican congress. The congress was dominated by the PRI for most of the twentieth century. However, in 1997 the party lost its majority for the first time.

Minor Opposition Parties

In addition to the three major political parties in Mexico there have been a number of minor parties, most of which have had close links to the PRI and presented little threat to it.

The Partido Popular Socialista (PPS; Popular Socialist Party) was founded in 1948 by a radical sector of the PRI led by Vicente Lombardo Toledano. Despite its Marxist orientation, the PPS supported the PRI until 1988. The PPS presented its own candidate, Marcela Lombardo, at the 1994 presidential election but made little impact.

In 1952 dissident PRI members established the Partido Auténtico de la Revolución Mexicana (PARM; Authentic Party of the Mexican Revolution). The PARM had a strongly nationalistic platform and maintained its minority representation in the lower chamber until 1994.

The Partido del Frente Cárdenista de Reconstrucción Nacional (PFCRN; Cárdenas Front of the National Reconstruction Party) was established in 1973. After backing Cuauhtémoc Cárdenas's bid for the presidency in 1988, the PFCRN ran its own candidate in 1994. However, Rafael Aguilar received less than 1 percent of the vote.

Other parties that registered for the 1994 election included the Partido Verde Ecologista Mexicano (PVEM; Mexican Green Ecologist Party) and the Partido del Trabajo (PT; Labor Party). The PT's Cecilia Soto received more than 3 percent of the vote. Both parties are represented in congress, receiving their main support predominantly from urban areas. A total of eight political parties registered to compete in the 2003 mid-term elections.

At the end of the administration of Manuel Ávila Camacho (1940-1946) the party's military sector was abolished and the popular sector was enlarged. On January 18, 1946, the PRM was renamed for the last time as the Partido Revolucionario Institucional, a party of civilians reorganized into labor, agrarian, and populist sectors. Miguel Alemán became the first PRI presidential candidate, adopting the motto "Democracy and Social Justice."

Internal structure of the PRI

Since the PRI's creation, its executive organization has been pyramidal in structure, headed by a party leader and a secretary general who direct the National Executive Committee (CEN). At the party base there is a National Assembly, which meets every six years to review the party's platform and to formally nominate the candidate for the national presidency. In practice, however, the assembly has only ratified the candidate handpicked by the existing president through a system known as *dedazo* ("finger-pointing"), a custom followed by all presidents. The informal right to name his successor has given the Mexican president considerable power within the party.

Since the late 1930s there have been few episodes of large-scale political upheaval in Mexico, despite considerable economic strains in the 1970s and a period of economic austerity in 1982. During this time the PRI has distributed political positions to the different sectors in accordance with each group's relative strength.

During the PRI's long history there have been occasional attempts to democratize the party. In 1965 party leader Carlos Madrazo suggested changing the way that mayoral candidates were chosen. He also proposed that people should become members of the party by individual affiliation, rather than the traditional system of membership through sectors. Sectorial and local leaders objected to these measures and Madrazo was forced to resign; only a few months later he died in a plane crash.

During the presidency of Miguel de la Madrid (1982–1988) the PRI started to change its nationalist agenda and adopt free-market policies. These changes produced an internal split within the party. In 1986, the Corriente Democrática (CD; Democratic Movement) was founded within the PRI by Porfirio Muñoz Ledo, a former PRI secretary general, and Cuauhtémoc Cárdenas, the son of former president Lázaro Cárdenas. This left-wing faction criticized "neoliberal" policies and called for a return to the party's traditional platform.

Two years later, the nomination of Harvard-educated political economist Carlos Salinas as the PRI candidate for the 1988 presidential election triggered the final rupture between these two groups. Cárdenas left the party to run as an independent in the 1988 presidential race. A broad coalition of leftist parties and other political organizations supported his candidacy.

In 1988, the PRI received its lowest margin of victory ever, and for the first time it lost more than one-third of the seats in the lower chamber. Toward the end of his term Salinas started negotiations for the NAFTA agreement with the United States and Canada. In 1994 the vote for the PRI was reduced to roughly 50 percent. In a contest where voter turnout reached 77 percent, the PRI's Ernesto Zedillo was elected president but was quickly enveloped in a profound economic crisis. In 1997 the opposition parties won the majority in the lower chamber and several governorships.

Prior to the 2000 presidential elections the PRI decided to make the procedures for choosing the party's candidate more open and democratic. Millions of Mexicans took part in the process, which resulted in the selection of Francisco Labastida as PRI candidate for president. Labastida lost the 2000 election with 36 percent of the vote against 42 percent for the PAN's Vicente Fox, who was supported by the Alliance for Change coalition.

This 1934 poster was produced to publicize the economic program carried out by Mexican president Lázaro Cárdenas. At this time the Mexican political system was completely dominated by the PRI.

The Partido Acción Nacional

For most of the twentieth century Mexico's main opposition party was the Partido Acción Nacional, founded in September 1939 by Manuel Gómez Morín. Gómez Morín and his supporters objected to President Cárdenas's radical policies, in particular his agrarian reform program, oil expropriation, land confiscations, and insistence on secular public education. The PAN's early support derived from three main groups: Catholic activists, professionals and intellectuals, and leaders of the business and industrial sector. Other groups that felt alienated by the dominance of the central state also participated in the party's foundation.

For the first 40 years of its history the PAN represented only a nominal challenge to the ruling party because the PRI blatantly manipulated the electoral process to its own advantage. However, despite widespread ballot-rigging and intimidation, the PAN did manage to make some inroads. In 1946, for example, four federal deputies took office. The mid-1940s also brought the first PAN municipal and state legislature victories, in Oaxaca and Michoacán.

In the 1960s, the PAN began to put increasing pressure on the government to make the electoral process more open and democratic. The party denounced the violation of civil liberties in some local elections and attempted to bring the issue into the international arena. Limited electoral reforms followed in 1963 and these opened some spaces for opposition representation in congress. At the end of the 1970s the PAN demanded that the composition of all electoral bodies be decided by proportional representation. When this attempt failed the PAN opted for a more gradual route to achieve democratic change, focusing first on the lowest levels of government.

During the 1980s the PAN assumed a new importance as it came to represent the interests of business leaders opposed to the nationalization of the banks. Nationalization had been instigated by President José López Portillo in response to a profound economic crisis that had struck the country at the time. Many of these business leaders were based in the prosperous northern states of the country, and the area became a PAN stronghold.

In the 1988 presidential election the PAN candidate, Manuel Clouthier, gained the largest number of votes ever received by the party. However, Clouthier came only third, behind the PRI's candidate, Carlos Salinas, and the rebel independent, Cuauhtémoc Cárdenas. Like many before it, the election was plagued with irregularities. Cárdenas, with some justification, claimed that he was the real victor of the election. The PAN agreed to recognize Salinas's presidency, but only if he would work with them on the issue of electoral reform. Salinas acquiesced to the PAN's demands and also recognized PAN victories in Baja California and Chihuahua. Guanajuato, meanwhile, became PAN's third governorship after a controversial state election in which the PRI candidate was initially declared the victor.

During the 1990s the PAN consolidated its role as the main opposition. After its second place in the 1994 presidential elections, the party won gubernatorial elections in Jalisco and Guanajuato in 1995. In 1997 the PRI lost its majority in the chamber of deputies for the very first time in its history. Finally, in the 2000 elections, the PAN won in Morelos but, more important, its candidate Vicente Fox won the presidency.

Opposition from the left

For most of the history of postrevolutionary Mexico, any left-wing opposition to the ruling PRI has had to operate in an atmosphere of secrecy and governmental hostility. The Partido Comunista Mexicano (PCM; Mexican Communist Party) was founded in 1919. Although it did have periods of influence, they alternated with times when the party was brutally suppressed.

For most of its history, the PCM was not allowed to compete in elections. The only way in which it could influence the electoral process was by supporting one faction or another in internal power struggles within the PRI. However, electoral reform carried out in 1977 allowed the PCM and other independent left-wing parties to compete legally in elections. Among them were, in 1982, the Partido Socialista de los Trabajadores (PST; Socialist Workers Party), and, in 1985, the Partido Mexicano de los Trabajadores (PMT; Mexican Workers Party). In the 1980s the parties of the left began to converge in a unification process. In 1981 the PCM went into voluntary dissolution, joining with other left-wing organizations to form the Partido Socialista Unificado Mexicano (PSUM; Unified Mexican Socialist Party). The PSUM later evolved into the Partido Mexicano Socialista (PMS; Mexican Socialist Party), which, in 1987, was joined by the registered PMT and other nonregistered parties.

Cárdenas's challenge

The birth of this new party coincided with an internal crisis within the PRI that created the Corriente Democrática (CD). The PMS was broadly sympathetic to the aims of the CD and when Cuauhtémoc Cárdenas left the PRI to run against the party in the 1988 presidential elections, the PMS was one of several parties that supported his candidacy. Together these parties formed a coalition called the Frente Democrático Nacional (FDN; National Democratic Front).

After Cárdenas took second place in the presidential election, leading figures within the FDN attempted to consolidate their success by transforming the loose coalition into a bona fide political party. The Partido de la Revolución Democrática was founded in May 1989 with Cárdenas as its leader. The party's membership represented a diverse selection of political views, but generally the PRD's program emphasized social welfare concerns and strongly opposed the free-market economic program of the governing PRI. The PRD was also opposed to the ecclesiastical, agrarian, and electoral reforms approved during Salinas's presidency.

The PRD failed to build on Cárdenas's success in the 1988 presidential election and soon lost its position as the main opposition party to the PAN. However, in the late 1990s the party began to enjoy some degree of electoral success. In 1997 Cárdenas won the mayoral election for Mexico City before resigning to run, unsuccessfully, for the presidency in 2000. Since then, the PRD won the governorships of Zacatecas and Tlaxcala in 1998 and Baja California Sur in 1999, retained Mexico City in 2000, and won the governorship of Michoacán in 2001. In March 2002 the PRD held open elections to decide who should lead the party. Almost a million people participated in the democratic process, which led to the selection of Rosario Robles as PRD president.

Susana Berruecos García Travesí

SEE ALSO:

Communism and Marxism; Elections in Mexico; Partido Acción Nacional; Partido de la Revolución Democrática; Partido Revolucionario Institucional; Presidency, Mexican.

Political Parties in the United States

Historically the two major U.S. political parties have taken a variety of stances toward Mexico and Mexican Americans. Presently, the Democratic Party attracts over 60 percent of the Mexican American electorate. This is due partly to the party's identification with the working class and ethnic minorities since the 1930s. In principle the Democrats also support an activist state that enforces civil rights. The Republican Party, however, is making a strong pitch to woo Mexican American Democrats. The Republicans point to polls showing that the majority of Mexican Americans hold conservative (Republican) views on issues such as supporting family values and prayer in schools, and in opposing abortion.

Democratic presidential nominee Al Gore vied for the Hispanic vote during the 2000 general election.

Both the Democrats and Republicans realize that, though a small percent of the total regular voters, the Mexican American electorate can affect close races. This is particularly true in states such as California, Texas, and Illinois, with large numbers of both electoral votes and Mexican American voters.

Mexican American involvement in party politics dates to the 1880s, when several elite Mexican landholders served in state governments in the Southwest. During the early 1900s the Democrats in Texas imposed reforms that masked racist views and eliminated, via the poll tax, nonwhite voters.

The Democratic Party operated differently on the East Coast. In the early 1900s the Democrats attracted immigrant voters through urban political machines that offered employment and other inducements in return for votes. Republicans mounted a good government campaign during the Progressive Era that led to civil service reform. In 1928 New York Democratic governor Al Smith, while running for president, began alluring immigrant voters into national elections. The Republican Party was identified as the party of business, employers, and civil-service reform, and in the 1920s the party backed immigration restrictions.

After Congress passed several restrictions on Asian and eastern and southern European immigration in the late nineteenth and early twentieth centuries, farmers in the West began recruiting Mexicans to harvest crops. Between 1900 and 1930 more than one million Mexicans immigrated to the United States. They came to work in agriculture, on the railroads, and in factories.

As Mexican immigration increased, Republican critics called for restrictions. The Immigration Act of 1924 virtually excluded Asian immigration and greatly reduced European immigration. The 1924 law also attempted to restrict Mexican immigration by requiring immigrants to undergo a literacy test, a medical examination, and to pay both a $10 visa fee and an $8 head tax. The 1924 law also created the Border Patrol, which enforced the new rules. However, the Border Patrol was understaffed and the border remained virtually open to new immigrants from Mexico.

The Great Depression (1929–1939)

During the 1930s Democrats solidified their hold on working-class whites, blacks, Mexican Americans, and immigrant voters. At the onset of the Great Depression in 1929, the Republican Party led by

President Herbert Hoover (1929–1933) appeared unresponsive to the unemployed. Also in the early 1930s, Hoover and the Republicans launched a repatriation campaign that resulted in the return of over one million Mexicans and some Mexican Americans to Mexico. While some unemployed Mexicans returned voluntarily, many left because they feared being arrested and deported by U.S. authorities. In contrast, Hoover's successor, Franklin Delano Roosevelt (1933–1945), a Democrat, expanded government involvement in the economy and launched so-called New Deal programs that created employment opportunities. Roosevelt also severely curtailed the deportation of immigrants.

Early political activism

In the 1920s increased nativism and the growth of an urbanized middle class led Mexican Americans to form their first significant political association, the League of United Latin American Citizens (LULAC). LULAC celebrated the Mexican American community's loyalty to the United States in the face of nativism and communism. LULAC provided education in the English language, promoted citizenship, and denounced radical unions and communists while filing lawsuits against school segregation and fighting other forms of discrimination. LULACers, as members were called, strongly supported the Democratic Party and encouraged participation in the electoral process.

At the other end of the political spectrum during the 1930s, the Communist Party helped organize Mexican migrant workers throughout the Southwest. Migrant workers were frequently used as strike breakers, and the American Federation of Labor (AFL) ignored them. Whereas the Congress of Industrial Organizations (CIO) made some attempts to organize Mexican workers in the 1930s, the Communist Party made an even stronger push by supporting the formation of El Congreso, which advocated improved pay and working conditions for Mexican workers in the factories and fields and strongly supported unionizing Mexican workers.

World War II (1939–1945)

Increased demand for workers during World War II created a labor shortage throughout the United States. Many Americans abandoned low-paying jobs and headed to cities to work in defense plants. The resulting shortage of migrant laborers led western farmers to lobby for the temporary importation of workers from Mexico. Both Republicans and Democrats in Congress supported the Bracero Program that began in 1942.

Following the war, farm owners pressured Congress to continue the Bracero Program as a way to help provide food during the rebuilding of Europe and the Korean War (1950–1953). Again, Democrats and Republicans both supported the continuation of the Bracero Program. However, Republican criticism of illegal immigration mounted during the 1950s, when fears of communist subversion increased throughout the United States. In this climate, foreigners came under intense suspicion of being communist spies. These fears, coupled with an economic downturn in 1954, resulted in a renewed program to deport illegal immigrants. In 1954 the Immigration and Naturalization Service (INS) deported over one million Mexicans in what became known as Operation Wetback.

Despite this hostile political climate, many Mexican American voters, and particularly the members of LULAC, continued to support the Democratic Party. However, Mexican Americans were becoming more politically active and their support for the Democrats helped elect John F. Kennedy as U.S. president in 1960. The Mexican Americans organized "Viva Kennedy Clubs" throughout the Southwest, which mobilized Mexican Americans to vote for the Catholic Democrat.

The new anti-immigrant movement

Immigration, legal and illegal, surged following termination of the Bracero Program in 1964. The Immigration Act of 1965 was passed by a Democrat-dominated Congress and reflected the strong economy of the 1960s. The act eliminated the quota system that had been in place since the 1920s and admitted immigrants based on family ties, job skills, and refugee status. It also granted the countries of the Western Hemisphere a total annual quota of 120,000, of which Mexicans made up the bulk of the new arrivals.

During the 1970s under the Republican presidents, Richard Nixon and Gerald Ford, and the one-term Democrat, Jimmy Carter (1977–1981), affirmative action became a dominant issue concerning ethnic minorities, including Mexican Americans. In response to their growing importance each administration appointed more and more Mexican Americans to high-profile government jobs. For example, in 1974, Nixon appointed Mexican Americans as federal judges, and President Carter later gave federal positions to around 200 Mexican Americans. Nevertheless, immigration remained the main point of contention for Mexican American voters.

While Mexican immigration to the United States surged in the 1970s, an economic downturn in the early 1980s brought renewed efforts to restrict immigration. President Ronald Reagan (1981–1989), a Republican, claimed that the surge in Latin American immigration was the result of the spread of communism and that stopping immigration required U.S. aid for anticommunist forces in Central America. Democrats generally did not support U.S. involvement in those military conflicts. In 1986 Democrats and Republicans united in Congress to pass the Simpson-Rodino Act, also called the Immigration Reform and Control Act

(IRCA), which required undocumented workers to register for amnesty by proving they had lived in the United States continuously since January 1982. If so, applicants could receive an 18-month temporary residency, after which they could apply for permanent status. The act also cracked down on employers hiring undocumented workers. Under the act, employers who hired undocumented workers faced large fines and possible jail sentences.

Immigration in the 1990s

In the 1990s the Republican Party once again sought to take advantage of the immigration issue. In 1994 Republicans in California rallied support for the passage of Proposition 187, which prohibited undocumented immigrants from receiving basic education and medical care. In 1996 the state's Republican Party also backed Proposition 209, aimed at ending affirmative action in California. Moreover, throughout the country Republicans were more

The Influence of Chicano Activism

Despite the Viva Kennedy Clubs and the strong support of Mexican American voters for John F. Kennedy during the 1960 general election, the Democratic Party's response to Mexican Americans in the early 1960s was disappointing. Kennedy and later Lyndon B. Johnson, president from 1963 to 1969, picked few Mexican Americans to serve in their administrations. This brought criticism of the Democrats by a new generation of Mexican Americans, the so-called Chicano generation. Influenced by both the anti-Vietnam War and African American civil rights movements, this new generation of usually student activists rejected assimilation into either the Democrat or Republican parties, or indeed into U.S. Anglo society as a whole, and identified with nonwhite Americans and Third World liberation movements occurring around the world. Increasing numbers of Mexican Americans began calling for militant actions to achieve social justice.

The Chicano movement's growing frustrations with both the Democrats and Republicans led José Ángel Gutiérrez, a student activist and president of the Mexican American Youth Organization (MAYO), to organize El Partido de la Raza Unida (PRU; United People's Party) in

Crystal City, Texas, in 1970. Originally numbering only 300, the PRU soon spread to communities throughout the Southwest. The PRU nominated candidates to run for city councils and school boards and drew support from disaffected Mexican American voters, including college students and community activists. The party's most significant electoral achievement was the domination of both Crystal City's school board and city council in the early 1970s.

However, problems with internal dissension and regional differences soon divided the PRU, and by the mid-1970s, after failing to make an electoral dent outside of Texas, the party began to wane. Nevertheless, the political and cultural impact of the PRU and the Chicano movement galvanized many Mexican Americans, even if they did not always agree with the more radical agenda.

Most Mexican Americans, such as César Chávez, the cofounder of the United Farm Workers union, remained staunch supporters of the Democratic Party throughout the 1970s and 1980s, and some Mexican American Democratic politicians even won federal elections. These included congressmen Edward Roybal from California and "Kika" de la Garza of Texas.

likely to support English-only initiatives. In the 1980s the surge in immigration from Asia and Latin America led conservatives to launch a movement to make English the official language of government and organized against the use of bilingual ballots.

In the 1990s western growers continued to lobby for a renewed Bracero Program. However, immigration opponents pressured for a decrease in both legal and illegal immigration. Both parties supported increasing the budget of the INS, which faced a mounting backlog of immigration cases.

Reform Party attacks

Growing numbers of Hispanics had registered to vote as Democrats in the 1980s and 1990s. As a result, by the late 1990s, Republicans had somewhat toned down anti-immigrant and English-only rhetoric. However, such rhetoric still emanated from third-party politicians. During the 1992 and 1996 general elections the Reform Party candidate, Ross Perot, criticized the North American Free Trade Agreement (NAFTA) by claiming it would encourage employers to vacate the United States for low-wage labor in Mexico. Mexicans viewed Perot's statements as overly critical of Mexico and Mexican labor, alienating many Mexican Americans. In 2000 the Reform Party candidate, Patrick Buchanan, campaigned for severe immigration restrictions and the rescinding of NAFTA, positions that again alienated many Mexican American voters.

With more than 20 million Mexicans and Mexican Americans in the United States, Democrats and Republicans could ill-afford to engage in anti-immigrant or English-only rhetoric. The anti-immigrant movement remained active, yet it lost significant support among some union leaders who sought to organize immigrants. Whole sectors of the economy have been dependent on immigrant labor. While some elements of the Republican Party continued to call for immigration restrictions, business owners dependent on immigrant labor have opposed such initiatives.

Moreover, some aspects of the Republican agenda appeal to Mexican Americans, and more affluent Mexican Americans identify with the Republican Party, particularly with its strong support for socially conservative issues such as family values and anti-abortion. Recent overtures toward improving relations with Mexico have included talks between U.S. president George W. Bush and Mexican president Vicente Fox.

Voting issues

While the number of Mexican Americans elected to federal, state, and local offices increased after the 1960s, several factors have continued to limit their political power. First is the lower rate of Mexican voter participation. The Mexican population is young, and the young are generally less likely to vote. Also, 30 percent of those with Mexican origins in the United States are not citizens and thus are ineligible to vote. Other factors include gerrymandering (the manipulation of voting district boundaries) and at-large elections, both of which dilute the Mexican American vote and discourage participation. Also, the poor and poorly educated tend to vote less often, and many Mexicans fall into those categories. Also, any change of residency requires re-registering and that discourages voting by workers who migrate frequently. Intimidation at the polls also discourages voting, and convicted felons cannot vote, two further factors that limit the Mexican electorate.

Among those who do vote, a majority cast ballots for the Democrats, whom Mexicans perceive as more responsive to the needs of the poor, workers, minorities, and immigrants. The Democratic Party has been more supportive of immigrant civil rights, bilingual education, and affirmative action, and is less likely to support English-only laws.

Immigration post–September 11

The terrorist attacks on the United States of September 11, 2001, led to renewed calls for stricter policing of the U.S. border to curb the immigration of suspected terrorists. Republicans and Democrats alike criticized the INS for lax enforcement of immigration laws and for the backlog of naturalization applications leading up to September 11, even though during the 1990s the number of border agents had doubled to nearly 20,000 and the INS budget had doubled to nearly $5 billion.

In 2002 both parties were treading carefully, trying to balance the security demands for stricter enforcement of the U.S.-Mexico border, the economic reality of employer dependence on immigrant labor especially in the border region, and the political reality of a large Mexican American vote.

Joseph A. Rodriguez

SEE ALSO:

Affirmative Action; Bracero Program; Bush, George W.; Civil Rights in the U.S.; Elections in the U.S.; González, Henry B.; Great Depression; Presidency, U.S.; Roosevelt, Franklin D.; Voter Registration.

Bibliography and Other Resources

Nonfiction Studies

Bailey, John. *Governing Mexico: The Statecraft of Crisis Management*. London: Macmillan Press, 1988.

Bruhn, Kathleen. *Taking on Goliath: The Emergence of a New Left Party and the Struggle for Democracy in Mexico*. University Park: Pennsylvania State University Press, 1997.

Cameron, Maxwell A., and Brian W. Tomlin. *The Making of NAFTA: How the Deal Was Done*. Ithaca: Cornell University Press, 2002.

Centeno, Miguel Angel. *Democracy within Reason: Technocratic Revolution in Mexico*. University Park: The Pennsylvania State University Press, 1994.

Chapa, Juan Bautista. *Texas and Northeastern Mexico, 1630–1690*. Austin: University of Texas Press, 1997.

Cook, Maria Lorena, et al. *The Politics of Economic Restructuring: State-Society Relations and Regime Change in Mexico*. San Diego: The University of California at San Diego, 1994.

Davis, Mike. *Magical Urbanism: Latinos Reinvent the U.S. Big City*. London: Verso Publications, 2000.

Dent, David W. *The Legacy of the Monroe Doctrine*. Westpoint, Conn.: Greenwood Press, 1999.

Foster, William C. *Spanish Expeditions into Texas, 1689–1768*. Austin: University of Texas Press, 1995.

Halperín Donghi, Tulio. *The Contemporary History of Latin America*. Durham: Duke University Press, 1993.

Kopinak, Kathryn. *Desert Capitalism: Maquiladoras in North America's Western Industrial Corridor*. Tucson: University of Arizona Press, 1996.

Krauze, Enrique. *Mexico, Biography of Power: A History of Modern Mexico, 1810–1996*. New York: Harper Perennial, 1998.

Leonard, Thomas M. *United States-Latin American Relations, 1850–1903: Establishing a Relationship*. Tuscaloosa: University of Alabama Press, 1999.

Lorey, David E. *The U.S.–Mexican Border in the Twentieth Century: A History of Economic and Social Transformation*. Wilmington, Del.: Scholarly Resources, Inc., 1999.

Mabry, Donald J. *Mexico's Acción Nacional: A Catholic Alternative to Revolution*. New York: Syracuse University Press. 1973.

Mayer, Frederick. *Interpreting NAFTA: The Science and Art of Political Analysis*. New York: Columbia University Press, 1998.

Meyer, Michael C., William L. Sherman, and Susan M. Deeds. *The Course of Mexican History*. New York: Oxford University Press, 1999.

Nkrumah, Kwame. *Neocolonialism: The Last Stage of Imperialism*. New York: International Publishers, 2001.

Noriega, Chon A. *Shot in America: Television, the State, and the Rise of Chicano Cinema*. Minneapolis: University of Minnesota Press, 2000.

Rodriguez, Jaime E., and Kathryn Vincent (eds.). *Common Border, Uncommon Paths: Race, Culture and National Identity in U.S.-Mexican Relations*. Wilmington: Scholarly Resources Inc.,1997.

Ruiz, Ramón Eduardo. *On the Rim of Mexico: Encounters of the Rich and Poor*. Boulder: Westview Press, 2000.

Scott, Mainwaring, and M. Shugart. *Presidentialism and Democracy in Latin America*. New York: Cambridge University Press, 1997.

Skerry, Peter. *Mexican Americans: The Ambivalent Minority*. New York: Free Press, 1993.

Skidmore, Thomas E., and Peter H. Smith. *Modern Latin America*. New York: Oxford University Press, 2001.

Smith, Marian L. *Overview of INS History: A Historical Guide to the U.S. Government*. New York: Oxford University Press, 1998.

Smith, Peter H. *Talons of the Eagle: Dynamics of U.S.–Latin American Relations*. New York: Oxford University Press, 1996.

Spicer, Edward H. *Cycles of Conquest*. Tucson: The University of Arizona Press, 1992.

Weber, David J. *The Spanish Frontier of North America*. New Haven: Yale University Press, 1992.

Wilson, James Q., and John J. Diiulio, Jr. *American Government: The Essentials*. Boston: Houghton Mifflin, 2001.

Wright, Bill. *The Tiguas, Pueblo Indians of Texas*. El Paso: Texas Western Press, The University of Texas at El Paso, 1993.

Fiction Writing

Acosta, Oscar Zeta. *The Autobiography of a Brown Buffalo*. New York: Vintage Books, 1989.

Anaya, Rudolfo. *Bless Me Ultima*. Berkeley: Quinto Sol Publications, 1995.

Bellow, Saul. *The Adventures of Augie March*. New York: Knopf, 1995.

Burroughs, William. *Queer*. New York: Viking Press, 1995.

Ford, Richard. *The Ultimate Good Luck*. New York: Vintage Books, 1987.

Gonzales, Rodolpho "Corky." *Message to Aztlán: Selected Writings*. Houston: Arte Publico Press, 2001.

Gómez-Peña, Guillermo. *Warrior for Gringostroika: Essays, Performance Texts, and Poetry*. St. Paul: Graywolf Press, 1993.

——. *The New World Order: Prophesies, Poems & Loqueras for the End of the Century*. San Francisco: City Lights Books, 1996.

——. *Dangerous Border Crossers: The Artist Talks Back*. New York: Routledge, 2000.

——. *Codex Espangliensis: From Columbus to the Border Patrol*. San Francisco: City Lights Books, 2000.

Hinojosa, Rolando. *Becky and Her Friends*. Houston: Arte Publico Press, 1995.

McCarthy, Cormac. *The Border Trilogy: All the Pretty Horses, the Crossing, Cities of the Plain*. New York: Knopf, 1999.

McMurtry, Larry. *Lonesome Dove*. New York: Pocket Books, 1991.

Michener, James. *Mexico*. New York: Crest, 1994.

Nichols, John Treadwell. *The Milagro Beanfield War*. New York: Owl Books, 2000.

Niggli, Josefina. *Mexican Folk Plays*. Manchester: Ayer Company Publishers, 1976.

——. *Mexican Village*. Albuquerque: University of New Mexico Press, 1994.

Traven, B. *Treasure of the Sierra Madre,* New York: Hill & Wang Publishers, 1996.

Mexican American Movies

American Me. Director: Edward James Olmos, 1992.

Aqueda Martínez: Our People, Our Country. Director: Esperanza Vásquez, 1977.

Born in East L.A.. Director: Cheech Marin, 1987.

Chicana. Director: Sylvia Morales, 1979.

I am Joaquin. Director: Luis Valdez, 1969.

Luminarias. Director: Jose Luis Valenzuela, 2000.

My Family. Director: Gregory Nava, 1995.

No Movie. Director: Harry Gamboa, 1976.

La Raza Nueva (The new race). Director: Salvador Treviño, 1969.

Salt of the Earth. Director: Herbert Biberman, 1954.

Stand and Deliver. Director: Ramon Menendez, 1988.

Y Soy Chicano (I Am Chicano). Director: Salvador Treviño, 1972.

Zoot Suit. Director: Luis Valdez, 1981.

Web sites

Barrio Life.com
http://www.barriolife.com

Centro Virtual Cervantes (Spanish language site)
http://cvc.cervantes.es

Discover Southeast Arizona: Spanish Missions
http://discoverseaz.com/History/Missions.html

The Handbook of Texas Online
http://www.tsha.utexas.edu/handbook/online/

Hispanic Agenda for Action
http://www.haa.omhrc.gov

Hispanic Magazine Online
http://www.hispaniconline.com/magazine

MANA: A National Latina Organization
http://www.hermana.org

Mexican Population Figures
http://www.geohive.com/cd/mx

Mexico Connect: A general guide to people, places, and history of Mexico
http://www.mexconnect.com

Music of Mexico: An Introduction
http://www.ethnomusic.ucla.edu/ethnomusicology/Ensembles/Mexico/Mexico.htm

National Latina Organization
http://www.hermana.org

PEMEX.com (Spanish language site)
http://www.pemex.com

Population Research Center, University of Texas at Austin
www.prc.utexas.edu/hispanic

United States Embassy in Mexico
http://www.usembassy-mexico.gov/

United States Immigration and Naturalization Service
http://www.ins.gov/

Vicente Fox (Spanish language site)
http://www.vicentefox.org.mx

Index